Contemporary Philosophy and Social Science

Also available from Bloomsbury

The Bloomsbury Companion to the Philosophy of Science, edited by Steven French
The History and Philosophy of Science, edited by Daniel McKaughan and Holly VandeWall

Contemporary Philosophy and Social Science

An Interdisciplinary Dialogue

Edited by
Michiru Nagatsu and Attilia Ruzzene

BLOOMSBURY
NEW DELHI • LONDON • OXFORD • NEW YORK • SYDNEY

BLOOMSBURY INDIA
Bloomsbury Publishing India Pvt. Ltd
Second Floor, LSC Building No. 4, DDA Complex, Pocket C–6&7,
Vasant Kunj, New Delhi 110070

BLOOMSBURY, BLOOMSBURY ACADEMIC INDIA and the Diana logo are trademarks of Bloomsbury Publishing Plc

First published in India 2025
First published in Great Britain 2019
Reprinted by Bloomsbury Academic 2019

Cover image: Mimi Haddon / Getty Images

This edition published with permission from Bloomsbury Publishing Plc,
50 Bedford Square, London, WC1B3DP, UK

A catalogue record for this book is available from the British Library.
Library of Congress Cataloging-in-Publication Data

ISBN: 9789-3-61318-69-6

Typeset by Newgen KnowledgeWorks Pvt. Ltd., Chennai, India
Printed and bound in India by Replika Press

To find out more about our authors and books
visit www.bloomsbury.com and sign up for our newsletters

Contents

Illustrations

Figures

Tables

Contributors

Daniel Breslau is Chair of the Department of Science, Technology, and Society at Virginia Tech. He is the author of many articles and book chapters on the social sciences in their role of constituting modern institutions. His current work investigates economics and engineering in the politics of electricity markets.

Nicolas Brisset is associate professor at the Université Côte d'Azur (GREDEG-CNRS), France, and associate member of the Centre Walras-Pareto of the University of Lausanne, Switzerland. His areas of specialization are the philosophy of social sciences, history of economic thought, and economic sociology. He recently published *Economics and Performativity, Exploring Limits, Theories and Cases.*

Raffaella Campaner is Associate Professor of Philosophy of Science at the Department of Philosophy and Communication of the University of Bologna. Her research interests include causation, scientific explanation, and modeling, and she has specialized on topics in philosophy of medicine. She is currently working on models of mental disorders.

Mikael Carleheden is Associate Professor, Department of Sociology, University of Copenhagen; coordinator of the Centre for Anthropological, Political and Social Theory (CAPS), Faculty of the Social Sciences, University of Copenhagen; editor of *Distinktion: Journal of Social Theory* and Board member of Research Network Social Theory, European Sociological Association.

Nancy Cartwright works at both Durham University in the UK and at University of California at San Diego in the United States. She specializes in philosophy of natural and social science with special interests in philosophy of economics, modeling, causal inference, objectivity, and evidence.

Mathieu Charbonneau is a philosopher of science and technology, currently a postdoctoral researcher at the Social Mind Center, at the Department of Cognitive Science, Central European University (CEU). He is also affiliated with the Department of Philosophy and the Social Studies Program at the CEU.

C. Tyler DesRoches is Assistant Professor of Sustainability and Human Well-Being and Assistant Professor of Philosophy at Arizona State University. Tyler has published articles in the *Australasian Journal of Philosophy*; *History of Political Economy*; and *Ethics, Policy & Environment*. His monograph, *Sustainability without Sacrifice*, is under contract with Oxford University Press.

Jay Fogelman received his BA from Lake Forest College and did his graduate study in philosophy at the Johns Hopkins University. For eight years he was a faculty member at the Business School of the Central European University. He is now retired and resides in Copenhagen.

Tom L. Green is an ecological economist based in Vancouver, Canada, working on climate policy with the David Suzuki Foundation and formerly associate professor at the University of Rosario in Bogota, Colombia.

Glenn W. Harrison is the C.V. Starr Chair of Risk Management & Insurance and Director of the Center for the Economic Analysis of Risk, Georgia State University. He is also affiliated with the School of Economics, University of Cape Town. His current research interests span risk management and perception, experimental economics, behavioral econometrics, behavioral welfare economics and the costs of smoking.

Christophe Heintz is Associate Professor of cognitive science at CEU, Budapest, Hungary. He is studying how human cognition, characterized as adaptive, shapes social behavior, economic choices, and cultural practices. He has published on pro-social choice, the principles of cultural evolution, and the cognitive history of science.

Andre Hofmeyr is Senior Lecturer and the Undergraduate Convenor in the School of Economics at the University of Cape Town. He is an experimental economist who specializes in game theory and the application of behavioral and experimental methods to health issues.

S. Andrew Inkpen is Assistant Professor of history and philosophy of science at Brandon University in Manitoba, Canada. He writes on issues surrounding the human-natural distinction and about ecological function and health.

Daniel Little is the Chancellor for the University of Michigan-Dearbon and Professor of Philosophy. He also serves as Professor of sociology at the University of Michigan, Ann Arbor. His books include *Varieties of Social Explanation* and *New Directions in the Philosophy of Social Science.*

Michiru Nagatsu is Associate Professor in Practical Philosophy and Helsinki Institute of Sustainability Science at the University of Helsinki. He works on foundations of human sociality and on the methodology of interdisciplinary research, in particular environmental and behavioral sciences.

Wendy Olsen works as Professor of Socio-Economics at the University of Manchester. She has taught development studies, sociology, and development economics. Olsen does research on employment, informal labor, gender, and labor markets in India and South Asia, as well as the UK. She has created new "mixed methods," cutting across the qualitative-quantitative divide.

Cédric Paternotte is Assistant Professor in philosophy of science at Sorbonne University (Paris). His work focuses on sociality in general, which includes: joint action, explanations of cooperation, social norms, collective reasoning, social epistemology and collective agency.

Don Ross is Professor and Head of the School of Sociology, Philosophy, Criminology, Government and Politics at University College Cork; Professor in the School of Economics, University of Cape Town; and Program Director for Methodology at the Center for Economic Analysis of Risk, J. Mack Robinson College of Business, Georgia State University.

Attilia Ruzzene is a philosopher of the social sciences with a major interest in qualitative methodology. She currently holds a post-doc scholarship at the University of Bergamo where she works on the use of visuals and visual analysis to study phenomena related to organizational identity and family entrepreneurship.

Daniel Steel is an associate professor in the Centre for Applied Ethics at the University of British Columbia. His research focuses on the intersection of values and science in the context of environmental and/or public health issues. Current research includes a project on different concepts of diversity, and how these are relevant to explanations of how diversity can generate better science or better science-informed policy.

Stephen Turner is Distinguished University Professor in Philosophy at the University of South Florida. He has written extensively on the history and philosophy of social science, especially Weber and Durkheim. His most recent book is *Cognitive Science and the Social: A Primer* (2018).

Charlotte Vangsgaard is managing partner at ReD Associates, where she handles marketing- and pharma-related projects for consumer goods and healthcare companies. She holds an MBA in International Business and Marketing and a masters in Political Science. She has a strong analytical background in social theory and business strategy.

Tommaso Venturini is Advanced Research Fellow of the French Institute for Research in Computer Science and Automation (INRIA) and founder of the Public Data Lab (publicdatalab.org). He has been lecturer at the Department of Digital Humanities of King's College London and coordinator of the research activities at the médialab of Sciences Po, Paris.

David Waldner (PhD, University of California, Berkeley) is an Associate Professor in the Department of Politics at the University of Virginia. He teaches courses on democracy and development as well as courses on research design and methodology.

Nathaniel T. Wilcox studied Economics and Psychology at the University of Chicago and received his PhD in Economics from there in 1992. His research interests are decisions, beliefs, learning, experimental methods, and applied econometrics and statistics. He serves on the editorial boards of the *Journal of the Economic Science Association* and the *Journal Experimental Economics*. He is professor of economics at Chapman University's Economic Science Institute in Orange, California.

Michael Woolcock is lead social scientist in the World Bank's Development Research Group, where he has worked since 1998, and a Lecturer in Public Policy at Harvard Kennedy School. His current research focuses on strategies for enhancing state capability for implementation, and assessing "complex" development interventions.

Petri Ylikoski is Professor of Science and Technology Studies at University of Helsinki. His research interests include theories of explanation and evidence, science studies, and social theory. His current research focuses on the foundations of mechanism-based social science, institutional epistemology, and the social consequences of artificial intelligence.

Preface

Some years ago, Colleen Coalter from Bloomsbury approached one of us inviting to compile a handbook on the philosophy of the social sciences. The proposal sounded exciting but also challenging since several similar books in the form of readers, handbooks, and anthologies had been published. We feared that the marginal return from adding another similar volume to this already rich and comprehensive array of texts was diminishing (another Companion from Routledge appeared in 2017 while preparing this book). Hence our decision to give a new twist to the whole endeavor: our counterproposal to Bloomsbury was to base our book on a kind of performative experiment, in which we would encourage philosophers of social science to directly engage with contemporary social scientific practices. We envisioned that this trial would bring two research communities closer, as well as deliver some insights into how philosophers respond to new turns in the social sciences and into the challenges ahead.

This experiment has spent a long time in gestation and demanded effort and patience from the people involved. We want to thank first Colleen Coalter, Helen Saunders and Becky Holland, the editors of Bloomsbury, for accepting our unusual proposal and waiting for the results patiently. We thank all the contributors from the social sciences who generously shared their practical and theoretical insights with us. We also thank the philosophers who provided commentaries, all of which proved the fruitfulness of philosophical engagement with social scientific practices in different ways. Several scholars helped this accomplishment by reviewing chapters before philosophical commentaries: Sonja Amadae, Alkistis Elliott-Graves, Osvaldo Feinstein, Raul Hakli, Phyllis Illari, Tuukka Kaidesoja, Aki Lehtinen, Miles MacLeod, Werner Reichmann, Federica Russo, and Mikko Salmela. We also thank three anonymous reviewers of the book proposal, as well as another reviewer of the introduction, for their encouragements and suggestions. Finally, we thank Francesco Guala and Don Ross for their unswerving support throughout the project.

Michiru Nagatsu has received support in various forms from TINT, Academy of Finland Center of Excellence in the Philosophy of the Social Sciences (2012–17), as well as from his Academy Fellowship (No. 294545).

Michiru Nagatsu and Attilia Ruzzene

Venice, 2018

Introduction

Michiru Nagatsu and Attilia Ruzzene

Philosophy of social science is a small but vibrant field, which is attested by the number of handbooks and companions: Turner and Roth (2003), Jarvie and Zamora Bonilla (2011), Kincaid (2012), Kaldis (2013), and McIntyre and Rosenberg (2017). The maturity of the field is suggested by the standard textbooks that have been continuously revised—Hollis (1994, revised and updated in 2002), Elster (2015, originally published in 1989), and Rosenberg (2016, 5th edition, originally published in 1988)—as well as standard readers, both classic (Martin and McIntyre 1994) and contemporary (Steel and Guala 2011). Two edited volumes from Cambridge (Mantzavinos 2009) and Oxford (Cartwright and Montuschi 2014) have been recently added to these collections.

One will notice in this literature a gradual shift of focus from the demarcation question of whether social science can be a proper science—despite the peculiar nature of the mental and the social—to the questions concerning actual social scientific practices, such as experimentation, model-building, problem-solving, and evidential reasoning. This shift is in line with the so-called practical turn in the philosophy of science. Accordingly, some philosophers have started adopting a range of empirical approaches including bibliometric, ethnographic, case-based, and experimental methods to study practices. We can call this an empirical turn. Although the practical and empirical turns are sometimes misleadingly interpreted as sociological turns, these turns have not changed philosophers' main interests in ontological, conceptual, and methodological issues in science; rather, they have enriched empirical bases for philosophizing by enriching the kinds of methods to obtain data.

Ambitions of the empirical philosophy of social science in practice thus construed include informing and improving social scientific practices. However, there has not been a systematic effort on the part of philosophers to increase direct engagement with practicing social scientists. This book is a modest attempt to initiate such a move. Specifically, it does so by adopting a dialogical template: we invited philosophers and social scientists to engage each other and see in what form and to what extent they could be partners in the same conversation. Admittedly, the dialogical format is not new in the philosophy of social science (e.g., Little 1995; Mantzavinos 2009). However, this book is different from these precedents in a crucial respect. While Mantzavinos (2009) and Little (1995) had social scientists comment on philosophers' views on social sciences, we decided to reverse the roles. Chapters are written by social scientists with the purpose of showcasing their innovative research, while philosophers partake in the exchange by providing commentaries (all commentaries, except one, are written by philosophers). Social scientists thus offer an entry point for the conversation. We hoped that this "social science first, philosophy second" approach would elicit a different kind of dialogue between the two research communities. In particular, we hoped that it would encourage philosophers to engage with scientific practices head-on, more directly, thoroughly, and seriously than when they are free to philosophize about social science.

Have our expectations been met? What kind of materials have social scientists brought to the table? And what kind of responses have philosophers provided? In what follows, we summarize our findings in the form of a quasi-scientific report.

Methods

We identified an initial pool of approximately twenty social scientists on the basis of our background knowledge, interests, and networks, whose work we thought was suitable and exciting because of its theoretically and methodologically innovative features. We approached them by e-mail, explicitly requesting them to expose the innovative aspects of their work. They were also informed that a philosopher who specializes in relevant fields would provide a detailed commentary. Thirteen social scientists out of this initial pool showed interest in our initiative and accepted to participate in it. One scholar agreed to contribute, but never followed up. One had to be excluded due to misunderstandings about the focus of the chapter. As a result, we obtained eleven manuscripts. The manuscripts went through anonymous reviewing processes and a round or two of revision, some minor and others major. After the manuscripts have been completed, we asked philosophers of social sciences with relevant expertise to provide critical commentaries. We the editors substituted as commentators on two chapters for which we could not find philosophers suitable to the task or willing to participate. The editors have reviewed and commented on the commentaries, which have been finalized after a round or two of revision (each editor's commentary was reviewed by the other).

Results

What kind of trends did we find in this exchange? First, we found that some of the social scientists have well-articulated philosophical concerns. They grapple with the same philosophical and methodological questions that philosophers of social science discuss, such as the ontology of the social world or the methodology of causal inference. In these domains, philosophical and social scientific questions largely coincide. The exchange between social scientists' contributions and philosophers' responses is, as a result, not only smooth but also mutually enriching since it provides partly different answers to what are in fact very similar questions. Thus, the philosopher and the social scientist talk to each other in a way that enables them to advance a shared agenda. We see this kind of exchange exemplified, for instance, by David Waldner and Daniel Steel who provide alternative interpretations of process tracing while trying to resolve what they both recognize as the problematic aspects of a specific practice. In a similar vein, Nancy Cartwright argues for an extension of Michael Woolcock's proposal to use mixed methods in policy evaluation so as to include a broader population of interventions.

These productive exchanges suggest that philosophers are already informing and improving scientific practices in some domains, together with social scientists. The two research communities happily overlap in such domains. This overlap is due partly to philosophers' increasing attention to scientific practice, but also due to the problems in question being inherently philosophical, disposing the social scientists to adopt philosophical approaches in formulating or framing the problem they are working on.

In a second, perhaps more traditional, kind of exchange, philosophers elaborate, clarify, or even correct social scientists' characterizations of their own practices. Sometimes the philosopher provides a sort of philosophical backbone to the interpretation outlined by the social scientist. This would be, for instance, the case of Stephen Turner commenting on Michael Carleheden's discussion on the role of social theory in sociology. Other times the philosopher provides a rationale for the practice at hand, clarifying the methodological and theoretical import of the innovation advocated by the social scientist. Exemplary of this type of exchange is Daniel Little's commentary on Wendy Olsen's discussion of the role of critical realism in social statistics. In yet other cases, the philosopher, while seeing the reasons and goals behind a given practice, points out underlying misunderstandings that could impair or obfuscate its potential. This is illustrated by Petri Ylikoski's commentary on the discussion of temporal modeling by Tommaso Venturini. In all these cases the philosopher's contribution amounts to sharpening the philosophical underpinning of the practice in a way that not only makes it philosophically sounder but also clears the path where further benefits and developments could or should be sought.

In these cases, we find that some of the standard analytic and conceptual tools developed in the philosophy of (social) science have proved useful. These tools—realism, the micro-macro distinction, social ontology, under-determination, scientific pluralism, interpretivism versus positivism, and so on—do not directly solve social scientific problems, but they are useful in helping us better understand practice.

Discussion

In this section, we briefly address some of the limitations of our study and suggest an area we think philosophers of social science need to study. As noted in the beginning, the main goal of our project was to facilitate a new kind of dialogue between social scientists and philosophers led by the former. This design probably created a self-selection bias toward those social scientists who are more likely to be philosophically minded than the average researcher in their field. We think that this bias served our purpose, namely to initiate and facilitate collaborative and critical interactions between the two communities. But in general, an empirical study of social scientific practices should pay attention to the self-selection bias.

Potentially problematic is our selection of the target social science disciplines and fields. Our selection is by no means a balanced and comprehensive sample from the state of the art in the social sciences. It has a clear bias toward economics and related fields, such as business research, econometrics, evaluation of development policies, ecological economics, and, to a less extent, sociology and political science. Other fields such as anthropology, psychology, social epidemiology, and so on are absent. This is partly due to the bias in the editors' areas of expertise, but also it reflects the bias of the current philosophy of social science in general.[1] We have no intention to endorse such a bias as a good thing. Rather, we simply acknowledge that we, as the editors, are part of the bias and encourage the reader to consult the handbooks and edited volumes mentioned in the introduction that address this selection bias to some extent.

Whereas the biases discussed above can be justified by appealing to the primary purpose of the book and the path-dependence of the literature in which the project is embedded, there is another, more important, limitation that we should address here: we could not cover many of the emerging new methodological innovations that are somehow philosophically relevant and likely to trigger the interest and reactions of philosophers of the social sciences in the near future, if they haven't done so already. Below we would like to briefly discuss one such area of relevance, big data, to indicate that there is much more uncharted area of potential mutual engagement between social scientists and philosophers.

The digital revolution and the advent of big data generated changes across social sciences. Specialized journals have been founded (e.g., *Big Data and Society*) and established journals have guested special issues dedicated to the topic (e.g., *International Journal of Sociology, Journal of Psychological Methods, Journal of Business & Economic Statistics, Political Science & Politics*, just to name a few). This turn has caused a broad range of novelties. First, the most tangible and immediate effect is that a massive amount of data, which are different in relevant respects from traditional data (Leney 2004; Kitchin 2014; Leonelli, 2014; Kitchin and McArdle 2016), have become available, constituting an additional source of evidence for the phenomena and processes that have been already studied, for example, use of web search data to estimate unemployment: Ettredge et al. (2005); D'Amuri (2009); Fondeur and Karamé (2013); and Askitas and Zimmermann (2015) Second, the turn has generated novel social, economic, and political phenomena worth investigating in their own right. Consider as an example the work of political scientist Jonathan Bright (2018), who studies how political fragmentation in social media increases radicalization and how social media affect patterns of news sharing (Bright 2016), or the work of media scholar Zizi Papacharissi (2010), who theorizes on how digital technologies have shifted civic engagement from the public to the private sphere and introduces the concept of affective publics to explain how social movement use digital media to generate engagement and make their voice matter in politics (Papacharissi 2015). The third novelty concerns methodology. The digital revolution makes the traditional tools of research more powerful and also generates new ones, giving rise to new fields such as digital humanities. Finally, the digital revolution has stimulated the critical approach in the social sciences. For example, the Gender and ICT research group at the Open University of Catalonia was established in 2006 to study data intensive research methods from a feminist perspective. One of its goals is to investigate the ways in which new data conceptualizations, technologies, and related social practices can be used for transformative societal changes.

Philosophers of science have only recently started paying attention to the digital turn in the sciences (with the notable exception of Sabina Leonelli, who has published extensively on the advent of digitization and big data mainly in the biological sciences). Other philosophical contributions have so far focused on big data as forecasting tools (Hosni and Vulpiani 2017), theory-ladenness (Pietsch 2015), epistemology and causality (Canali 2016), modeling in data-intensive science (Pietsch 2016), and philosophy of information (Floridi 2012). However, contributions focusing on the social sciences are still scant. Much more investigation is needed into how social mediatization contributes to the dissemination of scientific knowledge and its transformation (e.g., by reducing its complexity), and how this will affect society and policy making at large.

As the big data case indicates, social scientific practices are changing in response to the technological and societal changes. Philosophers and social scientists can work together to understand and respond to these changes. We hope this book will help facilitate a collaborative dialogue between the two communities.

How to Use This Book

We will close this introduction by offering some guide on how to use this volume in courses on the philosophy of social science. The instructor can use this book as a philosophical guide to three salient trends in social sciences in practice: issues raised by the plurality of approaches, disciplines, and theories (Part One: Chapters 1–3); debates over choices of one method over another and the need to mix multiple methods (Part Two: Chapters 4–8); and issues around the methodology and foundation of social scientific explanation and theorizing (Part Three: Chapters 9–11). Alternatively, the reader can organize chapters according to the philosophical concepts that have been used by commentators. For instance, mechanism and social causation (Chapters 7, 8, and 11), causal inference (Chapters 4, 5, and 9), theory choice (Chapters 3 and 10); scientific pluralism (Chapters 1 and 2), and interpretivism (Chapter 6). In either way, we recommend the instructor to require students to read a chapter and its commentary as a set and have them discuss whether the philosopher and the social scientist talk past each other, or their exchange is fruitful.

We have two cautions. The book highlights the domains where we think potential gains from exchange between social scientists and philosophers are high, rather than evenly covering all the areas in the social sciences. The second caution concerns the level. Some chapters and commentaries presuppose some familiarity with technical details of theories, methods, and philosophical concepts. The instructor may want to provide introductory materials before assigning those chapters to students.

Note

1 For example, Philosophy of Economics is by far the biggest subcategory under the category Philosophy of Social Science at PhilPapers.org (11,324 entries out of 59,698 as of September 2018). Note that the other bigger two subcategories, Philosophy of Education (27,438) and Philosophy of Law (17,915), are usually not considered to be part of the Philosophy of Social Science.

References

Askitas, N., and K. F. Zimmermann. 2015. "The Internet as a Data Source for Advancement in Social Sciences." *International Journal of Manpower* 36 (1): 2–12.

Bright, J. 2016. "The Social News Gap: How News Reading and News Sharing Diverge." *Journal of Communication* 66 (3): 343–65.

Bright, J. 2018. "Explaining the Emergence of Political Fragmentation on Social Media: The Role of Ideology and Extremism." *Journal of Computer-Mediated Communication* 23 (1): 17–33.

Canali, S. 2016. "Big Data, Epistemology and Causality: Knowledge In and Knowledge Out in Exposomics." *Big Data & Society* 3 (2): 205395171666953.

Cartwright, N., and E. Montuschi, eds. 2014. *Philosophy of Social Science: A New Introduction*. Oxford: Oxford University Press.

D'Amuri, F. 2009. *Predicting Unemployment in Short Samples with Internet Job Search Query Data*. Italy: University Library of Munich.

Elster, J. 2015. *Explaining Social Behavior: More Nuts and Bolts for the Social Sciences*. 2nd ed. London: Cambridge University Press.

Ettredge, M., J. Gerdes., and G. Karuga, 2005. "Using Web-based Search Data to Predict Macroeconomic Statistics." *Communications of the ACM* 48 (11): 87–92.

Floridi, L. 2012. "Big Data and Their Epistemological Challenge." *Philosophy & Technology* 25 (4): 435–7.

Fondeur, Y., and F. Karamé. 2013. "Can Google Data Help Predict French Youth Unemployment?" *Economic Modelling* 30: 117–25.

Hollis, M. 1994. *The Philosophy of Social Science: An Introduction. Cambridge Introductions to Philosophy*. London: Cambridge University Press.

Hosni, H., and A. Vulpiani. 2017. "Forecasting in Light of Big Data." *Philosophy & Technology* 31 (4): 557–69.

Jarvie, I. C., and J. P. Zamora Bonilla, eds. 2011. *The SAGE Handbook of the Philosophy of Social Sciences*. London: SAGE.

Kaldis, B., ed. 2013. *Encyclopedia of Philosophy and the Social Sciences*. Volume 2. London: SAGE.

Kincaid, H., ed. 2012. *The Oxford Handbook of Philosophy of Social Science*. Oxford: Oxford University Press.

Kitchin, R. 2014. "Big Data, New Epistemologies and Paradigm Shifts." *Big Data & Society* 1 (1): 205395171452848.

Kitchin, R., and G. McArdle. 2016. "What Makes Big Data, Big Data? Exploring the Ontological Characteristics of 26 Datasets." *Big Data & Society* 3(1): 205395171663113.

Leney, T. 2004. *Finnish. Teach Yourself.* Chicago, IL: McGraw-Hill.

Leonelli, S. 2014. "What Difference Does Quantity Make? On the Epistemology of Big Data in Biology." *Big Data & Society* 1(1): 1–11.

Little, D., ed. 1995. *On the Reliability of Economic Models: Essays in the Philosophy of Economics.* Volume 42. Germany: Springer Science & Business Media.

Mantzavinos, C., ed. 2009. *Philosophy of the Social Sciences: Philosophical Theory and Scientific Practice.* Cambridge: Cambridge University Press.

Martin, M., and L. C. McIntyre, eds. 1994. *Readings in the Philosophy of Social Science.* Cambridge, MA: MIT Press.

McIntyre, L., and A. Rosenberg, eds. 2017. *The Routledge Companion to Philosophy of Social Science.* London: Routledge.

Moffatt, P. G. 2016. *Experimetrics: Econometrics for Experimental Economics.* London: Palgrave.

Papacharissi, Z. 2010. *A Private Sphere: Democracy in a Digital Age.* Cambridge: Polity.

Papacharissi, Z. 2015. "Affective Publics and Structures of Storytelling: Sentiment, Events and Mediality." *Information, Communication & Society* 19 (3): 307–24.

Pietsch, W. 2015. "Aspects of Theory-ladenness in Data-intensive Science." *Philosophy of Science* 82 (5): 905–16.

Pietsch, W. 2016. "The Causal Nature of Modeling with Big Data." *Philosophy & Technology* 29 (2): 137–71.

Rosenberg, A. 2016. *Philosophy of Social Science.* 5th ed. London: Taylor & Francis.

Steel, D., and F. Guala, eds. 2011. *The Philosophy of Social Science Reader.* London: Routledge.

Turner, S. P., and P. A. Roth, eds. 2003. *The Blackwell Guide to the Philosophy of the Social Sciences.* Malden, MA: Blackwell.

Part One

The Plurality of Approaches, Disciplines, and Theories

Summary of Chapters

The focus of the first three chapters is how approaches, disciplines, and theories are related to each other in the social sciences. Examining this set of relations raises distinctive philosophical issues about pluralism, interdisciplinarity, and theory choice.

The chapter by Christophe Heintz, Mathieu Charbonneau, and Jay Fogelman discusses the integration of multiple approaches and theories from different social sciences. The authors address crowd dynamics as a target phenomenon common to psychology, rational choice, and network science. They argue that the plurality of causal factors leading to crowd formation and maintenance requires a plurality of explanatory tools from a variety of fields while potentially leading to incompatibility between the different approaches. Heintz et al. advocate integrative pluralism as an epistemic stance oriented not only to reducing emerging incompatibility between approaches but also, more positively, to pursuing three epistemic virtues—consistency, consilience, and complementarity. The authors envisage that integrative pluralism will eventually yield more comprehensive explanations of social phenomena by addressing the multiplicity of causal factors involved. Pluralism of various strands has been advocated in recent philosophy of science, largely concomitant with an increasing interest in the special sciences and their practice. By highlighting key differences in different strands of scientific pluralism, Raffaella Campaner's commentary provides epistemological tools to better understand the specificity of the approach of Heintz et al.; at the same time, she outlines a framework in which questions about the ultimate desirability and fruitfulness of an integrative stance in the social sciences can be addressed.

The chapter by Tyler DesRoches, Andrew Inkpen, and Tom L. Green focuses on model-building in economics and ecology and calls for fruitful interdisciplinary exchange between these two disciplines. The authors consider the restrictions on the exchange between ecology and economics resulting from the commitment to the ideal of disciplinary purity, that is, the view that each discipline is defined by an appropriate, unique set of objects, methods, theories, and aims. The authors problematize the "artificial-natural distinction" that has underwritten the disciplinary purity of economics and ecology. They argue that this distinction is no longer tenable conceptually and that models linking anthropogenic (i.e., "artificial") and non-anthropogenic (i.e., "natural") factors provide epistemic and policy-oriented benefits. Furthermore, they predict that in the current age of the Anthropocene ecology and economics may relinquish global relevance if they don't make room for adequate interdisciplinary exchange. In his commentary, Michiru Nagatsu provides a context in which this issue can be discussed in the philosophy of social science, such as its relation to performativity; he also critically analyzes the case of DesRoches et al., drawing on his own case study of economics and ecology interactions in renewable natural resource management.

The chapter by Andre Hofmeyr and Don Ross narrows down the focus to inter-theoretical relations within economics, specifically between different game-theoretic explanations of pro-social behavior. The authors consider the motivations leading individuals to participate in multiple levels of economic agency. One of these levels is characterized in terms of utility to social groups with which people identify. Hofmeyr and Ross review and assess two theoretical approaches to pro-social behavior, namely Bacharach's account of "team reasoning" (2006) and Stirling's account of "conditional games" (2012). While they regard Bacharach's conceptualization as useful, they argue that its application is limited to processes supported by deliberation. Since this is, however, only one of the causal mechanisms underlying pro-social behavior, they regard a more general account as desirable, and argue that Stirling's (2012) achieves the desired generalization. Paternotte's commentary critically analyses the assumed notion of generality of theories in terms of explanatory power, explanatory potential, and assumptions about agents. Paternotte argues that, if one takes these dimensions into account, neither conditional game theory nor team reasoning is more general than the other. Correspondence in this chapter shows that philosophy of science, while unable to give the final verdict, can elucidate relevant methodological and epistemic considerations underlying scientific disagreements over theory choice.

1

Integration and the Disunity of the Social Sciences

Christophe Heintz, Mathieu Charbonneau, and Jay Fogelman

1.1 Introduction

There is a plurality of theoretical approaches, methodological tools, and explanatory strategies in the social sciences. Different fields rely on different methods and explanatory tools even when they study the very same phenomena. We illustrate this plurality of the social sciences with the studies of crowds. We show how three different takes on crowd phenomena—psychology, rational choice theory, and network theory—can complement one another. We conclude that social scientists are better described as researchers endowed with explanatory toolkits than specialists of some specific social domain. Social scientists' toolkits are adapted for identifying and specifying the role of specific causal factors among the multiple factors that produce social phenomena. These factors can be, in a nonexclusive way, economic incentives, psychological processes, the ecology, or aspects of the social and cultural environment.

The plurality of methods and theories in the social sciences flies in the face of the project to unify the sciences associated with the positivists of the nineteenth and twentieth centuries. Yet, the compatibility and consilience of theories and practices still have epistemic value: they enable the development of more powerful and robust theories and they allow the advent of interdisciplinary studies. We present the integrative stance as the will to improve compatibility and consilience across fields, yet recognize that the plurality of causes of social phenomena invite a diversity of methodological and theoretical tools. We conclude by characterizing naturalism as an integrative stance applied to fields that belong to the social sciences *and* to the natural sciences.

1.2 The Unity of the Social Sciences: A Failed Project

The strong unity model associated to positivists such as Carl Hempel and Ernst Nagel holds that social facts reduce to facts about individuals, which in turn can be reduced to biological, chemical, and ultimately physical facts. Disciplinary boundaries do not necessarily correspond to the organization of nature; they are arbitrarily drawn by scientists. Furthermore, the methods and aims of the social sciences should be modeled on those of the natural sciences, as ultimately everything could be explained in physical terms. Although this view has generally fallen into disrepute, its specific answers to the ontological, disciplinary, and methodological objectives remain hotly debated. For instance, some social scientists would advocate methodological individualism in the social sciences, arguing that social phenomena should be explained in terms of individual behaviors and their aggregation. But some other social scientists recommend methodological holism—social facts can appear in scientific explanations (Zahle 2016).

In spite of these attempts to single out the specificity of the social sciences, explanations of social phenomena remain very diverse. For instance, an explanation in economics relies on modeling an economic agent as a rational individual maximizing her own expected utility. Such assumption is at odds with standard explanations in sociology, which appeal to the social milieu as a determinant of individuals' behaviors. It is hard to find a methodological principle and/or a theoretical claim that would characterize or unify all explanations in the social sciences. What is in fact striking is the diversity of methods and theories in the social sciences compared to the relative unity of other scientific disciplines. Given the lack of consensus, the social sciences have *de facto* followed a generally pluralistic philosophy: Different social sciences develop their own methods for studying the social world, yet often with their disciplinary boundaries overlapping in such a way that the very same social phenomena are investigated and explained in radically different ways.

Contrary to this stance of "default pluralism," we argue in favor of a methodological pluralism: make the most of different approaches, as they can bring explanatory insights, and yet strive for integration. Successful integration makes apparent the complementarity of different theories and methods for explaining a given social phenomenon. We argue that deploying a plurality of methods and theories for studying, understanding, and explaining some social phenomena and asking different questions is often justified because social phenomena result from a multiplicity of causal factors. Different methodologies and theories might be needed for identifying and describing these causal factors. When that is the case, the methods and theories are complementary to one another, giving a richer, deeper understanding of the social world. We illustrate this diversity with explanations of crowd phenomena.

1.3 Explanations of Crowds

How, why, and when do crowds form and dissipate? Crowds are the archetype of social phenomena. At first glance, it seems that crowds would form a well-identified and characterized object of scientific investigation—a social kind, so to speak. It turns out, however, that there is no satisfactory scientific characterization of crowd. There are no constitutive factors or defining traits for identifying a category of social phenomena whose extension would cover our intuitive notion of crowds. The notion of crowd is, in that respect, similar to the notion of tree. One is very able to recognize a tree, but there is no scientific category for trees. In spite of this, scientists can well describe why a birch or an oak is the way it is. Likewise, social scientists can investigate the causes of a specific crowd formation. In this section, we show that an understanding of any specific crowd is likely to require drawing on very diverse explanatory tools. In Sections 1.4 and 1.5, we examine how different approaches studying a same phenomenon yet with different tools and theories can be integrated and provide a richer understanding of the phenomenon.

1.3.1 Crowd Psychology: Imitation and Contagion

The classical accounts of crowding developed at the turn of the nineteenth century (Le Bon 1896; Tarde 1901, 1903; Trotter 1916; Freud 1989). These accounts appeal to psychological concepts like contagion, herd instinct, imitation, and group mind. Each of these concepts has been invoked to explain the commonality of sentiment and behavior that seem to be at the root of crowding. For instance, "contagion" is a metaphor for the transmission of ideas or behavioral inclinations among agents, much as disease is transmitted through a population. But how? Through what mechanism? Some authors appeal to the effect of facial expressions on others, some to chants; some appeal to the herd instinct, which purportedly drives humans to cluster together into ever-larger groups. These psychological notions point to the relevance of mental phenomena in producing the behavior that eventually constitutes a crowd. Crowds appear when people do the same things at the same time—marching, chanting, and having aggressive or fearful behaviors. The similarity can arise because of similar reaction to a single event: for instance, a fire might cause people to flee from the burning building independent of the fact that others similarly flee. In many cases of crowds, however, the behaviors are interdependent: the choices and emotions of one individual influence the choices and emotions of the others. This strong social influence has been grasped by the authors mentioned above.

While studies of crowd behavior started at the beginning of the twentieth century with thought-provoking speculations on its psychological bases, current studies of the relevant psychological underlying mechanisms involve laboratory experiments testing hypotheses specified with the technical vocabulary of cognitive science. The specification of the herd instinct and dispositions to imitate, as psychological traits shared by all humans, has led to numerous work in psychology, especially when investigating what, in human psychology, allows for the emergence of culture (Tomasello 2009; Mesoudi 2016). The existence of a herd instinct and "compulsive imitation" has, however, been largely challenged by other authors working on cultural evolution and its psychological foundations (Morin 2015). Crowd behaviors such as marching or breaking things together are some type of joint actions. Recent cognitive studies investigate to what extent these can be caused by processes of "entrainment," simultaneous affordance, simulation mechanisms, joint attention, and so on (see Knoblich and Sebanz 2008). Crowd behavior might also involve the rapid spread of emotions. Cognitive science, again, investigates with laboratory experiment how and why emotions can spread in crowd contexts: the emotions can result from the social connectedness of doing things together (Marsh et al. 2009) and it can be rapidly transmitted through face perception (Dezecache et al. 2013). The investigations are enabled by the methodological tools of behavioral experiments but also by conceptual and interpretive tools from larger psychological theories, such as theories of embodied cognition and social cognition. For instance, Dezecache, Jacob, and Grèzes (2015) use evolutionary psychology to interpret results and formulate hypotheses about emotional contagion.

Although enlightening, there are several limits to explanations of crowd phenomena on the basis of contagion of emotions and automatic imitation of others' behaviors. For one, participation to crowd might be motivated by reasons rather than induced by spontaneous cognitive processes such as compulsive imitation. For another, the environmental factors are neglected in the merely psychological explanations. We now turn to these other factors, which can contribute to the formation of crowds.

1.3.2 Rational Choice: Unintended and Intended Crowd Formation

Rational choice theory remains one of the main tools of the social sciences. It includes a set of assumptions about how agents make decisions: they are rational, which means they make the best choices for achieving their goals, given their limited knowledge. Sometimes, the rationality assumptions are supplemented with the presumption that economic agents' goal is to maximize material gains. Rational choice theory is strongly criticized by both sociologists and psychologists on the ground that it includes false assumptions about human decision-making: contrary to the model of rational choice, humans are often not able to select the best means for achieving their goals. Kahneman and Tversky's work in behavioral economics provided strong evidence that people's choices often depart from what the theory of rational choice would predict (see, Gilovich, Griffin, and Kahneman 2002). Still, there remains several ways to use rational choice theory as a tool for explaining social phenomena. One way is to interpret rational choice models of specific phenomena as "as if" models. This interpretation favors predictive power over explanatory value, since it does not identify the actual causes of the phenomena.

A second way is to use rational choice theory as providing a well-justified baseline for the study of human behavior because animal cognition, human or not, is adaptive. Cognition is a function of some organisms that consists in processing information so as to produce behavior that increases fitness. It is therefore likely to select the best means for achieving goals that are themselves proxy for maximizing fitness (sexual desires, for instance). In that sense, rational choice theory can be a useful tool for the study of nonhuman behavior as well as human behavior. It is not necessarily a good description of the psychological mechanisms, but it is likely to be a good first approximation.

A third way to interpret and use rational choice theory consists in making the minimal assumption that, in the specific case at hand, the choices of agents are motivated. The choices are sensitive to incentives. The use of rational choice theory is, in such case, not a set of axioms for formalizing social phenomena, but a heuristic way to formulate empirical hypotheses, which are then put to the test. This heuristic is justified because of the second point mentioned above: cognition is adaptive. So far, a minimal core of rational choice theory has often proved to be true: economics has provided a rich set of cases showing that people's choice are best explained as being sensitives to incentives and risk. The popular book *Freakonomics* (Levitt and Dubner 2005) provides beautiful illustrations of such explanations, enabling to uncover the surprising effect of some incentives.

For this chapter, we will focus on the insights that rational choice theory brings for explaining crowd formation. One such illustration is the crowd forming in one restaurant, while the restaurant next door remains empty. The cognitive and social processes go as follows: passers-by want to eat in a good restaurant but have no knowledge about whether the restaurant on the right is better than the restaurant on the left. The first group decides at random; it goes to the restaurant on the right. The second group then decides on the basis of the fact that the restaurant on the right has clients while the one on the left has none. Without further information, the best bet is to rely on the choices of others and go to the restaurant on the right. This is what the second group does. The same thing happens again and again, so that the restaurant on the right becomes crowded and the one on the left remains empty. People end up all doing the same thing and forming a crowd, in spite of the fact that they have no interest in doing so. Still, people make the best decision given that the information they have is only, or mainly, derived from their observation of the choice of others. Such phenomena, called information cascade, provide an example of crowding because of the rational choice of people who do not want to create a crowd. It is based on the testable hypothesis that people take these specific decisions (going to a restaurant in our illustration, but other actual phenomena) on the basis of information that they derive from observing the behavior of others. There are other conditions where crowds appear as unintended consequences of people making the best choice for themselves. The Braess's paradox, for instance, describes the conditions in which traffic jams are caused by actually improving on the available roads and creating highways. One situation for this to happen is pictured in Figure 1.1: there are 4,000 people commuting from one city (start) to the other (end) every morning, and these two cities are connected by two roads. The traveling time is forty-five minutes for covering one trunk of the road (a small road) plus the number of users of travelers on the other trunk, divided by 100. Because of rational choice, half of the population takes one road, while the other half takes the other road. It thus takes sixty-five minutes to go from start to end. However, one improvement in the road structure—building a highway between A and B—leads commuters to take one path and neglect the alternatives, which are now comparatively longer. They do so because they want to minimize their commuting time, but the

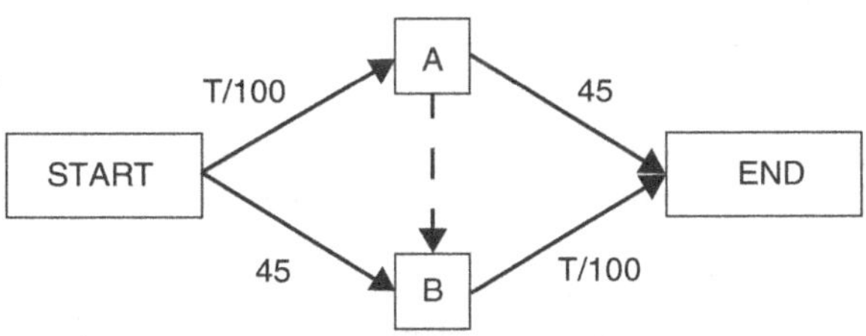

Figure 1.1 Illustration of the Braess's paradox.

unintended consequence is that the road is crowded. With all people taking the same road, the travel time is now eighty minutes.

There are also cases where a crowd is formed because people do actually want to form a crowd. In such cases, rational choice theory helps specifying the cognitive problems that need to be solved in order to coordinate for forming a crowd. The problems occur when many people are motivated to participate to a crowd, yet these people know that there is no such crowd to participate to. Thus, in spite of their desire to come together to form a crowd, they fail to do so. How is this problem solved in real life? An example is provided by the Arab Spring, a set of revolutions that took place in North Africa in the years 2010–12. One key event of the Arab Spring is the crowd that gathered in Tahrir Square, in Cairo. This crowd formed for expressing their preferences for a change of regime. Yet, the preference for changing the regime of Mubarak and the willingness to express this preference did not come from one day to the other. The motivation for participating to a demonstration and forming a crowd was present throughout the Egyptian population for some time, but the coordination problem prevented the formation of a crowd. Indeed, expressing one's disagreement with the regime was not without danger; yet it could be done with more safety as a collective action. A first problem, in collective action, is to agree on a time for action. When people cannot talk and agree on this matter, this is a hard task. One salient event can provide the required information: now is the good time! This salient event enables solving the coordination problem—it is a Schelling point (Cronk and Leech 2012). In the Arab Spring, the salient event was provided by the events in Tunisia, which was the first of the North African countries to undergo a successful uprising, with the fall of Ben Ali in 2011. The action of Mohammed Bouazizi, a Tunisian street vendor who self-immolated, might also have provided the first coordinating signal that it was now time to demonstrate (Howard and Hussain 2011).

The crowd in Tahrir Square was first and foremost caused by a desire, shared by many, to express their dissatisfaction with the Mubarak regime. However, an analysis of coordination problem with the tools of rational choice theory points out that this desire is not enough. Beliefs about what others will do are crucial, as revealed by a rational choice theory analysis.

1.3.3 Network Science and the Ecology of Crowd Formation

The above explanations make one causal factor of crowd formation apparent: the means of communication and how they connect people. The Arab Spring has often been qualified as Twitter or Facebook revolutions. Some have argued that one key feature of the Arab Spring was the reliance of the demonstrators on New Information Technology (Howard and Hussain 2011; Stepanova 2011). Some others have argued that social media had a modest impact, while television and word of mouth were the most important source of information (Williams Associates 2011; Friedman 2011). The penetration of Twitter in Egypt around the time of the revolution was low: about 12,000 subscribers out of a population of 80,000,000. At the same time, there were 3.5 million Facebook users: a 4.5 percent penetration rate (Dunn 2011). Still, the penetration of internet users in Egypt had skyrocketed in the decade leading up to the Arab Spring, with 17 million users online by May of 2011, about 21 percent of the population (Stepanova 2011).

Le Bon and Tarde did, in their time, already mention the role of mass communication (LeBon 1896, 137; Tarde 1901, 7–11), but the recently developed field of network science makes its systematic study possible. Network science applies mathematical analysis for describing patterns of interconnections among a set of things. Relying on the mathematics of graph theory, it conceives connections as vertices in a graph and the connected things as nodes of that graph. Network science can be used for the analysis of diverse phenomena, such as the modeling of the spread of disease in an epidemic and the spread and containment of forest fire (Porterie et al. 2007). For us, however, the relevant applications of network science concern the "connectedness" of social agents and the spread of specific behavior. In this context, connections might be communication links, "friend" relation in Facebook, or physical connections.

We saw in the previous section that crowds might arise when a coordination problem that involves a large number of people is being solved. Coordination can be achieved when the same action-triggering information is distributed to many people in a short time. Network science shows that it is possible when the network of communication allows for rapid spread of coordinating information. What types of network allow for this rapid spread? This is made possible when a few nodes are extremely popular and thus able to distribute the information at once to many other nodes. In other words, the existence of hubs—highly connected nodes—can play a crucial role in crowd formation and maintenance. Thus, during the Arab Spring, the Facebook account of Wael Ghonim played the role of a hub for distributing coordinating information. In a demonstration, this role of distributing coordinating information can be taken by the person who holds the megaphone: the network, in that case, is constituted of nodes that represent members of the demonstration and links that represent who hears whom.

One observation made by early scientists of crowd (LeBon 1896, 34–5) was that crowds seemed to be answering the will of one single individual—the leader—or at least one "idea." We interpret this intuition about crowds as related to the coordinated action of people forming a crowd. Network science can therefore specify this intuition: the leader, if any, is not necessarily an individual with official leadership. It is the individual that is a hub. Also, the ideas that seem to belong to the crowd in virtue of holding it together are coordinating ideas that are shared by the participants of the crowd.

Another property of networks can provide insights in the formation and maintenance of crowds. When links in a network express hyperlinks in the web, friendship, or any type of social connection, the number of links connecting a node provides a measure of popularity of that node. For instance, there are many more links to the pages of Wikipedia than to the ResearchGate homepages of this chapter's authors. The former is more popular than the latter. Networks that express popularity evolve: new links are created, and some are deleted. One factor for the creation of a new link toward a node is how much this node is already connected. Indeed, an individual with many friends is more likely to meet new people, by means of his existing friends, than someone with few friends. Likewise, well-connected websites are more likely to be visited than others. Thus, the very structure of the network—who is connected to whom—partially determines how this network evolves, in such a way that the nodes already rich in connections, get richer. The consequence of this type of evolution is that the popularity is distributed following a power law, which means that very few nodes are extremely popular while the rest of the nodes have very little popularity.

Such a process can cause the advent and maintenance of crowds. For instance, if people prefer to go to a disco where there already are people, then they will crowd in one disco and let the other empty (note that this is different from the restaurant story, where people did not want to be together but did end up doing so deriving information from the presence of others). Likewise, crowds can happen on the internet, when people visit the same webpage at the same time. An illustration of this effect is the crowd of 80 million YouTube users who, on December 7, 2009, chose to watch Britney Spears's video " 'Womanizer." A key factor of the rush was its appearance as the first recommendation for the YouTube users watching "Toxic," an already popular video. Being already rich from this very valuable link, "Womanizer" gathered more links and references. As with the disco example, there is a process of preferential attachment, where past success determines future success. The analogy between crowds on the internet and crowds in public spaces makes sense because similar principles—features of the network driving the influence of a behavior on others—can lead to both types of "crowds." Interestingly, the evolution of unequal distribution of popularity can be boosted or moderated by hugely popular nodes, which regulate access to other nodes. The best illustration of this fact is search engines: insofar as answers to queries are ordered list of websites, which is determined by popularity (this is what Google's algorithm PageRank does), it will boost the rich-get-richer effect of networks. On the other hand, the rich-get-richer effect is moderated by the role given to keywords and by the personalization of results implemented by search engines: these processes promote websites that might not be so popular but which respond to specific interests.

The management of crowds during mass gathering, and the prevention of crushing deaths during evacuation is a problem that city and building architect have to face. Indeed, dramatic events can be avoided with good egress design. A historical example is the Italian Hall disaster of 1913 (described in Tubbs and Meachan 2007): the evacuation of partygoers directed to inward-swinging doors, which could not be opened due to the physical pressures exercised by the evacuating occupants. The crowd formed making it impossible to open the door and causing the death of seventy-two people by crushing and suffocation. This provide dramatic examples of the role of the environment on crowd formation, which are now studied with several tools, including models about how crowd are most likely to behave given external constraints such as fire escape route.

1.4 Diversity of Explanatory Tools and the Integration of Theories

The above illustrations show that diverse methods, theoretical resources, and conceptual tools can be fruitfully used for explaining crowd formations. In general, social scientists benefit from using a rich toolkit of explanatory techniques. This is because social phenomena, including crowd formation, arise from diverse causes, ecological or psychological, related to motivations or to other cognitive processes. Thus, a different selection of tools will be appropriate for identifying the role of different causes of social phenomena.

1.4.1 Fields in the Social Sciences as Explanatory Toolkits

In some mythical academic world, each discipline corresponds to a well-specified domain of study, which is best explained on the basis of a unified theory and investigated with some dedicated methods. In that world, all studies happen within a paradigm. The above examples—explanations of crowds—show that the social sciences do not resemble this mythical world. A first difference with the mythical academic world is that there is rarely any agreement about how to define the domain of investigation. Crowds, for instance, might seem to form a rather well-defined social kind. They are the subject of many books and papers and are being modeled with computer simulation. Yet, there is no necessary and sufficient condition for a social phenomenon to qualify as a crowd. The archetypical crowd is a gathering of a large number of people at the same location and at the same time. But the sorites paradox applies when looking for specific criteria: how many people does it take to make a crowd? Also, people packed in a place do not make an archetypical crowd if they do not influence each other's behaviors. Conversely, the folk notion of crowd can be extended to cases where people are not physically next to each other but influence each other at a very rapid rate: that is the case of the crowding on the internet mentioned above.

The problem of circumscribing domains is pervasive in the social sciences. Social and cultural anthropologists, for instance, disagree on the very notion of culture (Boyer 2014) and other key notions (e.g., religion). This is not a weakness of the social sciences compared to the "natural sciences": notions that supposedly identify fields in natural sciences, such as genes and life, are also hotly debated. Most scientific fields do not carve the world at its joints. Still, social scientists do specialize. The specialization is, however, more a question of focus on different aspects of the same phenomena than the study of different phenomena that would presumably belong to different domains. Most importantly, social scientists differ from field to field in that they have at their disposal different explanatory tools. During training and practice, they come to master methodologies and theories, which they diligently put to work for explanation. Thus, fields are not defined in terms of a domain of explananda, but rather through means of explaining and type of explanantia. This raises an important challenge: checking that for a given explanandum, social scientists do not provide incompatible explanations. This does not imply unifying the social science in the sense specified in the first section, but it does imply some interdisciplinary work.

When explaining crowds, social scientists are, thanks to a sufficiently rich explanatory toolkit, able to identify a set of diverse factors that will influence the causal processes that lead to crowd phenomena. The tools put to work for explaining that we mentioned above include the cognitive studies of transmission and imitation, the study of motivated behaviors and how they aggregate, with rational choice theory, and the description of infrastructure for transmission—network science. Each explanatory tool provides a means to identify causes of crowd formation and maintenance and describe their specific effects. Each explanatory tool provides elements of explanation that are not necessarily incompatible with the other explanations. The fact is that crowds result from the conjunction of multiple causes.

Network science is an explanatory tool for identifying ecological factors of crowd formation: they allow the description of structural elements that will direct the distribution of information. But, of course, the content of the distributed information will make a difference. To what extent, for instance, is it coordinating information? Answering this question might require the tools of rational choice theory (including game theoretical notions such as the Schelling point). Likewise, the rich-get-richer structural process might need to be complemented with other factors to explain why one rather than the other item or node became hugely popular. Bianconi and Barabási 2001 have talked about cultural fitness or a node's fitness, which is "its ability to compete for links at the expense of other nodes". Invoking cultural or node's fitness itself does not provide a causal explanation, but it calls our attention to what needs to be further explained: the residue that is not predicted by structural aspects of the network. These further factors are mainly psychological factors. These might involve different types of preferences and motivations, as specified in subsection 1.3.2. or this might involve psychological mechanisms of transmission, as specified in subsection 1.3.1. Thus, combinations of the tools for analyzing the diversity of causal factors will be called for in the study of plausible causal mechanisms and for identifying their causal role in each particular case.

1.4.2 Integration and Pluralism

As the case studies described above show, there is a plurality of methods and explanatory strategies that can be relied upon to understand the different aspects of crowd phenomena. One way to react to such plurality is to take it as a defect of a field which needs to be fixed. This was the goal set by advocates of the unity of science that we mentioned in the introduction. We saw, however, that the disunity does not arise from a lack of understanding of the relations between well-defined domains. Rather, it arises from the multiple means for investigating different causal factors. The causal roles of the factors are best explained with psychology, rational choice theory, network science, and so on. In the face of a plurality of causal factors contributing to a phenomenon, and with factors that are best studied by different approaches, we seem to be left with scattered and possibly incompatible explanations. One could be tempted to stop here: acknowledge the diversity and disunity of the social sciences and resign to their apparent incommensurability as an inevitable outcome of the social world. In contrast, an integrative stance approaches explanatory plurality in the social sciences as raising questions of compatibility and interactions: the goal, then, is not unity and reduction, but the search for more integration, enabling interdisciplinary research.

The integrative stance is an epistemic *attitude* that involves investigating how the plurality of causal factors interact and differentially contribute to some phenomenon. The integrative stance involves allowing multiple apparently incompatible perspectives to cohabit, interact, and enrich one another by offering tools to study different aspects of the same phenomenon. We advocate adopting the integrative stance because it is a way to pursue three epistemic values: consistency, consilience, and complementarity.

Consistency refers to the fact that two different approaches to a same phenomenon are not contradicting one another.

Two approaches are *consilient* when they can identify, and agree on, the role of the causal factors that each of them study. For instance, in the Braess's paradox, the psychological factor is the willingness to shorten as much as possible one's commuting time. The ecological factor is the size of the road, determining how many cars can go at what speed. These two approaches, one analyzing the psychology of drivers and the other the flow of cars, are consilient because one can identify the causal role of each factor in forming traffic jams. Consilience consequently implies that there exists a set of terms common to the consilient approaches and describing the explanandum. In the Braess's paradox, for instance, both approaches agree on one way to describe the explanandum, namely, the time it takes to commute. Note that consilience does not imply commensurability in the classical use of the term: there does not need to be a single overarching theory, a unifying language or common criteria for assessing the scientific validity of an explanation. The diverse explanantia, which identify psychological or ecological causal factors, need not rely on common terms and measures. The commensurability is local: just at the points where the approaches can fruitfully interact and be combined.

Finally, an integrative pluralism celebrates the division of scientific labor so long as *complementarity* is pursued. Complementarity means that what serves as a black box for one approach is an explanandum for another. As each approach focuses on specific causal factors and using special methods devised to understand the causal roles of these factors in bringing about some phenomenon, it is inevitable that other aspects of the phenomenon are either ignored or simplified. However, by dividing the study of the causal factors of some phenomenon, the blind spots of one approach can productively be complemented by the tools of another, thus leading to more comprehensive explanations of the phenomenon. For instance, Barabasi analyzes the causal factors leading to success or popularity that are in the network, but he identifies one variable that network science cannot explain. This variable is black boxed under the term "cultural fitness." A successful complementarity approach would have another approach—a psychological one in that case—taking over and specifying the causes of cultural fitness. What is likely to happen, however, is that the approach called in specifies what it is that they can and cannot explain. Thus, a preliminary work improving consilience might be needed to achieve complementarity.

Adopting an integrative stance does not imply a reductionist perspective where one approach would have to be modified in order to become coherent with the other (e.g., making the social sciences coherent with the natural sciences, which suggests a directionality in the coherence assessment). Instead, an integrative attitude aims at developing better interfaces between the different approaches in order to allow their mutual enrichment and a co-development of their respective research methodologies. Note that we are not describing principles of the scientific method aimed to ground the reliability of science. We are more modestly emphasizing the epistemic value of consistency, consilience, and complementarity and drawing consequences on interdisciplinarity. Likewise, Popper's falsificationism is better understood as an attitude of scientists toward possible refutations, rather than as a principled characterization of "the scientific method" or an order to abandon theories in view of data incompatible with the theories' predictions. To adopt an integrative stance is thus to open the investigation of a particular phenomenon to the possibility that its constitutive elements and causes may be better understood by interdisciplinary efforts. This does not mean that interdisciplinarity should be pursued at all costs. Integration is worth pursuing when and because a richer understanding of a phenomenon benefits from conciliating different approaches together.

Here are examples of the problem of integration involved in the studies of crowd.

- First example, sociological studies of crowd, especially early ones, have often attributed ideas and emotions to the crowd itself. However fruitful this metaphor might be, it prevents consilience with psychology. One field is using the term in one sense, and the other is using the term with another sense. Consilience can be improved by either avoiding the attribution of mental states to sets of people, or by redefining the concepts of ideas and emotions, to the satisfaction of both sociologists of crowds and psychologists. So far, it seems that the best option is the former rather than the latter. In this case, the effort for consilience has to be done by sociologists. Yet, the other option might also be fruitful: for instance, Chalmers and Clark (1998) have been advocating a notion of cognition that is not limited to the bounds of the skull. Memory for instance, could be ascribed to a system that include both a human agent and his notebook containing some relevant information. In that case, the effort for consilience has to be done by both cognitive scientists and sociologists.
- Second example: Economists, including behavioral economists, have been keen to develop models that rigorously describe the observed behavior and have some predictive value—this is rational choice theory. The models can be interpreted in at least two ways. In one interpretation, the models are precise mathematical redescription of observed patterns of behaviors. In another interpretation, the models describe some psychological processes. Thus, an essential variable of models in rational choice theory refer to individual preferences, which is quantified in terms of "utility." The variable can be used eithe to describe behavioral data assuming that agents are rational or to make empirical claims about the actual motives that cause people to make the choices they do. Both usages are consistent with psychology, which can either develop independent theories of motivation or theories that are compatible with, and building upon, findings in experimental and behavioral economics. The interpretation of preferences as psychological facts might be the solution for making economics consilient with current cognitive psychology. Since the 1970s the field of behavioral economics has worked on the consilience between economics and psychology. This effort was celebrated with the prize in economic sciences in the memory of Alfred Nobel delivered to Kahneman and Smith in 2002. In our example of the crowd gathering at Tahrir Square, we do really want to talk about underlying motives as having a causal role in crowd formation.

- Third example: The network science analyses of popularity explicitly state that they identify one factor in the growth of popularity and the consequent distribution. Features of the sociocultural phenomena that cannot be explained with the structure of the network are residual and in need of some other type of explanation. In this way, network science is striving for compatibility with other scientific approaches. But there remains more work to be done for consilience: we want to know how the ecological factors related to the network interact with the psychological factors. For instance, why and when are people led to use and trust the results of search engines?

1.5 Naturalism as an Integrative Stance

The integration advocated above has focused on integration among fields in the social sciences. However, the integrative stance can be applied to fields coming from both the social and natural sciences. As a case of integration in the natural science, Mitchell (2002) documents explanations of the division of labor in social insects. She shows how different approaches—such as evolutionary theory, behavioral genetics, behavioral ecology, and animal learning—are not understood as competitive explanations but can be integrated together to explain both the patterns of division of labor together with their plasticity and apparent self-organization. Closer to the social sciences is the case of archaeology and explanations of site formation, which often involves articulating theories and methods from anthropology, geology, taphonomy, nuclear chemistry, osteology, and many more (Renfrew and Bahn 2008).

We think of naturalism in the social science as the stance of valuing consilience between the social and the natural sciences. It is thus an integrative stance, but one that goes against the historical divide between the social and natural sciences. Naturalism is therefore different from reductionism. For instance, neuro-economics, insofar as it aims to explain economic behavior with the sole means of brain science, is a reductionist project. But it is not consilient with psychology. It bypasses it and thus loses the ability to describe how multiple causes such as beliefs, evolved and learned skills, individual history, motivation, and so on might interact for producing a given behavior. Reductionist projects run the risk of making oversimplification because social phenomena are likely to result from multiple causes of different types. Naturalistic projects, not so much.

Naturalism does not consist either in mimicking or drawing on the methods of natural science. For instance, theories of cultural evolution have made an analogy between the processes of biological evolution and cultural changes (Mesoudi, Whiten, and Laland 2006). This motivated some authors to draw on the models of biological evolution (Boyd and Richerson 1985). The analogy might be justified and fruitful, but it does not make the project a naturalistic one. It does not make biological and cultural theories consilient because it does not matter to theories of evolutionary biology that their models might work for explaining culture and, reciprocally, it does not matter to theories of culture that the model they use comes from evolutionary biology or from elsewhere.

Dan Sperber (1996) is explicitly aiming at developing a naturalistic approach in the social science. He presents a framework theory that allows distributing questions across several fields: to psychology as a most relevant field, but also to any other relevant field able to describe the causes of cultural phenomena. For instance, the chemistry of chert explains its hardness and brittleness, which in turn explains aspects of the production of arrowheads in the Neolithic (Charbonneau 2015). Likewise, crowd formation often results from both intentions, such as the intention to escape, and nonpsychological factors, such as inward rather than outward swinging doors—as illustrated by the Italian Hall disaster. Sperber has especially worked on ways to make cultural anthropology consilient with cognitive psychology. For this, he specified how and when mental representations are causally involved in social and cultural phenomena. He then points out the work that the cognitive revolution and evolutionary psychology have done for making psychology consilient with the natural sciences—investigating, respectively, the material implementation of cognitive processes and the biological evolution of cognitive capacities.

1.6 Conclusion

Following the failure of the unificationist program of the logical positivists and of the reductionist approach, it seems that the social sciences are to remain divided and their different approaches and disciplines insulated. In this chapter, we have argued in favor of an integrative pluralistic stance, where the specificity of the different approaches in the social sciences is celebrated, but where interdisciplinary cohesion and cooperation are strived for. Indeed, the best ways to promote integration and naturalism as we characterized them in this chapter is to focus on causal explanations. Since social phenomena result from multiple causes, the best explanations will make use of the relevant explanatory tools of the fields and disciplines, whether they come from the social or natural sciences.

The integrative pluralism developed here is based on the toolbox metaphor: since social phenomena result from many different causal factors, it is worth having a set of explanatory tools that best afford the production of satisfactory explanations. In our illustrations, we mentioned the following causal factor of crowd formation and maintenance: the psychology of crowd behavior such as the transmission of emotions, incentives for making the choices that lead to crowding, the network, and a multitude of ecological factors. For each of these causal factors, one approach was best endowed for analyzing its role in producing the crowd phenomenon. Our approach to pluralism is a pragmatic one: there exist a set of explanatory tools, let the scientists use the ones that better fit their specific explanatory purposes.

Integrative pluralism promotes an active cooperation and co-development of theories and methodological approaches between the different social sciences. In this, it is different from the many competition-centered approaches of theory-choice that view the coexistence of different theories and methods explaining a same phenomenon as the grounds for the falsification (e.g., Popper), elimination (e.g., Paul Churchland), and/or simply abandonment (e.g., Kuhn) of the "weaker" ones. An integrative pluralism is also distinct from an epistemic anarchism that aims to normatively impose a plurality of scientific approaches in order to stimulate scientific progress (Feyerabend 1975; Chang 2002). Nor, in fact, does it entail that different approaches are inevitably incommensurable, as staunch relativists would have it. Instead, we acknowledge the existence of different explanatory frameworks and argue that interdisciplinary dialogue can obtain when the identification of the causal factors underlying a phenomenon serves as a common epistemic goal. Finally, our defense of pluralism does not rest on a rejection of the metaphysical assumption of monism—that is, that the world is itself one, united thing—nor does it entail that we need to grant reality to various types of entities (Dupré's 1993; "promiscuous realism"). Rather, we argue for an *epistemic* pluralism, the benefit of which is cashed in terms of a complementarity between approaches leading to a more comprehensive understanding of some phenomenon.

Our view of pluralism is in line with Peter Galison's view on scientific disunity and pluralism in the physical sciences. In his *Image and Logic*, Galison (1997) argues for a pluralistic view of physics, showing how theoreticians, experimentalists, and instrument-makers often have very different problems, methods, and languages when working on some common project. However, this plurality becomes productive as the different traditions develop what Galison terms "trading zones," that is, a minimal language that allows the different traditions to exchange and jointly solve problems. The languages so developed are not universal and englobing, the different approaches are not unified, but the benefits of interdisciplinarity are achieved by establishing a common epistemic space of interaction between the traditions. Similarly, we argue that the integration of multiple approaches should rely on three epistemic values, that of consistence, consilience, and complementarity. Instead of striving for a unified theory that would englobe the different methods and theories of the social sciences, aiming toward these epistemic values has the benefit to offer a more comprehensive understanding of the contributions of the different causal factors producing a phenomenon under study.

References

Barabasi, A.-L. 2003. *Linked: How Everything Is Connected to Everything Else and What It Means for Business, Science, and Everyday Life*. New York: Plume.

Bianconi G., and A.-L. Barabási. 2001. "Competition and Multiscaling in Evolving Networks." *EPL* (Europhysics Letters) 54: 436.

Boyd, R., and P. J. Richerson. 1985. *Culture and the Evolutionary Process*. Chicago, IL: University of Chicago Press.

Boyer, P. 2014. "What Scientific Idea Is Ready for Retirement? Culture." *Edge*, available at https://www.edge.org/response-detail/25388.

Chang, H. 2012. *Is Water H20? Evidence, Realism, and Pluralism*. Dordrecht: Springer.

Charbonneau, M. 2015. "Mapping Complex Social Transmission: Technical Constraints on the Evolution Cultures." *Biology & Philosophy* 30: 527–46.

Chwe, M. S.-Y. 2000. "Communication and Coordination in Social Networks." *The Review of Economic Studies* 67: 1–16.

Clark, A., and D. Chalmers. 1998. "The Extended Mind." *Analysis* 58 (1):7–19.

Cronk, L., and B. L. Leech. 2012. *Meeting at Grand Central: Understanding the Social and Evolutionary Roots of Cooperation*. Princeton, NJ: Princeton University Press.
Dezecache, G., P. Jacob, and J. Grèzes. 2015. "Emotional Contagion: Its Scope and Limits." *Trends in Cognitive Sciences* 19 (6) (June 2015): 297–9.
Dezecache, G., L. Conty., M. Chadwick, L. Philip, R. Soussignan, D. Sperber, and J. Grèzes. 2013. "Evidence for Unintentional Emotional Contagion beyond Dyads." *PLoS One* 8 (6): e67371.
Dunn, A. 2011. "Unplugging a Nation: State Media Strategy during Egypt's January 25 Uprising." *Fletcher Forum of World Affairs* 35: 15.
Dupré, J. 1993. *The Disorder of Things: Metaphysical Foundation of the Disunity of Science*. Cambridge, MA: Harvard University Press.
Fahim, K., and M. El-Naggar. 2011. "Emotions of a Reluctant Hero Galvanize Protesters." *The New York Times*, February 8, 2011.
Feyerabend, P. 1975. *Against Method*. London: New Left Books.
Freud, S. 1989. *Group Psychology and the Analysis of the Ego*. New York: Norton.
Friedman, T. 2011. Tulane University—2011 Speaker—Thomas Friedman.
Galison, P. 1997. *Image & Logic: A Material Culture of Microphysics*. Chicago, IL: University of Chicago Press.
Gilovich, T., D. Griffin, and D. Kahneman. 2002. *Heuristics and Biases: The Psychology of Intuitive Judgment*. Cambridge: Cambridge University Press.
Granovetter, M. 1978. "Threshold Models of Collective Behavior." *American Journal of Sociology* 83 (6): 1420–43.
Howard, P., and M. Hussain. 2011. "The Role of Digital Media." *Journal of Democracy* 22: 35–48.
Knoblich, G., and N. Sebanz. 2008. "Evolving Intentions for Social Interaction: From Entrainment to Joint Action." *Philosophical Transactions of the Royal Society of London B: Biological Sciences* 363 (1499): 2021–31.
Le Bon, G. 1896. *The Crowd: A Study of the Popular Mind*. London: T. Fisher Unwin.
Levitt, S., and S. Dubner. 2005. *Freakonomics: A Rogue Economist Explores the Hidden Side of Everything*. New York: William Morrow.
Little, D. 1991. *Varieties of Social Explanation*. Boulder, CO: Westview.
Marsh, K. L., M. J. Richardson, and R. C. Schmidt. 2009. "Social Connection through Joint Action and Interpersonal Coordination." *Topics in Cognitive Science* 1 (2): 320–39.
Mesoudi, A. 2016. "Cultural Evolution: Integrating Psychology, Evolution and Culture." *Current Opinion in Psychology* 7: 17–22.
Mesoudi, A., A. Whiten, and K. N. Laland. 2006. "Towards a Unified Science of Cultural Evolution." *Behavioral and Brain Sciences* 29 (4): 329–47.
Mitchell, S. D. 2002. "Integrative Pluralism." *Biology and Philosophy* 17: 55–70.
Morin, O. 2015. *How Traditions Live and Die*. Oxford: Oxford University Press.
Popper, Karl R. 1968. "Remarks on the Problems of Demarcation and of Rationality." In *Problems in the Philosophy of Science*, ed. I. Lakatos, A. Musgrave. Amsterdam: North-Holland.
Porterie, B., N. Zekri, J. P. Clerc, and J. C. Loraud. 2007. "Modeling Forest Fire Spread and Spotting Process with Small World Networks." *Combustion and Flame* 149 (1): 63–78.
Renfrew, C., and P. Bahn. 2008. *Archaeology: Theories, Methods and Practice*. London: Thames & Hudson.
Sperber, D. 1996. *Explaining Culture: A Naturalistic Approach*. Oxford: Blackwell.
Sperber, D. 2001. "Conceptual Tools for a Natural Science of Society and Culture." *Proceedings of the British Academy* 111: 297–318.

Stepanova, E. 2011. "The Role of Information Communication Technologies in the 'Arab Spring.'" *PONARS Eurasia Policy Memo* 159: 1–6.

Tarde, G. 1901. *L'Opinion et la Foule*. Paris: Félix Alcan.

Tarde, G. 1903. *The Laws of Imitation*. New York: Henry Holt.

Tomasello, M. 2009. *The Cultural Origins of Human Cognition*. Cambridge, MA: Harvard University Press.

Trotter, W. 1916. *Instincts of the Herd in Peace and War*. London: T. Fisher Unwin.

Tubbs, J. and B. Meacham, 2007. *Egress Design Solutions: A Guide to Evacuation and Crowd Management Planning*. Hoboken, NJ: John Wiley.

Williams Associates. 2011. Egyptian Public Opinion Survey, April 14–27.

Zahle, J. 2016. "Methodological Holism in the Social Sciences." In *The Stanford Encyclopedia of Philosophy* (Summer 2016 Edition), ed. Edward N. Zalta. https://plato.stanford.edu/archives/sum2016/entries/holism-social/. Metaphysics Research Lab, Stanford: Stanford University.

Commentary: Plurality and Pluralisms for the Social Sciences

Raffaella Campaner

Heintz, Charbonneau, and Fogelman present plurality as a hallmark of the social sciences. Taking investigations on crowd formation and dissipation as relevant case studies, they argue for methodological pluralism, claiming that an integrative stance encompassing a range of different approaches is the best strategy to address the multiplicity of causes and varied aspects of social phenomena. Pluralistic views have met with growing consent in recent philosophy of science, largely concomitant with an increasing interest in the special sciences, their specific methodologies and conceptual tools, and in scientific practice. By highlighting a few differences in possible ways of being pluralists, this contribution aims to provide some epistemological tools to further detail the authors' discourse on pluralism, and to question if it can qualify as a permanent stance for the social sciences.

1. Plurality and Pluralism

Philosophical reflections on pluralism have given rise to myriad views in the last few decades, touching upon a whole range of—largely interrelated—issues from scientific theories to causation, explanation, and evidence. Some of these views have tackled science and scientific method as such, while others have addressed specific disciplinary fields and the special issues they face.

While both "plurality" and "pluralism" are the leitmotifs of much current philosophical work on the scientific enterprise, they must not be confused. Pluralist positions stem from the acknowledgement of a plurality of elements related to the construction of scientific knowledge in a given domain, but they do not coincide with it. Many scientific fields—some would argue all of them—display a plurality of methodologies, explanatory accounts, theories, and conceptual tools. Disciplines can exhibit plurality at different stages of their development in time, or when dealing with different sorts of phenomena, or different aspects of the same phenomena, or when pursing different research programs, when having different epistemic aims, or when different groups of researchers are at work. The elaboration of *pluralistic* positions has specifically to do with philosophical considerations over the implications that such *pluralities* might have with respect to our expectations on the goals science should have, over whether or not science must aim at a single method, at universal laws, single explanatory and predictive procedures, and general shared concepts. Pluralism has to do with our orientations and commitments on scientific discourse and the forms of plurality it might exhibit.

Acknowledgment of the variety of natural phenomena and their features, for example, of complexity in the biological world (see Mitchell 2003), has been accompanied by claims on separateness and disunity in nature (see Dupré 1993; Cartwright 1994, 1999). Without entering into metaphysical issues, I will focus here on epistemological problems and discuss different ways of tackling plurality from pluralistic standpoints, in line with the methodological concerns expressed by Heintz, Charbonneau, and Fogelman (henceforth HCF). Once the distinction between plurality and pluralism has been clarified, we shall reflect on how pluralism can be defined, what it exactly amounts to, and what basic ideas most pluralists would generally agree upon. What all "pluralisms" seem to share is not just the acknowledgment of a range of different possible epistemic tools but an *explicit endorsement* of the multiplicity of perspectives, notions, and methodological approaches. Not only is there a plurality of methods and theories in scientific research and practice, but this is an added value, and should be strongly preferred over monistic attempts to reduce, neglect, or overcome plurality.

Pluralism implies some positive evaluation of present plurality. It will not take some single view to be clearly the best in all respects, and it will not condemn all those not conforming to some established "orthodoxy" as somehow inferior. The next section examines how different views on what pluralism amounts to can take different stances with respect to not only how scientific research is currently pursued but also how it should be pursued, and ultimately with respect to the very "fate of [scientific] knowledge" (Longino 2002).

2. Varieties of Philosophical Pluralism

Without aspiring to provide an exhaustive list of the perspectives available in the current philosophical debate, I will present some of the leading and most successful views on pluralism, outlining their characterizing features and general implications.[1]

Among the most prominent pluralist positions, Sandra Mitchell's *integrative pluralism* (Mitchell 2002, 2003) emphasizes explanatory issues and possible complementarity among different approaches. Previous works by Mitchell (Mitchell 1992; Mitchell et al. 1997) distinguish between *competitive* and *compatible pluralism*. The competitive approach takes the competition between different theories or research programs as the best strategy to test them severely and thereby enhance scientific progress. It helps scientific communities face problems related to theory choice given available evidence and the fact that currently accepted theories might not be those deserving the highest epistemic trust in the future in light of further evidence (see Kitcher 1990). Competitive pluralism can be seen as strategic, and merely temporary, to be employed as a means to achieve the acceptance of a single true theory in the long run. Compatible pluralism, on the other hand, sees alternatives as not mutually exclusive, and has been widely recognized—especially in the biological sciences—with respect to different explanatory accounts and different levels of analysis. While grasping some real features of biology, this approach might fail to entertain a crucial insight of pluralism, namely the role of various alternatives in tackling *one and the same* feature of a given phenomenon. In the end, it might isolate single levels of analysis, neglecting the wealth of mutually interacting processes and separating disciplinary fields and research groups. In other words, compatible pluralism runs the risk of turning into *isolationist pluralism*.

As a way to overcome the ambiguities of pluralistic standpoints and to analyze how various models of the same phenomenon are related, Mitchell puts forward *integrative pluralism* to distinguish between theoretical modeling and the application of models to specific complex phenomena. "At the theoretical level pluralism is sanctioned," while "at the concrete explanatory level … integration is required," since "however many contributing causes participated, there is only one causal history that, in fact, has generated a phenomenon to be explained" (Mitchell 2002: 66). Pluralism will continue to hold in modeling potential contributing causes, but not in the application of such models in specific explanations, where they must be integrated: "pluralism with respect to models can and should coexist with integration in the generation of explanations of complex and varied biological phenomena" (68). In between integrative and isolationist pluralism, *interactive pluralism* has been advocated, which claims that "satisfactory explanations can also be obtained without integration of multiple levels" and, while not establishing an integration imperative, "does not discourage interaction as, in some instances, interaction and integration do lead to better explanations" (van Bouwel 2014: 109).

Pluralism can be taken as an overall attitude to science as such, how it should be pursued and what we can expect from it, but—as has just emerged—it also addresses more specific issues, such as explanation and causation. *Explanatory pluralism* argues for the rejection of a winner-takes-all view, in favor of the employment of different explanatory approaches, taking different features of the explananda and different relations holding among them as explanatorily relevant.[2] Different explanatory accounts may be adopted according to the specific kind of phenomenon we are dealing with, the features of the phenomenon or the levels of organization we are tackling, the researcher's background knowledge and that of those to whom the explanation is to be conveyed, the final purpose of the explanation, and our further epistemic aims. For explanatory pluralism to be genuine, we always have to make sure that the competing explanatory accounts are actually addressing the same object and the same explanatory question. Otherwise, available explanations will not be genuinely different explanations of the same explanandum, and the plurality of explanations will not be much of an issue. *Causal pluralism* has, in turn, been presented in various guises. Generally speaking, it argues that there is no such thing as *the* causal relation: when talking about causation, we deal with different kinds of relations in different systems and/or different concepts and theories to capture them. Causation can be conceived in terms of, for example, productive, difference-making, and probability-raising relations and can be analyzed by mechanistic, manipulative, and counterfactual theories. Causal pluralism can be advanced into ontological, conceptual, and epistemological versions and questions, among others, whether causal discourse can be tackled in the same terms across different fields.[3]

Is pluralism here to stay? This is one of the crucial questions to address when discussing different forms of pluralism: does pluralism have to do with some provisional feature of our construction of knowledge, to be eventually overcome by changes in, for example, methodological, experimental, and conceptual tools, or does it stand as a permanent perspective whose fate will persist over time? Different answers are provided. The so-called *moderate pluralism* implies a temporary copresence of alternative theories aimed at achieving some form of unity in the long run. Other views stress how pluralism seems to persist in disciplines that have significantly progressed, as a symptom not of the allegedly immature character of investigations, but rather of the complexity of the systems under enquiry and of the interfield work addressing them. Hasok Chang advocates pluralism as a permanent feature of scientific endeavour we should all, normatively, strive for. His *active normative epistemic pluralism* claims that different approaches must be enhanced insofar as they address different epistemic aims (e.g., describing, explaining, predicting, measuring, classifying, etc.) and satisfy different—sometimes divergent—epistemic values (e.g., simplicity and completeness). Pluralism offers twofold benefits: toleration amounts to "insurance against unpredictability, compensation for the limitations of each system, and multiple satisfaction of any given aim," while interaction includes "the integration of different systems for specific purposes, the co-optation of beneficial elements across systems, and the productive competition between systems" (Chang 2012: 253). Chang stresses how pluralistic science does *not* abdicate its freedom and responsibility to interpret and evaluate scientific work, dissipate resources, admit of *any* simultaneous contribution whatsoever, and end up in relativism.[4] It is not the pursuit of some "anything goes" kind of trend, but the commitment to promote a motivated and justified "many things can go" attitude.

Pluralism is also related to the social nature of scientific investigations. Longino (2002) has stressed how researchers working, for example, in the biological sciences, present a wide array of different expertise, employ different theories and methodological approaches within open debate, and are subject to critical review, with no primacy of a specific subfield or standpoint over the others. Research being pursued in multiple directions is required to proceed transparently, making use of processes of peer review, and can provide simultaneously independent and/or interconnected views in a multidisciplinary context. Scientific communities benefit from entertaining numerous perspectives to investigate phenomenal intricacy, and the social nature of scientific activity is held to further support epistemological pluralism. Epistemological reflections thus bring with them considerations on the relations between science and politics—more specifically between democratic societies and the construction of pluralistic knowledge.[5]

3. Crowd Formation and Methodological Pluralism

Let us now turn to the case study discussed by HCF and to their epistemological concerns. HCF's discourse starts off with the recognition that the social sciences are characterized by "a plurality of theoretical approaches, methodological tools, and explanatory strategies," and that "different fields rely on different methods and explanatory tools even when they study the very same phenomena" (HCF: 11). Pluralism is introduced because "the plurality of causes of social phenomena invite for a diversity of methodological and theoretical tools" (HCF: 11). Different toolkits are needed in order to grasp the multiplicity of causal factors bringing about social phenomena, and pluralism is given a disciplinary flavour, showing how crowd phenomena are investigated by psychology, rational choice theory, and network theory—which are claimed to provide complementary explanatory accounts.

Crowds are presented as the objects of quite distant investigations. Psychology and cognitive science study them in terms of "contagion" of ideas, behavioral inclinations, emotions, and the herd instinct, responsible for making people gather in large groups, as when marching or chanting together. Rational choice theory, on the other hand, focuses on unintended and intended crowd formation and explains it on the basis of information cascade, where the crowd is the unintended consequence of what people take to be the best choice for themselves—for example, crowd forming in a restaurant, while the one next door remains empty—or the intended consequence of motivated behaviors that aggregate starting from a first salient event—for example, crowds forming for revolutionary purposes, as during the Arab Spring. Yet another view is provided by network science, which aims to model connections among people accounting for the distribution of coordinating information and the maintenance of virtual crowds, analyzing infrastructure for transmission (e.g., the distribution of website popularity).

To evaluate the meaning and role of pluralism as a theoretical option, we shall first of all establish what exactly we are being pluralists about. In discussing crowd formation and maintenance, do the different accounts actually address *the same* phenomena? Do psychology, rational choice theory, and network theory tackle *the same explanandum*? Are we identifying different causes of the same phenomenon, due to different standpoints or different epistemic aims, or are we considering different phenomena altogether, and providing answers to different why-questions? A careful elaboration of a fruitful pluralist approach preliminarily means drawing the boundaries within which our pluralistic perspective is put to work. We shall hence make clear, for instance, to what extent such phenomena as intended and unintended crowds, marching and sitting in a restaurant, promoting a revolution or a website can be taken as the same object of investigation on which alternative accounts are provided.

Once we establish exactly which object pluralism is targeting, we need to consider in which sense it can count as explanatory pluralism. According to HCF, "social scientists benefit from using a rich *toolkit of explanatory techniques*. This is because social phenomena, including crowd formation, arise from *diverse causes*, ecological or psychological, related to *motivations* or to other *cognitive processes*. Thus, a different selection of tools will be appropriate for identifying the role of different causes of social phenomena" (HCF: 18–19, italics added). As already stressed, multiple possible causes are per se neither necessary nor sufficient to force pluralism and to abandon the search for some unique overarching explanatory account. Pluralism is selected here as the most fruitful option to do justice to a variety of elements, which, while related, should not be conflated. What we are presented with is a wide field of investigation—the social sciences—with a plurality of explanatory methodologies, dealing with different kinds of causes, in the light of various motivations and epistemic interests. Accordingly, explanatory pluralism can be understood as having multiple facets. It might regard which different core *relations* are to be taken as explanatory, whether, for example, causal, unificationist, functional, or other, and, if causal, which relation is deemed to be at play (e.g., mechanistic or manipulative-counterfactual). If it is the diverse causes we are focusing on, pluralism will be dealing not only or primarily with explanatory relations but also with different kinds of *relata*. Moreover, HCF acknowledge an important role played by motivations and final *epistemic aims*, that is, the reasons we are looking for an explanation and what in the end we will use the explanatory content for. What is worth stressing is that explanatory pluralism itself has to do not just with the plurality of causes and current variety of methods devised to tackle them, but with the very idea of what "explaining" amounts to. It can involve the relata of the explanatory relation and the ways to identify them, the very nature of the explanatory relation, the purpose for which the explanation is sought, and the epistemic values by which the adequacy of the explanation will be evaluated.

4. On the Integrative Stance: From Plurality to Pluralism, and Back

HCF take pluralism to have a specific epistemic purpose, advocating an "integrative stance" to improve compatibility and consilience among fields, and to foster interdisciplinarity. To fully understand HCF's position, we shall ask whether this is a provisional proposal, or whether embracing a whole range of separate and distinctive methods is conceived as a permanent approach. How can integrative pluralism be implemented? Can it eventually be resolved, with some unitary picture to emerge in the long run, or is pluralism here to stay?

HCF do not defend just tolerant pluralism, that is, mutual respect and the coexistence of different approaches, or interactive pluralism, where different views are encouraged to cross-fertilize the soil, but *integrative* pluralism, which asks for some *joint* bloom to blossom out. Integration, it is argued, "involves allowing multiple apparently incompatible perspectives to cohabit, interact, and enrich one another by offering tools to study different aspects of a same phenomenon" (HCF: 20–21). The integrative stance is specifically advocated to pursue three epistemic values: consistency, consilience, and complementarity. Consistency has to do with the different approaches not contradicting each other; consilience with the role of the causal factors they study—with just local commensurability; complementarity with the division of scientific labour, with each field of expertise focusing on a few factors, simplifying or bracketing the others; and then all covering each other's blind spots.

With respect to crowd formation, HCF recommend interdisciplinary integration between disciplines belonging in principle to both the social and the natural sciences, to make the most out of the different causal explanatory approaches developed within different fields. They advocate an integrative pluralistic stance to ensure interdisciplinary cohesion and cooperation by focusing on causal explanations. Different explanatory tools are adopted for the integration of theories in order to avoid epistemic anarchism, staunch relativism, or strong incommensurability, and to favour "a *complementarity* between approaches leading *to a more comprehensive understanding* of some phenomenon" (HCF: 25, italics added). While coherence and consilience seem less problematic, I believe integration through complementarity merits further reflection and constitutes a critical aspect to fully grasp the whole perspective HCF suggest.

In the first place, we shall make clear on which features explanatory integration shall focus. For integration to be fruitful, we should start by positing some common language and conceptual toolbox between the fields of enquiry involved, to allow a shared terrain of communication and exchange. Building on that, some insights should be provided regarding the level of description of the exact object of the purported integration. It should be specified whether we are supposed to integrate explanations of some "archetypical crowd," like the simultaneous gathering of a very large number of people at the same (real or virtual) location, in very general terms, or some more specific phenomenon, like virtual crowding on the internet or, rather, people converging in a square for political reasons, or, even more specifically, some instantiation of a crowd, for example, during the Arab Spring in Egypt. Is explanatory integration to be pursued in accounts at the type or token level? HCF state: "combinations of the tools for analyzing the diversity of causal factors will be called for in the study of plausible causal mechanisms and for identifying their causal role in each particular case" (20). For integration—and not just compatibility—of causal explanations and mechanistic accounts to take place, the boundaries of the target system and the graininess of the analysis must be very carefully specified.

Second, should we believe that integration would necessarily and always lead to better explanations? How can we be sure it will always yield the most adequate answer to a given question? As highlighted, motivations and final epistemic purposes affect the choice of a given explanatory account as the most adequate in a given context. Furthermore, for integration to be pursued, explanatory models must be commensurable, which might not always be the case. Thus, while it is worth testing compatibility between different explanations to see whether fruitful *interactions* between them can be performed, that *integration* will always be possible and always constitute the preferred strategy to fit specific explanatory purposes is debatable, and cannot just be assumed as an uncontroversial starting point.

Third, how can we combine the idea that we are not striving for a single unified theory, yet at the same time argue for an epistemic pluralism the benefit of which is given by a complementarity between approaches leading to a *more comprehensive understanding* of the phenomenon at stake? What would a "more comprehensive understanding" consist in, and with respect to which aims should it be measured? Would a more comprehensive understanding of crowd formation and dissipation be, for instance, more inclusive, or more detailed, or carry higher predictive power? And should we then take integration to be progressively pursued toward some sort of "*most comprehensive* understanding"? Both the second and third points raised here seem to suggest that an interactive pluralism should rather be preferred over an integrative one if the variety of approaches in the social sciences and their genuinely specific features are to be both respected and cultivated—if, so to speak, after going from plurality to pluralism, we want to endorse pluralism in order to preserve the richness of plurality.

Concluding, I'd like to stress that HCF's proposal includes different suggestions that might elicit different reactions. The advocacy of different methods and kinds of explanations to study different aspects of the same phenomena, the claim that different explanations can be compatible, and the plea for interdisciplinary work all seem straightforward and agreeable. Whether they also, and necessarily, commit us to integration, and how that shall be achieved merit, instead, a qualified reading and might need further reflection. The challenge HCF must meet is how to have not only interaction, but integration, while bearing in mind that "the degrees of integration, like the degrees of accuracy and simplicity, will be a function both of what is possible and of the purposes to which we intend to put the knowledge" (Longino 2005: 193), with no guarantee that integration can be achieved, and no expression of faith to be made in that respect. Given the reasons that motivate it, pluralism must be promoted as a way to enhance plurality and its role, over and above any specific, "winning" position related to a single epistemic aim, even were it integrative.

Notes

1 For possible taxonomies of pluralism, see, for example, Kellert, Longino, and Waters (2006); Mitchell (2009); and van Bouwel (2014).
2 Explanatory pluralism has also been addressed with a specific focus on the social sciences (Little 1991; van Bouwel 2004; van Bouwel and Weber 2008), and with disciplines at the crossroads of the natural and the social sciences, such as psychiatry (see Kendler 2008; Campaner 2014).
3 See, for example Cartwright (2004), Campaner and Galavotti (2007), Godfrey-Smith (2009), and Psillos (2009).
4 Let us stress that relativism, in turn, does not per se imply pluralism: relativism demands that *actually existing* alternatives are all treated on a par, but does not commit to any requirement that a multiplicity of alternatives *should be* in place.
5 See also Longino (1990) and Kitcher (2001).

References

Campaner, R. 2014. "Pluralism in Psychiatry: What Are We Pluralists about, and Why?" In *New Directions in the Philosophy of Science*, ed. M. C. Galavotti, D. Dieks, W. Gonzalez, S. Hartmann, and T. Uebel, 87–103. Dordrecht: Springer.

Campaner, R., and M. C. Galavotti. 2007. "Plurality in Causality." In *Thinking about Causes*, ed. P. Machamer and G. Wolters, 178–99. Pittsburgh, PA: Pittsburgh University Press.

Cartwright, N. 1994. "Fundamentalism vs. the Patchwork of Laws." *Proceedings of the Aristotelian Society* 94: 279–92.

Cartwright, N. 1999. *The Dappled World: A Study of the Boundaries of Science.* Cambridge: Cambridge University Press.

Cartwright, N. 2004. "Causation: One Word, Many Things." *Philosophy of Science* 71: 805–19.

Chang, H. 2012. *Is Water H_2O? Evidence, Realism and Pluralism*. Dordrecht: Springer.

Dupré, J. 1993. *The Disorder of Things: Metaphysical Foundations of the Disunity of Science*. Cambridge, MA: Harvard University Press.

Godrefy-Smith, P. 2009. "Causal Pluralism." In *The Oxford Handbook of Causation*, ed. H. Beebee, C. Hitchock and P. Menzies, 326–37. Oxford: Oxford University Press.

Heintz, C., M. Charbonneau, and J. Fogelman. This volume. "Integration and the Disunity of the Social Sciences." 11–27.

Hitchcock, C. 2003. "Of Humean Bondage." *British Journal for the Philosophy of Science* 54: 1–25.

Kellert, S., H. Longino, and K. Waters, eds. 2006. *Scientific Pluralism*. Minneapolis: University of Minnesota Press.

Kendler, K. 2008. "Explanatory Models for Psychiatric Illness." *APA* 165: 695–702.

Kitcher, P. 1990. "The Division of Cognitive Labor." *Journal of Philosophy* 87: 5–22.

Kitcher, P. 2001. *Science, Truth, and Democracy*. New York: Oxford University Press.

Little, D. 1991. *Varieties of Social Explanation*. Boulder, CO: Westview Press.

Longino, H. 1990. *Science as Social Knowledge*, Princeton, NJ: Princeton University Press.

Longino, H. 2002. *The Fate of Knowledge*, Princeton, NJ: Princeton University Press.

Longino, H. 2005. "Complexity and Diversity All the Way." *Metascience* 14: 185–94.

Mitchell, S. 1992. "On Pluralism and Competition in Evolutionary Explanations." *American Zoologist* 32: 135–44.

Mitchell, S. 2002. "Integrative Pluralism." *Biology and Philosophy* 17: 55–70.

Mitchell, S. 2003. *Biological Complexity and Integrative Pluralism*. Cambridge: Cambridge University Press.

Mitchell, S. 2009. *Unsimple Truth. Science, Complexity and Policy*. Chicago, IL: University of Chicago Press.

Mitchell, S., L. Daston, G. Gigerenzer, N. Sesardic, and P. Sleep. 1997. "The Why's and How's of Interdisciplinarity." In *Human by Nature: Between Biology and the Social Sciences*, ed. P. Weingart, S. Mitchell, P. Richerson, and S. Maasen,103–50. Mahwah, NJ: Erlbaum Press.

Psillos, S. 2009. "Causal Pluralism." In *Worldviews, Science and Us: Studies of Analytical Metaphysics: A Selection of Topics from a Methodological Perspective*, ed. R. Vanderbeeken and B. D'Hooghe, 131–51. Singapore: World Scientific Publishers.

Van Bouwel, J. 2004. "Explanatory Pluralism in Economics: Against the Mainstream?" *Philosophical Explorations* 7: 299–315.

Van Bouwel, J. 2014. "Pluralists about Pluralism? Different Versions of Explanatory Pluralism in Psychiatry." In *New Directions in the Philosophy of Science*, ed. M. C. Galavotti, D. Dieks, W. Gonzalez, S. Hartmann, and T. Uebel, 105–19. Dordrecht: Springer.

Van Bouwel, J., and E. Weber. 2008. "A Pragmatic Defense of Non-relativistic Explanatory Pluralism in History and Social Science." *History and Theory* 47: 168–82.

2

The Eroding Artificial-Natural Distinction?

Some Consequences for Ecology and Economics

C. Tyler DesRoches, S. Andrew Inkpen, and Tom L. Green

2.1 Introduction

Since the publication of Thomas Kuhn's *The Structure of Scientific Revolutions* (1962), historians and philosophers of science have paid increasing attention to the implications of disciplinarity. For Kuhn, rigid disciplinary training was essential for progress within periods of "normal" science. "A commitment to a discipline," as Andrew Barry and colleagues put it, "is a way of ensuring that certain disciplinary methods and concepts are used rigorously and that undisciplined and undisciplinary objects, methods and concepts are ruled out" (Barry et al. 2008). This "ruling out" is valuable as it discourages intellectual wandering or false-starts, but it is also, and necessarily, normatively restrictive: the ideal of disciplinary purity—that each discipline is defined by a commitment to an appropriate, unique set of objects, methods, theories, and aims—has powerful implications for the structure and practices of many sciences, including life sciences, such as ecology, and social sciences, such as economics. This ideal has governed, and continues to govern, what ecologists and economists do, since it serves as a normative guidepost that establishes, in particular, which objects of study are appropriate and endogenous: pure ecologists are to study non-anthropogenic or "natural" factors, and economists are to study a specific set of anthropogenic causal factors, or an aspect of what might be termed the "artificial" realm.

While articulating the historical formation and full set of connections between the artificial-natural distinction and ideals of disciplinarity in ecology and economics is beyond the scope of this chapter, we provide evidence below to support the claims that (1) historically, the objects of ecology have been "natural" and those of the political economy "artificial" (in the sense that the causes are exclusively human) and that (2) this has been one important factor hindering interdisciplinary exchange (though, obviously, it hasn't made exchange impossible).[1] Attempting to sever the connection between the artificial-natural distinction and proper practice in these sciences, we argue that this distinction is conceptually and empirically problematic. We recognize that the artificial-natural distinction can be drawn in a number of ways, but argue that if this distinction is interpreted as dividing all phenomena into two sui generis categories—artificial versus natural objects of study—then the distinction, along with a commitment to it as defining appropriate objects of study, is problematic. In other words, this distinction should no longer serve as the mechanism that determines the objects of study for ecology and economics.

What, then, are the appropriate objects of study for ecology and economics? We claim that, in many cases, such objects are better viewed as a blend of the artificial and the natural, or what one might describe as *entangled phenomena*, rather than phenomena that are merely natural or merely artificial. Because entangled phenomena are a *shared* object of study, it remains an open question whether it is best for each science to operate independently or engage in interdisciplinary exchange. We argue that, if the goal of ecology and economics is to develop stronger predictions and explanations, and to develop better policy prescriptions, then the evidence suggests that interdisciplinary exchange is preferable, for epistemological and policy-oriented reasons, to these two sciences acting independently. Entangled phenomena, and the transdisciplinary questions they encourage, require interdisciplinary treatments.

The arguments of this chapter are divided into four additional sections. In Section 2 we draw selectively on a long philosophical tradition of analyzing the artificial-natural distinction in order to argue that the distinction is conceptually problematic, if understood as a binary; it should, instead, be understood as a continuum. In Section 3 we demonstrate that the objects of ecology have been "natural" and those of the political economy "artificial," and that this has been one factor hindering interdisciplinary exchange. In Section 4 we empirically problematize the artificial-natural distinction by providing recent case studies that highlight the benefits of treating objects of study as entangled phenomena. In the final section we draw out some of the implications of our analysis. Our main point is this: if disciplinary purity rests on the artificial-natural distinction, then it is in trouble for both conceptual and empirical reasons.

2.2 The Artificial-Natural Distinction?

The artificial-natural distinction is problematic in two senses that are relevant for the sciences of ecology and economics. We can think of these two senses as two separate questions: a conceptual question (can the distinction be clearly drawn?) and an empirical question (is it useful to draw the distinction?). These questions come apart insofar as it may be useful to draw the distinction *even if* it is ultimately conceptually problematic (e.g., it might be useful to categorize landscapes as artificial or natural for practical purposes, even if urban landscapes are also, in a widely accepted sense, natural). In this section we address the conceptual question and argue that relying on this distinction is a questionable strategy. This literature has become so vast that, in this section, we can only briefly consider some of the ways in which the distinction, particularly that originally developed by Aristotle and promulgated by John Stuart Mill ([1874] 2006), has been problematized.

For Aristotle, the concept of "nature" has several meanings (Kelsey 2003; DesRoches 2014). His most prominent concept denotes an inner principle of change that is characteristic of self-moving things. Unlike artificial objects, natural objects are involved in a process of growth, change, and flux. Nature, in this sense, is deeply intertwined with how things behave when left to themselves, free from intentional human agency.

In Book II of the *Physics*, Aristotle gives the famous example of a wooden bed. While the shape and structure of the bed has been fashioned by an intentional human agent, the carpenter, this formal cause is merely "human impositions on the unchanged matter that remains a natural product" (Bensaude-Vincent and Newman 2007: 5). If one were to plant the bed in the ground and that bed were to sprout anything at all, it would not generate beds, but trees. In this case, the inner principle of change or motion is independent of the form that is imposed on it by the carpenter and the nature of the object is associated with the unchanged matter. In this sense of "nature," the natural world would be one that owed its entire existence to natural causes and, therefore, would exclude all intentional human activity. This world would be one populated by objects, whether biotic or abiotic, without any forms imposed on them from without. It would be a world that was left entirely to itself, independent of human agency. With this concept of nature, one can easily imagine a contrary world, where there is no biotic or abiotic items that are left to be naturally expressed, where every last object and bit of material has been subject to the intentional activity of human agents.

There is perhaps no greater classical authority on the artificial-natural distinction than John Stuart Mill ([1874] 2006). In his *Three Essays on Religion*, Mill considers a variety of possible meanings of "nature," but eventually boils his analysis down to two distinct concepts, one of which is clearly inspired by the Aristotelian concept of nature described above. Mill states,

> In one sense, [nature] means all powers existing in either the outer or inner world and everything which takes place by means of those powers. In another sense, it means, not everything which happens, but only what takes place without the agency, or without the voluntary and intentional agency, of man. ([1874] 2006: 375)

In this quotation, Mill's first concept of nature denotes everything actual and everything possible, including human agents and their intentional activities. The second concept of nature, the one that Mill himself prefers, drives a wedge between intentional human agency and that realm of phenomena that has not yet been affected by human agency (Schabas 1995). On this account, human beings and their intentional activities are, in some sense, special. They are the only creatures in the universe that are beyond or "outside of" nature.

Our claim is that the idea of disciplinary purity exemplifies Mill's second concept of nature since it alone provides the resources for making a distinction between nature and nonhuman nature, as objects that are different *in kind*. Pure ecologists exclude human beings and their intentional activities from their models and theories, because they are not believed to be a part of nature (in Mill's second sense). The object of study for pure economic theory is a subset of intentional human activity or anthropogenic causal factors. Mill's second concept of nature has the resources to explain and justify why there would be such separate sciences: there are different objects of study to which each science applies. Mill's first concept of nature, by contrast, denies the possibility of this kind of exclusion since nothing, including human beings and their intentional activities, can be unnatural.

But, while this second Millian concept of nature may help to explain the idea of disciplinary purity as it applies to ecology and economics, the concept is far from unproblematic. For one, the extension of this concept appears to be empty. Strictly speaking, there is no longer any part of the earth's surface that remains completely unaffected by human technologies (Bensaude-Vincent and Newman 2007; Wapner 2010). In his *The End of Nature* Bill Mckibben states,

> An idea, a relationship, can go extinct just like an animal or a plant. The idea in this case is "nature," the separate and wild province, the world apart from man to which he has adapted, under whose rules he was born and died. In the past we have spoiled and polluted parts of that nature, inflicted environmental "damage" ... We never thought we had wrecked nature. Deep down, we never really thought that we could: it was too big and too old. Its forces, the wind, the rain, the sun—were too strong, too elemental. But, quite by accident, it turned out that the carbon dioxide and other gases we were producing in pursuit of a better life—in pursuit of warm houses and eternal economic growth and agriculture so productive it would free most of us for other work—*could* alter the power of the sun, could increase its heat. And that increase could change the patterns of moisture and dryness, breed storms in new places, breed deserts. Those things may or may not have begun to happen, but it is too late to prevent them from happening. We have produced carbon dioxide—we have ended nature. We have not ended rainfall or sunlight ... But the meaning of the wind, the sun, the rain—of nature—has already changed. (Mckibben 1990: 43–4)

Of course, Mckibben's (1990) claim that nature is dead is not meant to suggest that there is nothing left that is actual and possible—Mill's first concept of Nature—but simply that there is no longer any part of the earth's surface that can be truly described as completely detached from human agency.

Ever since McKibben's influential discussion of nature, the idea that humans play a dominant role in the world's ecosystems has been continuously and strongly reinforced. Moreover, we are, since 2000, increasingly inundated by a burgeoning literature on "the Anthropocene," which holds that human presence in the natural world is so pervasive it marks a new geological epoch (Bensaude-Vincent and Newman 2007; Steffen et al. 2011; Sarkar 2012; Church and Regis 2012; Kaebnick 2014; Vogel 2015). It is now estimated that 75 percent of ice-free land on Earth has been transformed by humans, changing ecosystem patterns and processes across the terrestrial biosphere (Vitousek et al. 1997; Ellis and Ramankutty 2008; Martin et al. 2012; Ellis et al. 2013). Paul Wapner (2010), in his recent book *Living through the End of Nature*, writes, "the wildness of nature has indeed largely disappeared as humans have placed their signature on all the earth's ecosystems" (2010: 19). He continues,

> a growing human population, unparalleled technological prowess, increasing economic might, and an insatiable consumptive desire are propelling us to reach further across, dig deeper into, and more intensively exploit the earth's resources, sinks, and ecosystem services … the cumulative force of our numbers, power, and technological mastery has swept humans across and deeply into all ecosystems to the point where one can no longer easily draw a clean distinction between the human and nonhuman realms. (Wapner 2010: 4)

Beyond planet Earth, the technology of our species is now so vast that it has extended past the sublunar region to include the Cydonia (the region of Mars) (Bensaude-Vincent and Newman 2007).

It would appear that the claim that there is some pure realm of phenomena on Earth that remains unaffected by human agency is false since there is nothing left on Earth that remains unaffected by human agency. Mill's two concepts of nature appear to present us with a dilemma. Accepting Mill's second concept of nature appears to explain the idea of disciplinary purity, but it also requires us to recognize the claim that everything on Earth is, in some sense, artificial because the whole planet has been, directly or indirectly, affected by human activity. Mill's first concept of nature, on the other hand, presumes that all humans and their intentional activities are part of nature, but it is not capable of selecting the supposedly distinct objects of study for the sciences of ecology and economics, respectively.

Fortunately, this dilemma is more apparent than real. The way out of this rabbit hole is to concede that while everything, metaphysically, is natural (i.e., naturalism is true), we can still operationalize the concept of "nature" for our purposes by insisting that those items that remain *relatively detached* from human agency, those items that do not possess *significant* features caused by intentional human agents, are natural. What counts as "relatively detached" and "significant" will depend on specific research contexts. In taking this pragmatic approach, we are following Sahotra Sarkar when he states,

> Even if humans are conceptualized as part of nature, we can coherently distinguish between humans and the rest of nature. There is at least an operational distinction; that is, one that we can straightforwardly make in practical contexts. We can distinguish between anthropogenic features (those largely brought about by human action) and non-anthropogenic ones. (2012: 19)

By making this operational distinction, Mill's two concepts of nature are treated as compatible since one does not necessarily preclude the other. The first concept is more fundamental since even the most artificial of objects, such as atomic bombs, personal computers, and jumbo jets, are judged to be natural. On the other hand, for practical purposes, these same items are deemed artificial since they were intentionally built by human agents and they possess a variety of anthropogenic features. Be that as it may, in light of the claim that characterizes the Anthropocene—that no phenomena is completely insulated from human agency—it is always a question about the *relative detachment* that the objects of study (for ecology and economics) have in relation to human agency.

On this view, the natural and artificial can be positioned along a continuum, in which the most natural objects are those that remain relatively detached from human agency, and the most artificial objects being those that have been built and constructed by intentional human agents. It should be clear that, on this account, there is no sui generis difference between artificial and natural objects since the difference is always a matter of degree. In other words, there is a blending of the natural and the artificial, which we describe as *entangled objects*. This approach to the natural-artificial distinction has the virtue of preserving the practically significant distinction between, for example, intentionally modified environments, such as city centers, and environments that have been subject to relatively little human agency, such as remote uninhabited islands that were recently generated by natural causes in the Pacific Ocean. The point is that the artificial-natural distinction is conceptually problematic if understood as a binary, and so we advise understanding this distinction as a continuum.

2.3 Disciplinary Purity and the Artificial-Natural Distinction

In this section we show that ideas of disciplinary purity have been underwritten by the artificial-natural distinction. We argue that the objects of ecology have been "natural" and those of the political economy, "artificial," and that this has been one factor hindering interdisciplinary exchange. Although this distinction is conceptually problematic if understood as a binary, it, as we showed in Section 2.2, might still be empirically useful to draw the distinction in some contexts. We turn to this question in Section 2.4.

2.3.1 Ecology and Nonhuman Nature

Ecologists have, in general, largely ignored anthropogenic factors and discounted human activity as external to ecosystems (O'Neill and Kahn 2000; Martin et al. 2012; Worm and Paine 2016; Inkpen 2017, forthcoming). Ecologist James Collins and colleagues write, for example, that "from the perspective of a field ecologist examining a natural ecosystem, people are an exogenous, perturbing force" (Collins et al. 2000: 416). Boris Worm and Robert Paine agree that "humans have historically been treated as an externality, as if their effects belong in a separate category compared to other species and their interactions" (2016: 604).

We can divide the claim that humans are an externality into three categories, which we will characterize as *empirical*, *explanatory*, and *methodological* claims. As an *empirical* claim, one might hold that humans are not a major (causal) influence in ecological systems at most levels of ecological organization. Of course, they have a large influence over the structure of urban and agricultural spaces, but these spaces are inconsequential when compared to the diversity of other systems that ecologists study. This reason seems hardest to accept today, given the recent widespread agreement that humans are pervasive (considered below), but was influential in the early twentieth century.

As an *explanatory* claim, one might hold that human-disturbed nature is simply not worth studying or trying to explain. For example, the nineteenth-century biologist Thomas Henry Huxley argued that because man was a living creature, he and "all his ways" should properly be considered under the province of biology; yet, biologists, he felt, are a "self-sacrificing" bunch, for whom nonhuman nature is sufficient disciplinary territory (Huxley [1876] 1897: 270–1). Other ecologists have viewed human-disturbed nature as oxymoronic, as not really nature, and thus as not worth studying. Ecologist Mark McDonnell explains that, "for much of the twentieth century the discipline of ecology contributed relatively little information to our understanding of the ecology of human settlements ... some biological researchers viewed cities as 'anti-life' (i.e., without nature) for they supported few plants and animals" (McDonnell 2011: 7).

As a *methodological* claim, one might hold that not including humans in one's models is the best starting place for an analysis of any ecosystem. This methodological claim has been held for a number of reasons. Some ecologists have felt that not including anthropogenic factors is the simplest, and thus best initial, step to take when trying to understand the dynamics of an ecological system. As one ecologist recently remarked, "Our understanding of even the basic characteristics of major areas, like the Congo Basin, are missing ... Adding direct human impacts to studies requires a certain initial understanding first" (Corbyn 2010). In other words, to begin by including humans is experimentally and computationally intractable. In the future, one might aim to build models that do include humans, but for now there is a pragmatic justification (of complexity) for not including them. Other ecologists have felt that human activity is too unpredictable, contingent, or whimsical to be captured by ecological theory. For example, the urban ecologist Herbert Sukopp wrote that, for a long time "it was assumed that few plants or animals could survive in an urban setting and that urban animal and plant communities were products of coincidence. Attempts to discover patterns or reasons for such patterns were regarded as futile" (Sukopp 1998: 3–4).

Regardless of the reasons justifying it, the disciplinary practice of treating anthropogenic factors as externalities has given rise to two patterns of restriction in the science of ecology. A restriction on the choice of research site (that is, where ecologists conduct their research) and a restriction on the sorts of systems that are considered relevant for theory development and application.

With regard to the choice of research site, a recent meta-analysis of the ecological literature, attempting to quantify such trends in current ecology, showed a strong bias in favor of studies performed in "protected" areas (Martin et al. 2012). The authors argue that this trend is partly the result of an implicit bias among ecologists that nonhuman environments "better represent ecological and evolutionary processes and are therefore better objects of study" (Martin et al. 2012: 198). In other words, ecologists favor nonhuman environments because they take them to be the target of their analyses. Hobbs et al. (2006) provide anecdotal evidence of this trend when they report that a reviewer of their article about "novel ecosystems"—assemblages of species not previously occurring and often created through human-induced environmental changes—"indicated a lack of willingness to accept such ecosystems as a legitimate target for ecological thought or management action" (2006: 5).

The way that theory is developed and applied also shows the effects of treating anthropogenic factors as externalities. A good example of this is model-building and application in the renewed interdisciplinary field of urban ecology, which we further discuss below (Cittadino 1993; McDonnell 2011; Cadenasso and Pickett 2013). These ecologists are confronted by the challenge of building into their models the decision-making capacities of humans, which partly govern and determine the "shape" of urban ecosystems (Grimm et al. 2000; Marzluff et al. 2008; Pickett et al. 2001, 2008, 2011; Swan et al. 2011). They often lament the fact that many classical ecological models are poorly suited to their needs because such models were not developed to account for human-disturbed systems, like an urban center or its surrounding agricultural land, or anthropogenic factors at all (Collins et al. 2000; Alberti et al. 2003).

Traditional models of biological community formation and development, for example, include biotic variables such as the foraging and dispersal strategies of the species involved. These strategies are predictable enough that ecological community development follows a gradual and somewhat predictable series of changes known as succession. Humans, however, make this succession much less predictable from a traditional ecological standpoint, since their actions are often governed by individual whim or social forces—whether cultural, political, or economical—that are on a different disciplinary and explanatory level from what we commonly think of as ecological variables. In a seminal paper, Collins et al. (2000) write,

> An abandoned home site may begin to fill with plant growth—vegetative succession, to an ecologist—but redevelopment typically truncates the process that might otherwise fill the patch with trees and animals. Such redevelopment is an example of the single most important force of landscape change in urban areas: land conversion, driven by institutional decisions, population growth and economic forces… . Both the temporal and spatial scales of patterns in human-dominated ecosystems are likely to emerge from social forces far removed from foraging and dispersal strategies. (2000: 421, 423)

To ecologists, systems involving humans can appear unpredictable from an ecological standpoint because the variables that explain the dynamics of such systems are not a part of—not endogenous in—traditional ecological models. As with the choice of research site, it is well documented that restrictions on which target systems are considered relevant for theory development and application are underwritten by the artificial-natural distinction.

2.3.2 Economics and Human Society

Compared to ecologists, economists have frequently made an inverse restriction on which systems and factors are considered relevant, especially when it comes to the development of *pure* economic theory. In the Millian tradition, at least, the object of study was limited to a specific set of human or anthropogenic causal factors. Among most classical political economists, natural factors were invariably treated as "fixed" and, throughout much of the mid-twentieth century as well, such factors were, for a number of different reasons, omitted from aggregate production functions.

In *On the Principles of Political Economy and Taxation* ([1817] 1951), David Ricardo famously treated nonhuman factors as fixed and exogenously determined; in doing so, he arguably inaugurated the trend to discount the significance of nonanthropogenic factors in economic models and theories. In this work, Ricardo depicted "land" or "Nature" as an original and indestructible factor of production that was incapable of depreciation, and, unlike manufactured capital, did not require a period of production. His "corn model" in particular showed that scarcity in an economy was due partly to the diminishing returns to land, which he assumed was, although improvable with the requisite technology, both permanent and fixed in supply.

When John Stuart Mill ([1848] 2006) endorsed the Ricardian view of land in his *Principles of Political Economy*, the most influential text in political economy during the nineteenth century, he went a step further than Ricardo, driving a wedge between the social and natural realms by repositioning the entire core of phenomena studied by economists such that human agency is the proximate cause (Schabas 2005). Prior to Mill, political economists, such as Ricardo and Adam Smith, had characterized land in ways that made it a distinctive factor of production, but they still regarded the target phenomena of political economy to be part of the same natural world that was to be studied by natural philosophers (Davis 1989).

Mill's ([1848] 2006) basic analytical model was profoundly Ricardian. The science of political economy was to trace the laws of certain phenomena of society, which arose from the combined operations of human beings in the production of wealth. Pure political economy was to be inexact and separate, and its theorists were to employ the a priori method, or reasoning from assumed hypotheses. Because human beings were to be treated as creatures that solely desire to possess wealth, political economy abstracted from every other human passion and motivation, except for those perpetually antagonizing principles to the desire of wealth, such as the aversion to labor and the desire of the present enjoyment of costly indulgences. The reason for excluding natural factors, such as nature's "spontaneous productions," was mostly empirical. Toward the beginning of his *Principles of Political Economy*, Mill cites a variety of nature's products generated by purely natural causes, including the bees that produce honey and some caves that would be used by people for shelter. He states,

> It is to be remarked, that some objects exist or grow up spontaneously, of a kind suited to the supply of human wants. There are caves and hollow trees capable of affording shelter; fruit, roots, wild honey, and other natural products, on which human life can be supported; but even here a considerable quantity of labour is generally required, not for the purpose of creating, but of finding and appropriating them. In all but these few and (except in the very commencement of human society) unimportant cases, the objects supplied by nature are only instrumental to human wants. ([1848] 2006: 25)

While Mill was certainly familiar with the existence of original or natural objects, and how they grew up spontaneously, he believed that they were, on the whole, scant and relatively unimportant for the pure science of political economy. Nature's productions almost always require a significant amount of human labor to not only locate but also prepare and process for human consumption. On this account, aside from accommodating Ricardian land, other natural causes were not sufficiently efficacious to be considered a proper object of study. Pure social scientists were to account for a subset of intentional human activity, to the exclusion of every other social and natural factor. As Margaret Schabas (2005) has argued, Mill's economic theorizing rendered explicit the role of intentional human agency as the framework for standard economic analysis, a central feature of economic theorizing that was then perpetuated well beyond the neoclassical revolution.[2]

Not only have natural factors been generally excluded from *pure* economic theory in the Millian tradition, but it is well-known that during the latter half of the twentieth century, the majority of aggregate production functions and economic growth models posited two and only two factors of production: capital and labor (Solow 1957). This convention was enshrined in the Cobb–Douglas production function where the formula $Y = K^{\alpha}L^{\beta}$ represents total aggregate production (Y) that depends on capital (K) and labor (L). As for the status of land, a mainstay of classical political economy, this factor was eliminated from such formulations under the implicit assumption that manufactured capital could always serve as a substitute for any such natural factors. As the economists Klaus Hubacek and Jeroen van der Bergh observe, "by the second half of the twentieth century land or more generally environmental resources, completely disappeared from the production function and the shift from land to other natural inputs to capital and labour alone" (2006: 15). In fact, it had been tacitly assumed by economic theorists that reproducible capital was a near-perfect substitute for land (Nordhaus and Tobin 1972). Because capital is universally viewed as a factor of production that human agents produce, such formulations portrayed the production of all economically valuable goods and services as emerging from human agency alone. Even after the aggregate variable "resources" was introduced to such production functions after the oil shock of 1973, when economists were genuinely concerned with the question of sustained economic production in the face of a declining stock of fixed resources, this variable was largely taken to represent a conglomerate of inert materials that were capable of producing only when conjoined with the other two factors of production, capital and labor (Solow 1974; Dasgupta and Heal 1979).

To be clear, our claim is not that every economist has always wished to exclude natural factors from their theories or models. In fact, today, many have begun to wrestle with their Ricardian inheritance. The Cambridge resource economist, Partha Dasgupta, states that economists can no longer afford to assume that "Nature" is an "indestructible factor of production" (2010: 6). Moreover, there is growing transdisciplinary field of research known as "ecological economics" that has always emphasized the significance of including social and ecological factors in coupled or ecological-economic models for the purpose of prescribing public policy (Christensen 1989; Costanza 1989; van den Bergh 2001; Røpke 2005; Martinez-Alier and Røpke 2008). Rather, our claim is that pure economics, like pure ecology, has been defined around an appropriate set of objects of study, and that this seemingly innocuous decision concerning disciplinary boundaries has powerful implications for the structure and practices of the social science. Pure economics in the Millian tradition has chiefly focused on a specific set of human or artificial causes, but in Section 2 it was shown that the very distinction upon which the boundaries of this set depends—the artificial-natural binary—is problematic, both empirically and conceptually. Without this distinction, it remains an open question whether the objects of study traditionally analyzed by economists should remain limited to human factors alone.

2.3.3 Bringing Things Together

A useful exercise at this point is to imagine a world in which ecology and economics get on quite well without one another. This is a world that is made up of relatively independent human and natural systems: one set of systems, the object of ecology, consists of nonanthropogenic or "natural" factors; another set, the object of economics, consists of anthropogenic or human factors. In such a tidy world, these sciences, when operating effectively, make successful predictions and prescribe policy interventions without the need for interdisciplinary exchange.

Throughout much of the twentieth century, this imaginary world seems to have been implicitly assumed, as we have just shown. As ecologist Robert O'Neill and economist James Kahn wrote in 2000,

> The current paradigm in ecology considers humans not as a keystone species [a dominant species on which other species within an ecosystem depend] but as an external disturbance on the "natural" ecosystem... . The problem with this approach is that human beings are, in fact, another biotic species within the ecosystem and not an external influence.
>
> But the artificial isolation of humans from their ecosystem is not due only to the ecologists' paradigm. In the economic paradigm as well, human society, with all of its self-organization and self-regulatory activity, is represented as a separate "system." The ecosystem is viewed as external to society, providing goods and services, unoccupied territory in which to expand, and assimilative capacity to handle by-products... . The ecological paradigm isolates human activity in a box labeled "disturbances." The economic paradigm, in turn, isolates ecosystem dynamics in a box labeled "externalities." (O'Neill and Kahn 2000: 333)

Of course, this imaginary world is just that, a fiction. The real world is messy. Strictly speaking, there is no longer any part of the earth's surface that remains completely detached from human technologies, as we said above. The world today is a blend of anthropogenic and nonanthropogenic factors and prima facie this seems like a world in which exchange between ecology and economics would be a prerequisite to successful science.

2.4 Case Studies of Entangled Phenomena

Let's take stock. We've argued that, as a binary, the artificial-natural distinction is conceptually problematic, and so it must be understood as a continuum—that is, the world is populated by entangled phenomena that are more or less natural. We've argued that the distinction might still be worth drawing if doing so is empirically useful in particular research contexts. In the last section, we argued that ecologists and economists do, in fact, draw this distinction when choosing objects to study that are relevant for theory development and application and we've suggested that this has hindered interdisciplinary exchange. In this section we aim to undermine the usefulness of drawing this distinction. Because entangled phenomena are a *shared* object of study, it remains an open question whether it is best for each science to operate independently or engage in interdisciplinary exchange. Here, we argue that, if the goal of ecology and economics is to develop stronger predictions and explanations, and to develop better policy prescriptions, then the evidence suggests that interdisciplinary exchange is preferable, for epistemological and policy-oriented reasons, to these two sciences acting independently.

2.4.1 Biodiversity: Urban Ecology and Biogeography

Acknowledging the now pervasive influence of humans on the planet, many recent ecologists have begun to include human activity in their models. They want an ecology that applies to human-disturbed as well as undisturbed landscapes, but this forces them to take into account economic processes (Alberti 2008). We will consider two subfields where this interdisciplinary exchange is occurring: in urban ecology and in island biogeography.

A central problem for mid-to-late twentieth-century ecology has been biodiversity and its conservation. Understanding how to conserve biodiversity in urban areas is now recognized as a pertinent but complex problem. As a recent issue of *Science* dedicated to urban systems highlights, human urban populations are expanding in many of the world's richest biodiversity hotspots at an increasing rate (*Science*, May 20, 2016). Urban ecologists aim to mitigate the loss of native biodiversity by attempting to determine the conditions under which it could continue to flourish in human environments.

In "pristine" environments—and thus also in traditional ecological theory—spatial variation in plant diversity is often a product of heterogeneity in resource availability, importantly water and other nutrients (Hope et al. 2003). In arid landscapes, like Arizona, these resources are strongly influenced by geomorphic controls, like elevation. But in cities, such controls would seem to be much less powerful, since resource availability reflects social, cultural, and economic influences on urban land use (particularly as people create small "urban oases"). Ecologist Diane Hope and an interdisciplinary team at Arizona State University confirmed this prediction (Hope et al. 2003). Plant diversity throughout the greater Phoenix area was driven largely by socioeconomics.

One interesting trend they discovered was what they dubbed: the "luxury effect." This was that median family income was highly predictive of variation in the biodiversity of plants in gardens. Plant diversity was on average double in neighborhoods with incomes above median compared to those neighborhoods with incomes below median. They also found that overall, such trends had increased total biodiversity for the region and increased diversity between sites (called "beta diversity"), but that this was largely due to native species being replaced by exotics introduced in urban areas.

Explaining trends in biodiversity in an urban setting—such as "the luxury effect"—requires building in anthropogenic factors, like the development and use of urban land. Without scientific representations that contain such factors, ecologists would not be able to explain these systems. But let us turn to a second example before drawing conclusions.

This example involves a less obviously human-disturbed system, and is important for this reason. The theory of island biogeography has long been the foundation for estimating extinction rates, predicting changes in biodiversity, and making policy recommendations (Diamond 1975; He and Hubbell 2011; Mendenhall et al. 2013; Thomas 2013). This theory explains and predicts the species richness (that is, number of species) that will be found on an island at equilibrium (that is, when rates of species immigration to the island and species extinction on the island balance out) (MacArthur and Wilson 1967; Diamond 1975).

The theory predicts that islands that are larger and nearer to the mainland will contain more species than islands smaller and further from the mainland. In a recent paper, Matt Helmus and colleagues (2014) tested the predictions of this theory for the distribution of Anolis lizard species among Caribbean islands. The theory predicts that a strong negative relationship will be found between species richness and geographic isolation: as a result of decreased inter-island immigration, more isolated islands will contain fewer species than less isolated ones.

This prediction is, however, false for Caribbean Anolis lizards because geographic isolation no longer solely determines immigration of new species. Instead, economic isolation mainly does so. Why? Because islands that receive more cargo shipments are more likely to contain lizard migrants from other islands, as the lizards move from island to island as stowaways on cargo ships. The result is that, for Caribbean lizards, geographic isolation is of less influence on biodiversity than economic isolation. Estimating economic isolation from global maritime shipping-traffic data, Helmus and colleagues found that when economic isolation was substituted for geographic isolation, the new biogeographic theory fit with their data: anole species richness was a negative function of economic isolation. They concluded that

> Unlike the island biogeography of the past that was determined by geographic area and isolation, in the Anthropocene ... island biogeography is dominated by the economic isolation of human populations. [And] Just as for models of other Earth systems, biogeographic models must now include anthropogenic [variables] to understand, predict and mitigate the consequences of the new island biogeography of the Anthropocene. (Helmus et al. 2014: 543, 546)

Building anthropogenic factors into their biogeographic model also gives Helmus et al. a way to predict the effects of increasing economic traffic. If the goal is to protect exotic species from immigration of non-native species, then strategies for doing so will be ineffective unless they account for anthropogenic factors. Traditional theories of island biogeography alone do not provide helpful resources because the variables that make a difference are not included in the model. And models that account for anthropogenic factors are capable of novel predictions. For example, they predict that a removal of the US trade embargo on Cuba would result in the addition of one or two species of non-native lizards, a prediction that could not be made with traditional biogeographic theory.

What can we learn from these two examples? We don't think that the lesson is that ecologists should always take anthropogenic factors into account. Rather, that (1) there are cases in which not taking anthropogenic factors into account can be epistemically disadvantageous, it can diminish our ability to predict the dynamics of certain systems, and (2) that such cases are not limited to urban or agricultural settings, but range over cases of "pristine" ecology such as the distributions of Anolis lizards on Caribbean islands.

Many of the world's ecological systems are entangled phenomena, and to capture the features that are relevant to the processes and events we want to understand, and on which we want to be able to intervene, we have to represent the interaction between anthropogenic and non-anthropogenic factors. Although there will surely be cases in which excluding anthropogenic factors will be innocuous, entanglement implies that the question of whether anthropogenic factors should be included has to, at the very least, be asked.

2.4.2 Invasive Species in Yellowstone National Park

Nowhere are the epistemological and policy benefits of including ecological factors in economic models more evident than in the case of managing invasive species in Yellowstone National Park, Wyoming. When Yellowstone Lake was invaded by an exotic lake trout (*Salvelinus namaycush*), managers were worried that the growth of this species would significantly reduce the population level of the Yellowstone cutthroat trout (*Oncorhynchus clarkii bouvieri*), a native species that supports an inland fishery and a variety of nonhuman species, such as ospreys, pelicans, river otters, and grizzly bears. Chad Settle et al. (2002) specified a model for two separate systems: the economic system in Yellowstone National Park and the ecosystem in and around Yellowstone Lake. They asked whether their model, which combines details of an economic system and an ecosystem with explicit feedback links (economic and ecological factors are jointly determined) between them, yields significantly different results than a model that ignores those links. Their economic-ecological model, predicted that when ecosystems change, people will change their economic behavior, which in turn affects the ecosystem; correspondingly, any alterations in the ecosystem affects human economic behavior, including economic production possibilities.

Settle et al. (2002) ran three different scenarios with their model. The best-case scenario is a hypothetical one, when the lake trout are costlessly eliminated from

Yellowstone Lake. Under this optimistic scenario, the cutthroat trout would return to the lake as if the lake trout had never invaded in the first place. The worst-case scenario occurs if the lake trout are left to their own devices, which would have the effect of producing the smallest viable population of cutthroat trout. Their third policy scenario involved the National Park Service gillnetting the lake trout in order to reduce the risk to cutthroat trout populations.

Their results showed that a dynamic model that integrates ecological and economic systems *with feedback links between the two systems* yields significantly different results than when one that ignores these links. In every scenario they outline, cutthroat trout populations differ in both magnitude and survival rates once feedback is allowed between the two systems. For both the best-case and policy scenarios, Settle et al. (2002) predicted the steady-state population of cutthroat is lower without feedback than with feedback. Given the worst-case scenario, however, ignoring feedback leads to estimating a relatively high cutthroat population. Settle et al. concluded that "basing policy recommendations in Yellowstone Lake on data from models without feedback puts cutthroats at greater risk than would be true if feedback was explicitly considered" (2002: 309). In this case, the policy recommendations derived from a model without ecological factors would be worse than those derived from a model that connects the economic system to an ecological system with explicit feedback links.

As with the case of Helmus et al., the "exchange gain" of including an ecological system with explicit feedback links in the cutthroat trout example can be purchased rather cheaply. The latter does not require the development of a completely new theory of bidirectional collaboration between economists and ecologists. Instead, the model of Settle et al. merely required the addition of feedback variables that link two jointly determined systems. In this case, the economic variable that constitute the economic system is not jettisoned or even supplanted by another variable. Rather, the traditional economic theory, in this case, is retained, but in supplementary form.

2.5 Conclusion

Ideas of disciplinary purity have long reinforced a divide between the natural and social sciences. In this chapter, we have argued that, when it comes to the objects of study in ecology and economics, ideas of disciplinary purity have been underwritten by the artificial-natural distinction. We have tried to problematize this distinction, and thus disciplinary purity, both conceptually and empirically.

If we accept that a central goal of ecology and economics is to develop stronger predictions and explanations, and to develop better policy prescriptions, then a commitment to disciplinarity purity—for the sake of purity—can be a bad thing. Our two case studies have shown that an inflexible commitment to purity can entail predictions that are worse than those provided by interdisciplinary science. There are at least some cases in which interdisciplinary exchange between ecology and economics is preferable, for epistemological and practical reasons, to these two sciences operating independently. Our hypothesis is that, in a growing number of cases, entangled phenomena will require an interdisciplinary treatment.

To be clear, our aim has not been to argue that we should revolutionize the divisions of science, but to simply urge that they do not always reflect the evidence we have about our current world, and thus that the divisions themselves should not structure or determine interactions across disciplines. As Banu Subramaniam has recently written, disciplinarity tends to "obfuscate the inconvenient, avoid the uncomfortable, and promote ignorance about the profoundly powerful insights of interdisciplinary thinking" (Subramaniam 2014: 225). We agree with ecologists Boris Worm and Robert Paine that "the recognition of a novel geological epoch might also provide a new focus for ecology and the study of humans as a primary and dominant component of contemporary ecosystems," but we'd add that this will require interaction with social scientists, including economists (Worm and Paine 2016: 601). And, the reverse is true as well: it is to be expected that, in a growing number of cases, economics will need ecology, too. Indeed, in the age of the Anthropocene, without interdisciplinary exchange it is to be expected that ecology and economics would relinquish global relevance because the distinct and separate systems to which each pure science applies will only diminish over time.

Notes

1 Our modest claim is that the artificial-natural distinction makes interdisciplinary exchange less likely.

2 The Millian view of classical political economy has not only been significant for the trajectory of contemporary neo-classical economics but it has also been central to the works of leading contemporary philosophers of economics, such as Dan Hausman (1981) and Nancy Cartwright (see Hartmann et al. 2008) as well.

References

Alberti, M. 2008. *Advances in Urban Ecology: Integrating Humans and Ecological Processes in Urban Ecosystems*. New York: Springer-Verlag.

Alberti, M., J. Marzluff, E. Shulenberger, G. Bradley, C. Ryan, and C. Zumbrunnen. 2003. "Integrating Humans into Ecology: Opportunities and Challenges for Studying Urban Ecosystems." *BioScience* 53: 1169–79.

Bensaude-Vincent, B., and W. R. Newman. 2007. *The Artificial and the Natural: An Evolving Polarity*. Cambridge: MIT Press.

Cadenasso M. L., and S. Pickett. 2013. "Three Tides: The Development and State of the Art of Urban Ecological Science." In *Resilience in Ecology and Urban Design: Linking Theory and Practice for Sustainable Cities*, ed. S. Pickett, M. Cadenasso, and B. McGrath. New York: Springer.

Christensen, P. P. 1989. "Historical Roots for Ecological Economics—Biophysical versus allocative approaches." *Ecological Economics* 1: 17–36.

Church, G., and E. Regis. 2012. *Regenesis*. New York: Basic Books.

Cittadino, E. 1993. "The Failed Promise of Human Ecology." In *Science and Nature: Essays in the History of the Environmental Sciences*, ed. M. Shortland. Oxford: British Society for the History of Science.

Collins, J., A. Kinzig, N. Grimm, W. Fagan, D. Hope, J. Wu, and E. Borer. 2000. "A New Urban Ecology: Modelling Human Communities as Integral Parts of Ecosystems Poses Special Problems for the Development and Testing of Ecological Theory." *American Scientist* 88: 416–25.

Corbyn, Z. 2010. "Ecologists Shun the Urban Jungle." *Nature News*, July 16, 2000.

Costanza, R. 1989. "What Is Ecological Economics?" *Ecological Economics* 1: 1–7.

Dasgupta, P. 2010. "Nature's Role in Sustaining Economic Development." *Philosophical Transactions of the Royal Society: Biological Sciences* 365: 5–11.

Dasgupta, P., and G. Heal. 1979. *Economic Theory and Exhaustible Resources*. Oxford: Cambridge University Press.

Davis, J. B. 1989. "Distribution in Ricardo's Machinery Chapter." *History of Political Economy* 21: 457–80.

DesRoches, C. T. 2014. "On Aristotle's Natural Limit." *History of Political Economy* 46 (3): 387–407.

Diamond, J. 1975. "The Island Dilemma: Lessons of Modern Biogeographic Studies for the Design of Nature Reserves." *Biological Conservation* 7: 129–46.

Ellis, E., and N. Ramankutty. 2008. "Putting People in the Map: Anthropogenic Biomes of the World." *Frontiers in Ecology and the Environment* 6: 439–47.

Ellis, E., J. Kaplan, D. Fuller, S. Vavrus, K. Goldewijk, and P. Verburg. 2013. "Used Planet: A Global History." *Proceedings of the National Academy of Science* 110: 7978–85.

Grimm, N., J. Grove, S. Pickett, and C. Redman. 2000. "Integrated Approaches to Long-term Studies of Urban Ecological Systems." *BioScience* 7: 571–84.

Hartmann, S., C. Hoefer, and L. Bovens. 2008. *Nancy Cartwright's Philosophy of Science*. London: Routledge.

Hausman, D. 1981. "John Stuart Mill's Philosophy of Economics." *Philosophy of Science* 48 (3): 363–85.

He, Fangliang, and S. Hubbell. 2011. "Species-Area Relationships Always Overestimate Extinction Rates from Habitat Loss." *Nature* 473: 368–71.

Helmus, Matthew R., D. Luke Mahler, and J. Losos. 2014. "Island Biogeography of the Anthropocene." *Nature* 513: 543–6.

Hobbs, R., S. Arico, J. Aronson, J. Baron, P. Bridgewater, V. Cramer, P. Epstein, J. Ewel, C. Klink, A. Lugo, D. Norton, D. Ojima, D. Richardson, E. Sanderson, F. Valladares, M. Vilà, R. Zamora, and M. Zobel. 2006. "Novel Ecosystems: Theoretical and Management Aspects of the New Ecological World Order." *Global Ecology and Biogeography* 15: 1–7.

Hope, D., C. Gries, W. Zhu, W. Fagan, C. Redman, N. Grimm, A. Nelson, C. Martin, and A. Kinzig. 2003. "Socioeconomics Drive Urban Plant Diversity." *Proceedings of the National Academy of Sciences* 100: 8788–92.

Hubacek, K., and Jeroen C. J. M. van den Bergh. 2006. "Changing Concepts of 'Land' in Economic Theory: From Single to Multi-disciplinary Approaches." *Ecological Economics* 56: 5–27.

Huxley, T. H. [1876] 1897. "On the Study of Biology." In *Collected Essays*, Vol. 3 of *Science and Education*. New York: D. Appleton.

Inkpen, S. A. 2017. "Are Humans Disturbing Conditions in Ecology?" *Biology and Philosophy* 32: 51–71.

Inkpen, S. A. Forthcoming. "Demarcating Nature, Defining Ecology: Creating a Rationale for the Study of Nature's 'Primitive Conditions.'" In *Perspectives on Science* 25 (3) (May–June 2017): 355–92.

Kaebnick, G. 2014. *Humans in Nature*. Oxford: Oxford University Press.

Kelsey, S. 2003. "Aristotle's Definition of Nature." *Oxford Studies in Ancient Philosophy* 25: 59–87.

Kuhn, T. S. [1962] 1996. *The Structure of Scientific Revolutions*. 3rd ed. Chicago, IL: University of Chicago Press.

Laura, M., B. Blossey, and E. Ellis. 2012. "Mapping where Ecologists Work: Biases in the Global Distribution of Terrestrial Ecological Observations." *Frontiers in Ecology and the Environment* 10: 195–201.

MacArthur, R., and E. O. Wilson. 1967. *The Theory of Island Biogeography*. Princeton, NJ: Princeton University Press.

Martinez-Alier, J., and I. Røpke, eds. 2008. *Recent Developments in Ecological Economics I*. Northampton: Edward Elgar Publishing.

Marzluff, J., E. Shulenberger, W. Endlicher, M. Alberti, G. Bradley, C. Ryan, C. ZumBrunnen, and U. Simon. 2008. *Urban Ecology*. New York: Springer.

Mckibben, B. 1990. *The End of Nature*. New York: Viking.

McDonnell, M. 2011. "The History of Urban Ecology: An Ecologist's Perspective." In *Urban Ecology: Patterns, Processes, and Applications*, ed. J. Niemelä. Oxford: Oxford University Press.

Mendenhall, C., D. Karp, C. Meyer, E. Hadly, and G. Daily. 2013. "Predicting Biodiversity Change and Averting Collapse in Agricultural Landscapes." *Nature* 509: 213–17.

Mill, J. S. [1874] 2006. "Nature." In *Collected Works of John Stuart Mill*, Vol. 9, ed. J. M. Robson. Indianapolis, IN: Liberty Fund.

Mill, J. S. [1848] 2006. "Principles of Political Economy." In *Collected Works of John Stuart Mill*, Vol. 2, ed. J. M. Robson. Indianapolis, IN: Liberty Fund.

Nordhaus, W., and J. Tobin. 1972. "Is Growth Obsolete?" In *Economic Research: Retrospect and Prospect, Volume 5, Economic Growth*, General Series No. 96, 1–80. New York: National Bureau of Economic Research.

O'Neill, R., and J. Kahn. 2000. "Homo Economies as a Keystone Species." *BioScience* 50: 333–6.

O'Neill, J., A. Holland, and A. Light. 2008. *Environmental Values*. London: Routledge.

Pickett, S., M. Cadenasso, J. Grove, C. Nilon, R. Pouyat, W. Zipperer, and R. Constanza. 2001. "Urban Ecological Systems: Linking Terrestrial Ecological, Physical, and Socioeconomic Components of Metropolitan Areas." *Annual Review of Ecology and Systematics* 32: 127–57.

Pickett, S., M. Cadenasso, J. Grove, P. Groffman, L. Band, C. Boone, W. Burch, C. Grimmond, J. Hom, J. Jenkins, N. Law, C. Nilon, R. Pouyat, K. Szlavecz, P. Warren, and M. Wilson. 2008. "Beyond Urban Legends: An Emerging Framework of Urban Ecology, as Illustrated by the Baltimore Ecosystem Study." *BioScience* 58: 139–50.

Pickett, S., M. Cadenasso, J. Grove, C. Boone, P. Groffman, S. Kaushal, V. Marshall, B. McGrath, C. Nilon, R. Pouyat, K. Szlavecz, A. Troy, and P. Warren. 2011. "Urban Ecological Systems: Scientific Foundations and a Decade of Progress." *Journal of Environmental Management* 92: 331–62.

Ricardo, D. [1817] 1951. "On the Principles of Political Economy and Taxation." *Works and Correspondence*, ed. P. Sraffa. Cambridge: Cambridge University Press.

Røpke, I. 2005. "Trends in the Development of Ecological Economics: From the Late 1980s until the Early 2000s." *Ecological Economics* 55: 262–90.

Sarkar, S. 2012. *Environmental Philosophy: From Theory to Practice*. Malden, MA: John Wiley and Sons.

Schabas, M. 1995. "John Stuart Mill and Concepts of Nature." *Dialogue: Canadian Philosophical Review/Revue canadienne de philosophie* 34(3): 447–66.

Schabas, M. 2005. *The Natural Origins of Economics*. Chicago, IL: University of Chicago Press.

Settle, C., T. D. Crocker and J. F. Shogren. 2002. "On the Joint Determination of Biological and Economic Systems." *Ecological Economics* 42: 301–11.

Solow, R. M., 1957. "Technical Change and the Aggregate Production Function." *The Review of Economics and Statistics* 39: 312–20.

Solow, R. M. 1974. "Intergenerational Equity and Exhaustible Resources." *Review of Economic Studies* 41: 29–46.

Steffen, W., J. Grinevald, P. Crutzen, and J. McNeill. 2011. "The Anthropocene: Conceptual and Historical Perspectives." *Philosophical Transactions of Royal Society A* 369: 842–67.

Subramaniam, B. 2014. *Ghost Stories for Darwin: The Science of Variation and the Politics of Diversity*. Urbana: University of Illinois Press.

Sukopp, H. 1998. "Urban Ecology: Scientific and Practical Aspects." In *Urban Ecology*, ed. J. Breuste, H. Feldmann, and O. Uhlmann. Berlin: Springer-Verlag.

Thomas, C. 2013. "The Anthropocene Could Raise Biological Diversity." *Nature* 502: 7.

van den Bergh, J. C. J. M. 2001. "Ecological Economics: Themes, Approaches, and Differences with Environmental Economics." *Regional Environmental Change* 2: 13–23.

Vitousek, P. M., H. A. Mooney, J. Lubchenco, J. M. Melillo. 1997. "Human Domination of the Earth's Ecosystems." *Science* 277: 494–9.

Vogel, S. 2015. *Thinking like a Mall: Environmental Philosophy after the End of Nature*. Cambridge, MA: MIT Press.

Wapner, P. 2010. *Living through the End of Nature*. Cambridge, MA: MIT Press.

Worm, B., and R. Paine. 2016. "Humans as a Hyperkeystone Species." *Trends in Ecology and Evolution* 31: 600–7.

Commentary: Toward a Philosophy and Methodology for Interdisciplinary Research

Michiru Nagatsu

1. Introduction

As DesRoches, Inkpen, and Green (DIG hereafter) point out, philosophers of science have been thinking about the nature and functions of scientific disciplines since Kuhn, but it is only recently that they started to systematically study how disciplines interact with each other. Not only historical but also other empirical methods such as qualitative case studies and quantitative methods (e.g., bibliometrics) have been utilized for this. However, few studies focus specifically on interdisciplinary interactions between economics and ecology, the practical relevance of which should be obvious to those who consider sustainability as a major challenge of our time. This chapter by DIG is thus a timely contribution both theoretically and practically. Since the chapter is well organized and its gist clear, in this commentary I will focus mainly on complementing and challenging its arguments.

In this commentary I will do two things: first, since interdisciplinarity is a relatively new topic in philosophy of social science, I will relate it to the existing debates in the field to guide the reader. I will argue that DIG's artificial-natural ontological distinction cannot be operationalized based on the "distance from human cause." Rather, specific ways in which human cause is special need to be unpacked. Second, I will highlight some ambivalence in their methodology of interdisciplinary research and suggest a more explicit (and perhaps conservative) methodology of interdisciplinary model-building, drawing on an ongoing study of interdisciplinary environmental sciences I have been working on with Miles MacLeod.

2. The Artificial-Natural Distinction

Disciplinary purity of economics and ecology that DIG highlight is closely related to the general problem of the social-natural distinction that philosophers of social science have been debating over many decades. Does social science have to be somehow different from natural science because of the ontological peculiarities of the human and the social, vis-a-vis the natural? As DIG state (p. 7), Mill's first concept of nature suggests a negative answer by noting that everything is natural including human agents and their intentional activities. This position corresponds to the underlying metaphysics of naturalistic philosophy of social science, which rejects any ontological divide between the natural and the social, and as a corollary, rejects any methodological divide between the two sciences. In contrast, Mill's second concept of nature isolates human agents and their activities as belonging to a specifically agential domain, thereby allowing the nonnaturalists to argue for a distinct methodology to study them, such as introspection and hermeneutic interpretation. I consider the standard strategy to ease this methodological tension is to say that the general standards of scientific reasoning such as rigorous causal inferences and severe testing of hypotheses apply to all sciences (since everything they study is natural in Mill's first sense), while at the same time accepting different methods to be epistemically fruitful in different domains, depending on their specific features. In short, the strategy is to erase the dichotomous artificial-natural distinction and redraw more fine-grained distinctions between different domains of science (see Mitchell 2009). This strategy is reflected in the current practice of many philosophers specializing in particular sciences (philosophy of biology, philosophy of economics, philosophy of physics, etc.), who work more or less independently from each other.

In philosophical and methodological discussions of interdisciplinarity, however, it becomes necessary to explicitly compare the domains of different sciences in question and their methodological ramifications. The challenge here, however, is not to demarcate scientific disciplines from unscientific ones or to rank them in terms of scientific rigor (as assumed in the naturalism vs. anti-naturalism debate in philosophy of social science) but rather to figure out epistemically gainful ways of linking distinct but closely related sciences. DIG's approach to this theoretical-methodological problem is pragmatic: they take the natural-artificial distinction to be a matter of degree, defined by "the *relative detachment* that the objects of study ... have in relation to human agency" (p. 8, original emphasis). That is, the more remote the object is from human agency, the more natural and less artificial it is, and can be studied accordingly.

This pragmatic approach will probably suffice in most contexts, but it misses an important question of why the relative detachment from human agency matters in the first place. Take, for example, atomic bombs, one of the examples DIG give. The authors claim that atomic bombs are "deemed artificial since they were intentionally built by human agents and they possess a variety of anthropogenic features"(p. 8). In this sense atomic bombs are very close to human agency, but this proximity to human agency does not imply that the mechanisms of those bombs have to be studied differently from those of naturally occurring objects. Laws of physics should apply to both (in fact, first atomic bombs were invented by physicists such as von Neumann). Using proximity to human agency as a degree of artificiality is misleading if the natural-artificial distinction (or continuum, as suggested by DIG) is supposed to imply different methodological practices. One should ask why agency is special as a cause in the first place.

In this regard, philosophy of social science has several conceptual resources to offer. Take, for example, the distinction between interactive and indifferent kinds made by

Hacking (1999). Indifferent kinds include tigers and gold, which are traditionally called natural kinds, and called as indifferent because the categorized objects do not intentionally respond to the categorization. In contrast, interactive kinds include homosexuals and housewives, which, while having somewhat stable clustering properties, can change their behavior in response to the very categorization either by conforming to or deviating from it, thereby affecting the validity of the original categorization. More generally, the reactivity of human agency to scientific theorizing and manipulation, and its methodological implications, have been discussed in the literature (Cooper 2004; MacKenzie, Muniesa, and Siu 2007; Jimenez-Buedo and Guala 2016).

Game theory may also offer a useful perspective to understand the natural-artificial distinction. In game theory, an interaction between agents is modeled as a game consisting of players, their alternative actions, and outcomes as combinations of these actions. The crucial insight is that the outcomes for one player is affected not only by what she chooses but also by what others do, and vice versa. In contrast, Nature is used as a metaphorical figure whose actions are stochastically selected, independent of what other players think or do. In this framework, the fact that human agency affects Nature means that human players change Nature's available "actions" by modifying her conditions, as well as the probability distribution of which options she "chooses" in the future. But still her course of choices will not be affected by other players' preferences over outcomes and expectations about her choice because she has no beliefs nor preferences. As a result, human-Nature interactions are not fully analyzable by game theoretic concepts such as Nash equilibrium. But to the extent that human interactions mediated by such changes in Nature are the focus, game-theoretic analysis may be useful (cf. Bailey, Sumaila, and Lindroos 2010, review the use of game theory in fisheries management). In fact, human interactions mediated by technological changes (such as the invention of atomic bombs) have been intensively studied by game theorists. In this regard, it is probably not a coincidence that Thomas Schelling, the prominent game theorist who worked on the Cold War conflicts, was in his later career interested in how the geo-engineering technologies affect the politics of climate change.

The point of these examples is not that reactivity or intentionality crucially demarcates the artificial from the natural. Rather, the point is that there are different mechanisms through which agency affects the object of study, and that it is these specific mechanisms that pose specific methodological challenges. Reactivity or performativity of agents to social (scientific) categorization is one such mechanism.

In considering methodological and empirical implications of the Anthropocene, one should thus carefully consider the ways in which human agency makes a difference in the natural domains, and what kind of repercussions that difference has in the artificial or social domains. The Anthropocene might require natural scientists to pay more attention to human agency and how it affects their theorizing about the nature. Conceptual resources provided by the philosophy of the social sciences in the debates over the social-natural divide may be useful in this new challenge.

Another important dimension along which to distinguish the natural from the artificial is the relevance of values. In social sciences, values—what they are, how people try to achieve them, and whether a given means to realize them is optimal—have been central objects of inquiry. In contrast, in natural sciences human values have been always in the background of their modeling practice. Of course, philosophers of science have discussed value neutrality of natural science (Nagel 1979), more recently in the context of inductive risks and related discussions of epistemic roles of non-epistemic values (Douglas 2000). However, in these contexts values are categorized as external constraints on objective epistemic activities, rather than the main object to study and control. Can we maintain this division of labor in the Anthropocene?

Let's consider the case of ecology and economics. Can ecologists focus on empirical issues of how ecosystems operate while economists handle value-related issues of how to govern them? The current controversy around ecological economics seem to challenge this division of scientific labor. Economists have been criticized for treating natural capital as infinite and perfectly substitutable with capital and labor, following Ricardo, as DIG point out. Note, however, that the issue here is strictly empirical, that is, that natural capital is not infinite. And judging whether or not this is the case seems to belong to the expertise of ecologists, not economists, and therefore this critical interactions between ecologists and economists do not violate the abovementioned division of ecology and economics along the no value-value line.

A more substantial challenge to the division is found in ecological economists' work on the value of ecosystem services, which has been criticized by economists for being conceptually confused (Costanza et al. 1997, 2014). In this controversy, ecologists (or ecological economists) have directly dealt with the measurement of values (specifically, the dollar value of the planet Earth), which has invited economists' criticism about how they go about in this business. Generally speaking, economics has well-articulated and systematized models and methods to calculate and evaluate (and sometimes optimize) anthropocentric values as preference satisfaction from actual as well as potential use of the environment, while ecology does not have such an articulate system of valuation. Ecologists might even have an implicit notion of valuation that is at odds with economists' anthropocentric approach. And yet ecologists are increasingly aware of the need of more systematic ways of modeling values and trade-offs of competing values, in particular, in the context of natural resource management (Stephenson et al. 2017).

Why is the clear division of labor between natural and social scientists—the former study natural systems while the latter study value systems—being challenged? Perhaps, this is where the natural-artificial continuum helps us clarify what is going on. That is, since the environment is becoming more and more artificial in the sense of being affected and modified by human agency, it becomes necessary to explicitly evaluate its values in relation to what we can do to it. Even the most untouched wilderness needs to be valued in this way because our alternative actions make a difference to its destiny. If, in contrast, something is really natural in the sense that it is beyond human agencial cause, then there is no need for valuing it because its destiny is beyond our control. We now know that nothing is that natural on Earth.

To sum up this section, I discussed two implications of DIG's natural-artificial distinction-continuum. In terms of empirical methodological repercussions, this distinction does not seem to have much bite. It is more important to look at exactly how human agency is special as a natural cause, rather than how far things are from it. And debates in the philosophy of social science may provide useful empirical and conceptual resources. In contrast, the distinction-continuum is more directly relevant to social scientists' traditional monopoly of value-related investigations. As the environment becomes more artificial, the impact of human agency on it looms larger. Accordingly, natural scientists may need to explicitly evaluate consequences of human actions, or social scientists may need to incorporate unanticipated consequences of human actions down the causal chain in their valuation of alternative actions. Alternatively, they can engage in interdisciplinary research in which their expertise complements each other. I will discuss the methodology for this in the next section.

3. Methodology of Interdisciplinary Science

The main theses of DIG are that the current divisions of science, in particular between economics and ecology, "do not always reflect the evidence we have about our current world [the Anthropocene], and thus that the division themselves should not structure or determine interactions across disciplines" (p. 25). This is a variation of prevalent calls for interdisciplinary research. According to the widely cited definition, interdisciplinary research is

> a mode of research by teams or individuals that integrates information, data, techniques, tools, perspectives, concepts, and/or theories from two or more disciplines or bodies of specialized knowledge to advance fundamental understanding or to solve problems whose solutions are beyond the scope of a single discipline or field of research practice. (National Academy of Sciences 2005: 26)

According to this definition, two key rationales for interdisciplinary research are epistemic and practical. The epistemic rationale, simply put, is that since the world is not chopped up in a disciplinary way, fundamental understanding necessitates knowledge integration across disciplines. The practical rationale, in a similar fashion, states that since the real-world problems and concerns do not correspond to the academic disciplinary structure, real solutions need to come from research that cut across the disciplines.

These lines of reasoning can easily lead to a radical recommendation to dissolve disciplinary structure altogether, which has been criticized by sociologists of science such as Jacobs (2013). DIG clearly do not endorse such a radical position, but there is some ambivalence in their chapter. On the one hand, they propose a new ontology—the natural-artificial entanglement—as the basis for criticism of the status quo. And they favorably cite ecological economics as a "transdisciplinary field"—the term associated with radical knowledge integration that sits at the top of epistemic hierarchy, above inter-, multi-, and cross-disciplinarity in interdisciplinarity studies' parlance. On the other hand, DIG's actual examples of ecology-economics interdisciplinary exchange seems less radical. What do they have in mind when they say existing disciplinary divisions of labor should not structure or determine interactions between disciplines? What should substitute them?

In this regard, DIG's examples of methodologically "cheap" exchanges are suggestive. Despite their potentially radical call for interdisciplinarity, their cases that show tangible exchange gains are cases in which methodological costs of bilateral interactions are kept low. This suggests how difficult it is in practice to come up with completely new interdisciplinary models. In general, cognitive obstacles arising from ontological, conceptual, and methodological mismatches between disciplines make interdisciplinary research difficult (MacLeod 2018). Given such obstacles, using cheap exchanges to gain tangible epistemic and practical benefits is an effective and legitimate interdisciplinary model-building strategy.

MacLeod and Nagatsu (2018) call this strategy substitutive model-coupling. Substitutive model-coupling occurs when two fields share model templates of roughly similar structure for solving given classes of problems but use simplified methods and representations for components of those templates, which another field can handle with much more sophistication. MacLeod and Nagatsu (2016) have closely studied interactions between ecologists and economists addressing renewable natural resource management problems. Concerning modeling of values, ecologists use what economists would consider unreflective optimization criteria, with a history of relying on maximum sustained yield (MSY), which omits crucial economic considerations such as discounting of future value. Economists instead use as a management goal the maximum economic yield (MEY), that is, net present value of a flow of a given stock over an infinite time-horizon, taking more economic variables into account. Concerning modeling of tree growth, economists traditionally use crude biomass models for representing tree growth, which can then be replaced with more realistic process-based models with more variables and structure.

We find that substitutive model-coupling (including DIG's cases of variable substitution) can be a very effective interdisciplinary platform if it leverages off preexisting relations between variables to join components from different disciplines. Since, for the most part, the components are already in spatial and temporal alignment within the existing frameworks, scale problems do not arise. Furthermore, model construction tasks largely remain within the domain of each discipline, and thus under governance of their own disciplinary methods and standards. Since the modeling components are well integrated and relationships clear, feedback between components can be used to help better design components using information from across disciplinary boundaries.

There are a couple of differences between our case and that of DIG. First, our case involved coupling of models, not just substitution of variables. This means that the seemingly simple borrowing involved substantial mutual adjustments of details of models from ecologists and economists. In this sense, substitutive model-coupling is not as cheap as it seems. Second, and as a result of the first point, our case demonstrates tangible mutual epistemic gains, while the cases of DIG seem more like those of unilateral knowledge transfer than interdisciplinary exchange. We observed that economists' optimization became more realistic, and biologists' tree-growth model, which replaced economists' simpler biomass model, has also received corrective feedback from the economic model as a result of model integration. These differences in detail notwithstanding, our case and that of DIG both suggest that interdisciplinary exchange (or collaboration in our case) can yield tangible epistemic benefits with relatively low costs of model adjustments while maintaining the existing division of cognitive labor under favorable conditions such as relative similarity in modeling scales and concepts between disciplines.

Now, coming back to the other side of the ambivalence, namely DIG's radical proposal to go beyond the current disciplinary structure in interdisciplinary research, it seems that their cases do not motivate such a radical move. MacLeod and Nagatsu (2018) identify other types of integrative model-building strategies (modular model-coupling, integral modeling, and data-driven modeling), with their own affordances and limitations, but none of them support such a radical proposal, either. More generally, we argue that the convergence of interdisciplinary model-building strategies into these four types reflects a disciplinary way of effectively organizing problem-solving activities around a limited number of model-templates. We need to take such cognitive functions of disciplinarity more seriously.

I would like to add a final observation, which goes beyond the considerations of cognitive obstacles in interdisciplinary exchange. As I mentioned briefly in Section 2, economics and ecology may be different not only in epistemic standards but also in their value orientations. The latter kind of differences might, in distinct ways, make it difficult for the two disciplines to use common models. For example, MSY, which seems an unsophisticated management goal to economists, is still commonly used in fisheries science and in policy. Although there are probably cognitive (e.g., inertia) and many other contingent factors, differences in value orientations (e.g., economists' commitment to anthropocentrism and/or ecologists implicit rejection of it) may be one of the factors that need to be addressed. Although philosophers of science have studied the plurality of epistemic values, they have not systematically studied the plurality of non-epistemic values and how they affect epistemic activities, disciplinary or interdisciplinary. The interactions between economics and ecology provide fascinating cases to be explored for this purpose.

4. Conclusion

DesRoches, Inkpen, and Green's chapter is a fresh contribution to the growing field of philosophy of interdisciplinarity. Its virtues include (1) its explicit discussion of the history of the natural-artificial distinction and (2) its hands-on focus on concrete cases of interdisciplinary exchange between two practically relevant fields, economics, and ecology. Although much of conceptual issues—what interdisciplinarity is, how it is different from cross-, multi-, and transdisciplinarity (Huutoniemi et al. 2010), as well as what interdisciplinary exchange is and what this metaphor implies—are in the background and not explicitly discussed (see Grüne-Yanoff and Mäki 2014), DIG's focus on concrete and practical cases is informative. I see the future of philosophy of interdisciplinarity in this type of work, and in particular I suggest differences in value orientations across disciplines and their epistemic implications as an important topic to be explored in the future.

References

Bailey, M., U. R. Sumaila, and M. Lindroos. 2010. "Application of Game Theory to Fisheries over Three Decades." *Fisheries Research* 102 (1): 1–8.

Cooper, R. 2004. "Why Hacking Is Wrong about Human Kinds." *The British Journal for the Philosophy of Science* 55 (1): 73–85.

Costanza, R., R. d'Arge, R. de Groot, S. Farber, M. Grasso, B. Hannon, K. Limburg, S. Naeem, R. V. O'Neill, J. Paruelo, R. G. Raskin, P. Sutton, and M. van den Belt. 1997. "The Value of the World's Ecosystem Services and Natural Capital." *Nature* 387 (6630): 253–60.

Costanza, R., R. de Groot, P. Sutton, S. van der Ploeg, S. J. Anderson, I. Kubiszewski, S. Farber, and R. K.Turner. 2014. "Changes in the Global Value of Ecosystem Services." *Global Environmental Change* 26: 152–8.

Douglas, H. 2000. "Inductive Risk and Values in Science." *Philosophy of Science* 67 (4): 559–79.

Grüne-Yanoff, T., and U. Mäki. 2014. "Introduction: Interdisciplinary Model Exchanges." *Studies in History and Philosophy of Science Part A* 48: 52–9.

Hacking, I. 1999. *The Social Construction of What?* Cambridge, MA: Harvard University Press.

Huutoniemi, K., J. T. Klein, H. Bruun, and J. Hukkinen. 2010. "Analyzing Interdisciplinarity: Typology and Indicators." *Research Policy* 39 (1): 79–88.

Jacobs, J. A. 2013. *In Defense of Discipline: Interdisciplinarity and Specialization in the Research University*. Chicago, IL: University of Chicago Press.

Jimenez-Buedo, M., and F. Guala. 2016. "Artificiality, Reactivity, and Demand Effects in Experimental Economics." *Philosophy of the Social Sciences* 46 (1): 3–23.

MacKenzie, D., F. Muniesa, and L. Siu. 2007. *Do Economist Make Markets? On the Performativity of Economics*. Princeton, NJ: Princeton University Press.

MacLeod, M. 2018. "What Makes Interdisciplinarity Difficult? Some Consequences of Domain Specificity in Interdisciplinary Practice." *Synthese* 195 (2): 697–720.

MacLeod, M., and M. Nagatsu. 2016. "Model Coupling in Resource Economics: Conditions for Effective Interdisciplinary Collaboration." *Philosophy of Science* 83: 412–33.

MacLeod, M., and M. Nagatsu. 2018. "What does Interdisciplinarity Look Like in Practice: Mapping Interdisciplinarity and Its Limits in the Environmental Sciences." *Studies in History and Philosophy of Science Part A* 67: 74–84.

Mitchell, S. D. 2009. "Complexity and Explanation in the Social Sciences." In *Philosophy of the Social Sciences*, ed. C. Mantzavinos, chapter 5, 130–45. Cambridge: Cambridge University Press.

Nagel, E. 1979. *The Structure of Science*. Indianapolis, IN: Hackett.

Stephenson, R. L., A. J. Benson, K. Brooks, A. Charles, P. Degnbol, C. M. Dichmont, M. Kraan, S. Pascoe, S. D. Paul, A. Rindorf, and M. Wiber. 2017. "Practical Steps toward Integrating Economic, Social and Institutional Elements in Fisheries Policy and Management." *ICES Journal of Marine Science* 74 (7): 1981–9.

3

Team Agency and Conditional Games

Andre Hofmeyr and Don Ross

3.1 Introduction

All of economics is concerned with how some *agent* could do something better or best, in response to choices of other agents, resource constraints, and incentives defined as such by reference to the agent's goals. It is appropriate to refer to "agents" rather than to "people," because in many economic models the agents are firms, or households, or governments, or teams. Indeed, the overwhelming majority of economic applications concern aggregated responses (Ross 2014, chapter 5). Notwithstanding this fact, economics is frequently associated, both by its critics and by many of its leading practitioners and textbook authors, with individualism, the view that individual people are in some sense the fundamental sites of agency on which others are dependent.

Economists typically do not give individualism an ontological interpretation, that is, as reflecting a metaphysical doctrine to the effect that all properties of nonindividual agents must decompose into, or be functions of, individual human (or other animal) agents. Even if some economists, when they dabble in philosophy, adhere to such social atomism, "official" individualism is usually held to be "methodological" and might be expressed as the following constraint on economic model-building: a sound economic model should not require any individual human agent to choose an action that is suboptimal for her, given the choices of the other agents, without some (good) explanation (Ragot 2012).

Stated this way, methodological individualism as expressed in game-theoretic applications is the assumption that the solutions of all models involving individual human agents, either explicitly or implicitly, should be compatible with a non-cooperative Nash equilibrium of a game, that also models the interaction,[1] and in which the individual people in question are the players. Binmore (1994) provides an explicit defense of this methodological principle.

Following Ross (2014), we distinguish two variants of substantive (i.e., not merely methodological) individualism. *Normative* individualism refers to the Enlightenment conviction that individuals, not groups, are the centers of human dignity and valuation that most *deserve* valorization. In modern democracies this is a premise that liberals and conservatives generally share. It is typically assumed in welfare economics. *Descriptive* individualism, by contrast, refers to the view that people acquire their preferences asocially. Descriptive individualism is, in general, false: most human preferences, and almost all of the most important ones, are copied from other people or shaped under their guidance and tutelage. Individual human distinctiveness merits valorization *because* its cultivation and maintenance is an *achievement* for members of a social species given to high levels of suggestiveness and conformity. Thus, far from being in tension with one another, normative individualism and descriptive anti-individualism make a naturally complementary pair.

The fact that people tend naturally to identify with social groups to which they belong, but simultaneously strive to operate and optimize individual utility functions, is a phenomenon that a fully adequate economic modeling apparatus should be able to represent. This is one of the aims of the *team reasoning* idea promoted by Martin Hollis (1998), Robert Sugden (1993, 2000, 2003), and Michael Bacharach (1999, 2006). In Bacharch's (2006) unfinished[2] treatise *Beyond Individual Choice: Teams and Frames in Game Theory*, he and his scholarly executors emphasize that most people are experienced in executing gestalt switches between individual and group agency, sometimes choosing in such a way as to maximize an individual utility function and sometimes choosing in such a way as to maximize the utility of a team with which they identify. Furthermore, people are often aware of this gestalt duality and can and do compare and weigh the alternatives suggested by each gestalt in specific circumstances.

Ross (2014) argues that this phenomenon is better characterized as team *agency* rather than team *reasoning*, because like most economic responses it only sometimes involves deliberate reflection. This is not to say that when people reflexively optimize the utility of a group rather than themselves this doesn't amount to a choice. There is generally *some* hypothetical incentive that could move a person to try, in a specific interaction, exclusively to optimize her self-interest. The point, then, is that some chosen identifications do not result from reasoning, even though by definition all choice is motivated. But Bacharach (2006) and his executors use the phrase "team reasoning" because they link the modeling problem to the rational solution of equilibrium selection problems in game theory.

In the chapter to follow, we will first summarize the team reasoning idea as Bacharach (2006) conceives it. However, we will then show that the effect of team reasoning on equilibrium selection in games is generalized, both conceptually and technically, by Wynn Stirling's (2012) modeling framework for *conditional games*. As with other games, conditional games might or might not be explicitly represented by their players; sometimes they might be selected and stabilized by processes of biological, but in humans more typically social and institutional, evolution. If Stirling generalizes Bacharach where game theoretic representation is concerned, this can be seen as supporting Ross's (2014) suggestion that team reasoning is at best one special mechanism that supports team agency. If team reasoning sometimes goes on, discovery of the mechanisms that implement it falls within the domain of psychology rather than economics. What economists need to be able to model is team agency; and thanks to Stirling they now can.

3.2 Equilibium Selection and Team Reasoning

Equilibrium selection problems in game theory arise from the fact that many games have multiple Nash equilibria (NE), but often some NE seem more "sensible" and people in fact converge on them, even though the formal theory of choice that is built into game theory[3] includes no axioms or principles that recommend it. This property of NE, taken as a problem, motivated the *refinement* literature of the 1970s and 1980s (Kreps 1990), which sought to add restrictive axioms to solution concepts and thereby rule out "inferior" NE as solutions. This approach threatened to degenerate into a programme for rationalizing every distinct situation as a sui generis game, thus eviscerating the explanatory and predictive power of NE, and so was largely abandoned in the 1990s in favor of evolutionary and behavioral approaches to equilibrium selection. Behavioral models tend to restrict solutions by motivating bounds on people's rationality, whereas evolutionary models hardwire agents with strategies and rely on evolutionary dynamics to provide estimates of the likelihoods with which various equilibria will be played in a particular population.

In contrast to these approaches, Bacharach (2006) argues that when "fully rational" individual people reason as members of teams, some equilibrium selection problems dissolve. He focuses on three types of game to illustrate and defend his general proposal.

The first type is the pure coordination game, for which the strategic form is presented in Table 3.1. Players 1 and 2 simultaneously choose "Heads" or "Tails." If the labels match (i.e., Heads and Heads or Tails and Tails) the players each receive their highest-valued outcome. If the labels do not match, each player receives an outcome with lower utility. The game has two pure strategy NE, (Heads, Heads) and (Tails, Tails). In experiments literally involving coins, people tend to converge on (Heads, Heads) (Mehta, Starmer, and Sugden 1994). This suggests that (Heads, Heads) tends to be salient in the sense of Schelling (1960). Salience, famously, operates exogenously and is not captured by NE as a technical solution concept.

The second game Bacharach considers is the Prisoners' Dilemma (PD), as shown in strategic form in Table 3.2. The PD's unique NE is (Defect, Defect), but the outcome when both players adopt their dominant strategies, (2, 2), is worse for both players than what they each would have obtained, (3, 3), had they adopted their dominated strategies instead.

Bacharach argues that the one-shot PD presents a problem for applied game theory because in experiments many pairs of human players arrive at the Pareto superior outcome.

Table 3.1 Pure Coordination Game

		Player 2	
		Heads	**Tails**
Player 1	**Heads**	1, 1	0, 0
	Tails	0, 0	1, 1

Table 3.2 Prisoners' Dilemma

		Player 2	
		Cooperate	**Defect**
Player 1	**Cooperate**	3, 3	1, 4
	Defect	4, 1	2, 2

Table 3.3 Hi-Lo Game

		Player 2	
		High	**Low**
Player 1	**High**	2, 2	0, 0
	Low	0, 0	1, 1

Bacharach argues that the third game he considers, the Hi-Lo game of Table 3.3, provides the most representative frame for understanding the general class of equilibrium selection puzzles for which pure coordination and PD games furnish special cases. Hi-Lo has two pure strategy NE, (High, High) and (Low, Low), where the former Pareto dominates the latter.

Hi-Lo raises the same kind of equilibrium selection problem, according to Bacharach, as a pure coordination game because NE as a solution concept does not prescribe play of one pair of equilibrium strategies over the other. But the indeterminacy in Hi-Lo seems particularly troubling because in actual applications people have no problem at all in coordinating on the (High, High) equilibrium.

If we are willing to incorporate bounds on people's rationality, then it is easy to explain the selection of (High, High): if each player assumes that the other assigns equal probability to both strategies, then High is a mutual best response. But given the simplicity of the game this approach is unconvincing. If a style of unbounded reasoning that would prescribe the choice of High in this game can be identified, then Bacharach argues that it might also account for the solution principles apparently used by many or most human players of pure coordination games and one-shot PDs. Bacharach's (2006) theory of *team reasoning* is intended to identify such a general solution.

In motivating his proposal, Bacharach also directs attention to non-toy examples such as the "offside trap" in football (soccer) where defenders simultaneously run forward so that the other team is caught offside when it tries to attack the goal. Each defender has two strategies: she can try to steal the ball from the attackers and block the goal, or she can rush forward. If all defenders choose the second strategy, they might catch the attackers offside. The first strategy, Bacharach argues, is akin to playing Low in Hi-Lo while the latter is equivalent to playing High, because when everyone adopts the offside trap defense, the likelihood of success is greater. Such play is routinely observed in experienced teams. Can game theory be used to play any role in explaining this achievement?

Team reasoning, according to Bacharach, provides the answer. Players using such reasoning find the strategy profile that yields the highest possible payoff for the team, and then the players adopt the strategies which, in combination, produce the profile.

To develop the idea, we begin with what Bacharach refers as a *simple coordination context*. Assume that there is a set T of n agents, with a set of feasible profiles of options O, and a shared ranking of these profiles as embodied in the payoff function U.[4] Thus, a simple coordination context is the triple (T, O, U). Bacharach argues that many non-toy situations have the properties of a simple coordination context, and directs attention to hypothesized causal processes or *choice mechanisms* that determine the actions of agents in these contexts. One such choice mechanism, which Bacharach calls *simple direction*, has the following features. Let o^* be the profile o that yields the highest value of U. Under simple direction, we assume that a $(n + 1)$ agent, the *director*, works out o^*, identifies the agents in control of the constituent components of o^*, tells each agent i to execute her component o_i^*, and the agents then perform the directed actions. If all the members of T are influenced by simple direction, then o^* is implemented and U is maximized.

Team reasoning, Bacharach (2006: 123) argues, is "do-it-yourself direction." Agents in a simple coordination context team reason about choice problems as follows: each computes the optimal profile o^*; each identifies their component o_i^*; and each reasons that she should perform o_i^* because that is the component of the optimal profile over which she has control. Clearly, if everyone in T team reasons, then the optimal profile o^* is implemented and team welfare, as embodied in U, is maximized.

Team reasoning is thus a two-step process. The first step involves reasoning at the *group level* so as to identify the optimal profile o^*. The second step involves reasoning at the *individual level* so as to select and implement o_i^*, the individual's component of the optimal profile o^*. When the agents in T execute the profile o^*, Bacharach refers to the mechanism by which they do so as a *team mechanism* and the members of T as a *team*.

If we apply the logic of team reasoning to Hi-Lo, we see that the equilibrium selection problem dissolves. If the players of Hi-Lo team reason, they will identify (High, High) as the optimal profile (step one), and they will then each execute High, as this is each player's action from the optimal profile under her control (step two).

What should we expect when T includes team reasoners and non-team reasoners? And what happens when one cannot determine with certainty who is a team reasoner and who is not a team reasoner? These cases lead Bacharach to the notions of a *restricted coordination context* and *unreliable coordination context*, respectively.

A restricted coordination context occurs when there is common knowledge among the agents as to who team reasons and who does not team reason in a particular group. The latter agents are referred to as the *remainder* and they are assumed to adopt a fixed sub-profile f of actions, which is known to the team reasoners. The team reasoners in the group apply *restricted team reasoning*, the goal of which is to maximize U subject to the constraint that the non-team reasoners will adopt f. A restricted coordination context is arguably more realistic than a simple coordination context, but a generalization of both of these interactions is an unreliable coordination context.

The scope of a restricted coordination context is limited by two assumptions. The first is that there is common knowledge concerning those agents who comprise the remainder. In most coordination contexts there is likely to be uncertainty about who team reasons and who does not. The second assumption is that the agents in the remainder adopt a fixed sub-profile f. It may be the case, however, that members of the remainder have strategic inclinations of their own which produces a noncooperative game between the team reasoners and the remainder. Bacharach refers to this case as the *strategic remainder* problem; it is discussed in detail in Bacharach (1999). We will focus on the limitations engendered by the first assumption, which Bacharach terms the *unknown remainder* problem.

Assume that membership of the remainder is determined by a random process. That is, let M be a mechanism governing team choice, and assume that every agent functions under M with probability ω, which is common knowledge among the group. Assume further that if agent i turns out to be in the remainder, she adopts option f_i, where f_i is referred to as her *default choice*. We can describe this *unreliable coordination context* by the collection (S, ω, O, U, f), where S represents the set of n agents, ω is the probability of functioning under M, O is the set of feasible profiles of options, U is the shared payoff function, and f is the profile of default options. T now represents the subset of agents from S that function under M, and $R = S - T$ denotes the remainder.

In an unreliable coordination context, the crucial issue is how a team defines an optimal profile given the probability ω of functioning under M. The first-best profile o^* is unlikely to be attained because that is only possible when all agents function under M. The optimal profile in this context will be the one that maximizes the *expected value* of U and thereby takes into account the probabilities of functioning and failing under M. This particular profile is labeled o^{**}, and it is to be understood as the profile that maximizes the expected value of U given that each agent i will choose o_i with probability ω and f_i with probability $1 - \omega$.

In an unreliable coordination context, the interpretation of a *team mechanism* is one where the agents adopt o_i^{**} if they function under the mechanism, such that the mechanism delivers the profile o^{**}. A *team* is therefore defined as those agents in S who function under the mechanism M, which implies that T is a random set of agents. The definition of team reasoning in this context follows naturally from the definition given earlier: each agent i in T (i.e., an agent that functions under M) determines o^{**}, and then identifies and implements o_i^{**}. Bacharach refers to team reasoning in this unreliable coordination context as *circumspect team reasoning*. This mode of reasoning is efficient, in the sense of maximizing the expected value of U, even when there is uncertainty about which agents will function and fail under the mechanism.

A reader who finds this framework useful for analysis is bound to wonder what conditions, in general, tend to generate team reasoning. Bacharach argues that *group identification* primes team reasoning and he refers to this as the *reasoning effect* of group identification.

This brings us squarely to the question of how we identify human game players with (economic) agents. When we attribute agency to an individual person, it is natural to think about the person's options and his or her ranking of alternatives. In this case, one asks questions of the form, "What should *he* or *she* do?" But when we attribute agency to a group of people, the focus can shift to the profiles which the group can enact, and to the group's ranking of the outcomes. Then the question of interest might change to, "What should *they* do?" Note that this latter question exemplifies the first step of a director's reasoning. Bacharach's core intuition is that as the focus shifts from the options that an individual can choose to the profiles that groups can implement, the answers to these should-do questions change from being indeterminate (as in the equilibrium selection problem) to determinate.

Suppose that instead of simply attributing agency to a group from the outside (i.e., the case of the director), members of the group come to self-identify with the team. In this case, the relevant question changes from, "What should *they* do?" to, "What should *we* do?" Bacharach argues that when people start to ask these questions they undergo a two-part transformation: they experience not only a *payoff transformation* (seeking to promote U rather than u_i) but also an *agency transformation*—each person thinks of herself as a component part of the team's agency. Then just as the director engages in the first step of director reasoning so the team member engages in the first step of team reasoning, identifying the profile that maximizes U.

Bacharach argues that the likelihood of group identification is a function of a range of factors, some of which may be identifiable characteristics of a strategic interaction. One such characteristic is *strong interdependence*: each player realizes that she will do well from framing her decision in terms of team agency only to the extent that she can be assured that her similarly motivated partner takes a particular action, and there is uncertainty as to whether the partner will take the action in question. In coordination games, PDs, and Hi-Lo games, solving for equilibria of the interactions among players optimizing their individual preferences does not provide such assurance.

Bacharach refines this notion of strong interdependence to define the *interdependence hypothesis*. Consider the profiles S and S^*, where S is a solution to the game when players reason individualistically, e.g., (Defect, Defect) in a PD, and S^* is optimal for the group, e.g., (Cooperate, Cooperate) in a PD. Strong interdependence implies that, given S and S^*, the players have common interest in, and copower for, S^* over S, while recognizing that S is a solution to the game that will obtain if the players reason individualistically. The interdependence hypothesis is that group identification is stimulated by perception of strong interdependence.

Bacharach then argues that the salience of strong interdependence, the lack of countervailing pressures to self-identify, and the degree of strong interdependence are likely to affect the tendency to group identify, as implied by the interdependence hypothesis. Finally, he argues that when endogenous group identification occurs, the shared payoff function U will respect *unanimity*: if u_i and u_j, $i \neq j$, share the same ranking of profiles, then U will embody this ranking.

We are now in a position to state Bacharach's proposed resolution of the selection problem that seems to leave the game theorist unable to apply the Hi-Lo game analysis reasonably to applications with human players. In strategic interactions that fit the Hi-Lo specification, strong interdependence is highly salient and the payoff assignment indicates that there are no countervailing pressures to self-identify. As the players' preferences are in perfect alignment, u_i and u_j will share the same ranking of profiles and, by unanimity, the group payoff function U will embody this ranking.

Consequently, the tendency for players to group identify will be strong, and, if this occurs, it sets in motion the process whereby players team reason, identify (High, High) as the best profile, and then implement the action that falls to them as part of the optimal profile, that is, play High.

Bacharach argues that this theory has a far wider scope than coordination games. Specifically, strategic interactions, such as Stag Hunt, Battle of the Sexes, and PD, which embody mixed motives, are likely to prime group identification and prompt team reasoning. However, these games differ in important ways from coordination games. In mixed-motive games, there are countervailing pressures to self-identify, which, therefore, imply reduction in the salience of strong interdependence. Consequently, one expects team reasoning and attainment of the optimal profile for the team to be less prevalent in these interactions than in coordination games. People might waver between the gestalts of self-identification and team-identification.

In mixed-motive games, the link between the group payoff function U and the individual payoff functions u_i and u_j is more complex than in games where players' utilities are perfectly aligned. Bacharach argues that when endogenous group identification primes team reasoning, the shared payoff function U will respect unanimity in u_i and u_j and symmetry between individual payoffs. That is, in the PD example below, we only need to specify u_F to account for the strategy profile when one player cooperates and the other defects, rather than use two variables to index the outcomes in which one player cooperates and one defects.

Consider Table 3.4 below, which represents a generic PD, where C stands for Cooperate and D stands for Defect. The following inequalities must hold for the game to be dominance-solvable: $a > b > c > d$. In addition, for (C, C) to be Pareto optimal, $b > [(a + d) / 2]$. Now suppose that we want to find mechanisms which maximize U, where U is defined as a sum of agents' payoffs, and assume that anyone in the remainder plays D as her default choice. Assume further that the players interact in an unreliable coordination context and will engage, therefore, in circumspect team reasoning.

The first-best profile o^* is (C, C) and if $\omega = 1$, this profile will be enacted. But if $\omega < 1$, then matters are more complicated. Let $u_C = 2b$ represent the sum of individual payoffs when both players cooperate, $u_D = 2c$ represent the sum of individual payoffs if both players defect, and $u_F = a + d$ represent the sum of individual payoffs if one player cooperates while the other player defects; the subscript F refers to free-riding. Given the inequalities above, $u_C > u_D$ and $u_C > u_F$.

Now consider the profile (C, C). With probability ω^2 both players will adopt the profile and u_C will result; with probability $2\omega(1 - \omega)$ one player will play C while the

Table 3.4 Generic Prisoners' Dilemma

		Player 2	
		C	**D**
Player 1	**C**	b, b	d, a
	D	a, d	c, c

other plays D and u_F will result; and with probability $(1 - \omega)^2$ both players will play D and u_D will result. Thus, the expected value of U for the profile (C, C) is $EU(\text{C}, \text{C}) = \omega^2 u_C + 2\omega(1 - \omega)u_F + (1 - \omega)^2 u_D$.

Now consider the profile (D, D). As D is the default choice of both players, they will adopt the (D, D) profile with certainty and u_D will result. Finally, consider the two profiles (C, D) and (D, C). As one of the players is always playing D, the expected value of U from these profiles is: $\omega u_F + (1 - \omega)u_D$.

To determine o^{**}, the profile which maximizes U in an unreliable coordination context, we must consider two cases. The first is where $u_F \geq u_D$. In this case, $EU(\text{C}, \text{C}) = \omega^2 u_C + 2\omega(1 - \omega)u_F + (1 - \omega)^2 u_D > \omega u_F + (1 - \omega)u_D = EU(\text{C}, \text{D}) = EU(\text{D}, \text{C})$ for all values of ω and (C, C) therefore defines the profile o^{**}.

The second case is where $u_D > u_F$. In this situation, the optimal profile o^{**} depends on the value of ω. To see this, normalize $u_C = 1$ and $u_D = 0$ and note that $u_F < 0$. Then, $EU(\text{C}, \text{C}) = \omega^2 + 2\omega(1 - \omega)u_F > 0 = EU(\text{D}, \text{D}) \Leftrightarrow \omega > [2u_F / (2u_F - 1)]$. The reverse holds if $\omega < [2u_F / (2u_F - 1)]$. In words, at high values of ω (i.e., when the likelihood that agents function under M is high) the optimal profile o^{**} is (C, C), but when the value of ω is low, the optimal profile o^{**} is (D, D). Thus, the PD can be averted when the probability that agents team reason is relatively high.

In summary, Bacharach's theory structures models in which individuals may undergo payoff and agency transformations when strategic interactions are characterized by strong interdependence. Such interdependence prompts group identification and team reasoning, which together entail identifying the optimal profile and then reasoning to the conclusion that each player should adopt her component of the optimal profile.

Bacharach's project reflects the assumption that to explain the outcome of an interaction by identifying it with the equilibrium of a game requires specifying a path of reasoning that would select the outcome in question. This leaves open the possibility that people sometimes reach the outcomes that team reasoners would by other means—say, emotional identification with symbols of fused agency. In such instances, Bacharach's account encourages the judgment that game theory has nothing to contribute to the explanation. The agents in this kind of case don't decide that it is best to reason as a team, but simply do fuse their agency; if they participate in any processes usefully modeled as games, these will be interactions of their team with other agents (including, perhaps, other teams).

Following Coleman (1990), Ross (2014) argues for wider applicability of game theory. The mathematics of games is the basis for more than models of rational choice based on deliberation; it is also a technology for modeling social group formation and maintenance. Evolutionary game theory is one widespread approach to this project, but it abstracts from the context of choice altogether; individuals in evolutionary games simply express strategies selected by fitness competitions. If people can in fact switch between individually framed and team-framed agency in the course of their strategic interactions, as Bacharach suggests and as observation supports, then it is natural to ask whether game theory can contribute anything to our understanding of this. If, in fact, it can, then a second question arises: might the strategic principles that govern team framing itself also help to explain the relative stability of the equilibria at which teams arrive?

The issue at hand transcends questions about the reach of game theory. Bacharach defends a deontological interpretation of team reasoning as a driver of behavior. Once an individual has identified the optimal team profile and her component in it, he insists, she is rationally obliged to execute her component. Bacharach refers to this as the *projection feature* of profile-based reasoning, arguing that, "The underlying general principle is that I cannot coherently will something without willing what I know to be logically entailed by it" (2006: 136). It seems plausible that people sometimes reason in this way. However, we are sceptical of a claim to the effect that when people identify with teams and choose actions accordingly, they *typically* do so by means of reasoning or are much influenced by "logical compulsion." Game theory, like economics, is concerned with choices. If choice is *defined* in terms of outputs of reasoning processes, it follows that an account of team agency must be an account of reasoning. It might not necessarily be an account of actual deliberation in which people consciously engage, but rather an ex-post rationalization of behavior that serves as a "stand-by" or "back-up" to more common behavior-generating processes, as per the account of Pettit (2001). However, in our view, a general theory of an aspect of agency, particularly economic agency, should reflect the more deflationary account of choice that, as argued by Ross (2014), partly distinguishes economics from psychology, both methodologically and in terms of explanatory domains. According to this deflationary view, a behavior is chosen just in case it is subject to influence by incentives, regardless of whether the causal channel that links incentives and behavior involves deliberation. For example, if people spontaneously copy the behavior of higher-status, kin-bonded, or apparently successful people without thinking, this behavior can still be regarded as chosen because counter-incentives could dampen it, even though by hypothesis it does not result from reasoning.

An empirical basis for doubting that team reasoning is the only, or even principal, basis for team agency among people is drawn from developmental psychology. In efforts to shed light on the evolutionary depth of human altruism, researchers have compared spontaneous prosocial behavior in human and chimpanzee infants (Warneken and Tomasello 2006, 2007, 2009a, 2009b). Much of the focus has been on sharing, which does not necessarily implicate team agency. However, one of the primary alleged sites of difference between young humans and young chimpanzees has been based on observations of spontaneous assistance provided to adults who feign difficulty in completing tasks. The claim that young chimpanzees do not do this has been called into question (Horner et al. 2011); but the claim that humans as young as fourteen months join the projects of others without direct inducement by contingent reward is well established. This is at least prima facie evidence that team agency in humans is a natural propensity, rather than behavior that depends on deliberate reasoning. If young chimpanzees in fact show the same proclivity, at least under certain conditions, this would provide further grounds for seeking a more general theory.

Thus there are both theoretical and empirical motivations for seeking a more general game-theoretic account of team agency. A theory of team reasoning would then be a special application of this more general theory that could augment the relative stability of team solutions in groups of agents who are overwhelmingly motivated by rational deliberation. Wynn Stirling (2012)[5] has recently provided a formal theory that

Ross (2014, chapter 5) conjectured as filling just this role. In the next section, we first summarize Stirling's construction, and then confirm Ross's conjecture.

3.3 Conditional Game Theory and Social Agency

The avowed aim of Stirling (2012) is to develop a concept of group preference, which is not simply an exogenous aggregation of individual preferences, but which arises endogenously as social influences propagate through a group. Stirling's framework is a strict generalization of orthodox, non-evolutionary game theory that incorporates the influence of social bonds through the technology of *conditional preferences.*

To illustrate the intuition we employ an example due to Ross (2014). Consider a Board of Directors that must decide whether to engage in a risky hostile takeover bid. There are at least two ways in which the views of the board can be elicited. Under process (1), the chair sends out a detailed risk analysis of the costs and benefits of the proposed takeover prior to the board meeting. Under process (2), the chair, citing security concerns, presents the same information to the board but only after they have assembled in the boardroom. The question of interest is whether these two processes should be expected to yield the same outcome.

Process (1) encourages the Board members to form unconditional preferences prior to the meeting, which they might then defend against other members' arguments. Process (2), by contrast, may induce members to monitor one another while they decide which option is best and may lead them to modulate their preferences on the basis of the preferences of others. Under both processes, differing individual preferences are likely to be expressed through nonunanimous votes. But the distribution of these preferences might vary across the two scenarios because process (2) encourages revelation of preferences that are influenced by information about the preferences of others, which thereby affords more opportunity for preference calibration.

The starting point of Stirling's analysis is the distinction between what he terms *categorical* and *conditional* preferences. Categorical preferences *unconditionally* define an agent's ranking of all possible outcomes, regardless of other agents' preferences, whereas conditional preferences are based on influence flows that propagate through a group and define agents' rankings of alternative outcomes as *conditional* on the preferences of others. This propagation of influence flows, which is modeled using graph theory, defines a social model that enables agents to jointly consider individual and group interests, as in Bacharach's framework, but without requiring us to leave the Nash constraint.

Building on the earlier example, but simplifying to the case of the chair and one board member, assume that each player has two actions[6]: support (S) the takeover bid or do not support (NS) the takeover bid. Thus, the outcome space for this game is (S, S), (S, NS), (NS, S), (NS, NS), where the chair's action is listed first and the board member's action is listed second. Assume further that the chair has categorical preferences over the action profiles but, as suggested earlier, the board member's preferences may be influenced by the chair's. Specifically, suppose that if (S, S) is the chair's optimal profile, the board member will define his ranking of the alternatives on the basis of this hypothesis. By contrast, if (NS, NS) is the chair's optimal profile then the board member may define a different preference ordering. Given the four possible outcomes of this game, the board member can define different preference orderings that are conditional on his conjecture concerning the preference ordering of the chair.

Stirling's intuition is that as social influence propagates through a group and players modulate their preferences on the basis of other players' preferences, a complex notion of group preference may emerge. This notion may not directly provide the basis for action, but rather serve as a social model that incorporates all of the relationships and interdependencies that exist among the agents. Stirling refers to this concept as *concordance* and it captures the extent to which a conjectured[7] set of (categorical or conditional) preferences yield controversy within a group. Crucially, concordance does not refer to the goals of a group nor to the goals of the individuals who comprise it, but rather to the level of discord that hypothetical propositions concerning players' preferences engender among members of the group.

For example, consider the following joint conjectures for the chair and board member: $\mathbf{a}_1$ = {(S, S), (S, NS)} and $\mathbf{a}_2$ = {(S, S), (NS, NS)}. Assume that under $\mathbf{a}_1$, the chair's conjecture (S, S) is best for her and next-best for the board member while the board member's conjecture (S, NS) is best for him but next-best for the chair. By contrast, assume that under $\mathbf{a}_2$, the chair's conjecture (S, S) is, once again, best for her and next-best for the board member while the board member's conjecture (NS, NS) is worst for both players. Which conjecture is likely to entail a greater level of controversy among the players? The joint conjecture $\mathbf{a}_1$ involves different conjectures by the two players but they do not include the players' worst outcome. The joint conjecture $\mathbf{a}_2$, by contrast, incorporates a conjecture (S, S) that might be satisfactory to either player but one (NS, NS) which is the worst for both players. Consequently, we might expect $\mathbf{a}_2$ to produce more severe dispute among the players than $\mathbf{a}_1$ and an ordering over these joint conjectures that is sensitive to these varying levels of controversy encodes the concept of concordance.

The level of concordance varies with the specific strategic interaction under study. In games where players' interests are perfectly aligned, the extent of controversy will be minimized when players conjecture identical action profiles. In zero-sum games, by contrast, a low degree of controversy is more likely when conjectures are diametrically opposed. In a penalty shootout in soccer, for example, success for the group (i.e., the two teams together) requires fierce competition and rivalry, so if the goalkeeper were to favor a conjecture similar to the striker, this would undermine competition and produce a high level of controversy. As Stirling (2012: 40) notes, "even antagonists can behave concordantly."

While the concept of concordance may provide the basis for an emergent notion of group preference, its value derives from the extent to which it is determined by the individuals who make up a group. In other words, concordance should not be imposed exogenously on a group from the outside but should instead be determined by the social linkages and influence flows among members of a group. Stirling refers to this principle as *endogeny*. It is among the building blocks of his *aggregation theorem*, which in turn provides a model of the social relationships and interdependencies of members of a group, and a device for simultaneously representing individual and group agency.

To develop a concordant ordering that respects the principles of conditioning (i.e., that players' preferences may be conditional on the preferences of others) and endogeny, Stirling employs the logic of multivariate probability theory in a *praxeological* context. He urges us to understand praxeology on the basis of an analogy with epistemology. Whereas epistemology is concerned with the nature and scope of knowledge and classifies propositions on the basis of their veracity, praxeology classifies propositions on the basis of their efficacy and efficiency.

In probability theory, given a set of two discrete random variables $\{X, Y\}$, the conditional probability mass function $p_{Y|X}(y \mid x) = P(Y = y \mid X = x)$ is a measure of the likelihood that the random variable $Y = y$ given that, or conditional on, the random variable $X = x$. This conditional probability mass function is defined as the ratio of the joint probability of X and Y and the marginal probability of X or $p_{Y|X}(y \mid x) = p_{XY}(x, y) / p_X(x)$. Solving this expression for $p_{XY}(x, y)$ as the subject of the formula (i.e., $p_{XY}(x, y) = p_{Y|X}(y \mid x) \times p_X(x)$) it is clear that the joint probability of X and Y can be derived from the conditional probability of Y given X and the marginal probability of X. In other words, probability theory provides a framework for combining information from different sources—in this instance, the conditional probability of Y given X and the marginal probability of X—to determine the joint likelihood of an event.

In the praxeological framework, Stirling's goal is to derive a concordant ordering for the group that combines the conditional and categorical preferences of members of the group, in much the same way as the joint probability of an event is determined by conditional and marginal probabilities. Working directly with preference orderings quickly becomes cumbersome, so Stirling seeks to derive utility functions that represent the players' categorical and conditional preferences and the group's concordant preference ordering. The existence theorem for a utility function that represents categorical preferences is well known, so we will focus on the derivation of a conditional utility function and the principles which must hold so as to permit aggregation of categorical and conditional preferences to derive a concordant utility function.

Let $\{X_1, \ldots, X_n\}$, $n \geq 2$, represent a set of n players, and let A_i denote a finite set of actions available to player i from which he or she must choose one element to instantiate. An action or strategy *profile* is an array $\mathbf{a} = (a_1, \ldots, a_n) \in A_1 \times \ldots \times A_n$. Under classical game theory, players have categorical utility or payoff functions defined over strategy profiles: $u_i: A_1 \times \ldots \times A_n \to \mathrm{R}$.

In the context of conditional preferences, it is useful to define the parent set $pa(X_i) = \{X_{i1}, \ldots, X_{in}\}$ as the n_i-element subset of players whose preferences influence X_i's preferences. Assume that X_{ij}, the jth parent of X_i, forms the hypothetical proposition that profile $\mathbf{a}_{ij}$ will occur. This hypothetical proposition is termed a *conjecture*. Thus, let $\mathbf{a}_i = \{\mathbf{a}_{i1}, \ldots, \mathbf{a}_{in}\}$ represent the *joint conjecture* of $pa(X_i)$. Then there exists a function that maps action profiles, *conditional* on the joint conjecture of $pa(X_i)$, to the real line R, which represents X_i's preferences: $u_{Xi \mid pa(Xi)}(\cdot \mid \mathbf{a}_i): A_1 \times \ldots \times A_n \to \mathrm{R}$. Note that if $pa(X_i) = \varnothing$ then the conditional utility $u_{Xi \mid pa(Xi)}$ becomes the categorical utility u_i. Given the existence of a conditional utility function which represents players' conditional preferences, the collection $\{X_i, A_i, u_{Xi \mid pa(Xi)}, i = 1, \ldots, n\}$ constitutes a finite, normal form, noncooperative *conditional game*.

Returning to our example of the chair (C) and the board member (B), the conditional game consists of two players $\{X_C, X_B\}$, each with two actions $A_i = \{S, NS\}$, and the utility functions $u_C(\mathbf{a}_C)$ and $u_{B|C}(\mathbf{a}_B \mid \mathbf{a}_C)$, for the chair and board member, respectively.

Note that through appropriate normalization one can ensure that all utilities (i.e., categorical and conditional) are nonnegative and sum to unity, which implies that the utilities have all of the characteristics of probability mass functions. As discussed earlier, in an epistemological framework marginal and conditional probabilities can be combined to determine a joint probability: $p_{XY}(x, y) = p_{Y|X}(y \mid x) \times p_X(x)$. Consequently, if the praxeology-epistemology analogy is appropriate, it may be possible to aggregate the conditional and categorical utilities to define a group utility function that incorporates the social linkages and interdependencies of members of a group and thereby represents the level of concordance of the group. The benefit of showing that this praxeology-epistemology analogy holds is that it will then be possible to apply concepts from multivariate probability theory, such as Bayes's rule and marginalization, in a praxeological context and derive game-theoretic solution concepts that incorporate both individual and group interests.

Returning to our example, the goal is to combine the categorical preferences of the chair with the conditional preferences of the board member to produce an emergent preference ordering for the group. The requirement is to prove that the group or concordant utility $U_{CB}(\mathbf{a}_C, \mathbf{a}_B) = u_{B|C}(\mathbf{a}_B \mid \mathbf{a}_C) \times u_C(\mathbf{a}_C)$. In words, the concordant utility U is the product of the board member's conditional utility and the chair's categorical utility.

In assembling the basis for such a proof, Stirling adopts three further assumptions or *principles*. The first is *acyclicity*, which means that no cycles can occur in the social influence relationships among players. In other words, if the chair influences the board member, then the board member cannot influence the chair. The problem with cyclical influence relationships is that they raise the possibility of indirect self-influence: the chair influences the board member, who in turn influences the chair, which leads to a nonterminating cycle. Clearly, this limits the generality of the model, and in so doing raises the stakes on its capacity to generalize the idea of team agency. As we shall see below, however, the restrictive power of acyclicity is countered elsewhere in the theory. An implication of acyclicity is that influence relationships are hierarchical and that at least one player in a strategic interaction must possess categorical preferences. Another implication is that social influence relationships can be represented using a directed acyclic graph (DAG).

The second principle is *exchangeability*, which Stirling and Felin (2013) refer to as framing invariance. This principle requires that if a strategic interaction can be framed in different ways but there is no loss of information under the different framings, then all framings must produce an identical concordant ordering. What this principle implies is that players must be willing to take into consideration the preferences of others when defining their own preferences, even if only to a small degree, and that the same information is available to the players under alternative framings.

In an epistemological context, framing invariance is a natural restriction because it implies that $p_{XY}(x, y) = p_{Y|X}(y \mid x) \times p_X(x) = p_Y(y) \times p_{X|Y}(x \mid y) = p_{YX}(y, x)$. For framing invariance to hold in a praxeological context, the concordant utility must satisfy the following conditions: $U_{CB}(\mathbf{a}_C, \mathbf{a}_B) = u_{B|C}(\mathbf{a}_B \mid \mathbf{a}_C) \times u_C(\mathbf{a}_C) = u_B(\mathbf{a}_B) \times u_{C|B}(\mathbf{a}_C \mid \mathbf{a}_B) = U_{BC}(\mathbf{a}_B, \mathbf{a}_C)$. In words, the concordant utility U_{CB}, which combines the conditional preferences of the board member and categorical preferences of the chair, must be the same as the concordant utility U_{BC}, which combines the categorical preferences of the board member and the conditional preferences of the chair. This principle mitigates the restrictive force of acyclicity with respect to the range of interactions we can use the theory to model.

The final principle required to derive a concordant utility function that has all of the characteristics of a joint probability mass function is *monotonicity*. This is a natural restriction on the concordant utility function, which ensures that no individual's preferences will be arbitrarily subjugated by the group. Specifically, if an individual or subgroup prefers option A to B and the other players are indifferent among them, then the group must not prefer B to A. Thus, if the chair prefers S to NS and the board member is indifferent, the group must not prefer NS to S.

Stirling (2012: 59–60) proves that if the principles of *conditioning*, *endogeny*, *acyclicity*, *exchangeability*, and *monotonicity* hold, then a concordant utility function exists that represents the social relationships of the group, and is derived from the conditional and categorical utility functions of its members. The most general form of the concordant utility function is

$$U_{X1 \ldots Xn}(\mathbf{a}_1, \ldots, \mathbf{a}_n) = \Pi^n_{i=1}\, u_{Xi \mid pa(Xi)}(\mathbf{a}_i \mid \mathbf{a}_i)$$

This expression shows that the concordant utility function, which combines information in a praxeological domain, shares exactly the same syntax as a joint probability mass function that combines information in an epistemological domain. Consequently, the full power of multivariate probability theory (particularly Bayes's rule and marginalization) can be applied in a praxeological context to determine effective and efficient action when social influences propagate through a group.

Marginalization is an important operation in the praxeological domain because it allows the analyst to extract players' ex-post preferences once social influence has permeated the group. A player's ex-post *unconditional* preferences are extracted in the following manner:

$$u_{Xi}(\mathbf{a}_i) = \Sigma_{\sim \mathbf{a}i}\, U_{X1 \ldots Xn}(\mathbf{a}_1, \ldots, \mathbf{a}_n),$$

where $\Sigma_{\sim \mathbf{a}i}$ means that the sum is taken over all arguments except $\mathbf{a}_i$. Note that these ex-post categorical utilities represent the players' preferences after taking into account the social relationships and interdependencies that exist in the group. As the preferences are unconditional, standard solution concepts such as dominance and NE can be applied to them.

The preceding discussion is summarized in Figure 3.1. As social influences propagate through a group, players define their conditional preferences. Through the process of aggregation these social linkages and interdependencies lead to an emergent notion of group preference: concordance. Finally, through the process of marginalization, the analyst extracts the players' ex-post categorical preferences.

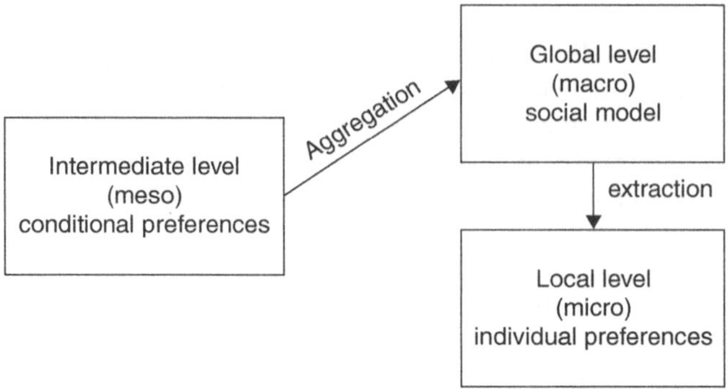

Figure 3.1 Conditioning, aggregation, and extraction.

Source: Stirling (2012: 19).

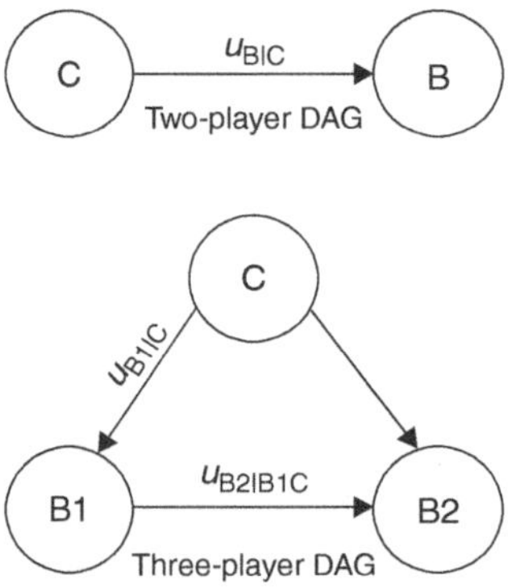

Figure 3.2 Directed acyclic graphs.

Acyclicity implies that social influence relationships in conditional games can be modeled using a DAG. A DAG is a *graph* made up of *vertices* or *nodes*, which in a praxeological context represents the players, and *directed edges* or *links*, which capture the influence relationships between the players. If one player, C, influences another player, B, we write C → B, where C is referred to as the *parent* of B and B as the *child* of C. The set of parents of B is denoted *pa*(B) and the set of children of B is denoted *ch*(B). If a vertex has no parents, *pa*(C) = ∅, then it is called a root vertex. Figure 3.2 shows the DAG for the chair and board member example and the case where there is a chair and two board members.

In the two-player DAG, the chair influences the board member but, given acyclicity, the board member does not influence the chair. The board member's conditional utility $u_{B|C}$ is represented by the edge between the nodes C and B. In the three-player DAG, the chair influences board member B1 and board member B2, and board member B1 influences board member B2. The influence flow between C and B1 is captured by the conditional utility $u_{B1|C}$ and the influence flows between C and B1 toward B2 are captured by the conditional utility $u_{B2|B1C}$. The associated concordant utility for the three-player DAG is

$$U_{CB1B2}(\mathbf{c}, \mathbf{b}_1, \mathbf{b}_2) = u_C(\mathbf{c}) \times u_{B1|C}(\mathbf{b}_1, \mathbf{c}) \times u_{B2|B1C}(\mathbf{b}_2 \mid \mathbf{c}, \mathbf{b}_1)$$

This expression combines information from the categorical and conditional utilities to define the concordant utility in much the same way that a Bayesian network, which can also be represented in a DAG, combines information from marginal and conditional probabilities to determine a joint probability. Thus, a DAG provides a graphical method to represent the influence flows, and associated conditional utilities, of a conditional game.

The three-player DAG in Figure 3.2 shows that B2 does not directly influence B1 and that neither B1 nor B2 directly influence C. However, this does not imply that B1 and B2 have no influence on C whatsoever. Recall that the exchangeability constraint means that a social model should be invariant to the way in which the information about linkages and influence flows is aggregated. This implies that once the concordant utility has been defined, we can apply Bayes's rule to extract reciprocal influence relationships. Specifically, suppose that B1 conjectures $\mathbf{b}_1$ and we want to determine the influence of this conjecture on the chair's preference for $\mathbf{c}$: $u_{C|B1}(\mathbf{c} \mid \mathbf{b}_1)$. The answer follows directly from Bayes's rule:

$$u_{C|B1}(\mathbf{c} \mid \mathbf{b}_1) = [u_{B1|C}(\mathbf{b}_1 \mid \mathbf{c}) \times u_C(\mathbf{c})] \;/\; u_{B1}(\mathbf{b}_1),$$

where $u_{B1}(\mathbf{b}_1)$ is derived by marginalizing the concordant utility.

We can also determine the influence that B1 and B2 exert on C and the influence that B2 exerts on B1 by computing the appropriate conditional and categorical utilities using Bayes's rule and marginalization. The crucial idea here is that once the concordant utility has been defined, exchangeability implies that many hierarchical structures are compatible with the social model of the group. In other words, the social model is framing invariant.

Stirling then extends—as opposed to refines—the standard solution concepts of dominance and NE, to apply over group-level preference orderings. His approach is to extract a marginal utility for the group in much the same way as a marginal utility for each player was extracted from the concordant utility. A crucial assumption behind the procedure is that, given that players can only control their own actions, each player will make conjectures over her own action sets and not those of other players.

Thus, let a_{ij} denote the *j*th element of $\mathbf{a}_i$, where $\mathbf{a}_i$ is X_i's conjecture profile. Now form the action profile $(a_{11}, \ldots, a_{nn})$ by taking the *i*th element of each X_i's conjecture profile. Finally, sum the concordant utility over all elements of each $\mathbf{a}_i$ except a_{ii} to form the group utility or welfare function:

$$V_{X1\ldots Xn}(a_{11}, \ldots, a_{nn}) = \Sigma_{\sim a11} \cdots \Sigma_{\sim ann} U_{X1\ldots Xn}(\mathbf{a}_1, \ldots, \mathbf{a}_n)$$

As Stirling notes, the group does not act as a single entity and it cannot, therefore, instantiate its own preferred alternative, but the group utility provides a metric by which individual players determine the impact of their choices on the group. In much the same way as players can extract their marginal utilities from the concordant utility function, they can extract their own individual marginal welfare functions from the group utility. Specifically, the marginal individual welfare function v_{Xi} of X_i is the *i*th marginal of $V_{X1 \ldots Xn}$:

$$v_{Xi}(a_i) = \Sigma_{\sim ai} V_{X1 \ldots Xn}(a_1, \ldots, a_n)$$

The existence of group and individual welfare functions allows Stirling to derive a solution concept that allows us to formally integrate consideration of the interests of the group with consideration of the interests of the individual players. This solution concept relies on the maximum individual and group welfare solutions.

The maximum group welfare solution is:

$$\mathbf{a}^* = \arg\max_{\mathbf{a} \in A1 \times \ldots \times An} V_{X1 \ldots Xn}(\mathbf{a})$$

The maximum individual welfare solution is

$$a_i^{\$} = \arg\max_{ai \in Ai} v_{Xi}(a_i)$$

If $a_i^{\$} = a_i^*$ for all $i \in \{1, \ldots, n\}$, the action profile is a *consensus* choice, meaning that group and individual welfare is maximized when **a** is instantiated. As Stirling notes, a consensus choice will often not exist, in which case players might be motivated to enter into negotiation to reach compromise. In a noncooperative game setting, the outcomes of such negotiations would need to be protected by commitment devices. This would signal a failure of team agency to form, though repeated interaction with the resulting new institutions might ultimately incentivize players to identify with them, and thereby create conditions for team agency later. For present purposes, however, it suffices to show that conditional game theory generalizes team agency in cases where consensus choice applies, because Bacharach's unanimity condition is a special case of it.

To show this, we begin with the PD. As Bacharach recognizes, one cannot obtain cooperation in a PD—in his framework, the conditions for team reasoning are not present—if no player cares about the welfare of the group at all. Thus, as established by Binmore (1994), if the preference structure of the PD describes *all* of the relevant preference information pertinent to the interaction, then general defection is the only outcome that a game theoretic model of it can predict. Binmore further insists that if the model does *not* incorporate all such information in the specification of preferences, then the game should not be characterized as a PD in the first place. However, admitting the mere *possibility* of team agency allows us to admit that more than one game structure might be relevant to modeling an empirical interaction. This situation is hardly unprecedented in economics. We are used to the idea, for example, that a plurality of models are useful for foregrounding different aspects of international trade, oligopoly, national production, and other phenomena. Stirling (2012: 80) draws a distinction between simple reciprocal altruism that transforms PDs into coordination games, and background representations of interaction structures in which players' models of their own and others' preferences are consistent with the PD structure, but they are also aware of preferences they *would* have *conditional* on the implementation of some degree of socially mediated agency. This is indeed the basis on which Stirling's general framework is given its name.

The machinery by which Stirling represents genuine PD structure simultaneously with scope for team agency representation are *cooperation and exploitation indices.* Specifically, Stirling endows each player X_i with a cooperation index $\alpha_i \in [0, 1]$ and an exploitation index $\beta_i \in [0, 1]$, where α_i represents the extent to which a player is conditionally willing to cooperate, and β_i represents the extent to which a player is conditionally willing to exploit his or her partner. Because these tolerances are conditional on the same model transformation, we impose a minimal consistency requirement by assuming that $\alpha + \beta < 1$. To respect acyclicity, assume further that X_1 has categorical preferences and that X_2's conditional preferences are conditional on X_1's.

Given the cooperation and exploitation indices, X_1's categorical utility is defined as follows:

$$u_{X1}(\text{C, C}) = \alpha_1 \qquad u_{X1}(\text{C, D}) = 0$$
$$u_{X1}(\text{D, C}) = \beta_1 \qquad u_{X1}(\text{D, D}) = 1 - \alpha_1 - \beta_1$$

In the PD representation of the interaction, $\beta_1 > \alpha_1 > 1 - \alpha_1 - \beta_1 > 0$, and X_2 has a categorical utility function such that $u_{X2}(\text{C, D}) > u_{X2}(\text{C, C}) > u_{X2}(\text{D, D}) > u_{X2}(\text{D, C})$.

For the conditional representation, we calculate $u_{X2|X1}(a_{21}, a_{22} \mid a_{11}, a_{12})$ by computing utilities for every possible conjecture that player X_1 can make. Assume that if X_1 conjectures either (C, C) or (D, D), then X_2 will place all of her conditional utility mass on the same action profile. In other words, if X_1 conjectures cooperation then X_2 finds it optimal to cooperate, but if X_1 conjectures defection then X_2 finds it optimal to defect. If X_1 conjectures (C, D), then X_2's utility mass will be apportioned according to her cooperation and exploitation indices. Specifically, X_2 will assign α_2 to (C, C), β_2 to (C, D), $1 - \alpha_2 - \beta_2$ to (D, D) and zero utility mass to (D, C) because this is the worst possible outcome for X_2. Finally, if X_1 conjectures (D, C), the worst outcome for X_2, X_2 should place zero utility mass on (D, C), α_2 and (C, C), β_2 on (C, D) and $1 - \alpha_2 - \beta_2$ on (D, D). The conditional utilities associated with each conjecture of X_1, represented in the columns, and every action profile, which can be instantiated by the two players, represented in the rows, are given in Table 3.5.

To compute the concordant utility, we combine X_1's categorical utility with X_2's conditional utility: $U_{X1X2}(\mathbf{a}_1, \mathbf{a}_2) = u_{X2|X1}(a_{21}, a_{22} \mid a_{11}, a_{12}) \times u_{X1}(a_{11}, a_{12})$. The result is shown in Table 3.6, where the rows index X_1's conjecture and the columns index X_2's conjecture.

Table 3.5 Conditional Utilities of the Prisoners' Dilemma

	(a_{11}, a_{12})			
(a_{21}, a_{22})	**(C, C)**	**(C, D)**	**(D, C)**	**(D, D)**
(C, C)	1	α_2	α_2	0
(C, D)	0	β_2	β_2	0
(D, C)	0	0	0	0
(D, D)	0	$1 - \alpha_2 - \beta_2$	$1 - \alpha_2 - \beta_2$	1

Table 3.6 Concordant Utilities of the Prisoners' Dilemma

			(a_{21}, a_{22})	
(a_{11}, a_{12})	(C, C)	(C, D)	(D, C)	(D, D)
(C, C)	α_1	0	0	0
(C, D)	0	0	0	0
(D, C)	$\alpha_2\beta_1$	$\beta_1\beta_2$	0	$\beta_1 - \alpha_2\beta_1 - \beta_1\beta_2$
(D, D)	0	0	0	$1 - \alpha_1 - \beta_1$

Table 3.7 Ex-post Payoff Matrix of the Prisoners' Dilemma

		X_2	
		C	D
X_1	C	$\alpha_1, \alpha_1 + \alpha_2\beta_1$	$0, \beta_1\beta_2$
	D	$\beta_1, 0$	$1 - \alpha_1 - \beta_1, 1 - \alpha_1 - \alpha_2\beta_1 - \beta_1\beta_2$

The concordant utility can now be used to extract the ex-post marginal utilities, the group welfare function, and the individual welfare function. X_1's ex-post utilities are equivalent to her categorical utilities, whereas X_2's ex-post utilities must be derived through marginalization: $u_{X2}(\mathbf{a}_2) = \Sigma_{\sim a2} U_{X1X2}(\mathbf{a}_1, \mathbf{a}_2)$. For example, u_{X2} (C, C) $= \alpha_1 + 0 + \alpha_2\beta_1 + 0 = \alpha_1 + \alpha_2\beta_1$. The ex-post payoff matrix for the PD is shown in Table 3.7.

The group welfare function for this two-player game is derived using the following expression: $V_{X1X2}(a_{11}, a_{22}) = \Sigma_{\sim a11} \Sigma_{\sim a22} U_{X1X2}(\mathbf{a}_1, \mathbf{a}_2)$. For example, V_{X1X2} (D, D) $= \beta_1\beta_2 + 0 + \beta_1 - \alpha_2\beta_1 - \beta_1\beta_2 + 1 - \alpha_1 - \beta_1 = 1 - \alpha_1 - \alpha_2\beta_1$. The full group welfare function is

$$V_{X1X2}(\text{C, C}) = \alpha_1$$
$$V_{X1X2}(\text{C, D}) = 0$$
$$V_{X1X2}(\text{D, C}) = \alpha_2\beta_1$$
$$V_{X1X2}(\text{D, D}) = 1 - \alpha_1 - \alpha_2\beta_1$$

Finally, the individual welfare functions are extracted from the group welfare function using marginalization: $v_{Xi}(a_i) = \Sigma_{\sim ai} V_{X1X2}(a_1, a_2)$. For example, $v_{X2}(\text{C}) = \alpha_1 + \alpha_2\beta_1$. Thus, the individual welfare functions are

$$v_{X1}(\text{C}) = \alpha_1 \qquad v_{X1}(\text{D}) = 1 - \alpha_1$$
$$v_{X2}(\text{C}) = \alpha_1 + \alpha_2\beta_1 \qquad v_{X2}(\text{D}) = 1 - \alpha_1 - \alpha_2\beta_1$$

To find the NE of this game after incorporating the social influence flows between X_1 and X_2, we work directly with the conditional and categorical utilities (Stirling refers to the equilibria identified using this method as *conditioned NE*) or the ex-post marginal utilities (Stirling refers to the equilibria identified using this method as *ex-post NE*). The two approaches yield identical solutions. Table 3.7 shows that (D, D) is a NE for all admissible values of α_i and β_i. Unlike the unconditional PD, (C, C) is a NE when $\alpha_i > \beta_i$. Furthermore, when $\alpha_i > \beta_i$, (C, C) is a consensus choice because it maximizes both group and individual welfare. In an unconditional representation of the play that will in fact be observed, this would be reflected in altered payoff rankings, making the empirically correct unconditional game an Assurance Game rather than a PD.

It is intuitive that if both players prefer cooperation to exploitation then (C, C) will be a conditioned or ex-post NE, but this result fails to highlight the role that social influences can play in this game. To see this, assume that $\alpha_1 = 0.6$ and $\beta_1 = 0.3$ and that $\alpha_2 = 0.3$ and $\beta_2 = 0.6$. Thus, X_1's cooperation index is twice as large as her exploitation index, but X_2's cooperation index is half as large as her exploitation index. So, in the absence of influence flows, X_1 is a cooperator and X_2 is an exploiter. But after X_2 takes into account X_1's preferences, X_2's penchant for exploitation is tempered by X_1's desire for cooperation and (C, C) is a conditioned NE.

While explaining cooperation in an empirical interaction that might be mis-predicted if we attend only to its unconditional model as a one-shot PD is an important accomplishment, we must keep in mind Bacharach's argument that the litmus test for an effort to represent team agency is that it furnish an explanation for High play in Hi-Lo. We now show that conditional game theory passes this test. In the discussion below, H stands for High and L stands for Low.

To allow social influences to affect the analysis of Hi-Lo, we endow each player X_i with a *High play index* $\alpha_i \in [0, 1]$ and a *Low play index* $\beta_i \in [0, 1]$, where $\alpha_i + \beta_i = 1$, because the players will assign zero utility mass to mis-matches, that is, (H, L) and (L, H). Assume again that X_1's preferences are categorical and that X_2's conditional preferences are conditional on X_1's.

Given the High play and Low play indices, X_1's categorical utility is defined as follows:

$$u_{X1}(\text{H}, \text{H}) = \alpha_1 \qquad u_{X1}(\text{H}, \text{L}) = 0$$
$$u_{X1}(\text{L}, \text{H}) = 0 \qquad u_{X1}(\text{L}, \text{L}) = \beta_1$$

To calculate $u_{X2|X1}(a_{21}, a_{22} \mid a_{11}, a_{12})$ it is necessary to compute utilities for every possible conjecture of player X_1. Assume that if X_1 conjectures either (H, H) or (L, L) then X_2 will place all of her conditional utility mass on the same action profile. That is, if X_1 conjectures High then X_2 finds it optimal to play High but if X_1 conjectures Low then X_2 finds it optimal to play Low. If X_1 conjectures (H, L) or (L, H), then X_2's utility mass will be apportioned according to her High play and Low play indices. Specifically, X_2 will assign α_2 to (H, H), β_2 to (L, L), and zero utility mass to (H, L) and (L, H) because these are the worst outcomes for X_2. The conditional utilities associated with each conjecture of X_1, represented in the columns, and every action profile which can be instantiated by the two players, represented in the rows, are given in Table 3.8.

To compute the concordant utility, we combine X_1's categorical utility with X_2's conditional utility: $U_{X1X2}(\mathbf{a}_1, \mathbf{a}_2) = u_{X2|X1}(a_{21}, a_{22} \mid a_{11}, a_{12}) \times u_{X1}(a_{11}, a_{12})$. The result is

Table 3.8 Conditional Utilities of the Hi-Lo Game

		(a_{11}, a_{12})		
(a_{21}, a_{22})	**(H, H)**	**(H, L)**	**(L, H)**	**(L, L)**
(H, H)	1	α_2	α_2	0
(H, L)	0	0	0	0
(L, H)	0	0	0	0
(L, L)	0	β_2	β_2	1

Table 3.9 Concordant Utilities of the Hi-Lo Game

		(a_{21}, a_{22})		
(a_{11}, a_{12})	**(H, H)**	**(H, L)**	**(L, H)**	**(L, L)**
(H, H)	α_1	0	0	0
(H, L)	0	0	0	0
(L, H)	0	0	0	0
(L, L)	0	0	0	β_1

shown in Table 3.9 where the rows index X_1's conjecture and the columns index X_2's conjecture.

The concordant utility can now be used to extract the ex-post marginal utilities, the group welfare function, and the individual welfare function. As X_1's preferences remain categorical, her ex-post utilities are her categorical utilities, whereas X_2's ex-post utilities must be derived through marginalization: $u_{X2}(\mathbf{a}_2) = \Sigma_{\sim\mathbf{a}2}\, U_{X1X2}(\mathbf{a}_1, \mathbf{a}_2)$. For example, $u_{X2}(\mathrm{H, H}) = \alpha_1 + 0 + 0 + 0 = \alpha_1$. The ex-post payoff matrix for the Hi-Lo Game is shown in Table 3.10.

The group welfare function for this two-player game is derived using the following expression: $V_{X1X2}(a_{11}, a_{22}) = \Sigma_{\sim a11}\, \Sigma_{\sim a22}\, U_{X1X2}(\mathbf{a}_1, \mathbf{a}_2)$. For example, $V_{X1X2}(\mathrm{H, H}) = \alpha_1 + 0 + 0 + 0 = \alpha_1$. The full group welfare function is

$$V_{X1X2}(\mathrm{H, H}) = \alpha_1$$
$$V_{X1X2}(\mathrm{H, L}) = 0$$
$$V_{X1X2}(\mathrm{L, H}) = 0$$
$$V_{X1X2}(\mathrm{L, L}) = \beta_1$$

Finally, the individual welfare functions are extracted from the group welfare function using marginalization: $v_{Xi}(a_i) = \Sigma_{\sim ai}\, V_{X1X2}(a_1, a_2)$. For example, $v_{X2}(\mathrm{H}) = \alpha_1$. Thus, the individual welfare functions are

$$v_{X1}(\mathrm{H}) = \alpha_1 \qquad v_{X1}(\mathrm{L}) = \beta_1$$
$$v_{X2}(\mathrm{H}) = \alpha_1 \qquad v_{X2}(\mathrm{L}) = \beta_1$$

Table 3.10 Ex-post Payoff Matrix of the Hi-Lo Game

		X_2	
		H	L
X_1	H	α_1, α_1	0, 0
	L	0, 0	β_1, β_1

To find the NE after incorporating the social influence flows between X_1 and X_2, we work directly with the conditional and categorical utilities to identify the conditioned NE, or with the ex-post marginal utilities to identify the ex-post NE. As desired, the two approaches yield identical solutions. Table 3.10 shows that (H, H) and (L, L) are NE for all admissible values of α_1 and β_1.

When one focuses on the group and individual welfare functions, we see that group and individual welfare is maximized through the profile (H, H) when $\alpha_1 > \beta_1$. As this is the assumption in Hi-Lo, the profile that caters for the interests of the individuals and the group is (H, H) and this is a consensus choice. Consequently, we would expect this profile to be instantiated when players take into account their own individual interests and the interests of the group, as encoded in the social linkages among the players and expressed through the group welfare function.

3.4 Conclusion

Conditional game theory has full power to represent team agency using only resources that can be defined within standard game-theoretic formalism, and which can be represented using only standard solution concepts. It does not presuppose that players explicitly reason their way to solutions based on identification with teams, but it captures conditionalization of games by that mechanism, among others.

A conditional game-theoretic specification is also compatible with the hypothesis that people experience the sorts of gestalt switches between individual and team agency that Bacharach conjectures. Psychologists can contribute to our unified understanding of social behavior by investigating the frequency of such switches, in both directions, in different sorts of circumstances, along with general kinds of conditions that encourage or interfere with them. It might be the case that, in most interactions, people either simply assume group-level agency and stick to it, or play their unconditioned best responses without reflection. (These tendencies might likely be both statistical and context dependent). It might even be typically *best*—because of the importance of stability of strategic expectations—if gestalt switches are relatively unusual.

The strategic life of a social being is complicated, and one of the leading sources of this complication is multiple scales of agency. Game theory is up to the job of representing this multiplicity. The philosopher's task of assessing it through its many normative angles and shadows is much less likely to find straightforward resolution, but can benefit from the existence of a general technical framework in which to describe its structure.

Notes

1 We assume that because no model ever completely describes an economic interaction or situation, interactions and situations can have multiple models that should be compatible with one another where their applications overlap. In the kind of example emphasized by Binmore (1994), bargaining scenarios are modeled as both cooperative and non-cooperative games for different purposes; but the cooperative solution must correspond to one of the Nash equilibria of the non-cooperative model.

2 Bacharach was approximately halfway through composing the manuscript when he passed away unexpectedly in 2002. Sugden and Natalie Gold, one of Bacharach's PhD students at the time, edited his work and wrote introductory and concluding chapters so that it could be published post mortem.

3 See Binmore (2009).

4 Following Bacharach, we use U to refer to the shared or group payoff function and u_i to refer to an individual payoff function.

5 See also Stirling and Felin (2013).

6 *Actions* properly refer to the alternatives available to a player at an information set in the extensive form of a game, whereas a strategy is a complete plan of action, specifying the move that a player will make at each information set where he or she may be called upon to act. Stirling confines his attention to finite strategic-form games and employs the term "action" interchangeably with "strategy." Despite some discomfort with this louche talk, we will follow his usage here.

7 The notion of a conjecture is familiar from Bayesian games, where each player is assigned a distribution of expectations over the elements of other players' strategy sets. In Stirling's framework, this idea is generalized so that a conjecture is a belief about the strategy profile that will be instantiated by *all* players, including the player to whom the conjecture is assigned. As will become clear, it is the recursive nature of equilibrium determination in conditional game theory that allows for this.

References

Bacharach, M. 1999. "Interactive Team Reasoning: A Contribution to the Theory of Cooperation." *Research in Economics* 53: 117–47.

Bacharach, M. 2006. *Beyond Individual Choice: Teams and Frames in Game Theory.* Princeton, NJ: Princeton University Press.

Binmore, K. 1994. *Game Theory and the Social Contract, Volume 1: Playing Fair.* Cambridge, MA: MIT Press.

Binmore, K. 2009. *Rational Decisions.* Princeton, NJ: Princeton University Press.

Coleman, J. 1990. *Foundations of Social Theory.* Cambridge, MA: Harvard University Press.

Hollis, M. 1998. *Trust within Reason.* Cambridge: Cambridge University Press.

Horner, V., J. D. Carter, M. Suchak, and F. B. De Waal. 2011. "Spontaneous Prosocial Choice by Chimpanzees." *Proceedings of the National Academy of Sciences* 108: 13847–51.

Kreps, D. 1990. *Game Theory and Economic Modeling.* Oxford: Oxford University Press.

Mehta, J., C. Starmer, and R. Sugden. 1994. "The Nature of Salience: An Experimental Investigation of Pure Coordination Games." *American Economic Review* 84: 658–73.

Pettit, P. 2001. "The Virtual Reality of Homo Economicus." In *The Economic World View*, ed. U. Mäki, 75–97. Cambridge: Cambridge University Press.

Ragot, X. 2012. "The Economics of the Laboratory Mouse: Where Do We Go from Here?" In *What's Right with Macroeconomics?*, ed. R. Solow, and J.-P. Touffut, 181–94. Cheltenham: Edward Elgar.

Ross, D. 2014. *Philosophy of Economics*. Basingstoke: Palgrave Macmillan.

Schelling, T. C. 1960. *The Strategy of Conflict*. Cambridge, MA: Harvard University Press.

Stirling, W. C. 2012. *Theory of Conditional Games*. New York: Cambridge University Press.

Stirling, W. C., and T. Felin. 2013. "Game Theory, Conditional Preferences, and Social Influence." *PLoS One* 8: e56751. Doi: 10.1371/journal.pone.0056751.

Sugden, R. 1993. "Thinking as a Team: Towards an Explanation of Nonselfish Behaviour." *Social Philosophy and Policy* 10: 69–89.

Sugden, R. 2000. "Team Preferences." *Economics and Philosophy* 16: 175–204.

Sugden, R. 2003. "The Logic of Team Reasoning." *Philosophical Explorations* 6 (3): 165–81.

Warneken, F., and M. Tomasello. 2006. "Altruistic Helping in Human Infants and Young Chimpanzees." *Science* 311: 1301–3.

Warneken, F., and M. Tomasello. 2007. "Helping and Cooperation at 14 Months of Age." *Infancy* 11: 271–94.

Warneken, F., and M. Tomasello. 2009a. "The Roots of Human Altruism." *British Journal of Psychology* 100: 455–71.

Warneken, F., and M. Tomasello. 2009b. "Varieties of Altruism in Children and Chimpanzees." *Trends in Cognitive Sciences* 13: 397–402.

Commentary: Explaining Prosocial Behavior: Team Reasoning or Social Influence?

Cédric Paternotte

The problem of explaining cooperative and prosocial behavior has triggered or favored many developments of game theory. Reputation, punishment, and social preferences are but a few examples of explanatory concepts that have been successfully formally explored in games of incomplete information, repeated games, and evolutionary games. Nowadays, most game theoretical approaches focus on the evolution and dynamics of social behavior, especially on its possible emergence and stabilization. For all that, the project of providing rational justifications for social behavior has not vanished. Bacharach's study of team reasoning, which started about two decades ago, and Stirling's more recent work on conditional games offer two conspicuous cases that epitomize this rational take. However, these two approaches seem radically different, although they claim to illuminate similar behaviors. What is their relationship, if any? Is one more general than the other, and, if so, in which sense? Basically, does our prosocial behavior stem from our tendency to reason by adopting the perspective of groups, or from the fact that our tastes and preferences result from an interplay of mutual, social influences?

Hofmeyr and Ross precisely aim to answer such questions. By carefully describing and explaining Bacharach's and Stirling's formal models, they reach the conclusion that "the effect of team reasoning on equilibrium selection in games is generalized, both conceptually and technically, by [Stirling]'s modelling framework for conditional games" (3). To put it simply, Stirling's social influence approach fully encompasses Bacharach's team reasoning. As a result, "team reasoning is at best one special mechanism that supports team agency" (3), while "conditional game theory has full power to represent team agency" (24). However, the full understanding of the two formal approaches requires such a wealth of details that the authors have little space left for actually comparing them.

I aim to complete Hofmeyr and Ross's analysis by assessing the relative generality of the team reasoning and social influence approaches. In this commentary, I pinpoint several aspects on which they can be systematically compared, which allows for a more nuanced assessment and leads me to doubt that either of them enjoys a higher degree of generality.

The discussion unfolds as follows. First, I explain why we should expect the team reasoning and conditional preference approaches to be competing rather than complementary. Second, I compare them with respect to several criteria: the exogenous factors on which they rely, the range of behaviors they explain or exclude, the situations to which they apply, their psychological interpretation, the nature of the rationality they presuppose, and their epistemic assumptions. Overall, the links between the two approaches are much less straightforward than may appear at first glance; in any case, neither of them can be said to include or generalize the other. I conclude on the relation between these approaches and on group agency in general.

1. Social Preferences and the Explanation of Prosocial Behavior

Hofmeyr and Ross's (henceforth H&R) paper describes Bacharach and Stirling's accounts in detail. Let us highlight their main features so as to pave the way for their comparison. As a first common point, note that both approaches follow the tradition of explaining interactive behavior by relying on the concept of *social preferences*. This means that they both consider agents that are motivated partly by their own payoff and partly by that of others. This is a respectable option, which solves the problem of social dilemmas by transforming them: if people cooperate in situations in which traditional game theory says they should not, it is because they are motivated by more than their own material payoff—they are playing a different game than the one based on material rewards.

On this common basis, the two accounts offer different alternatives. Bacharach's explanation of interactive behavior by team reasoning follows three steps. First, in an interactive situation agents may identify with a team, that is, adopt the team's preferences. This identification will typically depend on psychological processes triggered by salient characteristics of the situation. Second, agents who have identified with the team work out what would be the best collective strategy for the team, taking into account the fact that the precise list of team members may be unknown and that agents only have a known tendency to identify with a team, depending on what is rational for the non-team reasoners. Third, team members do their part of the best collective strategy (which prescribes an action for each of them). In short, team reasoners do their part of what is best for the team with which they identify, where what is best depends on how likely others are to identify as well (for an elaborate description of the formalism and examples, see H&R, Section 3.2).

At first glance, Stirling's account is markedly different. It starts from the social influences that exist among agents, from which it builds their conditional individual preferences (conditional, because they depend on the preferences of the influencing agents), which can thus be labeled "social preferences." Agents then reason individually on the basis of these social preferences, according to the principles of classical game theory, in order to determine their choice of action. In addition, the set of social influences also allows one to derive the group and individual welfare functions, which, respectively, determine the combinations of actions that are most beneficial collectively and individually. This allows Stirling to determine the degree of consensus enjoyed by a collective welfare, which depends on the discrepancy between the collectively optimal strategy and the set of individually optimal ones. In situations where negotiation is impossible, a collective strategy could not be enforced unless it is also a consensus choice (see H&R, Section 3.3).

Before we compare Bacharach and Stirling's approaches, one may wonder why they should be considered as competing explanations in the first place. Indeed, they may appear as complementary—as focusing on two different aspects of interactive rational choice. Team reasoning operates on the basis of a predetermined collective utility function, which represents the group's goals, interests, or preferences. Team reasoners decide to do their part of the best collective strategy, which can only be worked out from the group utility. The social influence approach, however, starts from influence relations between individual agents that ultimately generate a collective utility function (the "group utility or welfare function," H&R: 35). So it seems that the two approaches deal with distinct aspects of interactive rational choice: social influences have to do with collective *preference formation*, while team reasoning determines the *decision-making process* that presupposes such collective preference.

However, this conclusion underestimates the generality of the social influence approach. For it does not stop at establishing collective as well as individual preferences; as illustrated by H&R in two examples (Section 3.3), it also produces claims regarding the rationality of strategies in a given formal situation—just as team reasoning does. For instance, the social influence and the team reasoning approaches both offer methods in order to determine whether, and if so in what conditions, the choice to cooperate in a Prisoners' Dilemma (PD) may be rational. The social influence approach is even more general, as it also determines whether a given set of individual strategies may be a "consensus choice," that is, whether "negotiation may be required to reach a compromise solution" (Stirling and Felin 2013).

We now understand why Stirling's approach may appear more general than that of Bacharach. This is because the former encompasses more aspects of interactive rational choice than the latter, namely the emergence of the decision context and the conditions of implementation of the decision identified as rational. However, that the domain of one account contains that of another one does not entail that the former generalizes the latter, as they may still significantly differ within their overlapping region. Accordingly, we now turn to their comparison.

2. Comparison

How do we compare formal accounts with overlapping target domains? There are many possible criteria. For instance, Kuhn famously mentioned five values that govern scientific theory choice: accuracy, consistency, scope, simplicity, and fruitfulness. However, this list was not intended to be exhaustive, and not all criteria are relevant to the case of social science. Moreover, these values can be interpreted in different ways and involve different subvalues. As I am primarily interested in H&R's claim regarding the respective generality of Bacharach and Stirling's accounts, I focus on three criteria, each encompassing two aspects, most of which are relevant to Kuhn's values of scope or of simplicity. First, competing models may differ with respect to their explanatory power—the range of behaviors they explain (akin to Kuhn's scope) and the amount of presuppositions or parameters needed for such explanations (involved in a measure of simplicity). Second, one model may be interpreted more generally than the other one, because it covers either more real-life situations or a broader class of psychological mechanisms (both relevant to scope again). This criterion seems favored by H&R, as they claim that the social influence approach generalizes the team reasoning one and applies to more real-life situations (whereas team reasoning applies only to deliberation). Third, different accounts may be more or less demanding regarding the epistemic or the rational assumptions they make about agents (all of which is related to simplicity). I now consider each criterion in turn.

a. Explanatory Power

Explanatory range. What kinds of behaviors are explained by our two accounts? Let me here focus on the category of cooperative and coordinated behaviors, a natural application for both accounts, and to which the examples described by H&R belong. Cooperation and coordination in one-shot (non-repeated) games are two stumbling stones of classical game theory: cooperation in social dilemmas is individually irrational, while efficient coordination is no more rational than inefficient coordination—while human individuals typically cooperate and coordinate efficiently. Bacharach's team reasoners escape both pitfalls. A team reasoner will cooperate in a social dilemma such as the PD, provided she is confident enough that others will identify with the team (Bacharach 1999: 126–7; H&R: 19–22). Individual reasoners endowed with social preferences may cooperate as well under even lower levels of confidence (see Bacharach 1999: 128). However, for team reasoners it may also be irrational to coordinate inefficiently (although this is always a rational option for individual reasoners, even with social preferences)—for efficient coordination is almost always collectively preferable to inefficient coordination. Indeed, Bacharach saw this justification of efficient coordination as the main advantage of team reasoning.

By contrast, Stirling's social influence account is less explanatory. It can still label cooperation as rational (H&R: 20–2). However, its balance sheet is less favorable in the efficient coordination case. Even with preferences derived from social influences, efficient and inefficient coordination are both equally rational (H&R: 22). Still, group and individual welfare may be maximized by efficient coordination under some conditions. This says little more than the fact that both the group and the individuals will be better off if agents coordinate efficiently rather than not. As a result, team reasoning singles out efficient coordination, while social influences and individual reasoning may justify inefficient as well as efficient coordination. Team reasoning thus enjoys a greater explanatory range.

Exogenous parameters. That a theory covers more phenomena than another one may not mean much if it contains so many parameters that it may be made to fit any circumstance. How easy is it to fit our two accounts to behavioral data? Bacharach's team reasoning depends on two kinds of exogenous parameters: the team's utility function and the probability that individuals identify with the team. The latter is not really a parameter, because the theory generates predictions regarding behaviors depending on the value of identification probability: it tells us what team reasoners would do and not do for all such values. By contrast, the team utility function is genuinely exogenous: Bacharach typically worked out his examples by equating it with the mean of individual utilities (probably for the sake of simplicity); but any function would be compatible with team reasoning. This may not be a problem, as it was enough for Bacharach to show that it was *possible* for inefficient coordination not to be rational (for one set of parameters).

Unlike Bacharach's account, Stirling's account allows one to fully generate the group utility function. It does so, however, on the basis of the influence relations that hold between agents. More precisely, to apply his model one must specify, for each "influenced" agent and each possible game outcome, what the agent's utility would be if other agents preferred this outcome. For a game with two agents and two actions each, this means that sixteen utility values must be specified (compare to the four utility values needed to specify Bacharach's team utility function). Overall, if I understand them correctly, the team reasoning model appears more explanatory than the social influence one (at least with respect to the domain of cooperative behavior): it explains more phenomena on the basis of fewer exogenous parameters.

b. Explanatory Potential

When comparing two formal accounts, one obvious move is to investigate whether one formally entails the other, that is, in the case of models of rationality, whether what counts as rational in one model is also necessarily deemed rational in the other. Unfortunately, no such result is currently available in our case. Even if the team reasoning and social influence models share no relation of formal entailment, their respective generality can be compared at the level of their real-world interpretation. Does one model fit more interactive situations than the other? Or does it fit more psychological processes of human agents? Note that explanatory potential differs from explanatory range: while the latter refers to the number of behaviors actually explained, the former concerns the kinds of situations and of agents that the model covers—for which it provides results, whether accurate or not.

Applicability. Team reasoning applies mainly to one-shot situations in which a team utility emerges from the context, whether it be salient or already known (for instance, in the case of preexisting teams). It is not clear how it would apply to dynamic or repeated interactions—team reasoners, for instance, may not stick to a plan and group identity may vanish if previous choices from others are incompatible with the team's best strategy. Social influence may arise just as generally: it may emerge from certain situations or exist before the interaction due to some past history shared by agents (even if it may be difficult to see why agents would be influenced by others in anonymous, one-shot laboratory interactions). Here, the fact that an account relies on more exogenous parameters may be an advantage, as it allows it to fit more situations (but will damage explanatory power, as seen above).

Note, however, that a formal aspect of Stirling's account complicates its real-life interpretation. For technical reasons, influences among agent may formally be represented only by acyclic graphs; this means that two agents cannot mutually influence one another. Formally, this is not an issue, because if agent A influences B in a model, the same results may have been obtained in an alternative model where B influences A (see H&R: 18). The crucial point is that in every model, at least one agent will have categorical (unconditional) preferences that depend on no one else's. As a result, the model cannot straightforwardly represent cases in which several agents mutually influence one another—where they all have final preferences that differ from their initial ones. In other words, the way in which the influences are formally represented does not necessarily match the real influences relations that hold between agents. This limits the applicability of the model.

Psychological generality. At the psychological level, both accounts are noncommittal. Team reasoning is based on the psychological process of group identification, by which an agent comes to conceive of her identity primarily as a group member. However, "group identification," notwithstanding its respectable history in psychology, is a bit of a portmanteau expression, which may cover a variety of causal processes—Bacharach (2006: 76) mentions eight possible causes and as many kinds of effects of group identification. Still, the process of group identification remains incompatible with some psychological facts such as the high sensitivity of our preferences to the expectations of others; here, approaches such as Bicchieri's (2005) social norms account fare better.

Similarly, Stirling's account fits several psychological mechanisms. Social influence may represent the effects of imitation or of learning from others, and stem from feelings such as admiration or even envy. I may want what I think others do because I realize they understand something I do not, because I want to resemble them or fit in ... the account is compatible with an impressive list of underlying motivations. However, it is also restrictive in the following sense. In the social account, an agent's preferences are only influenced by another agent's *preferred outcome*—not by her entire set of preferences over all possible outcomes. In a fully general account though, agents may be influenced not only by what others rank first but also by what they rank last, or by the way in which they rank alternatives in general (for instance). Of course, including such possibilities in Stirling's model would render the set of necessary exogenous parameters even less tractable. But this restriction on the possible influential factors makes it less adaptable to various psychological mechanisms.

c. Agent Properties

I finally turn to the discussion of the conditions under which agents may cooperate and coordinate according to the team reasoning and the social influence accounts. How rationally and epistemically demanding are these conditions?

Rationality. Our two accounts seem to equip agents with two different kinds of rationality. Stirling's is consistent with the individual rationality assumptions of classical game theory. The set of social influences leads to modified individual preferences and thus transform the initial game into a new one. Once these have been determined, one may determine the set of (individually) rational actions by finding the Nash equilibria (NE) of this transformed game (that is, the set of individual actions such that no one may have attained a preferred outcome by deviating unilaterally). Typical explanations of cooperative behavior based on social preferences follow precisely this move: transform the game first, and then apply the classical tools.

Bacharach's account posits a distinct type of rationality. For him, team reasoning is the result of not only a "payoff transformation" but also an "agency transformation" (H&R: 7)—the latter constitutes a novelty that is absent from typical social preference accounts. To recall, the agency transformation consists in the agent's determining the collectively preferable strategy before doing their individual part of this strategy. Agents then must check not only possible *individual* deviations (would she or he benefit from doing something else?) but also *collective* deviations (would the team benefit from a number of us doing something else?). So team reasoners must at least consider more alternatives and possibly perform more complex calculations than individual reasoners. Team reasoning is more cognitively demanding than individual reasoning. The former may also be irreducible to the latter (see Hakli et al. 2010), at least in the sense that they are not compatible with the same set of observed behaviors.

In addition, H&R claim that Bacharach's account is limited to cases that involve deliberation: either actual deliberation of agents, or "an ex post rationalization of behaviour that serves as a 'stand-by' or 'back-up' to more common behaviour-generating processes" (H&R: 10). By contrast, with respect to Stirling's account,

> If people spontaneously copy the behaviour of higher-status, kin-bonded, or apparently successful people without thinking, this behaviour can still be regarded as chosen because counter-incentives could dampen it, even though by hypothesis it does not result from reasoning. (H&R: 10)

But this underestimates the similarity of the accounts. Both contain a utility transformation part, and group identification involves as little deliberation as basic imitation or learning. Then, both accounts make rationality assumptions. However, the differences in terms of complexity and of forms of reasoning do not mean that they exclude deliberation (in particular ex-post rational justification). Team reasoning relies on a game-theoretic concept of equilibrium, just as social influence relies on NE. Both may be reached by nondeliberative agents and both may be justified as rational after the fact.

Epistemic assumptions. I finish with the epistemic demands of both accounts. In Bacharach's account, the exogenous parameters already discussed—the team utility function, the probabilities that agents identify with the team, and even the fact that these agents team-reason—are supposed to be common knowledge. Team and non-team members must agree on the preferences of those who identify with the team in order to work out the best collective strategy, either in order to do their part of it or to adapt their individual action to it (respectively). These are demanding conditions, although not radically more so than is usually the case in game theory.

What about Stirling's account? If agents must act according to a NE of the transformed game, then the new utility functions must be common knowledge. This means that the agents must be aware to some extent of the web of social influences that surrounds them (from which the final utility functions are derived). One does not need to know much in order to be influenced by someone, but he must know considerably more if he is to work out what others will do, will expect him to do, and so on. In Bacharach's account, the context is supposed to make a team and one of its many possible utility functions salient. For Stirling, only one set of individual and collective utility functions is possible: if they result from the choice of interactive agents, then they must be known at least approximately, and so must be the set of social influences. This strikes me as a considerably more demanding epistemic constraint.

3. Conclusion: Team Agency

Let us take stock. Regardless of the assessment of their respective explanatory power, explanatory potential and assumptions about agents, it should now be clear that neither the team reasoning approach nor the social influence can be deemed more general or more specific than the other. They formally represent different psychological mechanisms, are both applicable to overlapping but not identical sets of situations: one is more rationally demanding, the other more epistemically so. Team reasoning has more explanatory power (or so I have argued), but covers a smaller portion of group agency.

This last point may ultimately cause one to favor Stirling's account (if one really has to choose). "Group agency" refers to a set of complex, intertwined social phenomena that include group preferences, group intentions, group belief, group decision-making ... however imperfect it may seem, the social influence approach encompasses group preference formation, group decision-making, and even negotiation. A few years back, in a paper that brought together Bacharach's game-theoretic account with Tuomela's philosophical theory of joint intentionality, Hakli et al. (2010) stressed that future analyses should increase their focus on the emergence of group preferences. Among other things, Stirling's account is an attempt to do just that. Its relative neglect of rational aspects may leave some room for its combination with the "agency transformation" part of team reasoning. Only time will tell.

References

Bacharach, M. 1999. "Interactive Team Reasoning: A Contribution to the Theory of Co-operation." *Research in Economics* 53: 117–47.

Bicchieri, C. 2005. *The Grammar of Society: The Nature and Dynamics of Social Norms*. Cambridge: Cambridge University Press.

Hakli, R., K. Miller, and R. Tuomela. 2010. "Two Kinds of We-Reasoning." *Economics and Philosophy* 26 (3): 291–320.

Stirling, W. C., and T. Felin. 2013. "Game Theory, Conditional Preferences, and Social Influence." *PLoS One* 8 (2): e56751.

Part Two

From Methodological Choice to Methodological Mix

Summary of Chapters

The second part collects those chapters that place special emphasis on methodological innovations and their contribution to research progress. The research discussed is innovative because it employs novel methods, applies existing methods in new contexts, or uses these methods in a novel integrated form.

Glenn Harrison's chapter reviews the latest development in behavioral economics called behavioral econometrics. Behavioral econometrics is one part of what Harrison calls a methodological trinity that includes theory, data collection, and econometrics. Harrison reviews the various methodologies of behavioral econometrics, with illustrative case studies that showcase appropriate and inappropriate states of the art. The methodological upshot is that valid tests of behavioral models need to simultaneously handle theoretical, experimental, and econometric issues as an intertwined whole. Harrison sets higher standards for the next generation of behavioral and experimental economists; his methodological trinity thesis also challenges philosophers and methodologists to more critically engage with scientific debates, without confusing the popularity of a model with its confirmation. In his commentary, Nathaniel T. Wilcox brings four themes to the fore that together provide historical and methodological background against which Harrison argues for the methodological trinity in behavioral economics. Wilcox invites philosophers and historians of science to fully develop these fascinating themes.

Michael Woolcock defends the use of mixed methods for the evaluation of public policies, particularly in the field of international development. When policies are complex, says Woolcock, as they are in international development, any single method is by itself insufficient to address the evaluator's concerns regarding policy efficacy and effectiveness. They in fact generate highly variable impact across contexts, space, and time, and it is impossible to anticipate all the contingent events and decisions that take place during implementation. Assessing this type of interventions thus requires the evaluator to call upon the full arsenal of research tools available to social scientists. Mixed-method research, which consists in the integration of qualitative and quantitative approaches, permits to overcome the weakness inherent in either approach while taking advantage of the strengths of both. In her commentary, Nancy Cartwright reinforces and extends Woolcock's conclusion. In particular, she suggests that we should leverage the plurality of methods when we are interested in the effectiveness not only of complex intervention but of interventions of any kind.

Charlotte Vangsgaard presents the work done at ReD Associates, a strategy and innovation consulting company. Vangsgaard claims that current marketing research is deeply informed by a Cartesian worldview and largely draws on quantitative methods and economic models constructed on false assumptions about consumers' behavior. ReD Associates replaces the Cartesian-quantitative paradigm with an approach borrowed from the humanities and the social sciences which is deeply informed by Heideggerian philosophy. This alternative paradigm aims at providing a more integrated and comprehensive understanding of consumers' experience. By using qualitative-ethnographic research, ReD achieves a deeper understanding of the consumers' world and provide valuable marketing insights into people's behavior and their motivation. In her commentary, Attilia Ruzzene challenges the dualistic view described by Vangsgaard. She traces the roots of the approach adopted at ReD Associates in consumer behavior research dating back to the early 1980s. Following its evolution, one can see that, rather than crystallized into two antithetic paradigms, the field is torn by a permanent tension between unity and disunity: moments of opposition between (a plurality of) approaches alternated to moments where continuity was instead cherished and actively pursued.

In his chapter on versioning, Tommaso Venturini remarks that social theory privileges a kind of spatial thinking whereby individuals are separated from the aggregate; while the latter tends to be represented as fixed, the former move and change against the background of stable structures. Venturini defines this as the "fish tank complex," that is, a conceptual framing where social actors move against a static background, like the fish in a plastic aquarium. He proposes an alternative framing based on a conception of collective phenomena that privileges temporality and narrative unfolding over spatiality. He finds a promising modeling technique for this approach in versioning—an ensemble of conceptual and technical tools for comparing different editions of the same document to trace its evolution over time. Venturini stresses that versioning has far broader applications than software development as illustrated by the case of the Law Factory. In his commentary, Petri Ylikoski asserts that Venturini is too dismissive of the micro-macro distinction, which he regards as central, and inescapable, for social theorizing. He acknowledges, however, that structural change deserves more attention on the part of social scientists, and in this spirit welcomes modeling techniques such as versioning. This modeling strategy, Ylikoski insists, is not alternative to explanatory social models but serves instead different inferential purposes.

Wendy Olsen presents an approach to social statistics that is consistent with a form of critical realism. She expresses her preference for a methodology that requires a clear and ambitious ontological vision to illuminate and underpin the work of the statistician. This ontology recognizes the prominence of social structures, which, while not deterministic for events, are the site of causal mechanisms that affect the agency in a dynamic ongoing way. From this perspective, she reviews a number of current developments in social statistics that are shaped by the epistemological implications of a realist ontology. The goal is to show how the complex nature of reality influences ways in which social scientists attempt to describe it. This leads to a form of methodological pluralism whereby distinct ways of reasoning are combined and quantitative and qualitative approaches integrated. In his commentary, Daniel Little advances philosophical arguments that further tighten the connection drawn by Olsen between ontological vision and methodological agenda. Not only does the plurality characteristic of the social world require forms of methodological pluralism such as the ones described by Olsen, but also this plurality coheres rather than contradict with the ontology of critical realism that inspires her work.

4

The Methodologies of Behavioral Econometrics

Glenn W. Harrison

There is an essential methodological connection between theory, the collection of data, and econometrics. Theory can consist of simple or complex hypotheses, the comparative static predictions of structural theory, or the latent components of that structural theory itself. The collection of data might be as simple as using preexisting data, the development of survey instruments, or the design of controlled experiments. In many cases of interest to behavioral econometrics, the data consist of controlled lab or field experiments.

Most of the behavioral data encountered from controlled experiments is relatively easy to evaluate with known econometric methods. Section 4.1 reviews a range of methods for different types of experiments. In some cases simple, "agnostic" statistical modeling is appropriate, since the experiment "does the work of theory" for the analyst, by controlling for treatments and potential confounds. In other cases more nuanced structural modeling is appropriate, and we now have a rich array of econometric tools that have been applied and adapted to the specific needs of behavioral economists.

On the other hand, there is a methodological tension in the air, with widely differing statistical and econometric methods being applied to what looks to be the same type of inference. There are two major problems with the methodologies applied in behavioral econometrics. One is a separation of skills, with statistical and econometric methods just being appended as an afterthought.[1] The other is the simple misapplication of econometric methods, akin to the story that Leamer (1978: vi) told of his teachers preaching econometric cleanliness in the classrooms on the top floor of a building, and then descending into the basement to build large-scale macro-econometric models that violated almost every tenet from the classroom.

These problems are anticipated in the review in Section 4.1, and the illustrations of two methodological innovations in Sections 4.2 and 4.3. They are directly illustrated with some real case studies in Sections 4.4, 4.5, and 4.6, with emphasis on the measurement and analysis of risk preferences. Section 4.4 considers the empirical evidence for Cumulative Prospect Theory (CPT) and asks if anyone is even reading the evidence with any methodological care. Section 4.5 considers the empirical evidence for the Priority Heuristic (PH) from psychology and offers a sharp reminder of why we worry about the likelihood of observations from the perspective of theory. Section

4.6 considers empirical evidence for the notion of "source dependence," the hypothesis that risk preferences depend on the source of risk, and shows why we must not confuse point estimates with data. Section 4.7 draws some general conclusions, and a call to arms for methodologists.

4.1 Best-Practice Econometric Methods

There is a useful divide between nonstructural econometric methods and structural methods. The two should be seen as complementary, depending on the inferential question at hand.

4.1.1 Non-Structural Methods

It is appropriate to dispense with a structural specification when the experimental design has controlled for the factors of importance for inference. Obviously, a randomized treatment is attractive and widely viewed as facilitating identification of the treatment effect, and this has been long recognized in laboratory experiments as well as in field experiments. There is also widespread recognition that sometimes it is not as easy to fully randomize as one would want, and in this case one might resort to evaluating the "intent to treat" instead of the treatment itself. Or one might engage in some sort of modeling of the sample selection process, by which subjects present for the control or the treatments. These econometric methods are well known and understood.

Although it is popular to use Ordinary Least Squares (OLS) methods for nonstructural econometrics, there is a growing awareness that alternative specifications are just as easy to estimate and interpret, and can avoid some major pitfalls of OLS.[2] These issues arise when dependent variables are not real-valued between $\pm\infty$. The first item of business is to just plot the data, normally with a histogram or kernel density. The advantage of a histogram is that it might show a "spike" better, whether the spike is at some natural boundary or at some prominent value. These plots are not intended to see if the unconditional distribution is bell-shaped, since it is the distribution of the *residual* that we want to be Gaussian for the proper application of OLS. Unless the only covariate is a constant term, these are not the same thing.

Once the plot shows us if the data are bounded, dichotomous, ordered, or nominal (e.g., integer-valued), we all know what to do. In the old days it was not a trivial matter to compute marginal effects using proper econometric methods that kept track of standard errors, and allowed hypothesis testing, but those days have long passed. Marginal effects can be calculated using the "delta method," allowing nonlinear functional relationships of estimated parameters to be calculated along with the (approximately) correct standard error. An important extension is to evaluate marginal effects for all values of the remaining covariates, and average those estimates: these are commonly called "average marginal effects," and convey a better sense of the marginal effect than when that effect is evaluated at the mean of the remaining covariates.

One important insight from modern methods is to recognize the important distinction between a "hurdle specification" and a censored specification (e.g., a Tobit). Each of these arise in the common situation in which there is a spike in the data at some prominent value, typically zero. The classic example in economics is an expenditure on some good, and in health economics the utilization or expenditure on medical services. In this case the hurdle model recognizes that the data-generating process that causes the zero observations may be very different than the data-generating process that causes the nonzero observations. For instance, women may be less likely to go to hospital than men, but once there they may use more costly resources. Hence an Ordinary Least Squares (OLS) estimate of the effect of gender on health expenditure might see no net effect, but that is because the two data-generating processes are generating large gross effects that offset each other. Hurdle models can only ever improve inferences in settings like this, by allowing two latent processes to generate the data independently. Specifications that handle censoring, such as Tobit models, assume that there is one latent data-generating process, but that it is transformed into a zero or nonzero observation in some manner that is independent of covariates.

Hurdle models are extremely easy to estimate. Limited-information methods, where one estimates, say, a probit model for the zero or nonzero characteristics of the data, and then a constrained OLS for the nonzero level of the data conditional on it being nonzero, generate consistent estimates. Efficient estimates require maximum likelihood (ML) methods for the joint estimation of both the probit and constrained OLS, but these are trivial now. One can easily extend the specification to consider two-sided hurdles, two-step hurdles, and nonzero data-generating processes that are integer-valued or bounded. Again, marginal effects can be readily calculated to correctly take into account both stages of the generation of an observation, or just one stage alone if that is of interest.

Randomization to treatment is one way to try to ensure that the effects of heterogeneity are controlled for. If sample sizes are large enough, and assignment to treatment random enough, then many observable and nonobservable characteristics will be "balanced" and hence play no significant role as a confound for inference. There also exist techniques to "re-balance" the samples that are used in treatments with the samples that are in the control, so as to make inferences about treatment effect even more reliable. These techniques are most widely used in observational settings where no assignment to treatment has occurred, or cannot occur for ethical reasons. However, they may also be used to improve inferences when sample sizes do not allow one to rely solely on the effects of randomization.[3]

4.1.2 Structural Methods

Behavioral economics now provides a rich array of competing structural models of decision-making in many areas of interest. In terms of risk preferences, major alternatives to Expected Utility Theory (EUT) include Rank-Dependent Utility (RDU) and CPT. In terms of time preferences, major alternatives to Exponential Discounting include Hyperbolic Discounting and Quasi-Hyperbolic Discounting. We now also have rich, structural characterizations of attitudes toward uncertainty and ambiguity, as well as social preferences. All of these models consist of latent structures: they posit latent constructs that individuals behave as if they evaluate when making decisions. For example, in EUT the latent constructs consist of the utility of outcomes, the expected utility (EU) of lotteries of outcomes, and the difference in EU of alternative lotteries in a binary choice setting. In turn, these latent constructs can be characterized with parametric, semi-parametric, or nonparametric functional forms. Within the parametric family, there can be flexible functional forms that generalize many others, or there can be relatively restrictive functional forms. For simplicity, most of our remarks focus on risk preferences.

Sometimes one can avoid estimating the full structure by just studying comparative static predictions of different theories. Indeed, the vast bulk of the behavioral literature testing EUT consists of the careful design of pairs of lotteries that provide tests of EUT by just examining the patterns of choice: see Starmer (2000) for a masterful review. In the renowned Allais Paradox, for instance, observed choices between one lottery pair A and B lead to precise predictions over another lottery pair A* and B* that are transformations of A and B: if the subject picks A (B), then under EUT the subject must also pick A* (B*). If the purpose is to test EUT against an alternative, then one might just study patterns such as these for consistency.[4]

One immediate problem is that choice patterns might have extremely low power when it comes to testing EUT. The reason is that many of the popular tests, such as the Allais Paradox and Common Ratio (CR) tests, use lottery pairs where the individual might reasonably be close to indifferent between the two. To avoid this problem, Loomes and Sugden (1998) design an ingenious battery of lottery choices which vary the "gradient" of the EUT-consistent indifference curves within a Marschak-Machina (MM) triangle.[5] The reason for this design feature is to generate some choice patterns that are more powerful tests of EUT for any given risk attitude. Under EUT the slope of the indifference curve within an MM triangle is a measure of risk aversion. So there always exists some risk attitude such that the subject is indifferent, as stressed by Harrison (1994), and evidence of CR violations in that case has virtually zero power.[6]

The beauty of this design is that even if the risk attitude of the subject makes the tests of a CR violation from some sets of lottery pairs have low power, then the tests based on other sets of lottery pairs must have higher power for this subject. By presenting subjects with several such sets, varying the slope of the EUT-consistent indifference curve, one can be sure of having some tests for CR violations that have decent power for each subject, without having to know a priori what their risk attitude is. Harrison et al. (2007) refer to this as a "complementary slack experimental design," since low-power tests of EUT in one set mean that there must be higher-power tests of EUT in another set.[7]

This design illustrates how smart experimenters can mitigate "downstream" econometric problems, when they know the theory they are testing. But the need for structural estimation remains. We still need to know if the subject has sufficiently precise risk preferences to make any of these tests powerful. What if the subject does not have a temporally stable or deterministic utility function? If we can estimate an EUT model for each subject, we can then weight the evidence across a sample, where the greatest weight is given to those with relatively precisely estimated risk preferences.

There are four deeper methodological reasons why the need for structural estimation remains.

The earliest tests of EUT were tests of the point-null hypothesis of EUT against the composite-alternative hypothesis of "anything but EUT." In this setting the subject either behaved consistently with EUT or not, and that translated into non-rejection of the null or not. But the most interesting tests now are horse races of one specification against another: for instance, does EUT or RDU best characterize behavior? This happens to be an easy horse race to judge, since EUT is nested within RDU. So the goal becomes the estimation of a reasonably flexible RDU model, and then a test if the restriction to EUT is rejected or not at conventional statistical levels. Horse races of non-nested models involve more careful hypothesis tests or mixture models, discussed by Harrison and Rutström (2009), but the need for structural estimation remains.[8]

The second reason for structural estimation is to be able to compare the latent risk preferences generated by different elicitation methods. An unfortunate cottage industry designing new elicitation methods has grown up, and a natural question to ask is whether they generate the same latent risk preferences or not. There are any number of reasons why theoretically incentive-compatible elicitation methods might not elicit the same risk preferences: the most important behaviorally is that some tasks are easier to explain than others.[9] The point is not whether there is some pairwise correlation between observed choices or reports across elicitation methods, but rather whether they lead one to recover the same latent risk preferences. For this comparison one must specify a structural model for each method that connects observed responses to risk preferences, and then generate the likelihoods of each observation for that method. Then do the same for other methods, and then generate a grand model in which the likelihoods for both models are estimated simultaneously, allowing a direct test that one method generates different structural parameters.[10]

The third reason for structural estimation is to be able to characterize risk preferences for normative purposes. It is one thing to say that a subject is better characterized by EUT or RDU, and another thing to be able to evaluate the consumer surplus (CS) of observed choices, given the estimates of the risk preferences of the subject. In other words, when someone makes a risky choice, and we "know" their risk preferences from some other battery of risky choices and structural estimates, what is the *size* of the CS gained or foregone? Data on choice patterns is silent on this, even if we have intelligently designed a battery to tell us that some choices involve a larger CS, positive or negative, depending on the choice, than others. By themselves, choice patterns can only tell us the sign of the CS, not the magnitude. Section 4.2 provides a case study to illustrate the role of structural estimation in behavioral welfare economics.

The fourth reason for structural estimation is to be able to correctly infer some latent construct that depends on some latent characteristic of another construct. This seemingly abstract point is of great practical significance. For example, to estimate time preferences, where the discount factor is defined as the scalar that equates the present discounted utility of a larger-later (LL) amount to the present discounted utility of a smaller-sooner (SS) amount, one needs to know the utility function for the amounts. Concavity of the utility function has a first-order impact on inferred discount rates, as shown by Andersen et al. (2008), who introduced the idea of joint estimation and applied it to risk and time preferences. To correctly infer discount rates from observed choices over LL and SS outcomes, one must know or assume some value for U″, and this comes most easily from estimates of a parametric utility function.[11] Similar applications arise when estimating subjective probabilities, as shown by Andersen, Fountain et al. (2014), and when estimating the intertemporal risk preferences, as shown by Andersen et al. (2018). Section 4.3 reviews applications of joint estimation, and the methodological issues that arise.

4.2 Behavioral Econometrics and Behavioral Welfare Economics

Consider the evaluation of CS from a simple, full indemnity insurance contract, following Harrison and Ng (2016). We know from theory that a risk averse EUT agent should always purchase this product at premia equal or below the actuarially fair premium and would garner a positive CS from doing so. But how large a surplus? The agent will also purchase the product at premia with positive loadings, but CS drops as the loading increases, and at some point the product should not be purchased. But how quickly does the surplus diminish, and at what point should the agent decline to buy?

To answer these questions we need to know the risk preferences of the agent, and then use those to evaluate the CS of observed insurance choices. That surplus may be positive or negative, depending on whether the "correct" purchase decision is made, conditional on the risk preferences of the agent. The first step is to estimate risk preferences, the second step is to calculate CS conditional on risk preferences, the third step is to determine the best characterization of risk preferences for the agent, and the final step is to assess the impact on welfare.

4.2.1 Risk Preferences

There are now many published statements of the structural models of risk preferences underlying EUT and RDU models, starting with Harrison and Rutström (2008, §2). Appendix A (online) reviews the formal econometric specification. The latest generation of these models is now commonly estimated at the level of the individual, as demonstrated by Harrison and Ng (2016) and Harrison and Ross (2018). Assume that a subject has been classified as an EUT or RDU decision-maker, using these methods, and that we have estimates (point estimates and covariance matrices) of their risk preferences condition on the type of risk preferences.

4.2.2 Welfare Evaluation

If the subject is assumed to be an EUT type, the CS of the insurance decision is calculated as the difference between the certainty equivalent (CE) of the EU with insurance and the CE of the EU without insurance. CS is calculated the same way using the RDU instead of EU if the subject is classified as a RDU type.

Assume a simple indemnity insurance product, which provides full coverage in the event of a loss. We assume an initial endowment of \$20, with a 10 percent chance of a \$15 one-time loss occurring. If an individual purchased the insurance, she could avoid the loss with certainty by paying the insurance premium up front. There are four possible payoff outcomes. If no insurance is purchased, the individual keeps her \$20 if no loss occurs, but is only left with \$5 if there is a loss. If insurance is purchased, the individual keeps \$20 less the premium if no loss occurs, and still keeps \$20 less the premium if the loss does occur.

Using the decision-making models discussed above, the EU or RDU across the two possible states, loss or no loss, can be calculated for each choice, to purchase or not to purchase insurance. The CE from the EU or RDU of each choice can be derived, and the difference between the CE from choosing insurance and the CE from not choosing insurance is then the expected welfare gain of purchasing insurance for that individual. It is easy to demonstrate, as in Harrison and Ng (2016), that it is critical to not only identify the right type of risk preferences (EUT or RDU) for each individual but also to estimate specific parameters of those risk preferences, if one is to correctly identify the sign *and* size of welfare gain or loss from insurance choices.

4.2.3 The Welfare Metric

To evaluate RDU preferences one can estimate an RDU model for each individual. For the purpose of classifying subjects as EUT or RDU it does not matter which probability weighting functions characterize behavior: the only issue here is at what statistical confidence level we can reject the EUT hypothesis that there is no probability weighting. This hypothesis takes the form of testing $\omega(p) = p$, where $\omega(p)$ is some probability weighting function defined over objective probabilities p.

Of course, if the sole metric for deciding if a subject were better characterized by EUT and RDU was the log-likelihood of the estimated model, then there will be virtually no subjects classified as EUT since RDU nests EUT. But if we use metrics of a 10 percent, 5 percent, or 1 percent significance level on the test of the EUT hypothesis that $\omega(p) = p$, then Harrison and Ng (2016) classify 39 percent, 49 percent, or 68 percent, respectively, of 102 subjects with valid estimates as being EUT-consistent.

4.2.4 Welfare Evaluation

Expected welfare gain is foregone if the subject chooses to purchase insurance when that purchase decision has a negative CS, and similarly when the subject chooses not to purchase insurance when the purchase decision has a positive CS. For example, if we compare the expected welfare gain from each decision to the actual decisions made by subject 8 of Harrison and Ng (2016), based on her EUT classification, we find that the subject has foregone \$10.37 out of a possible \$31.36 of expected welfare gain from insurance. This subject's total expected welfare gain for all twenty-four decisions was \$10.62; hence the efficiency for this subject, in the spirit of the traditional definition by Plott and Smith (1978), is 33.9 percent. In this experiment the efficiency is the expected CS given the subject's actual choices and estimated risk preferences, as a percent of total possible expected CS given her predicted choices and estimated risk preferences. The efficiency metric is defined at the level of the individual subject, whereas the expected welfare gain is defined at the level of each choice by each subject. In addition, efficiency provides a natural normalization of expected welfare gain on loss by comparing to the maximal expected welfare gain for that choice and subject. Both metrics are of interest, and are complementary.

Expanding this analysis to look across all subjects, we find that 49 percent of decisions made resulted in negative predicted CS. Although the average expected welfare gain of $0.27 from actual decisions made is statistically greater than zero at a p-value of less than 0.001, there is still a large proportion of decisions where take-up is not reflecting the welfare benefit of the insurance product to the individual.

The efficiency of all decisions made is only 14.0 percent. The modal efficiency is slightly less than 50 percent, and a significant proportion of individuals make decisions that result in negative efficiency. In other words, these subjects have made choices that resulted in a larger expected welfare loss than the choices that resulted in any expected welfare gain.

One objective of this exercise is to define conceptually and demonstrate empirically how one could undertake a field evaluation of the welfare of insurance products. We also view the laboratory as the appropriate place to "wind tunnel" the normative welfare evaluation of new products or decision scaffolds. Estimated distributions of CS changes, or efficiency, stand as explicit, rigorous "target practice" for anyone proposing nudges or clubs to improve welfare from insurance decisions.

4.2.5 What Should the Normative Welfare Metric Be

Our statement of welfare losses takes as given the type of risk preferences each individual employs and uses that as the basis for evaluating welfare effects of insurance decisions: *periculum habitus non est disputandum*. One could go further and question if the RDU models themselves embody an efficiency loss for those subjects we classify as RDU. Many would argue that RDU violates some normatively attractive axioms, such as the independence axiom. Forget whether that axiom is descriptively accurate or not. If RDU is not normatively attractive then we should do a calculation of CS in which we only assume EUT parameters for subjects: we could estimate the EUT model and get the corresponding CRRA (constant relative risk aversion) coefficient estimate (we would not just use the CRRA coefficient estimate from the RDU specification). Then we repeat the calculations. For subjects best modeled as EUT there is no change in the inferred CS, of course.

This issue raises many deeper issues with the way in which one should undertake behavioral welfare economics, discussed by Harrison and Ross (2017, 2018) and Monroe (2017). For now, we take the agnostic view that the risk preferences we have modeled as best characterizing the individual are those that should be used, in the spirit of the "welfarism" axiom of welfare economics. Even though the alternatives to EUT were originally developed to relax one of the axioms of EUT that some consider attractive normatively, it does not follow that one is unable to write down axioms that make those alternatives attractive normatively.

We view this methodological issue as urgent, open, and important. There is a large, general literature on behavioral welfare economics. Our general concern with this literature is that although it identifies the methodological problem well, none provides "clear guidance" so far to practical, rigorous welfare evaluation with respect to risk preferences as far as we can determine. We know of no way to undertake robust, general welfare evaluations of risky decisions without knowing structural risk preferences.

4.3 The Many Applications of Joint Estimation

The idea of joint estimation, again, is that one jointly estimates preferences from one structural model in order to correctly identify and estimate preferences of another structural model. The need for joint estimation comes from theory—it is not just an empirical matter of attending to behavioral correlations. We review three applications here, and one open area for future research, limiting attention to nonstrategic settings.[12]

4.3.1 Time Preferences

In many settings in experimental economics we want to elicit some preference from a set of choices that also depend on risk attitudes. An example due to Andersen et al. (2008) is the elicitation of individual discount rates. In this case it is the concavity of the utility function, U'', that is important, and under EUT that is synonymous with risk attitudes. Thus the risk aversion task is just a (convenient) vehicle to infer utility over deterministic outcomes. One methodological implication is that we should combine a risk elicitation task with a time preference elicitation task, and use them jointly to infer discount rates over utility. Appendix B (online) presents the formal theoretical specification.

As one relaxes the assumption that the decision-maker has a linear utility function, it is apparent from Jensen's Inequality that the implied discount rate decreases if $U(M)$ is concave in M. Thus, one cannot infer the level of the discount rate without knowing or assuming something about the utility function. This identification problem implies that discount rates cannot be estimated based on discount rate experiments with choices defined solely over time-dated money flows, and that separate tasks to identify the extent of diminishing marginal utility must also be implemented.

Thus, there is a clear implication from theory to experimental design: you need to know the nonlinearity of the utility function before you can *conceptually* define the discount rate. There is also a clear implication for econometric method: you need to jointly estimate the parameters of the utility function and the discount rate, to ensure that sampling errors in one propagate correctly to sampling errors of the other. In other words, if we know the parameters of the utility function less precisely, due to small samples or poor parametric specifications, we have to use methods that reflect the effect of that imprecision on our estimates of discount rates.[13]

Andersen et al. (2008) do this and infer discount rates for the adult Danish population that are well below those estimated in the previous literature that assumed linear utility functions, such as Harrison, Lau and Williams (2002), who estimated annualized rates of 28 percent for the same target population. Allowing for concave utility, they obtain a point estimate of the discount rate of 10 percent, which is significantly lower than the estimate of 25 percent for the same sample assuming linear utility. This does more than simply verify that discount rates and diminishing marginal utility are mathematical substitutes in the sense that either of them have the effect of lowering the influence from future payoffs on present utility. It tells us that, for utility function coefficients that are reasonable from the standpoint of explaining choices in the lottery choice task, the estimated discount rate takes on a value that is much more in line with what one would expect from market interest rates. To evaluate the statistical significance of adjusting for a concave utility function one can test the hypothesis that the estimated discount rate assuming risk aversion is the same as the discount rate estimated assuming linear utility functions. This null hypothesis is easily rejected. Thus, *allowing for diminishing marginal utility makes a significant difference to the elicited discount rates.*

4.3.2 Subjective Probabilities

Exactly the same joint estimation methodology can be used to infer subjective probabilities over some binary event. Subjective probabilities are operationally defined as those probabilities that lead an agent to choose some prospects over others when outcomes depend on events that are not yet actualized. These choices could be as natural as placing a bet on a horse race, or as experimentally structured as responding to the payoff prizes provided by some scoring rule. In order to infer subjective probabilities from observed choices of this kind, however, one has to either make some strong assumptions about risk attitudes or jointly estimate risk attitudes and subjective probabilities. Joint estimation of a structural model of choice across the two types of tasks, one to elicit risk attitudes and the other to (recursively) elicit beliefs conditional on risk attitudes, allows one to make inferences about subjective probabilities from observed behavior in relatively simple choice tasks.

For quadratic scoring rules applied to elicit subjective probabilities of binary events, theory tells us that EUT subjects that are risk averse will report a probability closer to 0.5 than their true, latent probability. This is due to an aversion to variability of payoffs under the two states of nature: in the extreme, reporting 0.5 ensures the same payoffs under each state of nature. If we know how risk averse the individual is, we can infer what subjective probability rationally led them to make any observed report. Andersen, Fountain et al. (2014) show how to operationalize this logic econometrically and jointly estimate risk preferences and subjective probabilities if the subject is EUT. As expected, each subjective probability estimate comes with a standard error, and imprecision in estimating risk attitudes propagates, as it should as a matter of theory, to imprecise inferences about subjective probabilities.

The same logic extends to RDU models of risk preferences, although here one must account for the "first-order" effect of probability weighting, by effectively taking the inverse of the probability weighting function. This adds some complexity, particularly for reports close to 0.5, but it is also econometrically tractable, as demonstrated by Andersen, Fountain et al. (2014).

The same ideas extend to application of proper scoring rules to elicit beliefs over nonbinary events, or discrete representations of continuous events. In this case risk-averse EUT subjects will "flatten" their optimal reports over events they assign any subjective probability to: again, just reducing the variability of payoffs across events that have nonzero chance of occurring (see Harrison et al. 2017). RDU subjects will again have a more dramatic distortion of their reports than EUT subjects, although one can also recover their true, latent subject belief distributions (see Harrison and Ulm 2015).

4.3.3 Intertemporal Risk Preferences

Joint estimation scales "vertically upwards," as needed by theory. The concept of intertemporal risk aversion, also known as correlation aversion, is all about preferences over the *interaction* of risk preferences and time preferences. As such, one must jointly estimate atemporal risk preferences, time preferences, and the intertemporal utility function building on the joint estimation approach.

The concept of intertemporal risk aversion arises from theoretical deviations from an additively separable intertemporal utility function. Define the lottery ψ as a 50:50 mixture of {x, Y} and {X, y}, and the lottery Ψ as a 50:50 mixture of {x, y} and {X, Y}, where $X > x$ and $Y > y$. So ψ is a 50:50 mixture of both bad and good outcomes in time t and $t + \tau$; and Ψ is a 50:50 mixture of only bad outcomes or only good outcomes in the two time periods. These lotteries ψ and Ψ are defined over all possible "good" and "bad" outcomes. If the individual is indifferent between ψ and Ψ we say that he is neutral to intertemporally correlated payoffs in the two time periods. If the individual prefers ψ to Ψ we say that he is averse to intertemporally correlated payoffs: it is better to have a given chance of being lucky in one of the two periods than to have the same chance of being very unlucky or very lucky in both periods. The correlation averse individual prefers to have non-extreme payoffs *across* periods, just as the risk averse individual prefers to have non-extreme payoffs *within* periods. One can also view the correlation averse individual as preferring to avoid correlation-increasing transformations of payoffs in different periods.

To elicit intertemporal risk aversion one has to present subjects with choices over lotteries that have different income profiles over time. Proper identification of intertemporal risk aversion thus requires that one controls for atemporal risk aversion and the individual discount rate. All three of these parameters are intrinsically, conceptually connected as a matter of theory, unless one makes strong assumptions otherwise. The experimental design and econometric logic of Andersen et al. (2018) follow from this theoretical point. The experimental procedures needed are a direct extension of those employed by Andersen et al. (2008, 2014b).

One task elicited atemporal risk attitudes for lotteries payable today, as a vehicle for inferring the concavity of the atemporal utility function. Another task elicited time preferences over non-stochastic amounts of money payable at different times: in general, an SS amount and an LL amount. In some cases, the sooner amount was paid out today, and in some cases it will be paid out in the future. A third task, new to this design, elicited intertemporal risk attitudes by asking subjects to make a series of choices over risky profiles of outcomes that are paid out at different points in time. For example, lottery A might give the individual a 10 percent chance of receiving a larger amount L_t at time t *and* a smaller amount $S_{t+\tau}$ at time t + τ, (L_t, $S_{t+\tau}$) and a 90 percent chance of receiving the smaller amount S_t at time t *and* the larger amount $L_{t+\tau}$ at time t+τ, (S_t, $L_{t+\tau}$). Lottery B might give the individual a 10 percent chance of receiving L_t *and* $L_{t+\tau}$ and a 90 percent chance of receiving S_t *and* $S_{t+\tau}$. The subject picks A or B.

The econometric implications for joint estimation follow rigidly from the theory and experimental design presented above, as explained by Andersen et al. (2018) and reviewed in Appendix C (online).

The nature of the implied joint likelihood function is matched by the recursive experimental design. Ignoring the objective parameters of the tasks, the lottery choices over stochastic lotteries paid out today depend on atemporal risk preferences; the discounting tasks over non-stochastic outcomes paid out today or sometime in the future depend on atemporal risk preferences (via U″) and time preferences; and the discounting tasks over stochastic outcomes paid out today or sometime in the future depend on atemporal risk preferences, time preferences, and intertemporal risk aversion. Putting behavioral error terms aside, if we were to try to estimate atemporal risk preferences and time preferences using either the lottery choices over stochastic lotteries paid out today or the discounting tasks over non-stochastic outcomes, we would be unable to identify both parameters. Similarly, if we were to try to estimate atemporal risk preferences, time preferences and intertemporal risk preferences using only two of three tasks, we would face an identification problem.

These identification problems are inherent to the *theoretical* definitions of the discount rate and intertemporal risk aversion, and demand a recursive experimental design that combines multiple types of choices and an econometric approach that recognizes the complete structural model. The general principle is joint estimation of all structural parameters so that uncertainty about the parameters defining the utility function propagates in a "full information" sense into the uncertainty about the parameters defining the discount function and the intertemporal utility function. Intuitively, if the experimenter only has a vague notion of what the utility function is, because of poor estimates of risk preferences, then one simply cannot make precise inferences about time preferences or intertemporal risk preferences. Similarly, poor estimates of time preferences, even if U″ is estimated relatively precisely, imply that one cannot make precise inferences about intertemporal risk preferences.

This inferential procedure about intertemporal risk aversion does not rely on the use of EUT, or the CRRA functional form. Nor does it rely on the use of the exponential discounting function; the method generalizes immediately to alternative specifications that use alternative discounting functions, as illustrated in Andersen et al. (2014b).[14]

4.3.4 Social Preferences

It is a commonplace that individuals care about others. The concept of social preferences is a reflection of the attitudes that one individual has for the well-being of others, and the extent to which that trades off with the well-being of the individual.

Just as preferences over different commodities are a latent theoretical construct to explain observed choice behavior by an individual over those commodities, social preferences are a latent theoretical construct to explain observed choice behavior over allocations by an individual to others and the individual. But if we find it useful to think of the utility that commodities bring, it follows that social preferences defined over allocations of commodities might also usefully be defined in terms of the utility of those allocations. That is, someone might choose to allocate commodities to another person because they behave as if they care about the *actual utility* of the other person, and not because they care about the commodities received by the other person per se. But then I cannot make inferences about the social preferences of one individual without jointly making inferences about the utility function of that individual and the utility function of the other person.

Another implication of adopting this approach is that the social preference of an individual might take into account their *subjective perception* of the utility that allocations to others brings to the other person. Even if the individual knows what allocation is being made to the other person, they may not know the well-being that this allocation brings. To take an example, imagine that the allocation to the other player is a lottery: my perception of the income-equivalent of that allocation depends on what I believe to be the risk attitude of the other person. In this case, to make conceptually valid inferences about social preferences requires that one jointly estimate subjective beliefs about the risk preferences of others as well as my social preference toward that perceived EU for the other person.

Yet another reason for adopting this approach is that the social preference of an individual might utilize a *normative* utility function for allocations to others. I may know that my child is a risk-lover, but treat her as if she is risk-neutral or risk-averse when deciding on my allocations to her. Again, the challenge for joint estimation is to make inferences about my normative judgments of utility functions for others at the same time as making inferences about my social preferences.

In effect, we are proposing that one characterize social preferences the same way that we characterize social welfare functions, where the arguments are almost always the utilities of the affected individuals. In some sense the main insight from this change in characterization is the possibility of developing a structural model of different social preferences that accord with the way we characterize social preferences over income distribution for society as a whole. After all, the social preferences of an individual for one other individual, or a member of their household, is just a "little social welfare function" defined over those individuals. If we are attracted to assuming "welfarism" when characterizing social welfare functions, the assumption that social welfare is defined over individual welfare values, then the same should follow for social preferences. The three ways of thinking about the utility of the other person,[15] then, would be viewed as distinct social preference functionals, but would instead simply be viewed as different *arguments* of a single social welfare function.

The methodological point is that we cannot begin to discuss social preferences in any general form without worrying about the identification and estimation issues of jointly estimating those social preferences *and* the arguments of any social preference function.

4.3.5 A General Lesson

One general methodological lesson from these examples is that there is some considerable virtue in having experimental tasks that are "agnostic" about what latent structural model will be applied to them. We do not want an elicitation method for atemporal risk preferences that assumes EUT, RDU, or CPT, or any of the myriad of alternative possible models one could consider (e.g., Disappointment Aversion or Regret Theory). Nor do we want an elicitation method for time preferences that assumes Exponential discounting. Inferences about intertemporal risk aversion should not be held methodological hostage to elicitation methods that lock in one theoretical specification or another, unless there are good a priori reasons for doing so.[16]

4.4 Just Read the Literature: A Case Study of CPT

The key innovation of CPT, in comparison to RDU, is to allow sign-dependent preferences, where risk attitudes depend on whether the individual is evaluating a gain or a loss. Tversky and Kahneman (1992: 309) popularized the functional forms we often see for loss aversion, using a CRRA specification of utility: $U(m) = m^{1-\alpha} /(1-\alpha)$ when $m \geq 0$ and $U(m) = -\lambda[(-m)^{1-\beta} /(1-\beta)]$ when $m < 0$, where λ is the utility loss aversion parameter, and α and β are coefficients of utility curvature in the gain and loss frame, respectively. Here, we have the assumption that the degree of utility loss aversion for small unit changes is the same as the degree of loss aversion for large unit changes: the same λ applies locally to gains and losses of the same monetary magnitude around 0 as it does globally to any size gain or loss of the same magnitude. This is not a criticism, just a restrictive parametric turn in the specification compared to Kahneman and Tversky (1979).

Probability weighting for gains is identical to RDU, and the logic for losses is similar. Following Tversky and Kahneman (1992), one often sees the use of the inverse-S function, resulting in $\omega(p) = p^{\gamma+}/(p^{\gamma+} + (1-p)^{\gamma+})^{1/\gamma+}$ for $m \geq 0$ and $\omega(p) = p^{\gamma-}/(p^{\gamma-} + (1-p)^{\gamma-})^{1/\gamma-}$ for $m < 0$. The application of probability weighting for loss-frame and mixed-frame lotteries is not obvious and is spelled out by Harrison and Swarthout (2016, Appendix B). Probability weighting can easily lead to differences in the decision weights for gains and losses, and hence generate loss aversion or loss seeking, ceteris paribus values for α, β, and λ.[17] One can usefully refer to this source of loss aversion as *probabilistic loss aversion*, following Schmidt and Zank (2008: 213). Thus, loss aversion comes from *two* possible psychological pathways: utility loss aversion *and* probabilistic loss aversion. This is not a radical interpretation of CPT but a direct consequence of the general form of CPT. The upshot is that the conventional CPT model can be defined by parameters α, β, λ, $\gamma+$, and $\gamma-$, although extensions are easy to consider (e.g., to the Prelec (1998) probability weighting function, which significantly generalizes the Inverse-S function).

It is remarkable to see how light the existing evidence for CPT is when one weighs the experimental and econometric procedures carefully. Moreover, a recent trend seems to be to declare any evidence for probability weighting, even if only in the gain domain, as evidence for CPT when it is literally evidence for RDU. Harrison and Swarthout (2016) provide a detailed review of the literature, focusing only on controlled experiments, which has been the original basis of empirical claims for CPT. Here we focus on several of the more prominent studies.

Tversky and Kahneman (1992) gave their twenty-five subjects a total of sixty-four choices. Their subjects received $25 to participate in the experiment, but rewards were not salient, so their choices had no monetary consequences. The majority of data from their experiments used an elicitation procedure that we would now call a multiple price list, in the spirit of Holt and Laury (2002). Subjects were told the expected value of the risky lottery, and seven certain amounts were presented in a logarithmic scale, with values spanning the extreme payouts of the risky lottery. The subject made seven binary choices between the given risky lottery and the series of certain amounts. To generate more refined choices, the subject was given a second series of seven CEs for the same risky lottery, zeroing in on the interval selected in the first stage.[18] Furthermore, "switching" was ruled out, with the computer program enforcing a single switch between the risky lottery and the certain values.[19] All risky prospects used two prizes, and there were fifty-six prospects evaluated in this manner. One half of these prospects were in the gain frame, and one half were in the loss frame, with the latter being a "reflection" of the former in terms of the values employed.

A further set of eight tasks involved mixed-frame gambles. In these choices the subject was asked to Fill-In-the-Blank (FIB) by entering a value $x that would make the risky lottery ($a, ½; $b, ½) equivalent to ($c, ½; $x, ½), for given values of a, b, and c. The probabilities for the initial fifty-six choices over gain frame or loss frame choices were 0.01, 0.05, 0.1, 0.25, 0.5, 0.75, 0.9, 0.95, and 0.01, whereas the sole probability for the eight mixed-frame choices was ½.

Tversky and Kahneman (1992) estimate a structural model of CPT using nonlinear least squares, and at the level of the individual. Remarkably, they then report the *median* point estimate, for each structural parameter, over the twenty-five estimated values. So, over all twenty-five subjects, and using the earlier notation, the median value for α was 0.88, the median value of λ was 2.22, the median value of γ+ was 0.61, and the median value of γ- was 0.69.[20]

These parameter estimates are remarkable in three respects, given the prominence they have received in the literature. First, whenever one sees point estimates estimated for individuals, one can be certain that there are many "wild" estimates from an a priori perspective,[21] so reporting the median value alone might be quite unrepresentative of the average value and provides no information whatsoever on the variability across subjects. Second, there is no mention at all of standard errors, so we have no way of knowing, for example, if the oft-repeated value of λ is statistically significantly different from 1. Third, the median value of any given parameter is not linked in any manner to the median value of any other parameter: these are *not the values of some representative, median subject*, which is often how they are implicitly portrayed.[22] The subject that actually generated the median value of λ, for instance, might have had any value for α, β, γ+, and γ-.

These shortcomings of the study of Tversky and Kahneman (1992) have not, to our knowledge, led anyone to replicate their experiments with salient rewards and report complete sets of parameter estimates with standard errors. The fault is not that of Tversky and Kahneman (1992), who otherwise employed quite modern methods, but the subsequent CPT literature. Anybody casually using these estimates as statistically representative of anything must not care about rigor in empirical work.

Camerer and Ho (1994) was a remarkable study, with many insights. It was also one of the first to claim to estimate a structural model of CPT using ML (§6.1). The data employed were choice patterns from a wide range of studies, but the analysis was explicitly restricted to the gain frame (188). Hence it should be viewed as the first structural estimation of the RDU model, but not of a CPT model.

Bruhin, Fehr-Duda, and Epper (2010) estimated parametric models of CPT that assumed that the utility loss aversion parameter λ was 1, noting wryly that "our specification of the value function seems to lack a prominent feature of prospect theory, loss aversion ... " (1382). They did this because their design only included lotteries in the gain frame and the loss frame, and none in the mixed frame. Estimation of utility loss aversion is logically impossible without mixed-frame choices.

Nilsson, Rieskamp, and Wagenmakers (2011) utilized the same "slightly real" data of Rieskamp (2008) and applied a Bayesian hierarchical model to estimate structural CPT parameters. They recognized the identification problem with power utility specifications when $\alpha \neq \beta$ indirectly. They initially simulated data using the popular point estimates from Tversky and Kahneman (1992), to test the ability of their model to recover them. They found that their model underestimated λ and that α was estimated to be much lower than β, rather than $\alpha \approx \beta$. They concluded (89) as follows:

> It is likely that these results are caused by a peculiarity of CPT, that is, its ability to account for loss aversion in multiple ways. The most obvious way for CPT to account for loss aversion is by parameter λ (after all, the purpose of λ is to measure loss aversion). A second way, however, is to decrease the marginal utility at a faster pace for gains than for losses. This occurs when α is smaller than β. Based on this reasoning, we hypothesized that the parameter estimation routines compensate for the underestimation of λ by assigning lower values to α than to β; in this way, CPT accounts for the existing loss aversion indirectly in a manner that we had not anticipated.

Of course, this is just the *theoretical* identification issue that requires an "exchange rate assumption," discussed in Köbberling and Wakker (2005, §7) and Wakker (2010, §9.6). In any event, they optionally estimate all models with $\alpha = \beta$, and avoid this identification problem. Using the Inverse-S probability weighting function, they reported Bayesian posterior modes (standard deviations) over the pooled sample of $\alpha = \beta = 0.91$ (0.16), $\lambda = 1.02$ (0.26), $\gamma+ = 0.68$ (0.11), and $\gamma- = 0.89$ (0.19). Unlike Rieskamp (2008), they did not constrain λ to be greater than 1.

These estimates are the Bayesian counterparts of random coefficients: hence each parameter is a distribution, which can be summarized in several ways. Reporting the mode is a more robust alternative to the mean, given the symmetric nature of their visual display of estimates, and the standard deviation provides information on the estimated variability across the thirty subjects, each making 180 binary choices. They find no evidence for utility loss aversion. There is *very* slight evidence of probabilistic loss aversion for small probabilities, since there is slight risk loving over gains and extremely slight risk aversion for losses. For large probabilities this evidence suggests probabilistic loss seeking, albeit modest.

von Gaudecker, van Soest, and Wengström (2011) estimated parametric models of CPT that assumed a complete absence of probability weighting, on both gain and loss frames. They note clearly (675) that their specification entails

> departures from the original prospect theory specification. . . . it does not involve nonlinear probability weighting because our goal is to estimate individual-level parameters, and the dimension of the estimation problem is large already. Adding a parameter that is highly collinear with utility curvature in our experimental setup would result in an infeasibly large number of parameters, given the structure of our data. Furthermore, typical probability weighting functionals develop the highest impact at extreme probabilities, which are absent from our experiment.

Unfortunately, these justifications are tenuous. The fact that the goal is individual-level estimation does not, by itself, have any theoretical implications for why one can pick and choose aspects of the CPT model. Indeed, adding two parameters for probability weighting does add minimally to the dimensionality of the estimation problem. But numerical convenience is hardly an acceptable rationale for mis-specification of the CPT model.

Colinearity with utility curvature is actually a theoretical point of some importance, and to be expected, and not an econometric nuisance. Indeed, it extends to colinearity with the utility loss aversion parameter, unless one assumes away a priori the possibility of probabilistic loss aversion by not estimating any probability weights. If one parameter plays a significant role in explaining the risk premium for an individual, then assuming it away surely biases conclusions about the strength and even sign of other psychological pathways. The final point, about not having sufficient variability in probabilities to estimate probability weighting functions, is even less clear. Their initial lottery choices varied the probability of the high prize from 0.25 to 0.5, 0.75, and 1; then their second-stage choice interpolated the probability weights between one of these gaps (0 to 0.25, 0.25 to 0.5, 0.5 to 0.75, or 0.75 to 1) in grids of roughly 10-percent points. Even from the first-stage choices, if one assumes the popular Power or Inverse-S function, then formally one only needs one interior probability to allow estimation. In fact, their design always has three interior probabilities of the first stage and typically have refinements within one of those intervals. In sum, these arguments sound as though they were constructed "after the fact" of extensive numerical and econometric experimentation, and in the face of a priori unreliable numerical results.

Murphy and ten Brincke (2018) estimate parametric structural models of CPT at the individual level, using mixed estimation methods to condition individual estimates based on pooled estimates. They assume that $\alpha = \beta$ in order to avoid making any "exchange rate assumption," but, of course, that is an assumption nonetheless. Although they used the flexible Prelec (1998) probability-weighting function, they assumed the same probability-weighting function for gains and losses, another restrictive assumption; their rationale (fn. 4) was "parsimony and as a first pass, given the relatively low number of binary observations compared to the number of model parameters." They report (§6.1) values for λ of 1.11 and 1.18 in two sessions, one later than the other, but do not say if these were statistically significantly different from 1. Estimated distributions, "given by medians of estimates" (fn. 9) for the pooled sample, show that there appears to be no statistically significant loss aversion, with $\lambda \approx 1$, and virtually no probability weighting on average, with $\eta \approx \varphi \approx 1$.

4.5 There Is a Reason We Compute Likelihoods: A Case Study of the PH

One of the valuable contributions of psychology is the focus on the *process* of decision-making. Economists have tended to focus on the characterization of properties of equilibria, and neglected the connection to explicit or implicit processes that might bring these about (Harrison 2008, §4). Of course, this was not always so, as the correspondence principle of Samuelson (1947) dramatically illustrated. But it has become a common methodological difference in practice.[23] Brandstätter, Gigerenzer, and Hertwig (2006) illustrate the extreme alternative, a process model that is amazingly simple and that apparently explains a lot of data. Their "priority heuristic" is therefore a useful case study in the statistical issues considered here and the role of an ML estimation framework applied to a structural model.

The PH proposes that subjects evaluate binary choices using a sequence of rules applied lexicographically. For the case of two nonnegative outcomes, the heuristic is,

1. If one lottery has a minimum gain that is larger than the minimum gain of the other lottery by ω percent or more of the maximum possible gain, pick it.
2. Otherwise, if one lottery has a probability of the minimum gain that is at least $\acute{\omega}$ percent better than the other, pick it.
3. Otherwise, pick the lottery with the maximum gain.

The parameters ω and $\acute{\omega}$ are each set to 10, based on arguments (412ff.) about "cultural prominence." The heuristic has a simple extension to consider the probability of the maximum gain when there are more than two outcomes per lottery.

The key feature of this heuristic is that it completely eschews the notion of trading off the utility of prizes and their probabilities.[24] This is a bold departure from the traditions embodied in EUT, RDU, CPT, and even the SP/A (security-potential/aspiration) theory of Lopes (1984). What is striking, then, is that it appears to blow *every* other theory out of the water when applied to *every* conceivable decision problem. It explains the Allais Paradox, the Reflection Effect, the Certainty Effect, the Fourfold Pattern, the Intransitivities, and it even predicts choices in "diverse sets of choice problems" better than a very long list of alternatives. It is notable that the list of opponents arrayed in the dramatic figures 1 through 5 of Brandstätter, Gigerenzer, and Hertwig (2006) do not include EUT with some simple CRRA specification and modest amounts of risk aversion, or even simple EV (expected value) maximization.

However, there are three problems with the evidence for the PH.

First, one must be extraordinarily careful of claims about "well known stylized facts" about choice, since the behavioral economics literature has become somewhat untethered from the facts in this regard. Consider behavioral Ground Zero, the Allais paradox. It is now well documented that experimental subjects just do not fall prey to the Allais paradox like decision-making lemmings when one presents the task for real payments and drops the word "millions" after the prize amount: see Conlisk (1989), Harrison (1994), Burke et al. (1996), and Fan (2002).[25] Subjects appear to crank out the EV when given real tasks to perform, and the vast majority behave consistently with EUT as a result.[26] This is not to claim that all anomalies or stylized facts are untrue, but there is a casual tendency in the behavioral economics literature to repeatedly assume stylized facts that are simply incorrect. Thus, to return to the Allais paradox, if the PH predicts a violation, and in fact the data says otherwise for *motivated* subjects, doesn't this count directly as evidence *against* the PH?

The second problem with the evaluation of the performance of the PH against alternative models is that the *parameters* of those models, when the model relies on parameters, are taken from studies of different subjects and choice tasks. It is as if the CRRA of an EUT model from an Iowa potato farmer making fertilizer choices had been applied to the portfolio choices of a Manhattan investment banker. The naïve idea is that there is one, true set of parameters that define the model, and that is the model for all time and all domains.[27] This flies in the face of the default assumption by economists, and not a few psychologists (e.g., Birnbaum 2008), that individuals might have different preferences over risk. It is notable that many applied researchers disregard that presumption and build tests of theories that assume homogenous preferences, but at least they are well aware that this is simply an auxiliary assumption made for tractability (e.g., Camerer and Ho 1994: 186). In any event, in those instances the researcher at least estimates parameters afresh in some ML sense for the sample of interest.

It is a different matter to estimate parameters for a model from responses from a random sample from a given population, and then see if those parameters predict data from another random sample from the *same population*. Although this tends not to be commonly done in economics, it is different than assuming that parameters are universal constants. For example, Birnbaum and Navarrete (1998: 50) clearly seek to test model predictions "in the manner predicted in advance of the experiment" using parameters from comparable samples. One must take care that the stimuli and recruitment procedures match, of course, so that one is comparing apples to apples.

This issue is not peculiar to psychologists: behavioral economists have an embarrassing tendency to just assume certain critical parameters casually, relying inordinately on the illustrative estimates of Tversky and Kahneman (1992), *very* critically reviewed in §4. For one celebrated example, consider Benartzi and Thaler (1995), who use laboratory-generated estimates from college students to calibrate a model of the behavior of US bond and stock investors. Such exercises are fine as "finger mathematics" exemplars, but they are no substitute for estimation on the comparable samples. In general, economists tend to focus on in-sample comparisons of estimates from different models, although some have considered the formal estimation issues that arise when one seeks to undertake out-of-sample comparisons (Wilcox 2008; 2011). An example would be comparing behavior in one task context to behavior in another task context, albeit a context that is comparable.

The third problem with the PH is the fundamental one from the present perspective of thinking about models using an ML approach: it predicts with probability one or zero. So, surely, aren't there *some* interesting settings in which the heuristic must be completely wrong most or all the time? Indeed there are. Consider the comparison of lottery A in which the subject gets $1.60 with probability p and $2.00 with probability 1 – p, and lottery B in which the subject gets $0.10 with probability p and $3.85 with probability 1 – p. The PH picks A *every time*, no matter how low p is. The minimum gain is $1.60 for A and $0.10 for B, and 10 percent of $1.60 is $0.16, greater than $0.10.

At this point experimental economists are jumping up and down, waving their hands and pointing to the data from a massive range of experiments initiated by Holt and Laury (2002) with exactly these parameters. Their baseline experimental task presented subjects with an ordered list of ten such choices, with p ranging from 0.1 to 1 in increments of 0.1. Refer to these prizes as their 1x prizes, where the number indicates a scale factor applied to all prizes. Identical tasks are reported by Holt and Laury (2002, 2005) with 20x, 50x, and 90x prizes, and by Harrison et al. (2005) with 10x prizes. Although we will want to do much, much better than just look at average choices, it is apparent from these data that the PH must be in trouble as a general model. Holt and Laury (2005: 903, Table 1) report that the average number of choices of lottery A is 5.2, 5.3, 6.1, and 5.7 over hundreds of subjects facing the 1x task, 6.0 over 178 subjects facing the 10x task, and 6.7 over 216 subjects facing the 20x task, in all cases for real payments and with no order effects. The predicted outcome for an EUT model assuming risk neutrality is for four choices of lottery A, and a modest extension of EUT to allow small levels of risk aversion would explain five or six safe choices quite well. In fact, using the usual CRRA utility function, any RRA between 0.15 and 0.41 would predict five choices, and any RRA between 0.41 and 0.68 would predict six choices (Holt and Laury 2002: 1649, Table 3).

But using the metric of evaluation of Brandstätter, Gigerenzer, and Hertwig (2006), the PH would predict behavior here perfectly as well! This is because they count a success for a theory based on whether it predicts the *majority* choice correctly.[28] In the ten choices of the Holt and Laury (2002) task, imagine that subjects picked A on average 5.000000001 times. An EUT model, in which the CRRA was set to around 0.25, would predict that the average subject picks lottery A five times and then switches to B for the other five choices, hence predicting almost perfectly in each of the ten choices. But the PH gets almost four out of ten wrong *every time*, and yet is viewed as a 100 percent successful theory by this metric.

This example shows exactly why it is a mistake to casually use the "hit rate" as a metric of evaluation in such settings.[29] The likelihood approach, instead, asks the model to state the probability of observing the actual choice, conditional on some trial values of the parameters of the theory. ML then just finds those parameters that generate the highest probability of observing the data. For binary choice tasks, and independent observations, we know that the likelihood of the sample is just the product of the likelihood of each choice conditional on the model and the parameters assumed, and that the likelihood of each choice is just the probability of that choice. So if we have any observation that has zero probability, and the PH has many, the log-likelihood for that observation zooms off to minus infinity. Even if we set the likelihood to some minuscule amount, so we do not have to evaluate the logarithm of zero, the overall likelihood of the PH is a priori abysmal without even firing up any statistical package.

Of course, this is true for any theory that predicts deterministically, including EUT. This is why one needs some formal statement about how the deterministic prediction of the theory translates into a probability of observing one choice or the other, and then perhaps also some formal statement about the role that structural errors might play, as explained in Section 2.

4.6 Point Estimates Are Not Data: A Case Study of Source Dependence

Abdellaoui, Baillon, Placido, and Wakker (2011) (ABPW) conclude that different probability weighting functions are used when subjects face risky processes with known probabilities and uncertain processes with subjective processes. They call this "source dependence," where the notion of a source is relatively easy to identify in the context of an artefactual laboratory experiment, and hence provides the tightest test of this proposition. Unfortunately, their conclusions are an artefact of estimation procedures that do not worry about sampling errors.[30] These procedures are now often used in behavioral economics, and need to be examined carefully. In this case, they make a huge difference to the inferences one draws.

Consider the simple two-urn Ellsberg design, the centerpiece of their analysis. The known urn, K, has some objective distribution of balls with five colors. Design an experiment to elicit CE for a number of these urns, where the probabilities are generated objectively and vary from urn to urn. Assume the subject believes that.[31] The unknown urn, U, has some mix of balls of the same colors. Define some lotteries from the U urn, such as "you get \$100 if blue comes out, otherwise \$0 if any other color comes out" or "you get \$100 if blue or red comes out, otherwise \$0 if any other color comes out." Then elicit CE for these bets.

Now write out some models to describe behavior. For the K urn, which we call risk, and restricting to two prizes, X and x, for X > x, we have $w_K(p)\ u_K(X) + [1 - w_K(p)]\ u_K(x)$ for some objective probability p of the bet being true and the subject earning X. We assume some specific functional forms for the probability weighting functions and utility functions, and estimate those parameters. For the U urn, which we call uncertainty, we propose $w_U(\pi)\ u_U(X) + [1 - w_U(\pi)]\ u_U(x)$ for some subjective probability π of the bet being true and the subject earning X. So in the general models shown here the probability weighting function *and* the utility function are source-dependent. This is the model that ABPW propose: source-dependence in both utility and probability weighting functions, which seems reasonable to test.

On the basis of a priori reasoning, some have suggested instead that we only have source-dependence in the probability weighting function, so we would have $w_K(p)\ u(X) + [1 - w_K(p)]\ u(x)$ and $w_U(\pi)\ u(X) + [1 - w_U(\pi)]\ u(x)$. Of course, this is a testable restriction of the general model to $u_K(z) = u_U(z)$ for $z \in \{X, x\}$. There is an obvious, symmetric special case with source-dependence only in the utility function: $w(p)\, u_K(X) + [1 - w(p)]\, u_K(x)$ and $w(\pi)\, u_U(X) + [1-w(\pi)]\, u_U(x)$. Again this is a testable restriction of the general model to $w_K(p) = w_U(\pi)$ for $p=\pi$. Indeed, it is the alternative hypothesis offered by (Vernon) Smith (1969) in a comment on Ellsberg.

These models can be estimated using data generated from the "Ellsberg experiment" of ABPW. In this experiment each subject was asked to state CE for thirty-two bets based on the K urn, and thirty-two bets based on the U urn, generating sixty-four observations per subject. They propose a power utility function defined over prizes z normalized to lie between 0 and 1, $u(z) = z^{\rho}$, where the parameter ρ is allowed to take on different values depending on the source K or U. So if S is defined to be a binary variable such that $S = 1$ when the U process was used and $S = 0$ when the K process was used, one estimates ρ_K and ρ_U in $\rho = \rho_K + \rho_U\, S$ and then there is an obvious hypothesis test that $\rho_U = 0$ in order to test for source independence with respect to the utility function.

The probability weighting function is due to Prelec (1998), which exhibits considerable flexibility: $w(p) = \exp\{-\eta(-\ln p^{\varphi}\}$, where $w(p)$ is for choices from the K process. The same function $w(\pi)$ can be defined for the choices from the U process. It is similarly possible to estimate linear functions of the structural parameters φ and η to test for source-independence: $\varphi = \varphi_K + \varphi_U\, S$ and $\eta = \eta_K + \eta_U\, S$. The obvious hypothesis test for source independence in probability weighting is that $\varphi_U = 0$ *and* $\eta_U = 0$.

The experimental data of ABPW can be used to estimate these structural parameters and undertake the hypothesis tests for source independence. Each of sixty-six subjects was presented with thirty-two tasks in which they were asked to indicate "switch points" between a bet on some outcome from drawing a ball from the urn and a certain amount of money. Half of the bets were based on draws from the K urn, and half from bets based on the U urn. The CE were ordered increments between 0€ and 25€, using fifty rows in a multiple price list elicitation. The end-result for each subjective lottery is a certain amount of money evaluated as being just less valuable than the lottery, and a certain amount of money evaluated as being just more valuable than the lottery. The switch point is enforced for the subject and involves an increment of 0.5€. Thus we have sixty-four binary lottery comparisons for each subject over thirty-two tasks. Each subject was told that one of the thirty-two tasks would be selected for payment, thereby incentivizing them to respond truthfully. Appendix D (online) reviews these estimates, which show no support for the hypothesis of source dependence.

Although the evidence for source dependence is missing, this does not mean that the behavioral phenomenon is missing. Indeed, it is intuitively plausible once one moves to the domain of subjective probabilities, or where objective probabilities are presumed to arise from some inferential process.[32] But we should not mistake our intuition for the evidence, as comforting as that might be.

4.7 Conclusion: Where Are the Methodologists?

The overall methodological lesson is that one cannot do behavioral econometrics effectively without knowing structural theory, and one cannot design experiments efficiently without knowing structural theory, and having an eye to what identification issues will arise. Of course, "identification" is a matter for theory, as much as econometric method: it basically means the same thing as proposing an operationally meaningful theory. So there is a methodological trinity here.

There are some low-hanging methodological issues reviewed here, and some subtle issues. To take the low-hanging cases first, how have philosophers of science and methodologists allowed CPT to survive on the basis of the flimsy empirical evidence transparently before us? If it is not their job to maintain intellectual standards across erstwhile intellectual silos, then whose is it? One reasonable response is that this is what experimental economists should do, since they are the methodological bridge between theory and evidence. In effect, they have to operate at both coalfaces.[33]

The subtle methodological issues involve the selection of metrics for normative evaluation, now that behavioral economics has given us a rich array of alternative *descriptive* models to the traditional models.[34] It is not automatically true that the traditional models are the normatively attractive models, even if they are often mis-characterized as such. To motivate richer discussion of these issues we need more examples where "getting the positive economics right" matters for the welfare evaluation of policies of substance. Armed with normative tradeoffs of substance, rather than abstract constructions per se, we will then have to address the normative methodological issues.

Notes

1 Adam Smith preached the virtues of a division of labor, but only under the assumption that trade occurred to allow the efficiency gains to be realized.

2 Occasionally one encounters defenders of OLS, even when we know that the conditions for OLS are violated. None of these arguments hold much water when confronted. One argument is that it is "easier to interpret OLS estimates directly as marginal effects." Yes, but that is only because one has to assume away anything that might cause OLS to generate unreliable marginal effects. That is just circular reasoning. What might be easier, might just as well be wrong: ease of calculation and cognitive effort are not the same thing as validity of estimates. And modern software completely removes the ease argument. Another argument for OLS is that "you get the same results anyway." Really? In the old days one might have seen a wide table of OLS estimates, with gaps here and there to reflect specification searches, and one column in which estimates from the appropriate model are included. But not the myriad of specification searches using the appropriate model, the validity of ad hoc specification searches aside. So we do not know if the "robustness" shown with OLS is indeed a robustness that carries over to the appropriate model. Another argument for OLS, common in some finance journals, is that "I don't believe the results unless I see them in OLS." This is just bad epistemology, and should be called out as such. And if this is the theological ritual needed to get published, why not put the knowingly incorrect estimates in the online appendix? Another argument for OLS is that, "I checked and the average is in the interior of the natural boundary." Perhaps some share, bounded between 0 and 1, has an average of 0.24. But that is the average, which

is swept out by the OLS estimate (on a good day with respect to other assumptions). It says nothing about the residuals, which are the things we would like to be Gaussian, and lie unconstrained between $\pm\infty$. Are we just to ignore the residual that is below 0 or above 1? Finally, one sometimes hears, "well, everyone else does it," and surely that statement does not even need a rebuttal in scientific discourse.

3 One limitation is that the "treatment" has to be binary, continuous, *or* multilevel, but cannot be a mix of these. Unfortunately, many treatments of interest are best characterized by a rich mixture of all of these. Consider the evaluation of the effect of smoking on health expenditures. Smoking history might depend on whether the individual had ever smoked 100 cigarettes (binary), whether the individual currently smokes daily or occasionally (binary), whether the individual is a former smoker (binary), the number of cigarettes smoked per day (discrete, multivalued), and the number of years that current daily smokers have smoked (discrete, multivalued).

4 One issue here is that we cannot compare the choices over A and B of one subject with the choices over A* and B* of another subject, without making the unwarranted assumption that they have the same preferences over risk. In practice, the same subject can have both pairs presented in the context of a wider battery, and then direct comparisons can be made for each subject.

5 In the MM triangle there are always one, two or three prizes in each lottery that have positive probability of occurring. The vertical axis in each panel shows the probability attached to the high prize of that triple, and the horizontal axis shows the probability attached to the low prize of that triple. So when the probability of the highest and lowest prize is zero, 100 percent weight falls on the middle prize. Any lotteries strictly in the interior of the MM triangle have positive weight on all three prizes, and any lottery on the boundary of the MM triangle has zero weight on one or two prizes.

6 EUT does not, in these circumstances, predict 50:50 choices, as some casually claim. It does say that the expected utility differences will not explain behavior, and that then allows all sorts of psychological factors to explain behavior. In effect, EUT has *no* prediction in this instance, and that is not the same as predicting an even split.

7 The famous "preference reversal" experiments of Grether and Plott (1979), for instance, have virtually no power when the individual is risk neutral, since the lotteries in each pair were chosen to have roughly the same expected value. But a given subject cannot simultaneously have a low-power test of EUT from preference reversal choices *and* a low-power test of EUT from CR choices, assuming we have some reasonably precise estimate of the risk attitudes of the subject.

8 Mixture models change the language of horse races, in important ways, as well as allowing one to see how non-nested hypothesis tests have historically been "second best" alternatives to a fully specified mixture. Rather than posing these as binary outcomes, where one model wins and the other is rejected, mixture models estimate the weight of the evidence consistent with one model over the other. And that weight can vary predictably with demographic characteristics or task characteristics. As usual, Bayesians handle all of this in a natural manner, with posterior odds being the basis for assessing the weight of one model over another, and Hierarchical Bayesian methods allow meta-parameters to affect these weights. Mixture models also provide an insight into the use of multiple criteria by an individual decision-maker in a given choice, in the spirt of the SP/A model of Lopes (1984) from psychology: see Andersen et al. (2014a).

9 A classic example is the binary choice procedure, which is self-evidently incentive-compatible, compared to the Becker, DeGroot, and Marschak (BDM) (1964) elicitation

method. Although formally incentive compatible, the BDM elicitation method is widely avoided by experimental economists since subjects often fail to understand it without a great deal of hands-on training: see Plott and Zeiler (2005: 537). Moreover, even if subjects understand the incentives, the mechanism is known to generate *extremely* weak incentives for accurate reports: see Harrison (1992; 1994).

10 It is not a priori obvious that this exercise is interesting if one has access to a transparent elicitation method that is attractive by making minimal demands on the understanding of subjects. Arguably this is true of binary choice methods, even if other methods would provide greater information *if behaviorally reliable* (e.g., knowing a certainty equivalent takes one immediately to the risk premium).

11 Since risk attitudes only equate to U″ under EUT, it is a mistake to equate joint estimation in this application with "risk attitudes and time preferences being correlated."

12 The same concepts apply in strategic settings, but with the added complexity that the likelihood of behavior of all subjects in the game must be constrained by some equilibrium concept. Goeree, Holt, and Palfrey (2003) illustrate the joint estimation of risk attitudes for a representative agent playing a generalized matching pennies game, with a "quantal response equilibrium" constraint. Harrison and Rutström (2008, §3.6) illustrate the joint estimation of risk attitudes and bidding behavior in a first-price sealed-bid auction, with a Bayesian Nash Equilibrium constraint.

13 It is true that one must rely on structural assumptions about the form of utility functions, probability weighting functions, and discounting functions, in order to draw inferences. These assumptions can be tested, and have been, against more flexible versions and even non-parametric versions (e.g., Harrison and Rutström 2008; 78–9). A similar debate rages with respect to structural assumptions about statistical error specifications, as illustrated by the charming title of the book by Angrist and Pischke (2009), *Mostly Harmless Econometrics*. But it is an illusion, popular in some quarters, that one can safely dispense with all structural assumptions and draw inferences: see Keane (2010) and Leamer (2010) for spirited assaults on that theology.

14 The implication for the claim by Andreoni and Sprenger (2012) that "risk preferences are not time preferences" is immediate. If the intertemporal utility function that subjects use is actually nonadditive, then risk preferences over time streams of money need to be sharply distinguished from risk preferences over atemporal payoffs. In effect, there are two possible types of risk aversion when one considers risky choices over time, not one. To be more precise, if one gives subjects choices over differently-time-dated payoffs, which is what Andreoni and Sprenger (2012) did, one sets up exactly the thought experiment that *defines* intertemporal risk aversion. They compare behavior when subjects make choices over time-dated payoffs that are not stochastic with choices over time-dated payoffs that are stochastic, and observe different behavior. In the former case, virtually all choices in their portfolios were at extreme allocations, either all payoffs sooner or all payoffs later; in the latter case, they observed more choices in which subjects picked an interior mix of sooner and later payoffs, diversifying intertemporally. Evidence that subjects behave differently, when there is an opportunity for intertemporal risk aversion to affect their choices compared to a setting in which it has no role, is evidence of intertemporal risk aversion. It is not necessarily evidence for the claim that there is a "different utility function" at work when considering stochastic and non-stochastic choices. We do not rule out the latter hypothesis, but there is a simpler explanation well within received theory. Evidence for intertemporal risk aversion in experiments is provided

by Andersen et al. (2018), who also provide extensive cites to the older literature. Intertemporal risk aversion provides an immediate explanation for the observed behavior in Andreoni and Sprenger (2012). Just as atemporal risk aversion encourages mean-preserving reductions in the variability of atemporal payoffs (imagine lotteries defined solely over x and X or defined solely over y and Y), intertemporal risk aversion or intertemporal risk aversion encourages mean-preserving reductions in the variability of the time stream of payoffs (imagine lotteries ψ and Ψ defined above over x, X, y, and Y). Hence, when Andreoni and Sprenger (2012) claim that "risk preferences are not time preferences," one can restate this correctly as "a-temporal risk aversion is not the same as intertemporal risk aversion," and of course that is true whenever there is a nonadditive intertemporal utility function.

15 The actual utility of the other subject, the subjective perception I have about the utility of the other subject, or the normative utility I choose to apply to the other subject.

16 For example, I have seen so little evidence for CPT that I no longer automatically build in (longer) risk batteries with mixed frames or loss frames. Others might demur.

17 Imagine that there is no probability weighting on the gain domain, so the decision weights are the objective probabilities, but that there is some probability weighting on the loss domain. Then one could easily have losses weighted more than gains, from the implied decision weights.

18 This variant is called an *iterative* multiple price list by Andersen et al. (2006).

19 This variant is called a *sequential* multiple price list by Andersen et al. (2006).

20 They also estimated β and apparently obtained *exactly* the same median value as α, which is quite remarkable from a numerical perspective.

21 This issue is the focus of the use of "hierarchical" methods by Nilsson, Rieskamp, and Wagenmakers (2011) and Murphy and ten Brincke (2018), which are in principle well suited to handling this particular problem, which is not unique to CPT.

22 Tversky and Kahneman (1992: 312) do note that the "parameters estimated from the median data were essentially the same." It is not clear how to interpret this sentence. It may mean that the median certainty-equivalents for the initial fifty-six choices, and the median values of $x for the final eight choices, were combined to form a synthetic "median subject," and then estimates obtained from those data. The expression "median data" does not lead one to suspect that it was any one actual subject. Nor is there any reference to standard errors for these estimates. Glöckner and Pachur (2012) used the same unfortunate style of reporting results.

23 Some would seek to elevate this practice to define what economics is: see Gul and Pesendorfer (2007). This is simply historically inaccurate and unproductive, quite apart from the debate over the usefulness of "neuroeconomics" that prompted it.

24 Of course, there are many such heuristics from psychology and the judgment and decision-making literature, noted explicitly by Brandstätter et al. (2006: 417, Table 3).

25 This finding may be well documented, but it is apparently not well known. Birnbaum (2004) provides a comprehensive review of his own experimental studies of the Allais common consequence paradoxes, does not mention any of the studies referenced here, and then claims as a general matter that using real, credible payments does not affect behavior (105).

26 Another concern with many of these stylized examples is that they are conducted on a between-subjects basis, and rely on comparable choices in two pairs of lotteries. Thus, one must account for the presumed heterogeneity in risk attitudes when evaluating the statistical power of claims that EUT is rejected. Loomes and Sugden (1998) and Harrison et al. (2007) pay attention to this issue in different ways in their designs.

27 There is a folklore joke about how psychologists treat their models the way economists treat their toothbrush: everyone has their own. In this case, it seems as though an old, discarded toothbrush is getting passed around to brush dataset after dataset.

28 To see this, follow carefully the explanation in Brandstätter et al. (2006: 418) of how the vertical axis on their figure 1 is created. There are fourteen choice tasks being evaluated here. The PH predicted the *majority* choice in each of the fourteen tasks, so it is given a predictive score of 100 percent. The "equiprobable" heuristic predicted ten out of fourteen of the *majority* choices, so it is given a predictive score of 71.4% = (10 ÷ 14) × 100. The predictive accuracy measure is not calculated at the level of the individual choice but, instead, using a *summary statistic* of those choices.

29 There are some noncasual, semi-parametric estimation procedures for binary choice models that use the hit rate, such as the "maximum score" estimator of Manski (1975). The literature on this estimator is reviewed by Cameron and Trivedi (2005: 483ff., §14.7.2).

30 These estimation procedures are defended by Wakker (2010, Appendix A), so this is not just an inadvertent slip.

31 If there is even the slightest concern by the subject that the experimenter might be manipulating the unknown urn strategically to reduce payouts, the Ellsberg paradox is explained: see Kadane (1992) and Schneeweis (1973). This is why one should not rely on computer-generated realizations of random processes in behavioral research if at all possible. The experiment in ABPW was conducted entirely on a computer.

32 For example, by the application of Bayes Rule or the reduction of compound lotteries.

33 The point here is the role of methodologists in addressing these issues. It is descriptively easy to see the effects of negative externalities generated by the popularity of the "mostly harmless" school of econometrics (Angrist and Pischke 2009).

34 See Harrison and Ross (2017, 2018) for a statement of the philosophical issues raised.

References

Abdellaoui, Mohammed, Aurélien Baillon, Lætitia Placido, and Peter P. Wakker. 2011. "The Rich Domain of Uncertainty: Source Functions and Their Experimental Implementation." *American Economic Review* 101: 695–723.

Andersen, Steffen, John Fountain, Glenn W. Harrison, and E. Elisabet Rutström. 2014. "Estimating Subjective Probabilities." *Journal of Risk & Uncertainty* 48: 207–29.

Andersen, Steffen, Glenn W. Harrison, Morten I. Lau, and E. Elisabet Rutström. 2006. "Elicitation Using Multiple Price Lists." *Experimental Economics* 9 (4): 383–405.

Andersen, Steffen, Glenn W. Harrison, Morten Igel Lau, and E. Elisabet Rutström. 2008. "Eliciting Risk and Time Preferences." *Econometrica* 76 (3): 583–618.

Andersen, Steffen, Glenn W. Harrison, Morten I. Lau, and E. Elisabet Rutström. 2014a. "Dual Criteria Decisions." *Journal of Economic Psychology* 41 (April): 101–13.

Andersen, Steffen, Glenn W. Harrison, Morten I. Lau, and E. Elisabet Rutström. 2014b. "Discounting Behavior: A Reconsideration." *European Economic Review* 71 (November): 15–33.

Andersen, Steffen, Glenn W. Harrison, Morten I. Lau, and E. Elisabet Rutström. 2018. "Multiattribute Utility Theory, Intertemporal Utility, and Correlation Aversion." *International Economic Review* 59 (2): 537–55.

Andreoni, James, and Charles Sprenger. 2012. "Risk Preferences Are Not Time Preferences." *American Economic Review* 102 (7): 3357–76.
Angrist, Joshua D., and Jörn-Steffen Pischke. 2009. *Mostly Harmless Econometrics: An Empiricist's Companion*. Princeton, NJ: Princeton University Press.
Becker, Gordon M., Morris H. DeGroot, and Jacob Marschak. 1964. "Measuring Utility by a Single-Response Sequential Method." *Behavioral Science* 9 (July): 226–32.
Benartzi, Shlomo, and Richard H. Thaler. 1995. "Myopic Loss Aversion and the Equity Premium Puzzle." *Quarterly Journal of Economics* 111 (1): 75–92.
Birnbaum, Michael H. 2004. "Causes of Allais Common Consequence Paradoxes: An Experimental Dissection." *Journal of Mathematical Psychology* 48: 87–106.
Birnbaum, Michael H. 2008. "Evaluation of the Priority Heuristic as a Descriptive Model of Risky Decision Making: Comment on Brandstätter, Gigerenzer, and Hertwig (2006)." *Psychological Review* 115 (1): 253–60.
Birnbaum, Michael H., and Juan B. Navarrete. 1998. "Testing Descriptive Utility Theories: Violations of Stochastic Dominance and Cumulative Independence." *Journal of Risk and Uncertainty* 17: 17–49.
Brandstätter, Eduard, GerdGigerenzer, and Ralph Hertwig. 2006. "The Priority Heuristic: Making Choices without Trade-Offs." *Psychological Review* 113 (2): 409–32.
Bruhin, Adrian, Fehr-Duda, and Thomas Epper. 2010. "Risk and Rationality: Uncovering Heterogeneity in Probability Distortion." *Econometrica* 78 (4): 1375–412.
Burke, Michael S., John R. Carter, Robert D. Gominiak, and Daniel F. Ohl. 1996. "An Experimental Note on the Allais Paradox and Monetary Incentives." *Empirical Economics* 21: 617–32.
Camerer, Colin F., and Teck-Hua Ho. 1994. "Violations of the betweenness Axiom and Nonlinearity in Probability." *Journal of Risk and Uncertainty* 8: 167–96.
Cameron, A. Colin, and Pravin K. Trivedi. 2005. *Microeconometrics: Methods and Applications*. New York: Cambridge University Press.
Conlisk, John. 1989. "Three Variants on the Allais Example." *American Economic Review* 79 (3): 392–407.
Fan, Chinn-Ping. 2002. "Allais Paradox in the Small." *Journal of Economic Behavior & Organization* 49: 411–21.
Glöckner, Andreas, and Thorsten Pachur. 2012. "Cognitive Models of Risky Choice: Parameter Stability and Predictive Accuracy of Prospect Theory." *Cognition* 123 (1): 21–32.
Goeree, Jacob K., Charles A. Holt, and Thomas R. Palfrey. 2003. "Risk Averse Behavior in Generalized Matching Pennies Games." *Games and Economic Behavior* 45: 97–113.
Grether, David M., and Charles R. Plott. 1979. "Economic Theory of Choice and the Preference Reversal Phenomenon." *American Economic Review* 69 (September): 623–48.
Gul, Faruk, and Wolfgang Pesendorfer. 2007. "The Case for Mindless Economics." In *Handbook of Economic Methodologies*, ed. A. Caplin and A. Schotter. New York: Oxford University Press.
Harless, David W., and Colin F. Camerer. 1994. "The Predictive Utility of Generalized Expected Utility Theories." *Econometrica* 62 (6): 1251–89.
Harrison, Glenn W. 1992. "Theory and Misbehavior of First-Price Auctions: Reply." *American Economic Review* 82 (December): 1426–43.

Harrison, Glenn W. 1994. "Expected Utility Theory and The Experimentalists." *Empirical Economics* 19 (2): 223–53.

Harrison, Glenn W. 2008. "Neuroeconomics: A Critical Reconsideration." *Economics and Philosophy* 24: 203–44.

Harrison, Glenn W., Eric Johnson, Melayne M. McInnes, and E. Elisabet Rutström. 2005. "Risk Aversion and Incentive Effects: Comment." *American Economic Review* 95 (3): 897–901.

Harrison, Glenn W., Eric Johnson, Melayne M. McInnes, and E. Elisabet Rutström. 2007. "Measurement with Experimental Controls." In *Measurement in Economics: A Handbook*, ed. M. Boumans. San Diego, CA: Elsevier.

Harrison, Glenn W., Morten I. Lau, and Melonie B. Williams. 2002. "Estimating Individual Discount Rates for Denmark: A Field Experiment." *American Economic Review* 92 (5): 1606–17.

Harrison, Glenn W., Jimmy Martínez-Correa, J. Todd Swarthout, and Eric Ulm. 2017. "Scoring Rules for Subjective Probability Distributions." *Journal of Economic Behavior & Organization* 134: 430–48.

Harrison, Glenn W., and Jia Min Ng. 2016. "Evaluating the Expected Welfare Gain from Insurance." *Journal of Risk and Insurance* 83 (1): 91–120.

Harrison, Glenn W., and Don Ross. 2017. "The Empirical Adequacy of Cumulative Prospect Theory and Its Implications for Normative Assessment." *Journal of Economic Methodology* 24 (2): 150–65.

Harrison, Glenn W., and Don Ross. 2018. "Varieties of Paternalism and the Heterogeneity of Utility Structures." *Journal of Economic Methodology* 25 (1): 42–67.

Harrison, Glenn W., and E. Elisabet Rutström. 2008. "Risk Aversion in the Laboratory." In *Risk Aversion in Experiments*, Vol. 12, ed. J. C. Cox and G. W. Harrison. Bingley: Emerald, Research in Experimental Economics.

Harrison, Glenn W., and E. Elisabet Rutström. 2009. "Expected Utility and Prospect Theory: One Wedding and a Decent Funeral." *Experimental Economics* 12 (2): 133–58.

Harrison, Glenn W., and J. Todd Swarthout. 2016. "Cumulative Prospect Theory in the Laboratory: A Reconsideration." *CEAR Working Paper 2016-05*. Atlanta, GA: Center for the Economic Analysis of Risk, Robinson College of Business, Georgia State University.

Harrison, Glenn W., and Eric R. Ulm. 2015. "Recovering Subjective Probability Distributions." *CEAR Working Paper 2015-01*. Atlanta, GA: Center for the Economic Analysis of Risk, Robinson College of Business, Georgia State University.

Holt, Charles A., and Susan K. Laury. 2002. "Risk Aversion and Incentive Effects." *American Economic Review* 92 (5): 1644–55.

Holt, Charles A., and Susan K. Laury. 2005. "Risk Aversion and Incentive Effects: New Data without Order Effects." *American Economic Review* 95 (3): 902–4.

Kadane, Joseph B. 1992. "Healthy Skepticism as an Expected-Utility Explanation of the Phenomena of Allais and Ellsberg." *Theory and Decision* 32 (1): 57–64.

Kahneman, Daniel, and Amos Tversky. 1979. "Prospect Theory: An Analysis of Decision under Risk." *Econometrica* 47: 263–91.

Keane, Michael P. 2010. "Structural *vs.* Atheoretic Approaches to Econometrics." *Journal of Econometrics* 156: 3–20.

Köbberling, Veronika, and Peter P. Wakker. 2005. "An Index of Loss Aversion." *Journal of Economic Theory* 122: 119–31.

Leamer, Edward E. 1978. *Specification Searches: Ad Hoc Inference with Nonexperimental Data*. New York: Wiley.
Leamer, Edward E. 2011. "Tantalus on the Road to Asymptopia." *Journal of Economic Perspectives* 24 (2): 31–46.
Loomes, Graham, and Robert Sugden. 1998. "Testing Different Stochastic Specifications of Risky Choice." *Economica* 65: 581–98.
Lopes, Lola L. 1984. "Risk and Distributional Inequality." *Journal of Experimental Psychology: Human Perception and Performance* 10 (4): 465–84.
Manski, Charles F. 1975. "The Maximum Score Estimator of the Stochastic Utility Model of Choice." *Journal of Econometrics* 3: 205–28.
Monroe, Brian A. August 2017. *Stochastic Models in Experimental Economics*. PhD Thesis. South Africa: School of Economics, University of Cape Town.
Murphy, Ryan O., and Robert H. W. ten Brincke. 2018. "Hierarchical Maximum Likelihood Parameter Estimation for Cumulative Prospect Theory: Improving the Reliability of Individual Risk Parameter Estimates." *Management Science* 64 (1): 308–26.
Nilsson, Håkan, Jörg Rieskamp, and Eric-Jan Wagenmakers. 2011. "Hierarchical Bayesian Parameter Estimation for Cumulative Prospect Theory." *Journal of Mathematical Psychology* 55: 84–93.
Plott, Charles R., and Vernon L. Smith. 1978. "An Experimental Examination of Two Exchange Institution." *Review of Economic Studies* 45 (1): 133–53.
Plott, Charles R., and Kathryn Zeiler. 2005. "The Willingness to Pay–Willingness to Accept Gap, the 'Endowment Effect,' Subject Misconceptions, and Experimental Procedures for Eliciting Valuations." *American Economic Review* 95: 530–45.
Prelec, Drazen. 1998. "The Probability Weighting Function." *Econometrica* 66: 497–527.
Rieskamp, Jörg, 2008. "The Probabilistic Nature of Preferential Choice." *Journal of Experimental Psychology: Learning, Memory and Cognition* 34 (6): 1446–65.
Samuelson, Paul A. 1947. *Foundations of Economic Analysis*. Boston, MA: Harvard University Press.
Schmidt, Ulrich, and Horst Zank. 2008. "Risk Aversion in Cumulative Prospect Theory." *Management Science* 54: 208–16.
Schneeweiss, Hans. 1973. "The Ellsberg Paradox from the Point of View of Game Theory." *Inference and Decision* 1: 65–78.
Smith, Vernon L. 1969. "Measuring Nonmonetary Utilities in Uncertain Choices: The Ellsberg Urn." *Quarterly Journal of Economics* 83 (2): 324–9.
Starmer, Chris. 2000. "Developments in Non-Expected Utility Theory: The Hunt for a Descriptive Theory of Choice under Risk." *Journal of Economic Literature* 38 (June): 332–82.
Stott, Henry P. 2006. "Cumulative Prospect Theory's Functional Menagerie." *Journal of Risk and Uncertainty* 32: 101–30.
Tversky, Amos, and Daniel Kahneman. 1992. "Advances in Prospect Theory: Cumulative Representations of Uncertainty." *Journal of Risk & Uncertainty* 5: 297–323.
von Gaudecker, Hans-Martin, Arthur van Soest, and Erik Wengström. 2011. "Heterogeneity in Risky Choice Behavior in a Broad Population." *American Economic Review* 101 (April): 664–94.
Wakker, Peter P. 2010. *Prospect Theory for Risk and Ambiguity*. New York: Cambridge University Press.

Wilcox, Nathaniel T. 2008. "Predicting Individual Risky Choices Out-of-Context: A Critical Stochastic Modeling Primer and Monte Carlo Study." In *Risk Aversion in Experiments*, Vol. 12, ed. J. Cox and G. W. Harrison. Bingley: Emerald, Research in Experimental Economics.

Wilcox, Nathaniel T. 2011. "'Stochastically More Risk Averse': A Contextual Theory of Stochastic Discrete Choice under Risk." *Journal of Econometrics* 162 (1): 89–104.

Commentary: Reflections on Decision Research and Its Empiricism: Four Comments Inspired by Harrison

Nathaniel T. Wilcox

Generally I find Harrison's chapter cogent, interesting, and well-informed in details and particulars, and so do not speak of them. Instead, I reflect on four larger matters Harrison brings to my mind. These four matters are presented below as four separate sections, to be read as four separate and short comments (though the four sections do share a few threads).

1. Intuitions of Theorists

"In some cases simple, 'agnostic' statistical modeling is appropriate, since the experiment 'does the work of theory' for the analyst, by controlling for treatments and potential confounds," says Harrison in his introduction. In their manifesto of Bayesian statistics, Edwards, Lindman, and Savage (1963) put it in this famously entertaining way:

> It has been called the interocular traumatic test; you know what the data mean when the conclusion hits you between the eyes. The interocular traumatic test is simple, commands general agreement, and is often applicable; well-conducted experiments often come out that way. (217)

Later Edwards, Lindman, and Savage add that, "The rule was somewhat overstated by a physicist who said, 'As long as it takes statistics to find out, I prefer to investigate something else (240);'" and Ernest Rutherford allegedly said, "If your experiment needs statistics, you ought to do a better experiment." These are also the sentiments of many (perhaps most) decision researchers. I find these sentiments deeply interesting and in some respects puzzling.

What is the source of those sentiments? Consider these two quotes.

> I am about to build up a highly idealized theory of the behavior of a "rational" person ... when certain maxims are presented ... you must ask yourself ... how you would react if you noticed yourself violating them. (Savage 1954/1972; 7)
>
> The following was offered by L. J. Savage as a criticism ... Suppose that a boy must select between having a pony *x* and a bicycle *y* and that he wavers indecisively between them [the thought experiment is further developed to a telling outcome] ... If this can happen—and the introspections of several people suggest that it can—then the strong binary model is too strong to describe these preferences. (Luce and Suppes 1965)

Theorists may sometimes use their own intuitions (or introspections) as inspiration for those "maxims" Savage alludes to above (today we generally call such maxims "axioms"). But I am not a theorist and so hesitate to speak on that matter of private inspiration: Instead, I am interested here in the persuasive role played by shared intuitions. In their writings, decision theorists reveal that intuitions play two strong roles among the theorists. Axioms are the foundation of any formal decision theory, and particularly in the case of a normative theory, a theorist frequently appeals to another theorist's intuition, as Savage does in the first quote above. A theorist will frequently state axioms in two ways: Once mathematically (for formal proofs) and once verbally to aid and persuade other theorists' intuitions (concerning the normative status, and/or the likely descriptive validity, of a proposed axiom). Second, when a theorist suggests an outcome of her thought experiment and that suggested outcome is widely endorsed by other theorists' intuitions, that *consensus of intuitions* becomes convincing evidence concerning some theory, as Luce and Suppes admit in the second quote above. Most frequently, such evidence from thought experiments is negative, suggesting a counter-example that casts doubt on the descriptive adequacy of some theory. The thought experiments are generally presented simply and transparently—largely in verbal form, perhaps with a table or two illustrating concrete sets of alternatives, but almost never more formally than that (Debreu 1960 being a notable exception). The purpose is to aid and persuade the reader's intuition that the thought experiment indeed leads to outcomes contradicting some theory. In both these cases, a consensus of intuitions or *intuition consensus* is a highly prized coin of the decision-theoretic realm.

If you are very used to persuasion by means of transparent and simple verbal descriptions or thought experiments, you may (perhaps unfairly) devalue other less transparent kinds of evidence. Many new inferential techniques and demonstration methods—widely accepted among either classical or Bayesian statisticians—draw on our newfound bounty of computational power. The inferential techniques include simulated maximum likelihood, simulation-based Bayesian estimation, and so-called "bootstrapping" of the sampling variability of estimates. The primary demonstration method is Monte Carlo simulation, a well-established framework for examining estimators' behavior in finite samples. Here I share what one theorist said about the latter method as used in one of my own papers (Wilcox 2017):

> I am quite confident that [other scholars I respect] would not be satisfied with simulation results for a claim that could perhaps be proved analytically. I am aware of the fact that simulations are being extensively used, but I tend to believe that people resort to these methods when there is no hope of obtaining an analytical result.

Analytical results on the finite sample behavior of most nonlinear estimators are only rarely forthcoming, and only in very simple circumstances.

For whatever reasons, simulations (computation-based existence demonstrations) are a kind of evidence contemporary theorists do not find compelling. I suspect this is because simulations don't lend themselves to intuition consensus in the same way the normative status of an axiom does, or the negative outcome of a thought experiment does (nor is it an analytical proof—which, of course, the theorists find convincing too). Presented with flair, a reader can usually grasp the *results* of a simulation with no serious problem. However, if the inferential or demonstration *process* of simulation is not part of your own methodological toolbox, the process remains a kind of black box to you.

I fear that fairly or not, there is only one inferential technique that stands a chance of generating intuition consensus among the theorists: It is the interocular trauma test, which, by definition, is intuitive—"the conclusion hits you between the eyes." Edwards, Lindman, and Savage (1963) warn that "the enthusiast's interocular trauma may be the skeptic's random error. A little arithmetic to verify the extent of the trauma can yield great peace of mind for little cost (217)." Simulation-based inferences and demonstrations take us well beyond "a little arithmetic." One might say they are just hundreds of millions of instances of "a little arithmetic" assembled with care, but truly such quantity has a nontransparent quality all its own.

Aside from simulation itself, Harrison's preferred style of statistics (and it is mine too) also depends on millions of computations assembled with care: Complex, highly nonlinear likelihood functions don't get maximized without the considerable computational muscle of a computer. The output will never have the same transparency as a comparison of sample means, or the inspection of other simple sample moments. Like Harrison (see in particular his Section 4.5), I have argued that simple sample moments can be highly misleading to decision researchers (Wilcox 2008: 224–31; Wilcox 2017), but the (apparent) transparency of (potentially misleading) simple sample moments seems irresistible.

2. Estranged Siblings

Among the decision theorists, McFadden (1974, 1981) arguably had the single largest impact on *empirical* social and behavioral scientists who work with *naturally occurring* "field" data (as opposed to laboratory data): Such field researchers are the overwhelming majority of empirical economists. In his Nobel Prize lecture, McFadden (2001: 351) prominently recognized nine scholars, very much a mix of decision theorists and econometricians:

> Nine other individuals who played a major role in channeling microeconometrics and choice theory toward their modern forms, and had a particularly important influence on my own work, are Zvi Griliches, L. L. Thurstone, Jacob Marschak, Duncan Luce, Amos Tversky, Danny Kahneman, Moshe Ben-Akiva, Charles Manski, and Kenneth Train.

During those remarkable twenty years from Savage ([1954] 1972) to McFadden (1974), a brisk traffic of ideas traveled between the decision theorists and the econometricians: For instance, Luce (1959) and Luce and Suppes (1965) are absolutely central to McFadden (1974), who additionally cites Block and Marschak (1960) and Tversky and Russo (1969).

In the decades since McFadden (1974), prominent decision theorists such as Fishburn (1978) and Machina (1985) also turned their talents to the apparently probabilistic nature of discrete binary choice—with no discernable impact on econometricians. And in the decades since Manski (1975), econometricians such as Cosslett (1983) and Horowitz (1992) turned their own talents to the same subject—with no discernable impact on decision research. Focus now on two papers published a quarter century ago: This gives us plenty of time to see their impact. Busemeyer and Townsend (1993) is a landmark contribution to probabilistic decision theory: It offers a very precise decision-theoretic model of both the econometric link function and index function. It is clearly influential with 569 total SSCI (Social Science Citation Index) citations, but gets zero citations from theoretical econometricians (though a handful of citations from applied econometricians). Published in the same year as Busemeyer and Townsend, most would call Klein and Spady (1993) an important milestone in econometric theory: It can free the researcher of assumptions concerning link functions—at the cost of strong assumptions (but short of linearity, and this was a major contribution to semiparametric estimation) concerning index functions. It too is clearly influential with 226 total SSCI citations, but just one (Donkers, Melenberg, and Van Soest 2001) is a decision research paper and none are decision theory papers. The sad truth is that over the quarter century since 1993, these two communities of scholars (the decision researchers and the econometricians) share about as much as the Dance and Physics Departments. Those remarkably cross-fertile years from 1954 to 1974 are well over: Econometrics and decision research went their very separate ways.

To see the ways they went, consider the probabilistic model Harrison specifies for Expected Utility Theory (EUT) in eq. (4), $\Pr(R) = f\,(\nabla EU)$. This is just a specific instance of the more general model $\Pr(R) = F(D(R,S\,|\,\theta))$, where F is any link function and $D(R,S\,|\,\theta)$ is any theoretical representation of the comparison between lotteries R and S—to the econometrician, the index function with parameters θ. It's fair to say many econometricians are perfectly happy to require linearity (in the parameters θ) of $D(R,S\,|\,\theta)$: They just want to estimate θ without assumptions concerning F, the link function. From the viewpoint of decision theory, making $D(R,S\,|\,\theta)$ a linear function of θ essentially takes the Prince of Denmark out of *Hamlet*: A representation without nonlinear entities in $D(R,S\,|\,\theta)$ just isn't worth discussing or thinking about. It's fair to say the decision researchers (Harrison and I, and at least some theorists such as Busemeyer and Townsend 1993) are fine with specific assumptions about F, if it buys us the ability to estimate the nonlinear entities in $D(R,S \mid \theta)$ with few extra assumptions. So decision researchers and econometricians have found themselves at cross-purposes since the days of McFadden and Manski.

3. All the Horses Are Dead, Long Live the Horse Race

A decision theory τ is (usually) an axiom set such as $A^{\tau} = \{A_1^{\tau}, A_2^{\tau}, \ldots, A_k^{\tau}\}$ generating a representation (such as EUT) that applies to some prespecified set Ω of lottery pairs $\{R,S\}$. There are two empirical strategies as regards skepticism concerning such theories. The more common strategy takes a narrow focus on one or another of the axioms in A^{τ}, over some subset $E \subset \Omega$: Here E is a special slice of Ω, for instance, a "common ratio group" of lottery pairs in some experiment designed to interrogate A_i^{τ} (e.g., the Independence Axiom of EUT). Generally Ω is an infinite set, so that special slice E is a very small fraction of Ω. When this empirical strategy rejects axiom A_i^{τ} on subset E, we do learn something important and especially useful to decision theorists in the here and now: They may now craft a replacement for A_i^{τ}, hopefully leading to an improved theory.

But we need to keep clear that we learned little about the theory's performance on the set $\Omega - \mathrm{E}$. We might be better off with a different sort of experiment: some kind of broad sampling of Ω instead of a specially contrived slice of Ω, and then a contest between the theories themselves rather than specific axioms. This less common empirical strategy (practiced by Harrison, myself and others such as Hey and Orme 1994) interrogates the *collective wisdom* of whole axiom sets A^{τ} by means of horse races between their representations—generally speaking with a rather less special slice of Ω as the experimental pairs. My firm conviction is that every descriptive decision theory is a dead horse walking—if we insist on its slaughter should it fail to describe every preference over all pairs in Ω for every decision maker. It is much more reasonable to race the horses (the theories, in competition with one another) and ask which ones win a noticeable fraction of the races (in other words, best explain the behavior of a noticeable fraction of our subjects on broad collections of decision problems). Harrison has this in mind when he discusses mixture models.

From both economic and evolutionary game theory we have good reason to expect living populations are *mixtures of types* (today this is well known to the point of banality). This is a primary reason (among others) why the "hypothetico-deductive" science model has limited usefulness for the *empiricism* of the biological and social sciences. I congratulate physicists for their clever selection of (mostly) the easiest possible populations (homogeneous ones) to work with, but someone has to meet the theoretical and empirical challenges of mixed populations with deep and pervasive heterogeneity. Given those types of populations, simple hypothesis-testing is potentially counterproductive. Suppose theory τ's axiom A_j^{τ} survives a narrow hypothesis test in set E for (say) 70 percent of subjects. But also suppose that in a competitive tests against (say) two other theories, on a broad sample of set Ω, theory τ best accounts for the behavior of just 20 percent of the subjects. I have little hesitation saying that the former test of axiom A_j^{τ} is at best a distraction and at worst highly misleading. When we concentrate on relative success rather than absolute null hypothesis-testing, we're in a different world of measures of predictive success such as likelihoods, information criteria, estimated type shares in the population, and so forth. It is not a world of simple sample moments and interocular traumas.

4. Do as Theorists Say (Not as Empiricists Do)

"It cannot be said ... that a rational man must behave according to the Bernoulli principle," Allais (1953: 505) concluded in the English Summary of his celebrated *Econometrica* article (in French). As Ellsberg (1961: 646) could have put the argument on Allais' behalf, "One could emphasize here ... that the postulates ... failed to predict reflective choices." Yet listen in today among the conferees at any decision research conference: Most regard "the Bernoulli principle" as definitive of rational decision-making under uncertainty and, in this and many other ways, we are all Savage's ([1954] 1972) children. To us, "Allais' Paradox" is a finding that subjects' decision behavior violates Subjective Expected Utility Theory (SEUT) and is therefore *not* rational (*pace* Allais and Ellsberg). As Harrison mentions, SEUT has other prominent normative Discontents (Loomes and Sugden 1982; Machina 1982; Schmeidler 1989; Epstein 1992)—Allais and Ellsberg are just the two most familiar names. But if pressed I think a majority of the conferees would agree that SEUT *is* rational choice under uncertainty.

Savage has other children: Bayesian statisticians (Box and Tiao 1973; Gelman et al. 2004), Bayesian econometricians (Zellner 1971; Geweke 2005), and Bayesian psychometricians (Kruschke 2011; Lee and Wagenmakers 2014). Edwards, Lindman, and Savage (1963) published perhaps the first manifesto of Bayesian statistics, contrasting "such procedures as a Bayesian would employ in an article submitted to the Journal of Experimental Psychology, say, and those [classical procedures] now typically found in that journal (195);" and in concluding said, "Bayesian procedures are not merely another tool for the working scientist ... as we saw, evidence that leads to classical rejection of the null hypothesis will often leave a Bayesian more confident of that same null hypothesis than he was to start with (240)." They squarely address the *statistical practices of researchers* and offer the new Bayesian alternative *to those researchers' classical data analysis*. They are not talking about modeling subject behavior. Yet most citations of the manifesto borrow its mathematical results as *descriptive models of subject behavior*—to be followed, with high likelihood, by classical hypothesis-testing using the experiment's data. Uncharitable people might say normative hypocrisy has been perfected in decision research: Scholars born of Savage's seismic advance ask why subjects don't do as theorists say (not as empiricists do). Just a half dozen years ago Matthews (2011: 843) could fairly say "Judgment and decision making research overwhelmingly uses null hypothesis significance testing as the basis for statistical inference" and ask "What might judgment and decision making research be like if we took a Bayesian approach to hypothesis testing?"

Harrison argues (I think fairly) that decision research does its classical statistics with sometimes questionable rigor. But why would decision researchers do classical statistics at all, if we really believe that obedience to SEUT and Bayes' Rule is rationality in the face of uncertainty? This question is wholly unoriginal: From conversations, I know it nags many other classical empirical economists. But in decision research, perhaps this question ought to elicit particularly sheepish grins? Or should we take our cues from Emerson and Whitman—not insisting on foolish consistency, and accepting that we contain multitudes? These are matters best addressed by philosophers, historians, and methodologists.

References

Allais, M. 1953. "Le comportement de l'homme rationnel devant le risque: Critique des postulats et axiomes de l'Ecole Americaine." *Econometrica* 21: 503–46.

Block, H., and J. Marschak. 1960. "Random Orderings and Stochastic Theories of Response." In *Contributions to Probability and Statistics*, ed. I. Olkin. Stanford, CA: Stanford University Press.

Box, G. E. P., and G. C. Tiao. 1973. *Bayesian Inference in Statistical Analysis.* New York: Wiley.

Busemeyer, J. R., and J. T. Townsend. 1993. "Decision Field Theory: A Dynamic-Cognitive Approach to Decision Making in an Uncertain Environment." *Psychological Review* 100: 432–59.

Cosslett, S. R. 1983. "Distribution-free Maximum Likelihood Estimator of the Binary Choice Model." *Econometrica* 51: 765–82.

DeBreu, G. 1960. "Review of Individual Choice Behavior: A Theoretical Analysis by R. Duncan Luce." *American Economic Review* 50 (1): 186–8.

Donkers, B., B. Melenberg, and A. Van Soest. 2001. "Estimating Risk Attitudes Using Lotteries: A Large Sample Approach." *Journal of Risk and Uncertainty* 22: 165–95.

Edwards, W., H. Lindman, and L. J. Savage. 1963. "Bayesian Statistical Inference for Psychological Research." *Psychological Review* 70: 193–242.

Ellsberg, D. 1961. "Risk, Ambiguity and the Savage Axioms." *Quarterly Journal of Economics* 75: 643–69.

Epstein, L. G. 1992. "Behavior under Risk: Recent Developments in Theory and Applications." In *Advances in Economic Theory*, ed. J.-J. Laffont, 1–63. Cambridge: Cambridge University Press.

Fishburn, P. C. 1978. "A Probabilistic Expected Utility Theory of Risky Binary Choices." *International Economic Review* 19: 633–46.

Gelman, A., J. B. Carlin, H. S. Stern, and D. B. Rubin. 2004. *Bayesian Data Analysis*, 2nd ed. Boca Raton, FL: Chapman and Hall.

Geweke, J. 2005. *Contemporary Bayesian Econometrics and Statistics.* Hoboken, NJ: Wiley.

Hey, J., and C. Orme. 1994. "Investigating Generalizations of Expected Utility Theory Using Experimental Data." *Econometrica* 62: 1291–326.

Horowitz, J. L. 1992. "A Smoothed Maximum Score Estimator for the Binary Response Model." *Econometrica* 60: 505–31.

Klein, R. W., and R. H. Spady. 1993. "An Efficient Semiparametric Estimator for Binary Response Models." *Econometrica* 61: 387–421.

Lee, M., and E.-J. Wagenmakers. 2014. *Bayesian Cognitive Modeling: A Practical Course.* Cambridge: Cambridge University Press.

Loomes, G., and R. Sugden. 1982. "Regret Theory: An Alternative Theory of Rational Choice under Uncertainty." *Economic Journal* 92: 805–24.

Luce, R. D. 1959. *Individual Choice Behavior: A Theoretical Analysis*. New York: Wiley.
Luce, R. D., and P. Suppes. 1965. "Preference, Utility, and Subjective Probability." In *Handbook of Mathematical Psychology*, ed. R. D. Luce, R. R. Bush, and G. Eugene, 249–410. Oxford: Wiley.
Machina, M. 1982. "'Expected Utility' Analysis without the Independence Axiom." *Econometrica* 50: 277–323.
Machina, M. 1985. "Stochastic Choice Functions Generated from Deterministic Preferences." *Economic Journal* 95: 575–94.
Manski, C. 1975. "Maximum Score Estimation of the Stochastic Utility Model of Choice." *Journal of Econometrics* 3: 205–28.
Matthews, W. 2011. "What Might Judgment and Decision Making Research Be Like if We Took a Bayesian Approach to Hypothesis Testing?" *Judgment and Decision Making* 6: 843–56.
McFadden, D. 1974. "Conditional Logit Analysis of Qualitative Choice Behavior." In *Frontiers in Econometrics*, ed. P. Zarembka, 105–142. New York: Academic Press.
McFadden, D. 1981. "Econometric Models of Probabilistic Choice." In *Structural Analysis of Discrete Data*, ed. C. Manski and D. McFadden, 198–272. Cambridge, MA: MIT Press.
McFadden, D. 2001. "Economic Choices." *American Economic Review* 91: 351–78.
Kruschke, J. K. 2011. *Doing Bayesian Data Analysis*. Burlington, MA: Academic Press.
Savage, L. J. [1954] 1972. *The Foundations of Statistics*, 2nd revised ed. New York: Dover.
Schmeidler, D. 1989. "Subjective Probability and Expected Utility without Additivity." *Econometrica* 7: 571–87.
Tversky, A., and J. Russo. 1969. "Substitutability and Similarity in Binary Choice." *Journal of Mathematical Psychology* 6: 1–12.
Wilcox, N. 2008. "Stochastic Models for Binary Discrete Choice under Risk: A Critical Primer and Econometric Comparison." In *Research in Experimental Economics Vol. 12: Risk Aversion in Experiments*, ed. J. C. Cox and G. W. Harrison, 197–292. Bingley: Emerald.
Wilcox, N. 2017. "Random Expected Utility and Certainty Equivalents: Mimicry of Probability Weighting Functions." *Journal of the Economic Science Association* 3: 161–73.
Zellner, A. 1971. *An Introduction to Bayesian Inference in Econometrics*. New York: Wiley.

5

Reasons for Using Mixed Methods in the Evaluation of Complex Projects

Michael Woolcock

5.1 Introduction

In the field of public policy in general—and international development in particular—project evaluations serve two core purposes. The first such purpose is to reach substantive conclusions, on the basis of formal empirical strategies, regarding the nature and extent of the net impact a specific project (or broader portfolio of interventions) has had on targeted populations, for example, in a particular country (or across a specific sector). Controlling for other factors, did this microfinance project for women in rural Bangladesh reduce poverty?[1] Do participatory programs in Indonesia empower otherwise marginalized groups (such as women) to have a greater influence on collective decision-making?[2] Does using contract teachers in Kenya improve student performance?[3] If the evaluation strategies used to address such questions meet certain professional standards, it is presumed that policymakers and project managers will be in a stronger position to determine whether or not the intervention in question has in fact "worked." The more sophisticated the evaluation, the more granular these decisions can be. Has the intervention been more (less) effective for some groups than others? Have particular *aspects* of a given intervention worked more effectively than others? Enhancing the frequency and quality of decisions made on this basis is the essence of widespread calls for taking an "evidence-based approach" to policy (Cartwright and Hardie 2012).

The second core purpose, which is an extension of the first, is to help decision-makers from different contexts draw inferences regarding whether to replicate a demonstrably "proven" intervention elsewhere, or to scale it up (either to larger numbers of the same target population or to new populations). If a pilot intervention in rural Bolivia seeking to reduce maternal mortality is deemed to have "worked," should it now be expanded to the cities? Do the "rigorous" positive findings from a deworming project in Kenya warrant its adoption in neighboring Tanzania? What about in Mongolia? Methodologically speaking, the first set of questions pertain to internal validity (or identification) concerns, while the second set to external validity (or generalization and extrapolation).[4] As we shall see, even carefully identified single-method assessments of what I will call "complex" interventions struggle to address key concerns pertaining to replication and scaling. Appropriately integrated, however, answers to both sets of questions can serve the broader purposes of enhancing "learning" (so that subsequent decisions regarding a project's design and implementation are made more prudently) and "accountability" (so that outcomes, such as they are, can be explained on a firm foundation to project recipients, managers, funders, and—if public money is being used—to taxpayers).

This is the conventional way in which evaluation work is framed and discussed, certainly among elite researchers (even if they give vastly more attention to internal validity concerns). Such discussions are necessary and important, and they elicit a range of methodological issues, the resolution of which, as we shall see, is likely to entail using a combination of qualitative and quantitative approaches—that is, mixed methods. Even so, all such approaches focus largely on assessing what Goertz and Mahoney (2012) call "the effects of causes": one starts with a given "cause" (e.g., a program to immunize babies) and then seeks to discern its net effects (e.g., on infant mortality). But many social problems don't (yet) have known solutions, and the most vexing of them are so idiosyncratic that it is highly unlikely that any putative solution deemed to work "there" would also work "here," meaning that considerable adaptation is likely to be required, both upfront and during the implementation process. Such projects are likely to yield widely divergent outcomes across time, place, and groups, and as a result require specific explanations for why some places or groups did so much better than others. In such instances, researchers are assessing "the causes of effects": beginning with particular outcomes and then working their way back up the implementation trail to discern when, where and how the critical junctures occurred. Here too, as we shall see, mixed-methods approaches are central to generating sound and useable answers.

To narrow our focus somewhat, our concern in this chapter is with such "complex" projects. In one sense, of course, all policies and projects are far from straightforward, and the methodological challenges outlined above are vexing enough even when it comes to assessing the impacts of relatively "simple" interventions, such as roads and bridges. For present purposes, such interventions are "simple" because, for the most part, they are characterized by (1) few ongoing interactions between people being required to realize the intervention's stated objectives (a bridge is inanimate); (2) interactions that do take place leaving little room for human discretion (toll collectors perform routine tasks); (3) problems that arise during implementation and maintenance having known (or readily discernable) solutions (fixing potholes, reinforcing girders); and (4) the service performed by the intervention (enhanced connectivity, vastly lower transportation costs), being welcomed by the vast majority of the target population, especially powerful elites.[5]

The very opposite of these four criteria characterize "complex" interventions such as taxation, justice, and social work. For example, if one is implementing a new program to enhance the welfare of children in "at-risk" households—one which may entail physically removing children from what are deemed to be unsafe family environments—the entire space is characterized by many interacting people, all of whom are exercising considerable discretion, deploying or living with the consequences of a "solution" whose efficacy is inherently imprecise, doing so in the face of (very likely strong and emotionally wrenching) resistance. What is the ethically sound "rigorous" methodology for assessing the virtues and limits of such a program? Whatever minimally serious evaluation strategy is deployed, its likely finding will be that—befitting the findings of other complex interventions—it worked wonderfully for some, had little effect on others, and was diabolically awful for still others. Even when carefully designed, fully supported (politically and financially), and faithfully implemented, complex interventions are characterized by the highly variable outcomes they generate over time, space, and groups—because the intervention's structural characteristics and implementation modality interact with "contexts" in inherently idiosyncratic ways. By construction one can create a mathematical "average" impact of such projects, but perhaps the more instructive statistic is the standard deviation—the variability around the average that, if carefully monitored over time, can be a fruitful basis of iterative learning. This monitoring itself, however, and accurately discerning the "lessons" from it, will require access to a broad array of theory and methods.

The central premise of this chapter is that complex interventions, as defined above, are best assessed by "mixed methods"—that is, an array of integrated qualitative and quantitative approaches to research design, measurement, analysis, and interpretation exploiting the comparative advantage of each approach in the joint pursuit of knowledge enabling real-time adjustments. Complex projects "learn" in a manner to which human learn complex tasks such as speaking a foreign language or playing a musical instrument: by extended trial and error. In the sections that follow, the strengths and weaknesses of stand-alone approaches to evaluation are outlined, along with a discussion of the importance of embedding empirical findings regarding project impacts in a theory of change that accommodates the likely trajectory of that impact over time. (Most of the examples come from international development, but they have been chosen because of the broader applicability of the common underlying principles.) Such analyses form the basis of a third section exploring the conditions under which empirical claims about the impact of a given complex intervention might be generalized to novel contexts, scales of operation, and implementing agencies. A concluding section reflects briefly on the rising and expanding role for complex policy interventions and the corresponding demand this will place on evaluators to become adept at assembling interdisciplinary teams (since it is unrealistic to expect any single evaluator to be fully competent in all methodological approaches).

5.2 The Complementary Strengths and Weaknesses of Different Methodological Approaches

Research and evaluation methods in the social sciences are typically categorized as either quantitative or qualitative, as are the data that these respective methods deploy (Hentschel 1999).[6] Quantitative methods, such as econometrics, use large amounts of numerical data derived from primary (e.g., household surveys) or secondary (government records) sources to draw inferences regarding relationships between categorical variables (e.g., age, occupation, income, health). Since it is rare to obtain such data on entire populations, careful attention is given to sampling concerns and specifying the confidence one has in both the strength of the measured relationships (net of other factors, such as non-random selection into groups) and the conditions under which these relationships might hold for the larger population. Largely because of this capacity to speak to trends and relationships in large populations, quantitative methods and data assume a privileged status in public policy deliberations. Qualitative methods, such as those of mainstream anthropology, focus on understanding the intricate details of the processes and meanings associated with social interactions within and between particular groups. As such, qualitative methods (interviews, observations, textual analysis) tend to be associated with qualitative data (words, images)[7]; less concern is given to demonstrating whether emergent findings (e.g., from a single village) are "representative" of the larger population from which they are drawn (e.g., a region or country) since such claims are rarely made or expected. Qualitative methods are especially useful when the interventions to be evaluated increase in complexity (i.e., require many discretionary and face-to-face transactions, and are contentious[8]), when the "context" itself is highly variable (and perhaps volatile), when the quality and availability of existing data is poor, and when insights are sought on specific types of impacts on specific groups (e.g., the effectiveness of a project for ethnic minorities, informal firms, or illegal immigrants, who may not be adequately represented in formal surveys). Qualitative methods can also be useful when evaluating small-N interventions such as regulatory reforms at the national level, or automation of procedures in one single agency.[9]

For the purposes of understanding the impact and generalizability of claims pertaining to complex projects, perhaps the simplest but most fruitful distinction between these quantitative and qualitative approaches is to argue that the former focus on "breadth" where the latter focus on "depth." The main rationale for the systematic integration of qualitative and quantitative methods in the evaluation of projects (of any kind) is that both approaches complement the others' limitations; this is particularly so with regard to the "breadth" and "depth" of information that together is needed to optimally describe and explain outcomes stemming from complex phenomenon. In this way, integrating qualitative methods in impact evaluation (IE) helps reveal the ways in which different causal mechanisms—singularly or in combination—generate observed outcomes and thereby enable evaluators to assess the intervention's broader theory of change[10]; that is, both whether and *how* impact is achieved in a specific instance, and also the conditions under which this impact might be expected elsewhere or at larger scales of operation (Bamberger et al. 2010; Clark and Baidee 2010). Table 5.1 summarizes the key ways in which both methodological approaches are used in the collection, design, analysis, and interpretation of data in project evaluations.

Another benefit of using qualitative and mixed methods in project evaluations is that they can enhance the robustness of the underlying model of causal inference (i.e., improve internal validity) and thereby diminish the influence of various sources of bias (e.g., selection bias, by observing "unobservable" factors shaping program placement and participation) and measurement error (e.g., discrepancies in terms of how survey questions are understood by respondents and researchers).[11] Results obtained from qualitative analysis may support the conclusions obtained from the

Table 5.1 Characteristics of Quantitative and Qualitative Methods in Project Evaluations

	Quantitative Methods	**Qualitative Methods**
Research Questions	Usually derived deductively (e.g., from knowledge gaps in the literature); seek to demonstrate "precise" causal effect (impact) of x on y for relatively large populations; can also draw on qualitative insights to refine/adapt questions for specific contexts	Usually derived inductively (e.g., by refining questions as they emerge in situ); focus on process concerns—how outcomes were attained, how different types and combinations of mechanisms generated different outcomes for different groups
Data Collection	Use data collection methods such as surveys with closed-ended questions; this standardizes but limits the depth and variability of the information obtained	Use data collection methods such as focus groups to capture in-depth, context-specific information; also used to ensure that questions in surveys are worded and sequenced in ways that all parties understand ("construct validity")
Evaluation Design	Seeks to reduce selection bias (and other confounding factors) and to ensure representativeness and comparability of project and non-project samples to enhance quality of statistical inference ("internal validity")	Can help to discern and discuss issues that are "unobservable" statistically (including identifying good instruments); weaknesses in "breadth" and representativeness are compensated for by strengths in "depth" and understanding of causal mechanisms
Analysis and Interpretation	Quantifies the magnitude of impact to try to determine *whether* an observed outcome can be causally attributed (probabilistically) to the intervention; but even the most "rigorous" ("well-identified") analysis rarely provides warrant for inferring that similar results will obtain elsewhere (or at larger scale) ("external validity")	Best suited to informing discussions regarding *how*, *why*, and *for whom* a given intervention worked (or not); thus can help explain (and foster learning from) variation in outcomes and/or implementation processes, and usefully contribute to discussions about the possible generalizability of given findings to novel contexts, populations, and scales of operation

Source: Alcántara and Woolcock (2014).

quantitative research but enable researchers to go beyond the measurement of impacts and provide specific evidence of *how* impact was achieved and for whom—that is, it can facilitate the exploration of variation across time, space, and groups by showing how local context characteristics and implementation dynamics interact. In a recent study of a national community development project in Indonesia, for example, even neighboring villages performed quite differently; a key factor shaping this variation was whether local leaders supported or resisted the project, even though these villages were participating in the same project being implemented by the same people (Barron et al. 2011).

In other instances, however, qualitative research might qualify or even contradict the findings emerging from quantitative approaches, in which case the research team needs to work together to resolve the anomalies; these deliberations, if done carefully, can serve to enhance the confidence the project team (and stakeholders in the reform process, including policy makers) has in the final conclusions and the policy implications to which they give rise (Woolcock 2009; Rugh et al. 2011). Results from a quantitative evaluation of a jobs program, for example, may show that wages significantly increased for program participants, and thus conclude that it was a success, while a qualitative assessment may find that program participants reported heightened levels of stress and health problems, and thus conclude that the program was a failure. Which interpretation is correct? Combining both findings may lead to a more nuanced and helpful conclusion, namely that real wage increases were achieved but at the price of considerable welfare declines for certain groups, enabling corresponding adjustments to be made in subsequent iterations of the program. Even when the empirical findings derived from different methods align, an iterative dialogue between qualitative and quantitative perspectives can contribute to a more comprehensive interpretation of the results – what they mean, and what their implications are for policy and practice (Shaffer 2011).

In short, the systematic combination of quantitative and qualitative methods helps evaluators to optimize the likelihood that their findings (and interpretations of those findings) will lead to accurate inferences about the effectiveness of interventions and how this effectiveness varies across time, contexts, and target groups. It achieves this primarily by using the strengths of one approach to offset the weaknesses of the other (Rao 2002; Rao and Woolcock 2003). Other instances where quantitative and qualitative methods can be combined in the evaluation process include the following:

1. Generating hypotheses about an intervention's effectiveness from theory, experience, and qualitative research and then testing their ability to be generalized with quantitative techniques.
2. Identifying contextual factors, processes, and causal mechanisms via qualitative methods and assessing them further via quantitative methods (e.g., Ludwig et al. 2011) and/or additional qualitative analysis.
3. Applying quantitative sampling techniques to units of qualitative data collection, and/or findings from qualitative analysis and using them to inform the design of quantitative data collection tools (i.e., household or firm surveys).
4. Using qualitative findings to see if they support, explain, qualify, or refute quantitative findings regarding an intervention's impact (Rao et al. 2017).

I address these and related issues in more detail below.

Even though the deployment of mixed-method approaches has been increasing in economic development IEs, most notably in health, to date relatively few IEs can be identified as truly using a mixed-method approach. For example, only 3 percent of the IE portfolio has used a mixed-method approach,[12] and neither J-PAL nor World Bank databases formally record whether mixed methods were used in a given evaluation. In the following sections we provide some examples of how qualitative methods have been deployed in each stage of the standard evaluation cycle. Although these studies did not use a systematic integration of methods, they are useful to showcase the fruitfulness of deploying mixed methods in specific stages of the evaluation. It bears repeating that, ideally, the most valid and useful findings are likely to emerge when both qualitative and quantitative methods can be integrated at different stages, enabling their systematic combination to exploit the strengths (and minimize the weaknesses) of using one method alone.

5.3 Understanding Impact Trajectories

Any hypotheses or claims about change processes must incorporate time (by when it is reasonable to expect that a net impact will be attained—six months, six years?) and the high likelihood that the trajectory of that change will be nonlinear (e.g., a J-curve or step function). Giving inadequate attention to changing circumstances and the possibility of nonlinear impact trajectories can lead to claims about impact that turn out to be premature, thereby forming an inaccurate basis for future projections. For example, a study that evaluated the impact of an export promotion-matching grant for small and medium-sized enterprises (SMEs) in Tunisia found that in the short term, beneficiary firms showed higher export growth and export diversification than those of the control group. However, in a subsequent study, it was found that the effects were not sustained over time, an issue that the authors highlighted as commonly overlooked in the literature (Cadot et al. 2012). The authors of the follow-up study even mention that these types of reforms have not been explored in the long term, questioning the sustainability of what in the short term was found to be "successful" (Cadot et al. 2012). Ravallion (2009) warns that the assessment of short-term impacts is common in IE, generating a "myopia bias" that can lead not only to erroneous conclusions but also to decisions to scale-up policies and programs without knowing the underlying factors of impact that can lead to negative spillovers.

How Impact Trajectories Shape Interpretations of Impact

Four months after planting, we do not conclude that the growth of oak trees (which takes years) is "less effective" than the growth of sunflowers (which takes weeks) because science and experience tell us what it is reasonable to expect by when. The same logic should apply to development interventions. The important implication is that when assessing an intervention at two points in time, evaluators must have (or build) a solid theory of change—on the basis of experience, evidence or theory—to specify the mechanisms (processes) by which they expect given inputs to generate observed outcomes, and over what time frame and trajectory it is reasonable for these outcomes to emerge (Woolcock 2009; 2013). Both qualitative and quantitative methods are needed to do this well. (Most complex to assess of all, of course, are those interventions that have no consistent impact trajectory.)

A central issue for both causal inference and policy extrapolation is that methods per se, no matter how "rigorously" and comprehensively they are applied, do not on their own provide a clear basis for discerning whether an intervention is working or is likely to do so in the future; for that, the empirical findings must be guided by theory and experience. Put differently, *the implications of evidence are never self-evident.*

Consider the figure below, which exemplifies four different impact trajectories and three different points in time at which an evaluation could be conducted: without knowledge of the likely impact trajectory associated with a given intervention (say, roads versus schools versus immunization versus land titling), and thus knowledge of what it is reasonable to expect by when, wildly inaccurate conclusions regarding the intervention's efficacy could be drawn. If the intervention was evaluated at point C, a fortuitously consistent story would emerge since all four trajectories converge on a similar net impact between "baseline" (t = 0) and follow-up (t = 1). (And the timing of the follow-up is largely determined by political and administrative imperatives, not scientific ones.) But if the intervention was evaluated at point A, four very different conclusions regarding the intervention's net impact—ranging from spectacular success to dismal failure—would be drawn, even if the intervention was being assessed via a randomized controlled trial (RCT). The shape of the trajectories, when extended into the future, has correspondingly important implications for the claims we make about the intervention's likely impacts down the road.

This dynamic can be seen in a World Bank–supported land reform project in Cambodia, which was hailed (rightly) as an initial success. But a mismatch between

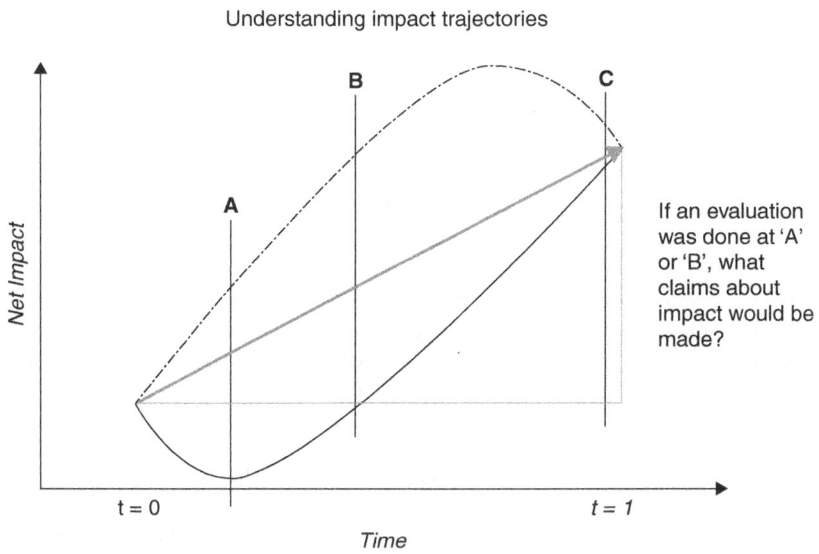

Figure 5.1 Understanding impact trajectories.

Source: Woolcock (2013).

the reform's expectations and the capacity of the administrative system to implement them on a larger scale, especially in sensitive peri-urban areas, generated stress on the demand side and weakened (in fact almost collapsed) the capacity of the system (Adler, Porter, Woolcock 2008; Biddulph 2014). Hence, generating in-depth contextual information is key to identifying the factors that are shaping the nature and extent of an intervention's impact trajectory (see Box 1), and to sustaining a commitment to equitably negotiating those aspects of implementation that may be contentious. Such information also plays a key role in decisions about whether, when, where, and how the intervention might be scaled up (or shut down, for that matter).

Hence, one important question that arises is: *when* should impacts be measured? By using qualitative methods to understand the context and by drawing on a range of experiences elsewhere, evaluators can derive informed knowledge of the change process (whether it be initiated by firms, governments, NGOs, or others), and thus help to more accurately specify what outcomes the intervention can be expected to generate over a given timeframe. Failure to do so can lead to claims about impact that are accurate only at a certain (often arbitrary) time period, when a fuller rendering of the path taken so far, and the path(s) that is likely in the future, is needed to guide decision-making.

5.4 Integrating Qualitative and Quantitative Methods into "Complex" Project Evaluations

As previewed above, qualitative analysis and data collection can complement quantitative techniques in the evaluation design to address common challenges such as identification (i.e., inference regarding causal relations), construct validity (assuring the quality of data itself), and model specification, but they are also crucial for understanding the role of implementation quality and "context," and interpreting extant empirical findings. These latter issues are especially salient in the evaluation of "complex" projects, such as those pertaining to governance and legal reform. I address these issues in turn:

(1) Identification: Qualitative data collection and analysis can be helpful in informing and selecting samples (whether of people, places, or issues) of interest. For example, in-depth interviews or focus groups might be used to identify firms or individuals with "entrepreneurial" behavior, or to identify what constitutes entrepreneurial behavior according to the context and prevailing social norms. Once firms are identified, quantitative methods can be applied to the population of interest to make the sample (more) representative. Another common identification strategy is selecting samples (or even stratified samples) of interest from the sampling list with specific characteristics; qualitative research can then be conducted on those selected individuals or units of interest to help explain common or different characteristics, or to explain variance or outlier behavior (Tedlie and Yu 2007). This technique is particularly useful when sample sizes are small.

Qualitative data collection methods have also been useful in refining the identification strategy and diminishing the risk of selection bias, especially for quasi-experimental studies where it is difficult to control for unobservable variables. An example is Bloom et al. (2013), who assessed the impact of management practices in firms' performance in India by conducting retrospective interviews and observation assessments at the factories of a representative sample of firms. Data gathered were used to confirm that there was no significant difference between the project and non-project firms. This study shows the importance of integrating both qualitative and quantitative sampling techniques to obtain a sample representative of the population with the specific desired characteristics. Such quantitative sampling techniques help to ensure that qualitative samples are adequately representative and contribute to ensuring that claims regarding the implications of these findings for wider populations are well founded.

(2) Construct Validity: Qualitative analysis may be useful to explore the dimensions of the indicators used in the design. Definitions of concepts such as "corruption," "justice," or "transparency" may vary widely across individuals, locations, or sectors. Exploring the meanings of indicators according to the context and incorporating them into the quantitative data collection methods is not only critical to obtain accurate data from surveys but also plays a key role in establishing and explaining causation.

As an example, the concept of "delay" in clearing goods in a border post may have different meanings depending on the sector and for people working at different points in the distribution channel. For importers of ultra-fresh products, a "delay" might be understood as more than one day, while for other sectors (e.g., processed food), it might represent more than three days. The definition may vary per location. A mixed-method approach can contribute to incorporating different dimensions of particular indicators (Shaffer 2013). Consider the concept of "human welfare." The most widely assessed measure of human welfare may be income (or expenditure), but if this was the only indicator chosen to assess a project's effectiveness at improving "human welfare," it would be considerably inadequate as a basis for an empirical conclusion if that conclusion had not been informed by insights from qualitative research potentially showing (say) that income gains were indeed attained, but at the price of increased stress and deteriorating mental health. Similarly, standard quantitative measurements of poverty such as consumption per capita can be weighted according to local or contextual definitions or perceptions of what "poverty" means (Kristjanson et al. 2010).

Understanding the dimensions of the indicators in their context (and for different personnel within a given context) is necessary to understand what is intended to be measured. Rao (2002) describes how a survey on the incidence of domestic violence in India generated rates far below expectations. Initial survey results suggested that the incidence of household violence in India was even lower than in the United States, but when researchers conducted qualitative analysis of this issue they found that domestic violence was understood differently relative to the context (e.g., a slap would not be considered as domestic violence by the average Indian household). Hence, the survey questions and results were inaccurate and did not reflect an accurate domestic violence situation. Even though quantitative approaches can be applied to measure changes in these outcomes, understanding the definitions of concepts as understood by different respondents is key to establishing valid quantitative measures for these concepts (i.e., to ensuring high "construct validity").

(3) Causation and Model Specification: By having detailed knowledge of a particular context, qualitative work can be helpful in solving endogeneity problems[13] and can reveal the direction of causality by identifying instrumental variables (Ravallion 2000; Rao and Woolcock 2003). (Some qualitative researchers also argue that techniques such as process tracing can be used to make causal claims of their own—e.g., Bennett [2010]—and note that case-study evidence is routinely the basis on which causal arguments are made and defended in real world settings such as court rooms—Honore [2010], Cartwright [2016]. However, I shall not address the details of such matters here.)

(4) Quality and Reliability of Data Collection: Understanding the context through qualitative analysis is not only useful with regard to knowing what should be assessed in a survey or what should be included in an equation. It also contributes insights as to how and to whom questions should be asked or assessed, given that the quality of the data obtained depends on the collection methods used with specific objectives in specific contexts. As an example, Sana et al. (2012) conducted a study in the Dominican Republic and found that respondents answered differently depending on the type of questions asked by type of interviewer (local or external). They found that respondents reported higher income and higher tolerance toward marginalized groups to external interviewers compared to the responses given to local interviewers. Hence, qualitative methods can help to improve the quality of the data by exploring the best ways in which a question should be asked, how and to whom it should be asked, and by whom.

Parallel qualitative data collection techniques such as those generated by participant observation or case studies can also help to assess the reliability and quality of the data collected through surveys. The IFC Lima Tracer Study, for example, which assessed the impact of firm formalization on the performance of micro firms in Lima, found significant divergence from survey responses when the team conducted in-depth interviews to try to understand the low demand for operating licenses. Researchers explain that this may happen because "questions involving a moral issue, such as complying with the law, tend to be answered 'correctly', but not necessarily honestly" (Alcazar and Jaramillo 2011).

(5) Implementation Factors: Qualitative data collection and analysis generally ask and answer different questions from quantitative approaches (when the aim of the mixed-method approach is not triangulation) in the process uncovering other factors that may be shaping observed impacts such as the institutional framework (i.e., formal laws and regulations, and informal customs and norms). Contextual analysis contributes to assessing the institutional capacity of local agencies involved in the project (i.e., financial resources, political support, power of implementation), the political economy, the forces supporting (or undermining) the reform, and so on. These factors, which are difficult to measure quantitatively, may influence the quality of implementation and outcomes/impact. Qualitative data collection assessing the process of implementation can provide insights of how and why outcomes and impact were achieved. One criticism of conventional IE is that when expected impacts are not found, given that there is a lack of process evaluation or monitoring, it cannot be inferred if the absence of impact was because of failure of the design/causal link or the failure of implementation (Bamberger et al. 2010; Rao et al. 2017).

Qualitative methods can be especially useful with regard to assessing the process and quality of implementation. For example, in implementing competition reforms, it has been found that larger impact in selected outcomes is achieved when effective enforcement is implemented (Kitzmuller and Licetti 2012). The implementation of effective enforcement could be analyzed starting from the political context through the analysis of secondary data such as newspapers, by conducting direct observation, or process tracing.[14] Results obtained from qualitative data collection methods may be transformed to variables that reflect these issues and can be incorporated into the econometric study, or they can be used in parallel to explain quantitative results.

(6) Data Analysis and Interpretation: Qualitative analysis can contribute to internal validity by verifying the connections between the causal mechanisms identified in a quantitative analysis. (Similarly, if its findings are contradictory, it may provide an alternative explanation or lead to further research.) As an example, in an evaluation assessing the demand for formalization among firms in Sri Lanka, researchers wondered if the large shifts in profits that few firms reported were attributed to formalization or were due to measurement error (De Mel et al. 2013). The researchers conducted case studies to ensure that the findings were not driven by measurement error and to articulate the mediating channels through which formalization helped the firms that benefitted most. The qualitative analysis supported the quantitative findings and confirmed the causal mechanisms demonstrating that formalization led to increased firm profits. The qualitative analysis shed light on how formalization helped firms by allowing them to issue receipts and thereby become suppliers in larger value chains—in a very effective way.

Another relevant example is again the Lima Tracer Study, in which researchers used as baseline data firms operating without a license and used incentives such as fee waivers for the treatment group. The analysis found no significant impact on outcome variables. In addition, it was noted that firms were not eager to take the incentives. Through a qualitative study applied to a smaller sample, it was possible to distinguish behavioral characteristics of entrepreneurs associated with license acquisition. Information obtained through in-depth interviews revealed that there are two distinct groups among the entrepreneurs—"typical entrepreneurs" and "survival entrepreneurs"—and that this distinction may be considered a determinant in the decision to obtain a license. In addition, managers from micro firms did not perceive important benefits from formalization and recognized that the cost of the license is a real barrier for the formalization process, but not the most important. These interviews led to the conclusion that, in fact, there is not a high demand for operating licenses, an issue that was not captured through surveys, which also explains the low take-up and impact obtained.

The qualitative analysis was not initially contemplated; the original design was mainly a quantitative approach. As many companies did not accept the incentives, the research institute (GRADE [Group for the Analysis of Development]) decided to conduct an in-depth study with a qualitative focus. Given the insightful findings obtained from the qualitative analysis, GRADE started using mixed methods in its IEs. The most common design now used is to initially conduct a qualitative study to understand the context and develop the questions for surveys and find insights regarding the outcome variables that should be taken into account. After the quantitative analysis is conducted, a second qualitative analysis is used to explain or dig deeper into the results found.[15]

An Example of Mixed-Methods Evaluation of a Complex Intervention

One example that illustrates the iterative systematic approach is an assessment of the Kecamatan Development Project (KDP, a national community-driven development program) in Indonesia on local conflict dynamics (Barron et al 2011). KDP's objective was to provide block grants to local communities, who would then allocate this money to those projects community members themselves deemed most pro-poor, sustainable, and cost-effective. This allocation process took place in community forums, but not every proposal was funded, generating the potential for conflict if villagers perceived that outcomes were a function of non-merit-based procedures (or worse). The evaluation's objective was to assess whether and how these forums improved local governance; the hypothesis was that participating in KDP creates robust civic spaces and deliberative skills, which enable local conflicts to be constructively addressed. One major challenge was that "conflict" is notoriously hard to measure, and what little data there were had been collected from village leaders (who had obvious incentives to underreport the incidence of conflict on their watch). A mixed-method approach was used to find a novel way to measure conflict (which included a comprehensive analysis of local newspapers) and the mechanisms by which it is initiated or resolved (discerned via key informant interviews). In addition, it was critical for the evaluation to understand the causal chain of events, which was only possible with a deep qualitative analysis (which was generated by collecting dozens of cases of conflict pathways in program and comparable non-program villages).

An iterative strategy for integrating the quantitative and qualitative analysis was used. An initial period of qualitative fieldwork was pursued for three months. The villages were selected using a quantitative sampling frame (using propensity score matching [PSM] techniques derived from nationally representative household surveys), but the final selection of the best match of program and non-program villages was made using detailed contextual knowledge (since a well-understood weakness of PSM is that it only matches on "observable" characteristics). This was critical to capture heterogeneity of the population and increase the validity of the results. This initial work contributed to the sampling of districts, research hypothesis formulation, and design of adequate survey questions. Once the identification of a "counterfactual" was done using qualitative analysis and supported by quantitative methods, data was collected from a survey administered to a larger sample of households and used to assess the generality of the hypotheses emerging from the qualitative work. In addition to the quantitative analysis, the analysis of case studies of local conflict, interviews, surveys, key informant questionnaires, and secondary data sources as newspaper evidence provided a broad range of evidence to assess the validity of the hypotheses stating the conditions under which KDP could (and could not) contribute to solve local conflict.

Another common situation in which the usefulness of mixed methods can be seen is small-N evaluations, such as the introduction of a business regulatory reform at the national or subnational level. Such reforms, by their very nature, make the construction of a counterfactual difficult or even impossible. In such circumstances, a process of elimination can be deployed to systematically identify and rule out alternative causal explanations of observed results. For example, firm performance could be attributed to the improvement of the business climate, but this could be happening in ways unrelated to the actual business entry reform, such as via improvements in infrastructure or more information being available on business opportunities. A thorough qualitative analysis of the processes by which positive outcomes were attained could enable one to establish a detailed causal chain and define how the specific context interacts with the reform and outcomes. Quantitative approaches can be used in parallel for triangulation purposes or can contribute by helping evaluators avoid some of the typical biases associated with qualitative analysis (such as selection bias), including selecting firms for in-depth analysis using randomization or purposive sampling techniques.

5.5 Assessing the External Validity of Complex Interventions

Heightened sensitivity to external validity concerns does not axiomatically solve the problem of how exactly to make difficult decisions regarding whether, when, and how to replicate and/or scale-up (or for that matter cancel) interventions on the basis of an initial empirical result, a challenge that becomes incrementally harder as interventions themselves (or constituent elements of them) become more "complex" (see below).[16] Even if we have eminently reasonable grounds for accepting a claim about a given project's impact "there" (with "that group," at this "size," implemented by "those guys" using "that approach"), under what conditions can we confidently infer that the project will generate similar results "here" (or with "this group," or if it is "scaled up," or if implemented by "those guys" deploying "that approach")? We surely need firmer analytical foundations on which to engage in these deliberations; in short, we need more and better "key facts" (Cartwright and Hardie 2012: 137) and a corresponding theoretical framework able to both generate and accurately interpret those facts.

One could plausibly defend a number of domains in which such "key facts" might reside, but for present purposes I focus on three[17]: "causal density" (the extent to which an intervention or its constituent elements are "complex"); "implementation capability" (the extent to which a designated organization in the new context can in fact faithfully implement the type of intervention under consideration); and "reasoned expectations" (the extent to which claims about actual or potential impact are understood within the context of a grounded theory of change specifying what can reasonably be expected to be achieved by when). I address each of these domains in turn.

5.5.1 Causal Density[18]

Conducting even the most routine development intervention is difficult, in the sense that considerable effort needs to be expended at all stages over long periods, and that doing so may entail carrying out duties in places that are dangerous ("fragile states") or require navigating morally wrenching situations (dealing with overt corruption, watching children die). If there is no such thing as a "simple" development project, we need at least a framework for distinguishing between different types and degrees of complexity, since this has a major bearing on the likelihood that a project (indeed a system or intervention of any kind) will function in predictable ways, which in turn shapes the probability that impact claims associated with it can be generalized.

One entry point into analytical discussions of complexity is of course "complexity theory," a field to which social scientists have increasingly begun to contribute and learn (see Byrne 2013; Byrne and Callighan 2013), but for present purposes, I will create some basic distinctions using the concept of "causal density" (see Manzi 2012). An entity with low causal density is one whose constituent elements interact in precisely predictable ways; a wrist watch, for example, may be a marvel of craftsmanship and micro-engineering, but its very genius is its relative "simplicity": in the finest watches, the cogs comprising the internal mechanism are connected with a degree of precision such that they keep near-perfect time over many years, but this is possible because every single aspect of the process is perfectly understood—the watchmakers have achieved what philosophers call "proof of concept." Development interventions (or aspects of interventions[19]) with low causal density are ideally suited for assessment via techniques such as RCTs because it is reasonable to expect that the impact of a particular element can be isolated and discerned, and the corresponding adjustments or policy decisions made. Indeed, the most celebrated RCTs in the development literature—assessing the effects of textbooks, deworming pills, malaria nets, classroom size, cameras in classrooms to reduce teacher absenteeism—have largely been undertaken with interventions (or aspect of interventions) with relatively low causal density. If we are even close to reaching "proof of concept" with interventions such as immunization and iodized salt, it is largely because the underlying physiology and biochemistry *has come to be* perfectly understood, and their implementation (while still challenging logistically) requires only basic, routinized behavior—see baby, insert needle—on the part of front-line agents. In short, when we have "proof of concept" we have essentially eliminated the proverbial "black box"—everything going on inside the "box" (i.e., every mechanism connecting inputs and outcomes) is known or knowable.

Entities with high causal density, on the other hand, are characterized by high uncertainty, which is a function of the numerous pathways and feedback loops connecting inputs, actions, and outcomes, the entity's openness to exogenous influences, and the capacity of constituent elements (most notably people) to exercise discretion (i.e., to act independently of or in accordance with rules, expectations, precedent, passions, professional norms, or self-interest). Parenting is perhaps the most familiar example of a high causal density activity. Humans have literally been raising children forever, but as every parent knows, there are often many factors (known and unknown) intervening between their actions and the behavior of their offspring, who are intensely subject to peer pressure and willfully act in accordance with their own (often fluctuating) wishes. Despite millions of years and billions of "trials," we have not produced anything remotely like "proof of concept" with parenting, even if there are certainly useful rules of thumb. Each generation produces its own best-selling "manual" based on what it regards as the prevailing scientific and collective wisdom, but even if a given parent dutifully internalizes and enacts the latest manual's every word it is far from certain that his/her child will emerge as a minimally functional and independent young adult; conversely, a parent may know nothing of the book or unwittingly engage in seemingly contrarian practices and yet happily preside over the emergence of a perfectly normal young adult.[20]

Assessing the veracity of development interventions (or aspects of them) with high causal density—for example, women's empowerment projects, programs to change adolescent sexual behavior in the face of the HIV/AIDS epidemic, social work—requires evaluation strategies tailored to accommodate this reality. Precisely because the "impact" (wholly or in part) of these interventions often cannot be truly isolated, and is highly contingent on the quality of implementation, any observed impact is very likely to change over time, across contexts and at different scales of implementation; as such, we need evaluation strategies able to capture these dynamics and provide correspondingly useable recommendations. Crucially, strategies used to assess high causal density interventions are not "less rigorous" than those used to assess their low causal density counterpart; any evaluation strategy, like any tool, is "rigorous" to the extent it deftly and ably responds to the questions being asked of it.[21]

By the definition of complexity offered in this chapter's introduction, problems are truly "complex" that are highly transaction intensive, require considerable discretion by implementing agents, yield powerful pressures for those agents to do something other than implement a solution, and have no known (ex ante) solution.[22] Solutions to these *kinds* of problems are likely to be highly idiosyncratic and context specific; as such, and irrespective of the quality of the evaluation strategy used to discern their "impact," the default assumption regarding their external validity, I argue, should be zero. Put differently, in such instances the burden of proof should lie with those claiming that the result *is* in fact generalizable. (This burden might be slightly eased for "implementation intensive" problems, but some considerable burden remains nonetheless.) I hasten to add, however, that this does not mean others facing similarly "complex" (or "implementation intensive") challenges elsewhere have little to learn from a successful (or failed) intervention's experiences; on the contrary, it can be highly instructive, but its "lessons" reside less in the quality of its final design characteristics than the processes of exploration and incremental understanding by which a solution was proposed, refined, supported, funded, implemented, refined again, and assessed—i.e., in the ideas, principles, and inspiration from which a solution was crafted and enacted.

5.5.2 Implementation Capability

As noted in the preceding section, another danger stemming from a single-minded focus on a project's "design" as the causal agent determining observed outcomes is that implementation dynamics are largely overlooked, or at least assumed to be nonproblematic. If, as a result of an RCT (or series of RCTs), a given conditional cash transfer (CCT) program is deemed to have "worked,"[23] we all too quickly presume that it can and should be introduced elsewhere, in effect ascribing to it "proof-of-concept" status. Again, we can be properly convinced of the veracity of a given evaluation's empirical findings and yet have grave concerns about its generalizability. If from a "causal density" perspective our four questions would likely reveal that in fact any given CCT comprises numerous elements, some of which are "complex," from an "implementation capability" perspective the concern is more prosaic: how confident can we be that any designated implementing agency in the new country or context would in fact have the capability to do so?

Recent research (Andrews et al. 2017) and everyday experience suggests, again, that the burden of proof should lie with those claiming or presuming that the designated implementing agency in the proposed context is indeed up to the task. Consider the delivery of mail. It is hard to think of a less contentious and "less complex" task: everybody wants their mail to be delivered accurately and on time, and doing so is almost entirely a logistical exercise[24]—the procedures to be followed are unambiguous, universally recognized (by international agreement) and entail little discretion on the part of implementing agents (sorters, deliverers). A recent empirical test of the capability of mail delivery systems around the world, however, yielded sobering results. Chong et al. (2014) sent letters to ten deliberately nonexistent addresses in 159 countries, all of which were signatories to an international convention requiring them simply to return such letters to the country of origin (in this case the United States) within 90 days. How many countries were actually able to perform this most routine of tasks? In twenty-five countries *none* of the ten letters came back within the designated timeframe; of the countries in the bottom half of the world's education distribution, the average return rate was 21 percent of the letters. Working with a broader dataset, Pritchett (2013) calculates that these countries will take roughly 160 years to have post offices with the capability of countries such as Finland and Colombia (which returned 90 percent of the letters).[25]

The general point is that in many developing countries, especially the poorest, implementation capability is demonstrably low for "logistical" tasks, let alone for "complex" ones. "Fragile states" such as Haiti, almost by definition, cannot readily be assumed to be able to undertake complex tasks (such as disaster relief) even if such tasks are most needed there. And even if they are in fact able to undertake some complex projects (such as regulatory or tax reform), which would be admirable, yet again the burden of proof in these instances should reside with those arguing that such capability to implement does indeed exist (or can readily be acquired). For complex interventions as here defined, high quality implementation is inherently and inseparably a constituent element of any success they may enjoy; the presence in novel contexts of implementing organizations with the requisite capability thus should be demonstrated rather than assumed by those seeking to replicate or expand "complex" interventions.

5.5.3 "Reasoned Expectation"

As discussed above, complex interventions are highly likely to unfold along nonlinear trajectories. Accordingly, any empirical claims about a project's putative impact, *independently of the method(s) by which the claims were determined*, should be understood in light of where we should reasonably expect a project to be by when. With variable time frames and nonlinear impact trajectories, vastly different accounts can be provided of whether a given project is "working" or not.

A study by Casey et al. (2012) embodies these concerns. Using an innovative RCT design to assess the efficacy of a "community-driven development" project in Sierra Leone, the authors sought to jointly determine the impact of the project on participants' incomes and the quality of their local institutions. They found "positive short-run effects on local public goods and economic outcomes, but no evidence for sustained impacts on collective action, decision making, or the involvement of marginalized groups, suggesting that the intervention did not durably reshape local institutions." This may well be true empirically, but such a conclusion presumes that incomes and institutions change at the same pace and along the same trajectory; most of what we know from political and social history would suggest that institutional change in fact follows a trajectory (if it has one at all) more like a step-function or a J-curve than a straight line (see Woolcock et al. 2011), and that our "reasoned expectations" against which to assess the effects of an intervention trying to change "local institutions" should thus be guided accordingly. Perhaps it is entirely within historical experience to see no measureable change on institutions for a decade; perhaps, in fact, one needs to toil in obscurity for two or more decades as the necessary price to pay for any "change" to be subsequently achieved and discerned[26]; perhaps seeking such change is a highly "complex" endeavor, and as such has no consistent functional form (or has one that is apparent only with the benefit of hindsight, and is an idiosyncratic product of a series of historically contingent moments and processes). In any event, the interpretation and implications of "the evidence" from any evaluation of any intervention is never self-evident; it must be discerned in the light of theory, and benchmarked against reasoned expectations, especially when that intervention exhibits high causal density and necessarily requires robust implementation capability.

In the first instance this has important implications for internal validity, but it also matters for external validity, since one dimension of external validity is extrapolation over time. The trajectory of change between the baseline and follow-up points bears not only on the claims made about "impact" but on the claims made about the likely impact of this intervention in the future. These extrapolations only become more fraught once we add the dimensions of scale (if x gets us y, will 10x get us 10y?), context, and implementation capability. Bruhn and McKenzie (2013), for example, show that a business registration program in Brazil that worked wonderfully as a pilot failed as a national project, because at scale citizens perceived it to be a surveillance tool designed by an overbearing state to monitor their business activities. Bold et al. (2013) show that an intervention (using contract teachers in schools) that worked well in Kenya when implemented by an NGO was unable to generate the same result when exactly the same intervention was implemented by the government of Kenya.

The abiding point for external validity concerns is that decision-makers need a coherent theory of change against which to accurately assess claims about a project's impact "to date" and its likely impact "in the future"; crucially, claims made on the basis of a "rigorous methodology" alone do not solve this problem. Incorporating an array of complementary theory and methods best suited to addressing these concerns into the evaluation's design and conduct offers the most promising path to more satisfactory inferences and extrapolations. Causal density, implementation capability, and reasoned expectations together comprise a basis for pragmatic and informed deliberations regarding the external validity of development interventions in general and "complex" interventions in particular. While data in various forms and from various sources can be vital inputs into these deliberations (see Bamberger et al. 2010), when the three domains are considered as part of a single integrated framework for engaging with "complex" interventions, it is extended deliberations on the basis of analytic case studies, I argue, that have a particular comparative advantage for delivering the "key facts" necessary for making hard decisions about the generalizability of those interventions (or their constituent elements) Widner, Woolcock and Ortega (forthcoming).

5.6 Conclusion

A defining characteristic of complex development interventions is that—even when carefully designed, politically supported, and faithfully implemented—they generate highly variable impacts across contexts, populations, and time. A second defining feature is that it is impossible to fully anticipate, up front, all the contingent events and decisions that will need to be made during implementation, meaning that learning in real time from this variation is itself necessary to ensure that positive impacts on target populations are maximized.[27] Discerning this variation, the sources of it, the reasons for it, and the implications from it, cannot be done using a singular method (no matter how putatively "rigorous") or the tools of a singular discipline; of necessity it requires, instead, the deployment of a mixed-methods approach.

From this standpoint, efforts to enhance development effectiveness through evidence derived from project evaluation need to move beyond debates pertaining to the "rigor" of isolated methods to more concerted attempts to understanding mechanisms driving impact trajectories over time, in different places, at different scales, and in accordance with how well they are implemented. Knowledge of exactly how, when, where and for whom this variance manifests itself is crucial for making accurate empirical evaluations of project/policy effectiveness. Doing this well requires, in the first instance, familiarity with the serious challenges associated with assessing complex interventions and awareness of the *array* of methods that exist to deal with them. It also requires a capacity to discern and to combine, and to work constructively in teams (since, given the degree of specialized knowledge required, it is unrealistic to expect a single person to be fully conversant across these different methodological domains).

Acquiring the knowledge necessary to assess complex interventions will not be a product of simply deploying what some deem to be 'gold standard' evaluation protocols per se, but rather deep engagement with the contexts and processes within which all projects are embedded, and calling upon the full arsenal of research tools (qualitative, quantitative, and comparative-historical) available to social scientists. The future will surely be more rather than less "complex"; evaluations of interventions addressing these issues must themselves be designed accordingly, rather than imagining that singular approaches can elicit the "key facts" they were not designed to elicit.

Notes

The views expressed in this chapter are those of the author alone, and should not be attributed to the World Bank, its executive directors, or the countries they represent. This chapter extends, summarizes, and updates work previously published in Woolcock (2009, 2013) and Alcántara and Woolcock (2014).

1 See, for example, Pitt and Khandker (1998). Needless to say, such evaluations invariably elicit criticism (legitimate and otherwise) on both methodological and political grounds (e.g., Roodman and Morduch 2014).

2 See Mansuri and Rao (2012) for a review of empirical findings (and associated policy claims) from studies from around the world assessing the effectiveness of various "participatory" development projects.

3 See Bold et al. (2013).

4 The distinction between internal and external validity (as well as construct validity—the extent to which the specific phrasing of concepts such as "welfare" in survey instruments accurately reflects how they are understood in everyday life) comes from Cook and Campbell (1979). Construct validity issues are discussed briefly below.

5 To be sure, the very existence of the bridge, or securing the land needed to make way for the road, may be deeply controversial, but the functional tasks these forms of infrastructure provide—namely, enhancing the ease and speed of travel, and lowering transportation costs—do not themselves provoke coordinated resistance, as does (say) efforts to regulate powerful financial companies. So, to be more precise, there may well be "complex" *aspects* of standard infrastructure projects (such as peaceably securing the land on which they will reside).

6 More nuanced distinctions include comparative methods as a separate third epistemological approach (e.g., Ragin 2014) but the use of such methods is relatively rare in project evaluation and thus are not discussed here.

7 A benefit of distinguishing between methods and data is that it creates a space for recognizing that quantitative methods can be used on qualitative data (e.g., assessing the frequency of certain words in books or newspapers over hundreds of years, as search engines now make possible) and that qualitative methods can be used to generate quantitative data (e.g., when medical anthropologists collect data on the height and weight of children in remote villages as a guide to assessing their overall health status). Qualitative methods (such as "anchoring vignettes"; see Hopkins and King 2010) can also be used to enhance inter-rater reliability in response to subjective questions in large-scale surveys. Space precludes exploring these particular types of approaches in this chapter, since they are the exception rather than the rule in terms of how most evaluations of complex projects are conducted.

8 Thus delivering the mail is a "simple" (logistical) task while promoting women's empowerment in rural Pakistan, or regulating powerful companies, is a highly "complex" one (see Andrews et al. 2017).

9 Small-N cases are those in which insufficient units are available to be assigned to comparison groups to get the sufficient statistical power to run an experimental or

quasi-experimental design. For a helpful discussion on this point, and how concerns surrounding it might be addressed, see Ruzzene (2012).

10 "Mechanisms" here refers to specific processes causally connecting discrete variables; "normal science" advances when these processes are understood ever more precisely and at smaller units of analysis. (A canonical example is the refinement of knowledge from "citrus fruits" to "Vitamin C" as the *mechanism* responsible for alleviating scurvy among sailors.) Strictly speaking, a true mechanism is time and context invariant—taking Vitamin C will always and everywhere reduce the likelihood of scurvy—though relatively few of these have been identified in the social sciences (for reasons partially articulated in Henrich et al. 2010). A "theory of change," on the other hand, is a broad (aspirational) statement asserting, on the basis of logic and reason, how the provision of certain inputs (e.g., cash given to poor households) will, through a long administrative implementation chain in a particular context, lead to outputs (increased school attendance) that, in turn, generate a desired policy outcome (e.g., enhanced learning) and impact (higher income, reduced poverty). A given intervention can "fail" because of breakdowns at any point along this implementation chain, which is why a comprehensive *theory of change* needs to be specified from the outset—the better to anticipate where such breakdowns might occur, and to respond accordingly.

11 Quasi-experimental designs, for example, present the risk of selection bias due to unobservable factors that affect participation and outcomes that are not easy to measure, are not known by the researcher, or are time variant. Using qualitative methods enables researchers to identify potential instrumental variables or identify those time variant and invariant unobservable variables.

12 Better Evaluation Blog, August 2013. "Mixed Methods in Evaluation Part 3: Enough Pick and Mix; Time for Some Standards on Mixing Methods in Impact Evaluation." Available at http://betterevaluation.org/blog/mixed-methods-part-3.

13 In evaluation, endogeneity problems stem from biased estimates of impact due to issues such as omitted variables or measurement error, which weaken the claims of attribution. In principle, experimental designs greatly reduce these problems by ensuring that any such biases are at least equally present in the treatment and control groups.

14 Process tracing is a tool of qualitative analysis that contributes to drawing descriptive and causal inferences from diagnostic observations undertaken chronologically (Collier 2011).

15 Information obtained from a telephone interview with Lorena Alcazar, November 2012.

16 This section draws on Woolcock (2013).

17 These three domains are derived from my reading of the literature, numerous discussions with senior operational colleagues, and my hard-won experience both assessing complex development interventions (e.g., Barron et al. 2011) and advising others considering their expansion/replication elsewhere.

18 The idea of causal density comes from neuroscience, computing and physics, and can be succinctly defined as "the number of independent significant interactions among a system's components" (Shanahan 2008: 041924). More formally, and within economics, it is an extension of the notion of "Granger causality," in which data from one time series is used to make predictions about another.

19 See Ludwig et al. (2011) for a discussion of the virtues of conducting delineated "mechanism experiments" within otherwise large social policy interventions.

20 Such books are still useful, of course, and diligent parents do well to read them; the point is that at best the books provide general guidance at the margins on particular issues, which is incorporated into the larger storehouse of knowledge the parent has gleaned from their own parents, through experience, common sense, and the advice of significant others.

21 That is, hammers, saws, and screwdrivers are not "rigorous" tools; they become so to the extent they are correctly deployed in response to the distinctive problem they are designed to solve.

22 In more vernacular language we might characterize such problems as "wicked" (after Churchman 1967); see also Andrews et al. (2017).

23 See, among others, the extensive review of the empirical literature on CCTs provided in Fiszbein and Schady (2009); Baird et al. (2013) provide a more recent "systematic review" of the effect of both conditional and unconditional cash transfer programs on education outcomes.

24 Indeed, the high-profile advertising slogan of a large, private international parcel service was, "We love logistics."

25 For a broader conceptual and empirical discussion of the evolving organizational capabilities of developing countries see Andrews et al. (2017).

26 Any student of the history of issues such as civil liberties, gender equality, the rule of law, and human rights surely appreciates this; such changes took centuries to be realized, and many of course remain unfulfilled.

27 Kauffman (2016: xiv) argues that such characteristics render the state of an emergent phenomena "unprestate-able"—an inelegant but technically accurate description. In these instances, he argues, "[n]ot only do we not know what *will* happen, we often do even know what *can* happen. If we cannot prestate what *can* happen, we cannot know what can happen and thus cannot reason about it. But we must live forward anyway" (emphasis in original).

References

Adler, Daniel, Doug Porter, and Michael Woolcock. 2008. *Legal Pluralism and Equity: Some Reflections on Land Reform in Cambodia*. Washington, DC: World Bank. Available at http://siteresources.worldbank.org/INTJUSFORPOOR/Resources/J4PBriefingNoteVolume2Issue2.pdf.

Alcántara, Alejandra Mendoza, and Michael Woolcock. 2014. *Integrating Qualitative Methods into Investment Climate Impact Evaluations*, Policy Research Working Paper No. 7145. Washington, DC: World Bank.

Alcázar Lorena, and Miguel Jaramillo. 2011. *Panel /Tracer Study on the Impact of Business Facilitation Processes on Microenterprises and Identification of Priorities for Future Business Enabling Environment Projects in Lima, Peru*. IFC Evaluation Report. Washington, DC: World Bank.

Andrews, Matt, Lant Pritchett, and Michael Woolcock. 2017. *Building State Capability: Evidence, Analysis, Action*. New York: Oxford University Press.

Baird, Sarah, Francisco Ferreira, Berk Özler, and Michael Woolcock. 2013. "Conditional, Unconditional and Everything in between: A Systematic Review of the Effects of Cash Transfer Programmes on Schooling Outcomes." *Journal of Development Effectiveness* 6 (1): 1–43.

Bamberger, Michael, Vijayendra Rao, and Michael Woolcock. 2010. "Using Mixed Methods in Monitoring and Evaluation: Experiences from International Development." In *Handbook of Mixed Methods in Social and Behavioral Research,* 2nd revised ed., ed. Abbas Tashakkori and Charles Teddlie, 613–41. Thousand Oaks, CA: Sage Publications.

Barron, Patrick, Rachael Diprose, and Michael Woolcock. 2011. *Contesting Development: Participatory Projects and Local Conflict Dynamics in Indonesia.* New Haven, CT: Yale University Press.

Bennet, Andrew. 2010. "Process Tracing and Causal Inference." In *Rethinking Social Inquiry*, 2nd ed., ed. Henry Brady and David Collier. Lanham, MD: Rowman and Littlefield.

Biddulph, Robin, 2014. *Cambodia's Land Management and Administration Project*, WIDER Working Paper No. 2014/086. Helsinki: UNU-WIDER.

Bloom, Nicholas, Benn Eifert, Aprajit Mahajan, David McKenzie, and John Roberts. 2013. "Does Management Matter? Evidence from India." *Quarterly Journal of Economics* 128 (1): 1–51.

Bold, Tessa, Mwangi Kimenyi, Germano Mwabu, Alice Ng'ang'a, and Justin Sandefur. 2013. *Scaling-Up What Works: Experimental Evidence on External Validity in Kenyan Education*, Working Paper No. 321. Washington, DC: Center for Global Development.

Bruhn, M., and D. McKenzie. 2013. *Entry Regulation and Formalization of Microenterprises in Developing Countries.* Policy Research Working Paper No. 6507. Washington, DC: World Bank.

Byrne, David. 2013. "Evaluating Complex Social Interventions in a Complex World." *Evaluation* 19 (3): 217–28.

Byrne, David, and Gillian Callighan. 2013. *Complexity Theory and the Social Sciences: The State of the Art.* London: Routledge.

Cadot, Olivier, Ana M. Fernandes, Julien Gourdon, and Aaditya Mattoo. 2012. *Are the Benefits of Export Support Durable? Evidence from Tunisia.* Washington, DC: World Bank. Available at https://openknowledge.worldbank.org/handle/10986/12189.

Cartwright, Nancy. 2016. "How to Learn about Causes in the Single Case." Paper prepared for Princeton—World Bank conference on The Case for Case Studies: Integrating Scholarship and Practice in International Development.

Cartwright, Nancy, and Jeremy Hardie. 2012. *Evidence-Based Policy: A Practical Guide to Doing it Better.* New York: Oxford University Press.

Casey, Katherine, Rachel Glennerster, and Edward Miguel. 2012. "Reshaping Institutions: Evidence on Aid Impacts Using a Pre-Analysis Plan." *Quarterly Journal of Economics* 127 (4): 1755–812.

Chong, Alberto, Rafael La Porta, Florencio Lopez-de-Silanes, and Andrei Shleifer. 2014. "Letter Grading Government Efficiency." *Journal of the European Economic Association* 12 (2): 277–99.

Churchman, C. West. 1967. "Wicked Problems." *Management Science* 14 (4): 141–2.

Clark, Vicki Plano, and Manijeh Baidee. 2010. "Research Questions in Mixed Methods Research." In *Handbook of Mixed Methods in Social and Behavioral Research*, 2nd revised ed., ed. Abbas Tashakkori and Charles Teddlie, 275–304. Thousand Oaks, CA: Sage.

Collier, David. 2011. "Understanding Process Tracing." *PS: Political Science and Politics* 44 (4): 823–30.

Cook, Thomas D., and Donald T. Campbell. 1979. *Quasi-Experimentation: Design and Analysis Issues for Field Settings.* Boston, MA: Houghton Mifflin.

De Mel, Suresh, David McKenzie, and Woodruff, Christopher. 2013. "The Demand for, and Consequences of, Formalization among Informal Firms in Sri Lanka." *American Economic Journal: Applied Economics* 5 (2): 122–50.

Fiszbein, Ariel, and Norbert Schady. 2009. *Conditional Cash Transfers: Reducing Present and Future Poverty*. Washington, DC: World Bank.

Goertz, Gary, and James Mahoney. 2012. *A Tale of Two Cultures: Qualitative and Quantitative Research in the Social Sciences*. Princeton, NJ: Princeton University Press.

Greene, Jennifer C., Valerie J. Caracelli, and Wendy F. Graham. 1989. "Toward a Conceptual Framework for Mixed-Method Evaluation Designs." *Educational Evaluation and Policy Analysis* 11 (3): 255–74.

Henrich, Joseph, Steven J. Heine, and Ara Norenzayan. 2010. "The Weirdest People in the World?" *Behavioral and Brain Sciences* 33: 61–135.

Hentschel, Jesko. 1999. "Contextuality and Data Collection Methods: A Framework and Application to Heath Service Utilization." *Journal of Development Studies* 35 (4): 64–94.

Honore, Anthony. 2010. "Causation in the Law." In *Stanford Encyclopedia of Philosophy*. Available at http://stanford.library.usyd.edu.au/entries/causation-law/.

Hopkins, Daniel J., and Gary King. 2010. "Improving Anchoring Vignettes: Designing Surveys to Correct Interpersonal Incomparability." *Public Opinion Quarterly* 74 (2): 201–22.

Kauffman, Stuart A. 2016. *Humanity in a Creative University*. New York: Oxford University Press.

Kitzmuller, Markus, and Martha Martinez Licetti. 2012. "Competition Policy: Encouraging Thriving Markets for Development." World Bank View Point Series. Available at http://siteresources.worldbank.org/EXTFINANCIALSECTOR/Resources/282884-1303327122200/VP331-Competition-Policy.pdf (accessed November 29, 2016).

Kristjanson, Patti, Nelson Mango, Anirudh Krishna, Maren Radeny and Nancy Johnson. 2010. "Understanding Poverty Dynamics in Kenya." *Journal of International Development* 22 (7): 978–96.

Ludwig, Jens, Jeffrey R. Kling, and Sendhil Mullainathan. 2011. "Mechanism Experiments and Policy Evaluations." *Journal of Economic Perspectives* 25 (3): 17–38.

Mansuri, Ghazala, and Vijayendra Rao. 2012. *Localizing Development: Does Participation Work?* Washington, DC: World Bank.

Manzi, Jim. 2012. *Uncontrolled: The Surprising Payoff of Trial and Error for Business, Politics, and Society*. New York: Basic Books.

Pawson, Ray. 2006. *Evidence-based Policy: A Realist Perspective*. London: SAGE.

Pitt, Mark, and Shahidur Khandker. 1998. "The Impact of Group-Based Credit Programs on Poor Households in Bangladesh: Does the Gender of Participants Matter?" *Journal of Political Economy* 106 (5): 958–96.

Pritchett, Lant. 2013. "The Folk and the Formula: Fact and Fiction in Development." Helsinki: WIDER Annual Lecture 16.

Ragin, Charles. 2014. *The Comparative Method: Moving beyond Qualitative and Quantitative Strategies*, 2nd ed. Berkeley, CA: University of California Press.

Rao, Vijayendra. 2002. "Experiments in Participatory Econometrics: Improving the Connection between Economic Analysis and the Real World." *Economic and Political Weekly* 22 (20): 1887–91.

Rao, Vijayendra, and Michael Woolcock. 2003. "Integrating Qualitative and Quantitative Approaches in Program Evaluation." In *The Impact of Economic Policies on Poverty and*

Income Distribution: Evaluation Techniques and Tools, ed. Francois J. Bourguignon and Luiz Pereira da Silva, 165–90. New York: Oxford University Press.

Rao, Vijayendra, Kripa Ananthpur and Kabur Malik. 2017. "The Anatomy of Failure: An Ethnography of a Randomized Trial to Deepen Democracy in Rural India." *World Development* 99 (11): 481–97.

Ravallion, Martin. 2000. "The Mystery of the Vanishing Benefits: An Introduction to Impact Evaluation." *World Bank Economic Review* 15 (1): 115–40.

Ravallion, Martin. 2009. "Evaluation in the Practice of Development." *World Bank Research Observer* 24 (1): 29–53.

Roodman, David, and Jonathan Morduch. 2014. "The Impact of Microcredit on the Poor in Bangladesh: Revisiting the Evidence." *Journal of Development Studies* 50 (4): 583–604.

Rugh, Jim, Michael Bamberger, and Linda Mabry. 2011. *RealWorld Evaluation: Working Under Budget, Time, Data, and Political Constraints*. Thousand Oaks, CA: Sage.

Ruzzene, Attilia. 2012. "Drawing Lessons from Case Studies by Enhancing Comparability." *Philosophy of the Social Sciences* 42 (1): 99–120.

Sana, Mariano, Guy Stecklov, and Alexander A. Weinreb. 2012. "Local or Outsider Interviewer? An Experimental Evaluation." Available at http://paa2012.princeton.edu/papers/122313 (accessed November 29, 2016).

Shaffer, Paul. 2011. "Against Excessive Rhetoric in Impact Assessment: Overstating the Case for Randomised Controlled Experiments." *Journal of Development Studies* 47 (11): 1619–35.

Shanahan, Murray. 2008. "Dynamical Complexity in Small-World Networks of Spiking Neurons." *Physical Review E* 78 (4): 041924.

Teddlie Charles and Fen Yu. 2007. "Mixed Methods Sampling: A Typology with Examples." *Journal of Mixed Methods Research* 1 (1): 77–100.

Widner, Jennifer, Michael Woolcock and Daniel Nieto Ortega (forthcoming) *The Case for Case Studies: Integrating Scholarship and Practice in International Development*. New York: Cambridge University Press.

Woolcock, Michael. 2009. "Toward a Plurality of Methods in Project Evaluation: A Contextualized Approach to Understanding Impact Trajectories and Efficacy." *Journal of Development Effectiveness* 1 (1): 1–14.

Woolcock, Michael. 2013. "Using Case Studies to Explore the External Validity of Complex Development Interventions." *Evaluation* 19 (3): 229–48.

Woolcock, Michael, Simon Szreter, and Vijayendra Rao. 2011. "How and Why Does History Matter for Development Policy?" *Journal of Development Studies* 47 (1): 70–96.

Commentary: Why Mixed Methods Are Necessary for Evaluating *Any* Policy

Nancy Cartwright

1. Introduction

Michael Woolcock distinguishes two purposes for public policy project evaluations: (1) to investigate "the net impact a specific project ... has had on targeted populations" and (2) "to help decision-makers from different contexts draw inferences regarding whether to replicate a demonstrably 'proven' project elsewhere." His focus is on (2). The central premise he aims to defend is that "complex interventions ... are best assessed by 'mixed methods.'" The principal reason is that complex projects of the kind he characterizes are likely not to "function in predictable ways" because they tend to interact with the context they are set in. He also makes what I take it will be seen as a highly unwelcome claim about impact evaluations of complex projects—one controverted by the very language of "What works": namely, that "the default assumption regarding their external validity ... should be zero ... [I]n such instances the burden of proof should lie with those claiming that the result *is* in fact generalizable."

I think these claims of Woolcock are correct, but they are far too constrained. I shall argue that *all* interventions are best assessed by mixed methods. That's because Woolcock's strong claim about external validity is true no matter whether the project evaluated is highly complex or exceedingly simple. Even if they do not *interact with* the context they are set in, the kinds of causal pathways necessary for public policies to succeed *depend on* those contexts and so claims to external validity for impact evaluations require knowledge about the structure of the target context[1] (including social, political, cultural, economic, institutional, moral, and religious norms) for their warrant. To defend this extension of Woolcock's arguments, I shall distinguish between two broad approaches to policy evaluation and prediction: the *intervention-centered* and the *context-centered.*

2. The Two Approaches

Both approaches aim to help policy makers pick policies that are reasonably likely to achieve their targeted outcomes. The *intervention-centered approach* focuses on features of the policies themselves, in particular, on whether they "work." It aims to find out what has worked elsewhere as a guide to what to do here. Much of the effort in evidence-based policy (EBP) then goes into accumulating and vetting evidence that a policy has worked somewhere. The *context-centered approach* focuses on the context where policies are to be implemented and on understanding what causal pathways to the targeted outcome it affords.

Box 1 Highlights of the Central Features of the Two Approaches[2]

I. The intervention-centered approach
   1. Focuses on characteristics of the policy
      - Does it work?
      - Moderator variables to answer "For whom, when, and where?"
      - What does it take to implement it?
      - How much does it cost?
      - What are the side effects?
   2. Studies
      - Repeatable causal processes.
      - Measurable outcomes.
   3. Requires evidence strong enough to support generalization or transfer of policy outcomes.

II. The context-centered approach
   1. Focuses on the structures of target contexts.
   2. Studies
      - What causal processes these afford.
      - What changes can be made in the structures so that they afford more desirable processes.
   3. Requires
      - A model of what's happening in the target context.
      - An understanding of how the structures there afford this.
      - A plan to change what's happening, via producing either
        - A new intervention, old structure, or
        - A new structure.
      - Evidence for all of this.

3. The Intervention-Centered Approach

This is by far and away the dominant approach in EBP. What it studies are cause-effect pairings. Consider a typical passage from London's EPPI (The Evidence for Policy and Practice Information and Co-ordinating) Centre "Quick Guide" … *Learning From Research: Systematic Reviews For Informing Policy Decisions* (Gough, Oliver, and Thomas 2013: 12),

> Each concept within the question has to be carefully defined, as this will affect which studies are included or excluded ...Thus a review on the effects of homework on children would require clarity of what was meant by both "*children*" and "*homework*," and also what "*effects*" were to be considered.

This cause-effect pairing suggests there is something special about *this* cause with respect to *this* effect, that the effect is the "natural" outcome of the cause, or as John Stuart Mill (1836) puts it, that the cause "tends" toward that effect. Although it is not trouble free, I adopt Mill's terminology for want of something better.

We see similar cause-effect pairings everywhere in EBP sites. Here are just a couple from the Campbell Collaboration's 2016 *Campbell Plain Language Summaries*:

> *Do business support services work?* On average, business support to SMEs [small and medium enterprises] seems to improve their performance, their ability to create jobs, their labour productivity and their ability to invest. The effects on innovation are unclear.[3]

> *How effective are PES [payment for environmental services] programmes?* There is evidence of moderate quality which suggests that PES programmes only have a modest effect on deforestation.[4]

Note that my focus is not on how well established some cause-effect pairing is nor on what the quality of the evidence is. What's to be noticed is the pairing itself and the assumption that there is something that can be said about it independent of, or across, contexts. There are three reasons to be suspicious of such pairings.

4. The Three Problems

i. The Long View Problem

There is always a gap in time between policy implementation and outcome, often a long one, which Woolcock highlights in his concerns about impact trajectories. Few outcomes of policy interest are achieved directly by the policy features but rather through a series of intermediate stages. These are described in the theory of change of the policy. The outcome will only be achieved if the causally relevant features at each step succeed in influencing the causally relevant features at the next as they should. If the outcome is to occur, the policy features implemented at the start must then be directed toward getting the very first step in the process in place, not the ultimate outcome. After that, the features that appear at subsequent steps take over, each in turn. The outcome is achieved not because the policy has an inbuilt tendency to influence it but because the policy has the power to kick off a process that the context[5] can sustain. For example, if deworming children increases their reading scores in some context, that is not because deworming has the tendency to influence reading but because deworming pills in the children's guts interfere with the proteins in the worms' intestines, which inhibits the worms' ability to absorb sugars, which kills the worms, which (thinking in bigger steps) influences the health of the children in that context, which influences their ability to attend school and their ability to think, which in that context improves their ability to read—as the theory of change for this policy suggests.

Apart from raising a serious problem for the supposition of cause-effect pairing at the core of the intervention-centered approach, my reminder about the many intermediate steps that need to succeed each other if the intervention is to lead to the targeted outcome directly underlines the usefulness of mixing methods.

It is typical to claim that randomized controlled trials (RCTs) are the gold standard for evidencing effectiveness claims. But even if we had an ideal RCT in which the intervention was genuinely orthogonal to the other causal factors, we only do an RCT on a given population once, and all that orthogonality ensures is that if we randomize infinitely often on that population the expectation of the results converge on the true effect size. And most policy RCTs are far from ideal: some are not blinded at all let alone at every stage that matters[6]; it is hard to police for systematic differences in what happens to the post-randomization of the two groups[7]; there are measurement errors, implementation failures, crossovers, dropouts, and so on. One does not need to take a stand on whether RCTs trump other methods of producing evidence to maintain that other evidence is always welcome and that we are in a far weaker position without it.

The theory of change for how the policy effects should evolve in a given context provides a framework for categorizing some of the relevant evidence. This includes evidence that

- each intermediate step occurs as expected.
- at each step the moderator (interactive) variables take appropriate values to allow that step to produce the next.
- each step occurs at the time and of the size appropriate for being the effect of the previous and for being the cause of the subsequent step.
- other possible causes that might produce the outcome are ruled out.[8]

How do we get such evidence? For a coarse-grained judgment about just input-output relations—"Did the intervention contribute to the targeted outcome in φ"—we can make a reasonable stab at a catalogue of methods: RCTs, quasi-experiments, causal Bayes nets, qualitative comparative analysis, instrumental variables, certain kinds of structural equations modeling, … where which can be used reliably depends on what data can be made available and what substantive knowledge can be drawn on. When it comes to evidence sourced by the theory of change, no such catalogues are available. The kinds of information that would be helpful are too varied, and so too are the methods that can provide evidence for them. What is clear is that, if we want to avail ourselves of this additional evidence—as we should—we shall have to employ a great variety of different methods.

ii. The Donald Davidson Problem

I name this problem after the philosopher Donald Davidson, who believed that causal claims can always be generalized. If an intervention x causes an outcome y in some context, then there are descriptions of x and y, say C and E, such that it is a universal truth that Cs cause Es. That's cause-effect pairing in spades! But, Davidson warned, the concepts that appear in the universal generalization may not be the ones we use to describe the intervention and the outcome. He urged, for example, that the events on page 1, column 2 of the *New York Times* yesterday may well have caused the events described in the continuation of that article on page 5, column 1—but not under those descriptions (Davidson 1993).

Consider the Rube Goldberg pencil sharpener, pictured in Cartwright and Hardie (2012: 77).[9] With this device in hand, flying a kite proves an effective way to get sharp pencils. We can understand why by taking short views. Flying the kite opens the door of a cage containing moths, opening the door frees the moths, the freed moths eat some flannel, the lightening of the flannel allows a boot hovering over a switch to turn on an electric iron, ... the pecking of the woodpecker sharpens the pencil.

But influencing cage-door opening is not a natural tendency of kite flying. Yet the door's opening is not a fluke. It is entirely predictable—given knowledge of the context. Because of the context, flying the kite is pulling up on the input end of a double-pulley rope. That has a natural tendency to raise objects on the output end. Raising an object at the other end is relevant because the structure of the context ensures that that is also lifting a door of a cage with moths inside. So, context matters. It is the structure of the context in which a cause operates that fixes what it can do.

iii. The Concatenation Problem

Consider the second step of the pencil-sharpening process. Opening a door does not normally free moths. It does so because, in this context, opening the door is breaching a closed container and this tends to allow mobile contents to escape. At this abstract level, we have a problem. At stage 1, pulling up on the input end of a double-pulley rope raises a weight at the output end, represented thus,

$$U \rightarrow R$$

At stage 2, breaching a closed container allows mobile contents to escape, represented thus,

$$B \rightarrow E.$$

These do not concatenate. How then does the kite flying (k) cause the moths' eating of the flannel, let alone the final sharpening of pencils?

The answer again lies in the structure of the context. R and B are different features. But, due to the structure, they are instantiated in the very same happening: the opening of the door. In this context, raising a weight at the output end of a double pulley (R) *is* the opening of the door (d) and the opening of the door (d) *is* the breaching of a closed container (B). That's how kite-flying (k) leads to the moths being free to eat the flannel (m):

$$U = k,\ U \rightarrow R,\ R = d,\ d = B,\ B \rightarrow E,\ E = m$$

Therefore: $k \rightarrow d \rightarrow m$.

5. Lessons from the Three Problems

The lesson of the first problem is that policy variables generally don't have a natural tendency to influence the policy outcomes we want them for. *Mass* has a natural tendency to influence the motion of other masses and *charge*, to influence the motion of other charges. But *deworming children* has no natural tendency to improve reading. The lesson from the last two problems is that the structures of the context into which a project is inserted are crucial to what outputs can be produced. This is true even for the pair "taking deworming pills—becoming worm-free." The only reason we can think of mebendazole as having a tendency to kill threadworms in people's guts is because we are dealing with contexts—people's digestive systems and threadworms living in their guts—with similar-enough structures to support the cause-effect pairing: consuming mebendazole-death of threadworms. These three problems together argue that the cause-effect pairings at the heart of so much "what works" efforts do not reflect natural tendencies. It is the structure of the underlying context into which a project is inserted that determines what causal pathways are possible for it.

Woolcock stresses problems that arise when "complex" projects interact with context. I use the Rube Goldberg machine to show that we have problems that require mixed methods far more broadly. The kite-flying intervention is simple; it satisfies all four of Woolcock's criteria. Nor is there anything messy about the context—it is completely stable and deterministic. There is nothing complex nor wicked here. Yet you would not know to expect sharp pencils unless you had

- studied the structure of the context in detail,
- understood some general principles that have nothing to do with the description we give of the intervention ("kite flying")—the laws of the double pulley, that breaching a closed container allows mobile contents to escape, and so on, and
- understood that those principles apply in the way they do, that is, that flying the kite is pulling up on the input end of a double pulley rope in this context, that opening the door is breaching a closed container in this context, and so on.

There is no way to do any, let alone all, of these with just one method.

Happily, there are cases where we can get away with less—though we can never make responsible outcome predictions with just one method, no matter how perfect the conditions for use of the method are and how well done it is. I turn to these next.

6. When Does the Intervention-Centered Approach "Work"?

Consider the central tool of the intervention-centered approach, the RCT. A standard account of how to interpret RCT results supposes that the measured outcome Y is determined for individuals i in the study population by a formula like the following, where X represents the intervention variable:

$$\text{RCT: In } \varphi, Y(i)\ c = \alpha(i)X(i) + W(i)$$

For policy purposes, we would like to know the *individual treatment effect* for each individual in the population, that is, how much difference having the intervention (X = 1) versus not having it (X = 0) would make to that individual. Clearly, this cannot be observed. The wonderful thing about RCTs is that they estimate the *average individual treatment effect* across the population in the RCT even though we can't observe the values to be averaged. It is easy to show that, for an ideal RCT,[10] the observed difference in average outcome values between treatment and control groups is an unbiased estimate of the average individual treatment effect in the population, *Exp α*.[11]

$$\text{Exp (O/T)} - \text{Exp (O/-T)} = \text{Exp } \alpha \text{ in the RCT population}$$

The intervention-centered approach hopes to use evidence about how an intervention has influenced the outcome in some study population/context,[12] φ, to predict outcomes of the intervention in new contexts. So, in what new context can an intervention contribute in the same way as in the study context? This is analogous to the question, "Where, besides my study, will flying a kite sharpen pencils?" If my arguments are correct, the answer is

> The same connection can hold between intervention and outcome in a new context as in φ if the structural features that afford this connection are sufficiently alike in the two.[13]

This catapults us straight into the context-centered approach. We need to understand the structure of the local context. That is extremely difficult. We have no standard methodology for what the relevant facts are and even were we to know them, it is difficult to figure out what causal relations they afford.

7. Voodoo

Happily, sometimes life is better for the intervention-centered approach. To see when, I detour through work by the philosopher Michael Strevens (2012). Like me (see Cartwright 1994), Strevens supposes that many of the cause-effect connections we observe hold only ceteris paribus (cp), and that one of the central references in the cp conditions is to the underlying structures that give rise to them. Strevens call these underlying structures "mechanisms."[14]

He claims, "When a causal hypothesis is framed it is supposed to make a claim about a particular contextually determined mechanism: the target mechanism," and renders

> Ceteris paribus, in conditions Z, Fs cause Gs

as

> By way of the target mechanism M, the conditions Z and the property F bring about the property G. (Strevens 2012: 661)

Stevens's paper is called "Voodoo that works". That's because the facts about the mechanism that make the cp claim true "are typically opaque to the very scientists who formulate and test them" (Strevens 2012: 652). They can refer to the mechanism but they often cannot describe what it consists in.[15]

This fact may seem not only miraculous but useless. What is the practical significance of knowing that an intervention produces the desired outcome "if M obtains" when we don't know what M is? This is where the real voodoo lies. The reference to mechanisms is opaque; nevertheless, we can put our cp claims to use—supposing we have sufficient *markers* and *cautions*:

- *Markers.* Often there are recognizable markers for when the relevant underlying structures obtain, markers that we can come to learn without understanding what the structures are. Toasters come with labels; acorns have a recognizable look to them. Common characteristics treated as markers in development studies include "democracy", "good governance," "growth/GDP," "women's participation," "foreign direct investment," and "capacity for enforcement." But getting the right markers and defending that they are right requires a lot of theorization and conceptual development, which is not at the fore in EBP.
- *Cautions.* We also come to learn some of the ways in which our interventions must be and must not be carried out if we are to avoid disturbing the arrangements that afford the intervention-outcome process. For example: Don't plant red acorns till the spring; don't drop the toaster into the dishwater; ... For a putative economics example, consider Robert Lucas's (1976) model of how the Phillips curve trade-off between inflation and unemployment arises from an underlying structure in which people maximize their utility according to their rational expectations. In this model, rising inflation induces employment in the short term because entrepreneurs mistake inflation for a rise in prices in their sector so hire workers to produce more of their product. But if the government tries to use inflation as a handle to improve employment, people will not be deluded. The government intervention will alter the underlying expectations that afford the trade-off—or, so says the Lucas model.

So, when does the voodoo of the intervention-centered approach to policy prediction "work" The answer is summarized in Box 2.

An intervention-centered approach is likely to produce reliable predictions if it uses reliable markers for picking populations in which to implement the policy and enough reliable cautions about how to implement it. We are justified in those predictions if we have good warrant that these markers and cautions are reliable.

The demands described in Box 2 are a tall order. But it is not out of the question that sometimes there is enough knowledge available to fill it, at least to some reasonable degree of certainty.

Box 2

Consider a fictional example from Nobel prize winning economist Angus Deaton (Deaton 2012). St. Mary's school is thinking of adopting a new training program for which there have been well conducted RCTs in schools somewhere else. A meta-analysis pooling results says that, on average, the training program improved test scores by some given amount across these schools. St. Joseph's, just down the road, adopted this program and got a significantly different outcome. What should St. Mary's do? Deaton notes that St. Mary's is not the mean, and may be a long way from it.[16] He argues "The mean is useful, and will be considered, but it is not decisive. St Joe's may be closer, more 'like' St Mary's, and may have got similar results in the past, [b]etter than an average over unlike schools." Here Deaton relies on a loose common sense evaluation of what kinds of things matter—what I have called "markers." He concludes that it is "[n]ot obvious, or clear that St Joe is not a better guide than the RCT, or indeed an anecdote about another school." (His overall recommendation, though leans to the context-centered approach: "Perhaps the board of St Mary's could go to St Joe's and see the new policy in action.")

The trick in all cases is to be able to defend these claims about markers and cautions. This is why I cited Strevens's "Voodoo that works." EBP is not supposed to be voodoo. Claims about policy effectiveness are supposed to be backed by good reasons, and at every stage. This is so no matter whether these are post hoc evaluations that serve Woolcock's first purpose or predictions about a new context that serve his second purpose. It is no use insisting on a lot of rigor in establishing effectiveness claims for study populations if we have little to say in defense of the markers we use to decide where to expect similar results.

8. The Context-Centered Approach

The context-centered approach takes on the difficult job that intervention-centering ducks: understanding the details of the new context well enough to figure out what causal pathways it can and cannot afford. Context centering can have real advantages. It should not only provide more reliable predictions about the effectiveness of the proposed policy in the new site; it can also ground new proposals for bespoke policies geared to the causal pathways available there. That is, it will have these advantages if we can do it. Which is a big if. Two things I know for certain. (1) To figure out what process of change a new situation can support requires a vast amount of different kinds of knowledge. (2) There's not likely to be any recipes for how to do it. But, on the optimistic side: perhaps a little good guidance could be developed if we put our efforts to it.

9. Conclusion

Whether we can rely on the intervention-centered approach or have to resort to detailed study of the context, for warranting effectiveness predictions, we cannot get by with any single method. For the intervention-centered approach, no matter how well documented it is that the policy has worked elsewhere, we need to identify and defend the markers and the cautions we use to decide to implement that policy in a new context. Alternatively, understanding the details of the context and what causal pathways it can afford is a complicated matter that requires knowledge, skills, and methods from multiple disciplines. In neither case is there a catalogue of which methods to use, nor, ipso facto, a guide to how to do it.

I close with a warning. Discussions of mixed methods tend to focus on empirical methods. But recall the UK Department for International Development's *tri*-partite categorization of research (Department for International Development 2014): (1) Primary, empirical research: observing first-hand, collecting or analyzing "raw" data; (2) Secondary research: interrogating findings from other studies; (3) Theoretical or conceptual studies: constructing and interrogating new concepts and theories. EBP must not neglect the third. We will not get substantially more reliable predictions without a great deal of improved conceptualization and theorization at all levels.

Notes

This material is based on work supported by the National Science Foundation under Grant No. SES-1632471, and from the European Research Council (ERC) under the European Union's Horizon 2020 research and innovation programme (Grant agreement No 667526 K4U). Much of the content of this paper was presented as the third Carus Lecture at the Pacific Division, APA, April 2017.

1 In order to avoid controversy or unclarity about what is going on in the cases discussed, I shall primarily use mechanical structures to illustrate. For an account of how the concept "underlying structure" can be characterized when it comes to social/political/economic/cultural contexts, see Seckinelgin 2017.

2 Woolcock distinguishes studies of the "causes of effects" from studies of the "effects of causes." The intervention/context distinction is not the same. Both approaches aim to identify the causes of targeted effects. The difference is in how they expect to find these: the intervention-centered approach, by studying the effects of causes in study settings in aid of identifying some causes that can generally be relied on to produce those effects across different settings; the context-centered approach, by identifying what causal pathways to the effect are locally possible.

3 "Business support services to small and medium enterprises seem to improve firm performance" (The Campbell Collaboration 2016).

4 "Payment for Environmental Services have only a modest effect on deforestation" (The Campbell Collaboration 2015).

5 This may include any changes to the context that are part of the implementation process, either at the start or ongoing.

6 Including study participants, those administering the intervention, those measuring the outcome, and those doing the statistical analysis.

7 Especially when we don't know what many of the other factors affecting the outcome are, which is when we most need random assignment.

8 All of these may be available for post hoc evaluation; for ex ante prediction, only some.

9 I use this example rather than a real policy case to focus attention on the basic argument and avoid controversy about the substance of the examples. What is happening in the Rube Goldberg pencil sharpener is entirely transparent and easy to agree on.

10 As before, "ideal" means that the orthogonality conditions $X \perp \alpha, W$ are satisfied, which is what we aim for with random assignment and blinding.

11 Note that the observed difference is an unbiased estimate of the average treatment effect does not imply that the observed outcome is anywhere close to the true average. For more on "Understanding and Misunderstanding Randomized Controlled Trials" see the joint paper of that title by Angus Deaton and me (Deaton and Cartwright 2016).

12 Or some set of study populations.

13 Note that for the same average treatment effect we need not only that the same RCT formula holds, as I discuss here, but also that the support factors (represented by so-called *moderator* or *interactive* variables) have the same average. What "same RCT formula" guarantees is that the intervention *can* help there if only the support factors are right.

14 Note that this is only one of the many ways the term "mechanism" is used in the natural and social sciences.

15 This, Strevens claims, is what a good scientific model that explains the cp regularity will do.

16 Recall that RCTs estimate the *average* treatment effect in study populations.

References

Cartwright, N. 1994. *Nature's Capacities and Their Measurement*. Oxford: Clarendon Press.

Cartwright, N., and J. Hardie. 2012. *Evidence-Based Policy. A Practical Guide to Doing It Better*. Oxford: Oxford University Press.

Davidson, D. 1993. "Thinking Causes." In *Mental Causation*, ed., J. Heil and A. Mele, 3–17. Oxford: Clarendon Press.

Deaton, A. 2012. "Searching for Answers Using RCTs?" at *NYU: Debates in Development: The Search for Answers* [PowerPoint], Princeton University. Available at http://www.rural.nic.in/sites/downloads/latest/Presentation_Prof_Angus_Deaton.ppt (accessed July 2, 2017).

Deaton, A. and N. Cartwright. 2017. "Understanding and Misunderstanding Random Controlled Trials." *Social Science and Medicine*, 210: 2–21.

Department for International Development. 2014. *How to Note: Assessing the Strength of Evidence*. London: Department for International Development. Available at https://www.gov.uk/government/uploads/system/uploads/attachment_data/file/291982/HTN-strength-evidence-march2014.pdf (accessed June 2, 2017).

Gough, D., Oliver, S., Thomas J. 2013. *Learning from Research: Systematic Reviews for Informing Policy Decisions: A Quick Guide* [ebook], A paper for the Alliance for Useful

Evidence, London: Nesta. Available at http://www.alliance4usefulevidence.org/assets/Alliance-FUE-reviews-booklet-3.pdf (accessed June 2, 2017).

Lucas, R. 1976. "Econometric Policy Evaluation: A Critique." In *The Phillips Curve and Labor Markets*, Carnegie-Rochester Conference Series on Public Policy, ed. K. Brunner and A. Meltzer, 1: 19–46. New York: American Elsevier.

Mill, J. S. 1836. "On the Definition of Political Economy and on the Method of Philosophical Investigation in that Science." *London and Westminster Review* 26: 1–29.

Seckinelgin, H. 2017. "The Politics of Global AIDS: Institutionalization of Solidarity, Exclusion of Context." *Social Aspects of HIV* [ebook], Switzerland: Springer International Publishing. Available at http://www.springer.com/gp/book/9783319460116 (accessed June 2, 2017).

Strevens, M. 2012. "Ceteris Paribus Hedges: Causal Voodoo That Works." *Journal of Philosophy* 109: 652–75.

The Campbell Collaboration. 2015. "Payment for Environmental Services Have Only Modest Effects on Deforestation." *International Development Plain Language Summary*. Available at https://www.campbellcollaboration.org/media/k2/attachments/EN-0176_PLS_effects_of_payment.pdf (accessed June 2, 2017).

The Campbell Collaboration. 2016. "Business Support Services to Small and Medium Enterprises Seem to Improve Firm Performance." *Campbell Plain Language Summary*. Available at https://www.campbellcollaboration.org/media/k2/attachments/CC_PLS_Impact_of_Business_Support_Services.pdf (accessed June 2, 2017).

Woolcock, M. 2013. "Using Case Studies to Explore the External Validity of 'Complex' Development Interventions." *Evaluation* 19 (3): 229–48.

6

From an Individual to a Holistic Lens: Reassessing Marketing Models to Deliver Impact

Charlotte Vangsgaard

The shortcomings of the quantitative, segment-based approach to marketing research have today become clear. The prevailing doctrine is based on a Cartesian worldview that postulates a number of erroneous assumptions about human beings: namely, that they are rational, predictable creatures in full control of their wants and desires; that the human experience of the world is atomizable; and that human behavior can be studied in an isolated and controlled environment. By contrast, a social science–based approach to consumer research aims to understand people and the products and services they use in the broader contexts of meaning they inhabit. With a strong theoretical foothold in Heideggerian phenomenology, this approach to consumer research holds that the behavior of human beings cannot be understood in isolation but only through an understanding of the series of different worlds they inhabit, defined by familiar objects, practices, people, and moods. This article outlines a critique of prevailing marketing practice and its theoretical grounding, offering instead a holistic approach to understanding consumers. Through a case study for a global athletic apparel company, we demonstrate how a holistic and ethnographic approach allows businesses to reframe their fundamental assumptions and adopt truly innovative marketing strategies. We conclude by defining the broader implications of our method for the practice of marketing.

6.1 Introduction

6.1.1 Marketing Needs a New Theoretical Starting Point to Deliver Bigger Impact

Any decision a company makes is a bet on human behavior. Marketing, from its very beginning as a field of study and practice, has aimed to deliver the best possible return on investments by making these bets as sound as possible. Over the years, as industries have shifted product development and sales toward a more "consumer-centric" approach, new emphasis has been placed on marketing as a gateway to better understanding consumers (Sheth, Sisodia, and Sharma. 2000; Coursaris and Hassanein 2002; Niininen, Buhalis, and March 2007; Carpenter 2013). Marketing departments are increasingly called upon to advise the rest of their company on what kinds of products they should offer their customers, and how and where to offer them.

While marketing has traditionally borrowed its methodology from quantitative disciplines (Franses and Paap 2001; Churchill and Lacobucci 2010), the limitations of this approach have recently become evident (Dib et al. 2006; Kotler and Keller 2006; Cai et al. 2009; Dunn and Halsall 2009). At ReD Associates, a strategy-consulting firm that draws upon methodologies and approaches from the social sciences and humanities, we look to philosophy and social theory to fill this gap. We believe that by studying the cultural contexts for human choices we can increase the likelihood that our clients will make the right bet.

In our work, we have observed that many clients suffer from a certain kind of tunnel vision. They face diminishing returns on their investments in bringing new products to market, marketing campaigns, and other market optimization strategies. A good example of this tendency is Procter & Gamble's (P&G) rising advertising costs. P&G's washing detergent "Tide" has been a major revenue driver for the company, dominating the American detergent market for decades. In 2013, sales of Tide fell by 9 percent (WSJ At P&G, New Tide Comes In, Old Price Goes Up, Feb. 10, 2014). At the same time, advertising costs for Tide have grown from US$102 million in 2011 to US$142 million in 2014 (Advertising Age; Kantar Media; ID 314855). Apparently, P&G are finding it hard to adapt to changing behaviors and changing markets.

One factor that contributes to the tunnel vision is the way that companies are applying the wrong methodologies to understand their customers. Their analytics rely heavily on economic models and behavioral sciences that do not capture the depth and nuance of consumer behavior needed to design new products, experiences, and campaigns that will engage consumers. This approach is keeping marketers and business leaders from understanding their customers—the frameworks guiding their decisions seem to be getting in the way.

In this chapter, we take a step back from the daily churn of business and make a case for using theories and methodologies from the humanities and social sciences to provide a new perspective on business. First, we begin with a critique of the prevailing approach to consumer research and demonstrate how it is rooted largely in a Cartesian view of the world that accounts for little of actual human behavior and experience. Next, we outline the holistic approach to consumer research that we adopt at ReD Associates, a strategy and innovation consulting company. As applied ethnographers, we turn to philosophers—particularly Martin Heidegger—and social theorists to inform our approach to business problems. In so doing, we move beyond conventional wisdom to unlock new insights about the behaviors, needs, and aspirations of consumers and show how this new perspective can bring about better products and marketing strategies. Following a discussion of the philosophical and ethnographic underpinnings informing our work, we then present the specific business case of a project we worked on for a global athletic apparel company. As we demonstrate, it was precisely our holistic approach that allowed our client to reframe their fundamental assumptions about running, resulting in an entirely new global marketing strategy.

In the conclusion, we explore the broader implications of our applied approach to the practice of marketing.

6.2 Status Quo: Today's Marketing Landscape

The prevailing approach to consumer research in large companies today reflects the kinds of questions marketing is meant to answer: Who are the most valuable consumers to target, how should they be targeted, and by what means? What makes these consumers high value? What resources should we allocate in targeting them? And how will this increase our return on investment? To answer these questions and focus marketing activities on high-value groups, marketers build complex segmentation models modeling consumer behavior.

These models of consumer behavior are premised on three key assumptions about human behavior: (1) that a hypothetical individual's daily experience can be broken down into discrete consumption occasions and categories of needs matched by sets of sought-after benefits; (2) that consumers are rational decision-makers with full awareness of, and access to, their inner needs, aspirations, and reasoning; and (3) that consumers can meaningfully and objectively report back on how these needs will drive their product choices and use.

These models define what data marketers look for in order to understand and leverage the high-value moments and emotions in people's lives. In practice, however, working alongside sophisticated marketing departments, we have found that this focus on market segmentation is more of an exercise in analysis and compartmentalization than a means of understanding the customer. As a result, it often ends up alienating marketers from the people they are trying to understand, creating a screen between marketer and customer rather than providing valuable insight into people's behaviors and motivations.

Much of the practice of marketing rests upon assumptions ultimately rooted in the ideas of the seventeenth-century philosopher René Descartes. Reduced to its core, the Cartesian worldview understands individuals as self-contained subjects existing apart from the world and its contents. The basic logic of this "subject-object distinction" is replicated in the rational, linear thinking of business science, which treats consumers and their actions, attitudes, and motivations as isolated data points. The result is a highly atomized view of the world.

Business science offers the alluring prospect of predictive accuracy; that is, that by developing sophisticated models (e.g., systems of interlocking consumer segmentations,[1] occasion models,[2] etc.) companies can target their consumers with precision, offering the right product at the right time, place, and price. Such efforts to develop consumer behavior models rest on the underlying postulates that (1) consumers can be understood in isolation and (2) their actions are predictable. This, in turn, leads to segmentation models designed to carve up the range and diversity of consumer experiences into discrete parcels. These could be attitudinal segmentations—dividing the customer base according to age, gender, interests, spending habits, and so on; occasion models, that is, the division of customers into groups according to specific occasions of purchase or product usage; or benefit frameworks, which is to say, the systematic way of identifying both functional and emotional customer benefits linked to product features or brands. All three options, however, assume that people are rational, self-contained actors who make choices about the products they buy, the people they marry, the car they drive, and so on in isolation from the world around them.

The Cartesian logic of a subject-object distinction shapes the practice of marketing research in a number of fundamental ways:

6.2.1 The Research Tools That Are Used to Gain Insight into Consumers' Needs and Motivations Are Often Asking the Wrong Questions

To understand consumer choices, marketers continue to rely on data collected using the traditional market-research toolbox of quantitative surveys, focus groups, perception analysis, brand tracking, and customer satisfaction questionnaires. Marketers use these methods to ask people directly about their desires and opinions, assuming that what they say aligns with their real-life behavior. Research tools like co-joint analysis, which tries to determine how consumers evaluate different attributes of a given brand or product, are based on the premise that consumers compare products in controlled decision-making situations.

All of these methodologies presuppose that individuals have transparent access to their own intentions, and that these intentions can be reported in such a way as to predict what they will do in the future. However, this is very often not the case. Many of the decisions we make—including our purchasing decisions—can only be understood in the context of our day-to-day lives. Is what a consumer says about a product in response to a survey question really the best indicator of how they will use the product in the real world? Or whether they will even buy it in the first place? It does not require a stretch of the imagination to see how many answers will misrepresent real behavior, either because the person is not comfortable with the reality (*in fact I only exercise once a week*) or because they have a hard time predicting what they will actually do in a purchasing situation further down the road (*Should I get the practical car or the sports car?*).

6.2.2 The Models That Are Built to Map Consumer Behavior Assume That the Human Experience Is Atomizable

Modeling human behavior has considerable appeal as a framework for estimating consumer decisions and reducing the perceived complexity of marketing decisions. These models make the complicated reality of consumers' lives feel more intelligible, predictable, and, therefore, targetable. Marketers take data gathered in market research and develop customer segmentation models, occasion mappings, emotional and functional benefit frameworks, purchasing funnels, and so on. The more detailed the model, it is assumed, the greater the precision of the marketing strategy, and the more likely that the resources allocated to reach those customers will be well spent.

But can customers' consumption decisions be properly understood as a collection of discrete data? Can the consumption decisions of consumers really be separated from one another? Take, as an example, attitudinal segmentation, which places individuals in different segments. It is not difficult to imagine that as individuals move through their day, they interact with the people and objects around them, and that through these interactions, they can cycle between any numbers of attitudinal segments in a day. These finely grained and multilayered segmentation models are based on a long series of approximations that, though they may make sense individually, when added up often lead to a significant percentage error in the end result—according to Harvard Business School professor Clayton Christensen, up to 85 percent of new product launches fail because of poor or ineffective market segmentation mechanisms (HBS Working Knowledge, Carmen Nobel 2011). These modeling errors are typically not described as errors, since that would be disconcerting. Instead, they are often referred to as "off-strategy consumption."

The root of this problem is that in standard market research, the individual is taken as the primary point of reference, which does not reflect the way people act in the real world. Marketers may have to accept that they cannot build models of consumer behavior premised on the idea of the rational individual consumer nor can they disaggregate individuals' experience of the world into discrete pieces.

6.2.3 The Expectations for How Consumer Understanding Can Be Used to Guide Marketing Activities Are Self-limiting

Consumer research is generally commissioned by marketers with a particular end in mind: to test a new innovation idea, refine an existing branded product, identify new sales channels or platforms to determine the most valuable consumer segments, or generate input for a new campaign. The scope of consumer research, therefore, is delimited at the very outset of the investigation: marketers test product A based on internal hypotheses that were created for segment B. By testing these hypotheses, the thinking goes, marketers can use research outcomes to guide decision-making. This reinforces preexisting categories and ideas (about consumer segments, the benefits a product delivers, how a brand is perceived, how a branded product should be positioned, etc.) in a company rather than delivering fresh insight into the world of the consumer, which might then be used to drive marketing activities in a new direction.

As an example, a large corporate client of ours in the consumer goods industry wanted to refocus their portfolio to better target one of their key high-value segments. Their marketers had invested a lot of resources defining the segment along a variety of demographic and psychographic parameters—their form of housing, the frequency with which they go out, their dreams, and so on. Internally they shared a strong visual and data-driven idea of who these consumers where. However, the study could not get off the ground. For weeks we tried to find qualified participants who belonged to the specified high-value segment, but came up empty handed. Not one of the hundreds of people we contacted fit the company's understanding of their core consumer. This "ideal customer" was an approximation of an approximation, sliced and diced into discrete checkboxes so many times that she no longer bore any resemblance to the real-life person the marketers needed to reach.

As this case illustrates, when consumer research originates from the company's own ideas about its brand, products, customers, and the market more broadly, marketers will not acquire deep insights into the worlds of their consumers.

This predicament is very common in the world of consumer research. Another of our clients, one of the most influential consumer goods companies in the world, uses an occasion model with over 1,000 unique occasions, inevitably resulting in a highly atomized look at customers' daily lives. Thirty years ago, marketers might have used a classic customer purchasing funnel, a model that has since been rejected and now serves primarily as a straw man. Today's models aim to map the full breadth and depth of consumer behavior, in minute complexity, in an effort to identify high-value opportunities. Many of these models could go the way of the funnel. They present a distorted view of individuals and the decisions they make that, at best, provides decision-makers with a false sense of security, and, at worst, leads to bad decision-making.

6.3 Moving Beyond the Cartesian Worldview

What would it mean for marketing if we were to take the view that the subject-object distinction is a false one? The challenge to the Cartesian worldview is a well-trodden path, and its implications have echoed through the humanities and social sciences.

When introducing our social science methodologies to business leaders, we are typically met with the response that these ideas belong to academia, that the insights into human behavior they offer have little direct relevance to business. But this attitude is changing rapidly as companies run up against the limits of their current methods—especially in a business environment that is rapidly growing in complexity. To manage this complexity, companies increasingly understand that they need to develop a meaningful picture of their customers. And this means questioning the underlying logic that marketing—and in fact all business science—uses to understand them.

6.4 Building Holistic Marketing Models

We believe that the world of business can gain new perspective on their customers by learning from the humanities and social sciences (including disciplines such as sociology, anthropology, political science, and philosophy). Using philosophy and social theory, we help our clients understand the worlds in which their products live and how consumption decisions are made (or not) so that they can deliver more meaningful experiences to their core customers and make better use of their marketing budgets.

Since the optimization logic prevalent in business has its origins in a Cartesian mindset, we find it useful to look to thinkers who have critiqued this view. Among the sharpest critiques of the subject-object distinction can be found in the work of the twentieth-century German philosopher Martin Heidegger. Before outlining Heidegger's opposition to the Cartesian perspective, however, it is important to have a clear sense of what exactly Descartes argued—in this way, we can better understand the meaning and force of Heidegger's critique.

For Descartes, everything physical that exists in the universe is a variation or form of what he (following, in this regard, if in few others, the Aristotelian tradition) termed substance, or *res extensa*. Descartes believed that there was only one substance in the universe—not one *type* of substance, but one substance full stop. Everything that physically exists in the universe is simply a modification of this one extended substance (Descartes, *Principles of Philosophy*, II: 64, 247). But Descartes also held that there is another category of stuff that exists in the universe, which he calls *res cogitans*, or thinking substances. This category is subdivided in two: there are finite thinking substances, that is, the mind or soul of human beings, and there is an infinite thinking substance, which is God. The human mind thus consists of a fundamentally different form of matter than the physical world around it. World (including our physical bodies) and mind are distinct and self-contained. This, in short, is the Cartesian doctrine of mind-body dualism.

In his groundbreaking 1927 work *Being and Time*, Heidegger aimed, among other things, to overthrow this belief. He noted that Descartes's notion of "*res cogitans* … does not coincide with *Dasein* either ontically or ontologically" (*Being and Time*, 95/66). This is Heidegger's way of saying that Descartes's conception of what it fundamentally is to be a human—*res cogitans*, a self-contained mind distinct from the world around it—bears no resemblance to Heidegger's own understanding of human being. Heidegger's term for people—*Dasein*, literally, "being there"—emphasizes both the ontological character of existence (its "being") and its situated-ness *in the world* (its "there"). The "there" of *Dasein* is a proximal there—it is a spatiotemporal orientation in the world.

For Heidegger, there is no such thing as an isolated mind that acts or thinks separately from the body or the world. Rather than understanding ourselves as detached from the world—that is, the people, things, social conventions, and so on—around us, Heidegger argues that human beings always inhabit what he terms a "with-world" [*Mitwelt*] (*Being and Time*, 155/118). To exist is to exist *with others*. Even when we are physically alone, Heidegger insists, we still inhabit a world shaped and made intelligible by other people and things. There is thus an inherent sociability to human existence. As Heidegger notes, again using his preferred term for humans, "Even Dasein's being-alone is being-with in the world" (156–7/120). To be a human being simply is to be implicated in the world around us.

For Heidegger, then, the subject-object split is an illusion. We are essentially in and of the world not only because we inhabit an environment populated by other people and things, but also because we are continuously interpreting and engaging with those people and things. In keeping with his phenomenological orientation, Heidegger argues that human beings are defined by their participation in the world. When we use what Heidegger calls "equipment"—a keyboard, say—we become absorbed in the world around us (*Being and Time* 98/68–9). Rather than consciously thinking of myself as a subject that is using an object that is distinct from me, my engagement with the keyboard transcends this artificial divide, leaving only an entity engaged in the performance of a given task.

To illustrate the point via Heidegger's famous example, when I use a hammer, I generally do not sit back and consciously reflect upon my use of an object that is *x* centimeters long, weighs *y* grams, and is made of wood and metal. Instead, I simply pick it up and use it. In part, this is a consequence of that fact that I inhabit a world that is constituted and realized through social interactions and everyday practices—other people define the reality of my world just as much as I do. If I want to insert a nail into a hard surface, I *just know* that I ought to use a hammer. As Heidegger points out, it is only when things *fail*—when the hammer I'm using breaks—that it "shows up" to my consciousness. But under normal circumstances, the subject-object distinction is elided by my absorption in everyday activities (*Being and Time* 98/69).

If we take from Heidegger that people inhabit a world in which the subject-object distinction makes little sense, what can this tell us about the way consumers interact with brands and products? How might we use this to better understand consumers' choices? Building on the idea that consumers are defined by how they engage with the world around them, we have developed a different approach to modeling consumer behavior. In our practice, we recommend that clients shift their strategy from an approach to marketing based on abstract consumer preferences to one based on a comprehensive understanding of the world of meaning and significance inhabited by both consumer and product. In other words, we believe that marketing ought to shift from an atomized, piecemeal approach to a more holistic one.

There are four building blocks to this holistic approach to modeling consumer behavior.

6.4.1 The World

If we want to acquire a meaningful conception of how consumers act, we need to study people and products in the context of their world and understand how they experience the world. So first we need to ask: What defines the consumer world into which a brand or product is distributed?

How do people experience the world around them? As Heidegger notes, it is not always through a cognitive or highly reflective process. Instead, it is a constant dialogue, much of it familiar: getting ready in the morning, having lunch, driving to work, meeting with friends, reading the news online, and so on. This experience of the world does not have an end goal—there is not always a job to complete, or a place to be. Instead, we experience the world around us more often as a familiar background, as something with which we engage in an ongoing process.

Each day, we move through a series of different worlds—essentially, phenomenological environments—that are defined by a set of familiar objects, practices, and people. Take the world of cooking, for example. You expect to see objects like a stove, or a coffee pot, or a bowl of fruit, while a toothbrush might seem out of place. You engage in certain practices in that world without even consciously thinking about them—making eggs in the morning, setting the table for dinner, or chatting with your spouse while you cook, thinking about a dish that you had at a restaurant recently that was particularly good.

There are meaningful differences between worlds—you would not behave in the same way, say, cooking for a wedding or office party as you would making dinner after work on a Wednesday evening in your own kitchen. Different contexts call for different moods, clothes, rituals, and practices. That this point is obvious is itself important: it is clear to people in a given world what is appropriate for that world. It is through the process of interacting with people and objects in a world that we attune ourselves to it.

6.4.2 The Aspects

It is through our engagement with the objects and people around us that we are who we are. Or rather, we are what we do. But the inverse is also true: we cannot understand the significance of a product or service without understanding how and why people use it.

When we look at a particular object, we do not regard it in terms of its physical properties. All objects have what can be called an "aspect": that is, the purpose for which we use the product. Knives are used to slice bread or chop vegetables, for example. This function is what I see when I look at a knife—it is primarily an object of use connected to some kind of human activity. Different knives may be used for different purposes—one may be used to slice sushi, while another may be more appropriate for cutting into a steak. This aspect of the knife is situational: a knife is not just sharp—it is sharp *for the consumer*, for the job for which she plans to use it, for the kinds of vegetables she needs to chop or the meat she needs to slice.

Consumers assess products to see if they meet their needs: Is the knife sharp enough to cut? They also assess the social appropriateness of using a given product for a given task: When is it socially appropriate to use a knife to cut food? It may be appropriate in one context to use a knife to cut food, but in another it might not be. We would not know whether or not using a knife were appropriate without taking account of our context, which can tell us whether it is more appropriate to eat with a knife and fork or our fingers. Products are thus never understood in isolation from the world around them. Different objects naturally relate to each other; they are intertextual and cross-referential.

6.4.3 The Mood

Although moods may strike us as a relatively simple and intuitive idea, the concept actually has a rich and varied history, especially within the German intellectual tradition. Moods are, for example, central to Heidegger's account of the lived experience of human existence provided in *Being and Time*. By paying careful attention to particular moods, Heidegger argues, we can become truly authentic selves. From the perspective of marketing, we believe that an accurate understanding of the mood of the particular world a product inhabits enables us to more accurately assess how consumers relate to that product.

For Heidegger, there are three crucial aspects to moods. First, they are prior to, or more "primordial" than, conscious thought. Moods are *had*, not *known*. Before thought enters the picture, we have a natural attunement to the world around us. Second, they are ubiquitous: we are *always* in a mood, whether we realize it or not. Much as he insists that even when we are alone we are actually with others; Heidegger also argues that what appears to be a lack of mood is itself a form of mood. We are always open to the world around us and influenced by it. This leads to the third basic characteristic of moods: although they may appear to be deeply individualistic, moods are, in fact, a fundamentally *social* phenomenon. Since this final aspect is so important to the point we are making here, it is worth going into a little more detail.

Against Descartes's view that we are private selves existing prior to the world—that is, that the self is more basic than the world—Heidegger argues that our experience of the world is public and shared. This is also true of moods. Although we might think of moods as in some sense "internal"—after all, what could be more personal than a mood?—such thinking, from Heidegger's perspective, entails a twofold error. First, from a methodological perspective, the language of "internal" states recapitulates precisely the Cartesian mind-body dualism Heidegger is so keen to overcome. Phenomenologically speaking, distinguishing between "internal" and "external" worlds is nonsensical: there is simply the world into which we are thrown and which we experience as a unified totality. Second, from an experiential perspective, Heidegger claims that moods are in fact always shared—recall that for Heidegger, the world we inhabit is a with-world constituted by and through others. Since, in a very real sense, there is no "world" without "we," our moods must by necessity be at least partially defined by others.

On a more basic level, too, we often cannot help but be caught up in the mood of those around us. Consider a wedding, for example: although you may arrive at the wedding venue feeling glum, you will likely to be overtaken by the joy and enthusiasm of the event. This is a response both to the social expectation that you as a wedding guest perform your duty of acting in a celebratory manner and to the influence of the mood in which you find yourself. Of course, it is always possible for a guest to resist the prevailing mood and remain out of sync with those around her—we've all seen (or perhaps been) the person retreating to the corner of the room and refusing to join in with the festivities (this, on a certain reading of Heidegger, could be interpreted as an act of authenticity). But—and this is crucial—even the act of refusing to submit to the mood around us is still an acknowledgement of the power and reach of that mood: our individual mood is defined *in opposition to* the prevailing mood. With the exception of certain medical conditions, we cannot remain oblivious to the given mood of our environment.

Of course, moods are mutable. One person can change the emotional tenor of a party from upbeat to sad, with obvious consequences for the mood of that party. Products can also shape how people respond to a given mood. For example, opening a bottle of champagne can lift the spirits or further excite the guests at a party. Similarly, it is easy to imagine that toasting a wedding with wine would not mark the occasion in the same way as toasting with champagne. As noted above, a glass of champagne in this context may not always transform a given person's mood. Perhaps they had a lousy day at work and cannot shake off their doldrums. Indeed, perhaps the champagne only reinforces how out of sync with the generally convivial atmosphere they feel at that moment. Despite this, the person will still feel the pull of the shared mood and cannot help but respond to it—even if that response is negative.

Moods are an ontological feature of our existence. They are fundamentally shared and they help us to make sense of a given context. When trying to get a better sense of the relationship between consumers and products, we need to understand not only the mood of the world a product is a part of but also how that product can shift and influence that mood.

6.4.4 The Meaning

We know already that people define themselves through their interactions with other people and objects—that we are what we do. But how do we make sense of the world, and of the things in it? We use objects for specific tasks and purposes, which give them meaning in a specific context. In performing these tasks, we acquire or assume an identity (or identities) as academics, carpenters, chefs, and so forth. A writer, for instance, may use a particular notebook in order to write, but it serves the additional function of solidifying her sense of herself *as a writer*. Objects and practices act as markers of identity.

The products in a person's life can provide the emotional resources to define the kind of person she wants to be. The challenge for those of us working in this particular subfield of the applied social sciences is to identify the shades of meaning a product or brand can offer the consumer. How might a consumer use a given product to tap into a certain identity? While it is useful to observe how consumers use a given product or brand, in our practice we try to go even further, uncovering the meaning that consumers using these products create for themselves. In the process, we open ourselves to the possibility of identifying a new meaning and purpose for the company's products.

6.5 Implications for the Practice of Marketing

By taking a holistic view of consumer worlds, we can achieve a fuller understanding of what motivates people to buy certain products or brands, and in what contexts. Companies can then use this knowledge to make more informed decisions about which tools to use, where to focus their resources, and which consumer behaviors to bet on. We believe the holistic approach has several important implications for the practice of marketing:

6.5.1 The Research Tools: Consumer Behavior Needs to Be Studied in Context

To develop an in-depth understanding of the world to which a company and its products belong, researchers need to observe the consumer in the context of the world that the offering is part of. Rather than administer a hypothesis-driven survey, run the numbers, or conduct carefully scripted focus groups, researchers can learn a great deal by diving deep into the world of their consumers, using methods developed in the human sciences.

Since a great deal of research has built on existing frameworks and notions of "how the industry works," most companies have strong ideas about what motivates consumers to buy and use their products. These assumptions are typically so embedded in the thinking of the company that they appear as "truths." We advise our clients to approach consumer research without preconceptions, instead gathering large quantities of information in an open-ended way. We believe that it is only through unprejudiced data gathering that one can gain real insight into the customer's experiences and understand the underlying values and systems of meaning that together constitute a particular world.

Methodologically, this means our process is iterative. We rigorously frame a research approach that will enable us to understand the phenomenon in a comprehensive and deep way, but allow for the assumptions and principles that govern that approach to be revised as we gather more data. This method is based on the "hermeneutic circle," a kind of dialectical epistemology that Heidegger developed in *Being and Time*. Heidegger conceives of the hermeneutic circle as an incremental process through which a new understanding of reality can only be achieved through a willingness to work back iteratively from the phenomenon to the fore-understanding of the phenomenon.

Let's take the example of a recent study we conducted on kitchens for a global appliances manufacturer. The research was initially framed around the phenomena of cooking and home-making, with the goal of understanding which aspects and functions of appliances could be enhanced to deliver more premium experiences to customers (e.g., How can the refrigerator make fruits last longer?). During our deep immersion in households across the United States, it quickly became apparent that people selected appliances in terms of how they fit into the larger "space-making" design of their homes, conceiving them more as furniture than functional entities (e.g. Does this appliance fit in my kitchen? Do the lines of this refrigerator fit with the rest of the cabinet?). Working backward, we integrated the phenomenon of space in our research framing, both by delving deeper into the themes of space and by interpreting existing data in light of it. In the analysis phase that followed our deep dive, space became an organizing principle for understanding people's perception of appliances as well as a lens for informing recommendations around design, sales, and customer loyalty programs.

6.5.2 The Role of Brands in an Age of "Co-ownership": Marketers Need to Think about the World in Which Their Brands Belong, in Order to Differentiate Their Products and Services from Others

The relationship between companies and their consumers has been transformed. Pushing products out using a top-down approach is proving increasingly difficult, especially as social media and online reviews make it nearly impossible for companies to maintain control of the narratives surrounding their brands. Consumers now "take ownership" of brands, while companies compete to design the most interactive campaigns. When companies depend on consumers to take ownership of their products and brands, the former's ability to understand and decode their customers' worlds becomes even more fundamental.

Companies may want to think together with consumers much of the time, but they are still concerned to find out exactly what those consumers think. In practice, this often means relying on old-school market research that tries to understand consumers by soliciting their views and then acting upon these self-reported views as truths.

We recommend that marketers approach the brand–consumer relationship differently, using a holistic lens. Which moods and practices are specific to a brand, and what differentiates it? And what are the meaningful differences in the world that the company wants to effectuate? Understanding the broader world a product is a part of—the world of celebration, say, or the world of mobility—can help marketers who work across brands acquire a general depth of knowledge about their customers.

6.5.3 The Role of Consumer Understanding in Business Strategy: Insights into the World of the Consumer Should Drive Decision-making

A holistic model of consumer understanding should challenge companies to examine things from their customer's point of view, rather than their own.

After a company determines the potential market and commercial prospects for a product, they will often commission consumer research to test and refine existing marketing strategies. The scope of the consumer research is narrowed at the outset, based on internal hypotheses, and defined by what the standard size-of-price analysis deems to be relevant. Zooming in on predefined target areas, companies set the parameters for these studies based on where they believe the most value can be created. While it may seem an efficient way to conduct research, this practice can in fact reinforce internal ideas rather than reveal new information.

The holistic approach we recommend provides a possible solution to the problem of dogmatism in consumer research by pushing companies to challenge their core business assumptions. It reveals those areas where the traditional thinking of a group, company, or industry is at odds with the observed behavior of consumers. By identifying these asymmetries, marketers have the opportunity to deliver better business strategy solutions, moving beyond conventional thinking to identify and capture new opportunity areas for their clients.

6.6 Case Study: Holistic Framework Applied to Running

To illustrate how our holistic methodology can be used to develop a marketing strategy that is based on a deep understanding of customers' lives, we would like to share a story from another client of ours, a global athletic apparel company. We recently worked with them on a project aimed at revamping their approach to marketing running gear.

Like most large corporations, they had carried out extensive research to construct complex consumer segmentations, occasion models, and benefit frameworks, which together served as the foundation for their global marketing strategy. But these models were not able to keep up with the rapid changes affecting the running market—namely, running's transition from being an elite, technical sport to a more democratic one. This shift prompted the company to take a fresh look at how they understood the market.

After gathering some basic facts about who was buying their running gear and when it was being used, we placed the phenomenon of how running culture is changing at the core of the research. We identified a number of themes to explore through open-ended interviews, participant observation, and artifact collection. Through these, we determined different functional running techniques, explored the aspirations of runners, and classified the sociality and goals of running. Throughout the research, we adjusted our conceptual frame and the focus and priority of our themes in light of the revelation that what a run *feels* like is more important to consumers than the different functions (i.e., speed, support, etc.). When we started organizing our findings according to the *moods* elicited by different types of runs, we found that our other findings could also be meaningfully categorized under this heading.

What we found was surprising at the time, but simple in retrospect: the meaningful differences in the market had much less to do with different types of runners (i.e., consumer segments), and more to do with different running *moods*. The company was able to identify a handful of distinct runs, each characterized by a mood—for instance, the "badass run," (think urban ninjas running and jumping through the city at night).

At this point, it is worthwhile highlighting how moods are distinguished from other ways of modeling differences within a market. First, moods are distinct from consumer segments because the same person can cycle between a number of different moods within a single day. Another key difference is that moods are things you are in, rather than things that are *in you* (in contrast to, say, emotions or aspirations). This linguistic point is important—it implies a set of contextual aspects that work together to influence the mood of the consumer. Moods bring together aspects of both occasion models (which account for contextual aspects) and benefit frameworks (emotional need states, etc.). What differentiates moods from both occasion models and benefit frameworks is that they consider context—what is happening around the person—alongside the consumer's individual desires and needs.

Categorizing the market in terms of moods rather than traditional marketing models helped to reorganize our client's strategy. Rather than targeting types of people (e.g., hardcore athletes vs. casual yoga moms), they targeted running moods. Each mood influenced the way people selected shoes, apparel, even music—or rather, these factors contributed to the consumer's experience of the running mood. Each mood also had a whole host of implications for product design, marketing, and communications. Since an individual will most likely inhabit different moods at different times, it is not hard to see how this idea also opens up the possibility of adding multiple outfits and different types of equipment for different moods. From a client perspective, this insight helps to expand their potential market not by recruiting more consumers but by deepening their engagement with each individual consumer.

Of course, moods are not necessarily the right model for every company. What the running example illustrates, however, is that there are alternative ways of modeling differences within a market that are better at accounting for consumer context. And context matters, because at the end of the day humans are much more than a collection of discrete, abstracted cells on a spreadsheet. What makes us human is the ways in which our individual selves (our aspirations, needs, and so on) interact with the contexts we find ourselves in. Building models that take this seriously is difficult, to be sure. But the upsides for marketing strategy are significant—the more accurately our models show the reality of people's lives, the more genuinely human-centric our work will be, and hence the more successful companies will be at connecting with consumers.

In this article, we have outlined how the prevailing approach to consumer research today fails to account for many of the nuances and complexities of human experience, which often leads to poor decision-making. We have then demonstrated how using frameworks from the social sciences and humanities can unlock new avenues for growth and profit, illustrated by our specific case for a global athletic apparel company. Finally, we have delved into the broader strategic implications of our human-centered approach for contemporary marketing strategy.

The challenge for our business clients is to take a step back and reconsider the assumptions guiding their decisions. In our work, we aim to facilitate new ways of thinking about the issues with which companies are faced in an ever-changing business environment. There is an untapped potential for social scientists and philosophers to apply their knowledge of human actions and motivations to the world of business. While this chapter has been centered on marketing strategy, shifting to a more humanistic mindset has the potential to positively impact other business areas as well, from human resources and information technology to research and development.

Notes

1 Customer segmentation consists in dividing the customer base into groups where the individuals that make up the group are similar in specific respects such as sex, age, spending habits, and so on.

2 Occasion models divide the market into specific events or occasions for which some products or services are seen as particularly appropriate.

References

Carpenter, G. 2013. "Power shift: The Rise of the Consumer-Focused Enterprise in the Digital Age." *Kellogg School of Management, 2013.*

Churchill, G. A., and D. Lacobucci. 2010. *Marketing Research: Methodological Foundations.* Mason, OH: Thomson South-Western Publishers.

Coursaris, C., and K. Hassanein. 2002. "Understanding M-Commerce: A Consumer-Centric Model." *Quarterly Journal of Electronic Commerce* 3: 247–72.

Davenport, T. H., J. G. Harris, and A. K. Kohli. 2001. "How Do They Know Their Customers So Well?" *MIT Sloan Management Review* 42 (2): 63.

Descartes, R. 1985. "Principles of Philosophy." In *Philosophical Works of Descartes*, Vol. 1, ed. J. Cottingham, R. Stoothoff, and D. Murdoch. Cambridge: Cambridge University Press.

Dunn, M., and C. Halsall. 2009. *The Marketing Accountability Imperative: Driving Superior Returns on Marketing Investments.* San Francisco, CA: John Wiley.

Franses, P. H., and R. Paap. 2001. *Quantitative Models in Marketing Research*. Cambridge: Cambridge University Press.

Heidegger, M. 2008. *Being and Time*. New York: Harper Perennial Modern Classics.

Kotler, P., and K. Keller. 2006. *Marketing Management*, 12th ed. Upper Saddle River, NJ: Prentice Hall.

Niininen, O., D. Buhalis, and R. March. 2007. "Customer Empowerment in Tourism through Consumer Centric Marketing (CCM)." *Qualitative Market Research: An International Journal* 10 (3): 265–81.

Nobel, Carmen. 2011. "Why Companies Fail—And how their Founder can Bounce Back." *HBS Working Knowledge*. Available at https://www.businessinsider.com/why-companies-fail-and-how-their-founders-can-bounce-back-2011-3?IR=T.

Sheth, J. N., R. S. Sisodia, and A. Sharma. 2000. "The Antecedents and Consequences of Customer-Centric Marketing." *Journal of the Academy of Marketing Science* 28 (1): 55–66.

Commentary: Unity and Disunity in Consumer Behavior Research

Attilia Ruzzene

In her chapter, Charlotte Vangsgaard presents the work done at ReD Associates, an innovation and strategy consulting company founded in 2005 by Christian Madsbjerg and Mikkel Rasmussen. ReD advises companies on how to improve their marketing strategy. To the outsider, ReD looks like a curiosity, if not an exception, in the market for management consultancy because of its overt appeal to the social and human sciences. Unlike the majority of its competitors, ReD's practice is informed by thorough time-consuming ethnographic inquiry and its recommendations to clients rooted in the qualitative insights of this investigation. The anthropologists who work at ReD follow the consumer up to the place of use and consumption, observe her behavior and the space she inhabits, record her discourse and her bodily language, collect details about her ordinary actions, and sometimes even actively join in the consumption experience.[1]

Vangsgaard argues that by taking seriously the complexity of consumers' world and actively engaging with it, ReD generates a deeper understanding of consumption behavior and provides insights that help companies reach their customers more effectively. The source of this comparative advantage would reside in ReD's distinctive approach that explicitly rejects the research practices prevalent in the field. Scholars in marketing research, Vangsgaard argues, tend to study consumers in isolation, chop the consumption experience in discrete moments, and treat subjects as rational agents who have access to their own intentions, report faithfully about them, and act consistently with them. These scholars, however, end up with the image of an ideal consumer that does not longer bore any resemblance to the real-life person the marketers needed to reach. ReD instead aspires to do justice to the "real consumer" by addressing the consumption experience in all its complexity and concreteness.

From Vangsgaard's analysis emerges a dichotomous view of marketing research that pitches two paradigms against each other: let's call them the Cartesian-positivist and the Heideggerian-interpretivist. The two paradigms have philosophical, theoretical, and methodological underpinnings that are largely antithetical. The former follows a dualistic logic that sees subject and object as sharply distinct, while the latter is informed by a holistic worldview. The former uses modeling strategies and quantitative techniques, while the latter studies consumption in the field and employs the ethnographic method. The former examines consumption decisions as part of a process of rational deliberation, while the latter focuses on the significance of the consumption experience for the subjects involved. Being construed on assumptions about human behavior that are erroneous, the former is said to have poor practical relevance, whereas the right marketing insights can be reaped through the alternative, more realistic, view.

Similar narratives are not hard to find in marketing research. The field is punctuated by contributions that more or less inadvertently reinforce the dualistic opposition between rival, allegedly antithetic, research traditions: positivist-quantitative on the one side and interpretive-qualitative on the other (Simonson et al. 2001). This cleavage is perpetuated by institutional factors, namely, the internal organization of marketing departments and by current research practice, whereby work informed by positivist principles tends to be associated with the use of quantitative methods whereas work informed by the interpretive tradition routinely employs qualitative methods (Arnauld and Thompson 2005). The static image of two monolithic paradigms rivaling in the field is, however, misleading: the two paradigms are not coherent wholes, and did not always stand in sharp opposition to each other. In this commentary, I thus try to deflate the dualistic view by showing some fuzziness underneath. I will do so by telling a story in three steps.

1. *Ex uno plures*

   In the 1980s, a new way of studying consumption behavior began in consumer research. Initially, it represented an extension of previous work. Later on, it crystallized in a plurality of views in opposition to the presumably dominant one.
2. *Ex pluribus unum*

   The plurality of views eventually gathered under the same theoretical umbrella: in 2005, Consumer Culture Theory (CCT) was born. While the constitution of a compact front was welcome, its distance from the dominant paradigm was also toned down.
3. *Plurality within unity*

   Even when unity is achieved in the field, plurality persists in its own special way. While CCT unites different approaches under the flag of practical relevance, each approach has its own distinctive way to attain it. *Pace* Vangsgaard, there is no unique set of right marketing insights.

This story in broad strokes tells two messages. First, the history of consumer research could be recounted as the alternation of moments of *continuity* to moments of *opposition* among approaches. And even when continuity prevails, plurality rather than dualism governs the field. I thus conclude that it is plausible to see the field as characterized by a permanent tension between unity and disunity, rather than by the static opposition between two opposing fronts.

1. Ex uno plures

Appealing to the ethnographic method and, more generally, to principles and practices that are philosophically alien to the Cartesian-positivist tradition might be unusual in business-oriented marketing research, as Vangsgaard remarks in Chapter 6.[2] It is, however, much more common in academic marketing research and particularly so in the sub-field of consumer behavior research. Consumer behavior research sprouted from academic marketing research in the 1960s and strived ever since for becoming an independent field of inquiry.[3] Originally, it aspired to scientify the study of consumption behavior and to liberate it from the practical orientation that used to characterize scholarly marketing research (Holbrook 1987). It is in this area of study that one can find the intellectual ancestors of ReD's approach. Since the 1980s, research on consumer behavior falling without the positivist paradigm has been steadily increasing. Twenty years later it came to represent about 20 percent of the articles published in the *Journal of Consumer Research* (Simonson et al. 2001).

ReD is thus the epigone of a scholarly tradition the roots of which can be traced back to a handful of contributions dating back to the early 1980s. The primary goal of these early works was broadening the scope of the field by including aspects belonging to the sphere of consumption that went so far neglected. On the one hand, scholars rejected the narrow focus on *purchasing* behavior that excluded relevant moments of the consumption experience. In particular, they advocated a shift of emphasis from the consumer understood as *buyer* to the consumer as *user* (Fennell 1985). On the other hand, they expanded the spectrum of objects of consumption under investigation by including intangible goods that were formerly excluded such as events, plays, services, art performance, entertainment, TV shows, and so on (Holbrook 1987). Focussing on goods that play mainly a hedonic function in the consumption experience, these scholars highlighted the multisensorial, imaginary, and emotive dimensions of product usage (Hirschman and Holbrook 1982).

These changes were not understood as a rupture with the past but as an "evolutionary progression" over traditional theories of consumption, chiefly represented by the information processing view (Hirschman and Holbrook 1982: 93). The hedonic perspective did not represent a replacement of these theories but their extension and enhancement. At this stage, the emphasis was thus placed more on the *continuity* between views rather than on opposition. While introducing novel variables to capture the subjective, subconscious, and emotive aspects of consumption, the hedonic view adopted a model where stimuli and output were mediated by a response system, as much as the information-processing view used to (Holbrook and Hirschman 1982). Similarly, while advocating openness to different data sources such as introspection data, Holbrook and Hirschman defended continuity also in methods. For instance, they claimed that the multivariate methods traditionally employed by the information-processing view will be even more fruitful for the study of hedonic consumption (Holbrook and Hirschman 1982: 134).

Despite this initial apperception, this strand of research manifested profoundly innovative, and somehow disruptive, potential already at this stage. Expanding the range of phenomena under investigation had in fact far-reaching implications at the theoretical, methodological, and also philosophical level. In order to examine disregarded aspects of the consumption experience, scholars had to adopt different theoretical frameworks, often borrowed from other disciplines. The work by Sidney Levy, which proved extremely influential in the field, highlights the symbolic and mythical aspects of consumption behavior under the influence of structural anthropologist Claude Lévi-Strauss (Levy 1981). Following a similar path, Dennis Rook studied the ritual dimension of consumption behavior inspired by the analysis of psychologist Erik Erikson, among others. Rook examines ordinary behavior such as grooming as a profane ritual where objects of consumption become artefacts involved in ritual practice, whereby they acquire symbolic, emotional, and psychological value (Rook 1985). These theoretical shifts demanded parallel methodological changes: "To study consumers' ritual behaviors challenge the research community to try more holistic, qualitative approaches. By its very nature ritual behavior invites field observation" (Rook 1985: 262).

Radical methodological changes were accomplished by what is probably the most innovative research project at this stage. The Consumer Behaviour Odyssey was launched by Russell Belk in 1985. It involved a small group of researchers traveling coast-to-coast the United States to document qualitatively various buyer and consumer behaviors via video-taped interviews, still photos, field notes, audio tapes, and impressionistic journals.[4] This naturalistic unstructured and open-ended inquiry bore important fruits. Among these is a stream of research papers on sacralization and desacralization in consumption behavior (Belk, Wallendorf, and Sherry 1989). This work developed insights present in Rook and Levi's work on the ritualistic and mythical aspects of purchase and consumption. It studied the shifting boundaries between sacred and profane where rituals are seen as processes by means of which ordinary objects of consumption are sacralized. Backed up by social and psychological literature, it extensively relied on the Odyssey's vast production of data by means of visual representation, in-depth interview, and participant observation.

This strand of research culminated in a sort of "paradigmatic upheaval" (Belk 2014) the moment it became philosophically sophisticated and expressed the ambition of constituting not merely an extension of the existing view but an alternative to it. When the first paradigm battles burst, however, the parties involved were many, not only two. The very moment it became a self-conscious alternative to the prevailing positivist approach, in fact, this strand of works crystallized in a variety of views. Thus were born to consumer research humanistic inquiry (Hirschman 1986), existential-phenomenology (Thompson, Locander, and Pollio 1989), naturalistic inquiry (Belk, Wallendorf, and Sherry 1989), semiotics (Mick 1986), critical relativism (Anderson 1986, 1989), and many others. These views were united by the common opposition to the positivist paradigm (Hunt 1991). At the same time, however, they were separated by distinctive theoretical and epistemic commitments and by the conviction of constituting autonomous and legitimate alternatives to that paradigm. Thus, disunity prevailed and subdued the unity which characterized the field till a decade before.

2. Ex pluribus unum

The disunity that characterized the field in the late 1980s in the form of entrenched theoretical-philosophical views fighting for prominence also turned out to be transitory. Influential scholars who attended the paradigm battles started adopting a more conciliatory tone and pointing a way out of the heated opposition. In his presidential address to the Association of Consumer Research in 1989, Richard Lutz claimed that the field was finding itself at a perilous point and had to make a choice between "complete schism and re-integration into some sort of pluralist paradigm," the former of which would be in his view "disastrous" (Lutz 1989). Meanwhile, prominent scholars in the positivist camp also tried to diffuse the tension and work for reconciliation between the parties involved. Shelby Hunt, for example, did so by systematically revealing all the "misses" (misconceptions, misunderstandings, misrepresentations, and mischaracterizations of the opponents' positions) which constituted "a divisive wall" separating consumer researchers and which partly "stemmed from the fact that the debate had been historically ill informed" (Hunt 1991: 32). His goal was reconciliation by "punching a hole" exactly in that wall (Hunt 1991: 33).

The "watershed event" was the publication of an invited article by two associate editors of the *Journal of Consumer Research* (Belk 2014). In this article, Eric Arnould and Craig Thompson coined the brand-term Consumer Culture Theory (henceforth CCT) to refer to what they perceived as a family of views (Arnould and Thompson 2005). CCT in fact gathered under the same umbrella all those views that shared the theoretical orientation toward the study of cultural complexity and focussed on the experiential, social, and cultural dimensions of consumption (Arnould and Thompson 2005: 868–9). In particular, it reconnected a multiplicity of scattered and disconnected works to a common research tradition encompassing a few related research programs: consumer identity projects, marketplace culture projects, studies of the socio-historic patterning of consumption, and studies of marketplace ideologies and consumers' interpretation strategies (Arnould and Thompson 2005: 871).

The constitution and institutionalization[5] of CCT thus helped overcome the fragmentation that kept separated those parties in the field who were fighting the positivist paradigm from the same front. Its founders' ambition was higher than that, though. On the one hand, they explicitly refused to unify the existing approaches into a single grand theory; even less they aimed at homogenizing them into a monolithic paradigm. CCT, said Arnould and Thompson, is an "interdisciplinary research tradition [which] represents a plurality of distinct theoretical approaches and research goals" (2005: 868–9). On the other hand, they advanced a new vision of the field: consumer research "can generate and sustain multiple theoretical conversations, each speaking to distinctive theoretical questions … Furthermore, the presence of different conversations does not preclude cross-paradigmatic engagement and enrichment" (2005: 876). Arnould and Thompson were thus pursuing a peculiar form of unity in the field of consumer research where a plurality of views could peacefully and fruitfully coexist.

Coexistence was possible because the difference between CCT and the positivist paradigm had been greatly exaggerated. The persistence of a few enduring myths perpetuated this state of affairs. First, CCT had been wrongly construed as studying specific contexts as an end in itself. Being not unlike the positivist paradigm in its theoretical aspiration, CCT studies *in context,* and does so with the ambition of formulating new constructs, generating theoretical insights and expanding existing theoretical frameworks (2005: 869). Second, it is commonly thought that the primary difference between CCT and other research traditions is methodological. Even though CCT has manifested a predilection for a qualitative mode of inquiry, this is a consequence of the aims that CCT tries to achieve, that is, studying the experiential and sociocultural dimension of consumption. However, CCT "neither necessitates fidelity to any one methodological orientation nor does it canonize a qualitative-quantitative divide" (2005: 870).

Finally, the third myth is the lack of practical relevance attributed to this research tradition. Initially, when the problem was demarcating boundaries, scholars found the hallmark of consumer research, *as distinct* from marketing research, in the absence of the preoccupation with practical impact. Consumer research, Holbrook and other influential names in the field maintained, focuses on consumption "independent of any relevance that subject might carry for marketing managers or, indeed, for any other external interests" (Holbrook 1987: 130). Be that as it may, as a matter of fact, the issues addressed by CCT happened to have vast influence on social, scientific, managerial, and public policy constituencies. Furthermore, methods that are routinely employed by CCT researchers, such as ethnographic inquiry, have become commonplace in applied marketing research (Arnould and Thompson 2005: 870). Moreover, throughout the 1990s, several contributors to the field started highlighting the distinctive marketing insights that could be gained through the various approaches to consumption research.

3. Plurality within Unity

In consumer research, the thrust for unification coexists with plurality as a persistent feature of the field. The type of plurality relevant here pertains to the different marketing insights that can be reaped through the variety of available approaches. In particular, CCT, the research tradition to which ReD's approach in fact belongs, is not monolithic when it comes to extracting lessons that are managerially relevant. Vangsgaard's chapter, instead, leaves us with the impression of a strong dualism also in this respect. In this section, I further deflate the opposition between rival paradigms by showing the underlying fuzziness. I will do so by citing instances of the practice of reaping marketing insights in consumer research. These examples will illustrate two points. First, the ethnographic method traditionally appointed as *the* method of CCT is sufficiently malleable to be used in a way that is affine to the positivist view. Thus, the ethnographic method does not require the philosophical assumptions adopted by ReD researchers to be practically relevant. Second, the interpretive tradition embraces a plurality of strategies sufficiently different to be able to garner distinct marketing insights. In what follows, I will offer an overview of this type of plurality.

Russell Belk (2013) discusses the case of Gilette Fusion ProGlide razor. The razor was a big success in the US market where it enjoyed a dominant 80 percent share, sold well among middle-class Indian men (about 50 percent) but couldn't reach poor urban and rural Indian men. P&G thus developed a less expensive razor, which tested positively among Indian students at MIT but turned out to be a failure when introduced to the general Indian market. P&G thus sent a troupe of ethnographers and designers to India. They did in-home observations, depth interviews, shop-alongs,[6] and test shaves (Belk 2013: 6). They found out that poor Indian men lacked running water and used to shave with a bowl of water, holding a small mirror, in poor light, with a 100-year-old technology of double-edged razor blade. In these circumstances, they did not shave every day and when they did the outcome was many nicks and cuts. P&G designers thus developed a plastic razor with a large comb that prevents cuts and allows easy cleaning (2013: 6).

Wallendorf and Arnould (1991) study the role of consumption during Thanksgiving Day celebrations. They use ethnography to generate five datasets, among which are a series of deep interviews, reports from native and nonnative participant observation exercises, and a collection of photographs and video tapes. The authors understand Thanksgiving Day as a collective ritual that celebrates material plenty. Central to it is the ideal of the household as a self-sufficient unit that meets amply its basic needs through its productive ability. The ritual is enacted in a way that embodies the ideal of *home-madeness* in the context of contemporary consumer culture, where households rely on mass-produced, commercially processed and delivered food products. That is, participants engage in practices oriented to *sacralize* branded products, such as consuming quintessential food, discarding packaging material and price tags, adding special ingredients to branded product, and serving the meal on special dishes (Wallendorf and Arnould 1991: 27–8). The ensuing marketing strategies aim at reinforcing the idea of home-madeness and responding to the desire for decommodification that permeates the feast (Arnould and Wallendorf 1994: 500).

Thompson (1996, 1997) studies consumption experiences of professional working women of the baby boom generation. He conducts phenomenological interviews, which employ few preplanned descriptive questions, with working women with children. The participants interpret their consumption experiences through a narrative of self-identity centered on the ideal of leading a *balanced* life, which is highlighted by a constellation of binary themes, such as caring for others versus being cared for, doing for others versus doing for oneself, being together versus being apart, being helped versus being nagged (1997: 446). The consumption experience can further (or hamper) the fulfilment of this ideal by helping women find the right compromise between these binary contrasts. Marketing actions should thus respond to this ideal by products and services that reduce daily stress of the participants' juggling life style, increase their sense of control, alleviate their concern about the negative effects of their life style on their children, and enable them to experience greater personal satisfaction from their effort to lead balanced lives (Thompson 1997: 450).

These three vignettes instantiate very different strategies for gaining marketing insights. An exhaustive analysis of the differences would require more space than I have. Since all strategies make use of in-depth interviews, I will limit myself to pointing out some differences in the way in which these interviews are used. In the first case, what matters about what participants say of their consumption experience is its veracity. In this case, researchers are ultimately interested in establishing variation in the circumstances that affect shaving behavior. The texts of in-depth interviews are treated as evidence of these circumstances. Hence, they are valued for their accuracy and assessed by way of triangulation with the results obtained through in-home observation, shop-alongs, and test shaves. Since it aims at establishing the conditions that are causally relevant to shaving behavior, the ethnographic method is here employed in a way that resonates well with positivist principles and goals.

In the second case, the researcher engages in an act of interpretation that consists in analyzing "disjunctures" in the data (Arnould and Wallendorf 1994). Disjunctures are a discrepancy between what the researcher records through participant observation and the texts of in-depth interviews. Here, the purpose is not validation but eliciting the meaning of the disjuncture. One of the hallmarks of disjunctures is glosses.[7] When describing Thanksgiving Day, participants frequently refer to food dishes that are "made from scratch" while what they actually do is removing cranberries from cans, disposing the turkey wrapping, or scraping off price tags and labels from wine bottles. What matters is not that reports are literally false, but the ideal that is disclosed by drawing together all the perspectives emerging from the various data sources, namely *home-madeness*. By analyzing disjunctures, ethnography elicits the cultural meaning of this consumption ritual and thereby informs marketing insights.

In the third case, in-depth interviews are interpreted through the lenses of narratological models. Participants are regarded as self-narrators, who, through consumption stories, situate particular consumption events within a broader narrative of self-identity with the help of historically available cultural myths and beliefs (Thompson 1997: 440). From a narratological perspective, these texts contain structural elements, the analysis of which helps the researcher discover patterns of meanings. One of these elements is the symbolic parallels that consumers establish between events otherwise unrelated. For example, one participant associates cooking dinner and being heavily immersed in the client-centered dimension of her job (1997: 445). Both experiences are seen as instances of "doing for others" rather than "doing for oneself," and as such require an act of balancing. In this case, the narratological framework sheds light on the personal, rather than cultural, significance that consumption experiences have for constructing consumers' sense of identity. The patterns of meaning that thus emerge eventually inform marketing insights.

***

The interesting approach to marketing research described by Vangsgaard offered the occasion for a tour through the field of consumer research. Vangsgaard characterizes the field as split between two rival approaches, the Cartesian-quantitativist and the Heideggerian-qualitativist, which she portrays as coherent monolithic paradigms. The story I tell challenges this dualistic view. From a historical perspective, the field has gone through moments where there is a tension toward unity and moments where, instead, disunity prevails. From an analytic perspective, plurality characterizes the field even when the thrust for unification becomes widespread. I focus here on plurality in the strategies to generate marketing insights. This analysis challenges once again the idea of monolithic paradigms. Ethnography, which is typically described as *the* method of the interpretive paradigm, is also employed successfully in a way coherent with the positivist approach. Furthermore, a variety of interpretive strategies coexist within the CCT tradition that elicit distinctive, and distinct, marketing insights.

Notes

1 For a vivid description of ReD Associates' research style, see Graeme Wood "Anthropology Inc.", *The Atlantic*, March 2013.
2 Examples of business-oriented marketing research of this kind are not that hard to find anyway. See, for example, the research described in Cayla, Beers, and Arnould, *MIT Sloan Management Review* (2014).
3 Malecka and Nagatsu (2017) and Maciniss and Folke (2010) argue that consumer behavior research still is a subdiscipline of marketing.
4 For an early report of the project, see Kassarjian, 1987. "How We Spent Our Summer Vacation."
5 The institutionalization of CCT was accomplished by the initiation of a series of conferences, the Consumer Culture Theory Conference series, the Consumer Culture Theory Consortium, the publication of conference proceedings, and other similar events (see Belk 2014).
6 Shop-along is a form of market research where the interviewer accompanies consumers while they browse and shop for items, asking questions as the experience moves along (see www.driveresearch.com).
7 Glosses are "informants' metaphors for depicting events or descriptions of actions entangled with their perspective of what the events mean" (Arnould and Wallendorf 1994: 491).

References

Anderson, P. 1896. "On Method in Consumer Research: A Critical Relativist Perspective." *Journal of Consumer Research* 13: 155–73.

Anderson, P. 1989. "On Relativism and Interpretivism—with a Prolegomenon to the 'Why Question.'" In *Interpretive Consumer Research*, ed. E. Hirschman, 10–23. Provo, UT: Association for Consumer Research.

Arnould, E., and T. Craig. 2005. "Consumer Culture Theory (CCT). Twenty Years of Research." *Journal of Consumer Research* 31: 868–82.

Arnould, E. and M. Wallendorf. 1994. "Market-oriented Ethnography: Interpretation Building and Marketing Strategy Formulation." *Journal of Marketing Research* 31: 484–504.

Belk, R. W. 2013. "Qualitative versus Quantitative Research in Marketing." *Revista de Negocios* 18: 5–9.

Belk, R. W., M. Wallendorf, and J. F. Sherry, Jr. 1989. "The Sacred and Profane in Consumer Behaviour. Theodicy on the Odyssey." *Journal of Consumer Research* 16: 1–38.

Belk, R. W., and L. M. Casotti. 2014. "Ethnographic Research in Marketing: Past, Present, and Possible Futures." *Brazilian Journal of Marketing* 13: 1–17.

Cayla, J., R. Beers, and E. Arnould. 2014. "Stories That Deliver Business Insights." *MIT Sloan Management Review* 55: 54–62.

Fennell, G. 1985. "Things of Heaven and Earth: Phenomenology, Marketing, and Consumer Research." *ACR North American Advances* 12: 544–50.

Hirschman, E. 1986. "Humanistic Inquiry in Marketing Research: Philosophy, Methods, and Criteria." *Journal of Marketing Research* 23: 237–49.

Hirschman, E., and M. Holbrook. 1982. "Hedonic Consumption: Emerging Concepts, Methods, and Propositions." *Journal of Marketing* 46: 92–101.
Holbrook, M., and E. Hirschman. 1982. "The Experiential Aspects of Consumption: Consumer Fantasies, Feelings, and Fun." *Journal of Consumer Research* 9: 132–40.
Holbrook, M. 1987. "What Is Consumer Research?" *The Journal of Consumer Research* 14: 128–32.
Hunt, S. 1991. "Positivism and Paradigm Dominance in Consumer Research: Toward Critical Pluralism and Rapprochement." *Journal of Consumer Research* 18: 32–44.
Kassarjian, H. 1986. "How We Spent Our Summer Vacation: A Preliminary Report on the 1986 Consumer Behavior Odyssey." *Advances in Consumer Research* 14: 376–7.
Levy, S. 1981. "Interpreting Consumer Mythology: A Structural Approach to Consumer Behaviour." *Journal of Marketing* 45: 49–61.
Lutz, R. 1989. "Presidential Address: Positivism, Naturalism, and Pluralism in Consumer Research. Paradigms in Paradise." *Association for Consumer Research.* Available at http://www.acrwebsite.org/search/view-conference-proceedings.aspx?Id=6871.
Macinnis, D., and V. Folkes. 2010. "The Disciplinary Status of Consumer Behavior: A Sociology of Science Perspective on Key Controversies." *Journal of Consumer Research* 36: 899–914.
Malecka, M., and M. Nagatsu. 2018. "How Behavioural Research Has Informed Consumer Law: The Many Faces of Behavioural Research." In *Research Handbook on Methods in Consumer Law*, ed. K. Purnhagen, A. Sibony, and H. Micklitz. London: Edward Elgar.
Mick, D. 1986. "Consumer Research and Semiotics: Exploring the Morphology of Signs, Symbols, and Significance." *Journal of Consumer Research* 13: 196–213.
Rook, D. 1985. "The Ritual Dimension of Consumer Behavior." *Journal of Consumer Research* 12: 251–64.
Simonson, I., Z. Carmon, R. Dhar, A. Drolet, and S. M. Nowlis. 2001. "Consumer Research: In Search of Identity." *Annual Review of Psychology* 52: 249–75.
Thompson, C. 1996. "Caring Consumers: Gendered Consumption Meanings and the Juggling Lifestyle." *Journal of Consumer Research* 22: 388–407.
Thompson, C. 1997. "Interpreting Consumers: A Hermeneutical Framework for Deriving Marketing Insights from the Texts of Consumers' Consumption Stories." *Journal of Marketing Research* 34: 438–55.
Thompson, C. J., W. B. Locander, and H. R. Pollio. 1989. "Putting Consumer Experience Back into Consumer Research: The Philosophy and Method of Existential-Phenomenology." *Journal of Consumer Research* 16: 133–46.
Wallendorf, M., and E. Arnould. 1991. " 'We Gather Together': Consumption Rituals of Thanksgiving Day." *Journal of Consumer Research* 18: 13–31.
Wood, G. 2013. "Anthropology Inc." *The Atlantic*, March 2013.

7

The Fish Tank Complex of Social Modeling

On Space and Time in Understanding Collective Dynamics

Tommaso Venturini

7.1 A Change of Speed

In the BBC documentary *The Blue Planet*, the British naturalist David Attenborough narrates marine life commenting on the "time-lapsed" images of a tropical reef. The images are beautiful and surprising. Played at accelerated speed, the sequences reveal corals for what they are: not minerals or plants, but animals who grow, crawl, hunt, and fight to survive. In sibling documentary, *The Frozen Planet*, Attenborough uses the same acceleration to show a crowd of starfish swarming over a seal corpse. In both cases, the effect is startling: the change of tempo shatters the relation between the action and its scenery. While the expected actors disappeared (as the fishes of the reef) or froze to death (as the seal), the theater wings suddenly come alive and take the center of the stage.

A similar effect, I hold, can be experienced in social phenomena by abandoning the spatial metaphors we traditionally use to understand them. Considering our collective existence, we often picture ourselves as *coming from* different cultural milieus, *crossing* social spheres, *entering or leaving* institutions, *following* norms and conventions. In all these expressions, individual movements are portrayed as occurring *on the background* of stable collective structures. Social theory has much encouraged such spatial thinking, separating individuals from aggregates and placing the firsts *inside* the seconds. I refer here to the classic *micro-macro* distinction, which not only distinguish actors from structures but also picture them as nested levels, with actors moving through structures as trains traveling through railways. To be sure, many theories admit relations between the two levels: agents are bound by structures, but also feed back into them; systems emerge from actions, but also inform them. Yet, relation does not question separation, and our imagination remains trapped in a sort of "fish tank complex"—a conceptual framing where social actors move against a static background, like fishes in a plastic aquarium.

The micro-macro separation, of course, has its use. In collective life, not everything changes at the same time and it may be convenient to take some things as settled, in order to highlight faster transformations. This approach is common in the formal modeling of collective phenomena. As I will try to show, most models of social life tend to rely on a strict separation between a local level, where exchanges take place, and a global level where results are observed. I call this approach "spatial" not because it refers to a geographical topography (though many models actually do), but because it is based on a "topological" distinction between levels. Convenient as it is, this simplification has several disadvantages that I will try to show. To overcome some of them, this chapter will propose an alternative approach based on a temporal conception of collective phenomena and on the technique of versioning.

This temporal approach has a key advantage—it remains open to graduation and change of speed. Social entities are not separated in actors and structures forcing their interaction to "jump" from one level to the other. Social change, on the contrary, can slow down or speed up and what seemed stable and structuring can suddenly transmute, as corals bleaching at the speed of ocean acidification.

7.2 The Spatial Framing of Collective Modeling

A good way to appreciate the inherent *spatiality* of our sociological imagination is to consider the ways in which collective dynamics are implemented in computer models. Modeling is instructive because the formalization of computer code forces scholars to be explicit about their theoretical premises and conceptual metaphors. The examples of such formalizations are not in shortage. In the last decade, a variety of models derived from biology, chemistry, and physics have been applied to social dynamics in the hope to harness their complexity (Gilbert and Conte 1995; Castellano et al. 2009; Vespignani 2011; Naldi, Pareschi, and Toscani 2010; and most articles in the *Journal of Artificial Societies and Social Simulations*).

These efforts have produced many interesting results, but (so far) no breakthrough. This modest yield, I believe, depends in part on the constraints that a spatial framing has imposed on collective modeling. Though the alleged aim of most models is to reproduce (and sometimes to predict) the *dynamics* of collective phenomena, close inspection reveals that temporal features are rarely salient in models. Most often, change is limited to local aspects of a globally static architecture. The critique addressed by Mustafa Emirbayer to social network analysis can be extended to most social models (cf. also Abbot 2001):

> Paradoxically (for a mode of study so intently focused upon processuality), relational sociology has the greatest difficulty in analyzing, not the structural features of static networks, whether these be cultural, social structural, or social psychological, but rather, the dynamic processes that transform those matrices of transactions in some fashion. Even studies of "processes-in-relations," in other words, too often privilege spatiality (or topological location) over temporality and narrative unfolding. (Emirbayer 1997: 305)

A discussion of the three most common modeling approaches will elucidate this point. For the sake of space, this review will be highly schematic. While interesting experiments that exceed the three approaches below exist (I will discuss one at the end of this chapter), they remain in the minority.

1. *Variation.* The first way of handling change is derived from mathematical analysis. In such approach, elements are fixed from the beginning and their relations are defined by a predetermined set of equations, which are computed until a stable equilibrium (or a repeating pattern) is reached. Nothing new can be created in the model, and its components cannot acquire novel properties or alter their associations. Most models of equilibria in economic (Nash 1951; Tobin 1969) and ecological (e.g., the "Lotka–Volterra equations" as in Hofbauer and Sigmund 1988) systems fall within this tradition. As the model consists in the parallel computation of equations, the only type of changes admitted is the increase or decrease of quantities. Though these models can be extremely sophisticated, the nature of change is generally determined from the beginning and the only surprise can come from the different equilibria produced by the interaction among the equations.
2. *Circulation.* The second modeling approach focuses on the flow of entities through a network connections (generally a grid). Such systems admit the existence of mobile components that move according to the system topology, the state of its connections, and the position of other components. Epidemics (Keeling and Eames 2005) and routing (Cordeau, Toth, and Vigo 1998) problems are generally modeled through this approach. Though these models allow some dynamism, both the configuration of the network and the nature of the movable items are essentially static. The vectors of the circulating entities can change, but the shape of the grid and the rules of movement are fixed from the beginning.
3. *Interaction.* A more sophisticated approach is implemented in agent-based models (Epstein 2006). In such models, change does not derive from general equations or from the overall configuration of the system, but from a multitude of local exchanges among myriad calculating agents. As the mobiles of the previous approach, the agents of these models move through the system, but in addition they also encounter and interact with each other. Faithful to the emergent nature of collective transformations, the evolution of these models cannot be analytically computed. The dynamism of these systems derives, however, from a restricted and constant set of interaction rules. The pride of these models is indeed to generate the maximum of global variability from the minimum of local instructions. Classic examples of such models are the analysis of urban segregation of Thomas Schelling (1971) or the evolution of cooperation by Robert Axelrod (1984). Connecting movement and interaction recursively, agent-based models capture some elements collective change. Transformation, however, does not concern the nature of the elements or the architecture of the system, which are never affected by the interactions they contain.

Despite their differences, all above approaches share the same *spatial framing of temporal phenomena* and constrain collective dynamics in a topological arrangement where interaction occurs locally and resulting patterns are consistently global. In contrast to this framing, this chapter proposes to shift the focus from the distinction between "local exchanges and global patterns" to the interaction between "things that change quickly and things that change slowly." Hopefully, this will help us to see social structures for what they are: not a static background, but a specific type of actor whose change is, most of the time, particularly slow.

7.3 The Shortcomings of the Micro-Macro Divide

The spatial framing encountered in collective modeling is largely inspired to the classic framing of social theory, where it is customary to assume a fundamental partition between a "microlevel" of local and ephemeral exchanges and a "macrolevel" of far-reaching and long-standing aggregates. Expressed in terms of levels, this distinction stages the study of collective life through a spatial metaphor in which "macrobehaviors" are aggregations of "micromotives" (Schelling 1978). Far from being limited to human phenomena, this framing has been applied to all sorts of collective behaviors, from social animals (Moussaid et al. 2009) to biological organisms (Dawkins 1982); from mental processes (Minsky 1988) to artificial entities living in silico (Epstein and Axtell 1996).

Though it is reasonable (and analytically convenient) to assume that, in collective existence, not everything changes at the same time and that some elements can be taken as fixed to highlight faster transformation, the micro-macro framing comes with two major limitations.

1. *Conceptually*, the micro-macro divide ends up framing research as the quest for the pathway leading from one level to the other. Are macro-structure mere aggregates or sui generis phenomena (Durkheim 1897)? How do global properties emerge from local interactions (Boudon 1981)? Is it possible to reconcile the two levels by an encompassing theory (Bourdieu 1972; Giddens 1984; Archer 1995)? By presupposing the existence of two levels, this framing takes as solved the very question that it should open to investigation: how are stability and evolution obtained by slowing down or speeding up the stream of collective change (Callon and Latour 1981; Latour 2005)? How are institutions established by the repetition of interactions, and innovations produced by the propagation of variations? How does time matter in shaping social structures (Abbot 2001)?
2. *Empirically*, by constraining change to local circuits and stability to global structures, the micro-macro framing privileges phenomena that fit its assumptions and confines modeling to phenomena where change is clearly circumscribed. These phenomena include, for instance, variations of values in markets with preset rules (Neumann 1945); spread of diseases (Daley and Gani 1999); or species (Bak and Sneppen 1993) in stable habitats; flowing and queuing in fixed networks (Gawron 1998); circulation of memes through media (Leskovec, Backstrom, and Kleinberg 2009); and other dynamics of such kind (Macy and Willer 2002). Even worse, wary of blurring the micro-macro border, models often abstract

from actual processes and focus on artificial simulations where actors and structures can be separated by construction (Venturini, Jensen, and Latour 2015). A particularly unfortunate choice in a time in which the traceability of digital media is increasing the availability of social data (Lazer et al. 2009; Rogers 2013).

These conceptual and empirical limitations illustrate what I call the "fish tank complex of collective modeling"—an analytical setting where social actors perform against a fixed background, like fishes swimming through a plastic aquarium (as opposed to actual sea reefs that evolve with the colonies they host). This "fish tank complex" may be adapted to study the situations in which collective institutions are relatively stable and actors move through them without affecting them substantially. Yet, it prevents modeling from addressing the situations of structural change, the moments where old institutions dissolve and new arrangements crystallize. The moments in which a new species transforms an ecological environment (Levins 1968; Gordon 2011); an innovation "creatively destroys" a market (Schumpeter 1976); a compromise defuses a social crisis (Callon, Lascoumes, and Barthe 2009).

These moments of radical change are not necessarily more important than the stabler phases of collective existence, in which individual behaviors occur in a non-changing structure. Yet, their existence challenges the traditional separation between agents and structures, as in these situations individual and institutional change seem to synchronize on the same tempo. The investigation of these moments draws attention to the ways in which transformation slow down or speed up and has produced interesting studies (for instance, in the "new institutionalism" tradition—see, Powell and DiMaggio 1991; Alston, Eggertsson, and Thrainn 1996), which could provide inspiration for the computer modeling of social phenomena.

7.4 Versions

Searching for a *natively temporal* modeling of collective dynamics, I found an interesting (and unexpected) inspiration in the field of software development. I refer here to *version or revision control*. Versioning—the ensemble of conceptual and technical instruments developed to compare different editions of the same documents and to track their evolution—is one of the most important and overlooked information techniques of modern collective life.

Versioning has been around since early modernity. According to Elisabeth Eisenstein (1980) the idea of "versions" emerged with mechanical printing, when the possibility of reproduced exact copies made Western societies sensitive to the variances between copies of the same manuscript. Filing cabinets, carbon papers, and Xerox machines traced for decades the evolution of legal, administrative, and commercial documents, but it is with the advent of digital technologies that versioning entered its golden age. The association of versioning and digitization goes both ways. On the one hand, digitization facilitates the tracking of an increasing variety of inscriptions (see the brilliant work of Ben Fry on Darwin's Origin of Species—http://fathom.info/traces). On the other hand, version control constitutes one of the pillars of digital editing. In digital environments, it is so easy to duplicate and modify documents that keeping track of changes becomes vital.

This is especially true for software, a peculiar a type of document whose extreme formalization implies that even a single-character transformation can be of great consequences. It is therefore not surprising that the first advanced systems for revision control were introduced by and for software developers. The first of such systems was the SCCS (Source Code Control System) developed by Marc Rochkind (1975) at Bell's Laboratories in the early 1970s. Some ten years later, Walter Tichy (1982, 1985) introduced the Revision Control System (RCS) and the idea of storing modifications as "deltas" from a "master version" (thereby saving storage space).

From the onset, digital versioning has been a social technology, aiming to support collaboration among code writers. At first, editing conflicts were avoided by a simple system of locks, preventing developers from modifying a file if someone else was already working on it. In the late 1980s, however, a more sophisticated approach was introduced through the Concurrent Version System (CVS) developed by Dick Grune and Brian Berliner (1990). CVS implemented a server-client system with a "central repository," containing the "root version" of documents, and personal workspaces, where developers could create "local branches." This allowed developers to work simultaneously, but required them to "commit" their changes by merging them to the master version on the server. Various technical problems connected to CVS (particularly connected to file naming and hierarchy), however, discouraged developers from using branching functionalities and locking was still largely used.

To address such problems various open-source and commercial systems were introduced (ClearCase, Perforce, Subversion, to name a few), but the real step forward came in 2005 with the release of Mercurial (by Matt Mackall) and Git (by Linus Torvalds, the father of Linux). Despite their differences, both systems make branching and merging easier by scaling down the unit of change from documents to commits and "changesets." A few years later, in 2008, Github was launched offering free online storage for Git-versioned projects and, more importantly, social-networking functionalities. The success of Github was massive, reaching over a million repositories by 2010 and 10 million by 2013.

Despite its importance, version control has so far received little attention from academic research and has generally been discounted as ancillary to software development. I found most of the information discussed above in the introduction of technical books or in developers' blogs. The details in which I described the history and the technical features of revision control may seem amiss in a book on social sciences. I believe, however, that the idea of versioning is highly relevant to the study of social life and for at least two reasons.

The first reason is that this technique has long exceeded the domain of software development and has started to impact a variety of collective actions. The most famous example of this extension is Wikipedia. Everyone knows how, in less than a decade, Wikipedia has radically revolutionized the encyclopedic genre and grown to be one of the most influential sources of information about virtually anything. There is little doubt that Wikipedia's success is due to its collaborative nature, which is in turn made possible by the revision control engine integrated in its infrastructure (Niederer and

Dijck 2010; Venturini 2006). Yet, little has been written about such function and how it has shaped the interaction in Wikipedia (even though scholars have extensively exploited Wikipedia versioning data—for example, Kittur and Kraut 2008; Viégas, Wattenberg, and Kushal 2004; Borra et al. 2015). This absence is noted by one of the contributors to the of the "Version Control" article:

> Integrated revision control is a key feature of wiki software packages such as MediaWiki, TWiki, etc. Comparison of wiki software lists revision control for several wiki packages. It's hard to imagine a wiki functioning very well without revision control; for example, the ability to revert a page to a previous revision is critical for defending a public wiki against vandalism and spam, to allow legitimate users to correct their mistakes, and to allow groups of editors to track each other's edits. I certainly think this warrants a mention in Version control, but on Wikipedia I must cite our sources. It's not enough for something to be true or even obviously true; it must have been written about in some reliable source. I.e., *I would need to find some reputable news article or scholarly paper which discusses the role of revision control in wiki software*, so I could cite it here. I also need to avoid self-references.
>
> Teratornis 22:11, July 4, 2007
> (Wikipedia "Talk:Version_control,"
> en.wikipedia.org/wiki/Talk:Version_control,
> accessed on March 10, 2016, emphasis added)

Wikipedia is the clearest example, but the effects of the generalization of revision control are worth studying. What happens to team work when everyone can easily know who modify which part of a document and when? What happens to co-authoring when the modifications can be easily reviewed and accepted or discarded? What happens to personal communication when one can save drafts of e-mails or SMS? And, more generally, what happens to society when "Undo" (Ctrl+Z or Cmd+Z) becomes a widespread function of collective life?

The second reason why social scientists should be interested in versioning is that its techniques address the same conceptual problems that challenge the understanding of collective life. How do aggregates maintain their identity when all their components change? Not a single line of code can be preserved from the first to last version of a program exactly as all members of an institution can change throughout its existence. How can we handle modifications overlapping at different scales and in different moments? The edits made on the way functions are invoked can trickle up to each of the function exactly as a constitutional amendment can trickle up to a variety of regional laws. How is structural coherence sustained when thousands of modifications are negotiated independently? Software can be developed by hundreds of coders contributing simultaneously to different parts of the codebase in a similar way to which international treaties are negotiated on multiple diplomatic tables.

The examples above should make clear the interest of versioning is not limited to the particular techniques currently in use. Rather, my point is that the technical and conceptual tools developed for version control can provide a useful inspiration to envision a more temporal approach to social modeling—for example, encouraging us to imagine how an "institution" can be versioned by tracing the changes of its internal members and its external partners.

7.5 The Example of the Law Factory

To illustrate how the concepts and the techniques of versioning can be imported in the social sciences, I will relate the example of a research project I observed and facilitated at Sciences Po Paris. The project "The Law Factory—Do Parliament Members lay down the Law?" was born from a collaboration between a French NGO (regardscitoyens.org), the médialab (medialab.sciences-po.fr), and the Centre d'Études Européennes of Sciences Po. The question set on the table by Olivier Rozenberg (our expert on political sciences) was to assess how much French laws are transformed by parliamentary debates. This is a classic question for political scientists who have long discussed the weight of the legislative branch in the balance powers. In particular, we wanted to know whether laws were substantially amended by the *Sénat* and the *Assemblée* or whether the parliamentary debate had only a symbolic function. As the subtitle of the project reads "Do Parliament Members lay down the Law?"

As it concerns the process by which norms are created, such a question could hardly be fit in a binary framing which opposes institutions and individuals. Lawmaking is supposed to be the very moment in which the members of a society decide (through their elected representatives) the rules of the collective game—the moment in which the structures are as flexible as the alliances and oppositions shaping them. The impossibility to cut parliamentary processes into a micro and a macro level was not only a theoretical problem. In practice, it also meant that both qualitative methods (customarily used to describe micro-interactions) and quantitative ones (generally used to aggregate macro-patterns) were unfit for this project. Yes, we could have dissected the parliamentary journey of a few bills to qualitatively observe their transformation, but how to know if results could be generalized? And yes, we could have devised some statistical measures of parliamentary transformation and compute them for all French laws, but how to know whether those metrics were not too simplistic and capable to differentiate between substantial and cosmetic modifications?

Eventually, our NGO friends (all coming from a software development background) came up with a more original solution. They observed that if "code is law" (according to the famous aphorism by Lawrence Lessig 1999), then law can also be treated as code. Following this intuition, they extracted from the websites of the *Sénat* and the *Assemblée* all information on the amendments submitted on the 300 laws discussed between 2008 and 2014 by the French Parliament. After an extensive cleaning, this information was coded in through Git versioning format, formalizing amendments as "commits" to laws "master version."

The formalization offered by Git allowed to create an extremely flexible interface allowing scholars, journalists, and citizens to explore the lawmaking process of the French Parliament (lafabriquedelaloi.fr). The exploration starts from a "distant reading" (Moretti 2013) of six years of parliamentary activities comparing how long different laws were discussed in different branches and how many words were changed through these discussions (see Figure 7.1a). It then allows users to drill down disaggregating the data and identifying how each article of each law was modified at each passage (see Figure 7.1b); to consider all amendments proposed by different political groups (see Figure 7.1c); and, finally, to read the transcription of each word spoken by each parliament member on each specific article at each stage of the discussion (see Figure 7.1d).

The objective of such interface was to allow scholars to navigate from general hypotheses about the functioning of modern democracies (e.g., laws are created by the executive decisions more than by parliamentary discussions) to the details of debates' minutes. But "La Fabrique de la Loi" is not only a tool for legal studies, it is also a proof of concept of how the possibility to move *in a continuous way* from one-figure metrics to debate minutes (and back), may dissolve all micro-macro separations and promote instead the observation of temporal dynamics. The different layers of the interface are designed in order to encourage a seamless navigation, allowing users to identify stable trends and turning points. And, the heart of this feat, are versioning techniques (see Figure 7.2).

7.6 Everything Needs to Change, so Everything Can Stay the Same

In this chapter, I claimed that our understanding of social phenomena is often constrained by a spatial framing unfit to render temporal dynamics. In different modeling approaches we encountered the same binary separation between local exchanges and global patterns—a separation that closely mirrors the micro-macro divide typical of classic social theories. Exiling actors and aggregates on two separated levels, such framing conceals the moments of structural change where individual and collective actions interfere directly. To overcome such spatial framing, I proposed a description of collective dynamics based on the notion of "versioning." Instead of opposing local and global levels, this approach draws our attention to the speeding up and slowing down of social processes and gives us a technical tool to trace how old arrangements liquefy and new ones crystallize.

Moving modeling away from simulation and toward versioning has analytical consequence. Aki Lehtinen, who provided an extremely useful review of the first version of this chapter, harshly criticized my proposal for voiding the classic "explanatory" objective of modeling:

> The author should understand that it is not possible to study two different questions simultaneously with a model: how the environment changes, and how the agents' behavior changes as a result of changes in the environment. Perhaps reading Kenneth Shepsle's old paper on 'Institutional equilibrium and equilibrium institutions' might help here ... The point is this: if one sets both the structure and the agents simultaneously in motion, there is no way of knowing what causes what.

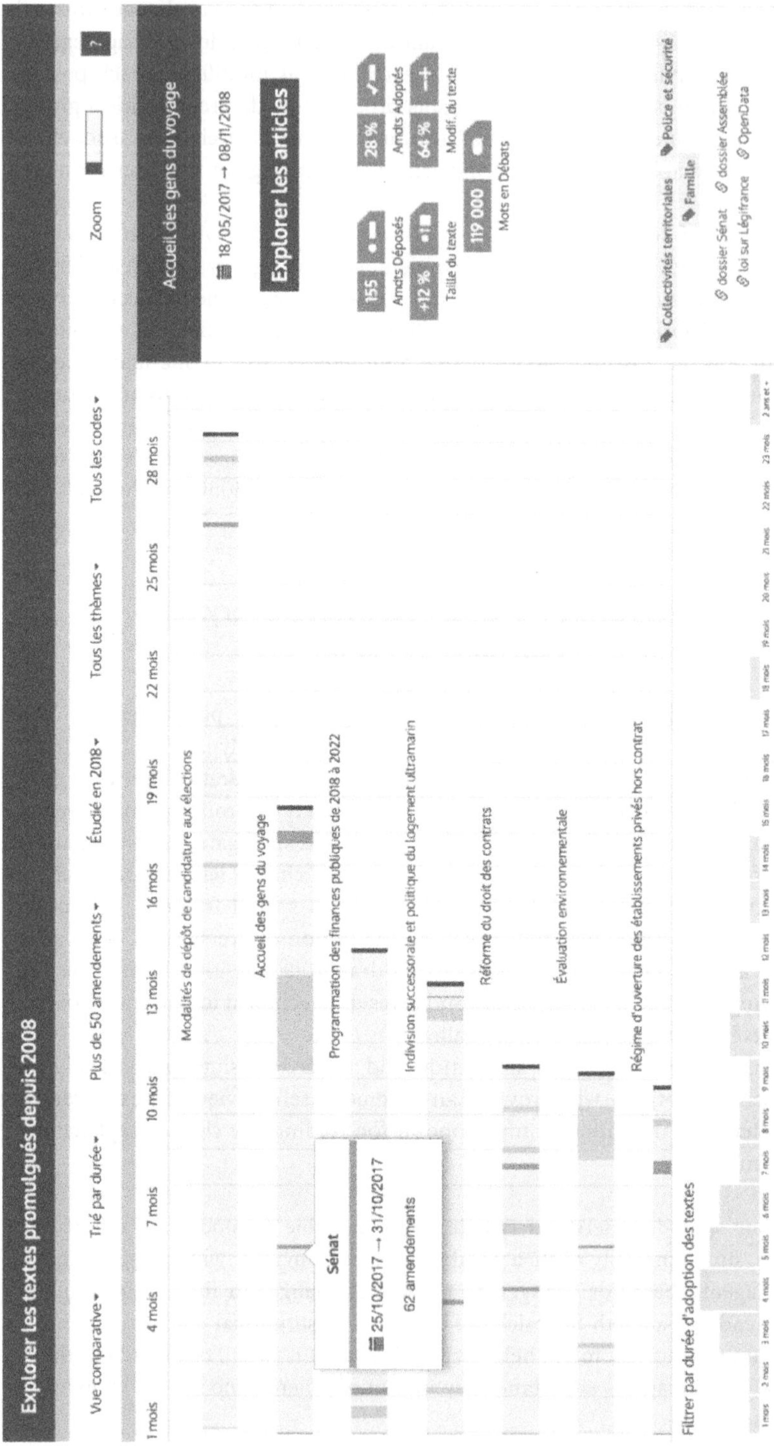

Figure 7.1 (a) Law-level interface.

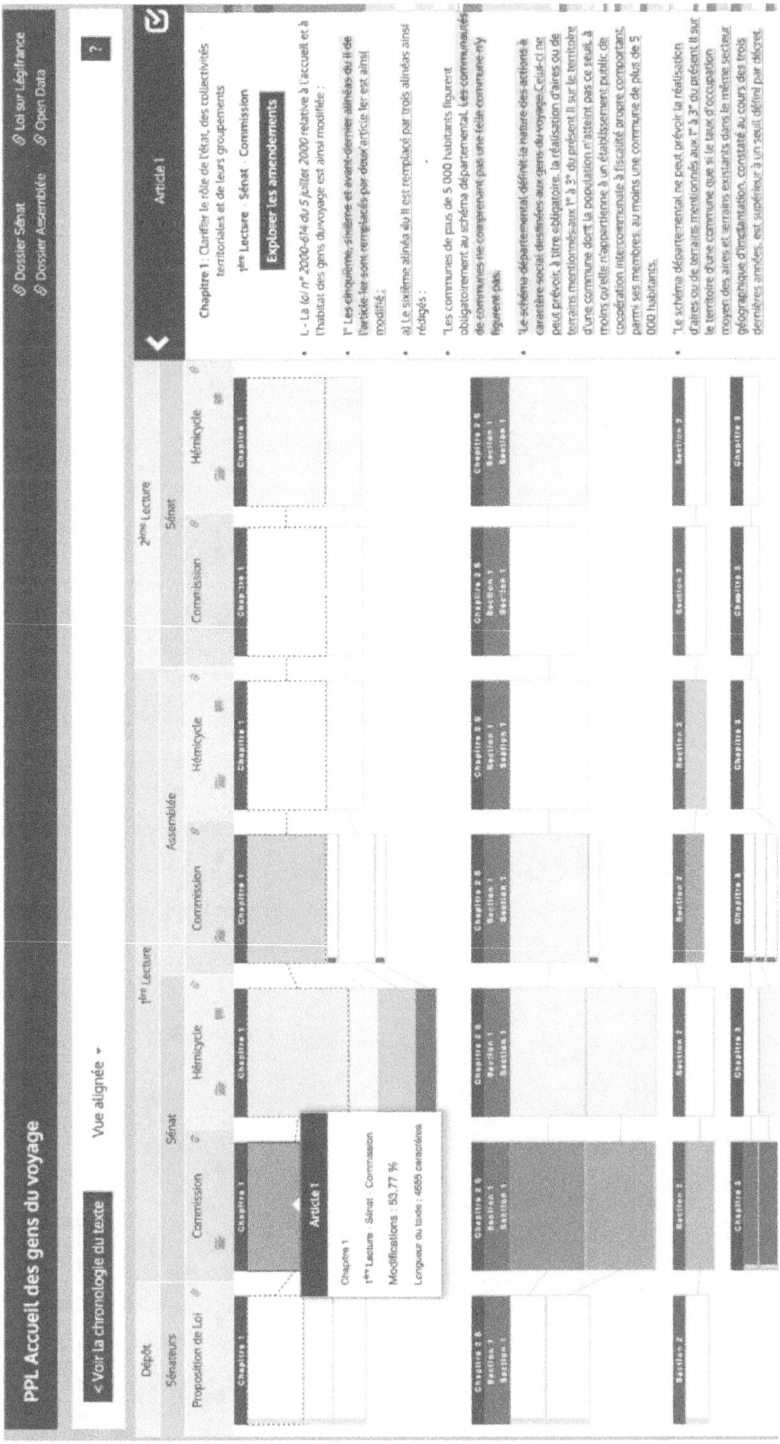

Figure 7.1 (b) Article-level interface.

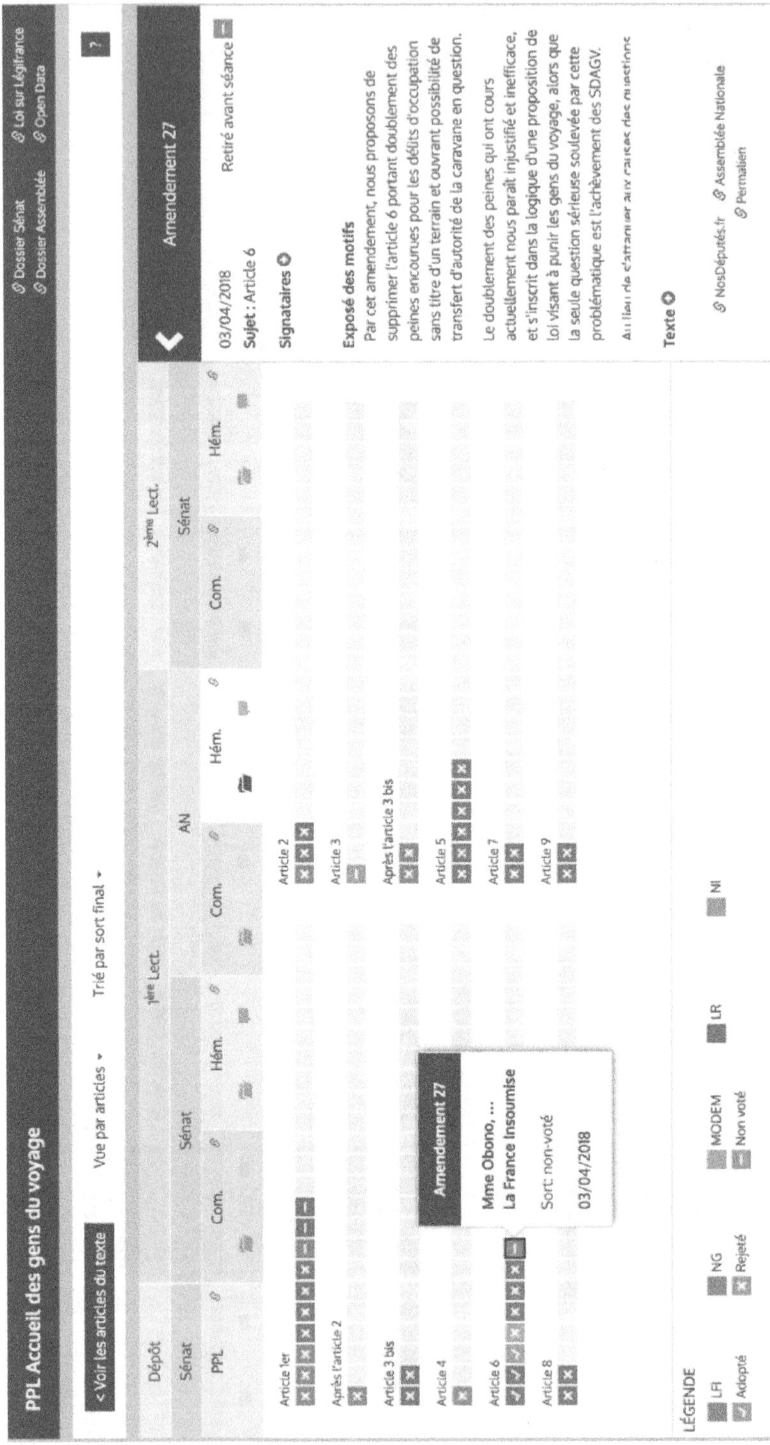

Figure 7.1 (c) Amendment-level interface.

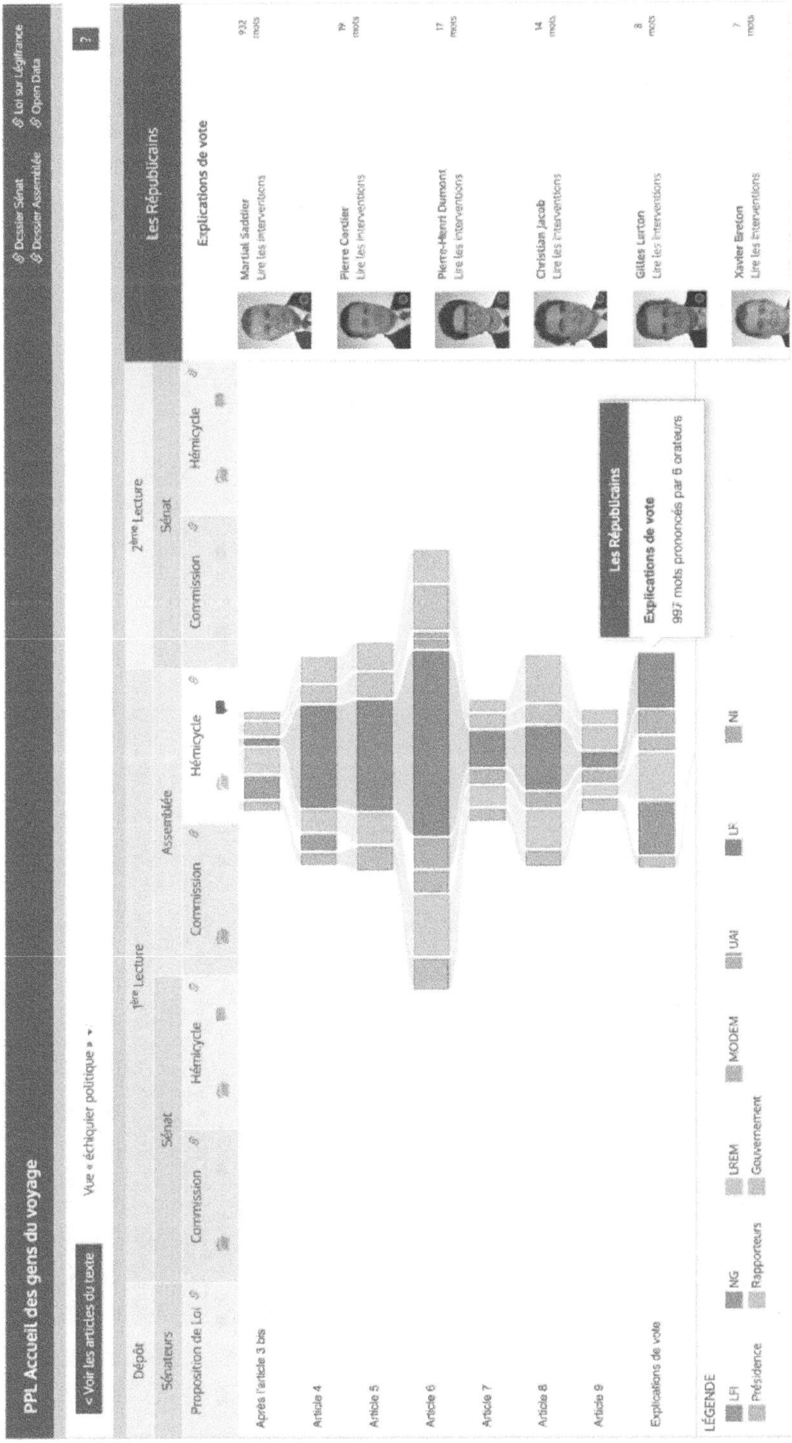

Figure 7.1 (d) Word-level interface.

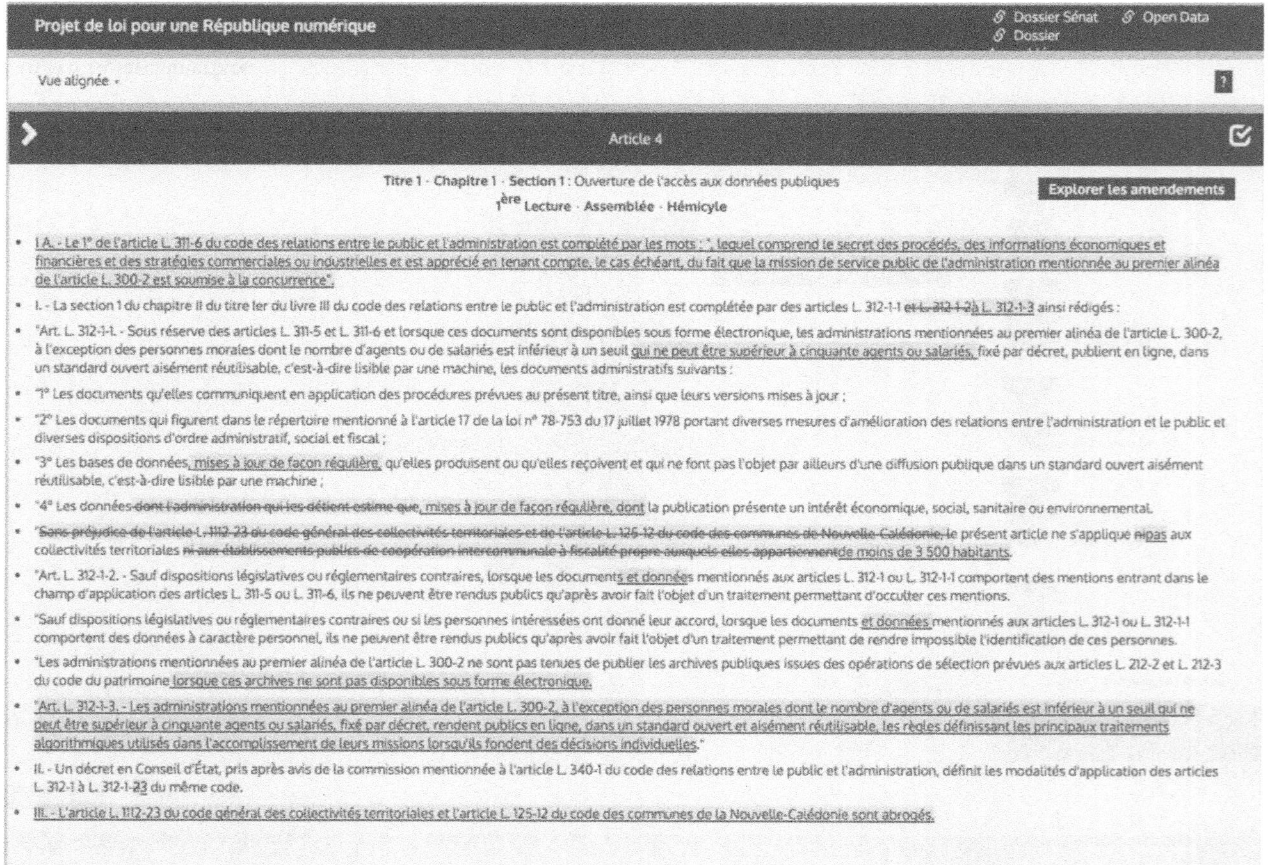

Figure 7.2 An example of visualization of law versioning.

This is a fair critique, but it sounds less fatal if one accepts that there might be more to modeling than deciding "what causes what." Causation, I believe, should not be investigated by simulation or analytical reflection, but by empirical enquiry. Kenneth Shepsle's researches on US parliamentary committees (1978) and institutional equilibria (1986) are perfect examples in this sense, for they suggest that institutional inertia is neither an ontological property of institutions nor a consequence of individual actions, but the result of a myriad of specific procedures for slowing down change (without making it entirely impossible). In a similar way, most collective dynamics are formed by the interaction of a multitude of factors acting in different but interfering ways. Reducing such richness to a micro-macro causation (actions cause structures or structures cause actions) would miss the interest of these delicate dynamics. See, for example, how Shepsle critiques "pure majority rule models" and argues instead for a detailed mapping of institutional practices:

> The PMR [pure majority rule] formulation, itself, is but a mere shadow of the complex procedures and structural arrangements of real decision-making bodies. Compare, for example, the preceding paragraph where PMR is described and the six-hundred-plus pages of Deschler's Procedures of the U.S. House of Representatives. (Shepsle 1986: 10)

A focus on change has also political consequences, which should be questioned. Such focus, it could be argued, may disguise the general stability in the distribution of resources (power and wealth in particular). Yes, collective existence can be constantly rebuilt by interactions operating at a variety of speeds and distances, but what is the advantage of such description if, ultimately, the same asymmetries are reproduced over and over again? Little good will come of the claim that everything can change *in theory*, if nothing changes *in practice*. At best, it will make sociological investigations uselessly complicated. At worst, it will blind individuals to the forces that exceed them and constrain their actions.

I cannot but disagree with this argument. The image of a structural apparatus (an overarching social system imposing its norms on individual actors) may encourage some to rebellion, but it also inflates the power of inertia. Let's go back to the example of collective modeling discussed above. Most formal models of social phenomena are borrowed from natural phenomena where global properties emerge from the blind interactions of local entities. It can be atoms generating material properties, molecules provoking chemical reactions, cells composing organs and organisms. All these cases have in common that the micro-entities have no clue of what is happening at the macro-level. They act (or rather "react") on the exclusive basis of the information in their immediate proximity. One of the most recurring metaphor is that of social insects: like ants moving sand grains and building their nest without the slightest idea of its global architecture—human beings would create their social structures without understanding them.

> Each ant lives in its own little world, responding to the other ants in its immediate environment and responding to signals of which it does not know the origin. Why

> the system works as it does, and as effectively as it does, is a dynamic problem of social and genetic evolution. How it works—how it is that the limited set of choices made by each ant within its own truncated little world translates, in the aggregate, into the rich and seemingly meaningful pattern of aggregate behavior by which we describe the society and the economy of the ant—is a question akin to the question of how it is that all the cows know how much milk is needed to make the butter and the cheese and the ice cream that people will buy at a price that covers the cost of maintaining and milking the cow and getting each little piece of butter wrapped in aluminum foil with the airline's own insignia printed on it. (Schelling 1978: 21, 22)

But human interactions are more sophisticated than those of ants (and ants' interactions, it seems, are more sophisticated than most entomological models, cf. Gordon 2015). Humans have developed all sorts of devices to extend the reach of their knowledge and action (Vinck 2012). Social organization is not the global effect of myriad local actions. It's a complex fabric whose threads extend at variable lengths; a story with a million themes, some of which star on a page, while others last through chapters and books; an ecosystem of species surviving or disappearing through evolution; a software with a million branching versions.

A temporal understanding of social phenomena focuses on stability as much as on transformation, but it draws attention to the fact that stability (exactly as change) is a consequence of collective action. The "constraints," that, according to Emile Durkheim (1966), constitute the essence of social facts are stable not because they exist in some higher layer, some macro-context shielded from micro-interactions. They are stable because the actions that uphold them last longer or are persistently repeated.

"Everything needs to change, so everything can stay the same," says Tancredi Falconieri, in *The Leopard* (*Il Gattopardo* 1958) of Giuseppe Tomasi di Lampedusa. With this line, the heir of Salina's princedom justifies his choice to join the cause of the Italian Unification even though this threatens the status of the Sicilian aristocracy to which he belongs. With ruthless political intelligence, the young Prince understands that his vantage is best preserved by aligning with the forces of change rather than resisting them. Power and privileges, he understands, are not structures sustained by an inherent logic, but arrangements that endure only when constantly updated. And the opposite, of course, is also true. Challenging traditional bias and asymmetries begins with understanding their history and dynamics "directing our attention not to the social but towards the processes by which an actor creates lasting asymmetries" (Callon and Latour 1981: 285, 286).

References

Abbott, Andrew. 2001. *Time Matters: On Theory and Method*. Chicago, IL: University of Chicago Press. Available at http://scholar.google.co.uk/scholar?hl=en&q=Time+Matters+author:abbot&btnG=Search&as_sdt=0,5&as_ylo=&as_vis=0#0.

Alston, Lee J., Thrainn Eggertsson, and C. North Douglass, eds. 1996. *Empirical Studies in Institutional Change*. Cambridge: University Press.

Archer, Margaret S. 1995. *Realist Social Theory: The Morphogenetic Approach*. Cambridge: Cambridge University Press. Available at http://www.amazon.com/Realist-Social-Theory-Morphogenetic-Approach/dp/0521484421 (accessed September 28, 2011).

Axelrod, Robert. 1984. *The Evolution of Cooperation*. New York: Basic Books.

Bak, Per, and Kim Sneppen. 1993. "Punctuated Equilibrium and Criticality in a Simple Model of Evolution." *Physical Review* 71 (24): 4083–6.

Berliner, Brian. 1990. "CVS II: Parallelizing Software Development." In *Proceedings of the USENIX Winter 1990 Technical Conference*, 352. Washington, DC: USENIX Association.

Borra, Erik, et al. 2015. "Societal Controversies in Wikipedia Articles." In *Proceedings of the 33rd Annual ACM Conference on Human Factors in Computing Systems—CHI '15*, 193–6. Available at http://dl.acm.org/citation.cfm?doid=2702123.2702436.

Boudon, Raymond. 1981. *The Logic of Social Action: An Introduction to Sociological Analysis*, trans. David Silverman. London: Routledge.

Bourdieu, Pierre. 1972. *Outline of a Theory of Practice*. Cambridge: Cambridge University Press.

Callon, Michel, Pierre Lascoumes, and Yannick Barthe. 2009. *Acting in an Uncertain World: An Essay on Technical Democracy*. Cambridge, MA: MIT Press. Available at http://www.worldcat.org/title/acting-in-an-uncertain-world-an-essay-on-technical-democracy/oclc/229467395 (accessed January 6, 2011).

Callon, Michel, and Bruno Latour. 1981. "Unscrewing the Big Leviathans How Do Actors Macrostructure Reality." In *Advances in Social Theory and Methodology. Toward an Integration of Micro and Macro Sociologies*, ed. Karin Knorr-Cetina and Aron Cicourel, 277–303. London: Routledge.

Castellano, Claudio, S. Fortunato, and V. Loreto. 2009. "Statistical Physics of Social Dynamics." *Reviews of Modern Physics* 81: 591–646. Available at http://rmp.aps.org/abstract/RMP/v81/i2/p591_1 (accessed September 12, 2012).

Cordeau, J.-F., Paolo Toth, and Daniele Vigo. 1998. "A Survey of Optimization Models for Train Routing and Scheduling." *Transportation Science* 32 (4): 380–404.

Daley, Daryl J., and Joseph Mark Gani. 1999. *Epidemic Modelling: An Introduction*. Cambridge: Cambridge University Press. Available at https://books.google.com/books?hl=en&lr=&id=DFrxpZHdz9UC&pgis=1 (accessed January 22, 2016).

Dawkins, Richard. 1982. *The Extended Phenotype*. Oxford: Oxford University Press.

Dawkins, Richard. 1996. *The Blind Watchmaker: Why the Evidence of Evolution Reveals a Universe without Design*. St. Louis, MO: Turtleback Books.

Durkheim, Emile. 1897. *Le Suicide*. Paris: Presses Universitaires de France.

Durkheim, Emile. 1966. *The Rules of Sociological Method*, trans. Sarah A. Solovay and John H. Mueller, ed. George E. G. Catlin. New York: Free Press.

Eisenstein, Elizabeth L. 1980. *The Printing Press as an Agent of Change*. Cambridge: Cambridge University Press. Available at http://books.google.com/books?id=0-FThHK2DNMC&pgis=1 (accessed November 4, 2014).

Emirbayer, Mustafa. 1997. "Manifesto for a Relational Sociology." *American Journal of Sociology* 103 (2): 281–317.

Epstein, Joshua. 2006. *Generative Social Science: Studies in Agent-Based Computational Modeling*. Princeton, NJ: Princeton University Press.

Epstein, Joshua M., and Robert L. Axtell. 1996. *Growing Artificial Societies: Social Science from the Bottom Up (Complex Adaptive Systems)*. Cambridge, MA: MIT Press. Available at http://www.amazon.com/Growing-Artificial-Societies-Science-Adaptive/dp/0262550253 (accessed October 14, 2011).

Gawron, C. 1998. "An Iterative Algorithm to Determine the Dynamic User Equilibrium in a Traffic Simulation Model." *International Journal of Modern Physics C* 9 (3): 393–407. Available at http://www.worldscientific.com/doi/abs/10.1142/S0129183198000303.

Giddens, Anthony. 1984. *The Constitution of Society*. Berkeley: University of California Press.

Gilbert, Nigel, and Rosaria Conte. 1995. *Artificial Societies: The Computer Simulation of Social Life*. London: Taylor & Francis.

Gordon, D. M. 2011. "The Fusion of Behavioral Ecology and Ecology." *Behavioral Ecology* 22 (2): 225–30. Available at http://www.beheco.oxfordjournals.org/cgi/doi/10.1093/beheco/arq172.

Gordon, Deborah M. 2015. "From Division of Labor to the Collective Behavior of Social Insects." *Behavioral Ecology and Sociobiology*: 70 (7): 1101–8.

Hofbauer, Josef, and Karl Sigmund. 1988. *The Theory of Evolution and Dynamical Systems: Mathematical Aspects of Selection*. London: Mathematical Society Student Texts. Available at http://www.amazon.com/The-Theory-Evolution-Dynamical-Systems/dp/0521358388 (accessed January 7, 2016).

John Nash. 1951. "Non-Cooperative Games." *Annals of mathematics* 54 (1): 286–95.

Keeling, Matt J., and Ken T. D. Eames. 2005. "Networks and Epidemic Models." *Journal of the Royal Society Interface* 2 (4): 295–307. Available at http://rsif.royalsocietypublishing.org/cgi/doi/10.1098/rsif.2005.0051.

Kittur, Aniket, and R. E. Kraut. 2008. "Harnessing the Wisdom of Crowds in Wikipedia : Quality through Coordination." *Proceedings of the 2008 ACM conference on Computer supported cooperative work*. Available at http://dl.acm.org/citation.cfm?id=1460572 (accessed May 9, 2014).

Latour, Bruno. 2005. *Reassembling the Social: An Introduction to Actor-Network Theory*. Oxford: Oxford University Press.

Lazer, David, Alex Pentland, Lada Adamic, Sinan Aral, Albert-László Barabási, Devon Brewer, Nicholas Christakis, Noshir Contractor, James Fowler, Myron Gutmann, Tony Jebara, Gary King, Michael Macy, Deb Roy, and Marshall Van Alstyne. 2009. "Computational Social Science." *Science* 323 (5915): 721–3. Available at http://www.pubmedcentral.nih.gov/articlerender.fcgi?artid=2745217&tool=pmcentrez&rendertype=abstract.

Leskovec, Jure, Lars Backstrom, and Jon Kleinberg. 2009. "Meme-Tracking and the Dynamics of the News Cycle." In *Proceedings of the 15th ACM SIGKDD International Conference on Knowledge Discovery and Data Mining*, 497–506. Paris, France: ACM. Available at http://portal.acm.org/citation.cfm?id=1557019.1557077 (accessed October 2, 2010).

Lessig, Lawrence. 1999. *Code and Other Laws of Cyberspace*. New York: Perseus Books.

Levins, Richard. 1968. *Evolution in Changing Environments: Some Theoretical Explorations*. Princeton, NJ: Princeton University Press. Available at https://books.google.com/books?id=ZSVJ8pA1RFIC&pgis=1 (accessed January 7, 2016).

Macy, Michael W., and Robert Willer. 2002. "From Factors to Factors: Computational Sociology and Agent-Based Modeling." *Annual Review of Sociology* 28

(1): 143–66. Available at http://www.annualreviews.org/doi/abs/10.1146/annurev.soc.28.110601.141117.

Minsky, Marvin. 1988. *The Society of Mind*. New York: Simon & Schuster.

Moretti, F. 2013. *Distant Reading*. New York: Verso Books.

Moussaid, Mehdi, Simon Garnier, Guy Theraulaz, and Dirk Helbing. 2009. "Collective Information Processing and Pattern Formation in Swarms, Flocks, and Crowds." *Topics in Cognitive Science* 1 (3): 469–97.

Naldi, Giovanni, Lorenzo Pareschi, and Giuseppe Toscani. 2010. *Mathematical Modeling of Collective Behavior in Socio-Economic and Life Sciences*. Germany: Springer Science & Business Media.

Neumann, J. V. 1945. "A Model of General Economic Equilibrium." *The Review of Economic Studies* 13 (1): 1–9.

Niederer, S., and J. Van Dijck. 2010. "Wisdom of the Crowd or Technicity of Content? Wikipedia as a Sociotechnical System." *New Media & Society*. Available at http://nms.sagepub.com/content/12/8/1368.short (accessed May 9, 2014).

Powell, Walter W., and Paul J. DiMaggio, eds. 1991. *The New Institutionalism in Organizational Analysis*. Chicago, IL: University of Chicago Press.

Rochkind, Marc J. 1975. "The Source Code Control System." *IEEE Transactions on Software Engineering* (4): 364–70.

Rogers, Richard. 2013. *Digital Methods*. Cambridge, MA: MIT Press.

Schelling, Thomas. 1971. "Dynamic Models of Segregation." *Journal of Mathematical Sociology* 1 (May): 143–86.

Schelling, Thomas C. 1978. *Micromotives and Macrobehavior*. New York: W. W. Norton.

Schumpeter, Joseph Alois. 1976. *Capitalism, Socialism and Democracy*. London: Routledge. Available at https://books.google.com/books?id=6eM6YrMj46sC&pgis=1 (accessed January 7, 2016).

Shepsle, Kenneth A. 1986. "Institutional Equilibrium and Equilibrium Institutions." *Political science: The Science of Politics* 51: 51.

Shepsle, Kenneth A. 1978. *The Giant Jigsaw Puzzle: Democratic Committee Assignments in the Modern House*. Chicago, IL: University of Chicago Press.

Tichy, Walter F. 1982. "Design, Implementation, and Evaluation of a Revision Control System." In *Proceedings of the 6th International Conference on Software Engineering*, 58–67. Los Alamitos, CA: IEEE Computer Society Press.

Tichy, Walter F. 1985. "RCS—A System for Version Control." *Software: Practice and Experience* 15 (7): 637–54.

Tobin, James. 1969. "A General Equilibrium Approach to Monetary Theory." *Journal of Money, Credit & Banking* 1 (1): 15–29.

Venturini, Tommaso. 2006. "Opera Aperta: Wikipedia E L'oralità Secondaria." *Magma* 4: 35–45. Available at http://www.doaj.org/doaj?func=abstract&id=286736 (accessed October 22, 2012).

Venturini, Tommaso, Pablo Jensen, and Bruno Latour. 2015. "Fill in the Gap: A New Alliance for Social and Natural Sciences." *Journal of Artificial Societies and Social Simulation* 18 (2): 11. Available at http://jasss.soc.surrey.ac.uk/18/2/11.html.

Vespignani, Alessandro. 2011. "Modelling Dynamical Processes in Complex Socio-Technical Systems." *Nature Physics* 8 (1): 32–9. Available at http://www.nature.com/doifinder/10.1038/nphys2160 (accessed August 23, 2012).

Viégas, F.B., Martin Wattenberg, and Kushal Dave. 2004. "Studying Cooperation and Conflict between Authors with History Flow Visualizations." In *Proceedings of the SIGCHI Conference on Human Factors in Computing Systems*, 575–82. Vienna: ACM. Available at http://portal.acm.org/citation.cfm?id=985692.985765&type=series (accessed October 2, 2010).

Vinck, Dominique. 2012. "Accessing Material Culture by Following Intermediary Objects." In *An Ethnography of Global Landscapes and Corridors*, 89–108. Available at http://www.intechopen.com/books/an-ethnography-of-global-landscapes-and-corridors.

Commentary: Versioning and Structural Change

Petri Ylikoski

Tommaso Venturini makes many claims in this provocative chapter, which focus mostly on three themes. First, there are arguments about the micro-macro distinction and its consequences for understanding social phenomena. I think Venturini has misunderstood the distinction and its purpose. The second theme is Venturini's observations about social scientific models and their shortcomings in understanding social change. I think here Venturini has identified some real limitations of current models, but he is not successful in diagnosing the reason for them. Finally, there are his suggestions about the possibilities of versioning in understanding social change. I think this is the most interesting part of the chapter, although I see the potential of versioning quite differently. In the following commentary, I will say something on each of these three themes.

1 The Micro-Macro Distinction

Venturini's central claim is that the spatial micro-macro focus of social scientific theorizing should be replaced with a focus on temporal analysis of change. I agree that there is a need for more attention on what is traditionally called the problem of *structural change*, especially in the modeling-oriented social sciences, but giving up on micro-macro issues would be a huge leap toward conceptual and empirical confusion. Thus it makes sense to try to reconstruct what leads Venturini to make this radical suggestion. I think the root of the issue is his understanding of the micro-macro distinction.

First, Venturini presents the distinction as being based on spatial metaphor. However, it is difficult to see in which way the distinction between large and small scale is metaphorical. Yes, this is spatial distinction that is based on part-whole relations, but there is hardly anything metaphorical in it. A family *consists of* its members, and there is nothing metaphorical about this. Similarly, families as households *are parts of* economic process in a fully nonmetaphorical sense. Thus the distinction itself is not metaphorical. Unfortunately, people often talk about it in a metaphorical way, for example, when they talk about it in terms of *levels*. As I have argued elsewhere, we should give up using this expression as it leads to conceptual confusion and pseudo-problems (Ylikoski 2012, 2014b, 2016).

Second, Venturini seems to confuse the micro-macro distinction with the agency-structure problem. While he might not be alone in this confusion, it is important to see these are two separate but related issues. The micro-macro problem is about the discontinuity between microscale and macroscale properties. The challenge is to understand how changes at the microscale are related to changes in macroscale, and *vice versa*. The distinction deals with the problems of complexity and emergence, although the latter term should be avoided as it tends to mystify things. If macro properties were mere aggregates of micro properties, we would not have this problem. The micro-macro problem is not unique to the social sciences: similar problems can be found, for example, in cell biology, neuroscience, and ecology. The agency-structure problem is quite different. Its starting point is the freedom and creativity of an individual agent and the things that are within an individual's control. This individual agency is contrasted with the structure, which usually generously refers to all relatively stable social matters that the agent experiences as external constraints (or enabling conditions). This opposition makes it possible to highlight the tension between two social scientific perspectives: on the one hand, an individual is a product of social influences and circumstances, but on the other hand, the whole of social reality is a product of agents' actions. Here, we see the fundamental difference between these two problems: the agency-structure problem is a problem because it is difficult or impossible to fully reconcile these general perspectives. In contrast, the problems with micro and macro are empirical and theoretical challenges of figuring out how small- and large-scale processes are related.

Venturini argues that "social structures ... are: not a permanently static background, but a specific type of actor whose change is, most of the time, particularly slow." It is important to see what is controversial or new in this statement. No sensible person would deny that social structures can change, or that the speed of this change can vary. The novelty in Venturini's thesis is calling a structure an actor. Is this a new idea that will allow major breakthroughs in understanding social dynamics? I doubt it. This is just a stipulation that expands the meaning of the term actor. This is a move to impoverish our philosophical vocabulary, not a conceptual breakthrough to expand our social scientific understanding. Of course, one could also try to suggest that only actors can be explanatory factors, but again, what would be the justification for this strange idea?

There are easier and more effective ways to dilute the agency-structure debate. The core issue often seems to be just a sociological version of the problem of free will that springs from a fear of sociological determinism (Loyal and Barnes 2001). After all, it sets social causality against human freedom in a way that gives an impression of deep theoretical problem. But it might also be that it is just a distraction and conceptual confusion produced by too abstract thinking. I don't have firm opinion on this and if Venturini wishes to dismiss the agency-structure problem as a distraction for empirical research I would not object. However, I think it is not possible to dismiss micro-macro issues in similar manner. The social sciences are interested in social phenomena at various scales and it is a key challenge to understand how these processes are related to each other. If we wish to understand social processes at various temporal scales, we should do that keeping an eye on micro-macro relations, not by ignoring them.

The digital humanities should consider what it can contribute to the common project rather than just ignore central questions in the social sciences.

Finally, it is surprising that Venturini does not even mention *history*, which has traditionally been the discipline that is especially focused on temporal change (Sewell 2005). In fact, many of the limitations of social scientific theorizing Venturini highlights could be seen as consequences of the dysfunctional division of labor between the social sciences and history. From this perspective, the social scientists often ignore temporal change, not because they are captivated by the micro-macro distinction, but because they presume that structural change is something historians will be taking care of. This suggests that an alternative strategy for making room for more temporal focus in the social sciences would be arguing that all social science should be historical. This line of argumentation will probably be more productive than an attempt to argue that one cannot, or should not, consider both scale and temporal change at the same time.

2 Representations of What?

Venturini discusses many sorts of models and representations. The article opens with a description of a TV-documentary that successfully represents slow changes in a coral reef in a manner that is appropriate for the attention span of the TV-viewer. Observing such "accelerated" change helps the viewer to rethink what a coral is. This is a very effective way to visualize long-term change. Similar representations have been used in the social sciences: one can, for example, use similar means to represent how a street corner changes over time, or how the city expands over the landscape or how buildings grow to fill the skyscape. One can only agree that we should have more of such representations and hopefully the development of digital technology makes preparing them less difficult and time-consuming.

The Law Factory research project is an ingenious example of what we can expect in the future. It helps to track and visualize how a proposed law changes from a draft to a final version. With the help of software it is possible both to zoom in to the minute details of changes and zoom out to whole process and observe large-scale patterns in the patterning of the revisions. This is a great tool. I can easily think of further applications for this approach. For example, one could study scientific article manuscripts in the same manner and observe how they change from the first draft to the published version. (Think how such a software could have helped Knorr-Cetina 1981, chapter 5.) With such tool and data one could start to compare research groups, disciplines, or publication forums and see whether there are some interesting differences in the ways in which the manuscripts are edited and by whom. So, if one has access to relevant data, the Law Factory approach is very useful both for managing the data and for finding and displaying patterns in the data. Especially, it is useful for capturing patterns that we might have otherwise missed.

Venturini is rightly proud of the Law Factory. However, I don't see why he sets it against social scientific models, especially those models that attempt to model micro-macro relations. To me, these two are very different sorts of representations. The Law Factory is a representation of a long-term change that allows describing the changes in various timescales. It does not aim to capture the dependencies in the relevant processes (i.e., it does not describe the negotiations and struggles behind the revisions, nor does it describe the institutional practices that are involved), but it captures the cumulative results of these processes. We could say that it is not an explanatory model, but a representation of a phenomenon that is a legitimate target for explanation. In other words, it is a representation of a social scientific *explanandum*.

In contrast, many of the models Venturini criticizes are explanatory models. They might be highly abstract and simplified, but the purpose of these theoretical models is to capture some important explanatory dependence. In other words, their purpose is to allow *what if*—inferences about the phenomenon of interest (Ylikoski 2014a; Ylikoski and Aydinonat 2014; Kuorikoski and Ylikoski 2015). The purpose is not to reproduce some empirical phenomenon in all its rich detail; rather, it is to capture a small set of explanatory dependencies that are assumed to be central. The idea is not that the model provides a full or complete explanation of a puzzling process or phenomenon. Rather, the suggestion is more modest: the model should capture an important, maybe even crucial, element that explains some important aspect of the phenomenon. These theoretical models are not to be confused with comprehensive theories about the phenomenon, they are inferential aids that facilitate inferences from the assumptions. Such tools are explanatorily valuable if they increase the range of correct *what if*—inferences that can be made about the phenomenon, make these inferences more reliable, or if they help to explicate the conditions under which such inferences can be made. One should not assume that this strategy will always work. Quite often, the models of this kind are mere sketches of how-possibly explanations, not actual explanations of anything (Ylikoski and Aydinonat 2014).

I find it puzzling that Venturini sets representations of temporal change and theoretical models against each other. These representations have so different purposes that regarding them as exclusive alternatives does not make much sense. No matter how failed the theoretical models are, or how brilliant and detailed the representations of change, the latter will never replace the former. They just have so different inferential purposes. However, there is one thing one could claim with some justification: most theoretical models in the social sciences do not address longer-term historical dynamics. I will finish my commentary by considering why this is so.

3 The Difficulty of Modeling Structural Change

Structural change is highly interesting, but also very difficult, topic for social scientific theorizing. I fully agree with Venturini that it deserves much more attention. However, we should consider what makes the problem of structural change so difficult. In fact, there are multiple reasons for this.

The first reason is the scarcity of detailed *explananda*. While we often have a generic understanding that some structural change has happened, only quite limited data on the details of the process are available. This lack of empirical data creates a great deal of indeterminacy for any attempt to model such a process. There are many alternative ways things might have worked out, which makes it difficult to justify specific modeling assumptions. No matter what one does, somebody will find the modeling choices arbitrary and without empirical data there is very little one can do to defend them. If the expected result will almost always be "a mere story," there is not much incentive to put much effort to more ambitious models or theoretical reasoning behind them. This is an area where versioning tools advocated by Venturini could be very useful. By providing detailed account of the dynamics of the process to be explained, they could make the target of explanation precise enough to serve as a testing ground for competing models. Explaining an empirically grounded pattern is quite different from trying to account for a half speculative historical scenario, so one could expect the interest in modeling structural change will increase as detailed and high-quality data become available.

The second reason for the limited attention to structural changes is the absence of a substantial theory. As the referee quoted by Venturini argues, individual models are tools for exploring consequences of certain structural assumptions and one cannot let everything change at the same time. Individual models are very limited and highly selective representations. To study more complex dynamics, one needs multiple models. And to justify the relations between these models one needs substantial theoretical ideas. I think this is one of the greatest problems with current social scientific modeling. Formal modeling is an excellent tool for theoretical thinking, but it is a mistake to identify modeling and theorizing. Models are tools for theoretical thinking, but there is a lot of theoretical thinking that goes in the background. Take agent-based simulation as an example. It is quite common to hear complaints that social scientific ABS-models are just fancy toys without much sociological relevance. While some of this frustration might derive from the difficulty of evaluating abstract models and seeing their possible explanatory relevance, the main basis for this sentiment is missing the theoretical motivation and context. This is a consequence of not explicitly discussing, or even thinking about, the background assumptions. I think the critics are right here: we need more than the conceptual exploration of possibilities of particular models, we need more developed theoretical context for them. And if simple models need theoretical context, it is even more needed in the case of more complex models that target structural change.

The structural change could be either exogenous or endogenous (Hernes 1976) with respect to the modeled variables. If the change is exogenous, one needs a theoretical idea of how structural assumptions of the models change in time. As there are often multiple exogenous variables that change at the same time, this problem is far from trivial. We no longer find monocausal theories of history credible, and things can be complex in so many ways. This should not prevent us from articulating such complex theories. On the other hand, if the structural change is endogenous, one needs theoretical ideas about these processes in order to model them. This case is even more difficult: the dynamics of the endogenous change might depend on the specific details of the process, which implies that one needs to have much more sophisticated models. This requires quite a lot of work. One can presume that one does not start developing such a model before one has quite clear idea of what to include. So, again the underdevelopment of theory is the bottleneck for the development of models of structural change.

4 Conclusion

In this commentary I have critically evaluated Venturini's critique of the micro-macro focus of social scientific modeling and his suggestion that versioning provides a fruitful alternative to agent-based simulation and other modeling approaches. I have welcomed versioning as an interesting tool for representing historical change, but suggested that there is no competition between simulation and versioning. The Law Factory and similar projects provide *explananda*, not *explanatia*. Thus simulation (and other forms of explanatory modeling) and versioning can be expected to complement each other. I have also argued against Venturini's critique of the role of micro-macro focus in social scientific theorizing. While he seems to think that paying more attention to structural change requires giving up micro-macro focus, I tend to think that in order to get to the root of structural change, we need to pay more attention to micro-macro issues. This is a quite substantial difference. However, both of us seem to agree that structural change deserves much more social scientific attention.

References

Hernes, G. 1976. "Structural Change in Social Processes." *American Journal of Sociology* 82 (3): 513–47.

Knorr-Cetina, K. 1981. *The Manufacture of Knowledge. An Essay on the Constructivist and Contextual Nature of Science*. Oxford: Pergamon Press.

Kuorikoski, J., and P. Ylikoski. 2015. "External Representations and Scientific Understanding." *Synthese* 192 (12): 3817–37.

Loyal, S., and B. Barnes. 2001. ""Agency" as a Red Herring in Social Theory." *Philosophy of the Social Sciences* 31(4): 507–24.

Sewell, W. H. 2005. *Logics of History. Social Theory and Social Transformation*. Chicago, IL: University of Chicago Press.

Ylikoski, Petri. 2012. "Micro, Macro, and Mechanisms." In *The Oxford Handbook of Philosophy of the Social Sciences*, ed. H. Kincaid, 21–45. Oxford: Oxford University Press.

Ylikoski, P. 2014a. "Agent-Based Simulation and Sociological Understanding." *Perspectives on Science* 22: 318–35.

Ylikoski, P. 2014b. "Rethinking Micro-Macro Relations." In *Rethinking the Individualism-Holism Debate. Essays in Philosophy of Social Science*, ed. F. Collin and J. Zahle, 117–35. Dordrecht: Springer.

Ylikoski, P. K. 2016. *Thinking with the Coleman Boat*. The IAS Working Paper Series, Vol. 2016, no. 1. Sweden: Linköping University Electronic Press.

Ylikoski, P., and E. Aydinonat. 2014. "Understanding with Theoretical Models." *Journal of Economic Methodology* 21: 19–36.

8

Social Statistics Using Strategic Structuralism and Pluralism

Wendy Olsen

8.1 Introduction

Social statistics is explanatory, follows a depth ontology, and is confident about validity without being deductivist. Perhaps this isn't how the statisticians you know operate, but in my view this approach to statistics is the best one. For example, some statisticians are confident about validity only when an argument is deductive in its form. In my statistical work I often use a survey dataset of one case per row, with many columns, to test a range of claims made prior to getting the data in such a situation. I am not using interview data or documents, although in practice I often do and I call that mixing methods. A related issue is what counts as evidence. Evidence refers not only to survey data but also to interview transcripts, documents, and historical records. Since evidence is so variegated, statistics can refer to many mathematical tools used in a clever combination with mental and discursive interpretations. Statistical research is dialogical, as D. Byrne said (2002).

A depth ontology refers to the existence of multiple linked levels in both society and nature, such as the ecosystem, the human social system, the weather system, and so on.

My own approach can easily be integrated with other sciences and has a coherent and explicit approach to knowledge (Olsen and Morgan 2005). In some statistical work, there is a notable dependence on deductive reasoning. We also see in some instances a fallacy of verification[1] (Sarantakos 1998). A fallacy of verification is where an argument is considered to be firm, because evidence that is introduced at the beginning does validate (or is consistent with) its conclusion; but if it hasn't critically assessed that evidence, then it may be a specious argument (Weston 2002). My approach is broadly structuralist. I find that it is better to use data harmonized over space, even if the harmonizing is done in a rough and ready way, than to use no survey data at all.

To harmonize the data, we backward translate the questions after translation to a new language, or, in general, we make sure the concepts used to create variables (columns in the survey data) are coherent and consistent with local usage over the whole space represented. The reasoning behind harmonization is that social structures are rather enduring and tend to exist in a social and physical space with boundaries that, in spite of being porous, can be known. Thus, my approach is rooted in a clear sense of what I mean by "structure(s)."

"Structure" is defined in such a way that the society is not seen as fixed or invariant (Outhwaite 1987). I see structures as the entities, involving sets of distinctive relationships between other entities, with the whole being more than the sum of its parts. Each structure, which we can describe, is a thing that is more durable in a specific society than other more ephemeral things, such as a love affair or a marriage. Each structure also has its own emergent properties. For example, there are structural properties of the marital system in a region. Another example: the legal system and its properties, which underpin the legal practices of a country. A third: the international structure of trade and trading relations.

In statistics, we often use variables and measures for each of a series of cases to reflect these highly institutionalized structural properties. It does not worry me to say "structures are structured"; it would worry me if we thought structures were fixed in place. For instance, the nuclear household is a socially and historically specific form of household found in particular places in certain eras.

Strategic structuralism refers to a researcher or an organization being strategic about how it plans and conducts survey research and statistical analysis about structures and their sub-entities. (Borsboom, Mellenbergh, and Heerden 2003 and Lawson 1997, 2003 explain the usage of "entities.") Strategic structuralism is "strategic" in the sense of considering a range of options to represent the society with some phenomena considered "given" and others more malleable. A strategic choice of variables will lead to new and useful knowledge. Although the precise findings cannot be predicted in advance.

I do not assume the structures are fixed or permanent. So I use a variety of types of evidence. I try not to fall into a naïve trap based on the empirical data. I tend to work from a realist starting point, because I am convinced that in reality, statisticians are strategic thinkers (Olsen 2010). We need to make warranted arguments in science (Fisher 1988). A warranted argument has links between its premises and its conclusions, and is a coherent complex statement. Others also argue strongly for multiple, mixed methods in social science (Roth 1987).

I usually aim to do my research in ways consistent with realism as described by Sayer (2000), Lawson (1997), Bhaskar (1998), and Archer (2000, 2015). Outhwaite (1987) described that realism is useful across the whole pantheon of social science, including constructionism, but he hardly mentioned statistical practices. Sayer wrote that extensive statistical studies using survey data ran a risk of overgeneralizing and making mistakes by being too abstract, but that has not been my experience. I have found it really valuable. For example, recently I found attitudes that center around social norms that we can measure, do vary considerably across the regions of India, but are coherently clustered within one region. A "region" has between 250 million and 550 million people, so these are large-scale structures that I'm studying. Attitudes, however, do not rigidly follow cultural norms, you see. Other structures, such as the social class structure, affect how individual attitudes deviate from local social norms.

My own particular take on social theory and knowledge, given that I am a realist, is to use structure-agency dynamics and mixed methods. The morphogenetic approach, which focuses on mechanisms of change and of reproduction in a society (as described by Archer 2010) is consistent with the realist use of social statistics.

Numerous authors may agree with me about the use of statistical data as part of mixed-methods research or triangulation; some disagree, due to the harmonization that is intrinsically part of doing survey research. I will deal with these as I go along.

The order of the paper is underpinnings, regression, an example from structural equation models, the fuzzy-set alternative to regression, F-tests, and some concluding comments. Overall, I show several ways in which the complex nature of reality shapes our attempts to describe it. Reality inhibits us from making false descriptions, and by making reference to specific aspects of reality. We also create new and strategically different, but still valid, arguments; in statistics a complex model is often superior to a simple model. I give examples of this and extend the argument to other forms of mathematical representations.

8.1 Strategic Structuralism

I have developed a methodology for integrated mixed methods using statistics as part of the evidence base for a study (Olsen 2012). This is one way to see realist statistics. We use a realist ontology and develop implications for epistemology. More importantly, by promoting this agenda, authors who are explicitly realist such as Blaikie (2013), Bryman (1988, 1998), D. Byrne (2002), and Williams (2000) have promoted mixed methods and rejected positivism without damaging our ability to use statistical data at all.

8.1.1 Inductive, Deductive, Retroductive, and Abductive

The first attempt at researching a new topic may use an inductive strategy (Blaikie 2000). Among statisticians, this usually refers to doing data collection without a clear theory, followed by analysis (notably "data mining"), then making generalizations about the social world. For me, induction would refer to the background reading, too; hence we all do a little bit of induction while getting well-informed about the topic. In naming some social statisticians who use inductive positivism, we would be focusing on Exploratory Factor Analysis (EFA) (Hair et al. 2005). As presented traditionally, the EFA is inductive and the Confirmatory Factor Analysis (CFA) is deductive, and both can lead to valid results—without any recourse to actual world experience, but simply by manipulating the data patterns (Tabachnik and Fidell 1996). Authors who open up the ground to confirmatory work, based on clear theorizing, include Long and Scott (1983), Bowen and Guo (2011), and B. Byrne (2011). A dualism is presented by Tabachnik and Fidell (2006) and by Hair et al. (2005). We also see it echoed in other texts on factor analysis. Yet, in recent years, a huge improvement moving toward a new approach has emerged, making many books out of date (Loehlin 2004; Bollen 1989), in spite of their eloquence and accurate mathematics. I will say a little about the excellent new approach to CFA later (see Ullman 2006).

A deductive strategy, as presented in this simplistic EFA/CFA dualism, works in the reverse order to induction. The researcher begins with an observed regularity or the existing literature about a regularity (e.g., suicide). A theory is constructed about that phenomenon, within this theory some hypotheses are deduced, and then each is tested using appropriate data.

This kind of statistical deductivism has axioms at the start, lemmas or hypotheses (null and alternative) in the middle, and firm accept/reject conclusions at the end. My view is that there is nothing wrong with using the EFA or CFA mathematics, but that the logic of research is more extensive, as Blaikie (2000), DeVaus (2001), and Bryman (1988, 2008) explain. We need diverse kinds of data, such as focus groups or interviews, to complement the statistical evidence. At least we can use the literature to get a sense of what is happening, then branch off into new learning. A *retroductive strategy* is a way of thinking, different from induction or deduction, where we ask why (or how) it is that the data look the way they do. None of the three categories of logic exhausts what a researcher will do. See Hunt (1994) for a clear discussion. We might apply each of them in turn, or iterate (Danermark et al., 2001). My book explains this using consistent wording, and presenting epistemological points alongside simple definitions of key terms (Olsen 2012).

We begin with an observed regularity, perhaps then generate a hypothetical model that is a theoretical model; from this, a theory of a mechanism is drawn as a more focused aspect, this theory is tested through an experiment or observation, and we draw conclusions. We seek to know *why* the data look as they do. We are particularly keen to find gaps or holes in the existing knowledge, so we generate claims (or hypotheses: these are not very different) which are new. There might be three theories once we have retroduced from data patterns and unique cases to what (historically, socially, or politically) may have caused them. We may gather extra data about these theories, and with regard to them, which is not the same as either induction, or deduction. Process tracing or fuzzy-set qualitative comparative analysis (QCA; Rihoux and Ragin 2009) are examples where one may decide to collect new data that augments the existing larger-scale survey data.

To reinforce my point, retroduction is defined as moving from what you have in front of you (e.g., empirical data; or data and existing literature) to the reality of what must be true or real in order for the data to appear as they do. It involves moving from data to findings. One does it via some mental machinations. It is a voyage of discovery or realization, different from deduction (from laws or premises to details) or induction (from detail to general). Retroductive arguments use evidence but are not generally deductive in the way that falsificationist arguments are. See Olsen and Morgan (2005) or Morgan and Olsen (2011a). An applied example is found at Morgan and Olsen (2011b).

I often use secondary survey data and government (administrative) data in a retroductive way. In such cases, one examines the headings and definitions carefully and then interprets them in terms of the social policy and political economy background. Statistical work does not exhaust what I do. Thus I am a pluralist in terms of theorizing and developing arguments.

I tried to publish a discussion of retroduction in Wikipedia, but this became embroiled in editorial debate, so is unpublished as yet. Jamie Morgan and I worked up these pointers. First, we distinguished ficts (e.g., numbers in a table) from reality.

"However the knowledge claims that we construct, using such numbers, may be argued to be true. The argument will combine induction (argument from evidence) with inference (argument which abstracts from the detail) and retroduction (argument which explains what conditions in reality may have or could have led to these observations)" (Olsen and Morgan, 2005: 275). As we noted, "methodological pluralism in general implies that data triangulation will be a welcome source of more rich retroduction, compared with simply using secondary survey data alone (Carter and New 2004)" (cited in Olsen and Morgan 2005: 279).

To complete the picture, the abductive strategy, as Blaikie (1993 and 2013) describes it, involves a description of social life in terms of the meanings and motives that social actors give to it. Validity arises one by one with strong correspondence to the world. The researcher seeks the best possible description of a process, ritual, or institution. We usually don't use social statistics for this purpose. Abduction per se, as currently construed, requires qualitative data and actual social experience. This usage differs from the historic usage in philosophy. Abduction can be combined with retroduction, induction, and/or deduction, if you go step by step.

Blaikie (2013) draws the ideal types too strongly. In recent years the "mixed-methods" approaches have enabled a more mixed, iterative, feedback-driven cycle of learning by gaining knowledge, testing claims, returning to the big picture, filling in pieces of a small section of that picture.

My preferred methodology requires that a clear and ambitious ontological vision illuminate and underpin the work of the statistician. Several options for such a vision arise in sociology and political science—in sociology, we have the theories of Archer and Giddens, new work by Scott (2011), approaches to transformative thinking by Bhaskar (1998), and my own work on strategic agency (Olsen 2009a; Morgan and Olsen 2007, 2008). These share most importantly a sense of the world as permeated by structures that are not deterministic for events, but instead are the site of causal mechanisms that affect agency in dynamic ongoing ways. To affect something is not the same as to "determine" an outcome. Figure 8.1 illustrates some of the key features of the kind of framework I like to use.

Here the structures are considered to be the most durable sets of entities. As structures have emergent properties, their component parts can change without the structure changing. Also, as a result, causal impact does not deterministically shape the future of structures. An example is ethnicity in an ethnically diverse society. Using Archer's helpful wording, the morphostatic part of the system perpetuates features like inequality, norms, and stereotypes that fit action (Figure 8.2). In an ethnicity example,

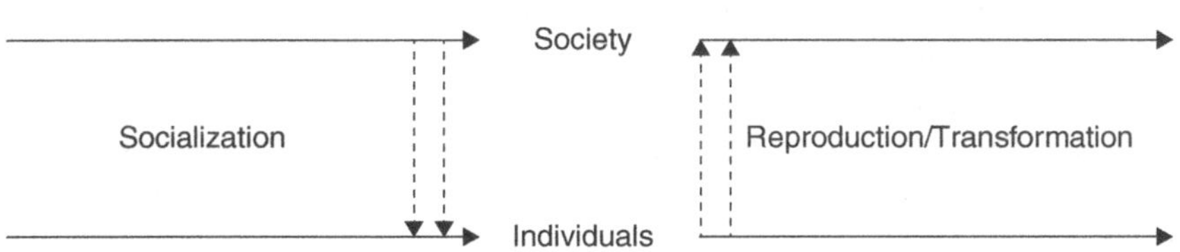

Figure 8.1 The transformational model of social action.

Source: Archer (1995: 155).

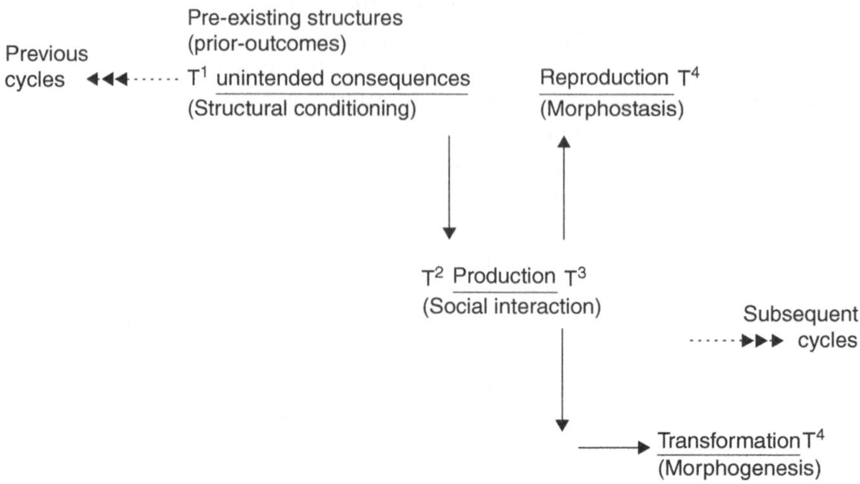

Figure 8.2 Structure and agency interact over time T.

Source: Archer, (1995: 158).

being in an oppressed minority may mean you are affected by stereotypes about your background, you are affected by your cultural background which has certain properties, and your actions may include in part conforming to dominant culture (morphostatic action) or in part resisting that culture (morphogenetic action; see Archer 1995: 158). Archer has shown that the morphogenetic (change-inducing) parts of this system require intervention of agents. In my view, the category "agents" refers not simply to individuals but also, often, to corporate entities. Entities like households also overlap and partly permeate individuals. There are strategic discussions among those who take part in the corporate entities. We recognize the cognitive inner debate and the pre-discursive role of human bodies and nature in shaping the way social debates about strategic action take place.

In summary, for me, a strategic agent is one who acts to change the society, not being perfectly aware of all features of the society but carefully picking their way through their knowledge base to influence the future institutions and future structures. A nonstrategic, or naive, agent might simply describe the scene and would tend toward a morphostatic or reproductive role (Olsen 2009a). It's really important to acknowledge all this so that the explanatory model for an outcome isn't attributing all causality to just one level of agent, nor simply to structure—we use a mixture of these, plus other causes.

In my past reading, critical realism authors expressed this solution clearly: they argued that there is an external reality that exists independently of the researcher, but that the researcher's knowledge generation will always be imperfect, and furthermore that people are embedded in the society at the same time they are attempting to describe it.

The realist approach to science is growing in popularity and can be described further as follows. Realism is a metaphysical stance arguing that when people describe things, there is some real world, or universe, to which they are making reference. Therefore it's obvious that the "subjective" and "objective" worlds overlap. For example, the knowing human is both a subject and potentially an object of knowledge. Second, claims about the world have a referential component (what they say about some referred-to parts of the world) while making oblique reference to the subject's desires, discourses, and interests. This is important for me, because when I study cultural norms and people's attitudes about the same matters, sometimes I have to reflect on my own norms and how they may either bias me, or blind me, or help me to understand deviants. As a feminist and a humanist, too, I try to be non-Eurocentric in studying values in various parts of the world. I consider all this normal for a statistician. It is all agreeable at the Royal Statistical Society, too.

I recognize that "evidence" is not always valid, that validity is not at all simple to establish, and that epiphenomenal evidence often gets taken as adequate representation. Here is an example of an "epiphenomenal" piece of evidence: a lie during an interview, or a masking statement in a survey. My research shows women in Asia often report "I am a housewife" and economically inactive, but later can be found reporting their many activities with livestock and informal cottage industries. Eight percent of UK workers stated they did household domestic tasks as their main labor status, but then also reported greater than 5 hours of paid work per week and a wage rate for that work (2014/15 Understanding Society data, my own calculations). So the epiphenomena are rather common.

I will give one more example of epiphenomena, this time rooted in a poor quality ontology. In water research, it would be naïve to consider an engineer's plans as an adequate account of a whole water supply system. The engineer may have drawn a map and built a model. It might be that engineers need to do planning to achieve what they aim for in their inventions. I believe the interlinkedness of the social world means we manage water along with affecting the *systemic basis* of the *water cycle* itself. Lemon (2003) wrote an overview of human-ecological systems, which I liked. He explicitly brought realism to the fore by insisting that water systems are so often misunderstood as human-produced systems by engineers. There is real complexity in the world. The huge interconnectedness of social and natural systems makes the best action hard to discern in water systems. A statistician working on water supply would want to be a strategic agent.

Other examples such as explaining divorce, working out what helps children learn to read, and so on, would all benefit from having a transdisciplinary theoretical framework. Yet, all are necessarily going to have imperfect, partial theories in order for theory to be tractable.

The reason that my ontic starting points are so important for social statistics is that we need to provide a basis for beginner, intermediate, and advanced statistical work in the interests of strategic, reflexive action. As I set out examples of each of these, the reader can see how helpful the framework is.

8.1.2 A Little Background on Realism in Social Science

Sayer (1992, 2000) explains what realism entails. We are committed to the existence of three domains of reality—the "real," actual, and empirical domains. The actual is a vast domain of both things and events. The empirical is that which is recorded. The "real" is a more encompassing set of things. The "real" is a complex reality that exists. As such it preconditions our scientific findings to an extent.

The real domain has structures whose composition may be a network, hierarchy, or other set of linkages. A realist seeks to know about generative causal mechanisms within an open system. The existence of causality in a particular case will need to be demonstrated, not assumed. Thus, retroduction may be useful as an investigative method to complement deduction and induction.

Realists seek, among other things, to know about the enduring structures but are interested in the institutions, norms, people, marriages, and many other things. Kinds of entity. Norms, marriages, and people are all different. Entity realism is a good point of entrée for statisticians into realism (Borsboom, Mellenbergh, and Heerden 2003). But there is much more going on: people's actual experience is too extensive to be described parsimoniously with any degree of accuracy (Quine 1951). Therefore, choice goes on in deciding how to describe a social phenomenon.

Realists say the data are not the same as reality. This difference is what makes operationalization possible, and it encourages our critical approach to evidence.

The analysis of generative causal mechanisms is widespread; a causal mechanisms such as a "treatment" or "intervention" can be studied in epidemiology or impact assessment terms. We also study "cases" which are ontically distinctive and may exist in nested sets, levels, or as unique ideographic one-off situations (Olsen 2009b).

The term "open system" stresses that causes don't work in isolation but may interact with other background factors. Downward and Mearman (2007) discussed the closed-model issue, urging that we use retroduction and mixed methods.

Structural factors are often referred to by realists. *A structure is a set of parts, all existing in relation to each other in enduringly patterned ways, such that the whole is an entity that has features beyond the characteristics of the parts*. Thus, a company has an organizational culture beyond the beliefs or attitudes of the employees. The class system may be exploitative even if individuals or companies do not think they are acting in directly exploitative ways. Structuralists are holistic. We avoid methodological individualism. Thus for me, because of being a realist, my research is at odds with individualistic forms of economics and atomistic forms of modeling. I worry about methodological individualism and atomism.

8.2 Realist Statistics: Simple Examples

A typical framework for regression by realists can look something like this.

$$\text{Outcome}_i = f\,(\text{structural, institutional, events, memberships, } \ldots) + e_i. \tag{1}$$

Here, a structural factor is exogenous to a current outcome (not caused by that outcome), and an event must be somewhat independent of each structural factor. For example, the person's household class, sex, marital status, and age group would be measurable structures. The institutional factors might include indicators of cultural affiliations such as religious background, regularity of worship, or which sexual orientation the people are currently declaring. Specific events relevant to the outcome, or memberships, can also be declared. Thus, while the outcome is recorded once per individual, the equation as a whole brings in elements from other types of entities in the transformational structure-agency framework (TMSA). An applied example of this kind is shown below:

$$Y^*_{i0} = \Sigma \boldsymbol{\beta}_0{}' \mathbf{X}_{i0} + \gamma_0 pov_i + u_{i0} \quad (2)$$

(Bridges, Lawson, and Begum 2011: 468; Bold indicates a vector)

Bridges, Lawson, and Begum offer a labor supply equation for Bangladesh. Bold indicates a vector. Here y^*_{i0} is the latent propensity to participate in the labor market, for case I (a person) in time 0. Pov_i indicates the poverty status of I and is structural. A vector **X** indicates other regression variables that affect labor-market participation (Bridges, Lawson, and Begum 2011). Age of the person, sex of the head of household, land holding, and local rainfall would be typical X variables. In their model, a secondary equation set helps discern factors that affect which sector a person works in: none, agricultural self-employment, nonagricultural self-employment, daily waged labor, or salaried employment (Bridges, Lawson, and Begum 2011: 469). Here,

$$Y^*_{im} = \boldsymbol{\beta}_m \mathbf{X}_i + \gamma_m pov_i + u_{im}, \ m = 0, 1, 2, 3, 4 \quad (3)$$

(Source: Bridges, Lawson, and Begum 2011: 469.)

A case is expected to participate in sector m if y^*_{im} is at its highest level for i in sector m. The predicted values of Y* are probabilities.

The e_i and the u_{i0} and u_{im} represent a stochastic element that is considered to have a particular distribution for each case; cases are assumed to be homogenous enough for the linear sum of terms to make sense in presenting us with a prediction or estimate for each case.

Although such equations do not exhaust what I can know, or say, about the labor markets, they help me understand what has been happening there in Bangladesh. Other statistical formulations describe cases of households, couples, schools, classrooms, student scores, and so on. The rural and urban sectors are structurally related and people operate differently in them, so we can introduce a Rural Dummy variable. We may interact each X variable with Rural to test whether there are response differences in the rural versus urban areas. In Bangladesh, typically there will be differences (Kabeer, Huq, and Mahmud 2013).

Equation (3) is from a good journal article. Yet, I feel driven to critically analyze the formulation by Bridges, Lawson, and Begum. Two criticisms arise—one from empirical evidence and the other from preferring a non-neoclassical theory that enables me to take a feminist and strategic approach to work issues. The first is that the sectors are considered as mutually exclusive but actual personal time-use diary data show them as overlapping. One may work in two sectors in the same season because of the great informality of the labor market. As a result, the use of the max-probability criterion in Eq. (2) can be questioned. It is a criterion based on the labeling approach to principal activity. It ignores subsidiary activities. It assumes the sectors' workers are in mutually exclusive groups.

The second critique is that if theory were restricted to a traditional neoclassical approach to labor (which says labor is drudgery, and people work because they're incentivized by human capital and opportunity-cost factors), we would be missing out on the labor obligations that arise from social roles, family norms, and gendered norms about the division of labor. Also, one can be both a worker and a housewife. I use a wide-ranging theory (Olsen et al. 2015) so that the labor "supply" function is redefined as a work-time function. The analysis can be similar to Bridges, Lawson, and Begum, but it now is multidisciplinary. The work has become economically "heterodox" in the choice of independent variables.

Some of the work can proceed according to textbook advice (De Vaus 2001). First, a beginner might run *t*-tests using survey data to test how influential each social structure is. Second, at the intermediate level a regression can use the S I M E method (Eq. 1) to name the exogenous variables, with an "action" or agentic positioning as a response variable.

Third, for more advanced work, invoking discourses that promote change as contrasting with those which preserve the current social scene, the mixed-methods researcher will examine—using qualitative data to explore selected spots—how the statistical findings illuminate strategies for change. An example might be to use data on child labor + focus groups of parents of child labor to help key stakeholders in the scene to reduce the willingness to send children out for full-time paid work; in the past, statisticians were not expected to be confident at handling groups of mixed stakeholders such as school principals, officers of local government or the Police, and child labor NGO activists. The new "impact" scene in UK research is a rich ground for getting social statistics more widely utilized.

If we suggest that there is a protocol, with steps in no particular order, so that iteration can occur, we are close to my and Danermark's approach. A summary might look like this (though it will differ, depending on the degree to which a topic is already studied, and how closely the boundaries around the study topic are drawn; see Box 9.1).

Box 9.1 Protocol for Realist Statistical Research (Which I Use Routinely)

Always start with a scholarly literature review.

(1) Induction → Theory 1 and Theory 2, perhaps Theory 3.

(2) Encompassing and pluralism: to what extent are these explanations overlapping, consistent, or mutually contradictory? In what way? What do we need to learn about? Can these be wrongly formulated? How? Critically assess the evidence, too.

(3) Deduction

- (3.1) If Theory 2 is true, what follows from that? Same for Theory 1.
- (3.2) We build the hypotheses.
  - (3.2.1) They each require some data.
  - (3.2.2) We then test each detailed H_0.
  - (3.2.3) Conclude within the model's overall formulation.

(4) Retroduction
  (4.1) Consider, "What do we now need to know more about? Why did these patterns occur?" See section on retroduction in Olsen (2012).
  (4.2) We gather more data, new data, new kinds of evidence (use mixed methods if time allows).
  (4.3) We use variables that might surprise the deductive statistician.
  (4.4) We draw conclusions → Theory 3.
(5) Iterate back to induction or deduction, as you feel appropriate
(6) Disseminate in a discussive, dialogical way to various audiences. Write up some findings.

8.3 Latent Variable Regression Models

Factor analysis offers good opportunities to illustrate strategic structuralism.

A number of authors have moved to end the debate between two polar opposites of CFA and EFA. (Confirmatory vs exploratory factor analysis.) The traditional approach was that a latent variable, lambda (λ), could reduce a set of variables to a single column in the data matrix. This data reduction was performed using Principal Components Analysis (PCA) for many years (Bollen 1989). The variance of the set of variables was parsed out into one or more factors. In PCA, it is unusual for a single factor to emerge, because the purpose is to exhaust all the variance. An underlying concept of the decomposition of the variance is implicit here.

The alternative method known as Confirmatory Factor Analysis does not require all the variance to be explained. Usually here the user decides how many factors they want to have emerge from the data-reduction step. Then the computer finds out which variables contribute to each factor, typically with three or more measures per factor, and often just one or two factors being sought.

Structural Equation Modeling (SEM) involves synthesizing regression and factor analysis. Some of the equations are listed to set up a relationship of each manifest (measured) variable with each latent variable (Borsboom, Mellenbergh, and Heerden 2003; B. Byrne 2011). For this part of a model there are as many equations as there are manifest variables. The relation we use is

$$Z = \Lambda_y W + \varepsilon_j \tag{4}$$

The measure (an index) is denoted by W, and Λ represents the factor loadings of the block of measured variables, Z, which might be five Likert Scales or some test scores. Thus there may be k equations. **W** (if written in bold) can be used to indicate a vector of latent variables (here, a vector would mean several indices, e.g., health well-being, a measure of personal autonomy, and psychological orientation). One may thus have three latent variables, each represented by four measures, of which a few measures overlap in relation to perhaps two or three latent variables rather than just one (Hair et al. 2005). The concept of these latent variables representing real entities in the world, such as personality characteristics, is explained by Borsboom, Mellenbergh, and Heerden by arguing the case for and against "entity realism." The case for realism of this kind is that the measures often have high correlations and that latent factors omit possible measurement errors. The case against is that many other kinds of things exist in the world, so that by "realism" we do not only refer to measureable entities; and furthermore, Borsboom, Mellenbergh, and Heerden (2003) say, processes are very complex and not even well conceptualized by the notion of entities. Look again:

$$Z = \Lambda_j W + \varepsilon_j \tag{4}$$

Here W is the continuous index that measures the attitude, perhaps an attitude about women's work; Z is the original measures available; and epsilon is a set of error terms, for j equations. There are j equations for j manifest variables. However, there are cases I, too (this subscript is hidden in our notation). I omitted an intercept term, which is implicitly present. The covariance matrix of the Z variables helps the machine optimally set the factor loadings to get small errors overall. In CFA, no rotation of the factors is undertaken. We set zeros into the matrix to represent the absence of a loading onto a factor W. I wrote Eq. (4) for a single factor, but if we write it with vectors we can have a complex range of loading patterns for indices W1 (attitudes to women's paid work), W2 (attitudes to women's domestic work), W3, and so on.

We now add to these equations some additional structural equations. Each of these reflects how a limited number of dependent and independent variables correspond to real relationships among the things (as represented by the variables). The part that measures the factor loadings is called the measurement model, and the rest of the equations is called the structural model.

$$Y_2 = a + bX_1 + cW + e_2 \text{ (sample of a simple structural equation)} \tag{5}$$

Examples of structural variables $X_1,\ldots,X_k$ would be age, type of housing, length of time spent in one job, and ethnic group of origin. This is another moment when structuralism comes to the fore. The strategic work of the researcher who has kept in mind the background reading, the audiences, and the other research they are doing, keeps the model simple and focused. I do not argue for parsimony in its own right. It is useful, though, to try to not have innumerable equations. Statistics tests—based on certain forms of classical statistics—argue this point from the standpoint of the identification problem. The identification problem would be having too few cases relative to the k + other variables, leading to non-identification and infeasibility of the model. I would argue for having few equations, furthermore, from the necessity and the usefulness of "abstraction" (Sayer 1992, chapters 1 and 2). Given a real referent, our aim is not usually to represent the whole system of real relationships. Instead, our aim is to tease out and study specific parts of the system.

We also do not try to generalize wholly about a locality or a social space. As Muthén (1983) took great pains to show, we can do group tests to find out how we might best split up the sample, and hence partition the represented locality or the represented social space, giving a good fit without creating too much omitted variable bias. A group test is a test of whether two distinct groups would be best modeled separately, or together.

It is usual these days to call the measurement model a CFA or a latent factor model. Maximizing the fit is only one of the criteria for a good measurement model. Coherence and plausibility are also important. Strategic choice of themes also influence what we highlight, such as a gender or ethnicity, which another scholar might have deployed.

A simple example can be used to illustrate how far the SEM with LFA (Latent Factor Analysis) methods have come. Far away from PCA, the authors of a project on farmer strategies notice a two-stage-norm formation process. (The authors used retroduction to theorize this.) They fit the data to this two-stage model using two equations, which I summarize here:

Step 1. Equation 1 for whether they engage in a practice.
Step 2. Equation 2 summarizing their norms for this practice.
Step 3. Insert the latent norm measure into the Step 1 regression.

See Fuller et al. 2002, as an example. One can also use SEM to engage with issues in the reverse order, or any combination of orders (see Muthén and Aspourhov 2009; Muthén and Muthén 2006; Muthén 1983, 1984, 1989, 1994; and Muthén and Kaplan 1985).

Step 1'. Equations that link variables to a single latent factor.
Step 2'. Equations that link the latent variable to a Y outcome.

Alternatives in the SEM tradition also include putting the latent variable W into the equation as a Y rather than explanatory variable. Mixtures are possible. Ordinal measurement of the underlying manifest variables can be handled using special software (MPLUS). The special treatment of the measurement "levels" in each ordinal variable is an efficient solution to the problem that typically arose in the 1980s–2000s in PCA. The following problems can be avoided: that we might assume:

(1) that the variables were continuously measured, for example, that a Likert Scale is a continuous variable;
(2) and/or that the variables' distributions lie on a normal curve.

For instance, MPLUS allows the user to handle these measurement issues with great dexterity. Maximum likelihood estimation, found in STATA and SPSS, also usually avoids the second problem. Many users, however, stick with SPSS or STATA software without these adjustments, not being aware of the solutions. At postgraduate level the synthesis makes more sense but has a relatively limited audience (Bartholomew, Knott, and Moustakis 2011). If the underlying distribution of the manifest variables is really like a normal distribution, that is, has only one peak and is fairly symmetrical, the results will not be very different. I find in many cases, however, that the data suggest the world of norms is much more nonsymmetric and complex. For example, some norms have a bipolar distribution when seen in a bar chart of a Likert Scale. Others are highly skewed. Therefore, I conclude that investing time in learning/using/disseminating MPLUS is worthwhile. It is a strategically worth addition to the statistician's repertoire.

An example can illustrate the MPLUS approach. I will cite a Structural Equation Model that I am currently working on. However, to keep it simple I have chosen to use STATA software not MPLUS, thus strategically widening my audience and enabling an international team to engage with the issues of causality.

Generalized linear modeling offers a framework into which all the possible regression and structural equation models can fit (Bartholomew, Knott, and Moustaki 2011; see also Kaplan, 2008). The traditional simpler models become subsets of this grand multiequation structural model. An example of a GLM helps to illustrate how notation can be quite general and very helpful (Dobson and Barnett 2008). To entice a wide range of readers I first place the computer syntax for two such models in Box 9.2.

Box 9.2 Two Structural Equation Models

Program A: SEM with no Latent Factor (STATA)

```
*run the global variable declarations
global hkvars "educ1 educ2 educ3 educ4" *declares certain dummy variables
global indepvar " landown age age2 wealth1 widow chronic " *holds more vars
** ***** *** ***********
*run a generalised structural equation model of 2 equations
gsem (microfin <- $hkvars $indepvar, probit) (worksum <- $hkvars $indepvar)
*Eq. 6
gsem (microfin <- $hkvars $indepvar, probit) (worksum <- microfin $hkvars $indepvar)
*Eq. 7
estat summ *Presents the N and Means of the variables within the estimation sample
estat vce *Covariance matrix of coefficients of gsem model
```

Programme B: SEM with a Latent Factor (MPLUS Combined with STATA GSEM)

```
runmplus decidel decided decidev, ///
 idvariable(serial) ///
 missing are . ; WEIGHT IS poolwgt; ///
 categorical(decidel decided decidev) ///
 ANALYSIS(TYPE = general; ) ///
 model(f1 by decidel decided decidev ; f1 on age age2 ) ///
```

```
    tech(1); ///
    savedata(save=fscores; file=C:\DATA\factor1.dat) ///
    savelogfile(C:\DATA\factor1)
  preserve
  runmplus_load_savedata, out(factor1.out) clear
  gsem (workmedium <- age age2 i.eduy hindu i.state
rural widow fhh F1 , probit) (F1 <- rural age age2
i.eduy fhh i.state), coeflegend nocapslatent
  estat ic
  *Simplify and compare the BIC, AIC for the model with/
without F1 in Eq 1.
  gsem (workmedium <- age age2 i.eduy hindu i.state
rural widow fhh , probit) (F1 <- rural age age2 i.eduy
fhh i.state), coeflegend nocapslatent
  estat ic
```

Notes: the STATA code calls up uses structural equation modelling (SEM) and generalized structural equation modelling (GSEM) in both examples, and it calls up MPLUS in a two-stage procedure in Programme B.
Key: hk = human capital, reflecting Theory 1 human capital theory; microfin = engaged in microfinance borrowing, reflecting a Theory 2 about this kind of peer-guaranteed borrowing and saving. Estat refers to a command that presents summary statistics for the above equation.

In the first SEM in Box 9.2, education is a human capital variable measured on four ordinal levels; land and other wealth indicate economic resources, "widow" reflects social norms about the paid work time (worksum) of widowed women, and "microfin" is a dummy reflecting whether or not they received a microfinance loan package. Many other modeling methods could represent this situation, for instance, a Heckman two-step model where the odds of a loan are passed through to the labor supply (worksum) equation, or a structural equation model in MPLUS with mixture modeling. In all three methods, it may be necessary to decide and declare which of the variables' covariances are to be determined, and which are to be assumed as a "zero." This key question influences the feasibility of the estimation because more "zeroes" imply a higher ratio of the information (cases) to the parameters (variables and other unknowns in the model). The variance of each variable is one of the parameters, excepting where it can be assumed known or set to equal some other parameter, such as another variance.

In the second example in Box 9.2, a measurement model for who makes household decisions about key purchases is combined with a labor supply model. At the end, a test is run to see if the latent factor for decision-making affects the labor supply outcome. The model's goodness of fit is measured using Akaike and Bayesian Information Criteria (AIC, BIC), first with and then without the latent factor in Eq. (1). The difference of the AIC is considered in relation to the change of 1 in the degrees of freedom.

We find a useful synthesis of such models in Bartholomew, Knott, and Moustaki (2011). Another option at a slightly easier level is Brown (2015); and a lucid simple introduction, which is quite encompassing in its coverage, is Bowen and Guo (2011). Further extensions can be modeled with hierarchies of nested cases, that is, multilevel models (Goldstein 2003; Snijders and Bosker 2011; and an integration offered by Kaplan 2008). For an example of multilevel regression, see Troncoso, Pampaka, and Olsen (2015). Here school scores in student tests reflect aggregate value-added from teaching, combined with background factors, in a linear model.

8.4 Criteria for Validity of Research Arguments

When statisticians test the goodness of fit of a model, they often use a p-value to measure how well the data fit a given model. There are alternative measures to p-values, such as the comparative fit index (CFI) and the root mean squared error of association (RMSEA). These are measures of goodness of fit used in SEM. Kaplan (2008) devotes a chapter to expounding on a range of these tests.

The p-value measure of fit has a specific wording and is usually expressed as follows. Assume (or assert) that the data are a random sample from a population whose boundaries and character are known, for example, adults in the UK. Then based upon this one sample, the data suggest that the probability would be p percent or less, for example, 3 percent or less, of a different result occurring if we had taken a large series of independently drawn samples of the same size and type from that population. This probability, the p-value, is usually derived using the Central Limit Theorem which in turn can be deduced from mathematical principles. To make it concrete, we usually have an accept-reject form of hypothesis before doing the test. We aim for a 95 percent confidence level, that is, a p-value of 5 percent. This implies that if we reject the null hypothesis, there is only a 5 percent or less risk of being wrong, as would be shown if we had multiple repeated independent samples from the same population (perhaps 1,000 samples, or 10,000 samples.)

To focus on one simple case, the dispersion of the distribution of estimates of the mean of a variable X, for example, measured by the standard error, can be firmly shown to be smaller than the standard deviation of the data for the same variable using a single sample. This particular result is typically proven in statistics textbooks first for a binomial variable and then for continuous variables. The wording is carefully developed. As I've expressed it here, the wording of this claim does not depend on either a real, or posited, normal distribution of the initial variable X.

Statisticians thus not only discern a key difference between standard errors and standard deviations but generally frame the results of such a study—known generally as a frequentist study—in terms that are rooted in a discourse and practice of random sampling.

When a statistician has data with a poor sampling frame, the logic of p-values does not fit well. Similarly, with population data or a small set of cases, chosen as a convenience sample, the logic of p-values does not fit well. In such cases it is useful to consider "what would the p-value tell us if this had been a random sample." The statistician is likely to consider this result unpublishable in peer-reviewed journals. Yet exceptions are made, notably in economics and social policy where a population of N = 16 countries or N = 109 countries is frequently considered a good enough sample (!) upon which to base frequentist statistics.

Validity criteria including tests of goodness of fit are presented in textbooks from a deductivist point of view. I am concerned about this deductivism because the scientist then hesitates to comment on anything outside their immediate experience. I think we need more warranted arguments. Warranted arguments is—among other authors—Fisher's technical term, which has been adopted by a large body of writers on critical thinking; see Fisher 1988, 2001. I found it a convincing way to go about setting up a research-based argument.

I therefore promote a widening of epistemological values beyond the issue of the validity of a numerical estimate such as a mean or a regression coefficient. The epistemological values act as criteria for good research (Olsen 2012). The values used traditionally include those shown at left in Table 8.1. My own values are phrased rather differently, and spread more widely, as shown at the right.

An interesting difference between the traditional scientific approach—"naturalism" (where social science can mimic natural science)—and a realist approach is that for the latter, many interpretations are going to be potentially acceptable in describing a given scene or a set of evidence. The role of facts is no longer to falsify all theories but only to help a researcher build an argument rejecting some theories, leaving us still with issues (or tasks) in setting out why one may prefer one theory (or explanation, or description) over another.

In my own work I try for deep linkage of the findings based on a mixture of evidence types: often I have qualitative data, survey data, and the results of NVIVO coding and quantitative transformations. I hope in future to add more from action research activities, too. Deep linkage refers to linking the data of both qualitative and

Table 8.1 Values and Validity in Two Forms of Social Science

Traditional Science Approach	*Situated Knowledge Approach*
Validity	Makes reference to recorded evidence Critical assessment of evidence
Replicability	Makes reference to contexts Makes reference to reality not merely to theory
Reliability	Offers transparency by offering some evidence for independent scrutiny Sophisticated and/or systematic data recording
Social science mimics natural science (naturalism)	Appreciates diverse standpoints as special feature of social science (reflexivity) and of society; the social scientist has a specially wide and deep knowledge Plurality of theories, and critical approach to theories of change Depth ontology involving nested and non-nested cases Authentic voices

Source: For a discussion of situated knowledge see Smith (1998).

quantitative types through arguments that, as interpretations of the data, do any or all of the following three triangulating things:

1. Corroborate arguments built upon different parts of the data.
2. Complement and build further upon these or other arguments.
3. Contradict existing theories, and set up problems to solve, offering insight across the different types of data.

Theory triangulation and methods triangulation are presupposed in this threefold distinction, as proposed also by O'Cathainn, Murphy, and Nicholl (2010: 147–8).

Mixed methods works best with critical realist underpinnings, rather than positivist methodological assertions.

8.5 Additional Use of Statistical Tests in Surprising Places

F-tests can be summarized as a simpler statistical test. An F-test in general tests whether one variance exceeds another; a common application is to test whether the variance of one variable from a random sample is higher than the variance of the variable from another random sample. The ratio of the two variances is used as the F value. In both numerator and denominator the value is typically adjusted for the fact that a sample estimate is being made. Two examples abound in statistical literature. The F-test of linear regression examines how far the explained variance exceeds the unexplained part of the total variance of the dependent variable (Elliot et al. 2016). The second common F-test is found in Analysis of Variance (ANOVA). Here,

$$F = \frac{\text{Mean Squared Error Between Groups}}{\text{Mean Squared Error Within Groups}}$$

It is key that the measure found in the numerator should not in a meaningful way be determined by the measure in the denominator. Other than that, however, the F-test can be adapted for other uses. I will explain a fresh use of F-tests. My new use is to examine how the results of a QCA give "distances" that deviate from a zero-distance of the data from a forecast data pattern based on a specific causal hypothesis (Stryker and Eliason 2009).

I developed simple software to carry out this F-test on each possible configuration of the variables with a vector of possible causal variables (see https://github.com/WendyOlsen/fsgof). I gratefully acknowledge the programming help of John McLoughlin with fsgof. The variables should reflect real causal mechanisms that do not necessarily work independently from each other. Using QCA, we focus on conjunctions of the X factors rather than making the typical frequentist assumption that all the components of **X** are independent of each other. Instead of exogeneity, we have complexity as a grounding assumption (Byrne 2002).

This "F-test for QCA" illustration shows that a specific statistical method using hypothesis-testing and p-values can be consistent with competing methodological underpinnings. I think it shows how pluralism may be viable in social statistics. Here by "pluralism" I now don't just mean using two contrasting substantive theories, as I did earlier. I mean using two very different methods. I will explain what QCA is (see also Rihoux 2006) and then show how the F-test works in terms of a retroductive and deductive logic. Earlier I meant by pluralism that a SEM could encompass three or more theories. Some people call that theoretical pluralism, while I'm now turning directly to pluralism of methods.

Comparative case studies are an extension of the single case-study method to examine the systematic analysis of patterns in groups of cases. Case-study research can involve qualitative in-depth investigation of how similar events are caused (often also involving some multilevel process tracing [Bennett and George1997; George and Bennett 2005]). Ontological depth in the casing is commonly one aim of the exploratory stage of research. For example, Lam and Ostrom (2010) looked at watershed sites in Nepal, along with doing a field study of households who used water for both consumption and agriculture. The systematic analysis approach known as QCA and fuzzy-set analysis use a range of binary indicators and ordinal rankings to draw contrasts (Ragin and Rihoux 2009). Fieldwork and documentary research are commonly used in QCA (Ragin 2006). One of the tricks of this process is fuzzy-set measurement. Fuzzy sets measure the degree to which a case meets the criteria for membership in a qualitatively defined (or simply real) set. QCA brings together the ideas of the case, its features, other cases that are either nested within, or non-nested relative to the original type of case, and measurement methods along with ideas about causality.

Fuzzy-set QCA (abbreviated fsQCA), in particular, is a promising and well-established systematic case-study method. Sometimes to keep it simple the researchers avoid fuzzy sets and use crisp sets only. More examples are found in the JISC online email list about fuzzy sets and QCA, QUAL-COMPARE (www.jiscmail.ac.uk), or see the COMPASSS web site [*sic*] www.compasss.org, which is dedicated to the needs of those who do research using small and medium numbers of cases. A crisp set is a 0/1 binary that indicates whether or not a case is in a set, and crisp set QCA is denoted csQCA.

Fuzzy-set social science and csQCA come under the umbrella of fsQCA, involving research designs that explicitly delineate a series of cases as single-level or multi-level, nested or non-nested units. Postal services, for example, include the government Post Office plus a variety of parcel delivery service companies. Bank customers include organizations and individuals. Case-based researchers make a virtue of comparing cases of varying types and sizes. The "casing" stage of the research involves discerning the cases (Ragin 2009).

It is useful to glance at a microlevel QCA dataset to see how easily it can be coded into a spreadsheet format. See Figure 8.3 which has only one level of detail.

In Figure 8.3, (A) represents whether a system has received infrastructure assistance since the competition of the WECS/IIMI project. (R) represents whether farmers on a

A	R	F	L	C	W
0	1	0	1	1	1
0	1	0	1	1	0
0	1	1	1	1	1

Etc. for a total of 19 rows, representing 19 watersheds.

Figure 8.3 A QCA dataset for watersheds in Nepal with crisp variates only.

Source: Lam and Ostrom (2010).

system have been able to develop a set of rules for irrigation operation and maintenance. (F) represents whether farmers have worked out provisions for imposing fines. (L) represents whether leadership in a system has been able to maintain continuity and to adapt to chaining the environment. (C) represents whether farmers have been able to maintain a certain level of collective action in system maintenance. (W) indicates whether watershed has a good water supply.

To become a "truth table," this table could be collapsed slightly and a column for "*N* = Number of cases" added. Then we seek evidence that the pattern of the data fits one of two hypotheses about causality.

First we test each column for necessary cause. Ragin showed that if all the Y's have the X attribute, then it can be argued that X is necessary for Y to have occurred.

The second test will be whether any of the $2^k - 1$ permutations of the *X* variables is sufficient for Y to have occurred. Each permutation is called a configuration and it may have $N > 1$. Therefore it can appear contradictory: some cases Yes on Y and some No on Y. However, if in all cases within a configuration, those which have high levels of X have just as high levels of Y, the pattern suggests that X is sufficient for Y; see Olsen (2014).

We can test a variety of X hypotheses, with X being a single variable or a multivariate vector, such as here ARF is sufficient for good water supply W. If any or all of these are necessary for Y = W = WATERSHED HAS GOOD WATER SUPPLY then we say X is necessary for Y.

Social scientists have debated whether the values X and Y take on a timeless, unchanging level, as suggested by Ragin, or whether, in fact, the models are restricted to a specific time period. Without panel data, some critics say the QCA method is fundamentally flawed. Ragin argues instead that the method focuses on essences, which are indeed historically contingent but which, by virtue of being structural over a specified period, can be examined as if they were constants. No one says we would predict from a QCA model. Instead, we go onward: we will retroduce after generating the initial model results. Even if it was so that an X caused a Y in the past, for N = 19 with the many sub-elements (farmers, consumers, etc.), it is not necessarily so in the future. Retroduction will tell us about what has happened, and what is now happening, that has created the patterns in these data, exceptions included.

The degree of apparent sufficient causality of a configuration for Y is measured by a ratio known as the inclusion ratio (Smithson and Verkuilen 2006). A cutoff level such as 0.75 or 0.8 is recommended by Ragin. My own research and the F-test based on Stryker and Eliason (2009) also validates the use of such a level.

Books on QCA aim not only at getting to this conclusion but aim at assisting in the further step of qualitative interpretation. Seminal papers like those of Snow and Cress (2000) give lengthy, detailed, ethnographically well-informed interpretation of each configuration. No matter how small or large N is, this method often results in a handful of interpretable (differentiated) configurations of the X factors. The method can also be run on various Y outcomes, which in Snow and Cress's case involve four measures of the success of social movement organizations. The results need not depend entirely on consistency but also on the interpretive judgments of the social scientists.

See Rihoux and Grimm (2006) for applications in social policy areas.

In summary, the results of QCA are not primarily numerical. They are primarily qualitative. The Q in QCA means Qualitative not Quantitative. It is a mixed method but more on the qualitative side, yet it uses some numerical data very easily. The researcher can easily mix QCA with other methods from a wide range of options.

8.6 Conclusions

I have set out some statistical models, and shown how they fit into wider scientific investigation strategies. I said these were often an expression of a strategic structuralism: a commitment to the reality of prior social structures along with a commitment to doing research aiming to root out problems, help tweak systems to improve them, and generally be aware of agency and avoid being too atomistic. There are commonalities with Flyvbjerg's phronesis (2001).

I always urge statisticians to reach out toward having good, morally helpful representations that are ethical. I try to be well-grounded in complex strategies to change the world. Thus, I argue that I do critical social science. You will find compatriots in Radical Statistics, a charity based in the UK (see URL www.radstats.org.uk). But aiming at good strategically focused representations is already rather widespread, because most humans try to do good in the world.

Acknowledgments

I am grateful to Patricio Ruiz-Troncoso, Maria Pampaka, and my department (Social Statistics) at the University of Manchester. I am grateful to the British Academy for its grant, under International Mobility Partnership funds, to work on mixed-methods research during 2014–17. Our grant is called "Innovation in Global Labour Research Using Deep Linkage of Mixed-Methods Data," Number PM140147.

This chapter is produced for the TINT/Finnish Centre of Excellence for the Philosophy of the Social Sciences, Social and Moral Philosophy/Department of Political and Economic Studies, University of Helsinki, Finland.

Note

1 A reviewer wrote, "Sarantakos has retained the rigour, content and 'flavour' of the earlier edition whilst adding relevant new and necessary content ... It is a well-balanced text that is both comprehensive and detailed. Above all, it is very readable and very understandable."—Rob O'Neil, Lecturer in Sociology, University of Western Sydney, quoted from Amazon website, https://www.amazon.co.uk/Social-Research-2nd-Sotirios-Sarantakos/dp/0333738683/ref=dp_return_2?ie=UTF8&n=266239&s=books (accessed September 2016).

References

Agresti, A. 2013. *Categorical Data Analysis*, 3rd ed. London: Wiley.

Archer, M. S. 2000. *Being Human: The Problem of Agency*. Cambridge: Cambridge University Press.

Archer, Margaret. 1995. *Realist Social Theory: The Morphogenetic Approach*. Cambridge: Cambridge University Press.

Archer, Margaret S. 2010. "Morphogenesis versus Structuration: On Combining Structure and Action." *The British Journal of Sociology* 61: 225–52.

Archer, M., ed. 2015. *Generative Mechanisms Transforming the Social Order*. Dordrecht: Springer.

Babbie, Earl. 2013. *The Practice of Social Research*, International Ed., 13th ed. London: Wadsworth Cengage Learning. Basic undergrad text. Necessary and suff. Cause defined by Babbie on pages 96–7.

Barr, T., and N. Lin. 2013. *A Detailed Decomposition of Synthetic Cohort Analysis*. IZA Discussion Paper No. 7743. Available at http://ftp.iza.org/dp7743.pdf.

Bartholomew, D., Martin Knott, and Irini Moustaki. 2011. *Latent Variable Models and Factor Analysis, A Unified Approach*. Chichester: John Wiley.

Bennett, A., and A. George. 1997. "Process Tracing in Case Study Research." MacArthur Foundation Workshop on Case Study Method, New York. Available at http://users.polisci.wisc.edu/kritzer/teaching/ps816/ProcessTracing.htm (accessed 2014).

Bhaskar, R. 1975. *A Realist Theory of Science*. Leeds: Leeds Books. Reprinted 2008, *A Realist Theory of Science*. London: Verso.

Bhaskar, R. 1990. *Reclaiming Reality. A Critical Introduction to Contemporary Philosophy*. New York: Routledge.

Bhaskar, R. 1998. *The Possibility of Naturalism: A Philosophical Critique of the Contemporary Human Sciences*. London: Routledge.

Billington, J., Simon Baron-Cohen, and Sally Wheelwright. 2007. "Cognitive Style Predicts Entry into Physical Sciences and Humanities: Questionnaire and Performance Tests of Empathy and Systemizing." *Learning and Individual Differences* 17 (3): 260–8.

Blaikie, N. W. H. 2000. *Designing Social Research: The Logic of Anticipation*. Cambridge: Polity Press.

Blaikie, N. W. H. 2003. *Analyzing Quantitative Data*. London: Sage.

Blaikie, Norman. 2013. *Designing Social Research*, 3rd ed. (2nd ed. 2009). Cambridge: Polity.

Blaikie, P. 1993. *Approaches to Social Enquiry*. Cambridge: Polity.

Bollen, K. A. 1989. *Structural Equations with Latent Variables* (Wiley Series in Probability and Statistics). New York: John Wiley.

Borsboom, Denny, Gideon J. Mellenbergh, and Jaap van Heerden. 2003. "The Theoretical Status of Latent Variables." *Psychological Review* 110 (2): 203–19. doi: 10.1037/0033-295X.

Bowen, Natasha K., and Shenyang Guo. 2011. *Structural Equation Modelling*. Pocket Guide to Social Work Research Methods Series. Oxford: Oxford University Press.

Bridges, Sarah, David Lawson, and Sharifa Begum. 2011. "Labour Market Outcomes in Bangladesh: The Role of Poverty and Gender Norms." *European Journal of Development Research* 23 (3): 459–87.

Brown, Timothy A. 2015. *Confirmatory Factor Analysis for Applied Research*, 2nd ed. New York: Guilford Press.

Bryman, A. 1988. *Quantity and Quality in Social Research*. London: Routledge.

Bryman, A. 1998. "Quantitative and Qualitative Research Strategies." In *Knowing the Social World*, ed. T. May and Malcolm Williams. Buckingham: Open University Press.

Bryman, A. 2008. *Social Research Methods*. Oxford: Oxford University Press.

Byrne, B. 2011. *Structural Equation Modelling Using MPLUS*. London: Routledge.

Byrne, D. 2002. *Interpreting Quantitative Data*. London: Sage.

Byrne, D., and C. Ragin, eds. 2009. *Handbook of Case-Centred Research Methods*, London: Sage.

Carter, B., and Caroline New, eds. 2004. *Making Realism Work: Realist Social Theory and Empirical Research*. London: Routledge.

Danermark, B. 2001. *Explaining Society: An Introduction to Critical Realism in the Social Sciences*. London: Routledge.

De Vaus, D. A. 2001. *Research Design in Social Research*. London: Sage.

Dobson, Annette J., and Adrian G. Barnett. 2008. *An Introduction to Generalized Linear* Models, 3rd ed. London: Chapman and Hall.

Downward, P., and A. Mearman. 2007. "Retroduction as Mixed-Methods Triangulation in Economic Research: Reorienting Economics into Social Science." *Cambridge Journal of Econoics* 31 (1): 77–99.

Elliot, Mark, Ian Fairweather, Wendy Olsen, and Maria Pampaka. 2016. *A Dictionary of Social Research Methods*. London: Oxford University Press.

Fisher, A. 1988. *The Logic of Real Arguments*. Cambridge: Cambridge University Press.

Fisher, A. 2001. *Critical Thinking: An Introduction*. Cambridge: Cambridge University Press.

Flyvbjerg, B. 2001. *Making Social Science Matter: Why Social Inquiry Fails and How It Can Succeed again*. Cambridge: Cambridge University Press.

Fuller, B., G. Caspary, S. L. Kagan, C. Gauthier, D. S. L. Huang, J. Carroll, and J. McCarthy. 2002. 'Does Maternal Employment Influence Poor Children's Social Development?' *Early Childhood Research Quarterly* 17: 470–97.

Goldstein, Harvey. 2003. *Multilevel Statistical Models*, 3rd ed., London: Oxford University Press.

Hair, J. F., R. E. Anderson, R. L. Tatham, and W. C. Black. 2005. *Multivariate Data Analysis*. Upper Saddle River, NJ: Prentice Hall.

Hunt, S. 1994. "A Realist Theory of Empirical Testing: Resolving the Theory-Ladenness / Objectivity Debate." *Philosophy of the Social Sciences* 24 (2).

Jann, B. 2008. "The Blinder–Oaxaca Decomposition for Linear Regression Models." *Stata Journal* 8: 453–79.

Kabeer, Naila, Lopita Huq, and Simeen Mahmud. 2013. "Diverging Stories of 'Missing Women' in South Asia: Is Son Preference Weakening in Bangladesh?" *Feminist Economics* 20 (4): 1–26. Available at http://dx.doi.org/10.1080/13545701.2013.857423.

Kaplan, David. 2008. *Structural Equation Modelling: Foundations and Extensions*, 2nd ed. London: Sage.

Lam, Wai Fung, and Elinor Ostrom. 2010. "Analyzing the Dynamic Complexity of Development Interventions: Lessons from an Irrigation Experiment in Nepal." *Policy Sciences* 43 (1): 1–25.

Lawson, T. 1997. *Economics and Reality*. London: Routledge.

Lawson, T. 2003. *Reorienting Economics*. London: Routledge.

Layder, D. 1993. *New Strategies in Social Research*. Cambridge: Polity Press.

Lemon, Mark. 2003. *Exploring Environmental Change Using an Integrative Method*. Hoboken: Taylor and Francis.

Loehlin, J. C. 2004. *Latent Variable Models: An Introduction to Factor, Path, and Structural Equation Analysis*, 4th ed. New York: Psychology Press.

Long, J. Scott. 1983. *Confirmatory Factor Analysis*, Series: *Quantitative Methods in the Social Sciences*. New York: Sage.

Morgan, J., and W. K. Olsen. 2011a. "Conceptual Issues in Institutional Economics: Clarifying the Fluidity of Rules." *Journal of Institutional Economics* 7 (3): 425–54. doi:10.1017/S1744137410000299.

Morgan, J., and W. K. Olsen. 2011b. "Aspiration Problems for the Indian Rural Poor: Research on Self-Help Groups and Micro-Finance." *Capital and Class* 35 (2): 189–212. doi: 10.1177/0309816811402646.

Morgan, J., and W. Olsen. 2007. "Defining Objectivity in Realist Terms: Objectivity as a Second-Order 'Bridging' Concept." *Journal of Critical Realism* 6 (2): 250–66. Available at http://www.equinoxjournals.com/ojs/index.php/JCR/).

Morgan, J., and W. Olsen. 2008. "Defining Objectivity in Realist Terms: Objectivity as a Second-Order "Bridging' Concept, Part 2: Bridging into Action." *Journal of Critical Realism* 7 (1): 107–32. Available at http://www.equinoxjournals.com/ojs/index.php/JCR/.

Muthén, B. 1983. "Latent Variable Structural Equation Modeling with Categorical Data." *Journal of Econometrics* 22 (1/2): 43–65.

Muthén, B. 1984. "A General, Structural Equation Model with Dichotomous, Ordered Categorical, and Continuous Latent Factors." *Psychometrika* 49: 115–32.

Muthén, B. 1989. "Latent Variable Modeling in Heterogeneous Populations." *Psychometrika*, 54: 557–85.

Muthén, B. 1994. "Multilevel Covariance Structure Analysis." *Sociological Methods and Research* 22: 376–98.

Muthén, B., and Tihomir Asparouhov. 2009. "Multilevel Regression Mixture Analysis." *J. R. Statistical. Society. A* 172 (3): 639–57.

Muthén, B., and Kaplan, D. 1985. "A Comparison of Some Methodologies for the Factor Analysis of Non-normal Likert Variables." *British Journal of Mathematical and Statistical Psychology* 38: 171–89.

Muthén, L. K., and B. O. Muthén. 2006. *MPLUS: Statistical Analysis with Latent Variables: User's Guide*, 4th ed. Los Angeles, CA: Muthén and Muthén.

O'Cathain, A., E. Murphy, and J. Nicholl. 2010. "Three Techniques for Integrating Data in Mixed Methods Studies." *British Medical Journal* 341: 147–8. doi: 10.1136/bmj.c4587.

Olsen, W. 2014. "Comment: The Usefulness of QCA under Realist Assumptions." *Sociological Methodology* 44: 101–7. doi: 10.1177/0081175014542080.

Olsen, W. K. 2009a. "Beyond Sociology: Structure, Agency, and Strategy among Tenants in India." *Asian Journal of Social Science* 37 (3): 366–90. Available at http://brill.publisher.ingentaconnect.com/content/brill/saj/2009/00000037/00000003/art00005.

Olsen, W. K. 2009b. "Non-Nested and Nested Cases in a Socio-Economic Village Study." In *Handbook of Case-Centred Research*, ed. D. Byrne and C. Ragin. London: Sage.

Olsen, W. K. 2010. "Realist Methodology: A Review." In *Realist Methodology, Benchmarks in Social Research Methods*, ed. Olsen, W. K., xix–xlvi. London: Sage.

Olsen, Wendy Kay. 2012. *Data Collection*. London: Sage.

Olsen, W. K., and J. Morgan. 2005. "A Critical Epistemology of Analytical Statistics: Addressing the Sceptical Realist." *Journal for the Theory of Social Behaviour* 35 (3): 255–84.

Olsen, W. K., Daniel Neff, J. Rangaswamy, and Vincent Ortet. 2015. "Strategies for Social Justice via Economic Theory." In *Economics of Social Justice: A Handbook for Students*, ed. Miriam Kennett, Iolanda Cum, and Sabeeta Nathan, 214–56. Reading: Green Economics Institute. ISBN 978-1-907543-46-3.

Outhwaite, W. 1987. *New Philosophies of Social Science: Realism, Hermeneutics and Critical Theory*. Basingstoke: Macmillan.

Potter, G. 1999. *The Philosophy of Social Science: New Perspectives*. Harlow: Longman.

Quine, W. V. O. 1951. *Two Dogmas of Empiricism from a Logical Point of View*. Boston, MA: Harvard University Press.

Ragin C. 1997. "Turning the Tables: How Case-Oriented Methods Challenge Variable Oriented Methods." *Comparative Social Research* 16: 27–42.

Ragin, C. C. 2000. *Fuzzy-Set Social Science*. Chicago, IL: University of Chicago Press.

Ragin, C. C. 2008. *Redesigning Social Inquiry: Fuzzy Sets and Beyond*. Chicago, IL: University of Chicago Press.

Ragin, C. C. 2009. "Reflections on Casing and Case-Oriented Research." In *Handbook of Case-Centred Research Methods*, ed. D. Byrne, and C. Ragin, 522–34. London: Sage.

Rihoux, B. 2006. "Qualitative Comparative Analysis (QCA) and Related Systematic Comparative Methods: Recent Advances and Remaining Challenges for Social Science Research." *International Sociology* 21 (5): 679–706.

Rihoux, B., and C. C. Ragin. 2009. *Configurational Comparative Methods: Qualitative Comparative Analysis (QCA) and Related Techniques* (Applied Social Research Methods). Thousand Oaks, CA: Sage.

Rihoux, B., and M. Grimm, eds. 2006. *Innovative Comparative Methods for Policy Analysis: Beyond the Quantitative-Qualitative Divide*. New York: Springer.

Roth, P. A. 1987. *Meaning and Method in the Social Sciences: A Case for Methodological Pluralism*. Ithaca, NY: Cornell University Press.

Sarantakos, S. 1998. *Social Research*, 2nd ed. London: Palgrave Macmillan.

Sayer, Andrew. 1992. *Method in Social Science*. London: Routledge.

Sayer, Andrew. 2000. *Realism and Social Science*. London: Sage.

Scott, J. 2011. *Conceptualising the Social World*. Cambridge: Cambridge University Press.

Smith, M. J. 1998. *Social Science in Question*. London: Sage.

Smithson, M., and J. Verkuilen. 2006. *Fuzzy Set Theory: Applications in the Social Sciences*. Thousand Oaks, CA: Sage.

Snijders, Tom A. B., and Roel Bosker. 2011. *Multilevel Analysis: An Introduction to Basic and Advanced Multilevel Modeling*, 2nd rev. ed. London: Sage.

Snow, D., and D. Cress. 2000. "The Outcome of Homeless Mobilization: The Influence of Organization, Disruption, Political Mediation, and Framing." *American Journal of Sociology* 105 (4): 1063–104.

Stryker R., and S. Eliason. 2009. "Goodness-of-Fit Tests and Descriptive Measures in Fuzzy-Set Analysis." *Sociological Methods & Research* 38:102–46.

Tabachnick, B. G., and L. S. Fidell. 1996. *Using Multivariate Statistics*. New York: HarperCollins.

Troncoso, P., M. Pampaka, and W. Olsen. 2015. "Beyond Traditional School Value-Added Models: A Multilevel Analysis of Complex School Effects in Chile." *School Effectiveness and School Improvement* 293–314. doi:10.1080/09243453.2015.1084010.

Ullman, J. 2006. Chapter 17 of Tabachnick and Fidell on structural equation models, NY: Harper Collins: Ullman, J. (2006), ch. 17 of Tabachnick and Fidell, 2006 edition of their 1996 book (online only). See also almost the same text as *Journal of Personality Assessment* 87 (1): 35–50, *Statistical Developments and Applications*, URL file:///C:/o/Te/LFA/Ullman%20%20Structural%20equation%20modeling.Ch17.Ullman2006.pdf, Accessed Sept. 2016. See also the earlier edition, where Ullman's chapter is printed with the rest of the book, Ullman, J. B. (2001). Structural Equation Modeling. In Tabachnick, B.G. & Fidell, L. S., (2001) Eds., *Using Multivariate Statistics* (4th Ed). Boston: Allyn and Bacon.

Weston, A. 2002. *A Rulebook for Arguments*, 4th ed. Indianapolis: Hackett.

Williams, M. 2000. *Science and Social Science: An Introduction*. London: Routledge.

Further Online References

JISC online e-mail list about fuzzy sets and QCA. See QUAL-COMPARE list at www.jiscmail.ac.uk

See COMPASSS web site [*sic*] www.compasss.org —Dedicated to the needs of those who do research using small and medium numbers of cases.

Commentary: Heterogeneity, Plasticity, and Mechanisms: Comments on Olsen

Daniel Little

Wendy Olsen is a social-science researcher trained in statistics and econometrics, but with a deep engagement with critical realism as well. She writes extensively on methodology, but she has also done primary research on gender, inequalities, economic development, and social attitudes in India and other parts of South Asia. Her book *Data Collection* (Olsen 2011) represents an extensive treatment of the methods of social inquiry that reflects both commitments, and the current chapter highlights many of the central findings of that book.

There are several things that I particularly appreciate about Olsen's work, both in the current chapter and elsewhere: her recognition of the importance of social ontology, her support for the ideas associated with critical realism, and her arguments for methodological and theoretical pluralism in social research. I will focus on these themes in my brief comments.

Some readers may find that abstract exposition of ideas about social ontology and epistemology is more difficult to follow than it needs to be. It is therefore useful to see how these ideas play out in a concrete case of social research. Fortunately, we can do that in the context of Olsen's empirical work. In fact, most of the ideas about social ontology that she expresses in the current chapter are illustrated in useful detail in her co-authored article with Jamie Morgan, "Entrapment of Unfree Labour: Theory and examples from India" (Olsen and Morgan 2015). In this research article Olsen and Morgan consider the phenomenon of unfree labor in India, and they emphasize the heterogeneity, plasticity, and contingency of the practices that fall under this social category. They make use of a method involving analysis of more than one hundred case studies, and they document many of the dimensions over which the reality of unfree labor shifts over time, space, and social location.

This research illustrates several important themes developed in the current essay. First, it gives concrete expression to the mantra of critical realism: that social relations and structures have a reality that is not fully observable, but that gives rise to the "generative mechanisms" that produce the social phenomena that are more directly accessible to research. The underlying reality of the social relations of unfree labor represents an important and clear example of the correctness of this view. Second,

Olsen's recommendation of making use of multiple methods and making systematic efforts to "triangulate" available evidence to arrive at well-justified conclusions is validated by the research presented in "Unfree Labor." In addition, several of the most basic ontological principles expressed in the current chapter (contingency, heterogeneity, plasticity) are illustrated in "Entrapment of unfree labor". (See my *New Directions in the Philosophy of Social Science* [Little 2016] for more detailed exposition of the major themes mentioned in here.)

Heterogeneity and Plasticity

Heterogeneity is a very basic characteristic of the domain of the social. And this makes a big difference for how we should attempt to study the social world "scientifically." The fundamental heterogeneity of the social world comes down to this: at many levels of scale we continue to find a diversity of social things and processes at work. A modern city represents a highly diverse set of social activities, purposes, and structures. Society is more similar to a modern city than a block of glass. Heterogeneity makes a difference because one of the central goals of positivist science is to discover strong regularities among classes of phenomena, and regularities appear to presuppose homogeneity of the things over which the regularities are thought to obtain. So, to observe that social phenomena are deeply heterogeneous at many levels of scale, is to cast fundamental doubt on the goal of discovering strong social regularities across groups of highly similar things.

This means that it is crucial to avoid the fallacy of reification of the social world onto a fixed set of entities, properties, and forces. Rather, the social world consists of a deeply heterogeneous mix of processes, some of which are better suited to an ethnographic or comparative approach, just as other processes may be best studied quantitatively. If one is interested in the topic of corruption, for example, he/she will need to be informed about institutions, culture, principal-agent problems, social psychology, and many other potentially relevant sociological factors. And these researches may well require a combination of statistical analysis, comparison across a select group of cases, and ethnographic investigation in a small number of specific cases and individuals.

The fact of heterogeneity has important implications for social research. Importantly, social causation is inherently multiple, with many kinds and tempos of social causation at work. It is therefore crucial that we avoid the impulse to reduce social change to a single set of underlying causal factors. The occurrence of a race riot at a time and place—Detroit 1967, Chicago 1968, Watts 1965—is partly caused by the instigating incident, partly caused by the long-simmering background conditions, partly caused by the physical geography of the city in question, and partly caused by a legal and political context far from the site of rioting. We sometimes describe this fact as the conjunctural nature of social causation. Second, social events, changes, and forms of stability depend on contingent alignments of forces and causes, which do not recur in regular sequences of Humean causation. Third, social causes are generally historically conditioned, with the result that we do not have a general statement of, same cause, same effect. We can summarize these points by saying that social causation is contingent, contextual, and conjunctural.

Olsen and Morgan's analysis of the complexity of the phenomenon of unfree labor illustrates this fact of heterogeneity in the social realm: the phenomenon of unfree labor exists, it is a profound disadvantage in the lives of the poor men and women whom it touches, and it works through multiple practices, norms, and mechanisms. So the social reality of unfree labor is not one unified and unchanging social structure or property, and we cannot give a simple and idealized definition of the phenomenon.

The features of plasticity and historicity that Olsen emphasizes are also very important aspects of social ontology. Upon careful examination, it is clear that virtually all social entities are "plastic": their properties change significantly over time, as a result of the purposive and unintentional behavior of the socially constructed individuals who make up a society. Organizations, labor unions, universities, churches, and social identities all show a substantial degree of flexibility and fluidity over time, and this fact leads to a substantial degree of variation among groups of similar social organizations and institutions. This points to a general and important observation about the constitution of the social world: The properties of a social entity or practice can change over time; they are not rigid, fixed, or timeless. They are not bound into consistent and unchanging categories of entities, such as "bureaucratic state," "Islamic society," or "leftist labor organization." Molecules of water preserve their physical characteristics no matter what. But in contrast to natural substances such as gold or water, social things can change their properties indefinitely.

This ontology emphasizes a deep plasticity in social entities over time. Organizations and institutions change over time and place. Agents within these organizations change their characteristics through their own behavior, through their intentional efforts to modify them, and through the cumulative effect of agents and behavior over time and place. Social constructs are caused and implemented within a substrate of purposive and active agents whose behavior and mentality at a given time determine the features of the social entity. As individuals act, pursue their interests, notice new opportunities, and innovate, they simultaneously "reproduce" a given institution and also erode or change the institution. So institutions are not fully homeostatic, preserving their own structure in the face of disturbances. Institutional arrangements and rules are a contingent and path-dependent result of the actions and mental frameworks of individuals and groups (past and present) who make up the institution, and they generally do not constitute a system in stable equilibrium.

Critical Realism

Olsen makes admirable efforts to incorporate the ontological insights of critical realism (including positions advanced by Bhaskar, Archer, and Elder-Vass) into a discipline that all too often presupposes an unsophisticated empiricism in its philosophy of social science and social knowledge. Critical realism maintains, most fundamentally, that social science requires the discovery of underlying generative mechanisms in order to explain social outcomes of interest. This is no less true in quantitative research than in other areas of social science. Olsen is right in arguing that statistical inquiry no less than other areas of social science needs to be framed by appropriate background theories and hypotheses about the way the social world works. Along the lines recommended by critical realism, statistical research needs to be guided by appropriate ontological assumptions about the nature of social entities and forces, and its methods and hypotheses need to be guided by ideas about the nature of those entities and forces. It is particularly valuable to examine in depth the ways in which statistical reasoning and analysis can be improved by attention to the theories of critical realism and this is precisely what Olsen encourages us to do.

As Olsen points out, Margaret Archer's development of the idea of morphogenesis is a particularly valuable bridge between abstract doctrines of critical realism and concrete efforts at social research. Archer summarizes her theory of morphogenesis in her contribution to *Late Modernity* (Archer 2014). Archer is consistent in referring to three "moments" of the social process, which she breaks into three phases T1, T2–T3, and T4:

T1 structural/cultural conditioning →
T2–T3 social interaction →
T4 structural/cultural elaboration or stasis

At the risk of over-simplifying, we might summarize Archer's view in these terms. Each phase involves constraints on action and interaction. T1 involves the large structural and cultural contexts in which individuals take shape and act. T2–T3 involves the interactions of individuals who bear interests and group identities and who strive to bring about outcomes that favor those interests and identities. And T4 represents a new formation (elaboration) of a complex of structural and cultural constraints. It is striking how closely this summary resembles the theory of strategic action fields put forward by Fligstein and McAdam (2012). This framework in turn gives more concrete understanding of what is needed on Olsen's requirement that statistical research design should seek out the underlying structures and actions that produce the social outcomes of interest. Researchers need to form hypotheses about the underlying mechanisms and processes that generate the social outcomes that are described in statistical terms within the study.

Key in Archer's approach is the idea of seeking out "generative mechanisms" of social change. What would be an example of such a mechanism? In her introduction to *Social Morphogenesis* Archer refers to "struggles for domination and control" (Archer 2013: 7) as a generative mechanism, and later she refers to "conflicting pressures of primary and corporate agency" (Archer 2013: 14). In each instance structures, rules, and organizations are understood as being malleable and subject to the pushes and pulls of actors within current circumstances.

There may seem to be a contradiction between the idea of social realism and the idea of heterogeneity. And yet both notions are key to Olsen's argument. Is the ontology of critical realism compatible with the idea of a highly heterogeneous social world? Or do Bhaskar and other critical realists presuppose social essences and universal causes in ways that are inconsistent with heterogeneity (Bhaskar 1975, 1989)? There are elements in Bhaskar's theory that point in both directions on this question.

His emphasis on the logic of experimentation is key to his transcendental argument for realism. But oddly enough, this analysis cuts against the premise of heterogeneity because it emphasizes exceptionless causal factors. He emphasizes the necessity of postulating underlying causal laws, which are themselves supported by generative causal mechanisms, and the implication is that the natural world unfolds as the expression of these generative mechanisms. This idea is plainly stated in *The Possibility of Naturalism* (Bhaskar 1989: 11). Second, his account sometimes seems to rest upon a kind of "mechanism fundamentalism"—the idea that there is a finite set of nonreducible mechanisms with essential properties (1989: 11). These are a few indications that Bhaskar's realism might be uncongenial to the idea of social heterogeneity.

More compelling considerations are to be found on the other side of the issue, however. First, Bhaskar's introduction of the idea of the social world as an "open" system of causation leaves space for causal heterogeneity.

Another reason for thinking Bhaskar is open to heterogeneity in the social realm is his position on reductionism. In a word, he rejects the idea that important features of the social world can be reduced to the fixed operations of a set of lower-level (individual-level) social mechanisms (Bhaskar 1975: 59).

Finally, his discussion of social structures in *The Possibility of Naturalism* as the social equivalent of natural mechanisms also implies heterogeneity over time:

> Social structures, unlike natural structures, may be only relatively enduring (so that the tendencies they ground may not be universal in the sense of space-time invariant). (1989: 49)

So on balance, we can reasonably conclude that Bhaskar's philosophy of social science is indeed receptive to social heterogeneity. And this in turn makes it a substantially more compelling contribution to the philosophy of social science than it would otherwise be, and superior to many of the positivist variants of philosophy of science that he criticizes. And this in turn enhances the coherence of Olsen's position in her work on social methodology and ontology.

Methodological Pluralism

A third important component of Olsen's philosophy of social science is her recommendation of a pluralistic method for social inquiry. As suggested here, the social world is heterogeneous, with multiple kinds of causes at work at any given time. So, as she argues in this chapter, we should embrace both theoretical and methodological pluralism. We should be open to multiple theories of social causation; we should be receptive to multiple forms of inquiry and evidence about the social world. This is associated with her defense of "triangulation"—the idea that we best understand a complicated social reality when we make use of multiple kinds of inquiry and evidence in arriving at ideas about the underlying social reality.

There are a number of fundamental reasons why the social sciences should be receptive to pluralism. Analysis of the situation of knowledge producers would suggest methodological pluralism. Multiple theories, perspectives, and methods lead to deeper insight into the social world.

More fundamentally, the complexity, contingency, and heterogeneity of the social world itself supports the need for multiple theories and methods in studying social phenomena. There is not one single kind of social process, for which there might conceivably be a uniquely best kind of method of inquiry. Indeed, Olsen is explicit in noting that there are multiple kinds of social causes and mechanisms at work in the social world, and she is equally explicit in noting that social structures persist but change over time. We should be open to a variety of tools and methods, and should design research in a way that is closely tailored to the nature of the empirical problem. And therefore sociologists should be encouraged to be eclectic in their reading and thinking; they should be exposed to many of the approaches, perspectives, and methods through which imaginative sociologists have addressed their problems of research and explanation.

In other words, there are very deep arguments supporting the value and epistemic suitability of methodological pluralism. And this in turn suggests that social science disciplines are well advised to incorporate a variety of methods and frameworks into their doctoral programs.

Let us reflect briefly on what the idea of methodological pluralism implies when it comes to using both quantitative and qualitative research methods. The social world is one reality, but the methodologies associated with quantitative and qualitative research are quite different. Quantitative research allows the researcher to discover patterns, associations, correlations, and other features of a population based on analysis of large numbers of measurements of individuals. Qualitative research usually involves studies of single individuals and situations, based on interviews and observations, with the goal of identifying their internal psychological and behavioral characteristics. Quantitative research is directed at identifying population characteristics, patterns, and associations. Qualitative research is directed at teasing out the mental frameworks and experiences of individuals within specific social and cultural settings. Qualitative researchers are generally not interested in discovering generalizations or regularities, and they are more interested in identifying particular features of consciousness, culture, and behavior. So how is it possible to integrate these disparate approaches into a single study? What kinds of interface or bridging are possible between these two levels of social research?

Take the example of race and ethnicity studies. Both qualitative and quantitative research studies have been conducted in this field, with the goal of shedding light on the phenomenon of race in American society. Quantitative research has often been concerned to identify the features of inequality which are associated with race within American populations, including income, wealth, education, health, employment, and other important features. For example, the National Survey of Black Americans provides voluminous data on a range of characteristics of African American individuals, with surveys extending from 1979 to 1992 (Jackson, Neighbors, and Gurin 1977 cont.). Several hundred research studies and reports have been completed making use of these datasets; for example, social psychologist James Jackson has made extensive use of datasets like these to probe health disparities by race. These quantitative studies permit the researcher to use advanced statistical tools to measure and evaluate the strength of associations among characteristics and to evaluate causal hypotheses about the linkages that exist among characteristics.

Qualitative research on race takes several forms. There are ethnographic studies, through which the researcher attempts to identify the phenomenology and lived experience of race. Here we can cite several important examples—Al Young's study of young inner city Chicago men (Young 2004), Loïc Wacquant's ethnographic study of a boxing club on Chicago's south side (Wacquant 2004), or Elijah Anderson's treatment of young black men in Philadelphia (Anderson 1999). There are theoretical studies exploring possible structures or mechanisms, which produce racial and racialized behavior and disparities. Here is a good example from Elizabeth Cole on the construct of intersectionality as a way of theorizing about racial and gender identities (Cole and Zucker 2007; Cole 2008). And there are studies of social psychology designed to identify the ways in which racial attitudes, presuppositions, and ideas contribute to behavior in American society. A nice example of such an analysis is provided by Lawrence Bobo and Cybelle Fox (2003).

It is clear that studies based on all of these methodologies are insightful and valuable. We will arrive at a better understanding of the meaning and causal importance of "race" through all these approaches. The question raised here remains an important one, however: how should we think about the relations among these bodies of inquiry and knowledge?

One possibility is that these different methodological approaches do not admit of "bridging" at all. Here the idea would be that these are fundamentally different forms of knowledge, and they belong in different parts of the toolbox. Sometimes this approach is taken by advocates of one methodology or the other in dismissing the scientific credentials of the other approach—quantitative researchers who dismiss qualitative research as anecdotal and qualitative researchers who dismiss quantitative research as positivist. This approach seems fundamentally wrong. We should look at the various ways of studying important aspects of social life as being complementary and fundamentally consistent.

Another way is to think in terms of *levels of analysis*: we might say that quantitative studies examine facts about race at a more macrolevel (large populations), whereas qualitative studies are more meso- or microlevel studies. This isn't a very satisfactory view, however, because each of these approaches is concerned about individual-level facts; what differs is the level of aggregation of those facts that is chosen.

An alternative approach seems more promising: to consider the suite of qualitative studies of race as being a tool box for identifying the *social mechanisms* through which the patterns and associations that are discovered at the large population level come about. Qualitative studies (studies aimed at discovering or theorizing the mentalities and behaviors through which race is constructed and carried out) permit us to understand racialized behavior in groups that in turn allow us to understand the population outcomes that quantitative studies identify.

Perhaps the most plausible approach is to think of the qualitative approaches as providing insight into how various social processes work; how it is that socially constructed actors bring about the patterns of behavior and outcome we observe at various levels of aggregation. A quantitative study of racial attitudes might suggest that cities with effective public transportation have higher (or lower) levels of racial mistrust across groups. We would want to be able to form some hypotheses about what the underlying behaviors and attitudes are that bring about this effect. What are the mechanisms through which access to public transportation influences racial trust? And for this kind of inquiry to be possible, we need to have some good empirical theories about racial identities and mental frameworks.

So it does in fact seem both possible and desirable to try to integrate the findings of both quantitative and qualitative studies of racial attitudes; this finding seems equally valid in almost all areas of the social sciences.

More generally, it is clear that there is no basic incompatibility between quantitative and qualitative methods. Each is amenable to the rigorous collection and assessment of empirical evidence. Each embodies well-established modes of inference through which the researcher can arrive at conclusions based on the evidence assembled. And most important, each kind of research has the potential for supplementing and extending the scientific understanding of social phenomena permitted by the other. Quantitative social scientists now commonly recognize that it is crucial to be able to identify causal mechanisms that give rise to the statistical associations that they discover. These mechanisms commonly have to do with patterns of human behavior and meaning which qualitative and comparative researchers are best situated to understand. So, quantitative research benefits by partnership with qualitative researchers. But likewise, the qualitative researcher who discovers a particular kind of mechanism in the limited domain of interviews and observations that he or she has performed on a given research topic will be well advised to attempt to find quantitative data sources that can help to support or limit the degree of generalizability that the qualitative findings have. Suppose, for example, that a qualitative researcher of youth recruitment into extremist populist movements in Stockholm finds that a common experience among new followers is a disrupted family life. It will be scientifically valuable to make use of European opinion surveys to attempt to determine whether there is evidence of this mechanism at work in other European cities as well. This shows in practical terms that both quantitative and qualitative methods are valuable tools for studying the complex forms of social behavior that are so important in understanding contemporary social change.

Conclusion

In short, Olsen is to be applauded for helping to focus some much-needed conversation within the social sciences on the importance of ontology, mechanisms, and pluralism for creating an adequate scientific understanding of the social world. The social world is too heterogeneous and contingent to permit us to maintain the illusion that master theories (rational choice theory, modernization theory, world systems theory, historical materialism) will permit us to derive important social outcomes. And this very heterogeneity and contingency also shows that a purely statistical and quantitative approach to social research will fail. We need hypotheses about generative mechanisms if we are to make sense of the wide range of data available to us about the social world. And this implies that it will be useful for quantitatively minded social scientists to spend some effort grappling with the philosophy of critical realism as they formulate their research hypotheses and methods.

References

Anderson, Elijah. 1999. *Code of the Street: Decency, Violence, and the Moral Life of the Inner City*, 1st ed. New York: W. W. Norton.

Archer, Margaret Scotford. 2013. *Social Morphogenesis*. New York: Springer.

Archer, Margaret Scotford. 2014. *Late Modernity: Trajectories towards Morphogenic Society, Social Morphogenesis*. New York: Springer.

Bhaskar, Roy. 1975. *A Realist Theory of Science*. Leeds: Leeds Books.

Bhaskar, Roy. 1989. *The Possibility of Naturalism: A Philosophical Critique of the Human Sciences*, 2nd ed. London: Harvester Wheatsheaf.

Bobo, Lawrence D., and Cybelle Fox. 2003. "Race, Racism, and Discrimination: Bridging Problems, Methods, and Theory in Social Psychological Research" *Social Psychology Quarterly* 66 (4): 319–32.

Cole, Elizabeth R. 2008. "Coalitions as a Model for Intersectionality: From Practice to Theory." *Sex Roles* 59 (5–6): 443–53.

Cole, Elizabeth R., and Alyssa N. Zucker. 2007. "Black and White Women's Perspectives on Feminity." *Cultural Diversity and Ethnic Minority Psychology* 13 (1): 1–9.

Fligstein, Neil, and Doug McAdam. 2012. *A Theory of Fields*. New York: Oxford University Press.

Jackson, James S., Harold W. Neighbors, and Gerald Gurin. 1977 cont. *National Survey of Black Americans Series*. Ann Arbor, MI: ICPSR.

Lerche, Jens. 2007. "A Global Alliance against Forced Labour? Unfree Labour, Neo-Liberal Globalization and the International Organization." *Journal of Agrarian Change* 7 (4): 425–52.

Little, Daniel. 2016. *New Directions in the Philosophy of Social Science*. Lanham: Rowman & Littlefield.

Olsen, Wendy. 2011. *Data Collection: Key Debates & Methods in Social Research*, 1st ed. Thousand Oaks, CA: Sage.

Olsen, Wendy, and Jamie Morgan. 2015. "Entrapment of Unfree Labour: Theory and Examples from India." *Journal of Developing Societies* 31 (2):184–203.

Wacquant, Loïc J. D. 2004. *Body & Soul: Notebooks of an Apprentice Boxer*. Oxford: Oxford University Press.

Young, Alford A. 2004. *The Minds of Marginalized Black Men: Making Sense of Mobility, Opportunity, and Future Life Chances, Princeton Studies in Cultural Sociology*. Princeton, NJ: Princeton University Press.

Part Three

Explanation, Theorizing, Performativity

Summary of Chapters

The third part of the volume shifts the emphasis from methods to theory. The chapters raise a range of philosophically challenging issues about the relations between theory and causal inference, the theoretical and the empirical, and theory and its performative effects.

David Waldner discusses process tracing as a method of within-case causal inference in political science. That process tracing plays an important role in social sciences is by now largely acknowledged, but it is still controversial how it functions exactly and how effective it is as a method of causal inference. Waldner has both a critical and positive outlook on process tracing. While acknowledging its potential, he claims that under the current understanding process tracing has not obtained yet the status of a defensible form of within-case causal inference. In his view, greater inferential leverage can be gained once the lesson and implication of a theory of mechanism is fully understood by political scientists. In their current practice, scholars do associate process tracing to causal theories of mechanism, but they fail to fully absorb them in their account and to effectively relate them to their method. Waldner provides a four-pronged standard of within-case causal inference so as to redeem justification of mechanism-based causal inference by way of process tracing. Daniel Steel, while sharing Waldner's diagnosis, sees his proposal as problematic because it fails to provide an account of how process tracing can actually solve the problem of unmeasured common causes. He provides a solution of his own that sees process tracing as using mechanisms as a heuristic to identify relevant variables to measure, variables that allegedly connect the putative cause to its effect, and, if measured, to reduce the underdetermination of causal hypotheses.

Mikael Carleheden discusses the role of social theory in scientific investigation and focuses on the case of sociology. He says that there are different meanings of social theory, and thus different answers to the question of what the role of social theory should be. Carleheden adopts a historical internalistic perspective that sheds light on the reasons why sociologists have shifted over time their conception of social theory. The author is particularly concerned with the distinction between the theoretical and the empirical, which has remained firmly in place despite the widespread recognition of the fact that theorizing is a significant part of doing empirical research. In his view, sociology tends either toward some forms of theoretical paternalism or some unquestioned scientistic conception of the empirical. Carleheden concludes by pointing to a third way that consists in a move toward immanence and toward theory as post-factum interpretation, or reconstruction. Stephen Tuner's commentary supplements Carleheden's account with a sort of philosophical backbone. He retells the story of sociology as proceeding from a condition of pluralism, through the attempt by Parsons and Merton to overcome it, and to the final return to it. In his view, the failure to overcome pluralism is caused by features of the subject matter—the limited applicability of social concepts as well as the underdetermination of theory by the data—that inhibits the success of any attempt at overcoming pluralism in sociology.

The final chapter by Daniel Breslau examines the performative role of economic theories and technologies in the formation of economic agents as "assemblages." The recent literature on performativity based on science and technology studies has incorporated the role of economic knowledge and technologies in the formation of economic agents as assemblages. Another strand of literature on the sociology of prices emphasizes political struggle in explaining the establishment of pricing systems. Using the case of recent reforms in the retail pricing of electricity, Breslau investigates the concurrent formation of a new price system and of the economic agents who are attuned to it. Through an analysis of a specific regulatory case, in which a new pricing framework was proposed, negotiated, and approved, he finds that not only the price system adopted is the outcome of a political struggle among actors with conflicting interests but also the consumers themselves, the kind of calculations they are able to make, and their ability to respond to those prices are outcomes of this process. As a result of the regulatory proceeding, the electricity consumer is reconfigured as a boundedly rational calculating economic agent. Nicolas Brisset in his commentary distinguishes two opposing ontological views underlying the literature on performativity—classical constructivism (Bourdieu) and decentralized constructivism (Actor Network Theory by Callon). While the former construes theory as part of causally potent macro structures, the latter interprets theory as part of technological devices that form a flat network of symmetrical agents involving both human and nonhumans. Brisset argues that decentralized constructivist ontology fails to help us identify the conditions under which a theory becomes performative. He commends Breslau for overcoming this problem by studying the political process through which a theory attains legitimacy to change the social world.

9

Causal Mechanisms and Qualitative Causal Inference in the Social Sciences

David Waldner

9.1 Introduction

Political scientists often want to answer questions like "What were the causes of World War I?" or "Why did the Egyptian military overthrow the democratically elected government in 2014?" To answer these questions, political scientists have developed a qualitative method called process tracing. Process tracing claims to "open the black box of causality," to move beyond correlations between causes and effects by investigating the process that connects a cause to its outcome. In effect, if one can observe traces of the process connecting X and Y, then one can be confident in the claim that X is the true cause of Y.

This essay adopts a sympathetic but critical stance toward process tracing. It intends to diagnose some problems in current understandings of process tracing, not to dismiss the method but rather to strengthen it. Process tracing needs further development to respond to two challenges, one internal to the method and one external to it. The internal challenge considers whether process tracing constitutes valid causal inference by its own explicit standards. Process tracing has two components, a set of procedures for empirical analysis—the core method—and a commitment to a mechanistic theory of causation. I argue below that the methods should be interpreted as a procedure for comparative hypothesis testing that overlaps considerably with a form of explanation called inference to the best explanation. While a valuable tool, inference to the best explanation is not equivalent to causal inference. Process-tracing methods might become strengthened when joined with a mechanistic theory of causation. I argue below that the mechanistic theory of causation favored by process tracers is under-developed and does too little work informing the empirical methods. The internal challenge, then, is that process-tracing methods are not yet defensible as a form of within-case causal inference.

The external challenge to process tracing stems from criticisms stemming from the Rubin Causal Model, (henceforth, RCM), which is the reigning theory of causal inference among quantitative social science methodologists. Advocates of the statistical analysis of causal relations deny that unit-level causal effects can be identified due to the "fundamental problem of causal inference," or the inability to observe simultaneously a unit's actual outcome under treatment and its counterfactual outcome under control. The claim that unit-level causal inference is impossible clashes with the process-tracing claim to derive causal claims from within-case analysis. Indeed, if the external challenge cannot be defeated, then process tracing can never become defensible as a form of within-case causal inference.

In this essay, I seek a principled intermediary position between conventional process tracers and those who deny the possibility of making causal claims at the unit level. I believe that meeting the challenge posed by the fundamental problem of causal inference is, in fact, feasible, in principle at least. Meeting this external challenge, even partially, promises to strengthen process-tracing methods, making them a more suitable instrument of causal inference. I argue below that updating the methods requires, in part, rethinking some features of mechanistic theories of causation. The essay thus embodies the importance of allowing empirical work to be motivated by philosophical inquiry; perhaps philosophers will find parallel lessons from the discussion of empirical methods.

I develop this argument in three main parts. The chapter begins with an introduction to process tracing, in part by way of two examples that are widely admired as successful examples of process tracing. This section then considers, in turn, process-tracing methods, which I argue are inadequate to causal inference, and the ways in which process tracers attempt to fortify their methods by drawing on a mechanistic theory of causation, an effort I consider to be largely unsuccessful. The second section introduces the RCM and the fundamental problem of causal inference. I consider some efforts by process tracers to avoid the fundamental problem of causal inference, but find them unpersuasive. The third section then outlines a modified approach to process tracing that, I argue, could in principle mitigate the fundamental problem of causal inference. This method combines causal graphs, event-history maps, and invariant causal mechanisms. A final section concludes by briefly considering some implications of the argument for theories of causation.

9.2 Process Tracing

The editors of an early and still influential collection of essays about qualitative methods defined process tracing as the "Examination of diagnostic pieces of evidence, commonly evaluated in a temporal and/or explanatory sequence, with the goal of supporting or overturning alternative causal hypotheses." A more recent collection of essays defines process tracing as "the examination of intermediate steps in a process to make inferences about hypotheses on how that process took place and whether and how it generated the outcome of interest." The key idea of process tracing shared by both definitions is to emphasize collecting diverse pieces of within-case evidence that shed light on the intervening processes connecting X and Y. Diverse evidence yields a range of opportunities for comparative hypothesis testing; some pieces of evidence will be highly dispositive, others less so. It is this differential dispositive value of evidence about intervening processes that is the core of process tracing and that distinguishes process tracing from standard statistical approaches that seek to establish correlations between X and Y while controlling for confounding variables.

The current state of the art of process tracing methodology is a three-legged stool consisting of (1) causal-process observations (CPOs), (2) hypothesis testing, and (3) Bayesian updating. CPOs are defined in contrast to dataset observations. The latter are the contents of cells in a rectangular dataset, based on the systematic coding or operationalization of variables for each unit as part of a statistical technique for establishing covariation. A CPO, on the other hand, is "an insight or piece of data that provides information about context, process, or mechanism, and that contributes distinctive leverage in causal inference" (Collier, Brady, and Seawright 2010: 277). James Mahoney (2012: 125–31) usefully distinguishes between three types of CPOs: (1) independent-variable CPOs, or data relevant to confirming the presence of a posited cause whose existence is controversial; (2) auxiliary-outcome CPOs, or data relevant to observable implications of a theory other than the main outcome of interest but which should be present if the causal relationship has been properly specified; and (3) mechanism CPOs, or data concerning posited intervening events and processes that a given theory leads us to expect link cause and effect.

These various CPOs are then used in a variety of hypothesis tests all derived from the hypothetico-deductive method. According to this method, each theory generates expectations about implied observations—predictions, in other words, of what the evidence must look like if the theory is true. Scholars of qualitative methods have worked out four permutations of this basic procedure.[1] Each prediction has more or less of two qualities: certitude and uniqueness. A prediction, or an expected observation given the posited truth of a hypothesis, is certain to the extent that the observation must be made to confirm the hypothesis, such that if the observation is not made, the hypothesis is falsified. A certain prediction, in other words, allows us to use the propositional logic of modus tollens:

$$P \rightarrow Q; \neg Q; \Rightarrow \neg P. \tag{9.1}$$

If, on the other hand, Q is observed, we are not permitted to infer backward to P: this is the logical fallacy of affirming the consequent. Consequently, tests based on the certitude of a prediction can disconfirm a hypothesis but not confirm one, as Popper long ago taught us. For this reason, process tracers call tests based on the certitude of a proposition "hoop tests" and have traditionally treated them as necessary but not sufficient for confirmation. Alternatively, a prediction may have the property of uniqueness, such that one and only one hypothesis predicts the existence of particular observations. Process tracers argue that these tests confer strong confirmation because observations consistent with the prediction can be derived from one and only one hypothesis. Hence, process tracers refer to these tests as "smoking-gun" tests. Predictions that combine the two attributes are "doubly-decisive tests," while prediction lacking both are "straw-in-the wind" tests that confer minimal confirmatory value.

Finally, Bayesian updating is used to interpret the results of these tests.[2] Given an estimated prior probability, p(h), we derive an updated probability conditional on the evidence, p(h|e) by estimating two likelihoods, the likelihood of the evidence given the truth of the hypothesis (the rate of true positives) and the likelihood of the evidence given the non-truth of the hypothesis (the rate of false positives), which together comprise the probability of the evidence. Given these three probabilities, we use Bayes' Theorem to update the probability of the hypothesis. Bayesianism allows us to quantify, albeit subjectively, the probative value of the evidence on the truth of the hypothesis.[3] With Bayesian analysis, we can drop the categorical logic of necessary and sufficient conditions for confirmation in favor of calculating continuous likelihood ratios, such that higher likelihood ratios correspond to stronger evidentiary tests (Humphreys and Jacobs 2013). This development frees us from the unrealistic assumption that certitude and uniqueness are binary variables.

Each of these three legs of the methodological triad of process tracing—CPOs, hypothesis testing, and Bayesian analysis—has been developed by following a descriptive path more than a prescriptive path. One or more examples of process tracing are taken to be "exemplars" that set the methodological standard for others to follow. Let's consider two such exemplars.

In perhaps the most widely discussed and admired example of process tracing, Henry Brady reconsiders the claim that in the American presidential elections of 2000, the premature announcement by network news shows that the Democratic candidate Al Gore had won the state of Florida before the polls had closed in the western panhandle of the state of Florida—which is on Central Time, one hour later than the rest of the state—dissuaded Republicans from voting, robbing the Republican candidate, George Bush, of at least 10,000 votes. This claim, derived from statistical analysis of data from four Florida elections, implied that even without the highly contentious recount of the 2000 Florida vote, George Bush should have been declared the winner in Florida. Brady uses diverse qualitative evidence to dispute this claim. He asks the basic question: if it is true that the premature declaration of Gore as the winner dissuaded more than 10,000 panhandle residents from casting ballots in favor of Bush, what else must be true of the causal process linking the network announcement to the decision to not vote? Simple logical deduction yields four questions: How many voters had not yet voted? Of those not-yet voters, how many heard the network announcement? Of those who heard the announcement, how many decided not to vote? And of the induced non-voters, how many would have voted for Bush over Gore?

Brady uses diverse sources of data to make the following claims. First, he estimates that about 300,000 residents of the Florida panhandle voted on election day. Second, he estimates that given the network announcement was made at 6:50 Eastern Time, leaving only ten minutes for the panhandle polls to remain open, no more than about 4,200 voters were likely to vote in the last ten minutes, given that the polls were open continuously from 7:00 a.m. to 7:00 p.m. This estimate would only be biased downward if there was an unusual rush to the polls in the last ten minutes, but diverse sources of evidence cast doubt on that proposition. Third, of the 4,200 potential voters, approximately 20 percent, or 840 people, would have heard the premature network announcement. Of these 840 people, how many were likely Bush voters? Brady estimates, once again drawing on diverse sources, that Bush would have received about 2/3 of the votes, or 560 Bush voters who had not yet voted by 6:50 p.m. likely heard the premature network announcement. Finally, of these 560 potential last-minute Bush voters, how many would have decided not to vote? Brady estimates a dissuasion rate of 10 percent, so 56 Bush voters would have decided to not vote at the last minute. But if we apply the same rate to last-minute Gore voters, 28 out of 280 votes would have been lost, yielding a final estimate of 28 net votes lost. Needless to say, this estimate is orders of magnitude lower than the figure of 10,000 estimated statistically precisely because process tracing is based on careful analysis of the causal process itself.

Brady's research is an exercise in falsification: in effect, he identifies a series of hoop tests that the network announcement hypothesis must pass, and then systematically demonstrates that the hypothesis fails every hoop test. What about using process tracing to validate a causal claim? A primary example is Nina Tannenwald's analysis of the nonuse of nuclear weapons after the Second World War, an outcome Tannenwald attributes to the development of a "nuclear taboo" that made their use unthinkable and so inhibited their use. From a process-tracing perspective, Tannenwald confirms this claim by considering "observable implications that should be true ... about the process through which the use of nuclear weapons should have been considered and rejected" (Bennett 2015: 277). One such implied observation would be that at least a subset of decision-makers considering the use of nuclear weapons would raise the nuclear taboo and in doing so would deter others who were more disposed toward their use. Clearly, this is a "hoop test": if nobody raised the nuclear taboo, then the nuclear taboo cannot have been the relevant cause. A second implied observation would be that those policy makers who favored the use of nuclear weapons protested the use of normative arguments to ultimately determine military strategy. Because no other theory predicts this observation, process tracers consider it a "smoking-gun" test. Hence, process tracers consider Tannenwald's argument to be confirmed because it passes both a hoop test and a smoking-gun test.

Process tracers have recently appended a Bayesian framework to this core procedure of looking for diagnostically dispositive evidence that confirms a causal hypothesis while casting doubt on its rivals. Bennett (2015) interprets Tannenwald's argument from a Bayesian perspective by proposing three reasonable probabilities: the probability that the theory is true, prior to looking at new evidence; the probability that we will observe the new evidence given that the theory is true; and the probability that we will observe the new evidence given that the theory is false, or the false positive rate. Bennett calculates that the passage of the hoop test and the smoking-gun test raises the probability that the theory is true from approximately 40 percent to about 75 percent, with most of the increase stemming from the smoking-gun test because it is highly unlikely that we would observe the new evidence if the theory were false. From a Bayesian perspective, Tannenwald's use of process-tracing methods results in a very high level of confidence that the nuclear taboo constitutes a valid causal explanation of the nonuse of nuclear weapons.

Each of these components of process tracing is a major advance in case-study methods, and taken together, they constitute a significant and invaluable set of claims about the procedures of within-case research. Yet it is my contention that a qualitative within-case study could faithfully execute these procedures without establishing a valid causal inference. To be concrete, I do not think that the passage of a hoop test and a smoking-gun test implies that the nuclear taboo is the cause of the nonuse of nuclear weapons. The hoop test, after all, is largely irrelevant to the causal inference. Causal inference begins when we observe some empirical association and we question whether it is a truly causal relationship. The passed hoop test merely establishes the association between the taboo and the outcome, establishing the existence of X. The smoking-gun test, on the other hand, does not appear sufficient to establish a causal relationship for it only tells us that some participants in the strategic debate objected on normative grounds to one type of argument made by other participants in the strategic debate. In fact, it is not self-evident that evidence about how losers in a debate complained about arguments made by winners should be interpreted as part of the process linking a cause to an effect.[4] Imagine an election won by candidate A after which candidate B complains about campaign statements made by candidate A: should we jump to the conclusion that these statements are the cause of the electoral victory? Should we then ignore macro-economic conditions, the distribution of partisan identities, and get-out-the-vote efforts, among other factors? Clearly, the bar for causal inference is set too low in this example because process tracers have substituted the criterion of uniqueness (does any rival theory predict this evidence) for the criterion of causal relevance.

Indeed, I wish to argue that a low-bar of causal inference is characteristic of process tracing. Consider each leg of the methodological triad in turn. The distinction between CPOs and dataset observations is an important insight into types and uses of evidence. Yet the distinction neither divides evidence into mutually exclusive categories nor exhausts all types of evidence. On the one hand, some dataset observations are surely relevant to causal processes. That observations have been systematically coded according to an explicit set of operational rules and that multiple observations have been systematically recorded, either across units or across time, or both, does not preclude the possibility that these observations are relevant to causal processes and contexts. The difference is that dataset observations are typically used to establish statistical associations but nothing precludes a researcher from extracting a dataset observation from a dataset and using it qualitatively as a CPO. On the other hand, and more importantly, surely there is evidence that is not formatted as a dataset observation but is also irrelevant to a causal process: these are non-causal, non-dataset observations. If this further distinction is not taken into account, then literally all non-dataset observations become, by default, CPOs, a conceptual equivalence that surely strips the concept of virtually any meaning or analytic utility. To be blunt: calling an observation a "causal process observation" cannot be allowed to license that observation as automatically establishing a causal relationship. To do so would be to confuse naming with inference.

Turn next to the quartet of tests—hoop tests of certain predictions, smoking-gun tests of unique predictions, and their positive and negative conjoining. Each test embodies the logic of the hypothetico-deductive method, which asks the basic question of what qualities a body of evidence must possess to confirm a hypothesis. Note that confirming a hypothesis partially overlaps with causal inference but does not exhaust the category of causal inference, for one can use evidence to confirm a non-causal hypothesis. We might test the hypothesis "All celestial bodies follow elliptical orbits" by appending the initial condition "The earth is a celestial body" and then deducing the observational prediction "The earth must follow an elliptical orbit." The reasoning is impeccable; the claim is non-causal. The method is, quite evidently, a standard procedure for testing a range of different types of hypothesis, including hypotheses about purely empirical or statistical associations; standard tests of statistical significance and the derivation of confidence intervals from standard errors all conform to the logic of a "hoop test," but none of these tests imply causal relevance per se.

Finally, adding Bayesian reasoning does not substantially alter this conclusion; to think otherwise would be to attribute to Bayesianism features that it does not possess. Bayesianism, after all, deals with inverse probabilities that, if given a uniform causal interpretation, would violate the key idea that outside of some areas of theoretical physics, causation has temporal direction. Thus, if A causes B and A precedes B in time, then B does not cause A; but both P(A|B) and P(B|A) are well-defined probabilities. Conditional probabilities permit symmetrical relations that are ruled out by causal relations (Gillies 2000: 129).

The claim is not that Bayesian reasoning is irrelevant to causal reasoning, but rather that using Bayesian reasoning (or other logics for reasoning about the relationship between hypothesis and evidence) by itself does not convert an empirical association into a causal relationship. Bayesianism has served two purposes. On the one hand, it is a theory of probability, distinct from a frequentist theory, one that allows us to take into account subjective prior beliefs when thinking about how to assign probabilities. On the other hand, it plays a role in a theory of confirmation, helping to solve some problems that would be created by an exclusive reliance on falsifiability as the criterion of confirmation. Neither of these functions directly speaks to the question of causal inference; most obviously, Bayesian can be used to reason through non-causal relationships. Suppose I tell you that I had a fascinating conversation with a stranger on a train. You wish to know whether the stranger was a man or a woman. Your prior probability that I spoke to a woman, based on known empirical distributions, is 0.5.[5] Next, I tell you that my conversation partner had long hair. Suppose, reasonably, that P(LH|W) = 0.75 and P(LH|M) = 0.15. Then a simple computation gives us the posterior probability, P(W|LH) = 0.83. The evidence use to update the reasoning was diagnostically relevant, but the procedure has nothing to do with causal inference. Put differently, some hypotheses are about causal relationships, some hypotheses are about statistical associations, and some hypotheses are about descriptive features of some unit or entity; Bayesianism itself does not distinguish these types of hypotheses and so its use cannot be the source of causal inference.

In its current state, process-tracing methodology is best understood, I contend, as a form of inference to the best explanation, as explicated most recently by Peter Lipton (2004). Given a body of evidence, it is entirely justifiable to reason about the underlying causal process that, if true, would best account for the evidence. If upon awakening to a layer of fresh snow on a large field, with one set of footprints to and from my doorway, and a fresh bottle of milk on my doorstep, it is entirely justifiable to reason that the milkman made an early morning delivery after the snow had stopped falling. The footsteps themselves count as a hoop test (presuming the milkman does not use drone-based delivery, although this scenario is rapidly becoming more plausible), while the presence of the bottle of milk, given background knowledge of the local delivery of dairy products, is a plausible smoking-gun test. Inference to the best explanation can yield plausible explanations, but we run into serious trouble if we allow plausibility to govern our judgments about valid causal inferences. For example, returning to the example of the nuclear taboo, one influential expositor of process tracing methods claims that Tannenwald's analysis calls attention to particular pieces of data (e.g., specific conversations among high-level decision makers) which suggest that sustained discussion and even consideration of nuclear use was inhibited by prevailing norms. In evaluating her argument, the critical issue is precisely whether the nuclear taboo actually exists; if it does, it seems quite plausible that it would affect decision-making about nuclear weapons. In fact, given how the concept of nuclear taboo is defined by Tannenwald, its presence almost by definition shapes decision-making concerning nuclear use. Tannenwald's study can thus be seen mainly as an effort to use independent variable CPOs in support of the idea that a nuclear taboo did in fact exist after the Second World War.

I think we should be concerned when the validity of a causal claim is settled with reference to plausibility and to purely conceptual analysis.

My claim to this point is the best-articulated procedures of process tracing as an empirical method are not sufficient to reliably produce valid causal inferences or explanations. Yet there is a second pillar of process tracing that should bear directly on the question of causal inference. It is quite common to see process tracers defend their method with reference to the philosophical literature on causal mechanisms. Alexander George and Andrew Bennett, for example, extensively discuss causal mechanisms in their chapter on case studies and the philosophy of science. This chapter includes a very insightful definition of mechanisms as "ultimately unobservable physical, social, or psychological processes through which agents with causal capacities operate … to transfer energy, information, or matter to other entities" (George and Bennett 2005: 137). They define process tracing as a method that "attempts to identify the intervening causal process—the causal chain and causal mechanism—between an independent variable (or variables and the outcome of the dependent variable."

Two problems stand between this very promising beginning and the full redemption of a mechanistic understanding of process tracing. First, while process tracers almost uniformly justify their use of the method by reference to the philosophical literature on mechanisms, this justification fails because, to date, process tracers have not fully absorbed the literature on causation and mechanisms and so their justifications are only partial and not fully coherent. As Illari and Russo (2014: 126–7) recently opined, "Arguably the social science literature has been preoccupied more with how mechanisms are found or theorized, and with the role they play in explanation and theory, and less with developing a definition that captures the essential elements of mechanisms or that applies to all scientific contexts." I extend these critical comments below.

The second problem is that as we turn from theory to methods, causal mechanisms tend to disappear. In the George and Bennett exposition referenced above, the discussion of mechanisms appears in a separate chapter from the discussion of methods. In a more recent collection of essays, the editors introduce ten "best practices" for process tracing. Remarkably, not one of these ten best practices explicitly refers to causal mechanisms, raising doubts about the ability of process tracing to redeem its promise to justify causal inference by identifying causal mechanisms. In effect, mechanisms are found in the philosophical preamble but not in the concrete methodological procedures. Insofar as mechanisms play any inferential role, it is a negative one; hypotheses that explicitly specify mechanisms are to be preferred to those rival hypotheses that do not specify a causal mechanism. But at best, this methodological guideline can be used to eliminate rival hypotheses. While this logic of elimination has long-standing value—it is, after all, but an extension of John Stuart Mill's Methods of Similarity and Difference or Michael Scriven's modus operandi method—it falls short of explaining how a mechanistic theory of causation justifies particular instances of causal inference. In effect, even when evoking causal mechanisms, process tracers have not moved far beyond inference to the best explanation.

It should be clear, then, that despite considerable progress, process tracing is not established upon a coherent theory of causal inference. This places process tracing in an unenviable and, I think, unsustainable position, for there exist far more developed theories of causal inference according to which process tracing cannot be a valid form of causal inference. Most importantly, according to the RCM, also known as the potential outcomes framework, unit-level causal inference is simply impossible due to the fundamental problem of causal inference. The next section explicates this theory of causal inference and the challenge it poses to process tracing.

9.3 Causation as Intervention and the RCM

To understand the significance of the RCM, let's begin with the standard statistical approach to causation, the conventional wisdom that has been superseded by the RCM. The standard approach begins with a dataset, a sample of observations drawn from a theoretically infinite population of potential data. Statistical models estimate coefficients or fixed parameters fitting a functional form determined by the researcher, such that observed values of the response variable are functions taking the general form

$$Y = \alpha + \beta X + \gamma Z + \epsilon \tag{9.2}$$

where Y denotes the response or outcome variable, β denotes the coefficient of the main causal variable of the hypothesis being tested, γ is a vector of coefficients on the vector of control variables, Z, and ϵ is a stochastic error term. The substantive interpretation of β is quite straightforward as a marginal effect: a one-unit change in X is associated with a β-unit change in Y. Control variables represent confounders, or variables correlated with both the main variable and the response variable such that their omission leads to biased estimates of the coefficient β. Conditioning on confounders yields the partial effect of X on Y. The stochastic error term represents an unknown combination of measurement errors and omitted variables that, by assumption, are not correlated with X and so do not produce biased estimates, though violation of this assumption is common. Standard practice requires the reporting of standard errors, confidence intervals, and p-values, each of which provides information on the probability of false positives produced by random sampling error. The p-value is the probability of the data given that the hypothesis is false: if it were the case that the true but unknown population-level parameter were 0, what is the probability of obtaining a sample of data from a nonzero coefficient derived?

There is no doubt that statistical models can be used for prediction: given our estimate of β, and holding all other variables fixed, we can predict outcomes for any level of X. But the development of the standard statistical approach has always been shadowed by debate over its appropriate causal interpretation. Assuming the proper functional form of the statistical model, the standard approach licensed a causal interpretation when three conditions were met: X unambiguously preceded Y in time, Y was not simply a function of its own lagged values, and the relationship between X and Y persisted after controlling for the relevant confounding variables. It should be clear that this causal interpretation of statistical models draws on Humean ideas about causation: finding a statistical relationship after controlling for confounding variables is nothing but a more sophisticated method for demonstrating constant conjunction.

Standard statistical models, however, provide absolutely no information about the results of an intervention to change X. It is for this reason that statistical theory draws a bright line between using statistics to study an empirical relationship and drawing causal conclusions from statistical models. David Freedman, for one example among many others, insists on the difference between "conditional probabilities that arise from selection of objects with X = x and conditional probabilities arising from an intervention that sets X to x. The data structures may look the same, but the implications can be worlds apart" (Freedman 2010: 260). Indeed, standard statistical models predict precisely because they assume fixed parameters, an assumption that stands in stark contrast to most contemporary discussions of causality that invoke counterfactual responses to intervention and manipulation, whether these interventions are real or hypothetical. Causal inference thus requires our thinking about what might have been observed under different circumstances.

This shift from a regularity theory of causation to an interventionist theory of causation is part of the motivation for the RCM, which explicitly defines causation and causal effects in terms of interventions. The RCM can be concisely explicated as follows. Let y_{it} denote the outcomes of unit i under one of two states of the world, with $T \in \{0, 1\}$. Assume that the two potential outcomes for unit i, y_{i1} and y_{i0}, are fixed prior to treatment; they might be genetically conditioned responses to a cancer treatment, for example. Define a causal effect as the difference for unit i of the outcome under treatment and control,

$$\delta_i = y_{i1} - y_{i0} \tag{9.3}$$

Measuring causal effects, then, requires a well-defined treatment and always implies a well-defined counterfactual. Consider Donald Rubin's (1974: 689) simple example of taking aspirin to treat a headache. For those taking the treatment, the relevant counterfactual is that "had I not taken two aspirin 30 minutes ago, my headache would not have disappeared," while for those in the control group, the relevant counterfactual would be "had I taken two aspirin 30 minutes ago, my headache would have disappeared." This measure of causal effects has natural affinity with a manipulation theory of causation, whereby X is a cause of Y just in case that intervening on X produces changes in Y without altering any part of the causal system not mediating the relationship between X and Y (Woodward 2003). Now let $\omega \in \{0, 1\}$ be an indicator variable for treatment status; then for a given assignment, we observe $y_i = \omega y_{i1} + (1 - \omega)y_{i0}$; but we do not observe $y_i = (1 - \omega)y_{i1} + \omega y_{i0}$. This is the fundamental problem of causal inference, which is an unavoidable missing-data problem.

One might think a simple before-and-after research design would mitigate the fundamental problem of causal inference: take one or more measures before and then after the intervention to investigate whether the intervention altered the underlying secular trend. If the headache persists unabated prior to taking the aspirin, and then begins to abate shortly after taking the aspirin, then it seems quite plausible that the aspirin caused the reduction of the headache. But the RCM defines a causal effect as the difference between two potential outcomes measured simultaneously. Furthermore, even if we relax the condition of absolutely simultaneous measurement, a before-after research design is fraught with inferential peril. Consider, as a first example, the problem of over-prescribed antibiotics: after a lingering episode of respiratory distress, some patients will be prescribed and will take a week-long course of antibiotics, following which the patient returns to full health. But we know all too well that in a large percentage of these cases, the underlying cause was viral and hence unaffected by the antibiotic. Second, for at least some children, receiving vaccinations precedes the onset of significant medical complications such as a diagnosis of autism, but the scientific consensus is that vaccinations are causally unrelated to these conditions. Research-design textbooks provide standard catalogues of these various threats to the internal validity of naive comparisons of pre- and posttreatment outcomes without randomized assignment and a control group (Shadish, Cook, and Campbell 2002, chapter 2).

Therefore, according to the RCM, while causal effects are defined on a single unit, we can only learn about causal effects by observing differences across multiple units. If this consequence is valid, then process tracers are committing an inferential felony when they base causal claims on single-unit, within-case analysis. Furthermore, consider the inferential challenge that attends learning about causal effects by comparing two or more units to one another. Ideally, we would derive an average treatment effect by observing a group of units under treatment and the same group under control,

$$E[Y_{i1} \mid \omega = 1] - E[Y_{i0} \mid \omega = 1] \tag{9.4}$$

Think of this quantity as the difference between a group of unwell people receiving medical treatment and the same group of people not receiving medical treatment even though their health status merits therapeutic intervention. But, of course, we do not observe the counterfactual condition $E[Y_{i0} | \omega = 1]$, as we can observe a group of units either under treatment or under control, but not under both states simultaneously. What we can observe is

$$E[Y_{i1} \mid \omega = 1] - E[Y_{i0} \mid \omega = 0] \tag{9.5}$$

Think of this as the difference between a group of people receiving medical treatment after having been assigned to treatment because they are ill and a second group of people not receiving medical treatment after being assigned to the control group and hence not receiving treatment because they are healthy. As we can easily imagine,

$$E\left[Y_{i0} \mid \omega = 1\right] \neq E\left[Y_{i0} \mid \omega = 0\right] \tag{9.6}$$

In other words, unhealthy and untreated people are not equivalent to healthy and hence untreated people, and so we cannot use a measure of healthy people not receiving medical treatment as a substitute for the counterfactual outcome of unhealthy people not receiving medical treatment without introducing nontrivial bias into our measure of the causal effect. This bias is commonly known as selection bias, or the bias incurred from the nonrandom selection of units to treatment status.

There are three basic ways to manage the problem of selection bias. In a random controlled experiment, subjects are randomly assigned to treatment and control groups after which the experimenter intervenes to administer the treatment. Random assignment ensures that the potential outcomes are statistically independent of treatment assignment, $(Y_{i1}, Y_{i0}) \perp\!\!\!\perp T$; in effect, those who receive treatment are not, on average, more likely to have either a higher-than average response or a lower-than average response. When working with nonexperimental or observational data, the RCM inspires design-based inferences. In one set of such designs, naturally occurring selection processes are reconstructed to demonstrate that they are effectively analogous to randomization; call this "as-if" randomization, the basis for natural experiments and regression discontinuity designs. In a second set of such designs, the scholar seeks to achieve a status known as conditional independence of assignment and treatment such that the potential outcomes are statistically independent of treatment assignment after conditioning on covariates, $[(Y_{i1}, Y_{i0}) \perp\!\!\!\perp T]|X$. Any of these three conditions—investigator-induced random assignment, "as-if" randomization, or posttreatment conditioning to mimic the effects of randomization (sometimes known as "as good as randomization")—can be used as foundation of an unbiased estimate of the treatment effect, and is known in related literatures as unconfoundedness, exogeneity, or strong ignorability of treatment assignment (Imbens and Rubin 2015, chapter 3). For most analyses of observational data, exogeneity requires relatively strong knowledge of the assignment mechanism, either to argue for a natural experiment, in which social processes effectively mimic random assignment, or to propose a statistical model of the assignment process and hence control for nonrandom assignment (Dunning 2012).

The RCM thus poses two daunting challenges to process tracing. The first challenge is the fundamental problem of causal inference, which denies the possibility of unit-level or within-case causal inference. The second is the problem of selection bias in observational data, a problem that can be mitigated only with appropriate research designs that induce some measure of exogeneity.

With few exceptions, process tracers have ignored the potential outcomes framework.[6] In their list of ten best practices, Bennet and Checkel (2015: 26–7) implore process tracers to "Make a justifiable decision on when to start." The ensuing discussion never mentions either exogeneity or the bias that results when exogeneity is not satisfied. The discussion focuses on the question of whether the starting point is "too far back or too proximate," and the key criteria invoked to determine the proper starting point appears to be relevant. More promising is their brief reference to "critical junctures," which might imply exogeneity, though again the relevance of this critical junctures is never made a methodological centerpiece.

Gary Goertz and James Mahoney (2012) provide a more sustained argument about the inapplicability of the potential outcomes framework to process tracing. In their account, users of quantitative methods and users of qualitative methods are members of distinct cultures and so the standards of each do not apply to the other. More specifically, users of qualitative methods have distinct objectives and hold a unique definition of causation, such that any implications of the potential outcomes framework is denied relevance. There are three main components to this claim. First, whereas quantitative methods seek general laws, expressed as average treatment effects or type causation, qualitative methods seek to explain particular outcomes, that is, unit-level effects or token causation. Second, whereas quantitative scholars base their research on "effects of causes," or efforts to measure the results of an intervention, qualitative scholars orient their research to "causes of effects," or the total set of causes responsible for a particular outcome. Finally, while the quantitative approach derives its views of causation from statistical theory and linear-additive models, qualitative methods derives its views of causation from set theory, leading to an emphasis on INUS conditions.

This stark division between quantitative and qualitative approaches is neither conceptually nor empirically justified. These days, political scientists are encouraged to use mixed methods that combine elements of formal, statistical, and qualitative analysis. The enthusiasm with which this recommendation has been followed belies the claim that scholars belong to one culture or the other; as in other parts of social life, many people are multicultural. But the claims are conceptually overstated as well. The potential outcomes framework necessitates a shift from unit-level causal inference to population-level causal inference not out of a preference for type-causation claims over token-level claims—on the contrary, Rubin's example of taking aspirin is clearly an example of a token-level claim about the effect of his taking aspirin on his headache. Rather, the move to average treatment effects is an unavoidable implication of the fundamental problem of causal inference that makes unit-level causal inference simply unattainable. To deny the fundamental problem of causal inference out of a preference for unit-level over average treatment effects is a nonresponsive response to the principled argument about why unit-level inference is impossible.

A similar two-pronged critique applies to the distinction between causes-of-effects and effects-of-causes. Empirically, it is clearly the case that many users of process tracing are interested in effects-of-causes. Confronted with the statistical claim that democracies seldom if ever fight wars with one another, for example, process tracers such as John Owen have enthusiastically investigated the causal links between mutual democracy and peace. In doing so, they explore the effects-of-causes, albeit of often implicitly (Owen 1994).[7] Sometimes, at least, process tracers ask about the effects-of-causes and so implicitly, at least, think of causation in terms of interventions and counterfactuals.

Conceptually, the bright line between effects-of-causes and causes-of-effects should be blurred a bit as well. After all, the pragmatic objective elected by a researcher cannot itself govern a view of causation. Specifically, while I might be interested in the complete set of causes that interact to produce a particular outcome, each member of that set must itself be a cause. Nothing about preferring causes-of-effects over effects-of-causes obviates the possibility that causes are things that exercise some effect on an outcome such that intervening on the cause produces a change in the outcome. This claim, of course, covers INUS conditions as well. When we claim that an electrical short circuit was an INUS cause of a house fire—the short circuit was neither necessary nor sufficient, but was rather an insufficient but nonredundant part of an unnecessary but sufficient condition—we are recognizing that the short circuit does not operate in an otherwise vacant causal field. But we might still claim, correctly, that intervening on INUS causes in the proper causal field can induce changes in the outcome variable.[8]

One last line of defense against the fundamental problem of causal inference might be the ubiquitous resort to mechanism-based inference. One might claim that a mechanism definition of causation supplants a manipulation definition of causation and so mechanism-based inference need not confront the implications of the potential outcomes framework. But this is not correct. The potential outcomes framework appears to be a natural ally of a manipulation theory of causation, but the relationship is not inseparable. Indeed, as I have argued elsewhere, a mechanistic definition of causation is the necessary presupposition of a manipulation theory of causation (Waldner 2012: 77–8).[9] X is a cause of Y, in the sense that manipulating X causes modification of Y, just in the case that one or more mechanisms links X and Y. Thus, invoking a mechanistic theory of causation does not invalidate an affiliated manipulation account of causation; indeed, the potential outcomes framework is best-understood as a theory of how to measure causal effects, not a theory of causation itself. Invoking mechanisms, then does not immunize process tracers from the fundamental problem of causal inference.

I conclude this section with the following challenge to process tracers: given that process tracing is an instance of unit-level causal inference, and given that the fundamental problem of causal inference gives strong reasons to believe that unit-level causal inference is not possible, what solution do process tracers have for the fundamental problem of causal inference?

9.4 Process Tracing with Invariant Causal Mechanisms

Rather than avoid the fundamental problem of causal inference, let's consider a potential process-tracing solution to the "aspirin" problem. As we have noted, the RCM claims that we cannot make unit-level causal inferences about treatments, such as taking aspirin for relief of a headache, because we cannot measure the response under treatment and the response under control simultaneously. A process-tracing response would have to claim that investigation of the intermediary causal connection would compensate for the inability to observe a unit under treatment and under control simultaneously. My claim is that a well-specified causal model of average treatment effects, evidence about specific events at the unit level, and knowledge of invariant causal mechanisms can, in tandem, mitigate but not eliminate the fundamental problem of causal inference. We can make valid causal claims at the unit level just insofar as a causal model with invariant causal mechanisms acts as a proxy for the missing data that constitutes the fundamental problem of causal inference. Put differently, with near-complete knowledge of the data-generating process, we can make reasonable inferences of what the data would have looked like had it been generated. Clearly, this claim places a tremendous epistemic burden on the combination of the causal model and the affiliated set of invariant causal mechanisms.

According to our current knowledge, a reasonably detailed model of the causal connections between aspirin and pain relief is depicted in Figure 9.1, in which the top panel represents the outcome under control and the bottom panel represents the outcome under treatment. The two figures depict a causal pathway formed by a series of neurochemical responses to injured cells. In the absence of aspirin, or a similar synthetic substance, the causal pathway terminates with pain and inflammation; the effect of the administration of aspirin is to break the causal connection at its midpoint. Note that the administration of aspirin is an ideal intervention, leaving all prior states of the system intact and altering only those parts of the pathway intermediate between the intervention and the outcome. Operationally, using bioassay techniques, we can identify the two states of the world for a given subject, even though one state of the world would remain a counterfactual. But more importantly, when the knowledge encoded in the two graphs is supplemented by parallel knowledge of the causal mechanisms forging the connections on the two causal pathways, we can use the causal model corresponding to the counterfactual state of the world as an inferential substitute for the missing counterfactual data.

This causal model of the effects of aspirin forms a template for process tracing. I propose a four-part standard of unit-level causal inference that elsewhere I have called the "completeness standard" (Waldner 2015a, 2015b). This standard is designed to fully redeem philosophical justifications of mechanism-based inference that have been significantly under-determined by the current state of the art of process tracing.

The four components of the completeness standard are (1) a complete causal graph, (2) a corresponding event-history map, (3) a complete set of descriptive inferences from event-history map to causal graph, and (4) a complete set of causal mechanisms that link nodes in the causal graph by way of invariant causal principles. I argue that qualitative research that meets this admittedly tough standard can claim to make valid causal inferences at the unit level; in other words, the standard is explicitly designed to meet the challenge of the fundamental problem of causal inference. Much or perhaps most qualitative research will not meet this standard; I contend, however, that work that makes considerable progress toward the standard will possess considerable inferential validity and explanatory adequacy. At minimum, such work could be considered under the standard of inference to the best explanation, as explained above. At worst, in other words, work that fails to fully meet the standard should perform at a high level according to current standards. By following the standard, we can do no worse and probably considerably better than under the current state of the art.

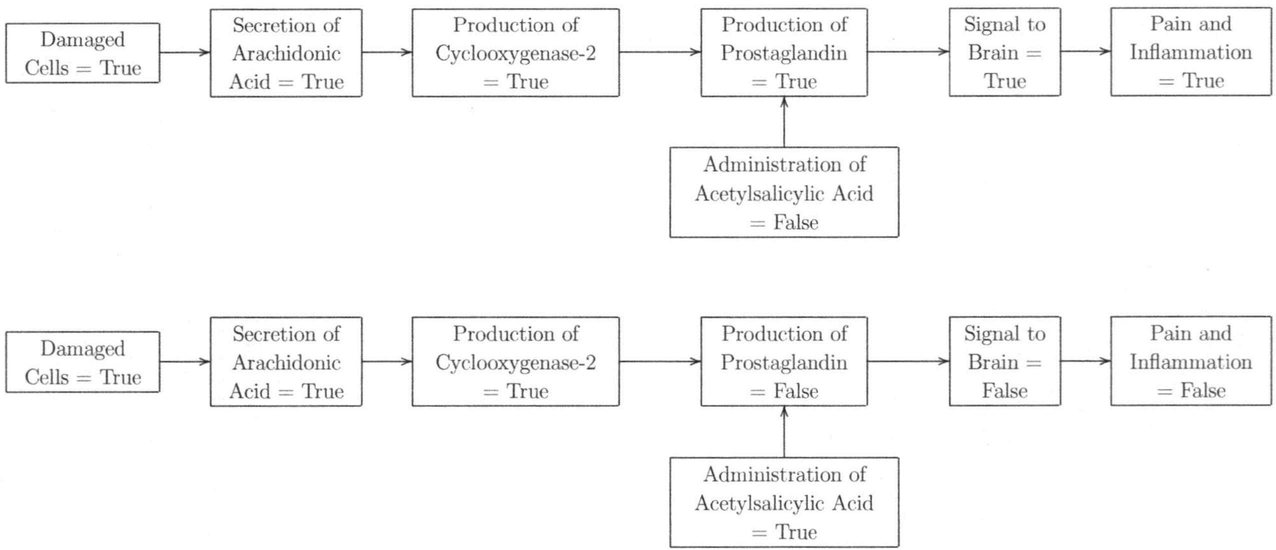

Figure 9.1 (a) and (b) Causal model of effect of aspirin.

Note: The figure shows two causal graphs depicting the effect of taking aspirin in the bottom graph (Figure 9.1b) and not taking aspirin in the top graph (Figure 9.1a). GT means the graph in which "treatment = true," that is, the bottom graph. GC means the graph in which "treatment = false," that is, the outcome under control in the top graph.

Causal graphs, also known as Bayesian networks and directed acyclic graphs, represent a system of probabilistic dependencies and independencies between random variables. Random variables are represented by nodes in the graph; relations of statistical dependence are represented by directed edges or arrows. These graphs are acyclic when no node has directed edge entering it from one of its descendants. In a slight deviation from normal practice, the completeness standard requires two graphs representing two discrete states of the system.

This pair of causal graphs performs multiple functions. First, it instantiates the abstruse but critical notion of a causal process. Early production accounts of causation that drew attention to the connection between cause and effect drew heavily on physicalist accounts of causation, as in Russell's causal lines, Salmon's transmission of marks, and Dowes' conserved quantities. Illari and Russo (2014: 115) note that these make sense in the physical world but not in other contexts; they make no sense at all in social contexts. Process tracers, on the other hand, have made little progress beyond relatively vague statements about intervening variables and events. Causal graphs precisely represent intervening variables while, crucially, adding much-needed structure to the resulting causal systems.

Second, causal graphs structure our accounts in part by focusing attention on relations of direct causation, as embodied in the Causal Markov Condition (CMC), which states that each node in the causal graph is independent of all non-descendants, conditional on its parents (Pearl 2000: 30). The key implication is that only direct causes matter, where a direct cause is defined such that an exogenous intervention on X will change the distribution of all descendants holding all other variables in the model fixed (Woodward 2003). In effect, while causal graphs by definition automatically satisfy the CMC, my proposal forces process tracers to justify theoretically the CMC, thereby constraining the structure of causal relations.[10]

Third, causal graphs draw our attention to the critical issue of exogeneity. An exogenous variable is one that has no directed edges entering the node representing it. Thus, in place of the vague criterion that process tracers must justify their starting point, causal graph theory informs us of the requirement that valid causal inference requires a causal graph with clearly defined and justified initial nodes (i.e., parents without ancestors).

Finally, the additional requirement of two-paired graphs representing different states of the systems is included because the paired graphs correspond to two potential outcomes (given binary variables), with each graph representing the counterfactual potential outcome of the other. It is precisely my claim that we can make unit-level causal inferences in such case that we can validly invoke the paired causal graph as representing the relevant counterfactual. In other words, the pairing of causal graphs will substitute for the missing data that lies at the heart of the fundamental problem of causal inference.

Causal graphs represent population-level inferences or what philosophers call type causation. Process tracing, on the other hand, is unit-level inference related to token causation. In effect, by demanding causal graphs, I obligate process tracers to first commit to type causation before making specific claims about token causation. Token causation takes the form of an event-history map. The component parts of the event-history map are the events that constitute realizations of the random variables represented in the causal graph, that is, a subset of the sample space. But they are also events in the ordinary-language sense of the word: a spatially and temporally localized occurrence of a change in some feature of an object. We do not observe causal graphs for two reasons; first, they consist of random variables that are only potential realizations of some underlying distribution, and second, they represent theoretical constructs like collective action and revolution, not concrete particulars. We observe events but we reason about causal relations between the random variables they realize. An event-history map is thus a pathway through a probability tree representing one of the possible realizations of the random variables in a causal graph (Shafer 1996).

The third component of the completeness standard is a complete set of inferences from event-history map to causal graph. Each node in the causal graph can be conceived as an independent hypothesis about the connection between two variables, thus forming one link in the overall causal chain. Each node in the event-history map is the evidence for or against that hypothesis. Thus, the apparatus of hypothesis testing and Bayesian updating discussed in the previous section is relevant here. But importantly, the apparatus of hypothesis testing and Bayesian updating is not the basis for causal inference; for that, we turn to the fourth component of the completeness standard.

Let us assume that we have completed steps 1–3 discussed in the previous section. We have theorized a set of random variables and their statistical dependencies and we have argued that the result is a causal graph, that is, it satisfies the CMC. Furthermore, we have constructed at least one event-history map, using the standard repertoire of hypothesis testing, as discussed above, to establish that observed events constitute a realization of the causal graph. At this point, although we have gone beyond the conventional wisdom in both theorizing a causal process and confirming a set of hypotheses, we are still in the domain of inference to the best explanation. What further steps would be necessary to make a valid claim of causal inference? Put differently, given that we are using process tracing on a case that corresponds to either GT and GC, on what grounds do we justify our estimate of $\delta_i = y_{i1} - y_{i0}$ based on reference to the counterfactual causal graph?

There are a variety of statistical solutions that would justify a claim of conditional independence, but as process tracing by definition is unit-level causal inference, these are not available to us. Our only remaining option is what Holland (1986: 948) refers to as the scientific solution, which relies on exploiting "various homogeneity or invariance assumptions." Laboratory scientists exploit a unit homogeneity assumption by carefully preparing two pieces of laboratory equipment so that they "look" identical in all respects except, of course, treatment exposure. Scholars using cross-case designs based on Mill's methods implicitly make use of this assumption, but its fragility is well known and it is not the basis of process-tracing claims. Alternatively, one can exploit invariance assumptions of temporal stability and causal transience, by using the same physical device to measure outcome under treatment and control and assuming that the two measures are not affected by the sequence of measures. Outside of the laboratory, we tacitly make these assumptions when we intervene on causal systems, such as flicking light switches to turn on a lamp.[11]

How can one make and justify an invariance assumption outside of physical devices that have been carefully prepared in the laboratory? My claim is that we can invoke an invariance assumption by supplementing our causal graphs with the full set of invariant causal mechanisms.

There is some tension between causal graphs, which treat causation as difference making, and causal mechanisms, which treat causation as production. Difference-making accounts of causation treat a cause as something that makes its effect more or less probable. Production accounts, on the other hand, "focus on the connection between cause and effect, rather than on causes making some kind of difference to their effects" (Illari and Russo 2014: 112, emphasis in original). Many accounts of mechanisms draw on graph theory to conceptualize mechanisms; as a result, they emphasize the difference-making aspect of causation at the expense of a production account. Knight and Winship (2013: 283, emphasis removed), for example, define mechanisms as "modular sets of entities connected by relations of counterfactual dependence." In this account, causal mechanisms are mediators, M, or intervening nodes in a causal graph such as X → M → Y. As Knight and Winship state, "we define a mechanism as a causal relationship involving one or more intervening variables between a treatment and an outcome." This definition emphasizes difference-making because it subsumes causation within a counterfactual dependence approach to causation, such that intervention on an intermediary node will alter the outcome. This graphical approach to causal mechanisms has its counterpart in the philosophical literature. Glennan (2002: S344) defines a mechanism for a behavior as "a complex system that produces that behavior by the interaction of a number of parts, where the interactions between parts can be characterized by direct, invariant, change-relating generalizations." Proponents of this approach often offer the toy model of a car's engine as a complex mechanism. As Gebharter (2014: 139) illustrates the model, "The question of why a car speeds up when the gas pedal is pressed can be answered by pointing at/describing the underlying mechanism (i.e., the motor and how it is connected to the gas pedal, the wheels, the gas tank, etc)." Two political scientists, Beach and Pedersen (2013: 30), offer the identical analogy, with X as the motor, Y the car's movement, and "the driveshaft and wheels can be thought of as the causal mechanism that transmits forces from X (motor) to produce Y (movement)."

Both approaches identify mechanisms with causal graphs themselves. Consider Figure 9.2. The top panel is a two-node causal graph, with a single cause and a single effect and hence no information about any intervening processes. The lower panel adds an intervening variable; the ensuing three-node model appears to fulfill the definitions of mechanism offered by Knight and Winship and by Glennan.

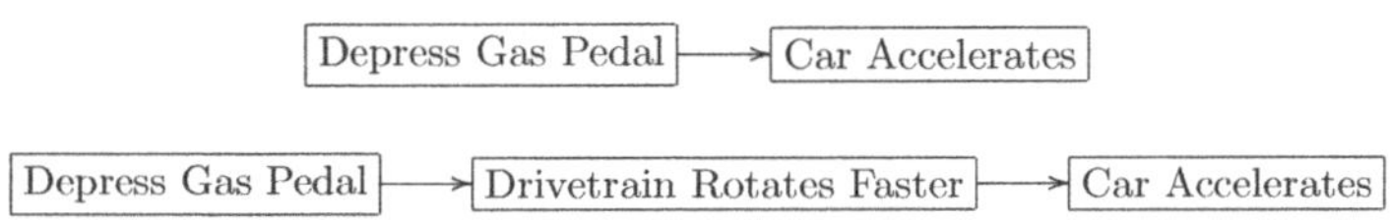

Figure 9.2 Mechanisms as intervening variables.

My claim is that a complex system of interdependent parts characterized by "direct, invariant, change-relating generalizations" is not sufficient to satisfy a unit-homogeneity assumption. Mechanisms cannot be reduced to either an individual intermediary note within a causal graph or to a set of nodes in a causal graph. Rather, mechanisms must be understood as independent of the causal graph and indeed as generating the causal graph. Most importantly, mechanisms are invariant in sense that one cannot use the "do" operator to set mechanisms to a different value. It is precisely this property of invariance by which mechanisms constitute a causal connection.

To make the case, let's continue working with the toy model of an automobile in our quest to understand why depressing the gas pedal causes acceleration. Next, let's introduce a factor omitted from the simple models discussed above: that factor is combustion. It is odd, after all, to explain acceleration without any reference to combustion, given that we are speaking about internal combustion engines. An advocate of a reductionist notion of mechanisms might respond that combustion can easily be added to the existing causal model, making a slightly more complex model that adds finer-grained detail and the more microlevel. Figure 9.3 depicts one section of the causal model that would result.

Something is clearly amiss in Figure 9.3. The three parent nodes are clearly random variables: one can remove fuel from a car, one can disable an ignition system, and one can take pressure off a gas pedal. But if these three parent nodes are all set as depicted in Figure 9.3, one simply cannot intervene directly on combustion to set it to off. We must take care to distinguish preventing combustion by removing its preconditions—fuel, oxygen, and heat above the flash point of the fuel-oxygen mixture—from turning combustion off given the existence of fuel, oxygen, and super-flash point heat. An intervention on combustion would mean to set it to a new value while leaving all of its ancestors unchanged. Such an intervention is clearly impossible. The invariance of combustion stems from two sources. At the macroscopic level, it has to do with how oxygen attacks hydrocarbon molecules, releasing energy when the weak bonds of a hydrocarbon molecule are replaced by the strong bonds of molecules of carbon dioxide and water. At the microscopic level, atoms of the original hydrocarbon molecules settle into "energetically more favorable arrangements" because of subatomic properties, including the spin and angular momentum of electrons of a dioxygen molecule.

My point is simply that while we can turn off random variables, we cannot turn off the invariant causal mechanisms that connect them. Here, I agree fully with

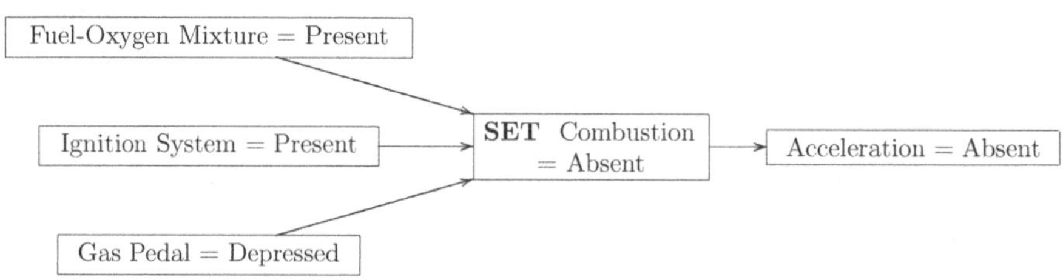

Figure 9.3 An invariant mechanism.

Beach and Pedersen (2013: 30) that mechanisms are not represented by the nodes of a causal graph but rather by the edges that connect random variables. Gebharter, however, insists that causal graphs have two types of edges, causal arrows, represented by dashed directed edges, and the standard arrows representing only relations of probabilistic dependence. In contrast, my claim is that every directed edge in a causal graph represents an underlying causal mechanisms whose invariant causal principle identifies how the two nodes are causally connected.

To understand the distinction between random variables and invariant causal mechanisms, we can draw on the distinction between causation and constitution as recently discussed by Petri Ylikoski (2012, 2013). Causation involves relations between events that are temporally extended, asymmetric, and involve changing properties. Constitution, on the other hand, relates properties, of which the most important appear to be the relation of the parts to the whole. These relations are not temporally extended processes and they are not asymmetric in terms of manipulation (but they are asymmetric in that parts constitute wholes); consequently, they are invariant in the sense that they cannot be manipulated.

Thus, we know that aspirin reduces headaches not only because we can produce causal graphs representing pathways from damaged cells to the production of a chain of enzymes to signals sent to the pain center of the brain, as in Figure 9.1, but also because we understand the nature of the neurotransmitters and other entities that manufacture the links between the nodes in the causal graph. As Machamer, Darden, and Craver (2000: 3) have argued, the activities of neurotransmitters are constrained by their fundamental structures, just as the behavior of a molecule of hydrocarbon is constrained by its constitutive structure. These invariant mechanisms in turn lead from one node in a causal graph to its descendant. Precisely because of this invariance, we know, with high confidence, that in the absence of aspirin, Cyclooxygenase-2 stimulates the production of Prostaglandin, while in the presence of aspirin, Prostaglandin is not secreted and hence the pathway to pain and inflammation is disrupted. It is this knowledge—highly reliable but, of course, not without some degree of uncertainty—that allows us to substitute the counterfactual causal graph for the missing data and hence mitigate but not eliminate the fundamental problem of causal inference.

9.5 Conclusion

The RCM assumes outcomes that are fixed prior to treatment, with one outcome under treatment and a second under control. Because we cannot observe both outcomes simultaneously, we cannot make unit-level causal inferences. This is the fundamental problem of causal inference and it clashes starkly with the claim by process tracers to make causal claims based on within-case analysis. The standard methodological repertoire of process tracing—causal process observations, hypothesis testing based on diverse evidence with differential probative value, and Bayesian updating—neither addresses the fundamental problem of causal inference nor on its own constitutes a method of causal inference. Rather, the standard methodology is best understood as permitting inference to the best explanation.

Invoking a mechanistic notion of causation does not immunize process tracing from the fundamental problem of causal inference. On the one hand, process tracers have not integrated the mechanistic perspective into their standard methodological procedures. On the other hand, the fundamental problem of causal inference, while often affiliated with a manipulationist conception of causation, is just as easily derived from a mechanistic conception of causation.

I have proposed that rather than avoiding the fundamental problem of causal inference, process tracers seek a process-tracing solution to it. The framework I have offered consists of causal graphs, event-history maps, and invariant causal mechanisms. This framework subsumes but goes beyond standard process-tracing methods. It is the invariant causal mechanisms that allow us to substitute the counterfactual causal graph for the missing data that is unavoidable given the inability to observe outcomes under treatment and under control simultaneously.

This chapter perhaps has some philosophical implications as well. First, the distinction between type and token causation is not fully sustainable; the methods proposed here obligate scholars who wish to claim token causation at the level of event-history maps to first commit to type causation in the form of causal graphs. Second, the distinction between causation as difference-making and causation as production is not fully sustainable; by combining causal graphs representing relations of probabilistic and counterfactual dependence, with causal mechanisms that generate causal links, the methods proposed here draw on both conceptions of causation. In effect, causes make a difference only if they are capable of producing effects. Finally, the methods proposed here ask us to consider two types of relations, of causation between events and of constitution between properties. Thus, while the chapter is largely an exercise in using philosophical considerations to inform empirical methods, it is hoped that some of the influence flows in the other direction as well.

Notes

1 Stephen Van Evera (1997) initiated explication of these tests. Further development of these basic ideas can be found in Bennett (2008), Bennett (2010), Mahoney (2010), Mahoney (2012), Beach and Pedersen (2013), and Collier (2011).

2 Two essays by Andrew Bennett (2008, 2010) are the foundational texts recommending the merger of process-tracing methods with Bayesian reasoning.

3 There is latent conflict, however, between the idea of tests of varying strength and Bayesian reasoning, what Mayo calls the "highly probed versus highly probable" debate. For detailed exposition, see Mayo (2005).

4 Nathaniel Beck (2006: 349) points out that by basing the claim exclusively on the evidence of the types of arguments made, Tannenwald substitutes an answer to the question "What did decision makers claim was important to them" for the stated research question "why did the US not use nuclear weapons." This sounds exactly right to me.

5 The global gender ratio is 102 males for every 100 females; in both the United States and the UK the ratio is 97.

6 Brady and Collier invoke the problem of nonrandom assignment to treatment to impeach the validity of standard regression models; they do not, however, consider how the same problem might affect process-tracing research.

7 See also Beach and Pedersen (2013) for an explicit statement of the intent to use process tracing to investigate the effects-of-causes such as the effect of democracy on interstate peace.

8 To be sure, there might be some operational implications of thinking of causes as parts of complex conditions; at minimum, it means that efforts to measure causal effects must be carefully designed so that the proper conditions—other relevant INUS conditions—are present as well. Medications, after all, do not produce an effect without a fully functioning circulatory system, but this in no way prevents researchers from designing experiments to measure their causal effects.

9 In fairness, I should confess that some of my earlier work (Waldner 2007) was prone to this sort of resort to the near-magical properties of mechanisms to refute methodological challenge to qualitative methods.

10 Furthermore, causal graphs satisfy what we might call the "continuity criterion," according to which "All the intervening steps in a case must be predicted by a hypothesis" (George and Bennett 2005: 207); see also Ruzzene (2014). This criterion has not been systematically explicated or satisfied in existing accounts, and indeed, the very notion of intervening steps is conceptually vague.

11 This appears as well to be what John Collier has in mind with the concept of an infomorphism, such that knowing the attributes of one object in a causal system provides reliable information about attributes of a second object in that systems—that is, knowing the position of a light switch tells you something about whether a bulb is illuminated. See the summary provided in Illari and Russo (2014: 140).

References

Beach, Derek, and Rasmus Brun Pedersen. 2013. *Process-Tracing Methods: Foundations and Guidelines*. Ann Arbor, MI: The University of Michigan Press.

Beck, Nathaniel. 2006. "Is Causal-Process Observation an Oxymoron?" *Political Analysis* 14 (3): 347–52.

Bennett, Andrew. 2008. "Process Tracing: A Bayesian Perspective." In *The Oxford Handbook of Political Methodology*, ed. Janet M. Box-Steffensmeier, Henry E. Brady, and David Collier. Oxford: Oxford University Press.

Bennett, Andrew. 2010. "Process Tracing and Causal Inference." In *Rethinking Social Inquiry: Diverse Tools, Shared Standards*, ed. Henry E. Brady, and David Collier, 2nd ed. London: Rowman & Littlefield.

Bennett, Andrew. 2015. "Disciplining Our Conjectures: Systematizing Process Tracing with Bayesian Analysis." In *Process Tracing: From Metaphor to Analytic Tool*, ed. Andrew Bennett, and Jeffrey T. Checkel. Cambridge: Cambridge University Press.

Bennett, Andrew, and Jeffrey T. Checkel. 2015. "Process Tracing: From Philosophical Roots to Best Practices." In *Process Tracing: From Metaphor to Analytic Tool*, ed. Andrew Bennett and Jeffrey T. Checkel, 3–37. Cambridge: Cambridge University Press.

Collier, David. 2011. "Understanding Process Tracing." *PS: Political Science and Politics* 44 (3): 823–30.

Collier, David, Henry E. Brady, and Jason Seawright. 2010. "Sources of Leverage in Causal Inference: Towards an Alternative View of Methodology." In *Rethinking Social Inquiry: Diverse Tools, Shared Standards*, ed. Henry E. Brady and David Collier, 2nd ed. Lanham, MD: Rowman & Littlefield.

Dunning, Thad. 2012. *Natural Experiments in the Social Sciences: A Design-Based Approach*. Cambridge: Cambridge University Press.

Freedman, David A. 2010. *Statistical Models and Causal Inference: A Dialogue with the Social Sciences*. Cambridge: Cambridge University Press.

Gebharter, Alexander. 2014. "A Formal Framework for Representing Mechanisms." *Philosophy of Science* 81: 138–53.

George, Alexander L., and Andrew Bennett. 2005. *Case Studies and Theory Development in the Social Sciences*. Cambridge: MIT Press.

Gillies, Donald. 2000. *Philosophical Theories of Probability*. London: Routledge.

Glennan, Stuart. 2002. "Rethinking Mechanistic Explanation." *Philosophy of Science* 69 (3): S342–S53.

Goertz, Gary, and James Mahoney. 2012. *A Tale of Two Cultures: Qualitative and Quantitative Research in the Social Sciences*. Princeton, NJ: Princeton University Press.

Holland, Paul W. 1986. "Statistics and Causal Inference." *Journal of the American Statistical Association* 81 (396): 945–60.

Humphreys, Macartan, and Alan Jacobs. 2013. "Mixing Methods: A Bayesian Unification of Qualitative and Quantitative Approaches." *Presented at the Annual Meeting of the American Political Science Association*, Chicago, IL: APSA.

Illari, Phyllis, and Federica Russo. 2014. *Causality: Philosophical Theory Meets Scientific Practice*. Oxford: Oxford University Press.

Imbens, Guido W., and Donald B. Rubin. 2015. *Causal Inference for Statistics, Social, and Biomedical Sciences: An Introduction*. New York: Cambridge University Press.

Knight, Carly R., and Christopher Winship. 2013. "The Causal Implications of Mechanistic Thinking: Identification Using Directed Acyclic Graphs (DAGs)." In *Handbook of Causal Analysis for Social Research*, chapter 14, 275–99. Netherlands: Springer.

Lipton, Peter. 2004. *Inference to the Best Explanation*. 2nd ed. New York: Routledge.

Machamer, Peter, Lindley Darden, and Carl F. Craver. 2000. "Thinking about Mechanisms." *Philosophy of Science* 67 (1): 1–25.

Mahoney, James. 2010. "After KKV: The New Methodology of Qualitative Research." *World Politics* 62 (1): 120–47.

Mahoney, James. 2012. "The Logic of Process Tracing Tests in the Social Sciences." *Sociological Methods & Research* 41 (4): 570–97.

Mayo, Deborah G. 2005. "Evidence as Passing Severe Tests: Highly Probable versus Highly Probed Hypotheses." In *Scientific Evidence: Philosophical Theories & Applications*, ed. Peter Achinstein, 95–127. Baltimore: The Johns Hopkins University Press.

Owen, John M. IV. 1994. "How Liberalism Produces Democratic Peace." *International Security* 19 (2): 87–125.

Pearl, Judea. 2000. *Causality: Models, Reasoning, and Inference*. Cambridge: Cambridge University Press.

Rubin, Donald. 1974. "Estimating Causal Effects of Treatments in Randomized and Non-randomized Studies." *Journal of Educational Psychology* 66 (5): 688–701.

Ruzzene, Attilia. 2014. "Process Tracing as an Effective Epistemic Complement." *Topoi* 33: 361–72.

Shadish, William R., Thomas D. Cook, and Donald T. Campbell. 2002. *Experimental and Quasi-Experimental Designs for Generalized Causal Inference*. Boston: Houghton-Mifflin.

Shafer, Glenn. 1996. *The Art of Causal Conjecture*. Cambridge: MIT Press.

Van Evera, Stephen. 1997. *Guide to Methods for Students of Political Science*. Ithaca, NY: Cornell University Press.

Waldner, David. 2007. "Transforming Inferences into Explanations: Lessons from the Study of Mass Extinctions." In *Theory and Evidence in Comparative Politics and International Relations*, ed. Richard New Lebow and Mark Lichbach. New York: Palgrave Macmillan.

Waldner, David. 2012. "Process Tracing and Causal Mechanisms." In *The Oxford Handbook of the Philosophy of Social Science*, ed. Harold Kincaid. Oxford: Oxford University Press.

Waldner, David. 2015a. "Process Tracing and Qualitative Causal Inference." *Security Studies* 24 (2): 239–50.

Waldner, David. 2015b. "What Makes Process Tracing Good? Causal Mechanisms, Causal Inference, and the Completeness Standard in Comparative Politics." In *Process Tracing: From Metaphor to Analytic Tool*, ed. Andrew Bennett and Jeffrey T. Checkel, 126–52. Cambridge: Cambridge University Press.

Woodward, James. 2003. *Making Things Happen: A Theory of Causal Explanation*. Oxford: Oxford University Press.

Ylikoski, Petri. 2012. "Micro, Macro, and Mechanisms." In *The Oxford Handbook of Philosophy of Social Science*, ed. Harold Kincaid, chapter 2, 21–45. Oxford: Oxford University Press.

Ylikoski, Petri. 2013. "Causal and Constitutive Explanation Compared." *Erkenntnis* 78: 277–97.

Commentary: An Alternative Hypothesis about Process Tracing: Comments on "Causal Mechanisms and Qualitative Causal Inference in the Social Sciences"

Daniel Steel

1. Introduction

Process tracing is an approach to causal inference that emphasizes careful attention to mechanisms linking causes and effects. Its appeal in the social sciences appears to be due to two factors. First, it is claimed to offer a solution to ever-present problems of unmeasured common causes that may be responsible for statistical associations between putative causes and effects. Second, process tracing can be used in the context of qualitative research, and therefore is an appealing approach for researchers who adopt qualitative methods. In his chapter, "Causal Mechanisms and Qualitative Causal Inference in the Social Sciences," David Waldner makes a number of interesting critical observations regarding process tracing, and advances a positive proposal about how the difficulties he highlights can be addressed. In this commentary, I express sympathy with Waldner's critical points but skepticism about his positive proposal, while suggesting an alternative account of process tracing of my own.

Waldner identifies three challenges confronting process tracing. Advocates of process tracing base their approach on philosophical literature on mechanisms that they (1) have not "fully absorbed," (2) have not specified adequate methods for discovering mechanisms, and (3) rarely engage with more recent developments in causal inference, such as approaches utilizing directed-acyclic graphs. Waldner's positive proposal is premised on a particular interpretation of process tracing as a method for answering questions about "unit causation," or what is also known as "token" or, more recently, "actual" causation.[1] That is, questions about what caused this specific event, or what effects did this particular cause have. Waldner then suggests four criteria for evaluating inferences of this kind.

I am sympathetic to the concerns raised about process tracing by Waldner, and have made similar claims in my earlier work. For example, I have argued that advocates of process tracing have not adequately explained how their approach avoids difficulties relating to unmeasured common causes, and my own positive proposals on the topic have often been conveyed with the assistance of directed-acyclic graphs (Steel 2004, 2008, 2011, 2013). Nevertheless, I think it is a mistake to limit process tracing to inferences about unit causation, because this fails to address questions about how causal inference is possible when unmeasured common causes may be present. Instead, such an approach assumes that this problem has been solved by other means and then uses causal generalizations as a basis for inferences about actual causes in particular cases. In contrast, I suggest an alternative hypothesis about the nature of process tracing. I propose that process tracing works by strategically enlarging the set of variables that are focus of the analysis by delving into the details of possible mechanisms that may link the cause to the effect. This approach enables a non-mysterious explanation of how process tracing might achieve its stated aims, an explanation that furthermore can be expressed within a directed-acyclic graph framework.

2. Is Process Tracing a Method for Inferring Unit Causation?

Waldner frames his discussion of process tracing in reference to Rubin's "fundamental problem of causation." The stock illustration of this problem is a person who has a headache, takes an aspirin, and whose headache subsequently goes away. The claim that the aspirin caused the headache to subside is naturally understood to entail that the headache would have lasted longer if the aspirin had not been taken. This counterfactual involves a comparison between two states (the person taking the aspirin and not taking it), only one of which is observed. Thus, it seems that we can never know whether the aspirin was really the cause of relief of the person's headache. In the best situation, one might estimate the average causal effect in a sample of people who are similar in all respects except for having been randomly assigned differing values of the suspected cause. Naturally, such ideal experimental conditions rarely, if ever, obtain in social science research, or indeed any research involving human subjects, which raises questions about what less stringent conditions might suffice for causal inference.

Waldner characterizes the implications of Rubin's fundamental problem of causal inference for process tracing as follows: "According to the [Ruben causal model], while causal effects are defined on a single unit, we can only learn about causal effects by observing differences across multiple units. If this consequence is valid, then process tracers are committing an inferential felony when they base causal claims on a single-unit, within-case analysis" (Waldner, this volume, p. 287). This statement implies that Waldner conceives of process tracing as a form of within-case inference, which is in turn assumed to be an attempt to draw inferences about the causes of single events (i.e., about unit causation). The link between process tracing and within-case causal inference derives from a recent volume on process tracing by Bennett and Checkel (2015), who "define process tracing as the analysis of evidence on processes, sequences, and conjunctures of events within a case for the purposes of either developing or testing hypotheses about causal mechanisms that might causally explain the case" (Bennett and Checkel 2015: 8). Bennett and Checkel contrast this definition with another that does not mention cases or limit process tracing to within-case inferences: "The essential meaning retained by the term 'process tracing' from its origins in cognitive psychology is that it refers to the examination of intermediate steps in a process to make inferences about hypotheses on how that process took place and whether and how it generated the outcome of interest" (Bennett and Checkel 2015: 6).

I suggest that the following two questions should be considered at this point. First, is within-case inference necessarily inference about unit causation? And second, should one accept Bennett and Checkel's proposal that process tracing be limited, by definition, to within-case inference? I propose answering *no* to both of these questions.

To tackle the first question, it will be helpful to say a bit more about what is meant by "case" and "within a case." Bennett and Checkel define a case as an instance of a broader class or social type (they give wars, revolutions, democracies, and capitalist economies as examples), and they "define within-case evidence as evidence from within the temporal, spatial, or topical domain defined as a case" (Bennett and Checkel 2015: 8).

Given these definitions, within-case causal inferences are not necessarily about unique occurrences because a case may include a sample of subcomponents. For instance, if capitalist economy is a social type, then a case study could examine a particular capitalist economy over the course of a century. Thus, the case might include a number of events of similar types (e.g., economic recessions), which could constitute a sample for within-case causal inference. Similarly, there may be subregions within the economy, such as provinces, states, counties, cantons, metropolitan areas, and so forth, and differences among these may also allow for useful comparisons and generalizations. Similar points can be made about other examples. Consider Donohue and Levitt's (2001) study of the effects of legalized abortion in the United States due to the *Roe v. Wade* decision in 1973 on the decline in crime rates that began there in the 1990s. Since some states had legalized abortion prior to *Roe v. Wade*, it was possible to ask whether early legalizing states experienced a decline in crime rates before late legalizers (Donohue and Levitt 2001). These observations show that the concept of a "unit" in unit causation does not always correspond to the notion of a case in case study. A unit is a single entity that, for statistical purposes, can be represented by one row on a spreadsheet. In contrast, cases typically mark out complex and multicomponent swaths of social reality consisting of many events, actors, institutions, locations, and time periods, any of which may be treated as units of analysis in their own right. Thus, even if one grants that process tracing is limited to within-case reasoning, it does not follow that it is necessarily a method for inferences about unit causation.

But why should one limit process tracing to within-case inferences in the first place? Granted, Bennett and Checkel suggest this, but is it a good idea? I think there are strong reasons for saying that it is not. Most importantly, it is unwise because it gives undue methodological significance to decisions about where to draw boundaries around cases. Decisions about the temporal and spatial extent of cases must be made, as well as decisions about who are the relevant actors, organizations, and institutions. While researchers' theoretical perspectives often influence such decisions, they can also be made for reasons of convenience or established by convention or tradition. To illustrate convenience, note that it is not unusual for a case study to end at the most recent date when data were available to the researchers. Thus, Donohue and Levitt's study of the effects of abortion legalization on crime in the United States was published in 2001 and hence does not include subsequent data, despite the fact that their hypothesis made predictions about them (e.g., that the decline in crime rates would continue). In general, it is inescapable that decisions about the temporal and regional scope of case studies will often be influenced by data availability. To illustrate the role of convention and tradition, consider that the scientific revolution is commonly taken to begin with the publication of Copernicus's *On the Revolutions of the Heavenly Spheres* in 1543 and to end with the appearance of Newton's *Mathematical Principles of Natural Philosophy* in 1687. Yet, there is nothing magical about either of these dates. Despite the undeniable importance of the two publications that mark them, the causes of the scientific revolution did not begin with Copernicus nor its impacts end with Newton and hence other time intervals might be plausibly associated with it.

The above is by no means a criticism of case study research. The necessity of practical decisions about the boundaries of case studies is a fact of life. But recognition of this fact counsels against placing any great methodological or philosophical significance on where such boundaries happen to be drawn. Yet this is precisely what defining process tracing as a species of within-case inference does. Since inferences within cases can involve systematic comparisons of and generalizations about subcomponents that constitute the case (subsidiary events, regions, time periods, actors, etc.), the distinction between within and across-case inference ultimately boils down to how social scientists decide to draw boundaries around the flow of social life. What is within-case inference given one way of carving things up is across case inference given another. For example, Donohue and Levitt's study on the effects of legalization of abortion on crime is within-case inference if the regional scope of the case is taken to be the United States as a whole, but it would be across case inference if each state were treated as a separate case. Basic questions about method and causal inference should not rest on arbitrary decisions about where to draw lines around cases.

Indeed, I think some of Waldner's criticisms of process tracing reflect the inability of a within-versus-across cases distinction to support a methodology of causal inference. One of Waldner's primary criticisms is that the best practices recommended in the name of process tracing by Bennett and Checkel (2015) do not seem specific to process tracing or mechanism-based causal inference. Instead, they consist of general advice relevant to almost all forms of scientific reasoning, for instance, that one should take care to eliminate plausible alternative hypotheses. Yet Waldner's positive proposal is also founded on the assumption that process tracing is a method for inferring unit causation within cases, and as such it inherits the difficulties of this approach.

Consider the core of Waldner's proposal, four criteria for assessing attempts at process tracing that he collectively labels the "completeness standard."

> Process tracing yields causal and explanatory adequacy insofar as: (1) it is based on a causal graph whose individual nodes are connected in such a way that they are jointly sufficient for the outcome; (2) it is also based on an

> event-history map that establishes valid correspondence between the events in each particular case study and the nodes in the causal graph; (3) theoretical statements about causal mechanisms link the nodes in the causal graph to their descendants and the empirics of the case studies allow us to infer that the events were in actuality generated by the relevant mechanisms; and (4) rival explanations have been credibly eliminated, by direct hypothesis testing or by demonstrating that they cannot satisfy the first three criteria listed above. (Waldner 2015: 128)

Waldner's completeness standard is very similar to previous accounts of process tracing that he criticizes.

For example, George and Bennett explain process tracing by means of the following example:

> The process-tracing method attempts to identify the intervening causal process—the causal chain and causal mechanisms—between an independent variable (or variables) and the outcome of the dependent variable. Suppose that a colleague shows you fifty numbered dominoes standing upright in a straight line with their dots facing the same way on the table in a room, but puts a blind in front of the dominoes so that only number one and number fifty are visible. She then sends you out of the room and when she calls you back in you observe that domino number one and domino number fifty are now lying flat with their tops pointing in the same direction; that is they co-vary. Does this mean that either domino caused the other to fall? Not necessarily. . . . You must remove the blind and look at the intervening dominoes, which give evidence on the potential processes. (George and Bennett 2005: 206–7)

It is not difficult to recast this example in very similar terms as Waldner's completeness criteria.

George and Bennett's example involves an implicit theory of dominoes (tipping the first in a chain causes the second to tip, and so on) that, to a first approximation, could be represented by a Bayesian network as follows. Let the variable D_i be a binary variable indicating whether or not domino i had tipped over, with 1 indicating that the domino is tipped and 0 that it is upright. Supposing there are five dominoes, the domino theory could be represented by a Bayesian network consisting of the directed acyclic graph (DAG) in Figure 9.4 and a joint probability distribution that decomposes as follows: $P(D_1,D_2,D_3,D_4,D_5)=P(D_1)P(D_2|D_1)P(D_3|D_2)P(D_4|D_3)P(D_5 \mid D_4)$.[2] Finally, we can suppose that the implicit domino theory entails that $0<P(D_1=1)<1$

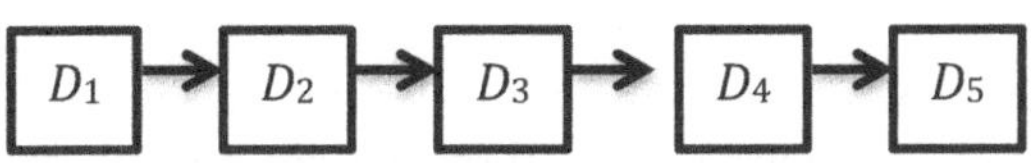

Figure 9.4 A DAG for the domino example.

and that, for every i, $P(D_i = 1|D_{i-1} = 1) = 1$. In other words, the theory doesn't tell us whether the first domino will be tipped, but it says that if it is, then all of the others will fall in turn. In George and Bennett's example, we observe that D_1 and D_5 both equal 1 (i.e., the first and last dominoes are tipped). If the domino theory explains these observations, then we would obviously expect that D_2 through D_4 all equal 1 as well (i.e., that they are all tipped). Thus, observing that this is the case would constitute further evidence that the domino theory is the correct explanation in this case, just as George and Bennett claim. George and Bennett's description of process tracing, then, invites a straightforward representation via Bayesian networks that satisfies the first two of Waldner's completeness criteria. That is, the proposed explanation about the case is related to more general theory represented by a DAG (criterion 1) and an "event-history map" that predicts values of the intermediate variables (criterion 2).

Waldner's criteria 3 and 4 have to do with whether the theorized mechanism rather than some alternative is the true explanation. George and Bennett also emphasize the importance of eliminating plausible alternative explanations, asking, "From the positions of all the dominoes, can we eliminate rival causal mechanisms, such as earthquakes, wind, or human intervention?" (George and Bennett 2005: 207). Representing the alternatives suggested by Bennett and George—for instance, that the dominoes were toppled by a gust of wind—would require more complex models in which the variables indicate not only whether each domino was tipped or not but also where the dominoes fell. The possibility that the same situation could be represented by different sets of variables will be an important point in the next section.[3] For now the relevant point is that there does not seem to be a substantive difference between Waldner's completeness criteria and the account of process tracing proposed by George and Bennett. The underlying concepts are the same, and the difference concerns the preferred mode of representation.

As a result, Waldner's completeness criteria confront many of the same difficulties as the approaches he criticizes. One of these is that both assume that relevant general causal knowledge exists without explaining how it was acquired. Yet the difficulty of gaining such knowledge in social science—especially due to the potential for unmeasured common causes—is one of the driving motivations for a focus on mechanisms and process tracing in the first place. The domino example, then, is misleading for conceptualizing process tracing in social science. In that example, ordinary experience provides knowledge of causes of toppling wooden tiles. We know that tipping the first in a row of otherwise stable dominoes will make the succeeding dominoes fall, and the only question is whether that is what happened in this instance. But for interesting social science examples, there is often great uncertainty about causality at a general theoretical level. To what extent does democratic government make a state less likely to go to war with another democracy? How effective is gun control legislation in reducing crime? And so on. In other words, process tracing à la Waldner asks: given general causal knowledge about a type of phenomena, what were the actual causes in a given case? But this evades the question of how such general causal knowledge is to be acquired in social science given familiar difficulties related to confounding.

3. An Alternative Hypothesis

In this section, I propose an alternative hypothesis about what process tracing is and how it works. The central idea stems from a simple observation about causal inference: the ability to learn whether X is a cause of Y can depend on what other variables one measures.

Let's begin by illustrating this with an approach other than process tracing, specifically, the method of instrumental variables. Suppose that random variables X and Y are probabilistically dependent, but independent conditional on Z. Then any of these three DAGs can explain the data: $X \rightarrow Z \rightarrow Y$, $Y \rightarrow Z \rightarrow X$, or $X \leftarrow Z \rightarrow Y$. In other words, if the set of measured variables is limited to $S = \{X, Y, Z\}$ and it is not possible to experimentally intervene on X, there is no way to know if X causes Y. But that does not eliminate the possibility of discerning whether X causes Y given some other set of variables. For example, the method of instrumental variables attempts to find a V that is a cause of X but otherwise unrelated to Z and Y. An instrumental variable, then, is a "natural experiment"—an exogenous influence on the putative cause lacking other links to the suspected effect. If such a V exists and can be measured, then given some commonly invoked assumptions about the relationship between causation and probability, it is possible to learn from probabilistic dependence relations among the set of variables $S^* = \{V, X, Y, Z\}$ whether or not X is a cause of Y.[4]

I suggest that process tracing also rests on a similar insight about the importance to causal inference of finding just the right set of variables to measure. The difference in the case of process tracing is that the emphasis is on variables that pertain to possible mechanisms linking the cause and effect. Indeed, this is one natural way to understand George and Bennett's domino example. If only the suspected cause (tipping of the first domino) and effect (tipping of the last) are observed, then the causal relationship between them is underdetermined by finding that they are associated. However, if potential intermediate variables are measured, then this underdeterminantion might be resolved, or at least lessened. In short, considered abstractly, the domino example says the following. Suppose variables X and Y are probabilistically dependent. Then the causal relationship between X and Y is underdetermined if $S = \{X, Y\}$ is the set of measured variables, but not necessarily underdetermined if the set of measured variables is $S^* = \{X, V_1, \ldots, V_n, Y\}$, where $V_1, \ldots, V_n$ include variables relevant to potential mechanisms linking X and Y. Process tracing, then, uses possible mechanisms as a heuristic for finding a set of variables that, if measured, would reduce the underdetermination of a causal hypothesis.

According to this proposal, process tracing is useful to the extent that it is easier to establish causal relationships among intermediate steps of a mechanism than to directly show that X causes Y. This might happen in several ways. There might be some relatively obvious or easily established immediate effects of X or similarly apparent immediate causes of Y. Moreover, "natural experiments" or instrumental variables may exist for variables representing intermediate nodes of a possible mechanism, but not for X. Or it might be possible to experimentally intervene on some of these intermediaries, but not on X. Or again, plausible confounding common causes may be easier to measure for intermediaries than for X and Y. Consider a simple schematic example to illustrate how process tracing, according to this proposal, might work. As before, assume that *X* is statistically associated with *Y*, but that it is unclear whether this association is due to *X* causing *Y* or to the presence of an unmeasured common cause. However, suppose that it is known from background knowledge that *X* is a cause of *Z*. Furthermore, suppose that in some populations it is possible to identify a variable *V* that is a cause of *Z*, but which is otherwise unrelated to *Y*. Thus, in this case, showing that *V* is associated with *Y* would (given the assumptions noted above regarding instrumental variables) show that *Z* is a cause of *Y*, and hence that the causal chain $X \rightarrow Z \rightarrow Y$ is present.

I suggest that this proposal has several advantages. Most of all, it makes process tracing non-mysterious. It depends on a basic insight about causal inference that grounds some other approaches, namely, that choosing the right set of variables is important for mitigating underdetermination of causal hypotheses. Process tracing is distinguished by its focus on possible mechanisms linking the suspected cause and effect, rather than, say, on controlling potential confounders or finding exogenous causes of the suspected cause as in the method of instrumental variables. And according to this proposal, process tracing can be explained and illustrated by means of the DAG framework that has become widespread for analyzing causal inference. Thus, the requisite assumptions in a specific application can be explicitly articulated and subjected to scrutiny. In short, process tracing is shorn of its air of hocus pocus and comes down to earth as one among several potentially useful means of causal inference that can be rigorously studied.

In addition, the proposal advanced here does not evade problems about causal inference posed by unmeasured common causes. As argued in the previous section, proposals to limit process tracing to inferences about unit causation have this feature. They assume that general causal knowledge about the phenomenon is given and ask about the actual causes in a particular instance. Yet, such an approach dodges the central problem of attempting to draw causal inferences in a context in which unmeasured common causes may be present. Without some way of addressing this problem, the project of using general causal knowledge to infer actual causes in particular cases cannot get off the ground. According to the proposal suggested here, process tracing begins with the problem of underdetermination stemming from confounding common causes and then suggests an approach that may be helpful for mitigating it in some cases.

Finally, the proposal advanced here does not put undue methodological or philosophical significance on the distinction between within- and across-case inference. Instead, it focuses on something that is undeniably important for the success of causal inference—careful selection of relevant variables to measure—and points out that consideration of possible mechanisms can be helpful in this regard.

Notes

1 For an entry into philosophical literature on actual causation, see Baumgartner and Glynn (2013).

2 That is, the probability distribution satisfies the causal Markov condition with respect to the DAG in Figure 9.4, since each variable is probabilistically independent of its non-descendants conditional on its parents.

3 In addition, one might check whether background conditions required for the operation of the theorized mechanism were present. For example, the domino theory assumes a stable platform, absence of interference (e.g., no one holds the second domino upright after the first is tipped), and so on.

4 For example, given the causal Markov and faithfulness conditions, then a probabilistic dependence between *V* and *Y* entails that *X* is a cause of *Y* (see Spirtes, Glymour, and Scheines 2001).

References

Baumgartner, M., and L. Glynn. 2013. "Introduction to Special Issue on 'Actual Causation.'" *Erkenntnis* 78 (1): 1–8.

Bennett, A., and J. Checkel. 2015. "Process Tracing: From Philosophical Roots to Best Practices." In *Process Tracing: From Metaphor to Analytic Tool*, ed. Andrew Bennett and Jeffrey Checkel, 3–37. Cambridge: Cambridge University Press.

George, A., and A. Bennett. 2005. *Case Studies and Theory Development in the Social Sciences*. Cambridge, MA: MIT Press.

Donohue, J., and S. Levitt. 2001. "The Impact of Legalized Abortion on Crime." *Quarterly Review of Economics* 116 (2): 379–420.

Spirtes, P., C. Glymour, and R. Scheines. 2001. *Causation, Prediction, and Search*, 2nd ed. Cambridge, MA: MIT Press.

Steel, D. 2004. "Social Mechanisms and Causal Inference." *Philosophy of the Social Sciences* 34: 55–78.

Steel, D. 2008. *Across the Boundaries: Extrapolation in Biology and Social Science*. New York: Oxford University Press.

Steel, D. 2011. "Causality, Causal Models, and Mechanisms." In *The Sage Handbook on the Philosophy of Social Science*, ed. Ian Jarvie and Jesús Zamora Bonilla, 288–304. London: Sage.

Steel, Daniel. 2013. "Mechanisms and Extrapolation in the Abortion-Crime Controversy." In *Mechanism and Causality in Biology and Economics*, ed. Hsiang-Ke Chao, Szu-Ting Chen, and Roberta L. Millstein, 185–206. Dordrecht: Springer.

Waldner, David. 2015. "What Makes Process Tracing Good? Causal Mechanisms, Causal Inference, and the Completeness Standard in Comparative Politics." In *Process Tracing: From Metaphor to Analytic Tool*, ed. Andrew Bennett and Jeffrey Checkel, 126–52. Cambridge: Cambridge University Press.

10

How to Theorize? On the Changing Role and Meaning of Theory in the Social Sciences

Mikael Carleheden

10.1 Introduction

In 1903, Charles Sanders Peirce held a lecture called "How to theorize?" He asked what role theory should have in scientific inquiry (Carleheden 2014; Swedberg 2014). Such a question is without doubt crucial also for the social sciences today. It concerns one of the most contested issues in the history of the social sciences. However, an investigation of the different positions in these debates makes it obvious that another contested issue always, more or less tacitly, is implicated; that is, the meaning of theory. An answer to Peirce's question presupposes a conception of what theory is. The debates about the role of theory are not seldom confusing just because the opponents mistakenly take for granted that they are referring to the same meaning of theory. If one takes a step back, it is easy to see that the meaning of theory is not one but many (Abend 2008).

This chapter deals with different meanings of social theory, which form the basis of different answers to the question of the role of social theory. I will proceed historically. The dominating conception of social theory has shifted over time. My investigation is restricted to transformations during the twentieth century. It will not be conducted in the manner of a sociology of science. The focus will be on reasons rather than causes of change. The general idea is that a historical investigation of such reasons is also the best way to be able to answer the normative question about what role theory should have today. An answer must be situated in the ongoing history of the social sciences, which in turn is related to social change in general. I will, so to say, "follow the actors," who in this case are social scientists debating theory of science. The focus will first and foremost be on the most recent development. My primary aim is to trace what I suspect to be an ongoing transformation of the conception of theory in contemporary social science. In the end, I will make a preliminary attempt to critically evaluate this ongoing transformation.[1]

To be able to investigate the historical transformation of social theory, some shared meaning of that subject matter is needed—at least on a general level. The first problem is then the differentiation within the social sciences between sociological, political, economic theory and so on. However, I will try to circumvent this problem to make the task manageable. I will simply take conceptions of theory in sociology as an example. Most often the terms social and sociological theory is treated synonymously. Sociologists have not seldom seen themselves as responsible for developing a general theory for the social sciences (e.g., Parsons and Mills). Further, sociology can be seen as an "extreme case" in a productive sense (Flyvbjerg 2006). While the dominating and subordinated positions have been more definite in other disciplines, the struggle has been fought on a more equal footing in sociology. Thus, one might suspect that this struggle has made the reasons behind different answers clearer.[2]

However, and as a consequence of what just has been claimed, the problem of finding a shared meaning of theory on some level turns up again within sociology. Sociology is a "hyperdifferentiated discipline" (Turner 2002: 6). Sociologists, "do not agree on what is real, what our core problems are, what our epistemology is, and what our theories should look like" (13). Nevertheless, it is possible to find a basic, common idea about what theory is. The theoretical must in some sense be understood in contrast to the empirical:

> "Theory is a generalization separated from particulars, an abstraction separated from a concrete case." (Alexander 1987a: 2)

> "At a very basic level, the different theoretical schools and disciplines are at least in agreement that theories should be understood as generalizations." (Joas and Knöbl 2009: 4)

In this basic sense it is easy to agree with Jeffrey Alexander that theory is "the heart of science" (1987a: 2). Most sociologists would actually also agree on taking a second step and claim that empirical generalization as such is not sufficient to qualify as theorizing. We need also to generalize in a certain way. However, this is as far as we get. As soon as we go hyperdifferentiation breaks out.

Surprisingly, there are rather few systematic overviews about what hyperdifferentiation means in the context of theorizing.[3] I will take my point of departure in a classic article by Robert Merton. He distinguished between six "types of analysis" (Merton 1945: 462) that the term sociological theory has been used to refer to and which have "significantly different bearings upon empirical social research" (463). He names them "methodology, general orientations, conceptual analysis, post factum interpretations, empirical generalizations, and sociological theory." Merton imagined that the struggle between these different types "has come to a well-deserved close" (1948: 164). The last type, that is, his own "theories of the middle range," had finally won and was to be seen as the only one that truly deserved the title "sociological theory." From the perspective of today it is easy to smile at such a statement, but in its historical context it was rather accurate. As we will see, he formulated the dominating understanding of how to theorize in that period.

I will use Merton's types of theorizing, but in contrast to him historicize them. Some of his types are in a historic perspective more useful than others and most often we have to combine them in different ways.[4] This approach presupposes the possibility of making divisions in the historical transformation of sociology. Such divisions unavoidably lead to simplifications and exclusions but can be defended as long as the approach facilitates the purpose of clarifying the meaning and role of theory. I will take my point of departure in the following rough divisions:

- Classical sociology: the founding fathers (around 1900).
- First phase of postwar sociology: Scientization (from 1945 until the beginning of 1960s).
- Second phase of postwar sociology: Interpretive turn, normative turn, return of Grand theory (from 1968 until the 1989).
- Contemporary sociology: A downward shift. Turn toward immanence.

Hence, even in sociology, some understanding of the discipline tend to be dominating for a period.[5] To be sure, such understandings might more or less influence what mainstream sociologists actually are doing, but in any case, my task is only to identify the conceptions of theorizing that are related to these dominating understandings.

10.2 Classical Sociology

Even though classical sociologists were engaged in establishing sociology as an acknowledged discipline among the social sciences, they were without doubt, more or less tacitly, deeply influenced by practical philosophy, first and foremost Kant and Hegel (Merton 1968: 46; Levine 1981; Mills 2000; Gangas 2007). Thus, they were theoretical in most senses on Merton's list, but seldom in the most important sense, according to him (Alexander 1987b). Much of their work was about conceptualization and categorization on both a micro- and a macrolevel (types of interaction, action, general social order, social pathologies, etc.). They certainly produced "general orientations toward substantive materials" rather than "specific confirmed hypotheses" (Merton 1945: 464). They tried to interpret social facts with the help of conceptual schemes without the intermediate step of formulating hypotheses and test them.[6] Because they tried to establish sociology as specific discipline, they spend much time on delimiting the subject matter of sociology: What is the social? What is modernity? Merton found all these kinds of analysis partly important but claimed that it was time to put them to the side and go on and produce "sociological theory."

However, in view of the influence of practical philosophy in the classical period, it is clear that theory in one important sense is missing in Merton's list, that is, normative or critical theory. In spite of the efforts that was made in order to make sociology an acknowledged value-neutral science, it is easy to see that some kind of normativity was a crucial, but more or less implicit, part of classical sociology. Donald Levine starts an article on Max Weber (and partly on Tönnies and Simmel) by quoting Hegel: "reason and freedom remain our principles" (1981: 5). C. W. Mills is quite explicit: "The role of reason in human affairs and the idea of the free individual as the seat of reason are the most important themes inherited by twentieth-century social scientists from the philosophers of the Enlightenment" (2000: 167). The conceptions of rationality and freedom in Weber's work were certainly not value neutral. His perhaps most well-known concept "the iron cage" must, for instance, be understood in relation to his understanding of reason and freedom. Weber was "a liberal in despair" (Mommsen 1974). Émile Durkheim's conception of the social pathologies of modernity must be understood in relation to a Kantian or even Hegelian understanding of freedom and reason (Gangas 2007). If we include Marx among the classic sociologists, this absence in Merton's list becomes obvious. In fact, a rejection of normative theory as a legitimate form of sociological theory has never been so hegemonic in the history of sociology as during the first postwar phase (Alexander 2000: 272).

10.3 First Phase of Postwar Sociology

A new conception of sociology included a move of its center from Europe to the United States. To be sure, Talcott Parsons's "Grand theory" was in many ways a continuation of classical sociology.[7] A change in the dominating understanding of theory should rather be attributed to the conception of sociology that Paul Lazarsfeld and Merton in cooperation developed at Columbia. On the basis of the development of quantitative methods and theories of the middle range, sociology became an established academic discipline—and only then also in Europe, in this new American form (Wagner 2001, chapter 1).

The successful institutionalization of sociology after the Second World War must be understood in view of the role that the discipline acquired in the second epoch of modernity—"organized modernity"—as an instrument of social planning (Wagner 1994): "The two great bureaucracies in America—the Warfare and the Welfare bureaucracy—were behind the spectacular development of empirical sociology" (Bauman in Cantell and Pedersen 1992: 143). Sociology became an "assistant science in service of administrations" (Habermas 1971: 299).[8]

To talk about theory in the sense of empirical generalizations was criticized by Merton. His conception of "theories of the middle range" should not—to use the terminology later developed by Mills—be placed between "abstracted empiricism" and "Grand theory" in the sense of scale. Merton developed it rather in contrast to both of them also in the more basic sense of a "type of analysis." Actually, in *Sociological theory* he did not even use the term middle range. Grand theory can be understood as a combination of what Merton called conceptual analysis, general orientations, and postfactual interpretation. The problem of empirical generalization, according to Merton, is that it is too descriptive. In a footnote he actually referred to John Dewey: Empirical generalization is "merely a set of uniform conjunctions of traits repeatedly observed to exist, without any understanding of why the conjunction occurs; without a theory which states its rationale" (Dewey in Merton 1945 :469). The decisive problem with both grand theory of the classical type and empirical generalization is that in neither of them are theoretical constructions of hypotheses seen as crucial. The task of a sociological theory is "to develop specific, interrelated hypotheses by re-formulating empirical generalizations in the light of these generic orientations", that is, specifying "relationships between particular variables" (Merton 1945: 464) and thus "the term sociological theory refers to logically interconnected sets of propositions from which empirical uniformities can be derived" (Merton 1968: 39).

Hence, theorizing is primarily about the art of constructing hypotheses. However, according to Merton, this art must be strictly regulated, because the hypotheses are to be constructed in such a way that they can be tested through some kind of experimental procedures. Thus, theory of the classical type must be abandoned. This testing (i.e., the context of justification) should be modeled after the natural sciences. Merton tried, successfully, to liberate sociology from its classical origin in practical philosophy and put it on a solid "scientific" base (Alexander 1987b). The idea that theories should be of the middle range is only a consequence of this conception of testing.

In this form sociology would be given a chance of attaining a share in the general legitimacy of the natural sciences. However, the price tended to be a loss in the significance of the hypotheses, which Merton himself was aware of (Merton 1945: 462). The scientistic restriction of the art of theorizing tended to lead to what critics later called "theoryless theories" (Gouldner 1970), that is, theories have to be rather simple to be testable. Merton also had to pay a second price, namely the price of a rather naive "methodological empiricism" (Merton 1945: 462). While all classical sociologists were well-educated Kantians, Merton simply seemed to take a dualistic relation between the theoretical and the empirical for granted. Reality was understood as something that exists "out there" in a "ready-made" form (Goodman 1978) independent of the theoretical. It is only possible to imagine that the theoretical and the empirical can be compared in clear-cut way under such a premise (Alexander 1987b).

This second conception of sociology was already challenged in the United States during the first phase of postwar sociology by outsiders and underdogs (Collins 1994: 262f, 266f). These alternative conceptions typically held on to the classical heritage of German idealism and did not accept the idea of a unified conception of science. The most important examples are symbolic interactionism and phenomenological sociology. Both had their origin in critical developments of Kant—by Peirce and Husserl—and were thus based on alternatives to empiricism already on a philosophical level. They both implicated a rejection of epistemological dualism by emphasizing the significance of meaning. These conceptions of sociology grew strong in the shadow of scientism and became eventually a part of the transformation to the next phase.

Meaning cannot, according to Herbert Blumer, simply be attributed to the object of study: "A tree will be a different object to a botanist, a lumberman, a poet, and a home gardener" (Blumer 1986: 11). Empiricists "regard meaning as intrinsic to the thing that has it" while idealists "regard meaning as a psychological accretion brought to thing by the person for whom the thing has meaning" (3–4). Symbolic interactionists, however, see "meaning as arising in the process of interaction between people" (4).

Alfred Schutz similarly saw reality as dependent on the social construction of meaning. He significantly developed Weber's subjective conception of the ideal type with the help of Husserl in order to clarify not only what sociologists should do when they theorize but also what goes on in everyday interaction (Schutz 1972). Schutz's version became under the third phase of sociology known as "double hermeneutics" (Giddens 1993), that is, social scientists have to—in contrast to natural scientists—construct typifications in order to understand the typifications of everyday life. Thus, Schutz reintroduced the need for conceptual analysis as a crucial form of theorizing. Further, because of the special demands on social science, general discussions about the subject matter of sociology must restart and new methods of meaning interpretation must be developed.

It should be added that Mills, just as Merton, tried to find a third position between "abstracted empiricism" and "Grand theory." However, his suggestion was certainly not "theories of the middle range." Rather, he argued for a sociology that was able to relate "personal troubles" and "structural transformations" (Mills 2000). Further, his sociological alternative was based on a critique of society that partly was inspired by both Marx and the Frankfurt school. Thus, in the works of Blumer, Schutz, and Mills we already find reasons behind both the interpretive and the normative turn of sociology.

10.4 Second Phase of Postwar Sociology

The rise of a third phase is often understood in terms of a crisis of sociology (Carleheden 1998). It is to be linked to the surge of academic Marxism, which in turn, had its social background in the 1968 movement and the crisis of the welfare state (Wagner 1994; Boltanski and Chiapello 2005, chapter 3). However, it was only a crisis for the conception of sociology that was hegemonic in the preceding phase. It opened up for other conceptions, not least for a reconnection to the classics. In 1982, Alexander claimed that there had been a "rehabilitation of the theoretical" (Alexander 1982: 30), and some years later Quentin Skinner edited a volume named *The Return of Grand Theory in Human Sciences* (Skinner 1985). In this book we find chapters about many of the most influential social theorists of the time (Gadamer, Kuhn, Derrida, Habermas, Rawls, Foucault, Althusser, Lévi-Strauss). In retrospect Patrick Baert and Filipe da Silva write about the significance of such scholars (adding Bourdieu, Giddens, and Luhmann) and call this period "the age of the golden generation of twentieth-century European social theory" (Baert and Silva 2010). This generation played a significant role for the social sciences toward the end of the twentieth century and set "the agenda for what is to be studied" (Baert and Silva 2010).[9] However, to talk about social theory in the singular is, as we have seen, wrong. What happened was rather a rehabilitation of the classical kind of theorizing and the ascendance of the outsiders in the preceding phase to the forefront. Habermas, for instance, developed his theory of communicative action in conversation not only with Marx, Weber, and Durkheim but also with Mead and Schutz.

So why did this transformation of the theoretical occur and why did it become such an influential answer to the crisis of the first phase of postwar sociology?[10] How did the social theorists at the beginning of the last quarter of the twentieth century managed to break the earlier empiricist hegemony? As far as I know, this transformation has not systematically been studied by sociologists of social science. However, lacking studies from such an external perspective, I will try to explicate the rise of a third conception of theorizing from the internal perspective of theory of science.[11] From that perspective it is quite easy to explain why it occurred.

The two most influential twentieth-century theories of science—that is, the logical positivism of the Vienna circle and the critical rationalism of Karl Popper—understood science as an endeavor that aimed at liberating science from theory in the classical, "speculative" sense. They were both based on the empiricist notion that theories could be directly compared with the world and argued for a unified conception of science modeled after natural science. The logical positivism of the Vienna circle implied that sooner or later science would be able to grasp the whole complexity of the world using the methods of natural science. Even in everyday life prejudices and metaphysics would eventually be conquered and replaced by conceptions based on science in this sense.[12]

Popper was not a revolutionary thinker in this way, but a reformist ("piecemeal social engineering," as he put it). However, also he, in the last instance, took for granted that we are able to test theories by comparing them with a "ready-made" world out there (Goodman 1978).[13] Also his theory of science implicates that the theoretical component of our understanding of the world—the hypothesis—must be formulated in such a way that it can be tested against the empirical. The sharp distinction between the context of discovery and the context of justification is then fundamental. The theoretical constructions that take place in the former context must be subordinated to the demands of the latter context:

> It is irrelevant from the point of view of science whether we have obtained our theories by jumping to unwarranted conclusions or merely by stumbling over them (that is, by "intuition"), or else by some inductive procedure. The question, "How did you first find your theory?" relates, as it were, to an entirely private matter, as opposed to the question, "How did you test your theory" which alone is scientifically relevant. (Popper 1957: 135)

Such a conception of science makes it possible to defend research from theoretical critique in other senses than Merton's by claiming that "what you are suggesting is just another theory."[14] Theoretical discussions in other senses are then seen almost as a waste of time. All we can do with theories is to prepare them for testing. A meaningful scientific discussion is only possible in the context of justification.

Dewey—one of the classical thinkers who was rehabilitated in the second phase of postwar sociology—argued that such empiricist notions of science are based on a "spectator theory of knowledge" (Dewey 1984: 163), and Jürgen Habermas talked about a "copy theory of truth" (Habermas 1971: 69). Further, it was against the background of such a notion of theory that Theodor W. Adorno ironically concluded "thinking is unscientific" (Adorno 2005: 124). When Habermas later claimed, "That we disavow reflection is positivism," he was saying the same thing, but without the irony (Habermas 1971: vii).

The crisis of the first phase of postwar sociology meant that sociological theory in Merton's sense lost its dominating role. The struggle between different conceptions of theorizing was opened up. Most of these conceptions were based on some kind of "post-empiricism" or "post-positivism." This transformation of sociology was by then, as we have seen, already prepared on a philosophical level by Peirce and Husserl and, which should be added, by post-Tractatus Ludwig Wittgenstein.

Let me just quickly mention some of the most important post-empiricist names: In Germany, Hans-Georg Gadamer, Adorno and Habermas were all firmly based on

German idealism and used in the first case Heidegger and in the latter cases Marx to reconstruct this heritage (Adorno et al. 1976; Gadamer 1989).[15] Niklas Luhmann radicalized Talcott Parsons by emphasizing Husserl's concept of meaning. He claimed that the introduction of empirical methods had led to a "Theoriedesaster" (Luhmann 1992: 410). In the UK, Peter Winch (Winch 1958) made the later Wittgenstein relevant for the social sciences, and Anthony Giddens further developed not only Winch's work but used also phenomenological and hermeneutical thinkers in order to formulate his *New rules of sociological method* (Giddens 1993). Thomas Kuhn's critique of Popper was crucial, but in the United States not only Blumer but also Richard Rorty and Richard Bernstein rediscovered—as Karl-Otto Apel and Habermas had done in Germany—the American pragmatist tradition (Bernstein 1976; Rorty 1979). Further, Alexander rehabilitated Parsons' Grand theory approach—as Habermas and Luhmann had done in Germany. Schutz became influential through Peter Berger and Thomas Luckmann's work and Harold Garfinkel's ethnomethodology (Collins 1994). In France, Michel Foucault's (ironic) statement of being a "happy positivist" did not stop him from joking about scientific methods that seem to presuppose that "things murmur meanings our language merely has to extract" (Foucault 1972: 228), and Pierre Bourdieu dismissed what he called the "the illusion of immediate knowledge" (Bourdieu, Passeron, and Chamboredon 1991: 250).

This massive critique of empiricism was so uncompromising that it seemed to reaffirm Max Horkheimer and Adorno's dark thesis of a dialectic of the Enlightenment. What once was understood as a revolutionary scientific struggle against prejudice and metaphysics had become a new kind of metaphysics; a kind which later was to be called "metaphysical realism" (Putnam 1983). Furthermore, on the ground of the epistemological criticism of methodological empiricism, science itself became not only an object for social theory but also a target for normative criticism. The scientists, the heroes of the Vienna circle, were now pictured not only as equipped with their own particular interests and habits but also as a kind of colonizers of nature, societies, and souls, carrying "instrumental reason" as a destructive weapon in their hands. In seeing themselves as neutral observers of society, social scientists had historically not been able to acknowledge that science itself had become a major force in producing the kind of society that already Weber had called an "iron cage." Such normative and political implications of empiricist theories of science must not be underestimated in the attempts to explain the transformation of the theoretical. Critique of the political consequences of mainstream science became a significant part of the general critique of society at the end of the 1960s and became a part in the transformation of both society and social science.

Thus, the epistemological and normative critique of empiricism should be seen as the intellectual base for the transformation of social theory in the last quarter of the twentieth century. The general implication of post-empiricism can be caught by the last part of the old Kantian dictum, "Thoughts without intuitions are empty, intuitions without concepts are blind"(Kant 1998)[16] or, with the more recent dictum that facts (or observations or data) are always already theory-laden (Kuhn 1962).[17] We cannot, according to this view, even see the world without concepts, theories or paradigms. Thus we should, using the recent terminology of Luc Boltanski (2011), make a distinction between reality and world. The world is infinitely complex. In real life (including both everyday activities and research) we can never do without generalizations, abstractions, selections, interpretations, constructs, typifications, categorizations, classifications, paradigms, languages, perceptual habits, and institutions. As a consequence, there is no way of making any sharp distinction between theories and facts, and further, it seems impossible to compare such entities. We will always lack a theory-neutral language of observation. As soon as this post-empiricist view was formulated with enough precision and persuasive force by "the golden generation" (Baert and Da Salvia 2010: 286), the door opened up for a transformation of our understanding of theorizing. Conceptual analysis, general orientation, and postfactual interpretation became rehabilitated.

As long as we believe that it is possible to differentiate between and compare theories and facts in a clear-cut way, testing will be in the center of our conception of being scientific. It is then first and foremost a matter of using empirical methods in the right way. But this empiricist conception of science was shaken when a new generation of social scientists was successful in showing that such a conception of science has been impossible to realize in practice, was based on an unconvincing theory of science and had problematic political consequences. Facts, they claimed, are always already situated in a (common sense or reflexive) theoretical context. Theories are necessarily related to world views, normative reasoning, and everyday knowledge, which make it practically impossible to find empirical criteria, which in an unambiguous way would count as verification or falsification. We must give up the idea of some kind of crucial experiment, "that will make the decision for us"—as Joas and Knöbl (2009: 16) put it. They end their introduction to the twentieth-century social theory with a statement that might very well be interpreted as the "the golden generation's" basic understanding of theory:

> Theoretical issues thus range from empirical generalizations to comprehensive interpretive systems which link basic philosophical, metaphysical, political and moral attitudes to the world. Anyone wishing to be part of the social scientific world cannot, therefore, avoid engaging in critical debate on all these levels. Those hoping to stick with purely empirical theories will be disappointed. (Joas and Knöbl 2009: 17–18)

10.5 Contemporary Sociology

Almost thirty years after his proclamation of the rehabilitation of the theoretical, Alexander—together with Isaac Reed—describe contemporary social science as "post-theoretical" (Reed and Alexander 2009: 24). They claim that we have seen an "abandonment of theoretical discourse" and date the beginning of this end to the "late 1980s" (23):

> In social scientific practice—and in Anglophone sociology in particular—there has been a return to empirical studies of social life, a letting go of theoretical

> concerns. This is a broad trend, with many exceptions, but one which nonetheless can be felt in the bones of any young sociologist entering graduate school with the hopes of "writing theory." (Reed and Alexander 2009: 21f)

They are here using the term theory in the sense that was dominating during the second phase of postwar sociology. We find support for their claim in some innovative recent discussions. These discussions—in contrast to the quote above—generally focus on the opening rather than the end of something. They are conducted under labels such as "return to the empirical" (Adkins and Lury 2009: 6), "descriptive turn" (Savage 2009), "new empiricism" (Latour 2005; Gane 2009; Lash 2009), and "reconstruction" (Boltanski and Chiapello 2005; Honneth 2011). These discussions are interesting because they are directed against what is seen as problematic consequences of the way theorizing most often were pursued during the previous phase. Under these labels opponents to the "golden generation" are gathered. To be sure, it is difficult to say how much influence this new understanding of theory have had on research practices, but many have pointed toward the fact that some kind of "downward shift" (Reed and Alexander 2009: 24) seems to be occurring.

In a similar way as in the previous section, I will only investigate the internal arguments that might motivate a "downward shift." These arguments cannot be understood as a plea for a return to the empirical in the sense of the "theoryless theories" and the "abstracted empiricism" of the first phase of postwar sociology, but rather, and more interestingly, a plea for a second transformation of our understanding of the theoretical and its role in empirical research. I will take my point of departure in three different diagnoses of problems that can be seen as consequences of second-phase postwar sociology.

The first diagnosis is formulated by Stephen Turner and is based on the following claim:

> Social theory is not only a field but a mature one, one that is essentially complete and self- sufficient as a coherent and valuable form of intellectual activity, a voice in the conversation of mankind, with its own internal conversation of considerable complexity and depth. (Turner 2004: 141)

Turner even talks about "the mutual irrelevance of empirical sociology and social theory" (Turner 2004: 146) and goes on,

> *Theory Culture and Society* and the *American Sociological Review* are journals, that for all practical purposes are not only in different disciplines, but in disciplines that are more widely separated than, say, sociology and economics." (2004: 147)

In line with the "golden generation" he understands social theory as historicizing and situating concepts. "Commentary is the basic method of social theory" (156), he claims. Thus, theorizing is always conducted in conversation with other social theorists. This conception does not implicate—of course—that social theory in some sense could replace empirical sociology. Rather, social theory must be saved from "the dead hand of sociology" (146). The problem for social theory today, according to this first diagnosis, is the problem of a subfield, institutionalized as a part of sociology. Today social theory suffocates by being subsumed under empirical sociology. Thus, Turner's article seems to be a defense of the "classic" and "golden" conceptions of social theory, which today are being threatened by the downward turn. He does not really identify any internal problems within this kind of theorizing. The problem lies outside of social theory and the only solution seems to be to reclaim its status as an acknowledged subfield. Turner's sharp distinction between social theory and empirical sociology seems to implicate that his diagnosis is caught by the struggles that went on during the transformation from the first to the second postwar phase of sociology.

However, Turner's diagnosis of the current state of sociology seems to stand in contradiction to the self-understanding of both classical and, at least partly, second-phase postwar social theory. The classical sociologists did not make such a sharp distinction between theoretical and empirical sociology and the interpretative turn in the second phase of postwar sociology was intended, as we have seen, to change empirical sociology. This intention leads to the second diagnosis:

> The modern social sciences are characterized … by an extremely damaging division between theoretical and empirical knowledge. Something of a division of labour, as it were, has arisen between those who see themselves as theoreticians and those who view themselves as empiricists or empirical social researchers. As a result of this strict division of labour, these two groupings scarcely register each other's findings anymore. (Joas and Knöbl 2009: 3)

Joas and Knöbl confirm Turner's statement about a de facto mutual irrelevance of empirical social science and social theory in contemporary sociology, but unlike Turner they see this division as a major problem. The diagnosis implies that during the last quarter of the twentieth century social theory was transformed in such a way that the tight connection between the theoretical and the empirical, which Merton's conception allowed for, was broken:

> Just as some intellectuals and theorists deride the seemingly myopic and 'pedestrian' concerns of empirical researchers—particularly those of the empiricist variety who believe that the facts speak for themselves—the force of anti-theoretical sentiments deriving from other sources cannot be underestimated. (Layder 1998: 8)

This picture of the contemporary state of social theory has been reaffirmed over and again; "social theory increasingly has become a separate academic field" (Baert and Silva 2010: 2) and "the precise role of theory in empirical research has become increasingly uncertain" (285). Reed and Alexander (2009: 25) and Savage (2013) claim something similar. According to all of them the solution to the problem is to "reassess" their relation (Baert and Silva 2010: 285). Such reassessment seems to exclude both the solution implied by the first diagnosis and the empiricism of first-phase postwar sociology. Social theory and empirical research are interdependent, but the significance of theorizing cannot be reduced to the construction of middle-range hypotheses.

Baert and da Silva (2010: 291) describe a "representational" view on theory, which can be seen as an instructive example of a failed attempt to connect theory, in the post-empiricist sense, and empirical research. In this case empirical researchers do not test theories, but apply them on specific cases. They might, for instance, investigate whether Bourdieu's distinction between economic and cultural capital is not only applicable in Paris in the 1970s, but also in the Danish city of Aalborg today. This way of using theory is the opposite of the empiricist model. Grand theories almost become bibles, and concepts are given a kind of fetishist status. Empirical researchers choose a grand theory or an influential concept and apply it on a subject matter that has not been investigated before—at least not recently and at this or that particular place. Application of ready-made theory might then become a kind of theoretical colonization of the empirical. On the other hand, post-empiricist theorizing might also be instrumentalized by the empirical researcher. If a ready-made theory does not fit to the empirical data, the empirical researcher simply throws it overboard and looks for another ready-made theory to apply. In both cases theory and data remain external to one another and the theory-fact dualism is not overcome.

The first two diagnoses are basically positive to the way "the golden generation" theorized. Baert and da Silva, in spite of their statements quoted above, open their concluding chapter *Social Theory for the Twenty-First Century* by claiming: "Social theory is an increasingly important intellectual endeavor in the social sciences today" (2010: 285). Neither of the two first diagnoses are really implying any need for any radical change of the way social theory has been conducted in the previous phase. The problems they identify are related to the relation to empirical research. The third diagnosis, however, attributes the problem of contemporary sociology to the way of theorizing that characterized late twentieth-century social theory. I will use two different versions of French pragmatism as my main witnesses.

Bruno Latour, just like Reed and Alexander, implies that we should see the late 1980s as a turning point for social theory. 1989 was not only the year of the fall of the Berlin Wall but also the year of the first conferences about the state of the planet (Latour 1993: 8). These events symbolize for him both the failure and the end of the two central modern projects; in the first case, the emancipation from exploitation, and, in the second case, the human domination over nature. In both cases science has played a crucial role—including academic Marxism, which was instrumental for the second transformation of the theoretical in sociology. French pragmatists tend to see this transformation as reifying and paternalistic in both an epistemological and a normative sense. We should

> avoid both the arrogance of the expert adviser to the Prince and pontificator, and the irresponsibility of armchair revolutionaries … basing their power on a dual, "scientific" and "political" legitimacy—something which … has led to unprecedented forms of intellectual terrorism. (Boltanski and Chiapello 2005: xiv)

The remedy of this diagnosis of sociology, is to "follow the actors themselves" (Latour 2005: 12; Boltanski and Thévenot 2006: 12). Ordinary actors are perfectly capable to formulate their own "theories" or "metaphysics" (Boltanski and Thévenot 2006: 145).

Latour names such an approach "empirical metaphysics" (Latour 2005: 51). French pragmatists direct their critique of paternalism first and foremost against Bourdieu's critical sociology (Celikates 2006). They seem sometimes almost to equate Bourdieu's sociology with sociological "method" in general—or what Latour calls "sociology of the social," in contrast to his own method, which he calls "sociology of associations" (2005: 159–60). Master concepts like "social" and "society" must be put to the side. They have

> remained stranded like a whale, yes a leviathan, beached on a seashore where Lilliputian social scientists tried to dig a suitable abode. Of late, the smell of this decaying monster has become unbearable. There is no way to succeed in reviewing social theory as long as the beach has not been cleared and the ill-fated notion of society entirely dissolved. (Latour, 2005: 163–4)

Latour seems in this respect to be partly critical of his own early sociology of science and distances himself from social constructivism: "The question was never to get away from facts but closer to them, not fighting empiricism but, on the contrary, renewing empiricism" (Latour 2004: 231). Thus, from this perspective, late twentieth-century social theory has been too Kantian. This way of theorizing actually prevents us from seeing the world.

Latour and his followers explicitly argue for a downward shift in terms of "a return to the empirical" and "a descriptive turn." However, this is not to be understood as a step back to methodological empiricism of the first phase of postwar sociology, but rather as a step forward toward "second empiricism" (Latour 2004: 232) or "new empiricism" (Gane 2009). Second empiricism is not based on a conception of "things-in-themselves" (Latour 1993: 5). The objectifying gaze—*Das Tatsachenblick* (Bonβ 1982)—of abstracted empiricism does as much violence to the empirical as the "apriorism" (Lash 2009) of the armchair social theorist. Hence, Latour does not argue that we should conceive the world as matters of facts but rather as "matters of concern." To see the world as "matters of fact are totally implausible, unrealistic, unjustified definitions of what it is to deal with things" (2004: 244). Thus, the question of the meaning of the theoretical is closely connected to the question "what is the empirical?" (Adkins and Lury 2009).

All the three diagnoses implicate that the post-empiricist critique of scienticism was correct, but also that the transformation of the theoretical in the second postwar period actually never led to an abandonment of the fact-theory dualism—at least not in practice. According to the third diagnosis, we must acknowledge this failure and see that there are two different ways to theoretically reify the world. The first way is mainstream methodological empiricism, which involves a reduction of the empirical to matters of facts. The second one subordinates the empirical under some intellectual conceptual scheme. Instead, Latour calls for "a new respectful realism" (Latour 2004: 244): "If the sociology of the social works fine with what has been already assembled, it does not work so well to collect anew the participants in what is not—not yet—a sort of social realm" (Latour 2005: 12).

How should we then, according to Latour, "collect anew"? It is not easy to say, because he avoids to reflect on his own role as an actor. It is even unclear if Latour accepts the common point of departure that theory basically is to be understood as some kind of generalization (Albertsen 2008). Boltanski and Chiapello are more decided on this crucial point. Together with Thévenot, Boltanski developed a sociology of critique in order to come closer to the actors of everyday life. However, according to Boltanski and Chiapello, we cannot stay on "the plane of immanence." Everyday actors do not stay on "the plane of immanence" nor can social scientists. At some point we have to "reconstruct" and "recategorize," which presupposes a conception of reality as a "two-tier space" (Boltanski and Chiapello 2006: 107, 320, xxxiiiff.). One could understand Boltanski and Chiapello's distinction between "a regime of displacement" and "a regime of categorization" as an implicit critique of Latour.[18] A regime of categorization is about generalization (321ff.). By means of recategorization and reconstruction they aim to overcome the antagonism between critical sociology and sociology of critique. They seem to be heading in the direction of a "critical sociology of critique" (Albertsen 2008: 76), which includes both epistemological and normative reconstructions. However, they are rather ambivalent and have not explained this idea in any systematic way.

Just as in the French case, we find theoretical moves toward immanence in American and German social theory. Alexander (2000) discusses such moves by analyzing, on the one hand, the "liberal-communitarian debate" and, on the other, Axel Honneth's criticism of Habermas. Alexander also points at the same tendency toward immanence in the development of Rawls and Habermas's own thinking. However, I cannot here discuss these transformations. Rather, I will end with a short analysis of the method Honneth uses to develop a normative social theory of freedom. Also he uses the terms "reconstruction" and "immanent analysis" in contrast to "construction" (Honneth 2011).

Honneth's method should be understood as an alternative to the Kantian way (e.g., early Rawls) of establishing the meaning of justice purely philosophically and, so to say, from above. His point of departure is simply to assert that freedom is the fundamental normative ideal of Western modernity. A theory of justice must, according to him, be based on that immanent ideal. However, Honneth does not support this claim inductively as an empirical researcher would do (e.g., in way of the "world value studies"). Rather, he analyzes the meaning of freedom. His method of normative reconstruction is built on a kind of quasi-transcendental logic.[19] This logic of inquiry—to use Peirce terminology—is primarily neither inductive nor deductive, but abductive or retroductive. It is an "inference a posteriori" (Carleheden 2014). It is, using Merton's term, a postfactual interpretation. It goes backward and aims to explain the conditions of the possibility of a known fact—in this case, the hegemony of the ideal of freedom. Because his analysis is immanent, Honneth has to proceed historically and sociologically. His analysis of the meaning of freedom must in some way be in contact with the historic development of Western modernity. The major part of Honneth's book is dedicated to that task. This method certainly needs to be explicated and developed further also in Honneth's case.[20] However, the idea of epistemological and normative reconstruction points to a way of overcoming the problems of post-empiricist theorizing that the three diagnoses have identified.

This is how far I will go with my historical investigation. I will now end with an attempt—based on this investigation—to indicate in what direction we should go in order to answer Peirce's question that opened this chapter.

10.6 Conclusion

My investigation indicates that it is possible to see a reasonable historical development of conceptions of theorizing in twentieth-century sociology. Merton's conception was directed against both pure empirical generalization and general theory detached from the empirical world, but presupposed a rather naïve epistemology, tended to trivialize social theory and clear the way for a bureaucratization of the discipline. A normative and interpretive turn and a return to Grand theory seemed to be necessary. However, in spite of the general acknowledgment of the notion that facts are unavoidably "theory-laden," the dualistic distinction between the theoretical and the empirical has commonly remained in place. This dualism points toward a less reasonable development. In some sociological quarters, the conception of theory-ladenness tended to become an excuse for focusing exclusively on the theory-side. Thus, the risk of theoretical paternalism and of holding on to "zombie-categories" (Beck and Beck-Gernsheim 2002) increased. In the meantime, an unquestioned scientistic conception of the empirical could thrive in other quarters of the discipline. It might be that the kind of liberation of social theory from empirical research, which Turner asks for, has been a part of the problem rather than its solution. It might have reinforced an abstracted understanding of the empirical that in the next round struck back on social theory in just the way that Turner wanted to avoid.

The notion of the theory-ladenness of facts suggests that theorizing in a post-empiricist sense must be a significant part of doing empirical research. Hence, theorizing might also be seen as a special kind of empirical method. Overcoming the fact-theory dualism cannot only be about a theorization of the empirical but also be about an empiricalization of the theoretical. Social theory must also be understood as a method of interpreting the world.

In order to explicate this claim, it might be helpful to turn to Michael Oakeshott's concept "mode of experience" (Oakeshott 1933). We can then understand mainstream empirical methods as certain ways of seeing the world among others. They are attached to certain "knowledge interests" (Habermas 1971a). Accordingly, such empirical methods cannot be given a privileged ability to connect to the world, but are to be seen as particular modes of experiencing it. Thus, these empirical methods need to be disenchanted and cannot simply be understood as neutral tools of knowledge production (Law 2009; Savage 2013; Gobo 2016). They are based on specific cognitive and normative assumptions. Or, to use Latour's terminology, methods predetermine the way the world is assembled. From this point of view we can take another look at social theory. Not only do methods always already include particular theoretical conceptions, but theories always already include certain methods of experiencing the world. Theorizing must be understood as a certain way of making the world real; that is, making sense of the world.

In Turner's version, social theory might look like a kind of history of ideas, "exegesis" (Blumer 1986: 141) or *Bildung* (Savage 2013: 13). But this would be a misconception of both the golden and the classical generation. Their primary aim was not to develop theories about theories, but to use and develop them in order to understand modern society. They did that on the shoulders of other theorists or in oppositions to them. In either case, they used already developed ideas, concepts, and theories as partners in discussions of how to understand the world.

Thus, also post-empiricist social theorists study the world "out there" in order to understand it. But in contrast to ordinary empirical researchers, these social theorists have been skeptical about so-called scientific methods.[21] This disbelief goes back to the abovementioned critique of the social role of empirical research that accompanied the second transformation of social theory. The general suspicion was that methods instrumentalize and reificate the world (Carleheden 1998). Post-empiricist theorizing, on the other hand, opens for another kind of knowledge as compared to quantitative or qualitative methods. The possibility of a theoretical kind of method might be explained by the simple fact that social theorists actually do not spend their lives in armchairs. They are situated in the world as every other human being. Let me just mention the background of Habermas's social theory as an illustration. His theory of communicative action is without doubt related to his own experiences of growing up in Nazi Germany with a physical handicap (Habermas 2005, chapter 1; Müller-Doohm 2014, Part 1). This example indicates that being an innovative social theorist presupposes the ability of somehow being in contact with deep personal and emotional experiences. Mainstream methods might stand in the way for such a contact.[22]

From the above perspective, it is possible to reconsider Turner's claim. The fact that today it is accepted that quantitative and qualitative methods produce different kinds of knowledge, might also be used to support Turner's claim that social theory in some sense is "self-sufficient." The kind of knowledge that late twentieth-century social theory produced is knowledge, but a different kind as compared to the kind that mainstream empirical methods produce. Post-empiricist theory is related to the world in another way. None of these modes of experience (or methods) need to be seen as better or truer than the other ones, but simply as different in kind.

The question then arises how theoretical claims of knowledge can be seen as more or less valid. We can answer by referring to American pragmatism or phenomenological sociology. Theory—both in a scientific and in a common sense—is about generalizations and typifications and they can of course be better or worse. The answer of the question of specific forms of theoretical validity is actually not very different from the question how mainstream empirical methods can be seen as more or less valid. The post-empiricist social theoretical way of reducing the subjectivity of individual experiences and of common sense is to communicate with other theories and other theorists. It is "the community of inquiry" that allows social theorists to generalize their findings (Carleheden 2014: 439; Tavory and Timmermans 2014, chapter 7). In this community the danger of ready-made theories and frozen concepts can be counteracted.

The question of the relation between the theoretical and the empirical can now be reformulated in a more fruitful way: How should we understand the relation between reconstructive, quantitative, and qualitative methods? These methods allow us to see different dimensions of the world. They include their special ways of making the world real and use different means of justification. They can, on the other hand, all reify the world in their own way if they do not acknowledge their own limits and the value of other modes of experience. If one of the modes dominates over the others our knowledge of the world declines.

This suggestion of how to interpret, evaluate, and develop the ongoing turn to immanence is of course highly tentative. It implicates distinctions between different, equally legitimate modes of experiencing the world, but also a close interdependency between them, that is, between theorizing and qualitative and quantitative methods. Theorizing is also a kind of experience and a kind of method, but a specific one. It might be understood as quasi-transcendental reconstruction or—with Peirce—abduction/retroduction. Theorizing in this sense of postfactual interpretation have reconceptualization as its aim. Its postfactuality shows that it is dependent on the results of other methods, but the theory-ladenness of facts shows, on the other hand, that these other methods also are dependent on conceptualizations.

Acknowledgments

Thanks to Nikolaj Schultz, Bjørn Schiermer, Margareta Bertilsson, and Emma Engdahl and also to the participants in seminars in Copenhagen, Gothenburg, and Helsinki in which earlier versions of this chapter have been discussed.

Notes

1 This "immanent" method anticipates in a way, as the reader in the end will see, the conclusion.
2 On the productive role of nonviolent conflicts in clarifying justifications in nonacademic life, see Boltanski and Thévenot (2006).
3 There is of course an overwhelming amount of overviews regarding the content of different social theories, but not regarding different approaches to the question of how to theorize.
4 Merton was using the first five types only as contrasts in order to clarify the sixth. He did not make much effort to explicate the merits of the other conceptions. I will however, as we go along, give some more substance also to the other types.
5 However, the claim that we are entering a fourth period is very tentative.
6 Georg Simmel's article "How is society possible?" would be a good example of a postfactual interpretation.
7 However, see Turner (2004) who argues that also Parsons's social theory should be seen as a part of the scientization of sociology after 1945.
8 "Hilfswissenschaft im Dienste von Verwaltungen."

9 Thus, the center of sociology seemed to have returned to Europe but again in a new form.
10 The development of "qualitative methods" was another answer, which I cannot discuss here.
11 With "external" I refer to explanations that focus on interest, power, politics of higher education and research, and institutional and general social structures. With "internal" I refer to an investigation of the rational arguments that might have supported the change. In opposition to a pure sociology of science perspective I simply take for granted that reasoning must be given some explanatory force.
12 Compare the American sociologist George Lundberg's book "Can science save us?" (1947).
13 This is why also Popper's theory of science should be understood as a kind of empiricism (Joas and Knöbl 2009: 8ff).
14 This answer was once given to me by a rational choice sociologist. I was arguing that it is strange that rational choice theory takes "the prisoner's dilemma" as its basic point of departure because in ordinary life people are most often able to communicate with one another. Therefore, I continued, we should rather take communication as our basic point of departure.
15 Positivist debates, similar to the German one, went on in both Norway and Sweden under this period (Heidegren, 2016).
16 I am puzzled over the fact that "Anschauungen" is translated to "intuitions" and not "observations"; "Anschauungen ohne Begriffe sind blind" (Kritik der reinen Vernunft [KrV B75, A51]).
17 Popper acknowledged that in a later German version (1968) of *Logic of Scientific Discovery*; "There are no pure observations: they are pervaded by theories and guided by both problems and theories" (Translated in Joas and Knöbl 2009: 11).
18 Explicitly they are rather criticizing Deleuze's "ontology of force" (xxv). Compare Latour's critique of Boltanski as being "half-Kantian" (2005: 232).
19 In his critique of Habermas as a constructivist Kantian, Honneth surprisingly does not mention that Habermas already in the beginning of the 1970 discussed his own method in terms of "rational reconstruction."
20 There is a problematic tension between the immanent method and what seems to be a kind of a priori developmental logic that Honneth inherits from Hegel's *Philosophy of Right*.
21 Compare Gadamer's distinction between "truth" and "method" (1989). His work could have been used in order to make a similar point as I have made with the help of Oakeshott.
22 Compare the appendix in Mills (2000) on "intellectual craftsmanship."

References

Abend, G. 2008. "The Meaning of 'Theory'." *Sociological Theory* 26 (2): 173–99.

Adkins, L., and C. Lury. 2009. "Introduction: What Is the Empirical?" *European Journal of Social Theory* 12 (1): 5–20.

Adorno, T. W. 2005. *Minima Moralia: Reflections from Damaged Life*. London: Verso.

Adorno, T. W., H. Albert, R. Dahrendorf, J. Habermas, H. Pilot, and K. R. Popper. 1976. *The Positivist Dispute in German Sociology*. New York: Heinemann Educational Books.
Albertsen, N. 2008. "Retfærdiggørelse, ideologi, kritik." *Dansk sociologi* 19 (2): 65–84.
Alexander, J. 1982. *Theoretical Logic in Sociology*. Berkeley: University of California Press.
Alexander, J. 1987a. *Twenty Lectures: Sociological Theory since World War II*. New York: Columbia University Press.
Alexander, J. 1987b. "The Centrality of the Classics." In *Social Theory Today*, ed. A. Giddens and J. Turner, 11–57. Stanford, CA: Stanford University Press.
Alexander, J. 2000. "Theorizing the Good Society: Hermeneutic, Normative and Empirical Discourses." *The Canadian Journal of Sociology* 25 (3): 271–309.
Baert, P., and F. C. d. Silva. 2010. *Social Theory in the Twentieth Century*. Maiden, MA: Polity Press.
Beck, U., and E. Beck-Gernsheim. 2002. *Individualization: Institutionalized Individualism and Its Social and Political Consequences*. London: Sage.
Bernstein, R. J. 1976. *The Restructuring of Social and Political Theory*. New York: Harcourt Brace Jovanovich.
Blumer, H. 1986. *Symbolic Interactionism: Perspective and Method*. Berkeley, CA: University of California Press.
Boltanski, L. 2011. *On Critique: A Sociology of Emancipation*. Cambridge: Polity.
Boltanski, L., and E. Chiapello. 2005. *The New Spirit of Capitalism*. London: Verso.
Boltanski, L., and L. Thévenot. 2006. *On Justification: Economies of Worth*. Princeton, NJ: Princeton University Press.
Bonβ, W. 1982. *Die Einübung des Tatsachenblicks: Zur Struktur und Veränderung empirischer Sozialforschung*. Frankfurt: Suhrkamp.
Bourdieu, P., J.-C. Passeron, J.-C. Chamboredon. 1991. *The Craft of Sociology: Epistemological Preliminaries*. Berlin: Walter de Gruyter.
Cantell, T., and P. P. Pedersen. 1992. "Modernity, Postmodernity and Ethics: An interview with Zygmunt Bauman by Timo Cantell and Poul Poder Pedersen." *Telos* 1992 (93): 133–44.
Carleheden, M. 1998. "Another Sociology: The Future of Sociology from a Critical Theoretical Perspective." *Dansk sociologi* 9 (Special issue): 55–75.
Carleheden, M. 2014. On Theorizing: C.S. Peirce and Contemporary Social Science. In A. Laitinen, J. Saarinen, H. Ikäheimo, P. Lyyra & P. Niemi (eds.) Sisäisyys & suunnistautuminen: juhlakirja Jussi Kotkavirralle (*Inwardness and Orientation – Festschrift in Honor of Jussi Kotkavirta*) SoPhi 125 2014 Jyväskylän yliopisto (University of Jyväskylä) pp 128–159.
Celikates, R. 2006. "From Critical Social Theory to a Social Theory of Critique: On the Critique of Ideology after the Pragmatic Turn." *Constellations* 13 (1): 21–40.
Collins, R. 1994. *Four Sociological Traditions*. New York: Oxford University Press.
Dewey, J. 1984. *The Later Works of John Dewey, Volume 4, 1925–1953: 1929: The Quest for Certainty*. Carbondale: Southern Illinois University Press.
Flyvbjerg, B. 2006. "Five Misunderstandings about Case-Study Research." *Qualitative Inquiry* 12 (2): 219–45.
Foucault, M. 1972. *The Archaeology of Knowledge*. New York: Pantheon Books.
Gadamer, H.-G. 1989. *Truth and Method*. New York: Crossroad.
Gane, N. 2009. "Concepts and the 'New' Empiricism." *European Journal of Social Theory* 12 (1): 83–97.
Gangas, S. 2007. "Social Ethics and Logic." *Journal of Classical Sociology* 7 (3): 315–38.

Giddens, A. 1993. *New Rules of Sociological Method*. Stanford, CA: Stanford University Press.
Gobo, G.2016. "Glocalization: A Critical Introduction." *European Journal of Cultural and Political Sociology* 3 (2–3): 381–5.
Goodman, N. 1978. *Ways of Worldmaking*. Sussex: The Harvester Press.
Gouldner, A. W. 1970. *The Coming Crisis of Western Sociology*. New York: Basic Books.
Habermas, J. 1971a. *Knowledge and Human Interests*. Boston, MA: Beacon Press.
Habermas, J. 1971b. *Theorie und Praxis: sozialphilosophische Studien*. Frankfurt am Main: Suhrkamp.
Habermas, J. 2005. *Zwischen Naturalismus und Religion: Philosophische Aufsätze*. Frankfurt am Main: Suhrkamp.
Heidegren, C.-G. 2016. *Positivismstrider*. Göteborg: Daidalos.
Honneth, A. 2011. *Das Recht der Freiheit: Grundriß einer demokratischen Sittlichkeit*. Berlin: Suhrkamp.
Joas, H., and W. Knöbl. 2009. *Social Theory: Twenty Introductory Lectures*. Cambridge: Cambridge University Press.
Kant, I. 1998. *The Critique of Pure Reason*. Cambridge: Cambridge University Press.
Kuhn, T. S. 1962. *The Structure of Scientific Revolutions*. Chicago, IL: University of Chicago Press.
Lash, S. 2009. "Afterword: In Praise of the A Posteriori: Sociology and the Empirical." *European Journal of Social Theory* 12 (1): 175–87.
Latour, B. 1993. *We Have Never Been Modern*. New York: Harvester Wheatsheaf.
Latour, B. 2004. "Why Has Critique Run out of Steam? From Matters of Fact to Matters of Concern." *Critical Inquiry* 30 (2): 225–48.
Latour, B. 2005. *Reassembling the Social: An Introduction to Actor-NetworkTtheory*. Oxford: Oxford University Press.
Law, J. 2009. "Seeing Like a Survey." *Cultural Sociology* 3 (2): 239–56.
Layder, D. 1998. *Sociological Practice: Linking Theory and Social Research*. London: Sage.
Levine, D. 1981. "Rationality and Freedom: Weber and Beyond." *Sociological Inquiry* 51 (1): 5–25.
Luhmann, N. 1992. *Die Wissenschaft der Gesellschaft*. Frankfurt am Main: Suhrkamp.
Merton, R. K. 1945. "Sociological Theory." *American Journal of Sociology* 50 (6): 462–73.
Merton, R. K. 1948. "Discussion of Talcott Parsons 'The position of social theory'" *American Sociological Review* 13 (2): 164–8.
Merton, R. K. 1968. *Social Theory and Social Structure*. New York: Free Press.
Mills, C. W. 2000. *The Sociological Imagination*. Oxford: Oxford University Press.
Mommsen, W. 1974. *Age of Bureaucracy, Perspectives on the Political Sociology of Max Weber*. Oxford: Basil Blackwell.
Müller-Doohm, S. 2014. *Jürgen Habermas: eine Biographie*. Berlin: Suhrkamp.
Oakeshott, M. 1933. *Experience and Its Modes*. Cambridge: Cambridge University Press.
Popper, K. R. 1957. *The Poverty of Historicism*. London: Routledge & Kegan Paul.
Putnam, H. 1983. *Realism and Reason*. Cambridge: Cambridge University Press.
Reed, I., and J. Alexander. 2009. "Social Science as Reading and Performance: A Cultural-Sociological Understanding of Epistemology." *European Journal of Social Theory* 12 (1): 21–41.
Rorty, R. 1979. *Philosophy and the Mirror of Nature*. Oxford: Blackwell.
Savage, M. 2009. "Contemporary Sociology and the Challenge of Descriptive Assemblage." *European Journal of Social Theory* 12 (1): 155–74.

Savage, M. 2013. "The 'Social Life of Methods': A Critical Introduction." *Theory, Culture & Society* 30 (4): 3–21.
Schutz, A. 1972. *The Phenomenology of the Social World*. London: Heinemann Educational.
Skinner, Q. 1985. *The Return of Grand Theory in the Human Sciences*. Cambridge: Cambridge University Press.
Swedberg, R. 2014. *The Art of Social Theory*. Princeton, NJ: Princeton University Press.
Tavory, I., and S. Timmermans. 2014. *Abductive Analysis: Theorizing Qualitative Research*. Chicago, IL: University of Chicago Press.
Turner, J. 2002. "Sociological Theory Today." In *Handbook of Sociological Theory*, ed. J. Turner. 1–17. New York: Kluwer Academic.
Turner, S. 2004. "The Maturity of Social Theory." In *The Dialogical Turn: New Roles for Sociology in the Postdisciplinary Age*, ed. C. Carnic and H. Joas, 141–70. Oxford: Rowman & Littlefield.
Wagner, P. 1994. *A Sociology of Modernity: Liberty and Discipline*. London: Routledge.
Wagner, P. 2001. *A History and Theory of the Social Sciences: Not All That Is Solid Melts into Air*. London: Sage.
Winch, P. 1958. *The Idea of a Social Science and Its Relation to Philosophy*. London: Routledge & Kegan Paul.

Commentary: Social Theory and Underdetermination: A Philosophical History and Reconstruction

Stephen Turner

Mikael Carleheden has presented a concise historical introduction to postwar social or sociological theory. In what follows, I will try to retell this story from a philosophical point of view, or, to put it differently, to supply a philosophical backbone—a kind of rational reconstruction from the point of view of philosophical considerations. The course of events follows a particular path: the attempt to supplant the pluralism of prewar sociology, based on a model of "science" borrowed from physical theory, which failed to achieve its aims, leading to a return to pluralism. The philosophical error behind Parsons and Merton was central to this progression. They failed to recognize that pluralism was grounded in two features of the subject matter: the underdetermination of theory by data, which meant that "data" could not decide between the existing alternatives, and the fact that social concepts, including those of social "science," lost their applicability in new circumstances and required new concepts.

1 The Project of Behavioral Science

We can begin at more or less the same point, the pivotal postwar event in theory: the 1947 public confrontation at the then American Sociological Society meetings between Talcott Parsons and Robert Merton that produced the term "middle-range theory" (Parsons 1948; includes the Merton "Discussion," 1948: 164–8), and opposed it to what later became known, following C. Wright Mills polemic against it, as Grand Theory (1959: 25ff.). Their message was consistent with the big generational shift of students in the postwar period, and the rise of the idea of "the behavioral sciences." What the students believed in this period was that they were the generation that was going to make sociology a genuine science. For the younger generation, the message of Parsons and Merton was simple: science requires a single answer to its questions. This was an explicit rejection of the prewar situation in sociological theory, which was pluralistic and was taught by understanding the ideas of past thinkers. They also had a unitary conception of science, so they wanted this answer to be consistent with the rest of the "behavioral sciences," a term "virtually created" by Merton's protégé Bernard Berelson (Sills 1981: 305), which understood the various social science fields to have common ground in social psychology. Parsons went farthest in this direction: he created a new Department of Social Relations at Harvard that brought in much of psychology and cultural anthropology, and influenced political science and area studies.

There is a difference between what one might call the philosophical background to these efforts—their role as professional ideology—and their philosophical aspects. The case of Parsons's "philosophical" sources is clear. He adopted L. J. Henderson's key idea, that every science to be a science required a conceptual scheme, and that the history of science consisted in long periods operating under a particular conceptual scheme. Parsons took from this the idea that for sociology to be a science it too required a conceptual scheme, and moreover a univocal and exclusive one.

Henderson had another idea, which Parsons also absorbed. Henderson was fascinated with the problem of teleology, and rejected vitalism, but nevertheless sought to explain the phenomenon of stable equilibrating systems. Henderson found a model for dealing with the topic theoretically in the writings of the Yale physicist J. Willard Gibbs, who described such a system in a set of differential equations. Parsons was himself promising to replicate this feat in sociology, by providing a theory that was "the logical equivalent of simultaneous equations in a fully developed system of analytical theory" ([1945] 1954: 218). The idea provided Parsons with a model of what he thought was the only conceptual scheme appropriate for sociology: the idea of society as an equilibrating system and of functional explanations as the substitute for actual equations.

But why did Parsons think this approach was uniquely valid? Why did he think that he had surpassed the pluralism of prewar sociology and that as a consequence sociology stood on the verge of what he liked to call a "breakthrough"? He thought that two considerations made his conceptual scheme *the* "theory" above the others: his claim of the essential role of the normative in solving what he called the "Hobbesian problem" of order, and the systematic nature of his "theory." Why did he think his particular construction of these issues, his "conceptual scheme," was any better than the ones it replaced? This question requires a digression.

Parsons's various "theories," of action, of the social system, and of its various components, were very far removed from empirical constraints, and also very far removed from the form of "deductive" theory. The content of the theory was the AGIL framework, which provided a picture of the equilibrating society in terms of four major functions: Adaptation, which corresponded more or less to economics; Goal attainment, which meant mostly politics; Integration, which concerned sociology; and Latency or pattern maintenance, which was his term for culture. The "pattern variables" distinguished alternative solutions to these functional problems: they could be solved universalistically or particularistically, for example.

In reality it was a form of commentary on past theory. The "variables" were essentially taxonomic, built up from the analysis and refinement of previous taxonomic schemes, such as Tönnies's categories of *Gemeinschaft* and *Gesellschaft* (Community and Society), and reflected the distinction between modern and premodern social modes. Taxonomy of this kind has its uses, and in any case this reflected a long tradition that extended long before and long after Tönnies. Distinctions between folk and urban society; military and industrial organization; status and contract; feudalism and bourgeois society; traditional, charismatic, and rational-legal forms of authority; and so on were a staple of sociological thinking. The sheer diversity of these distinctions, each of which was useful in its own way and for their authors' own purposes, reflected the complexity of the social reality they were attempting to address, and underlined, in a practical way, the fact of underdetermination.

Weber had been a pluralist rather than an essentialist: he presented his own taxonomies not as distillations of essences but as pragmatically useful aids to understanding which had no grounding beyond this utility. Parsons's intent was different: to supersede the others and provide a final framework—or at least a conceptual scheme that would last for a long time. But it didn't: not only were many of the older distinctions still informative in ways that Parsons's were not—such as Henry Sumner Maine's term "status" and Weber's "charisma"—new terms and concepts were invented to capture new phenomenon—such as Zygmunt Baumann's notion of liquid modernity.

So what went wrong? Parsons got into difficulties over the problem of the logical form of the theory. His "system" was clearly not a "deductive" theory, nor was it "empirical" in the normal sense of being testable. His philosophical critics wondered if he was saying anything meaningful at all (Black 1961). And this was not his problem alone. The standard model of deductive theory promoted by Logical Positivism, which was being consolidated and promulgated to social science audiences contemporaneously with the development of Parsons's and Merton's views, was an ideal imported from physics that social science theories were unable to meet.

But beyond the problem of logical form was a bigger issue: underdetermination—the underdetermination of theory by data. In its most radical form the idea is that any theory, with sufficient manipulation of its premises, can be made consistent with any sort of data. In its more mundane form, it is a matter of there always being more than one theory consistent with the data. In this form the problem can be solved, temporarily: one simply finds new data that is consistent with one theory but not the other. This is only a temporary solution, however, because another alternative theory can be found that will be consistent with the new data, or the defeated theories can be reformulated to fit with the new data. There is, however, another "solution": to decide between the competing theories and their associated conceptual schemes on non-empirical grounds, such as by reference to theoretical desiderata such as simplicity.

How did Parsonsianism fit into this issue? Because it was a pure conceptual scheme, albeit with empirical illustrations, it made no predictions. Instead, it enabled one to provide an analysis of social institutions and phenomena in terms of their equilibrating effects. This was the Henderson model, with the difference that Henderson's equilibrating mechanisms could be studied experimentally. The case for Parsons's theory had to be a non-empirical one. So to overcome pluralism and the fact of underdetermination, the fact, in this case, that social phenomena could be, and were, described in terms of other conceptual schemes, he needed to appeal to theoretical desiderata. Simplicity was not an option. His scheme was more complex than his rivals, and that indeed was its attraction: it purported to systematically and rigorously encompass the whole theoretical domain of society. The result, however, was essentially circular: one needed to accept Parsons's own ideas of what a theory was, what systematicity was, and what the essential nature of society is, together with his ontology of the equilibrating society, in order to regard his conceptual scheme as uniquely superior.

Merton's middle-range theory strategy was designed to avoid the problem of underdetermination, but proceeded in a different way ([1949] 1968). It, or rather the Columbia model of theory construction that developed and crystallized in the 1950s, incorporated elements of the statistical practice that was the bread and butter of practicing empirical sociologists. The practices, and the expanding body of research, created a problem. There were plenty of findings—for example, as collected in Berelson and Steiner's inventory of behavioral science results (1964). And there were many more results as statistical methods borrowed from psychology shifted to becoming more permissive than before: 2 ′ 2 tables analyzed by Chi-Square and treated as significant against a null hypothesis became the norm, though there were many refinements. The problem for "theory" was what to do with this mass of results to make them theoretically significant. This was the problem that middle-range theory and the Columbia model of theory construction was intended to solve. Merton's idea was that theory at the level of the "middle range" would avoid the pluralism or underdetermination at the level of general theories of society, and implicitly avoid the chaos of low-level empirical findings without significance.

The Columbia model was propounded in two major edited texts, *The Language of Social Research* (Lazarsfeld and Rosenberg 1955) and *Continuities in the Language of Social Research* (Lazarsfeld, Pasanella, and Rosenberg 1972), but it was best articulated by Hans Zetterberg, who had come to Columbia in the 1950s, in his *On Theory and Verification* ([1954] 1965), which reproduced as its motto Merton's dismissal of the pluralism of the past:

> We may have many concepts but few confirmed theories; many points of view, but few theorems; many "approaches" but few arrivals. Perhaps a shift in emphasis would be all to the good. (Merton quoted in Zetterberg ([1954] 1965: v)

It also took another form: the "grounded theory" of Glaser and Strauss (1967).[1]

The announced goal of middle-range theory was to produce small-scale, topically limited, deductive theories which were consistent with empirical statistical findings. The strategy was to take a particular empirical result that was intelligible as an explanation, but framed in lower level or particularistic descriptive terms, and raise it to a more general level by restating the findings in more general terms, and testing the new "generalization." The motivating idea was that a relationship that could be generalized in this way was more real or more explanatory than statistical relations that could not.

The fatal logical flaw in this approach was this: statistical relations of the relevant kind could not be stated in a form that allowed for deductive relations. The standard form of the results—the rejection of a null hypothesis or a correlation—did not allow for deduction, or even, in most cases, inferences about transitively related correlations (Costner and Leik 1964). Deduction required real generalizations in universal form: all x are y, or some variant of this. There were no such generalizations to be had. Moreover, even by relaxing the notion of deduction it was impossible to construct many—if any—successful "theories" of this sort, though there were many attempts (Coser 1956; Randall Collins 1975). As a matter of logic, the idea of relaxing the notion of deduction made no sense: the whole point of deduction is that the validity of the logical argument from premise to conclusion is guaranteed by the logical form of the premises. This is exactly what treating statistical relations as though they were generalizations precluded.

A second flaw followed from the first: restricting theorizing to the middle range while relaxing the demand for deduction and treating correlation as empirical support for generalization merely recreated the original problem of underdetermination that the approach was designed to solve. For every middle-range topic, there developed multiple, conflicting "approaches" each of which could point to a few correlations in its favor. In the end, Merton, influenced by Kuhn, implicitly acknowledged the failure of his strategy by reconstructing his own contribution to sociology as having elaborated a "structural" rather than merely "structural functional" approach. But he acknowledged that this was one approach among others, precisely the outcome he had originally rejected (Merton 1975).

2 The Next Stage

As Carleheden observes, what happened next was a turn to interpretation and Grand Theory, a shift from the United States to Europe, a return to the classics, and a new interest in the normative significance of theories. Philosophically, the turn coincided with, and was partially motivated by, the philosophical critique of standard logical positivism, the influence of Kuhn, and the emergence, from the mid-1970s, of "post-modernism." The problem of underdetermination was radicalized into a kind of epistemic relativism: when the standards deriving from the "science" model of theorizing were challenged, it became evident that there were many possible standards, many possible metatheoretical approaches, and that these standards were partially realized by "theories" that were already available. It became accepted that, as a major textbook put it, sociology was a multi-paradigm science.

One of the implied features of the science model had been a certain view of the relation of measurement to ordinary language. As Lazarsfeld put it, dismissing ethnomethodology, the survey researcher already knew the subtleties of interpretation that resulted from the fact that agents couched their self-interpretations in their own explanatory language. For Lazarsfeld, this meant that one could just construct measures, for example, of attitudes, in survey research and treat the quantitative results as scientific variables, and forget the interpretive origins and therefore interpretive limitations of the measures.

The result of the critique of survey research mounted by ethnomethodologists and others, which problematized this assumption, was to make interpretation itself the starting point for social theory. The empirical content of sociology, and even mundane fact (Pollner 1987), was now seen to be socially constructed, that is to say the product of routines that concealed its constructed character, but which were open to investigation. This level of interpretation was thus more basic than "fact" itself. It appeared now, in retrospect, that the previous form of sociological theory associated with Parsons and Merton had simply glossed over their covert dependence on interpretation, and misappropriated the language of "observation" from science just as they had misappropriated the language of "theory."

So what was "theory" after this? Or before it? Carleheden quotes a passage from a paper of mine in which I comment that the basic business of social theory was commentary. This perhaps requires some clarification. The choice of the term "social theory" was intentional: something like "theoretical sociology," for example, the use of rational choice theory to explain statistical results, might be thought to be something other than commentary. But as the interpretivists showed, there was no escaping the dependence of "sociological" categories on the language of the agents—on their concepts of what they were doing, on their concepts of the larger world, including the social world, and so on, and even more fundamentally on our capacity to understand people as people. There were many possible ways to approach this core fact: ethnomethodology, with its emphasis on the routine local construction of mundane reality was only one.

This dependence meant that social theory would necessarily be a form of commentary. The issue is simple, and familiar from Weber: the concepts in which we couch our explanations of others and articulate our understanding of others are the concepts of our own self-understanding as well. These are historically variable, cultural, and not "scientific." Moreover, we not only stumble onto the fact that others understand the world differently, explaining this difference and making sense of their understanding is perhaps even the core of sociology.

When we arrive at a new setting in which our old concepts and understandings no longer apply—when we encounter people with, for example, a different vocabulary of motives—this is primary-level sociology, and requires analogical forms of understanding. The cases that occupy higher level social theory and motivate Grand Theory are cases where second-order concepts—concepts that participants employ when articulating their own understandings of the social world, concepts such as "the state" or "authority"—cease to apply in the way they formerly did. Some failures to apply were failures of prediction, when, for example, "class" no longer predicted lifestyle. Other failures were more diffuse, such as the inability of the traditional model of citizenship given by T. H. Marshall (1950) to provide an account of our obligations to refugees. Much of social theory is concerned with such changes, and in commentary on them, though the discussion often takes the form of third-order commentary—commentary on the social and political theories that explain and analyze the second-order concepts. Neil Gross has written an appreciation of Zygmunt Bauman, which he entitles "How to do Social Science without Data" (2017). This is not quite right—the data for Bauman is data available to everyone, not data from sociology. It is true that some things that pass for sociological theory purport to be "general," and aspire to a larger historical and cultural applicability. But they, as Weber mordantly observed a century ago, are subject to the same difficulties—things change and they fail to apply: the light of the great cultural concerns moves on (Weber [1904] 2012: 134–5).

Writings like Bauman's are subject to a further difficulty, which perhaps explains the turn away from such theorizing in conventional and especially American sociology departments. The theories, or commentaries, at this third-order level not only differ—they differ with respect to questions of what an explanation is, what a good theory is, and what a theory is supposed to do—be emancipatory, for example. This introduces an additional level of underdetermination to the underdetermination that exists between theories or explanations in each order of analysis: and in the end the deciding considerations, though they are constrained by the lower-level facts of interpretation, are far removed from them. Each has its own body of metatheoretical, fourth-order, justification and explanation. And in addition to the issue of the problematic character of these justifications, each runs into the same problem: they arrive at some point at which they cease to apply.

When there seemed—however illusory this was—to be a more or less clear idea of what a theory was, namely as Parsons put it, "a body of logically interdependent generalized concepts of empirical reference," it was possible to have a discussion of strategy. The problem was to decide whether a univocal result could be best achieved by striving, as Parsons did, for "a system [which] tends, ideally, to become 'logically closed', to reach such a state of logical integration that every logical implication of any combination of propositions in the system is explicitly stated in some other proposition in the same system" (Parsons [1945] 1954: 212–13), or to something more modest, such as theories of the middle range. When both of these strategies failed, it is no surprise that the basic ideas of what a theory was, and the meaning of "empirical," came under scrutiny. That this scrutiny led to conflicting ideas and thus reproduced the pluralism that Merton and Parsons sought to overcome is equally unsurprising. Underdetermination afflicts the relations between each of these levels; but at the same time it liberates theory from the ill-fitting straitjackets of the Parsons-Merton era, and the positivists' standard conception of scientific theory.

The task of understanding, however, does not disappear as a result of this pluralism: we still find ourselves in social worlds in which the old concepts and old expectations no longer apply: this is the source of the continuing demand for theoretical commentary, both on the concepts of the agents and on the concepts created at the second-order level to account for them—and inevitably on the third-order level of metatheory in which the adequacy of these second-order concepts are debated.

Note

1 Robert K. Merton to Barney Glaser, July 2, 1998. Columbia University Rare Book and Manuscript Library, Robert K. Merton Collection, Box 31, Folder 8.

References

Berelson, B., and G. A. Steiner. 1964. *Human Behavior: An Inventory of Scientific Findings*. New York: Harcourt, Brace & World.

Black, Max. 1961. "Some Questions about Parsons' Theories." In *The Social Theories of Talcott Parsons: A Critical Examination*, ed. Max Black, 268–8. Carbondale, IL: Southern Illinois University Press.
Collins, Randall. 1975. *Conflict Sociology: Toward an Explanatory Science*. New York: Academic Press.
Coser, Lewis. 1956. *The Functions of Social Conflict*. Glencoe, IL: The Free Press.
Costner, H. L., and R. K. Leik. 1964. "Deductions from Axiomatic Theory." *American Sociological Review* 29: 819–35.
Glaser, B. G., and A. Strauss. 1967. *The Discovery of Grounded Theory: Strategies for Qualitative Research*. Chicago, IL: Aldine Publishing Company.
Gross, Neil. 2017. "How to Do Social Science without Data." *The New York Times* Sunday Review, February 9. https://www.nytimes.com/2017/02/09/opinion/sunday/how-to-do-social-science-without-data.html?_r=0.
Lazarsfeld, Paul F., and Morris Rosenberg, eds. 1955. *The Language of Social Research: A Reader in the Methodology of Social Research*. Glencoe, IL: The Free Press.
Lazersfeld, Paul F., Ann K. Pasanella, and Morris Rosenberg, eds. 1972 *Continuities in the Language of Social Research*, New York: The Free Press.
Marshall, T. H. 1950. *Citizenship and Social Class: and Other Essays*. Cambridge: Cambridge University Press.
Merton, Robert. 1948. "Discussion of 'The Position of Sociological Theory'." *American Sociological Review* 13 (2): 164–8.
Merton, Robert. ([1949] 1968). "On Sociological Theories of the Middle Range." In *Social Theory and Social Structure*, enlgd. edn., 39–72. New York: The Free Press.
Merton, Robert. 1975. "Structural Analysis in Sociology." In *Approaches to the Study of Social Structure*, ed. Peter M. Blau, 21–52. New York: The Free Press.
Mills, C. Wright. 1959. *The Sociological* Imagination. Oxford: Oxford University Press.
Parsons, Talcott. [1945] 1954. "The Problems and Prospects of Sociological Theory." In *Essays in Sociological Theory*, rev. edn., 212–37. New York: The Free Press.
Parsons, Talcott. 1948. "The Position of Sociological Theory." *American Sociological Review* 13 (2): 156–71.
Pollner, Melvin. 1987. *Mundane Reason: Reality in Everyday and Sociological Discourse*. Cambridge: Cambridge University Press.
Sills, David. 1981. "Bernard Berelson: Behavioral Scientist." *Journal of the History of the Behavioral Sciences* 17 (3): 305–11.
Weber, M. [1904] 2012. " 'Objectivity' in Social Science and Social Policy." In *Max Weber: Collected Methodological Writings*, ed. H. H. Bruun and S. Whimster, trans. Hans Henrik Bruun, 100–38. London: Routledge.
Zetterberg, Hans. [1954] 1965. *On Theory and Verification in Sociology*, rev. edn. Totowa, NJ: The Bedminster Press. Available at http://zetterberg.org/Books/b64_Ver/b1964.htm (accessed February 2, 2017).

11

Assembling Economic Actors: Time-varying Rates and the New Electricity Consumer

Daniel Breslau

11.1 Introduction

One of the most important insights of sociological studies of markets is the artificiality of the rational economic actor described by economic theory, allowing its emergence and constitution to be posed as research questions. Karl Polanyi argued that the economic actor only operates under specific institutional conditions. Cross-cultural studies associated with substantivist economic anthropology further strengthened Polanyi's insight, with a vast variation in organization of economic action, showing that *homo economicus* is culturally specific, not an anthropological universal (Dalton 1977). Modes of economic action are paired with institutional settings, so that the rational maximizing agent is a creature of economic systems based on exchange. Similarly, a system based on redistribution, in which economic distribution is united with a political hierarchy, economic action is regulated by deference and tribute to a local leader and palace. Economies based on reciprocity, restricted or generalized gift exchange, require yet another form of economic action (Sahlins 1972). Comparative and historical studies in this tradition, along with anthropological studies of noncapitalist societies, are full of accounts of the emergence and operation of a range of institutional orders by which societies reproduce themselves materially.

More recently, the "performativity" literature, developed within the field of science and technology studies and extended to questions that had pertained to economic sociology and institutionalist economics, has augmented our understanding of the formation of economic actors and their institutions in two main directions. The first has been to recast the relationship of economics to its object. Rather than representing actual economic actors and institutions from a detached epistemic perch, economics participates in the constitution of markets and market actors, actively establishing the conditions for rational calculation. Even when elaborating theories, conducting measurements, evaluating models, and describing markets, the work of economists shapes economic reality (Muniesa 2014). The economy itself could not have become the massive object that conditions our lives without the theoretical work of economists, and the system of measurement that allows the theoretical economy to be experienced

(Breslau 2003; Mitchell 1998, 2002). Within the aggregated economy, economics "formats," to use Michel Callon's term, the agents and their activities (Callon 1998). A formula developed with the scientific goal of predicting the behavior of derivatives' prices under idealized market conditions is then used by participants in the market for interpreting prices and making buy and sell decisions. As a result, the observed behavior of prices in the market more closely approximate the theoretical predictions (D. MacKenzie and Millo 2003; D. A. MacKenzie 2006). While MacKenzie has drawn attention to the self-referential case, in which economic actors confirm predictions of economic theory because those very theories inform their actions, this is a special case of the broader category of performativity advanced by Callon. The latter includes the more ubiquitous use of economics to configure the rules and devices that comprise the conditions of the possibility of economic calculation, and that constrain market actors to confirm the predictions of economic theory. In another setting, involving trade in electrical power, market designers and regulators incorporate measurement of the deviation of a market from the behavior of an abstract ideal into the market as a regulative mechanism (Breslau 2013). If economic institutions are composed of legitimate rules, expectations, and practices that organize economic life (Hodgson 2006; Maucourant and Plociniczak 2013), then economics participates in, and is constitutive of those institutions. Performativity thus allows the methods of the social studies of science, or science studies, to be extended to the study of the social construction of the economy.

A second important set of insights to be derived from the performativity studies, at least for my purposes, is due to its rejection of a subjectivist definition of economic actors, and its replacement with an actor that is distributed across an "assemblage" of devices. Information technologies, which frame markets as arenas of action, also provide the means for calculating and choosing among alternative actions (Callon, Millo, and Muniesa 2007; Knorr-Cetina and Preda, 2007; Preda 2009). The agency of economic actors, including electricity consumers, is the result of an *agencement*, a joining of persons and devices to produce a characteristic agency that none of the elements are individually capable of on their own. The characteristics of the economic agent, that are described in demand curves and measurements of elasticity, are the result of *agencements*, not traces of an internal cognititive process. Even in markets where buyers and sellers are physically present in a designated space, the architecture of that space, in the way that it groups participants and affords lines of visibility and obstructs vision, formats the trades and the agency of those trading (Zaloom 2006; Garcia-Parpet 2007). The performativity literature has borrowed fruitfully from laboratory studies of science that locate the cognitive capacities of scientists in the arrangements of their laboratories and instruments, rather than between their ears (Latour and Woolgar 1979). Similarly, the capacity of economic agents to order choices and perform a rational calculation is not an inherent mental ability. It is a property of the assembled devices. This set of insights is particularly helpful in the study of a case like the one discussed below, of a project to reconfigure an economic agent through the use of a range of devices. Those projects are preoccupied with *agencements*, designing, and arranging devices and frameworks of knowledge to provoke or maximize a desired response.[1]

While providing an instance of the assemblage of an economic actor, this chapter modifies the performativity analysis in two important ways. First, it nests the process of performativity, the construction of economic actors, in a political understanding of economic institutions. It is therefore concerned with reconciling performativity with the political-economic understanding of market formation found in works of economic sociology (Bourdieu 2005; Fligstein 1990, 1996). Actors with a stake in the organization of markets engage in a political struggle to define rules of exchange, property rights, and even the cultural understandings of economic activity, Fligstein's "conceptions of control." Markets are political outcomes. The political interpretation of economic institutions extends to the formation of price systems of the kind considered in this chapter, extending Max Weber's discussion of the political determination of prices. In a study that is closely related to the case examined in this chapter, Yakubovich, Granovetter, and McGuire studied the emergence of a dominant system for pricing electricity in the United States in the early twentieth century (2005). The system that won out, the so-called Wright price system that is the predecessor to the systems that are undergoing reform today, was not superior in terms of a detached standard of efficiency. Rather, it was the set of interests that formed a network in favor of the Wright system, their economic power, and institutional position, which conditioned the outcome. The Wright system, though it yielded profit margins that were inferior to those of its competitor, the Barstow system, favored rapid growth in revenues and market share for the owners of central generating stations. These interests, as well as those of the manufacturers of the metering technology needed for the Wright system, succeeded in instituting a price system that sacrificed efficiency but facilitated their control over the market. The Wright system also provided the central generators a competitive advantage in relation to small generators. Their interests were henceforth embedded in an institution for setting prices, through the kind of mimetic processes described by institutional sociologists (DiMaggio and Powell 1983).

The second modification of the performativity perspective has to do with the rationality of that agent. As we will see in the case discussed here, the degree to which that agent represents the idealized rational maximizer of economic theory is itself subject to contention. There are indeed many possibilities for calculating actors. In this case, the outcome is a boundedly rational actor, whose scope for rational calculation is structured by a range of practices and technologies, including prices, information technologies, home automation, consumer education, and an extensive program of pilot studies and experimentation. Through these devices, the actor's deliberate calculations are confined to a small number of occasions, and can be ignored the rest of the time. And those calculations are applied to a highly constrained set of prices and choices. But the politics of performativity determine just how rare those moments of calculation are, and how narrowly circumscribed are the set of prices that must be taken into account. The specific configuration of the economic actor, like the price system it confronts, is the outcome of the politics of performativity.

Because it produces variable results, contingent on market politics, the analysis of performativity is incomplete unless it places the process of performing economics within that political context. My aim in this chapter is therefore to reconcile the political analysis of market formation with the performative analysis of the constitution of economic agents. I will show how the work of performing a new economic actor, the price-responsive electricity consumer, is driven by the regulatory politics of ratemaking. The intensive and adversarial bargaining over rates is the immediate motivator of the drive for new economies in the power system, and the project of constructing new, price-responsive consumers. Through an analysis of rate cases in which new pricing frameworks were proposed, negotiated, and approved, we find first that the price system adopted is the outcome of a struggle among actors with conflicting interests. Consistent with the sociology of prices, the new price systems are not the predictable result of market efficiency but are compromises reached through a political struggle. Generating companies, electric utilities that resell power to consumers, manufacturers of "smart grid" technologies, several categories of consumers, and their advocates, all press for pricing systems that favor their perceived interests. Second, it is not only the prices but the consumers themselves, the kind of calculations they are able to make, their ability to respond to those prices that are outcomes of this process. The same deliberations that result in price systems also include thorough discussion of the nature of electricity consumers. Participants in the rate-making process debate the behavior of consumers and their ability to respond rationally to price changes. But as a result of the regulatory proceeding, the electricity consumer is reconfigured as a calculating economic agent.

This chapter examines one case of the construction of a new type of actor in the energy economy, the rational price-responsive residential consumer. The innovations that bring this new actor into being are often treated as a matter of rate design, in particular, the introduction of new pricing schemes in which the price for power reflects the large temporal fluctuations in the wholesale price, or, in turn, marginal cost. With reference to the efforts to date in the United States to induce a responsive demand for electricity among residential customers, this paper will show that a pricing system is but one condition and an insufficient one. The rational calculating electricity consumer is the product of a range of technologies, consumer education and marketing, and a network of economic theory, simulation, and experimentation.

Although the new pricing schemes have emphasized industrial, institutional, and commercial consumers of power, I will focus on the residential consumers, who are much smaller and much more numerous. They have been the object of a number of more recent initiatives to introduce economic calculation, and the issue is perhaps more controversial with respect to them. It is in the case of residential consumers that market calculation is induced in a sphere that is expected to be, to some extent, outside the bounds of calculation, protected from the risks of price changes and spared the need to monitor prices on an ongoing basis. Here, the construction of the rational consumer is a matter of what Michel Callon calls disentanglement, the extraction of agents from and ongoing set of relationships, allowing them to perform impersonal market calculations. In this case, it is a matter of disentangling the use of electricity from the social routines in which domestic power consumption is embedded. With the freedom to adjust one's demand in response to price fluctuations comes new risks for consumers. The use of electricity is embedded in a totality of social practices, particularly those having to do with the diurnal routines of work and leisure, workplace and home, and the weather cycles over the seasons and over the hours of each day. The historic system of electricity pricing allows our use of power to be conveniently articulated with these cycles, with the rhythms of social life. Electricity consumers bear no risk by using power when it is socially necessary. Time-varying pricing, or what is more commonly termed dynamic pricing, asks consumers to adopt a different, reflexive, relationship to the timing of their electricity use, and therefore to the diurnal cycle of their activities. It brings the marketplace into the domestic sphere in a new way.

11.2 Economics and Dynamic Pricing for Electricity

Since the adoption of electricity rate systems along the lines of the Wright system in the early twentieth century, consumers have used electricity in blissful ignorance of market conditions and irresponsible indifference to the state of the power system. The demand for electrical power in the short term, at least from residential consumers, is thoroughly embedded in social life, entangled with the quotidian. The institutionalized daily cycle and conventional standards of work, sleep, self-care, and childcare massively determine electricity consumption, in conjunction with annual cycles of weather, determine how much power must be used to realize conventional expectations for indoor climate (Cooper 1998; Cowan 1983; Nye 1990). Limitations on consumption are mostly a function of the differential capacities of households to consume due to being equipped with different sets of technologies and possessing different quantities of space to heat or cool. Actual economizing behavior had at best a marginal impact on demand, and, more importantly for our discussion, was entirely unrelated to fluctuating aggregate demand for power and the consequent fluctuation in the cost of its production.

For nearly the first three quarters of the twentieth century, this type of consumer, socially embedded on one hand and oblivious to market conditions on the other, was not regarded as problematic outside of the writings of a small number of economists. In fact, it comprised an integral element of the socio-technical system of electric power in advanced countries (Hughes 1983). It fit the overall logic of a system that included central power stations, a high-voltage AC transmission grid, massive and ever-growing baseload generating stations, and diverse loads based not just on residential use, but industrial, commercial, and agricultural as well. The lopsided shape of residential "load" (as demand is known in the power industry), with small early-morning peaks, large late-afternoon peaks, and a much lower baseline during nighttime hours, was offset by steady and massive industrial consumption around the clock. The socio-technical system was also held in place by continual improvement in efficiency of generators and continuous reduction in costs of electricity throughout the first six decades of the century. As long as the market was growing, the grid was expanding, efficiency was increasing, and costs were declining, utility managers had no reason to question the insulation of consumers from real-time market conditions (Rose 1995). They had every reason to see it as a salutary feature of the system. Any price structure that passed peak generating costs on to consumers could slow the growth of demand that the profitability of the entire industry presupposed.

Beginning in the middle of the 1960s, this regime of growth in the electric power system in the United States reached an impasse (Hirsh 1999: 55–70; Lifset 2014). Improvements in efficiency had arrived at a plateau as generators approached the theoretical limit of 48 percent thermal efficiency. In an effort to wring more power out of each dollar invested, utilities attempted to construct ever-larger power plants, also finding a declining return as the larger designs raised new problems of maintenance and reliability. The "last hope" of a system founded on continual growth, nuclear power, likewise failed to sustain the trajectory of cost economies of previous decades as the cost of building nuclear plants rose multiplicatively. The environmental movement, which had its first successes in legislating protections by the late 1960s, introduced further limitations on the continuous growth model. Finally, the crisis in supplies of oil and natural gas brought higher costs of generating electricity, since generation using these two fuels had proliferated in the previous decade owing to the abundance and low prices of oil and gas.

With the electric energy crisis, elements of the socio-technical system that were taken for granted or simply tolerated during the years of growth and efficiency improvement became visible and problematic. One of these was the underutilization of installed generating capacity, as signified by the measure known as load factor. This indicator is equal to the average load during a given period divided by the peak load. It can be thought of as a measure of the "peakiness" of load, and subtracted from 1, provides an indication of the quantity of generating capacity that is idle most of the time. For a combination of reasons, the actual production is ordinarily far below the industry's capacity. Electric power cannot be stored economically on a large scale, with the consequence that production must equal consumption, or load, at every moment. In order to avoid interruptions in supply, the system must be able to produce power equal to the highest expected load. To the extent that load is "peaky," that the maximum load is only achieved briefly at a level that is much higher than the average load, much of the generating capacity in the system will be idle most of the time.

The characteristic load pattern in the industry, the customary load factor, the ratio between peak and average load, is the footprint of the socially embedded, irresponsible consumer. This large-scale feature of the system is not simply a consequence of the technologies used. It is the aggregate effect of countless consumers that activate an appliance or turn on a light without considering the state of the grid at that moment. But both that consumer and the macro-effects on the system were tolerated or even desirable during the sixty years of rapid growth. The rapid acceptance of electric power, first in cities, and eventually throughout the country, was aided by a pricing system that allowed it to be integrated into daily life without concern for the daily cycle of load, and indeed, the scarcity of power. And while utilities were continually realizing greater economies of scale, coupled with higher voltages and longer transmission distances, they tolerated a certain level of peakiness in load. And they tolerated the many megawatts of idle peaking generators that were a permanent feature of the system. The regulatory system cooperated as well, allowing utilities to recover the investment costs of generators scaled to meet peaks in demand that occurred for only a few hours on summer afternoons.

With the crisis in the power system in the late 1960s, and early 1970s, observers, reformers, and industry participants identified the low load factors, paired with the cost-insensitive consumer, as a structural problem. As thermal efficiencies had reached their limits, and with nuclear power failing to deliver the expected cost reductions, engineers and economists turned their attention to systemic inefficiency. They understood the assault on those inefficiencies as a way to moderate the rising costs of electric power, and to moderate the conflict between producers and consumers of power, played out in regulatory battles. If only the consumer of electricity could be refashioned to respond to prices, consumers themselves would be the beneficiary. If consumers were to adjust their electricity consumption in response to prices, higher during times of peak demand, the overall load profile would be less peaky, and the need for huge reserve margins of generating capacity would be reduced. By obviating the need for a large reserve margin of generating capacity, consumers would ultimately save themselves the expense of recovering the costs of the excess generators that would be rendered unnecessary.

So it is not entirely coincidental that reform writings on power systems at this time, primarily from economists and engineers, singled out the irresponsible power consumer. Alfred Kahn, in his monumental book on the economics of regulation, repeatedly noted the inefficiencies of sheltering the consumer from cost variation. Kahn's work was avowedly performative, targeting the ways that pricing of existing public utilities deviated from the efficient markets of economic theory (Kahn 1970). The economist William Vickrey expressed the theoretical motivations for real-time pricing in a 1971 paper in the Rand Journal of Economics, following the promotion of marginal-cost pricing advocated by his teacher, Harold Hotelling (Hotelling 1938; Vickrey 1971). Vickrey likened resistance to his proposal to an earlier opposition to the use of interest rates. The resistance is based on quaint moral inhibitions from which the pricing of electricity should eventually be freed: "It took several centuries to free the use of interest in economic calculations and pricing from the opprobrium attached to 'usury'; hopefully it will not take this long for responsive pricing of utility services to achieve respectability" (Vickrey 1971: 346). A few years later, a group of power system engineers at MIT, under the leadership of Fred Schweppe, likewise identified the load-following principle of power systems as the key obstacle, not only to efficiency but to social peace (Schweppe et al. 1988). Load was extrinsically determined, that is, it responded to social practices, and the power system was expected to follow it wherever it led. The Schweppe group proposed instead a system of "homeostatic control" in which consumers would be responsive regulators of the system, using prices as the signal to which they would respond (Schweppe et al. 1980).

While irresponsible consumers introduce enormous inefficiencies, their failure to adjust demand to market conditions produces a further cascade of pathologies in wholesale electricity markets. An unresponsive or "inelastic" demand, as described by economic models, increases opportunities for sellers of electricity to exercise market power. Producers of power who control the supply, either individually or in a small-enough number to allow collusion, can manipulate prices by withholding supply or through "economic withholding," simply bidding their power into the wholesale market at artificially inflated prices. The incentives to engage in such practices are much higher when retail consumers do not adjust their consumption in response, since the consumers will continue to consume, unaware of the artificially inflated wholesale prices. Additional market rules are usually devised to manage the risk of market power, by invoking "mitigation" measures, usually price controls that force bids to the producer's marginal cost of production in cases where they would otherwise have the ability to manipulate prices.

Low load factors and high peaks also induce a demand for capping the wholesale price of electricity, typically at $2000–$3000 per megawatt hour, varying across regional transmission systems. This amounts to about twenty to thirty times the average price. Some economists argue that, due to the unresponsive demand, the supply and demand curves in electricity markets theoretically do not intersect at all, meaning there is no price at which supply and demand meet (Stoft 2002). Regardless of how high the price goes, demand will still outstrip supply, forcing the price even higher, or else leading to a disastrous "loss of load," in other words, blackouts. But the remedy, namely price caps, introduces distortions of its own. Presumably, these devices would be unnecessary if demand was reduced in response to spiking prices, eliminating the need for price caps and possibly for mitigation of market power as well. Those parts of the industry, such as the wholesale market for electric power, which have been framed in market terms, are compromised by those sectors that continue to defy market logic. The retail pricing of electricity thereby become a "reverse salient," frustrating efforts to achieve legitimate, uncontested and naturally occurring market prices in the industry as a whole (Hughes 1987). The responsive consumer, at least in abstract economic models, brings truth and discipline to the market, in the form of prices that truthfully signal the short-term marginal value of electricity. Thus many economists involved in the issue of electricity pricing are advocates for the introduction of real-time prices that reflect the changing marginal cost of generating power. Opposition to such pricing is attributed to irrational adherence to myths that can be easily dispelled (Faruqui and Palmer 2011).

As Vickery pointed out, a system of time-variable pricing presupposes a time-variable technique for communicating prices to those making consumption decisions. The provision of the good or service had to be overlaid with an information technology that would serve as a price tag. For this reason, Vickery thought that the telephone network, what we would refer to now as telecommunications, was ripe for time-variable pricing, since the price of a call could be communicated through the same network that delivers the call itself. The communication system ideally had to operate on the same timescale as the price variability, so that a system of monthly billing for electricity could not support prices that varied by the hour. So it was not until proposals to pair the electric grid with a communications network, in the set of technologies now known collectively as the "smart grid," that reforms in the retail pricing of electricity were implemented on a significant scale in the United States. Smart meters, connected to data centers, with price data that could be relayed both to the consumer and to a billing system on a real-time basis, provided the technical conditions for time-varying prices. And the push for smart grid, or the consumer-facing side of smart grid called Advanced Metering Infrastructure (AMI) was conjoined with intensified calls for time-varying prices.

But the implementation of dynamic pricing had, and continues to have, a political dimension, and is subject to concerted resistance. The resistance is organized by agents and groups that are continuous with those that represent consumer interests in the regulatory politics of electricity prices, namely consumer advocacy organizations and publicly appointed consumer advocates, or their equivalent, that exist in nearly every state. Resistance is staged on behalf of residential customers, with an emphasis on those who, for various reasons, are vulnerable to changing and occasionally high prices for this essential commodity. The time-variable prices, whose advocates describe as liberating or empowering, can be coercive for those with strict budgetary constraints, and whose demand for electricity is based on necessity. Low-income, or elderly consumers have a pressing need for electricity that cannot be shifted to another time of day, paradigmatically to power air conditioners on summer afternoons. Those tend to be the times of highest demand, and therefore the times when a dynamic price is most likely to peak. The dynamic price may induce consumers to endanger themselves by turning off their air conditioner, because the price is ten times the usual rate. A more diffuse sort of opposition is directed at the performativity of price reforms, pointing to the inherent disadvantage of some consumers to adopt the required calculating agency. Mark Toney, who directs a grassroots consumers' organization, articulates a counter-performativity position:

> So part of the issue is, so, the first challenge to that in order for people to identify their economic self-interests when it comes to varying electricity prices, people need, there are a number of preconditions that have to exist. So one is people have to have basic arithmetic skills. OK, they've got to have math skills. They probably need to have pretty decent English language skills. They most likely need to have decent computer skills and equipment. And then they've got to have the time, and that's just even to be able to calculate their self interest. So, you know, our first thing, is within the large percentage of the population that simply won't get there.

The most influential organized group opposing the reforms is the AARP, the American Association for Retired People, whose representatives frequently testify at the regulatory hearings in which dynamic pricing is considered. And offices of consumer advocates, which were established in many state governments as an outcome of the consumer movement, have also insisted on protections from price risks.

11.3 Explaining the Emergent Price Regime

The pricing system adopted in US states, and the configuration of the calculating electricity consumer, is an outcome of a struggle over the new rates. Contrary to Vickery's expectations, real-time, marginal-cost-based pricing has not caught on for residential consumers in the United States. Despite the continuing implementation of "smart meters" and the "advanced metering infrastructure" that are the technological prerequisites for real-time pricing, fewer than one in ten thousand households are exposed to pricing that changes with the marginal cost of generating power. Nowhere in the United States is real-time pricing mandatory for residential consumers, and even where real-time pricing has been offered as an option, fewer than one percent of households have opted in. Nor is there an active proposal anywhere in the United States to extend such a pricing system.

Instead of the pricing that is deemed efficient in the economic literature, jurisdictions that are moving to some kind of time-sensitive pricing are increasingly adopting a small set of compromise arrangements. These are systems that limit the degree to which consumers must break with their existing routines, either to track prices, or to change their pattern of electricity use, requiring a narrow range of choices and only during relatively rare events. One example is a system known as "critical peak pricing." Customers under this system receive a slightly discounted, but fixed rate for most of the year. But during a limited number of summer afternoons in which demand, based mostly on weather forecasts, is expected to exceed a predetermined threshold, a "peak event" is called. The event is called a day in advance and customers are notified then. For those under the pricing system, the electricity rate will rise to a price that is as much as nine or ten times the off-peak rate. An example of this type of pricing is provided in Figure 11.1 which compares critical peak pricing on a day with a critical peak event, to a standard fixed rate. In many of the recent rate cases, critical peak pricing has been adopted only as an opt-in rate that customers must deliberately select, rather than as the default rate.

Also common in recent rate cases is a default rate system known as critical peak rebate pricing. Under this pricing regime, consumers can simply maintain their customary usage of electricity and will still pay the same regulated fixed rate that they paid previously, subject to future adjustments through the regulatory process. But when peak events are called, again due to weather-based expectations of peak demand

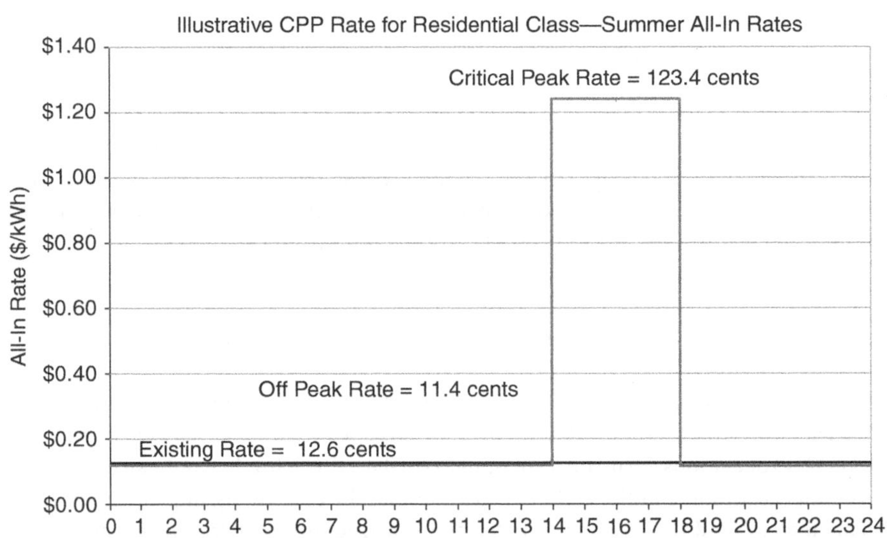

Figure 11.1 Critical peak pricing.

Source: Faruqui (2012: 6).

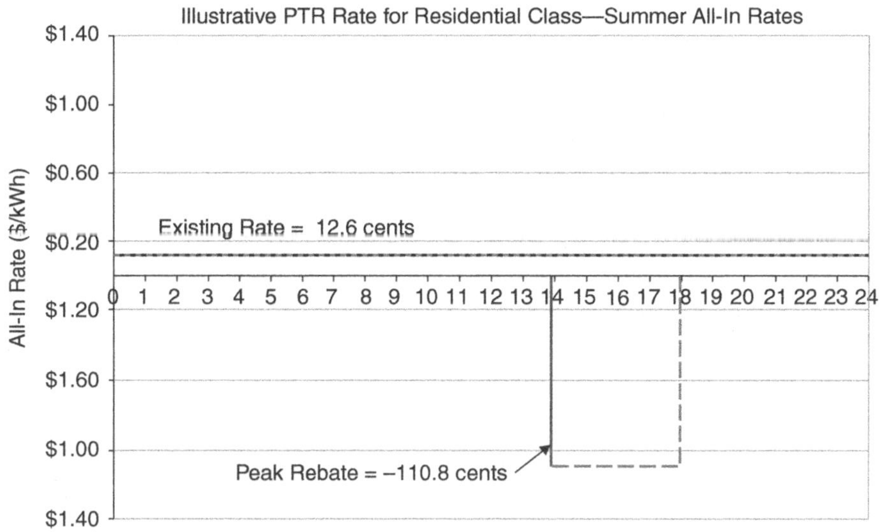

Figure 11.2 Critical peak rebate pricing.

Source: Faruqui (2012: 8).

on hot summer afternoons, they have a chance to earn rebates by reducing their consumption below a baseline determined by their historic consumption. Figure 11.2 shows how this regime works, with the red broken line representing the rebate paid for each kilowatt hour of load reduction during the hours of 2–6 p.m. for peak events. Rebate pricing is even more remote than critical peak pricing from the efficient ideal of economic theory. It delivers a price signal far weaker than the actual wholesale price of power, while providing a hedge in the form of the default price that allows consumers to ignore price signals with minimal consequences. The next section will describe the interests and stakes in the politics of electricity pricing reform, thus providing the context and motivation for the performativity of a new economic actor.

11.4 AMI Rate Cases

In order to account for the pricing reforms actually adopted in the United States, I will turn to the regulatory context in which these systems are proposed, debated and adopted. Typically, this takes place in the course of a business case before a state public utilities commission (or what may be called a public service commission or utilities regulatory commission, depending on the state). Utilities initiate these business cases, but not primarily because they are seeking to implement a new rate structure. Rather, they are requesting an increase in revenue to recover the costs of the metering system and the technological infrastructure that goes with it, usually called AMI, for "advanced metering infrastructure."[2]It is advantageous for utilities to gain approval for these large investments in capital, which can run into the billions of dollars, depending on the size of the utility's customer base. Approval of the investment means an increase in the value of their "rate base," meaning the amount of investment that they are allowed to recover, including a reasonable profit margin, through the rates they charge customers. Regulated utilities, including those involved in the Maryland case discussed here, no longer own power plants after being required to sell them off as the industry was "deregulated." One of their only avenues for increasing profits is through new capital investments, which, if approved by the regulator, can be recovered, amortized, in the rates charged to customers. By retiring the existing metering infrastructure, which is completely or nearly completely depreciated, and replacing it with a large investment that will earn a guaranteed return, they can greatly increase their profits beyond the small margin they collect on resale of electrical power itself. The adversaries of the utilities, such as the consumer advocate quoted here, are acutely aware of this motivation:

> The system of utility regulation continues at least in the distribution network, to reward investment. The profits continue to be estimated or allowed on the basis of return on plant investment. So the more investment the bigger the profits. (Interview with the author)

The analysis here will be based on the proceedings of a specific rate case, one initiated with a 2009 filing by the Potomac Electric Power Company, or PEPCO, before the Maryland Public Utility Commission, requesting that its planned AMI system be included in its rate base.

In order to win approval for cost recovery of the new investments, utilities must show that the new metering system will deliver cost savings to consumers, to offset the new costs of the AMI system itself. While in theory the desire for greater efficiency motivates the installation of the new metering technology, for the utilities the logic is reversed: their interest in winning approval for the new infrastructure investment drives their efforts to demonstrate improvements in efficiency and reduced consumer costs. Investments in AMI can save money by supporting the new, responsive electricity consumer. If sufficiently responsive, the consumer will reduce demand during times of peak demand, when prices are highest. This will immediately lead to lower costs to consumers simply as a result of their lower consumption. But, more profoundly and permanently, it will reduce the need to maintain expensive "peaking" generating capacity that is rarely used. Consumers will be spared the costs of maintaining decrepit peaking plants that can then be retired, and the cost of new plants, which will no longer be needed. Figure 11.3 shows a typical analysis presented in a business case, projecting the future consumer savings that will result from the new pricing system, made possible by AMI.

Consumer advocates, who are the main adversaries to the utilities in these business cases, sometimes as paid consultants to consumer-interest groups like the AARP, and sometimes with state agencies charged with consumer protection, dispute the claimed benefits to consumers. Thus in the Maryland case, the utility filed a request for expedited approval of the new infrastructure as a regulatory asset. But consumer advocates, from state agencies and NGOs such as the AARP, requested a full evidentiary hearing. As the Maryland People's Counsel put it,

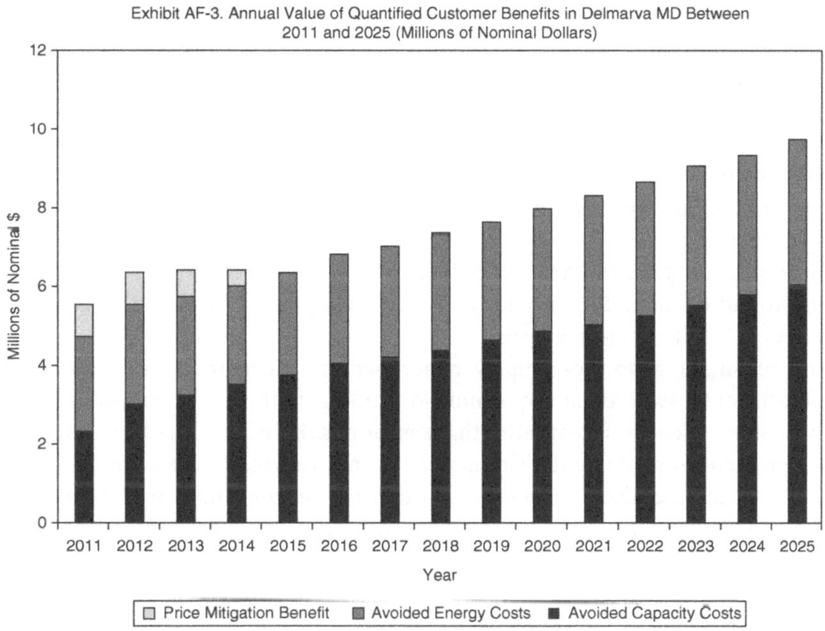

Figure 11.3 Presentation of consumer savings with AMI, presented in a business case.
Source: Farqui (2009: 168).

> An evidentiary proceeding is necessary to create a record to assure consumers that they are not being asked to pay for expensive, bright, shiny new toys that may not provide them any significant benefits or may become quickly obsolete in the long run.

Some part of the objection to the rate cases for AMI takes the form of skepticism regarding the utility's cost-benefit calculation. To be allowed to bill customers for the cost of the new meters and data infrastructure, the utility needs to show that the benefits of AMI will outweigh these costs. But measurement of the potential benefits requires a number of analyses, each susceptible to deconstructive criticism. These include the use of internal accounting data to estimate the operational savings of smart meters, such as labor costs saved through remote control and reading of meters.

But larger benefits have to do with estimating the effects of the new pricing systems on consumer behavior. Here, the benefit derives largely from projected reductions in peak load, consumption during times of highest demand. Reduced peak load reduces the amount of generating capacity that must be available, a quantity equal to the projected peak load plus a roughly 15 percent "reserve margin." The additional revenues needed to keeping this capacity online, beyond the higher wholesale prices of electricity during peak hours, is provided to generation owners through a capacity market, operated by the Regional Transmission Organization, PJM. Reductions in the amount paid through the PJM capacity markets are passed on to consumers as savings.

The utility also has the option of selling the projected consumer reduction in demand as a demand response resource on the capacity market, and thus "monetizing" the reduction in peak demand.

Each of these benefits depends on a set of analyses, simulations, and projections, each of which is fallible. In particular, the numbers rest on estimates of how the customers will be distributed across the various price schemes—the default of Critical Rebate Pricing, and the optional Critical Peak Pricing and Standard Offer Service pricing. Then projected reductions in demand are derived from estimates of price elasticities. In addition, the AMI Proposal in Maryland added a 1.5 percent reduction in year-round demand due only to the economizing effects of providing customers with feedback on their electricity use.

The consumer advocates employ a number of strategies to problematize the relationship of the experimental or simulation findings to the actual savings consumers might achieve. "Benefit to cost ratios that appear positive may in fact be negative [sic] if rosy predictions made by the Companies are not realized in actuality" (Brockway 2009: 11). If the predicted benefits do not materialize, consumers will still be liable for the AMI investments. As with any experiment, the extension of the experimental setup, under laboratory conditions, to the "field" is subject to contention, and cannot be resolved in principle (Collins 1992: 79–111). This provides an opportunity for the other side to suggest possible divergences between the conditions under which data for the estimates were gathered and the conditions to which the estimates are being applied. In this case, the pilot study from which demand elasticities were estimated, was carried out by Baltimore Gas and Electric in 2008. Both the $150 inducement payment and the significant dropout rate in the pilot study are cited by the consumer advocate as reason to suspect selection bias in the pilot.

With regard to the new rate systems themselves, the central objection of the consumer advocates has to do with the impact of those rates on "vulnerable" consumers: the poor, disabled, and elderly. These rates are marketed as ways to save money, and they are designed so that many customers will have lower energy costs over time under these rates even without changing their consumption profile. If they ordinarily do not use much more power during times of peak load, then their overall electric bill is likely to decline, as the lower price during roughly 95 percent of the time more than offsets the higher prices they would pay during the few annual hours of critical peak prices. But the consumer advocacy concern is that the much higher prices during critical peak events will compel the most vulnerable customers, many of whom live on very low incomes, to reduce their consumption when they need electricity most. The risk of high prices induces other, more serious, risks. Consumer advocates recast the freedom, control, and empowerment that the moral philosophy of dynamic pricing promises consumers, as coercive. They elaborate a freedom as freedom from risk, and control as the ability to adjust consumption to needs, especially for relief during heat waves, without taking price into account.

> I am concerned that some customers will select the CPP option under the impression that they will save money on their electricity bill and then take potentially unsafe and inappropriate actions to reduce electricity usage during

> hot summer afternoons. It is more likely than not that this group includes seniors who depend on electricity to run cooling systems that prevent the onset of hyperthermia or to operate medically required devices. Such customers may make inappropriate choices and fear the impact of the higher summer electricity bills if they do not take actions to avoid the very high prices during these peak summer periods. This Hobson's Choice will be even more dramatic when Maryland suffers a more normal summer season when very high temperatures and high humidity make the operation of air conditioning systems, whether central or window units, and fans even more important to the health and safety of elderly customers and those with special needs. (Alexander 2009: 21)

The testimony from the AARP consultant then cites the particular risks to elderly people during heat waves, and the vital importance of keeping air conditioning systems running during times of dangerously high heat. The testimony then mentions studies that have linked the high cost of cooling during summer heat among the elderly contributes to food insecurity. Food insecurity varies by season in relation to variation in home cooling costs.

Throughout the proceedings over AMI, consumer advocates have argued that reductions in peak usage can be obtained without AMI and the dynamic pricing that it makes possible. Here there are a number of arguments for a range of alternative means to reduce electricity consumption, and peak consumption in particular. One possibility is in-home display devices that do not require a networked metering system. Usage figures can be read directly from appliances or existing meters to allow consumers to monitor their use, without real-time price information.

11.5 Price System as Political Accommodation

Based on this cursory analysis of the AMI business case, the reasons that the regulatory process seems to gravitate toward pricing schemes like critical peak pricing and, especially, critical peak rebate pricing, are clearer. The utilities that develop and propose the rate system, are not interested in maximizing economic efficiency of pricing. They have little to gain as monopoly providers, since reduced consumption will yield lower revenues. Their interest, as described above, is primarily to win approval for investments in new infrastructure, and approval of rates that will allow them to recover the costs of those investments plus a profit margin. The greater the price differential between peak and off-peak pricing, and the greater the volatility of prices faced by consumers, the greater difficulty they will have in gaining approval for the new rates, and therefore for the entire AMI investment as well. Likewise, the more that the new regime requires consumers to extract themselves from their routines in order to keep up with prices, and to change the timing of their electricity use, the more consumer interests, and their allies, will oppose the proposed AMI investments. The utilities are constrained by the regulatory process, therefore, to seek a rate system, enabled by the technologies they want to install, that minimizes volatility and the differential between peak and off-peak pricing. In other words, it minimizes the coercive effects of the price signal, and the extent to which it requires consumers to be "disentangled" from their established routines of energy use. As has been the case throughout the history of their industry (something about load following and opposition to time-varying prices—the coalition between utilities and customers on this basis).

But because the utilities are also obliged to demonstrate a cost saving to consumers, they must also induce maximum consumer response to the limited price incentives that they are able to institute. And it is for this reason that reforms in rate structures are accompanied by a set of efforts to reconfigure the residential consumer as a calculating agent. The next section describes some of the technologies and practices that constitute the new electricity consumer.

11.6 Assembling the Consumer

Prices alone are insufficient to transform the passive electricity consumer into a responsive economic actor. In the Maryland business case discussed above, the utility also recognized that the time-varying rate they were proposing required a new kind of consumer that would be attuned to that rate. While consumers were only expected to respond to the critical peak events, which can be called a maximum of twelve times each year, this alone provided no assurance that they would actually pay attention to the peak periods and adjust their consumption patterns accordingly. While critical peak pricing and especially critical peak rebate pricing are designed to spare the customer the necessity of tracking electricity rates in real time, they cannot be counted on to break from their routines to discover when critical peak events would take place. The utility therefore proposed a set of technological supports for this purpose.

The principle behind the technological supports is to spare the consumer the cost and effort of seeking out and tracking price information. The utilities proposed a saturation of the consumer's attention with price information. The construction of the price system, with at most two or three discrete price levels simplifies the number of different price signals, the language of prices. The comparably severe temporal structure of peak pricing or peak rebates, likewise rigidly circumscribes the timing of price signals. The cost of generation changes constantly, but the consumer can expect changes only on twelve summer afternoons. The signaling is highly simplified. But when a price change takes place, it is brought into the consumer's sensorium through the technologies that already constitute their experience. Thus, the proposal states that customers would receive automated SMS text messages, e-mail messages, and phone calls beginning one day before the event, with follow-up notifications as the event's afternoon hours approached, and again as it was in progress. Additional devices have been proposed, and are provided in the Maryland demonstration, to bring the price signal into the physical living space. Thus a randomly selected subset of pilot participants will receive an "energy orb" to install in their home. The orb, illustrated in Figure 11.4, is a spherical lamp that can be set on a table in the consumer's living space. Connected wirelessly to the metering network, it glows different colors depending on the status of the electricity rate: blue indicates no event; yellow, that there will be an event the next day; pulsing yellow if an event will take place later the same day; red if a critical peak event is in

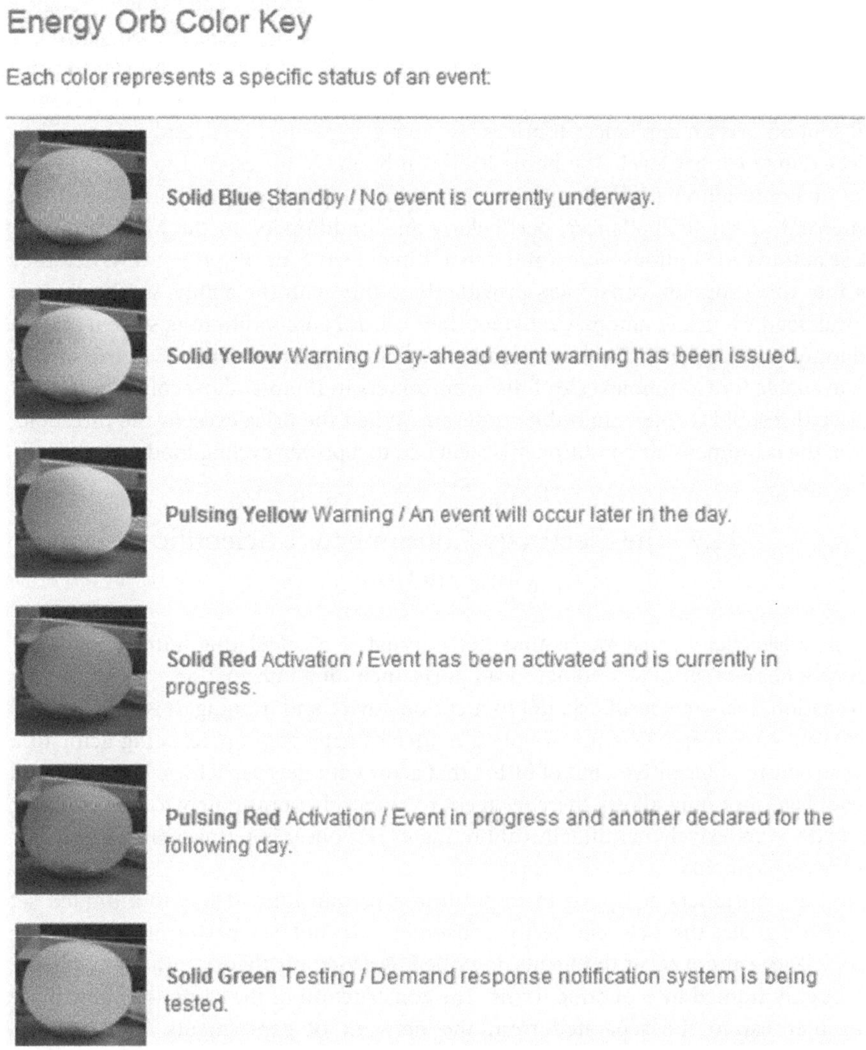

Figure 11.4 The energy orb.

Source: American Public Power Association (2011: 216).

progress. Thus the consumers will passively see all the price information, out of the corner of their eye, as they go about their daily routines. All of these devices are intended to relieve electricity consumers of the burden of seeking out prices, and are financed by the expected cost savings created by price-responsive electricity users.

While these devices serve as sensory prostheses, incorporating price information into consumers' daily experience, other technological supports allow them to delegate their agency, their electricity-using decisions, to nonhuman agents. Through various kinds of home automation, connected wirelessly to the metering infrastructure, consumers can more reliably and rationally respond to price signals without conscious attention to prices. They can fail to respond to price information, and can fail to engage in rational market calculation, but their failings can be bypassed if their agency is delegated to an algorithm. Control of their appliances can be linked directly to price information, so that a computer algorithm, which the consumer can set in advance, will shut off certain appliances if prices rise above a specified level, and resume when prices return to that level. The home itself can be made to respond to prices, in the case of home automation. But the most common forms of automation are those connected to single appliances, particularly air conditioners. In the Maryland case, home automation options were limited to a "direct load control" program. When they opt into this program, consumers provide the utility with the ability, strictly limited to peak load events, to automatically put their central air conditioning system into an economy mode, where it cycles on and off every fifteen minutes. Other systems, such as one available for Commonwealth Edison customers in Illinois, allow consumers to set a price threshold through an online program. When the price exceeds the threshold, again, the customer's air conditioner is switched to a power-cycling mode.

11.7 The Electricity Consumer as a Scientific Construction

The new electricity consumer is thus not internal to a calculating human actor, but incorporates a range of technological supports, including information systems, home-automation, real-time feedback, not to mention advice and training. It is a distributed agent, an assemblage. It is not simply a matter of exposing a preexisting actor to a new structure of incentives, but of fitting that actor with new capacities. This "material assemblage" not only allows the new agent to respond appropriately to price signals, but to do so reflexively, continually calibrating its responses in terms of their results for electricity payments.

But as consumers equipped to respond in a certain limited way to a limited set of price signals, the new electricity consumers are not yet performing economic theory. They cannot act as the agents described by economic theory without first being thoroughly framed in economic terms. The construction of the responsive electricity consumer cannot be separated from the network of experiments, pilot studies, demonstration projects, simulations, and economic theory, through which traces of its actions are aggregated, mobilized, and finally sedimented into the electricity market itself. As is often overlooked by the performativity studies, the intensive research scrutiny, and the embedding of local programs in systems of measurement and analysis, is itself an important way that a new economic institution is constituted. If we think of an economic institution as a system or rules, expectations, and their technological and material supports, the program of experimentation aims to build such an institution, guided by measurements of its effects. The behavior of the new agent is not a confirmation of the theory but the result of the use of the theory to reconfigure the electricity consumer in the ways described above.

Economic theory, measurement, experimentation, and simulation contribute to the construction of the new electricity consumer through two related activities. The first is the abstraction of consumers' actions from their local settings in the form of standardized measurements. The second is the assimilation of those measurements to an economic system, in which they can be expressed as a function of prices.

Performance is not restricted to overtly prescriptive statements and practices, decrees, rulemaking, and legislation. Acts of description, which assimilate the object described to a framework of reason and action, are not strictly descriptive. They would be superfluous if they were simply transmitting an already established state of things. The simulation or pilot study is, in Fabian Muniesa's terms, a provocation, designed to elicit a response (Muniesa 2014: 23–4). As an experiment provokes action on the part of the experimental apparatus, economic studies provoke the electricity consumer, and elicit its emergence as an actor. The price elasticity of demand is just such a provoked action, elicited when consumption and price data are used to evaluate an economic model. The consumer is not constituted simply in the myriad consumption decisions made when customers flip a switch.

The studies frame the introduction of dynamic pricing systems in terms of economic theory. The consumers are treated as interchangeable economic agents and their response to prices is measured as a parameter of an econometric model of the relationship of their electricity demand to price changes. Their response is made visible as the response of a calculating agent by estimating the price elasticity of the demand for electricity. This type of evaluation was used to gauge the effects of California's experimental Advanced Demand Response System (ADRS) in 2004 and 2005 (Faruqui and Sergici 2010). The system featured a dynamic price that was simpler than an hourly real-time rate design. The tariff featured three price levels: a default base rate, a higher price during peak periods defined as 2 p.m. to 7 p.m. on weekdays, and a "super peak" price three times the peak during the smaller number of events when demand spiked along with wholesale prices.

In the PEPCO case described above, a network of pilot research was central to making the case for the cost savings that the new rate structures would realize. The utility's filing included a study conducted by the same firm that ran the California demonstration described above. The analysis proceeded by using data from a 2008 pilot study in the Baltimore area to estimate the demand elasticities of customers. It then entered those elasticities into a simulation model of the entire electric system called the Pricing Impact Simulation Model or PRISM. The model is based on the pilot of pricing systems in California, and so is recalibrated, by changing values for the load shape, pricing system, weather, and central air conditioning saturation. Estimates are arrived at for what proportion of the customers will be under which price system. Then the reduction in demand is estimated. Reduction in peak demand per customer is estimated and then multiplied by the estimated number of customers under each rate design to get the aggregate reduction in peak demand. Then the amount of power purchase foregone and reduction in needed generating capacity are estimated and form the main part of the savings used to justify recovering the costs of the metering system from customers.

The experimental program leads to an iterative stabilization of the price-responsive consumer, by stabilizing and replicating a standard set of program features. But it also serves a second purpose, not of measuring effects, but of demonstrating effects. The economic/scientific framing of the new pricing regimes has transformed the terms in which the pricing of electricity to consumers is to be formulated and justified. Historically, rates were specified to realize a legal standard, codified in regulatory law, of "just and reasonable." That is, the satisfaction of a legal requirement that rates not include unfair markups, and that they allow consumers access to power whenever they want it without exposure to price spikes. The new pricing schemes introduce the measured effects on aggregate consumer behavior as the criterion for their justification. The criterion of satisfying legal requirements is replaced by the criterion of "what works." Combined with the set of technological supports and consumer information described above, the evaluation studies inquire simultaneously about the behavior of consumers and the effects of interventions. They do not simply ask how price-responsive electricity consumers are, but how responsive they can be made to be.

11.8 Conclusion

The economic actor that emerges from the struggles over electricity pricing is not the actor of neoclassical microeconomic theory. It is not an actor that seeks to maximize utility at every moment. Instead, it is a boundedly rational actor, only partially disentangled from its ongoing social involvements, choosing among a highly constrained set of choices, and then only during extraordinary periods. The capacity of this agent to exercise bounded rationality is not a mental capacity. As Herbert Simon developed the concept of bounded rationality, it was not necessarily innate, but was the result of learned routines, although still properties of the individual subject. (Simon 1957). But when rationality is bounded and enabled through an *agencement*, a set of devices for constructing decision spaces, making decisions, and analyzing those decisions, our attention is transferred from the formation of the subject to the configuration of those devices. The boundedness of the electricity consumer's rationality is structured through a political process in which opposed actors struggle over the extent to which the electricity consumer will be disentangled from its ongoing social commitments, and the extent to which it will be subject to changing electricity prices. Not just the price signal, but the technological supports that structure the new actor's perception and agency are outcomes of the politics of performativity. And the framework of measurement, simulation, and experimentation allows the agent to act as the agent described by economic theory, so it can have a measurable degree of responsiveness and an economic effect.

This paper is based upon work supported by the National Science Foundation under Grant No. 0620900. Any opinions, findings, and conclusions or recommendations expressed in this material are those of the author and do not necessarily reflect the views of the National Science Foundation.

Notes

1 Those familiar with the philosophy of mind will recognize an affinity of this approach with the "extended mind" thesis and related arguments for extended or distributed

cognition (Clark and Chalmers 1998; Rowlands 1999). While a full defense of that position is beyond the aims of this article, my account does nonetheless lend some reinforcement by showing that the inducement of a mode of economic action involves a transformation of devices, rather than simply offering a new environmental stimulus to the self-contained human organism. Callon, Millo, and Muniesa partially preempt the objections of critics of the extended mind thesis such as Adams and Aizawa (2010):

> But the notion of 'device' can also suggest a bifurcation of agency: the person on one side and the machine on the other, the trader on one side and the trading screen on the other, Bourdieu's *dispositions* on one side and Foucault's *dispositifs* on the other. In our view, this bifurcation needs to be avoided or, at least, handled with caution. Instead of considering distributed agency as the encounter of (already 'agenced') persons and devices, it is always possible to consider it as the very result of these compound *agencements* (and this applies to economic action in particular). (Callon, Millo, and Muniesa 2007: 2)

Indeed, one could argue that the positing of a self-contained mind (or agent) distinct from devices is an artificial move that serves only to preserve a prior commitment to that theory of mind (or agency).

2 AMI includes not just the meters, but also the data network for transmitting data, new billing systems, software, and data storage centers.

References

Adams, F., and K.Aizawa. 2010. *The Bounds of Cognition*, 1st ed. Malden, MA: Wiley.

Alexander, B. R. 2009. "Direct Testimony on Behalf of AARP," Case No. 9207.

American Public Power Association. 2011. *Energy Services that Work*. Arlington, VA: APPA.

Bourdieu, P. 2005. *The Social Structures of the Economy*. Cambridge: Polity.

Breslau, D. 2003. "Economics Invents the Economy: Mathematics, Statistics, and Models in the Work of Irving Fisher and Wesley Mitchell." *Theory and Society* 32 (3): 379–411.

Breslau, D. 2013. "Designing a Market-like Entity: Economics in the Politics of Market Formation." *Social Studies of Science* 43 (6): 829–51.

Brockway, N. 2009. "Direct Testimony on Behalf of the Maryland Office of People's Counsel," *Case No. 9207*.

Callon, M. 1998. "Introduction: The Embeddedness of Economic Markets in Economics." In *The Laws of the Markets*, ed. M. Callon, 1–57. Oxford: Blackwell.

Callon, M., Y. Millo, and F. Muniesa, 2007. *Market Devices*. Malden, MA : Blackwell.

Clark, A., and D. J. Chalmers. 1998. "The Extended Mind." *Analysis* 58 (1): 7–19.

Collins, H. M. 1992. *Changing Order: Replication and Induction in Scientific Practice*. Chicago, IL: University of Chicago Press.

Cooper, G. 1998. *Air-conditioning America : Eengineers and the Controlled Environment, 1900–1960*. Baltimore, MD: Johns Hopkins University Press.

Cowan, R. S. 1983. *More Work for Mother : The Ironies of Household Technology from the Open Hearth to the Microwave*. New York: Basic Books.

Dalton, G. 1977. *Tribal and Peasant Economies : Readings in Economic Anthropology*. Austin: University of Texas Press.

DiMaggio, P. J., and W. W. Powell. 1983. "The Iron Cage Revisited: Institutional Isomorphism and Collective Rationality in Organizational Fields." *American Sociological Review* 48: 147–60.

Faruqui, A. 2009. "Direct Testimony before Maryland Public Service Commission," Case Number 9207.

Faruqui, A. 2012. *Shaping Our Energy Future through Dynamic Pricing* [PowerPoint Slides]. Available at http://files.brattle.com/files/6598_shaping_our_energy_future_through_dynamic_pricing_faruqui_aug_21_2012.pdf.

Faruqui, A., and J. Palmer. 2011. "Dynamic Pricing and Its Discontents." *Regulation* 34 (3): 16–22.

Faruqui, A., and S. Sergici. 2010. *Household Response to Dynamic Pricing of Electricity: A Survey of the Empirical Evidence*. San Francisco, CA: The Brattle Group.

Fligstein, N. 1990. *The Transformation of Corporate Control*. Cambridge, MA: Harvard.

Fligstein, N. 1996. "Markets as Politics: A Political-Cultural Approach to Market Institutions." *American Sociological Review* 61 (4): 656–73.

Garcia-Parpet, M.-F. 2007. "The Social Construction of a Perfect Market: The Strawberry Auction at Fontaines-en-Sologne." In *Do Economists Make Markets? On the Performativity of Economics*, ed. D. A. MacKenzie, F. Muniesa, and L. Siu, 20–53. Princeton, NJ: Princeton University Press.

Hirsh, R. F. 1999. *Power Loss: The Origins of Deregulation and Restructuring in the American Electric Utility System*. Cambridge, MA: MIT Press.

Hodgson, G. M. 2006. "What Are Institutions?" *Journal of Economic Issues* 40 (1): 1–25.

Hotelling, H. 1938. "The General Welfare in Relation to Problems of Taxation and of Railway and Utility Rates." *Econometrica* 6 (3): 242–69.

Hughes, T. P. 1983. *Networks of Power: Electrification in Western Society*. Baltimore, MD: Johns Hopkins University Press.

Hughes, T. P. 1987. "The Evolution of Large Technological Systems." In *The Social Construction of Technological Systems: New Directions in the Sociology and History of Technology*, ed. W. E. Bijker, T. P. Hughes, and T. Pinch. Cambridge, MA: MIT Press.

Kahn, A. E. 1970. *The Economics of Regulation: Principles and Institutions*. New York: Wiley.

Knorr-Cetina, K., and A. Preda, 2007. "The Temporalization of Financial Markets: From Network to Flow." *Theory, Culture & Society*, 24 (7–8): 116–38.

Latour, B., and S. Woolgar. 1979. *Laboratory Life: The Construction of Scientific Facts*. Beverley Hills, CA: Sage.

Lifset, R. D. 2014. "A New Understanding of the American Energy Crisis of the 1970s." *Historical Social Research/Historische Sozialforschung* 39 (4): 22–42.

MacKenzie, D. A. 2006. *An Engine, Not a Camera: How Financial Models Shape Markets*. Cambridge, MA: MIT Press.

MacKenzie, D., and Millo, Y. 2003. "Constructing a Market, Performing Theory: The Historical Sociology of a Financial Derivatives Exchange." *American Journal of Sociology* 109 (1): 107–45.

Maucourant, J., and S. Plociniczak. 2013. "The Institution, the Economy and the Market: Karl Polanyi's Institutional Thought for Economists." *Review of Political Economy* 25 (3): 512–31.

Mitchell, T. 1998. "Fixing the Economy." *Cultural Studies* 12 (1): 82–101.

Mitchell, T. 2002. *Rule of Experts: Egypt, Techno-politics, Modernity*. Berkeley: University of California Press.

Muniesa, F. 2014. *The Provoked Economy: Economic Reality and the Performative Turn*, 1st ed. London: Routledge.

Nye, D. E. 1990. *Electrifying America: Social Meanings of a Mew Technology, 1880–1940*. Cambridge, MA: MIT Press.

Preda, A. 2009. *Framing Finance: The Boundaries of Markets and Modern Capitalism.* Chicago, IL: University of Chicago Press.

Rose, M. H. 1995. *Cities of Light and Heat: Domesticating Gas and Electricity in Urban America.* University Park: Pennsylvania State University Press.

Rowlands, M. 1999. *The Body in Mind: Understanding Cognitive Processes.* Cambridge: Cambridge University Press.

Sahlins, M. 1972. *Stone-Age Economics.* Chicago, IL: Aldine.

Schweppe, F. C., M. C. Caramanis, R. D. Tabors, and R. E.Bohn. 1988. *Spot Pricing of Electricity.* Boston, MA: Kluwer Academic.

Schweppe, F. C., R. D. Tabors, J. L. Kirtley, H. R. Outhred, F. H. Pickel, and A. J. Cox. 1980. "Homeostatic Utility Control." *Power Apparatus and Systems, IEEE Transactions on, PAS*-99 (3): 1151–63.

Simon, H. A. 1957. *Models of Man: Social and Rational- Mathematical Essays on Rational Human Behavior in a Social Setting,* 1st ed. New York: Wiley.

Stoft, S. 2002. *Power System Economics: Designing Markets for Electricity.* Piscataway, NJ: IEEE Press and Wiley-Interscience.

Vickrey, W. 1971. "Responsive Pricing of Public Utility Services." *The Bell Journal of Economics and Management Science* 2 (1): 337–46.

Yakubovich, V., M. Granovetter, and P. McGuire. 2005. "Electric Charges: The Social Construction of Rate Systems." *Theory & Society* 34 (5/6): 579–612.

Zaloom, C. 2006. *Out of the Pits: Traders and Technology from Chicago to London.* Chicago, IL: University of Chicago Press.

Commentary: Assembling the Economic Actors

Nicolas Brisset

Daniel Breslau studies the installation of a new type of electricity tariffing in the United States.[1] This tariffing system has been put in place to justify a large investment (a new metering system) that will allow a substantial increase in the profits reaped by the electricity utilities. To become integrated with the economic structure this tariffing system needs to be accepted by the society or, at least, not rejected outright. This acceptance rests on a certain world view, according to which this mode of tariffing will be advantageous for the consumer. How can this new tariff system be presented to consumers as benefiting them?

> The utilities that develop and propose the rate system are not interested in maximizing economic efficiency of pricing. They have little to gain as monopoly providers, since reduced consumption will yield lower revenues. Their interest, as described above, is primarily to win approval for investments in new infrastructure, and approval of rates that will allow them to recover the costs of those investments plus a profit margin. The greater the price differential between peak and off-peak pricing, and the greater the volatility of prices faced by consumers, the greater difficulty they will have in gaining approval for the new rates, and therefore for the entire AMI investment as well. (Chapter 11: 28–9)

A consumer with a "reasonable" behavior must get a better deal in the new technical configuration. Two aspects are important here. On the one hand, it is necessary to create the perception of a profit to consumer. This is linked closely to the concept of "rationality." Some experimental and simulation results are involved in order to show that the new game is worth the pain experienced by a "rational" consumer. As a consequence, there needs to be a consensus around the way that potential profits are considered. On the other hand, this perception has to involve the economic agents adopting the expected rational behaviors. This last aspect involves the effective construction of an active consumer based on an incentive system. The consumer must be encouraged to adopt a strategic behavior *vis-à-vis* the electricity pricing system. Here it is important to differentiate between perception of the new game proposed by the electricity supplier, and the way that the game is actually set up. The former is a necessary precondition for the latter. In other words, achieving social acceptance of the benefit is a felicity condition for the technical construction of a new type of economic agent.

The construction of a market is achieved here in part by using concepts and theories from economics. It is common today to refer to the "performativity of economic theories" to underline their influence in the construction of the real world. This idea has attracted much interest since its first theorization by Michel Callon (1998). Much has been written about the performativity of economics. It is one of the most exciting social science concepts to emerge since the late 1990s. Breslau's contribution is interesting insofar as it highlights the strengths of this concept while also trying to overcome its weaknesses. He tries to combine two different visions of the construction of markets: the performativist approach, and what he describes as "political-economic understanding of market formation," illustrated by the works of Bourdieu and Fligstein. This reference to Bourdieu is especially interesting since Callon builds his sociological theory as a kind of counterpoint to Bourdieusian sociology, which sets great store by the structuring of the social world via some important reflections on its "social field." Roughly, while the Bourdieusian perspective focuses on the way the economic theories spread some *representations* that support or call into question the general social representation (a symbolic order) on which power relationships are built, the performativist view is focused on the implication of economic theories into the making of singular socio-technical devices. The most famous example of such a perspective is the seminal work of MacKenzie and Millo (2003) on the way the Black-Scholes-Merton equation shaped the real financial markets since it served as blueprint both for some individual decisions making tools and for the structural organization of the markets.

These perspectives are ontologically radically different. On the one hand (the "political-economic understanding of market formation"), the economy is seen as embedded in a broad social structure that supports some macro-political struggles. On the other hand, the economy is a network made of human beings and technical devices in perpetual reconstruction. As we will see, these different views imply different visions on the capacity of economic theories to shape the social world: the Callonian social world is more plastic than the social world presupposed by the more classical constructivism to which Bourdieu belongs.

Breslau is taking a sort of middle way between performativist and the political-economic understanding of market formation: the performativity of economic theory through the setting of some specific technical devices necessitates the building of a consensus on these devices. This consensus emerges in a structured social world made up of divergent representations that must be understood. Building market structures, for example, a structure that enables price fixing, requires the construction of a socio-technical device, which contains pieces of some economic theories, and adopting a position in the social field that takes account of diverging views and political interests.

Since Breslau is positioning himself in the interstice between two radically different ways of thinking about the construction of markets, his text provides an opportunity to consider the ontological and epistemological characteristics of the theory of performativity proposed by Callon, with respect to the classical constructivist tradition. My purpose is to show how the performativity idea has been first well accepted by the constructivist tradition before being deeply questioned because of its strong ontological statement that led to the rejection of the distinction between theory and objective world.

1. Performativity: An Ontological Perspective

Since it was proposed by Michel Callon in 1998, the idea that economic theories are involved in the social construction of the world has flourished. In my view, one of the major reasons for its success is that at first sight, this assertion seems to fit with a strong tradition in social science which denaturalizes the objects of economic theory: market, capitalism, wage labor, and contracts are not objects of nature, are not potentially contained in all social systems but are the fruit of social, political, scientific constructions, and therefore, are located historically. This idea is at the heart of, for example, the work of Karl Marx. One of the young Marx's main objectives was to denaturalize the understanding of economic objects according to eighteenth- and nineteenth-century English classical economists. Marx writes at length in his *Economic and Philosophic Manuscripts of 1844* about the phenomenal order of the social world, how it is presented as intrinsically in conformity with the Robinsonades of classical theories. In contrast, Marx's objective is to relocate this social order (capitalism, market, etc.) in the long history of development of productive forces. Based on this reasoning, the social world has been built apparently in conformity with classical theories. However, Marx's teleological and essentialist world view remains the subject of debate among Marxist historians (Meiksins Wood 2002). Nevertheless, he opened the way to the notion of a constructivist stance, that is, the idea that the objects of an economy (the markets, the individuals signing contracts, the exchanges, the production, the consumption) are built socially and located historically. This idea has been well received in the social sciences: in economics (Polanyi 1947), in anthropology (Dalton 1977), and in sociology (Bourdieu 2000).

It is a small step to the conclusion that economic science relies on the plasticity of the social world to achieve an active and consequent construction of the real economy. This applies to the sociology of performativity and the writings of Michel Callon (1998). Of course, Marx and Polanyi underlined the role of economists in the journey to capitalism:

> It is therefore self-evident that only the political economy which acknowledged *labour* as its principle (Adam Smith), and which therefore no longer looked upon private property as a mere *condition* external to man—that is this political economy which has to be regarded on the one hand as a product of the real *energy* and the real *movement* of private property—as a product of modern *industry*—and, on the other hand, as a force which has quickened and glorified the energy and development of modern *industry* and made it a power in the realm of *consciousness*. (Marx 1844: 93).

Callon goes further in relation to form and substance. For Marx and Polanyi, the role of the economist is above all, ideological: Marx sees it as supporting economic forces while Polanyi sees it as supporting the process of liberalization of the markets (the process of disembeddedness of economy). While economists may pretend to discover the laws of the society, they in fact promote a particular behavior. As far as Callon is concerned, economic theory can be seen as one of the productive forces of the social world. For example, *homo economicus* is no longer a deformed vision of the reality that accompanies capitalism; rather, it shapes the economic reality (Callon 1998: 22). The theory of performativity belongs to the seminal constructivism tradition by promoting a singular kind of constructivism focused on a particular object: the link between theory and social reality. This is what explains its success. Nevertheless, there has been some strong resistance to this concept in particular due to its accompanying social ontology. The theory of performativity is rooted in, and shares the same ontology as, Actor Network Theory (ANT) (Callon 1986b; Latour 2005). Both ANT and performativity theory adopt a flattened vision of the social world, devoid of micro/macro, actors/institutions, human/nonhuman distinctions. Two ideas are important here. First, the Callonian ontology does not stop at humans but integrates nonhumans and all the technical devices enabling agents' decisions. Economic theories have an impact on social reality, since they become a part of the decision-making process through the calculation devices. In a seminal article, MacKenzie and Millo (2003) show that the Black-Scholes-Merton pricing model transformed the behaviors of traders to greater conformity with financial theory via the provision of calculating *dispositifs* that allowed them to calculate the theoretical prices of options.

The second important characteristic of this ontology is that it reduces the social world to a network linking human and nonhuman agents. Agents are defined by their networks and vice versa. This thesis known as "generalized symmetry," constitutes an important rupture with the Strong Program[2] (Collins and Yearley 1992; Bloor 1999). While the Strong Program insists on the sociocultural contexts in which the scientific facts and the scientific knowledge are built, ANT offers a vision of the world emptied of any macrostructure. There is no nature, society, institutions, nor is there capitalism; there are only some networks of symmetric agents (*actants*) in perpetual reconstruction.

The question of the role granted to collective entities has been well studied in social science. Debates often caricature the ontological positions constituting this debate; it is nevertheless clear that different ontological positions lead to very different results. The thesis of performativity follows directly in the steps of ANT by approaching the social world from the bottom, like the sum of singular acts of successive construction. We finally reach an important opposition regarding two kinds of constructivism we evoked in the introduction of this article. On the one hand, the idea of performativity offers a decentralized and technical constructivism. On the other, a huge amount of works (following Marx, Bourdieu, the Strong program, etc.) understand the construction of social reality by considering the social world as made of macrostructures (institutions, representations, interest struggles) that resist the different attempts to shape the world. This ontological position has important epistemological consequences.

2. From Ontology to Methodology

Any ontological opposition makes sense only if it yields different epistemological results. In fact, questions related to the constructivist stance are focused less on the facts and their construction than on the way that resistance is organized: what forces are opposed to the constructive (performative) processes. For Polanyi, the process of economicization is countered by the re-embeddedness of the economic sphere in the social sphere. Such an analytical framework requires determination of the nature of the social sphere which re-embeds economic practices. The "social" constitutes a set of conditions for the act of construction of the social world. Philosopher of language John Austin (1962) referred to "conditions of felicity" to mean the conditions that need to come together to allow an utterance to produce what the speaker intends to produce. What conditions need to combine to allow a particular form of economic configuration to take shape? By emptying the social world of part of its substance, performative sociology avoids consideration of part of the resistance against the performance of economic theories (Brisset 2016, 2018).

Breslau shows that one does not cause a new type of behavior in an empty and malleable social world. There are struggles among both peculiar interests and also their definition. However, concurrent perceptions do not arise from nowhere, and they need to be understood from a general point of view. In other words, it is necessary to understand the social embeddness of the economy. In Breslau's article, the whole process of market building is embedded in social representations about the rationality, about efficiency, about social welfare, about interest. Such a kind of holistic view of the influence of the economic theories on the social world is a priori rejected by the performativity thesis due to a radical ontological stance. Such a rejection has two closely intertwined epistemological consequences. The first one concerns the definition of a "true" theory. The other one is relative to the reception of these theories by the agents.

Since the constructivist stance as well as performativity theory call into question the naturalistic view of markets, this puts economics in an awkward situation. How can there be a "true" theory about a fluctuating object? The criterion of similarity between words and things disappears since economic theory leads its object to behave in accordance with its own statements. This is another area of debate in relation to the theory of performativity. Although it has come to be accepted that economic speech influences how the world operates, few intellectuals are ready to surrender to the idea that mainstream economic theories intrinsically describe the world badly (Miller 2002). Again, to take a canonical example, did the fact that Black-Scholes-Merton equations have an impact on the behaviors of agents make the financial reality in conformity with financial theories? Did these theories become true in the sense of there being a correspondence between the words and the things (Brisset 2017a)? If these questions would seem legitimate, sociologists of performativity refuse to address them since the performativity thesis rejects the separation between economic theories (their description) and the external world (Muniesa 2014). There is no such thing as an external social world. This represents a strong opposition to the constructivist approach à la Polanyi, à la Bourdieu. For Polanyi, although economic theory has an impact on the social world, the performative force is confronted by a social reality that resists this impact. This leads to an important question: is it possible to understand the participation of economic theory in the construction of the economic world without considering the congruence between the theory and the reality? This touches on the relationship between performativity and self-fulfillment. For Michel Callon (2006), all utterances are performative since every utterance can have an effect, can diffuse itself. From this perspective, the socio-technical diffusion is much more interesting than the question of the truth. However, despite these declarations of intent, the performativist literature is full of allusions to increasing congruence between the theories and reality. MacKenzie (2006: 31) distinguishes two kinds of performativity:

> ***Generic performativity***: "an aspect of economics (a theory, model, concept, procedure, data-set, etc.) is used by participants in economic processes, regulators, etc.";
> ***Effective performativity***: "the practical use of an aspect of economics has an effect on economic processes".

He considers *generic performativity* as not in itself of particular interest, and sees only *effective performativity* as inspiring. He also defines two subclasses of *effective performativity*:

> ***Barnesian performativity***: "practical use of an aspect of economics makes economic processes more like their depiction by economics"
> ***Counterperformativity***: "practical use of an aspect of economics makes economic processes less like their depiction by economics"

It is obvious that McKenzie's "Barnesian performativity" refers to self-fulfilling prophecy. Beyond the question of the growing similarity between a theory and the reality, it is important to understand the reasons why agents adopt and preserve a singular theory. The practical effectiveness of the theory used seems to be a significant component of this comprehension: agents preserve a theory if its use produces expected effects in accordance with some holistic social criteria (Brisset 2017a). This harks back to the question of the interest of social actors in adopting a technical device. This is a key issue in Breslau's article: to perform necessitates the building of a consensus around what we call "interest" and around the expected efficiency of the new device. This consensus emerges in a structured social world made up of divergent representations that must be understood in order to grasp the resistances against performative force of the economic theory.

3. Conclusion

In this short commentary, I tried to show how Breslau's article leads us to discuss ontological and epistemological perspectives upheld by the performativity theory à la Callon. These perspectives have implications on the way of thinking the construction of economic arena. We address these implications by re-situating the performativity theory within the constructivist tradition. I think that performativity à la Callon's is problematic for two reasons. First, it rejects the distinction between theory and objective world while still reverting to the question of the congruence between reality and theory. Second, the ontology on which this approach is built does not permit us to understand a set of conventional and political conditions under which a theory becomes performative. Breslau's approach overcomes the second problem by studying the political construction of the legitimacy of a piece of theory to change the social world.

To conclude, it should be noted that the concept of performativity is the topic of many contemporary works in various research areas (Muniesa 2014; Cochoy, Giraudeau, and McFall 2014; Boldyrev and Svetlova 2016). One cannot today reduce these studies of performativity to Michel Callon's theory, or to any unified theory of performativity. The concept has been defined and applied in multiple ways in different disciplinary fields: it is used within the framework of historical investigation (Pahl and Sparsam 2016), of broad theoretical reflections on the nature of the economy (Herrmann-Pillath 2012), of epistemological work related to the criteria for validating social theories (Herrmann-Pillath 2016; Brisset 2017a), of normative considerations (Roscoe 2016), and of debates relating to the philosophical definition of the concept (Mäki 2013; Brisset 2014, 2017b; Guala 2016).[3] In comparison, Breslau's text delivers a rather classical sociological concept of "performativity."

Notes

1 I deeply thank Michiru Nagatsu and Attilia Ruzzene for inviting me to contribute to this volume, and Judith Favereau for her valuable comments.

2 The Strong Program is one of the most influential forms of the sociology of scientific knowledge, also known as the Edinburgh School. The core idea of the Strong Program is to treat symmetrically the successful and the unsuccessful theories.

3 The concept of performativity comes originally from the philosophy of the language of John Austin. The question of the link between Austin's concept and Callon's concept is a matter of debate (Mäki 2013; Brisset 2014, 2017b; Guala 2016).

References

Austin, J. L. 1962. *How to Do Things with Words*. Cambridge: Harvard University Press.

Barnes, B. 2011. "Relativism as Completion of the Scientific Project." In *The Problem of Relativism in the Sociology of (Scientific) Knowledge*, ed. Richard Schantz and Markus Seidel, 23–39. Frankfurt: Ontos verlag.

Bloor, D. 1999. "Anti-Latour." *Studies in History and Philosophy of Science* 30 (1): 81–112.

Boldyrev, I., and E. Svetlova, eds. 2016. *Enacting Dismal Science: New Perspectives on the Performativity of Economics*. London: Palgrave Macmillan.

Bourdieu, P. 2000. *Les structures sociales de l'économie*. Paris: Seuil.

Brisset, N. 2018. *Economics and Performativity. Exploring Limits, Theories and Cases*. Routledge INEM Advances in Economic Methodology.

Brisset, N. 2016. "Economics Is not Always Performative: Some Limits for Performativity." *Journal of Economic Methodology* 23 (2): 160–84.

Brisset, N. 2017a. "On Performativity: Option Theory and the Resistance of Financial Phenomena." *Journal of the History of Economic Thought* 39 (4): 549–69.

Brisset, N. 2017b. "On The Future of Performativity." *Œconomia* 7 (3): 439–52.

Callon, M. 1986a. "Eléments pour une sociologie de la traduction. La domestication de coquilles Saints-Jacques et des marins-pêcheurs dans la bais de Saint-Brieuc." *L'Année Sociologique* 36: 169–208.

Callon, M. 1986b. "Some Elements of a Sociology of Translation: Domestication of the Scallops and the Fishermen of St Brieuc Bay." In *Power, Action and Belief: A New Sociology of Knowledge?*, ed. John Law, 196–223. London: Routledge.

Callon, M. 1998. "The Embeddedness of Economic Markets in Economics." In *The Laws of the Markets*, ed. M. Callon, 1–57. Oxford: Plon.

Callon, M. 2006. "La performativité de l'économie." *Le Libellio d'AEGIS* 2 (3): 21–8.

Callon, M., A. Barry, and D. Slater. 2002. "Technology, Politics and the Market: An Interview with Michel Callon." *Economy and Society* 31 (2): 285–306.

Cochoy, F., M. Giraudeau, and L. McFall, eds. 2014. *The Limits of Performativity. Politics of the Modern Economy*. New York: Routledge.

Collins, H., and S. Yearley. 1992. "Epistemological Chicken." In *Science as Practice and Culture*, ed. A. Pickering, 301–26. Chicago, IL: Chicago University Press.

Dalton, G. 1977. *Tribal and Peasant Economies: Reading in Economic Anthropology*. Austin: University of Texas Press.

Guala, F. 2016. "Performativity Rationalized." In *Enacting the Dismal Science: New Perspectives on the Performativity of Economics*, ed. I. Boldyrev and E. Svetlova, 29–52. London: Palgrave-MacMillan.

Herrmann-Pillath, C. 2012. "Institutions, Distributed Cognition and Agency: Rule-following as Performative Action." *Journal Economic Methodology* 19 (1): 21–42.

Herrmann-Pillath, C. 2016. "Performative Mechanisms." In *Enacting Dismal Science*, ed. Ivan Boldyrev and Ekaterina Svetlova, 53–86. New York: Palgrave.

Latour, B. 2005. *Reassembling the Social*. Oxford: Oxford University Press.

Latour, B., P. Jensen, T. Venturini, S. Grauwin, and D. Boullier. 2012. "'The Whole Is Always Smaller than Its Parts': A Digital Test of Gabriel Tardes' Monads." *The British Journal of Sociology* 63 (4): 590–615.

MacKenzie, D. 2006. *An Engine, Not a Camera*. Cambridge: MIT Press.

MacKenzie, D., and Y. Millo. 2003. "Constructing a Market, Performing Theory: The Historical Sociology of a Financial Derivatives Exchange." *American Journal of Sociology* 109: 107–45.

Mäki, U. 2013. "Performativity: Saving Austin from MacKenzie." In *EPSA11 Perspectives and Foundational Problems in Philosophy of Science*, ed. Vassilios Karakostas and Dennis Dieks, 443–53. Dordrecht: Springer.

Marx, K. 1844. *Economic and Philosophic Manuscripts of 1844*. New York: Dover Publications.

Meiksins Wood, E. 2002. *The Origin of Capitalism. A Longer View*. London: Verso.

Miller, D. 2002. "Turning Callon the Right Way Up." *Economy and Society* 32 (2): 218–33.

Muniesa, F. 2014. *The Provoked Economy*. New York: Routledge.

Muniesa, F., and M. Callon. 2009. "La preformativité des sciences économiques." In *Traité de sociologie économique*, ed. P. Steiner and F. Vatin, 289–324. Paris: Puf.

Pahl, H., and J. Sparsam. 2016. "The IS-LMization of the General Theory and the Construction of Hydraulic governability in Postwar Keynesian Macroeconomics." In *Enacting the Dismal Science: New Perspectives on the Performativity of Economics*, ed. I. Boldyrev and E. Svetlova, 151–81. London: Palgrave-MacMillan.

Polanyi, K. 1947. "On Belief in Economic Determinism." *The Sociological Review* 39 (2): 96–112.

Roscoe, P. 2016. "Performativity Matters: Economic Description as Moral Problem." In *Enacting Dismal Science*, ed. I. Boldyrev and E. Svetlova, 131–50. London: Palgrave-MacMillan.

Index

Page numbers in *italics* and **bold** denote figures and tables, respectively.